Monocacy and Catoctin

Additions and Corrections to the
History of Frederick County, Maryland
by
T. J. C. Williams and Folger McKinsey (1910)

VOLUME III

Calvin E. Schildknecht

Dedicated to Jacob M. and Edna M. Holdcraft
and to Althea J. Schildknecht

HERITAGE BOOKS
2007

HERITAGE BOOKS
AN IMPRINT OF HERITAGE BOOKS, INC.

Books, CDs, and more—Worldwide

For our listing of thousands of titles see our website
at
www.HeritageBooks.com

Published 2007 by
HERITAGE BOOKS, INC.
Publishing Division
65 East Main Street
Westminster, Maryland 21157-5026

Copyright © 1994 Calvin E. Schildknecht

Other books by the author:
Monocacy and Catoctin
Volumes 1 and 2

All rights reserved. No part of this book may be reproduced or transmitted in any form or by any means, electronic or mechanical, including photocopying, recording or by any information storage and retrieval system without written permission from the author, except for the inclusion of brief quotations in a review.

International Standard Book Number: 978-1-58549-291-6

CONTENTS

Introduction iii
About the Coauthors Williams and McKinsey 1
About Their History, Volumes I and II 5
Additions to Volume I 8
      - Pages 1-368 by Williams
      - Pages 369-622 by McKinsey
      - Pages 623-647 Census of 1790
      - Pages 648-656 Geology of Frederick County
Additions to Volume II (Biographical)...38
      - Pages 693-1623
Sources of Information with Abbreviations and Availability in Libraries 282

The History of Frederick County by Williams and McKinsey was reprinted by the Genealogical Publishing Company (Baltimore, MD 1979) (without illustrations)

INTRODUCTION

I have corrected some errors which occur in these two great and much used volumes of 1910, and have made additions especially to the earlier history and ancestors. These have been made possible by church, census, courthouse and other records. From the volumes of Names in Stone, by Jacob Mehrling Holdcraft, the years of birth and death have been added with places of burial. A past citizen's name is not complete without the years of living. Numerous gravestone dates differ from those of Williams and McKinsey by a year or more. Where earliest settlers have left no gravestones, the courthouse records such as settlements of estates, deeds and mortgages have been studied. Recent researches of origins in Europe, especially those by Annette K. Burgert, have been used as well as genealogies which have been written in intervening years. Assistance is acknowledged to the following: Norman C. Anders, Joseph H. Apple, IV, Raymond M. Bell, Dorothy G. Bentz, Linda K. Bischoff, William C. Birely, Robert D. Bittle, Angie Brosius, Velma Defibaugh, Bonnie Everhart, Alma M. Fogle, Mary Ann Frank, John Frye, Clement E. Gardiner, III, David C. Getzendanner, Nancy Gillette, Edward Helfenstein, Carroll H. Hendrickson, Jr., Dorothy T. and J. Richard Hershey, Edward J. Hogan, Mary H. Hoke, Stoll D. Kemp, Margaret Kwadrat, Jack and Betty Linton, Margaret E. Lough, Theresa M. T. Michel, Margaret E. Myers, Dorothy A. Nicodemus, Kent C. Nicodemus, Fred S. Palmer, Helen H. Ramsburg, Shirley Rohrbaugh, Althea J. Schildknecht, Christine Shryock, G. Helen Six, W. Cash Smith, Roy H. Wampler, Eileen R. Waesche, Mary Walters, Susan Hankey Weber, Richard R. Weber, Bryan T. Winter, Donald J. Wolf, F. Edward Wright and Lauren Wright.

THOMAS J. C. WILLIAMS, COAUTHOR

T. J. C. grew up in an environment of tobacco plantations in southern Maryland, being taught by his intellectual mother. He acquired a love of books and a large taste for historical reading. He entered Columbia College at Washington, D.C. but left because of financial difficulties. To support himself, he began to teach country school in Calvert County at age 16 while studying law with his brother Henry at Prince Frederick. He was admitted to the bar at Prince Frederick before he was 19 years of age. Young lawyer Williams was advised to leave the Calvert County of declining tobacco farms, from which slaves had been freed, and to try more promising Washington County, where he began law practice.

In 1872, he moved to Hagerstown where he was soon admitted to the bar. In 1874, he married Cora Marlin, daughter of Dr. Thomas and Mary (Maddox) Marlin. After briefly practicing law, Williams became a partner in printing the Hagerstown newspaper, *The Mail*, which initiated his 30 years in newspaper work and brought him into political activities. For five years Thomas and Cora lived at Woodlie Farm, south of St. James, where their first three children were born and Thomas became a vestryman at nearby St. Marks Episcopal Church. In 1880, they bought a cottage near St. James school and Thomas commuted to Hagerstown on the new Shenandoah Railroad.

In 1890 Williams founded the *Daily Mail*, but to obtain a better income, he left Hagerstown in November, 1891 to become an editorial writer for the *Baltimore Sun* newspaper until 1912. Williams kept up his contacts with Washington

County on summer vacations at Woodlie Farm. He became an editor of the *Baltimore Sun* and served as chief of its Legislative Bureau at Annapolis. In 1910 Williams was appointed Judge of the Juvenile Court of Baltimore; meanwhile, he served as vestryman of the Episcopal Church and somehow found time to publish four large volumes of *History of Washington County* (1906) and with McKinsey *History of Frederick County* (1910). In the former history, page 588, more information is given about the Williams family. Williams also left an autobiography of 39 pages which is in the files of the Historical Society of Frederick County. The obituary of Judge Williams appeared in the *Baltimore Sun* on December 12, 1929.

FOLGER MCKINSEY, THE BENTZTOWN BARD

Too often in our day, people of Frederick County speak of Williams' *History of Frederick County* forgetting that Folger McKinsey was the author of the part from the beginning of the Civil War in 1861 to 1910 of Vol. I. It is not clear how they divided editing of the biographical Vol. 2. McKinsey was much more closely associated and known in Frederick than Williams; he served as editor of the *Frederick Daily News* for 12 years. After leaving Frederick to pursue a newspaper career in Baltimore, he kept up his contacts with the Monocacy and Catoctin areas and continued using his pen name, the Bentztown Bard, acquired by living on West Patrick Street. There was deep emotional admiration between the Bard and people of the Frederick area, which has been recorded in newspapers and books, both in poetry and prose. A short biography is in Tercentenary History of Maryland, Vol. 4 (Baltimore, 1925).

Folger McKinsey was a distant relative of Jacob Mehrling Holdcraft as shown in a genealogy by Jacob's brother Rev. Paul E. Holdcraft (1954) (FH). Jacob Nickel (1810-1878), of Frederick, brother of Folger's mother, was a great grandfather of the Holdcraft brothers. Emigrant, John Adam Nickel (1781-1864) married Anne Elisabeth von Stouder (1793-1833). They came from Hirschberg near the Rhine River in 1821 to West Patrick Street in Frederick where they operated a florist business with adjoining greenhouse. Anna Elisabeth's daughter Catherine Nickel (1827-1918), born in Frederick, married James McKinsey. The latter left Frederick around 1845 to join the gold rush to California. Later they lived in Elkton, Maryland. James was appointed postmaster of Elkton by President Lincoln.

Folger McKinsey was born in Elkton, August 29, 1866. His early education was at private school operated by Miss Tably Jones and later he attended public school for a year. However, most of his education came from his literate mother. Folger started his newspaper career early by editing a weekly paper at Ocean Beach, near Belmar, NJ. Later he edited Elkton's newspaper the Civil Whig. In his youth, he visited Walt Whitman at Camden, NJ whom he greatly admired. He arranged for Whitman to give a lecture on Abraham Lincoln at Elkton.

At Ocean Beach, young Folger met Fannie H. Dungan of Philadelphia, a descendant of the theatrical Crabtree Family of Britain. After their marriage they decided to settle in Frederick where his parents had lived. Folger and Fanny had six children, of whom five were born in Frederick. In 1946, their living children were son Dungan in Covington, GA, Woerner of Westminster, Maryland, James of Baltimore, Mrs. Frank Williams of Baltimore, and Mrs. Orlando Rideout, III, of St. Margaret's, Maryland. In 1946, there were nine grandchildren. Fanny died in 1936, a month after their golden wedding anniversary.

Folger McKinsey was only 19 years old in January 1886 when William T. Delaplaine made him editor of the *Frederick Daily News*. He and bride Fanny moved into the house of former glove maker John Bentz on West Patrick Street beyond Carroll Creek, a part of so called Bentztown.

In 1898 the McKinsey family moved to Baltimore where Folger became Managing Editor of the *Baltimore News*. After the Baltimore fire of 1904, he served briefly the Washington Post and then joined the Baltimore Sun. Here his Good Morning Column appeared beginning in 1906 for nearly 40 years. In the period 1938-1941 the *Sun* published a remarkable series of his long articles about towns and villages of Maryland including pictures. Local history, architecture, occupations and personalities were emphasized in a glow of optimism and appreciation. A *Sun* editor stated that the Bard "elected to treat of homey matters and never permitted the taint of sophistication to confuse his public".

Besides writing up the half century of Frederick County History from the start of the Civil War for Vol. I of the history published in 1910, the Bard published three small books of poems: *A Rose of the Old Regime* (1907); *Other Poems of Home-Love and Childhood* (1908); and *Songs of the Daily Life* (1911). He won the prize for best four verses for a Baltimore City Anthem for which there were

800 entries. The song Baltimore, Our Baltimore, had its premiere at the Lyric Theater on Washington's Birthday in 1916.

Folger McKinsey kept up his interest in Frederick County by frequent visits. In 1945, he returned to Frederick for the Bicentennial of its founding by Daniel Dulany the Elder. At that time the *Sun* printed four articles about Frederick by the Bard. (FH).

The following poem was a favorite of Rev. Paul E. Holdcraft from the thousands of poems written by Folger McKinsey.

THE SUNSET HILLS OF FREDERICK

The sunset hills of Frederick---I see them in my dreams,
The valleys of the velvet bloom and of the winding stream.
The ridges of Catoctin, sweet in the twilight west,
And at their feet the happy town where hearts of dreaming rest:
> The sunset hills of Frederick,
> Ah, glow, dear dream, again
> As to and fro my way I go,
> Mid other times and men!

I hear young voices laughing where dancers in the night
Swing to the tune of silvery June far up on Braddock's Height;
Far down the dream town sparkles, the June time stars are sweet,
And love is in the moonlight spell, with moonbeams 'neath her feet:
> The sunset hills of Frederick,
> They call, and I am there,
> Wild as of old in June time's gold
> Of hill and stream and air!

See W&M-615 for his poems Catoctin Valley, Out of a Frederick Window, The Shadows of Catoctin and The Bells of Old St. John's.

In 1946, McKinsey retired from the *Baltimore Sun* to his home on the Magothy River where he died in July 1950. Funeral services were held at St. Margaret's Episcopal Church. His burial plot near Annapolis was surrounded by towering elms, sycamores and pines. He had always especially appreciated trees among the natural features of Maryland.

ABOUT VOLUMES I AND II

The title page of *History of Frederick County, Vol. I* states "From the Earliest Settlements, to the Beginning of the Civil War by T. J. C. Williams and continued from the Beginning of the year 1861 down to the Present Time 1910 by Folger McKinsey" (The Bentztown Bard).

Vol. II "A Biographical Record of Representative Families is prepared from data obtained from original sources of information". Most of these accounts apparently were written by members of families who showed wide variation in accuracy, details and objectivity. I do not know how Williams and McKinsey divided work and responsibility for editing Vol. II.

These two volumes make a remarkable collection of information about events, organizations and people of Frederick County during the late 1800's and early 1900's. They are said to be the books most used at the Public Library of Frederick. No comparable local books have been attempted since. The accounts regarding contemporary times and people are relatively accurate. In contrast, events, dates and people of the 1700's and early 1800's are often based on doubtful traditions and accounts in early books. I fear that Williams' statement that the biographical material came from original sources meant from the memories of people which often could not be trusted earlier than their grandparents.

Apparently Williams, McKinsey and most of their writers did not study courthouse records, church records, nor even gravestone records in order to verify early settlements and early ancestors. Such research seems not to have been customary at the time. A local historian such as Jacob Engelbrecht speculated about where the Monocacy German Settlement and Log Church might have been, but made no suggestion that land records in the courthouse might be helpful. One of the major errors of Williams is his repeated statements that Fredericktown was laid out by Patrick Dulany. A brief examination of the first index to deeds in the courthouse would have shown that Daniel Dulany, Sr. founded the town and that no Patrick Dulany is in the land records. This error and others apparently were copied from the History of Western Maryland by Scharf. A number of these errors have been repeated even in books published recently.

Histories of local churches apparently were accepted without investigation of claims to early dates and misleading traditions. In the biographical volume many of the repeated claims of ancestors as early settlers, and that three brothers emigrated from Europe, must be viewed with skepticism. I will not waste words to challenge all these but will give documented information when available. Among the repeated mistakes in Vol. II are claims that the local Buckey families are descendants of Col. Henri Bouquet of Switzerland and that the immigrant Kemp family settled first at Kemptown.

I make no claims for correcting all mistakes in Volumes I and II. From original sources and recent books based on original documentation, I have called attention to some of the questionable statements and given alternate information. In recent years growing interest in local history and genealogy has led to reprinting in books and pamphlets of many church and courthouse records, and also the unique volumes of local gravestone records, *Names in Stone* by Jacob Mehrling Holdcraft. Moreover, a great many printed and typed genealogies of local families have become available in libraries and historical societies, the greatest numbers being in the Library of Congress in D.C. and at the Historical Society of York County, at York, PA. The latter library also has the most complete collection of copies of publications on European origins of German speaking early settlers, many of whom came to Western Maryland. Similar abbreviations are used here for publications and library locations as already printed in our *Monocacy and Catoctin* Volumes I and II. I have included references to some of my articles in the *Frederick News and Post* available on microfilm (F).

In naming early ancestors the family accounts of Williams and McKinsey Vol. II often omit an early generation. This is not surprising since the first settlers usually buried their dead in family farm graveyards often without lettered gravestones. Many of these have been plowed over and stones lost. For these pioneers church, courthouse and family bible records often are useful. The Diaries of Jacob Engelbright are outstanding sources for later generations at Fredericktown.

My first additions to the biographical articles are the dates of death and where the couples were laid to rest. Locations of the cemeteries have been described by Holdcraft in *Names in Stone* Vol. I. The dates of life in parenthesis make an essential supplement to the personal names. If the months and days of birth and death were included, this whole effect would be lost. More precise dates can be found in Names in Stone or sources which I give.

It would be impractical to give complete accounts of the many recent descendants. I emphasize additions to earlier ancestors than those given in Vol. II. Suggestions for further research often are given with the overall genealogical picture from the known emigrating members of the particular family names. Locations in Germany have been corrected for example, where the old wide domains of Prussia and Bavaria do not apply today.

CEMETERIES. The Frederick County area is fortunate and unusual among U. S. Counties in having its gravestone inscriptions collected in the books *Names in Stone*, Vol. I and II, (1966) and More Names in Stone (1972) by Jacob Mehrling Holdcraft. In 1970 they were the only books of this type offered at Goodspeed Book Store in Boston. J. M. H. describes in Vol. I the locations with maps of those cemeteries and family graveyards which I mention here. By far the largest cemetery is Mt. Olivet on the south edge of Frederick with nearly 20,000 names in 1962. Second in size is the United Brethren with adjacent Blue Ridge Cemetery at Thurmont; third is Middletown Lutheran Cemetery. Approximate birth dates given with bc are from census records and from ages at death. Note that some villages such as Burkittsville, Creagerstown, Graceham Silver Run and Utica have only one principal cemetery so that church names are not essential. Reformed Churches have joined with Congregational to become United Church of Christ, UCC, also United Brethren and Methodist have become United Methodist.

With Holdcraft's excellent introduction, I must differ in only two matters. The earliest settlers were largely English speaking with a few of Scandinavian origin.

The earliest burial date remaining on gravestones of Frederick County is that of Ann Wheeler Elder, 1739, near Mt. St. Mary's.

The "Prefatory Notes" beginning Vol. II state that the material was compiled by T. J. C. Williams and Folger McKinsey." The biographical sketches were gathered from the most trustworthy sources by careful note takers." The typed biographies were submitted for correction and revision. It was stated that no charge was made for insertion of any reading matter contained in the works. The publishers, L. R. Titsworthy and Company, make special acknowledgement to ministers who supplied histories of churches. There was considerable variation in the accuracy of histories submitted by the pastors.

In large part William and McKinsey succeeded in obtaining representative families of our area including farmers. In the index of W&M, prepared by Holdcraft, the most frequent name in the two volumes is Smith followed in order by Thomas, Ramsburg (and related), Miller, Johnson, Zimmerman and Young. The underlined family names are particularly characteristic of Frederick County. In the Census of 1850 of Frederick County the order of frequency is Smith, Thomas, Miller with near a tie for fourth place among Ramsburg, Brown, Zimmerman and Young. A number of families of the 1850 census are underreported in Vol. II, such as Fox, Poole and Weller.

A number of prominent families in Frederick County history are not subjects of biographical articles in Vol. II of 1910, such as Beall, Beatty, Bentz, Biggs, Brengle, Delauter, Engelbrecht, Everhart, Hoffman, Link, Quynn, Scholl, Schorb, Shriver, Weller, Wetzel. I have added information on some of these.

The History of Williams and McKinsey shows great differences between Frederick County at the beginning of the 20th Century and that of the present, approaching the 21st Century. In 1910 the county still manufactured canned foods, meat products, fertilizers, bricks, leather goods, cigars, iron and steel products. In 1886 there were listed 75 shoemakers, nearly 100 millers of grain and timber and 25 carriage makers (D). Today, principally agricultural products with some lime, cement and stone manufacture remaining active. Aluminum production in the south of the county is carried on by French interests. Most manufactured goods are supplied from outside the county. Aside from agriculture, college and U. S. Government activities such as Fort Detrick and Fort Ritchie the county has become largely a bedroom community for commuters and retired persons. Manufactures of a few medical and photo-electronic products have been initiated.

The local heroes whom William and McKinsey honored by extended biographies usually were leaders of government and industry, also Sgt. Lawrence Everhart, Admiral Schley and of course Barbara Fritchie. In our so-called post-Industrial or Entertainment Age, our heroes and heroines, and those most rewarded financially, are more often leading entertainers of sports, films and T.V. Since 1910, progress has been made in one direction. W&M shows a male-dominated culture. Of the portraits in the printing of 1910 there were 157 of men and only 2 of women. Most of the accomplishments of the men were discussed before their marriages were mentioned. I have tried to give more attention to the wives.

The standard two-letter abbreviations of states are used, for example WV for West Virginia. Locations are in Maryland unless otherwise designated. Approximate years of birth taken from ages at death and from census data are preceded by b. c. (born about). Marriages are indicated by m. and deaths by d. The abbreviation d/o reads daughter of. County is abbreviated Co. and township by Twp. Volume numbers are marked Vol. or underlined. Other abbreviations are given with the Sources at the end of this book.

The census of 1790 giving heads of households in old Frederick County, including what later became Carroll Co., is given on pages 623-647 of Williams and McKinsey (W&M). The next census of 1800 was the first to indicate the approximate location of households in Frederick Co. (including what later was Carroll County). The election districts in 1800 were much larger than those later divisions having similar names. Thus in 1800 Liberty District included much of the adjoining area which later became Woodsboro and New Market. The districts of 1800, which I frequently cite in the biographical Section, were # 1. Southern Frederick county including Buckeystown area; #2. Central Frederick county including Fredericktown; #3. Western Frederick county (Middletown Valley); #4. Northern Frederick County including Emmitsburg and Creagerstown; #5. Taneytown District; #6. Westminster District; and #7. Liberty District including Woodsboro and New Market areas. The Frederick county census of 1850 is of special interest as the first one to give names and ages of all the people including infants.

ADDITIONS AND CORRECTIONS TO VOLUME I

W&M-1. In earliest European settlement of the Monocacy Valley scattered plantations of English speaking people from southern MD, Baltimore and Anne Arundel counties preceded the German speaking settlers from Pennsylvania.

Monocacy Manor was taken by Lord Baltimore but managed by Daniel Dulany and associates. Dulany patented nearby Dulany's Lot lying approximately from Ceresville to Mt. Pleasant, from which he sold early a large part to Susanna Beatty. Daniel Dulany, the elder, not his Irish cousin Rev. Patrick Dulany, acquired Tasker's chance and on its southern part laid out Fredericktown in 1745 (*Frederick News*, August 1, 1991). The Dulany family is discussed in the book *Pillars of Maryland*, by F. S. McGrath (Richmond, Va. 1950) (FH). and *Frederick News*, August 17 and September 24, 1992. Before Daniel Dulany laid out Frederick there were some indications that a town might be started in the area of Ceresville. The Old Annapolis Road was so directed and the Old English Graveyard was started east of the Monocacy River (used by Beatty, Graham and Cocke families) (*Frederick News*, August 8, 1985). For purchases of lots in Frederick 1748-1764, see Reed and Burns.

James Carroll did not take up his option for a tract in the Linganore Hills area.

Leonard Calvert died in 1649. It was Benedict Calvert who was associated with Gov. Thomas Johnson.

W&M-3. Monocacy Log Church of the German Monocacy Settlement was not near Creagerstown. This was first proved by Dr. Arthur Tracey in correspondence with Dr. A. R. Wentz. See M&C-I. As described in the Monocacy Lutheran Congregation Book the church was south of present Thurmont and just south of Big Hunting Creek and west of the German Monocacy Road (present Hessong Bridge Road). The location was confirmed by Moravian records and deeds, especially to the tract German Town found by myself. Edward T. Schulz who published the wrong location of Monocacy Church relied on false traditions and showed no evidence of having studied records.

It was Charles Carroll, the emigrant, (grandfather of Charles of Carrollton) who acquired c. 1720 the large tract in Monocacy Valley which became Carrollton Manor of Charles Carroll of Annapolis and later Charles Carroll of Carrollton.

It was John Digges who claimed land on Conestoga and Codorus Creeks which later became parts of Pennsylvania after establishment of the Mason-Dixon Line. Most of it lay between what is present-day Hanover and Littlestown, PA.

The main Monocacy Road southward continued east of Monocacy River until crossing the river at Hughes Ford east of Frederick. It did not cross the river near Creagerstown. The German Monocacy Road branched from the main Monocacy Road near Keymar and passed Rocky Ridge to Graceham then southward passing near Monocacy Church toward Lewistown by present Hessong Bridge Road and ending near Old Braddock where it met the road to what later became present-day Hagerstown. Thus the German Monocacy Road became a short cut toward the West bypassing Frederick.

W&M-4. Creagerstown was laid out by John Creager not Cramer (another inaccuracy from Schultz).

The Moravian pastors were Rev. George Nieke and Lawrence T. Nyberg.

Yost Hite (Jost Heit) born in Bonfeld, Germany, near Heilbronn, married Anna Maria Merckel (b. 1687) (from recent research in Virginia).

W&M-5. In the area of Monocacy Log Church lived Lutheran, Reformed and Moravian settlers. It was not correct to say "every resident belonged to the Reformed Church". However, at Fredericktown the Reformed Church was organized before the Lutheran congregation. Naturalization records prove that a Reformed Congregation was at Monocacy Church in 1743.

Burkittsville is west of Frederick, not north.

Fort Frederick was not rebuilt by Gen. Braddock, but after Braddock's death.

W&M-6. The Moravian Church site at Graceham was given by Maj. Joseph Ogle. The 10 acres from Charles Carroll of Annapolis was on Carrollton Manor south of Frederick.

The Schley party of less than 100 families arrived in Maryland around 1745. Maria Margaretha, daughter of Thomas and Margaretha Schley was born in Germany on May 22, 1743 (record of church at Billingheim). See *Frederick News*, September 7, 1991. Rev. Patrick Dulany of Ireland never visited America. Daniel Dulany, the Elder, named Patrick St. after his prominent theologian cousin of Ireland.

The baptism in 1737 of a son of Frederick Unsult by Rev. Wolf occurred in New Jersey and recorded in the Lutheran Monocacy Book in Monocacy Settlement.

W&M-6. Footnote: Michael, Steiner, Houck

W&M-8. The Harbaugh family, although of Swiss origin, emigrated from Germany, where George was born.

W&M-8. Footnote: Bietle or Beatly, later Beachley; Fearhake earlier Feuerhacker (both German in origin)

W&M-9. Early John Stull, leading early settler near what later became present-day Hagerstown, was not a German Stoll, but of English speaking origin.

W&M-10. Carrollton Manor was patented by Charles Carroll, emigrant from Ireland, grandfather of Charles Carroll of Carrollton. For distinguishing the many Charles Carrolls see my article in *Frederick News*, April 4, 1990.

W&M-11. William Elder who settled near Mt. St. Mary's about 1734 was born in Maryland, not England. His father emigrated from England.

Joseph Wood who settled on Monocacy Manor was not born in England. (See M&C-II).

Although All Saints Episcopal Congregation has been claimed to have organized early, the church building was not completed until after 1750. Quaker and Reformed church buildings were earlier in Frederick County.

W&M-10. Footnote: Dulany

W&M-12 to 18. For Indians, explorers and traders with the Indians see M&C-I. Maryland Historical Society in Baltimore has a collection of manuscripts on Indian Archaeology (MS 468). Indian artifacts collected early in Maryland were discussed by William B. Marye, MHM 33, 262 (1938).

The previously strong Susquehannock tribe was defeated and nearly exterminated by the Iroquois from the north in 1674. Survivors sought protection southward, building a fort settlement on Piscataway Creek. See MHM 36, 1 (1941).

Williams probably was correct that at the time of earliest white settlements there were few indians in the Frederick County area. Their clearings made by burning the woods were disputed hunting grounds of visiting Delaware, Susquehannock and the Seneca tribes (one of the Iroquois Five Nations). The Senecas seemed to predominate leaving their name frequently in Western Maryland. Before 1700 the Piscataways or Conoys moved up the Potomac and settled briefly on Conoy or Heater's Island (in sight of Point of Rocks). About the same time large numbers of Shawnees moved from the West to the Potomac and scattered quite peacefully in Maryland. After 1710 many Tuscarora Indians migrated through the Monocacy area to become the 6th nation of the Iroquois Confederation.

The Indian atrocities during and after the French and Indian War, 1755-1765, in Western Maryland were minimized by Williams. Apparently most of these were by Delaware Indians who had moved westward. Descendants of the Delawares today are proud that their ancestors defeated Gen. Braddock alongside the French. After Braddock's troops were so easily routed, Benjamin Franklin and others saw the feasibility of revolution against Britain. Note the works of E. Ralston Goldsborough on Monocacy Valley Indian archaeology in M&C-I, also William Marye MHM 33, 262 (1937). Indian archaeological sites in the upper Monocacy Valley in Adams County have been reviewed by S. W. Frost, Pa. Arch. 4, #4 (Jan 1935). Indian grave stone piles in Maryland were studied by C. A. Weslager MHM 42, 46 (March 1947). These usually were placed near a trail so that passing indians would add to the heap.

W&M-18. In the discussion of some customs of early settlers there is no mention of the folk art, so called fractur, of the Pennsylvania and Maryland Germans which flourished even into the early 19th century. These colored drawings of flowers, birds, also geometric designs (including barn signs) were used on gravestones, baptism and marriage certificates, also on furniture. Their forerunners in south Germany, Switzerland have been little appreciated except in a few museums, but in America they have been reproduced in beautiful books such as the following:

The Pennsylvania German Fractur, Vol. 1 & 2 compiled by Frederick S. Weiser and Howell J. Heaney (PA German Society, 1976)

Arts of the Pennsylvania Germans, by Scott T. Swank, et al of Winterthur Museum, DE (Norton, 1983).

The Pennsylvania German Chest, by Monroe H. Fabian (Universe Books, 1978). The Maryland and Pennsylvania German folk art, like earliest art of the Picts, early inhabitants of Scotland, has characteristics of Pre-Celtic art. Celtic, Viking and north German early arts usually are unrealistic, often grotesque and crowded with emphasis on warfare and fierce animals such as lions, serpents and dragons.

W&M-21. Conojohela where Cresap tried to settle was a short distance south of Wrightsville, Pa., west of the Susquehannah River. It was not near Peach Bottom which is much further south. Cresap was not victorious.

W&M-24 Relations between the earliest settlers and the Maryland government of the Calverts and Dulanys did not always go smoothly as shown in the following protest of German settlers: *The Archives of Maryland* records that on June 7, 1748 Gov. Samuel Ogle presented at Annapolis to his 11 Council Members, including Benjamin Tasker, Esq., Daniel Dulany, Esq., and Benedict Calvert, Esq., a complaint by Stephen Ramsberg about unfair treatment of settlers in Frederick County by Sheriff Bainbridge in collection of quit rents. As a result some settlers had left the state and others planned to do so. Also read was a statement by Col. Joseph Ogle supporting the German settlers. The Governor admonished the sheriff to deal more fairly in the future. the following early settlers were named: Jacob Fout, Peter Apple, Henry Trout, Melcar Warfield, Christian Thomas, Peter Hoffman, Christian Getzendanner, Henry Roads, Conrad Kemp, Francis Wise, Jacob and John Smith, George Loy, Isaac Miller, Thomas Johnson, Joseph, John and Jacob Brawner, Nick Frisk, Ken Backdolt, Nicholas Reisner, David Delauter, Martin Wetzel, Casper Windred, Peter Shafer, Jacob Brunner, Ignatius Digges, Nathaniel Wickham. (Some spellings modernized).

W&M-24. German settlers, Daniel Franz and John George Loy (Ley).

W&M-24. For the relation of Dulany families to Prospect Hall and Prospect Hill (here called Red Hill) see my article in the Frederick News, September 24, 1992. Patriot Benjamin Tasker Dulany, grandson of Daniel Dulany the Elder, lived there briefly.

W&M-24. (footnote): After the death of Daniel Dulany, Elder, in 1753 lots in Frederick were sold by his sons, Daniel II and Walter.

W&M-25. footnote: Hausihl or Hauseal

W&M-26. Parr's Spring (not Padd's) near present Ridgeville (south of Mt. Airy) was the landmark for county boundaries. It is a source of Patuxent River. Burnt House Woods was near what became present-day Taylorsville.

W&M-26. footnote: Joseph Chapline

W&M-29. The tiny house (pictured on page 232) formerly on West All Saints St. may indeed have been where Washington stayed, but it is more likely that a larger house or tavern accommodated Gen. Braddock and Benjamin Franklin at Frederick. Note that Franklin left Frederick before George Washington arrived. A short distance further west on All Saints St. was a blacksmith shop used by Washington according to tradition. The tavern site at Jefferson and West Patrick St. proposed in the book, *Ill Starred General*, by Lee McCardell is unlikely since it was far west of tiny Frederick in 1755.

W&M-31. Braddock's troops did not cross South Mt. at Turner's Gap, but further north at Braddock's Gap where highway I-70 now crosses the mountain. Henry Clay (1777-1852) married in 1799 Lucretia Hart. Note John C. Hart of Frederick in W&M-386.

W&M-46. Virginia Mills (earlier Bard's Mill) is a short distance north of Fairfield, PA, on the Bullfrog Road. It is just west of Carroll Tract Road (the road from Fairfield to Orrtanna, Pennsylvania).

W&M-64. Picture. Recent research makes it likely that Prospect Hall mansion was built by Col. John McPherson who owned the property in 1811-1844. It could not have been built by a Tory Dulany as claimed here. Most Dulanys of Maryland were neutral or patriots during the Revolution. See C.E.S. in Frederick News, August 17 and September 24, 1992.

W&M-68 and 70. The grant by King Charles I in 1625 to George Calvert, First Lord Baltimore, of land between the 40th parallel and the Potomac River contained the limitation to areas not previously cultivated by Christians. The Penn family researchers disclosed alleged Dutch settlements before 1625 near what became present-day Rehobeth, DE in order to draw the boundary further south. In fact the Dutch who landed early were most interested in trading for furs and in the Indian women, rather than in farming.

W&M-72. Col. Thomas Cresaps' disputed house was at Conojohela west of the Susquehannah River and south of what later became Wrightsville, Pennsylvania. Cresap's home and trading station at Old Town near the Upper Fork of the Potomac was more than a hunting cabin.

W&M-74. The original German spelling of Hager or Hagar is Heger as shown by many signatures of Jonathan Heger in Frederick County deeds to lots in early Hagerstown.

W&M-84. footnote: John Ramsburg.

W&M-85. In the list of signers at the meeting on January 24, 1776, the following additional names are given by Scharf in History of Maryland: Joseph Wells, David Moore, Joseph Wood, Norman Bruce and William Blair. A much longer list are those who took the Oath of Fidelity in 1778 in Frederick and Washington Counties in the book Revolutionary Records of Maryland by G. M. Brumbaugh et al (DC 1924) (GS). Footnote: Abraham Faw (not Paw) (M&C-I).

W&M-86. footnote: William Shields, Thomas Noland, Abraham Faw (not Paw) (M&C-I).

W&M-96. For the effects upon Dunkard settlers of the barbaric execution of pacifist Peter Suman and two other Brethren at Frederick in 1781, see the book *Allegheny Passage* by Emmert F. Bittinger (Camden ME, 1990) (FH). They were accused of planning to release prisoners in Frederick. Cf Dorothy M. Quynn, MHM 40, 201 (1945).

W&M-99. For German mercenary, troops, so called Hessian prisoners at the Barracks (later, the grounds of the School for the Deaf) see books and notes based on German Diaries such as a *Hessian Diary of the American Revolution* by John Conrad Doehla (Univ. of Oklahoma Press, 1990). For family data of German prisoners who settled in Frederick County, see (GM) also Frederick News October 22, 1990.

W&M-101. Yarmouth is in County Norfolk in southeastern England.

W&M-102. Louisa Johnson (b. 1775) a daughter of Joshua Johnson (brother of Gov. Thomas Johnson) became the wife of Pres. John Quincy Adams.

W&M-107. Gov. Thomas Johnson's emigrant grandfather, Thomas Johnson, was from near Yarmouth, not from Liverpool.

W&M-111. See book *The Life of Thomas Johnson* by Edward S. Delaplaine (NYC, 1927) (F). (FH)

W&M-131. For Nelson families see CES in *Frederick News*, July 7, 1990 and W&M-1122. Some were of English-speaking origin.

Sergeant Lawrence Everhart (Eberhardt) (1755-1840) was born at Hessheim, near Worms, Germany. See also W&M-183.

W&M-137. The visit of George and Martha Washington to Frederick on June 30, 1791 was described by Helen Urner Price in the Baltimore Sun on January 31, 1932 (FH). They passed through Frederick on their way from Mt. Vernon to Philadelphia. After breakfast at what is present-day Rockville they dined at Peter's Tavern 20 miles further and arrived at Frederick about sundown. According to Scharf the Washingtons were met south of town by a company of horsemen, prominent citizens headed by Major Mountjoy Bayley. According to questionable tradition President Washington was served coffee by young Barbara Hauer (later Fritchie) at a prominent tavern of uncertain name.

On April 20, 1923 bronze tablets on the two sides of a tall boulder of diabase rock were dedicated at the top of the first hill south of Monocacy River on Georgetown Pike (now route 355). The meeting with the Washingtons and on the other side the departure of Lafayette, 33 years later, were commemorated as follows: "On the 30th day of June, 1791, George Washington ascended this hill and looked over the beautiful Monocacy Valley. This farm was then owned by John Scholl. The mansion house is on the property of Mrs. Fanny McPherson Dennis. George Washington was met here by a cavalcade of horsemen from Frederick, Major Mountjoy Bayley, Chief Marshall; Col. John McPherson was one of the committee." On the other side: "In 1824 Lafayette was accompanied from Frederick this far by Dr. John Tyler and others, on his way to Washington D.C. Gen. Lafayette bid adieu and took his last look on South Mountain and the Frederick Valley".

In 1992 both bronze tablets had been stolen but the stone remained with fittings.

Records at the Taneytown Public Library and Washington's published diary show that George and Martha did not stay over night at Terra Rubra but at the Tavern of Adam Good in Taneytown (marked with bronze tablet).

W&M-141. (Lower right). St. Benjamin Church is on the western edge of Westminster, Maryland. The name St. Benjamin may come from a German church named before the Reformation.

W&M-147. Jonathan Heger signed his name to deeds as it was spelled in Germany. However, the dominant English speakers wrote Hagerstown. Jonathan wanted to call the town Elizabethtown after his wife.

W&M-163. Gen. James Wilkinson (1757-1825) whose court martial was held in Frederick was born in St. Mary's County, Maryland and died in Mexico. He was defended by Roger B. Taney and was acquitted. See NC Vol. I.

W&M-167. Footnote: John and Jacob Gonso; Henry and George Hauer; Abraham Neff.

W&M-183. Lawrence Everhart (Eberhardt) (1755-1840) who was honored by being seated opposite Lafayette in 1824 as Frederick County's outstanding hero of the Revolution from among the common people. He was born in Hessheim near Worms, Germany, in May 1755 to Christian Eberhardt (b. 1729) (son of Jacob of Hessheim and wife Maria Sibella (b. 1731 at Lansheim)). Lawrence had six brothers and seven sisters. He emigrated in 1764 to Middletown Valley and married in 1782 Anna Mary Beckenbaugh. In 1771 he is listed in the catechetical class of Frederick Reformed Church.

At the Battle of Brandywine Lawrence' assistance was given to wounded Lafayette and at the Battle of Cowpens in South Carolina, he is credited with coming to the rescue of Col. William Washington who was beset by a British officer and dragoons (See *Romance of the Revolution*, by Bunce). In 1832 a local rifle company commanded by Samuel Carmack was named the Everhart Greys. The Frederick chapter of the Sons of America Revolution is named after Lawrence Everhart.

In 1808 Lawrence Everhart of Middletown was ordained a minister of the Methodist Episcopal Church by Bishop Asbury. In 1815 Rev. Everhart bought for $40 lot 35 in Lewistown from Daniel Fundenberg and wife Rebecca. Also in 1815 Everhart, John Crouse and John Devilbiss bought lots 78-80 from Fundenberg for the Methodist Episcopal Church. Since Lawrence was a carpenter he may have worked on the church construction.

In his will probated in 1840 Lawrence named his friend of Middletown Valley, Jacob Flook of John, as executor. He willed wife Mary 18 acres, a cow of choice, the "choice of all my German books" and his pension of $1000 yearly. His daughters Elizabeth Jackson and Catharine Nickum lived in Indiana. Daughter Sarah married Henry Smelzer.

W&M-189. The author of the book *A Complete View of Baltimore in 1833* and the map of Western Maryland in 1808 was Charles Varlé. (The accented e is pronounced).

W&M-229. The B and O Railroad which reached Frederick from Baltimore in 1831, was the first built in the U.S. for general transportation of passengers and freight (Encyclopedia Britannica, 1929).

W&M-268. For early industries and owners of numbered lots in Frederick from 1748 to 1764 see Reed and Burns.

The New Bremen Glassworks of John F. Amelung was not the first in America, nor the first in Frederick County. In order to start production quickly Amelung bought the earlier glassworks near Sugar Loaf Mt. operated by Conrad Voltz and coworkers. In 1962 and 1963 the Corning Museum of Glass along with the Smithsonian Institution conducted an excavation of one of the Amelung glass houses under direction of Ivor Noel Hume, Chief Archaeologist of the Colonial Willamsburg Foundation. The results were reported by Dwight P. Lamon and others in 237 pages with illustrations in the Journal of Glass Studies Vol. 18 (1976). (F). (FH).

One of the most surprising discoveries of the Corning researchers came from the will of Conrad Voltz or Foltz, probated in 1784. It disclosed an earlier glasshouse near Sugar Loaf Mt. in Frederick County, which later was sold to Amelung and accounted for his speed in getting into production. Conrad Voltz, Balthasar Kramer and his brothers George, Martin and Adam Kramer arrived from Rotterdam on the ship Britannia at Philadelphia on September 18, 1773. By October 25, Baltsar, Martin and Conrad were on the payroll of Henry William Stiegel's glasshouse at Manheim, Pennsylvania near Lancaster. Within a year Stiegel's glasshouse closed and the Voltz-Kramer group moved south to Frederick County.

Not much is known about the Foltz-Kramer glasshouse which operated locally during the Revolution. Lamon concluded that their glasshouse was clearly an important stage in Amelung's development. Amelung sought to receive total credit for establishing the first glass making in Maryland. In his promotional publications he carefully omitted any reference to Foltz and the Kramers. Amelung also never disclosed the name of the skilled engraver who made the presentation goblets.

Conrad Voltz (1737-1784) was born at Voelklingen near Saarbruecken in southwestern Pfalz. In 1762 he married Susannah Margaretha Wagner of Saarbruecken-Burbach. Their daughter Maria married in 1763 George Cramer. Widow Susanna Margaretha in 1791 married widower Michael Roemer (Raymer) leader of the Frederick Lutheran Church.

After the failure of Amelung glass business the Kramer families moved to southwestern Pennsylvania around New Geneva. It is not clear whether some remained in Frederick.

From the same area as Voltz came Eberhardt or Everhart glassworkers for Amelung. These have been studied by Mrs. Bonnie Everhart of Gettysburg and later of Clinton, NC. Johann Frederick Adolphus Eberhardt, (1718-1770) of Karlsbrunn married Anna Katherine Elisabeth Reppert (1732-1784) who emigrated as widow and died at Frederick. She with sons Martin, Adolph and Ludwig Leonard arrived in 1773 on the same ship with her Kramer relatives. Karlsbrunn is the German town near Alsace from which Nicholas Eisenhauer, ancestor of President Eisenhower, emigrated.

At the reception of Lafayette at Talbott's Tavern the arrangement of the table was in charge of Mrs. Catherine Kimball, Frederick's outstanding early tavern keeper and business woman. Catherine (Grosch) Kimball died in 1831 and was buried at the Lutheran Church on East Church St. (*Frederick News*, March 9, 1991).

W&M-269. Bottom: Frederick was not established by Patrick Dulany, but by Daniel Dulany, the Elder.

W&M-283. Note that Frederick County native Zachariah Albaugh died in Licking County, Ohio, at 109 years.

W&M-284. Note that the first kerosene lamp was brought to Frederick in 1858. The oil was said to have been distilled from coal. Before my family at 714 N.

Market St. had electric lighting, about 1920, my mother sent me to the grocery store for "coal oil".

W&M-285. (Lower right) Kennedy Farrell; Capt. Nathaniel Wickham.

W&M-298. Daniel Dulany II or the Younger practiced briefly in Frederick as a lawyer after the Frederick County Court was organized in 1750.

W&M-299. The ancestor of Francis Scott Key was Philip Key (1696-1764) son of Richard and Mary (Cartwright) Key. Philip and family emigrated from Covent Garden, London, to St. Mary's County. See W&M-313 for more about Key ancestors.

W&M-321. Adamstown is south of Frederick.

Carrollton Manor tract was granted to Charles Carroll the emigrant, grandfather of Charles Carroll of Carrollton.

The first settlers in numbers, near Buckeystown were English speaking Quakers about 1725. George and Michael Buckey came much later. Their father Mathias Buckey was the emigrant. See W&M-853.

W&M-322 top. Trammelstown.

W&M-322. (Second Column): It is true that Gen. U. S. Grant met Gen. Sheridan at the later James Marshall home near Araby about a month after the Battle of Monocacy. An illustration from Leslie's news magazine shows them meeting at Frederick Junction Station. The visit of Grant to Frederick County seems to be little remembered locally. See later.

W&M-323. For Sgt. Lawrence Everhart, see W&M-183.

The town of Middletown was not laid out by Margaret Crone who lived much later. No record of Frederick Lauber has been found. Michael Jesserang sold at least 28 lots there by 1767. For early Middletown see Millard M. Rice in the book *New Facts and Old Families* (Redwood City, CA 1976).

Braddock Spring is east of the ridge of Catoctin Mountain.

Braddocks troops passed South Mt. at Braddock's Gap further north and would not have passed through Boonsboro.

W&M-323. For Emmitsburg history see the small book by James A. Helman (1906) and for Mt. St. Mary's see *The Story of the Mountain*, by Mary Miller Melins and Rev. Edward F. X. McSweeney (1911). For the early Elder settlers see William Elder Ancestors and Descendants by Sister Mary Louise Donnelly, Burke, Virginia, 1986. William Elder (1707-1775) was born in Maryland and moved from Mt. Calvert, Prince George's County to south of Mt. St. Mary's about 1734. He was a son of immigrant William Sr. and wife Elizabeth (Finch). William Jr's. first wife Ann (Wheeler) (1709-1739) was a daughter of Richard of Charles County. Ann's gravestone has the earliest death date discovered in Frederick County (Frederick News March 9, 1972). The second wife of William Elder, Jr. was Jacoba Clementina (Livers) (1717-1807) daughter of Arnold. Thomas Elder, (1740-1832) and family left Harbaugh Valley about 1810 to settle in Kentucky according to Sister Donnelly. Thomas and wife Elizabeth (Spalding) went to Cox's Creek settlement in Kentucky. Earlier James Elder, son of Guy (1761-1845) had been one of the first to move there from Emmitsburg area.

Mary Ann Elder daughter of Charles (b. 1730) and Julia (Wood) (1737-1814) married Charles Montgomery and they moved to Kentucky about 1795. For other Maryland families moving to Kentucky see the book *Catholicity in Kentucky*, by Ben J. Webb (Louisville, KY, 1884) (at Georgetown Univ. Library). About the same time Catherine (Ambrose) Weller, the widow of Reformed John Weller, and most of her children moved from near Apples Church to the area of Bardstown, Kentucky. (See M&C-II).

W&M-324. Attending church at Emmitsburg was the family of Dr. Alice Seabrook, pioneer woman medical doctor, whose parents farmed in nearby Liberty Township of Adams County. Dr. Seabrook designed the incubator for premature babies at Woman's Hospital in Philadelphia according to Beryl McPherson in the book *The History of Elias Lutheran Church*, by Rev. W. Ronald Fearer (1972).

James and Joseph Hughes were merchants and architects of Emmitsburg. Their ancestors had come from County Tyrone, Ireland via Massachusetts. James Hughes was Capt. of Militia of Emmitsburg who marched in the 1794 whiskey rebellion. James and Joseph were trustees of the Catholic Church in Emmitsburg. More about these families is in Helman.

W&M-325. Amelung Glassworks was not the first in America. See W&M-268.

W&M-326. Judge Joseph Wood of Cecil County, Maryland was born in America, a descendant of an emigrant from England (M&C II).

W&M-327. Daniel Dulany II was neutral and not a Tory during the Revolution. Monocacy Manor belonged to the Calverts, Lord Baltimore, and therefore was confiscated. Fredericktown was named for Frederick Calvert the last Lord Baltimore when he was a youth and before he acquired an unsavory reputation. See *Frederick News* August 17, 1792.

Leases on Monocacy Manor in 1767 and 1768 with names of earlier settlers are given by G. M. Brumbaugh in Maryland Records Vol. 2 (Lancaster, Pennsylvania 1928) (GS). Conococheague Manor of 1767, in what later became Washington County, is also recorded there.

W&M-334. There were settlers such as Jacob Weller in the area of what became Mechanicstown (later Thurmont) as early as 1738 but the town was formed much later, around 1800 led by Jacob Weller, blacksmith, a grandson of the first settler.

It was the grandfather of Jacob Weller BS, founder of Mechanicstown (later Thurmont) who had lived briefly in Berks County, Pennsylvania

W&M-335. Benedict Calvert and Thomas Johnson received a patent for land at Catoctin Furnace (earlier called Johnson's furnace).

The early steam operated pump brought from England was used at Arlington, northern New Jersey, west of New York City. The copper mine was not in New York state. I worked nearby for the DuPont Company at Arlington, NJ.

W&M-336. It is seldom recognized that James Rumsey's steam boat operated by jet propulsion, later applied to aircraft and space craft. For letters of Rumsey to George Washington see MHM 32, 28 and 136 (1937).

W&M-336. Alleged experimental iron axles made for Rumsey boats lie near the barn of late Ross Stull on Hessong Bridge Road. One is mounted upright at the intersection of this road with Little Hunting Creek. It is recorded in deeds as a surveyor's mark.

W&M-343 & 344. Lewistown District was not the birthplace of the celebrated Indian fighters Adam and Andrew Poe. They and their parents moved there from near Leitersburg in Washington County about 1762. See M&C-I. Most sources state that Lewis Wetzel the noted Indian fighter was a son of John Wetzel (born 1733 in Switzerland) who emigrated to Pennsylvania in 1747 and married Mary Bonnet. They went to Rockingham County, Virginia in 1756.

W&M-362. The Family of John Brown of Harpers Ferry:

In the 17 pages of *History of Frederick County*, by Williams and McKinsey devoted to John Brown and his raid on Harpers Ferry, very little is disclosed about the Brown family. Much of the following comes from a chapter by Robert E. McGlone in the book *Memory and American History* edited by David Thelen (Indiana University Press, 1990). The chapter emphasizes the tendency to rewrite and reconstruct history to comply with later desires. Contrary to later claims, not all of the Brown family supported John Brown's violent actions against slavery in Kansas and at Harpers Ferry.

John Brown (1800-1859) was born at Torrington, Connecticut, an alleged descendant of Peter Brown who came to America on the Mayflower. He was a grandson of Capt. John Brown who served in the Revolution. In 1805 John was taken by his parents, Owen and Ruth (Mills) Brown, to Hudson, Ohio, north of Akron. At age 18 John began to prepare for the Congregational ministry, but his attention was soon diverted by land surveying. He had grown up with the anti-slavery views of his father, "Squire" Owen Brown, who was a founder of two Free Congregational churches, at Hudson and at Oberlin. John tried tanning, sheep raising and the wool trade with little success. In 1842 he became bankrupt in Akron. In 1849, after living in Pennsylvania and Maine, he and second wife Mary Ann (Day) with nine children moved to North Elba, New York to farm and aid black settlers there.

John Brown by two wives had 20 children, 16 of whom reached maturity. By his first wife, Dianthe (Lusk) (d. 1832 in childbirth) there were six children, including John, Jr. and Jason (both returned from Kansas to Ohio); Owen who gave his father's causes most support; Frederick who was killed at Osawatomie, Kansas by a pro-slavery posse; and Ruth who married Henry Thompson. John Brown's second marriage was to Mary, aged 19 years who had 12 children in 14 years. At North Elba records show that Mary tried to persuade her sons against violence and she refused to join her husband at the Dr. Kennedy farm in Washington County near Harpers Ferry (then in Virginia). Son John, Jr. and Mary's sons Jason and Salmon also refused their father John's appeals to come to Harpers Ferry. In later historical writing this often was revised to claim that all family members gave support. The *Encyclopedia Britannica, 14th Edition*, states "His sons aided him in all his undertakings". Sons Watson and Oliver Brown died at Harpers Ferry and Owen escaped from the Harpers Ferry raid. John, Jr. claimed that he gave assistance by shipping to Chambersburg weapons disguised as mining equipment. William H. and Dauphin Thompson of New

York State were both killed in the raid on Harpers Ferry beginning in the early morning hours of October 16, 1859.

After John Brown's execution by hanging on December 2, 1859 at Charlestown, his body was taken by wife Mary for burial at North Elba, New York. Much less has been published about associates of John Brown who were executed at Charlestown.

W&M-369. This marks the beginning of the part of Vol. I written by Folger McKinsey, the Bentztown Bard. His writing seems to include fewer major errors than the writing by Williams. Most of the inaccuracies are in accounts of some of the pastors.

W&M-375. Correct dates for the Battle of Gettysburg are July 1, 2, 3, 1863. Below note Noland's Ferry.

W&M-377. McKinsey was a keen critic of the Barbara Fritchie story. He marks 16 lines of Whittier's poem in italics noting erroneous statements.

The ancestors of Barbara (Hauer) Fritchie have been traced recently to northern Alsace (B3). Otto Hauer, son of Peter and Catharina (Guth) had fourth child (Johan) Nicolaus (1733-1799) who emigrated in 1754 from Diedendorf. Nicholas and wife Catharine had the births of the following children recorded in the Reformed Church at Lancaster, Pennsylvania:

Catharine 1760	Daniel 1768
Jacob 1762	John Ludwig 1770
Maria Elisabeth 1765	Margaret 1773
Barbara 1766	John 1775

The family moved to Frederick where Barbara was confirmed at the Reformed Church and married Caspar Fritchie. See also Charles C. Hower, MHM 68, 94 (1973).

Note that Jacob Engelbrecht who lived near Barbara Fritchie heard or saw nothing of the flag incident with Confederate troops.

Daniel Hauer a brother of Nicholas emigrated in 1770 also from Diedendorf which is near Sarre-Union. Daniel (1748-1883) and wife Catharine (c. 1749-1834) had children: Nicholas (b. 1771), Magdalena (1775) and Anna Margaret (1785).

New England poet Whittier, who never visited Frederick, heard about the clustered spires of Frederick from author and philosopher Dr. Oliver Wendell Holmes who passed through Frederick enroute to Antietam battlefield looking in vain for his wounded son who later became Supreme Court Justice Oliver Wendell Holmes. The latter meanwhile was recovering in Hagerstown at the home of Howard Kennedy and wife Frances (Howell). See MHM 33, 109 (1938). Also CES in *Frederick News* June 13, 1991.

For the raid of Jeb Stuart in Western Maryland in June 1863 see George C. Keidel, MHM 34, 161 (1939). When the Baltimore and Ohio Railroad was occupied by the Confederates on June 29, rail traffic between Frederick and Baltimore was halted. Meanwhile, Stuart's cavalry was not at Gettysburg when needed by Lee's Confederates.

W&M-379. McKinsey omits the story of the lost Confederate command of Gen. Lee which was found before the Battles of South Mt. and Antietam. See the *Civil War, Vol. I* by Shelby Foote, page 670 (Random House) (N.Y.C. 1958). On the Best farm south of Frederick, Private B. W. Mitchell noticed in the grass on a former Confederate camp site an envelope containing three cigars wrapped in a sheet of official looking paper. The latter had a heading "Headquarters, Army of Northern Va., Special Order 1912". Plans with names of leaders and places followed and at the bottom was written "By command of General R. E. Lee, R.H. Chilton, Assistant Adjutant General". When Gen. McClellan saw this at first he thought it was a hoax, too good to be true. But a union officer who knew Chilton identified his handwriting. Thus McClellan learned that Lee planned to divide his army, sending Stonewall Jackson's troops to take Harpers Ferry. McClellan unwisely did not keep this knowledge secret, but declared to associates "Here is a paper with which, if I cannot whip Bobby Lee, I will be willing to go home".

Shelby Foote said the obvious thing for McClellan to do was to attack the half of the Confederate force around Boonsboro at once. Instead he delayed, allowing Jackson time to join in the battle of Antietam. One of the possible reasons for his delay was the enthusiastic reception of the Union Army by Frederick citizens with food and drink for the weary marchers. McClellan wrote to his wife that he was nearly overwhelmed and pulled to pieces by the greeting crowds at Frederick. He enclosed a little flag which an enthusiastic lady had thrust into the bridle of his horse.

W&M-380. McKinsey gives very little about the Battle of South Mountain on July 14, 1861 on the western edge of Frederick County from Crampton's Gap to Turner's Gap. Later the fighting around Fox's Gap on the Sharpsburg Road was especially fierce and bloody between Union General Jesse Lee Reno's 9th. Corps and the Confederate Division of General D. H. Hill. At its worst the fighting was hand-to-hand combat with clubbed rifles and bayonets. The Confederates withdrew after nightfall leaving their dead and dying. The next morning to clear the road near the summit the dead were thrown to the roadside in some cases piled higher than the stone fences. A monument marks where Gen. Reno was killed.

The horrible and gruesome aspects of the South Mt. Battles of Americans killing Americans were vividly told by Steven R. Stotelmyer in the *Blue and Grey* magazine of October, 1990. The regimental history of the 21st. Massachusetts Corps initiated the story that on the next day Daniel Wise who lived in the battle area was paid a dollar each for disposing of 58 Confederate bodies which he packed down his unused well. Stotelmyer found an earlier first hand report that on July 16 the odor of the Confederate bodies had become so offensive that the workers could only endure it by being half drunk. They filled a 60 foot well with bodies. Twelve years later, Henry C. Mumma of Sharpsburg, was paid $1.65 per head for removing the remains from the Wise well and burying them in Hagerstown's Confederate Cemetery with an inscription reading "29 boxes, 58 bodies unknown".

The Battle of South Mt. has been described also by John M. Priest in a book *Before Antietam, The Battle for South Mt.* (Shippensburg, Pennsylvania 1992), by Warren W. Hassler Jr. in MHM 52, 39 (1937) and by D. H. Strother in

Harpers Magazine 36, 275 (1868). McKinsey says about the Battle of South Mt. that "it was a terrific and splendid battle", thus following the post-Civil War fashion of glorification of battle and turning aside from the revolting horrors of war. It was at Turner's Gap on Old Route 40 that the Iron Brigade of soldiers from Michigan and Indiana received its name from McClellan.

W&M-382. Raids into western Maryland of the Confederate Cavalry of colorful Jeb Stuart have been reported by George C. Keidel in MHM 34, 161 (1939) and in the book Jeb Stuart by Burke Davis (Rinehart N.Y.C. 1957). Memorable was a Confederate ball on a moonlit night in an academy building at Urbana with music by the band of the 18th Mississippi Infantry. Decorations and other arrangements were made for Stuart by Prussian Major Heros von Borcke.

W&M-383. In his book of 1976, *Roads to Gettysburg*, Rev. John W. Schildt collected the many references of Union troops passing through Frederick County enroute to the battlefields of Gettysburg. After marching from near Fredericksburg, Va., they crossed the Potomac during three days on double pontoon bridges at Edwards Ferry south of Barnesville. Because it was expected that Lee's Confederates would attack through mountain passes in western Frederick County, some of the first union units were marched to Jefferson and Middletown before they trudged toward Gettysburg.

On Sunday evening June 28, 1863, the Union First, Fifth, Eleventh and Twelfth Corps were in and about Frederick. the Second Corps was south of Frederick while the Sixth was at Hyattstown and the Third Corps was near Woodsboro. At an early hour on that day near Prospect Hill, Gen. George Gordon Meade was awakened to learn that Lincoln had transferred supreme command to him from Gen Joe Hooker. Meade protested that Lincoln should have named Gen. John Reynolds. A Confederate spy named Harrison set off from Frederick at once with his news and positions of the Union Corps. This information supplied to Gen. Lee at Chambersburg led him to change his objective from Harrisburg to Gettysburg.

Author Schildt who grew up near Walkersville, has included many examples of cordial relations between the anti-slavery people in Frederick County and union troops. Unfortunately, some of his background history includes errors from Scharf and from W&M.

More about circumstances of Frederick's ransom payment of $200,000 to invading Confederates and about the Battle of Monocacy are given by Benjamin F. Cooling in the book *Jubal Early's Raid on Washington: 1864* (Baltimore 1989). Early made his temporary headquarters in the home of Dr. Richard Hammond at Second and Market St. Frederick's Mayor William G. Cole and City aldermen asked Gen. Early to reconsider the demand of $200,000, citing Hagerstown's ransom of only $20,000 to prevent burning the city. From its 8,000 citizens Frederick's annual tax revenue of only $8,000 was being received. However, by early afternoon of July 9, Frederick officials yielded. Banks as follows supplied the cash "as a loan to the city":

Frederickstown Savings Institution	$64,000
Central Bank	44,000
Frederick County Bank	33,000
Franklin Savings Bank	31,000

Farmers and Mechanics Bank 28,000

The baskets of greenbacks were hauled away by Confederate Quartermaster Maj. J. R. Braithwaite who with fellow officers celebrated by a victory meal with champagne and ice cream (while the Battle of Monocacy was in progress).

Efforts of Frederick to be reimbursed by the U. S. Government over the years have not been successful. By 1951, the debt with interest amounted to $600,000. In 1902, a booklet of 20 pages entitled The Appeal of Frederick City, Maryland to the Congress of the United States for Payment of Its Claim, etc. was prepared by Edward Y. Goldsborough. It consisted in large part of testimony by citizens who had been on the scene that as a result of payment, Early's army did not molest valuable government supplies remaining in storage in Frederick warehouses and ten or more hospitals were not disturbed. The booklet was reprinted recently by the Historical Society of Frederick County. Recently, Senator Charles Mathias gained approval of the Senate for payment to Frederick but it failed in the House of Representatives.

On the 100th anniversary of the Battle of Monocacy on July 9, 1964 a Maryland Civil War Marker, a bronze tablet, was dedicated on the field near Frederick Junction (Monocacy Junction). The Master of Ceremonies was Judge Edward S. Delaplaine. The program of the celebration stated that at first the Confederate attack north of Baltimore Road (near Jug Bridge) was repulsed by Union troops of Gen. Lew Wallace. However, Confederate Cavalry forded the Monocacy River near the Georgetown Pike and attacked the Union's left flank. The Union fell back outnumbered about 3 to 1 by Early's troops. About 2,900 men were killed, wounded or captured in the battle that saved Washington by delaying Early's march by a day while Union reinforcements reached Washington.

A portion of the Monocacy Battlefield near Araby was dedicated on July 13, 1991 as the Monocacy National Battlefield of the National Park Service (U. S. Dept. of Interior). A talk on the battle was given by Dr. B. Franklin Cooling, Historian of the Dept. of Energy. Invocation and benediction were given by Rev. John Schildt.

The Best farm owned by 12 descendants of Charles B. Trail, where part of the Battle of Monocacy was fought and where the "Lost Command" was discovered before the Battle of Antietam, was to be sold to the National Park Service. (*Gettysburg Times*, May 19, 1993).

Gen. Grant at Araby: An incident of the Civil War omitted in W&M and poorly reported by Scharf was the Council of War Between Gen. U. S. Grant, Gen. Philip H. Sheridan, Gen. David Hunter and others at the home of C. K. Thomas (1817-1889) of Araby southeast of Frederick. Grant arrived on August 5, 1864 nearly a month after the Battle of Monocacy. He came from his headquarters at City Point, VA, directly by railroad to Monocacy Junction south of Frederick without stopping at Washington.

When Confederate General Jubal Early returned to Virginia after the Battle of Monocacy, he remained in nearby Shenandoah Valley where food supplies were available and he could make raids again into Maryland. Grant was dissatisfied with the performance of General Hunter in keeping in touch and in opposing activities of Early. Hunter had brought his army to the Monocacy Junction area by the B & O Railroad. Grant called General Sheridan to come at once to Araby to take over command from Hunter. Grant stayed overnight with the Thomas family and on August 6 the council met in a room over the Thomas library.

Glenn H. Worthington in the book *Fighting for Time*, describes the meeting of Grant, Sheridan, Hunter, Horatio G. Wright, George Crook and several other Union Major Generals. To Grant's questions, Gen. David Hunter admitted that he did not know where Early's army was located, blaming his confusion on perplexing orders he had been receiving from Washington. Grant and Sheridan then planned a campaign in Shenandoah Valley which became successful. According to Edward J. Stackpole in the book *Sheridan in the Shenandoah* (Harrisburg, 1961) Hunter had placed his troops along the lower Monocacy River to protect Washington.

At breakfast the Thomas daughter Virginia aged 5 or 6 was asked by General Grant whether her parents were Rebels or Yankees. Her reply was satisfying to all, that her mamma was a Rebel but her papa was a Rebel to Rebels and a Yankee when Yankees were present. Grant laughed at the frank reply. Virginia's mother was Evelyn V. (1819-1899).

For Frederick County men who served as officers in the Union and Confederate Forces see (D).

W&M-402. Catoctin Furnace land was patented to Benedict Leonard Calvert and Thomas Johnson. For history of Catoctin Furnace see the book *Faith in the Furnace* by Elizabeth Y. Anderson (1984).

W&M-403. General James C. Clarke, railroad leader, attended school in Point of Rocks. Clarke Place in Frederick was named for him.

W&M-404. For a biography of George Alfred Townsend (b. 1841) of Gapland or Gathland see NC, Vol. 3.

W&M-404. Middletown Valley does not contain limestone and limestone soil. This valley with more acidic silica soil grows better cabbage than Monocacy Valley with limestone soil as noted by Engelbrecht.

W&M-405. With poetic admiration of Frederick County expressed here I hesitate to point out that White Rock is not a large boulder arising from the summit of Catoctin Mountain. It is an exposure of quartz formed from oldest seas. The mountain tops are more often of Catoctin Greenstone from ancient volcanoes.

W&M-406. There were no German settlers in Frederick County in 1710-1712. The first records of Europeans in the area around 1720 were non-Germans such as Anderson, Steelman, Nelson, Friend and Stoddard. The 1710 date may be based on false statements or misunderstanding of I. D. Rupp in the book *30,000 Immigrants* (1875). German settlers had reached the Conestoga area of Lancaster County, Pennsylvania soon after 1710 but did not reach the area of present-day Frederick County until later.

No records of churches as early as 1730-1732 have been found. First in 1743 are the records of the Monocacy Lutheran and Reformed Congregations.

The Monocacy Log Church was not near Creagerstown. See W&M-3.

The Thomas Schley party arrived no earlier than 1745. The immigrants settled on lands bought from Daniel Dulany, the Elder. See W&M-1.

W&M-407. Naturalization records show that Reformers worshipped at Monocacy Church by 1743. The Reformed congregation had built a church at Frederick by 1747. The Quaker congregation near Buckeystown began earlier, about 1725. An Episcopal Church was completed in Frederick after 1750.

W&M-408. Daniel Dulany, the Elder laid out Frederick. Rev. Theodore Frankenfeld was the first resident Reformed Pastor (See Glatfelter). The churches and other major buildings of Frederick City have been studied in history and detail in a thesis for the Degree Master of Arts by Diane Shaw Wasch at Smith College in 1982. Her title is *City Buildings in Frederick, Maryland* (FH). She found that the Roman Catholic Church of 1837 included features from Rome and from St. Louis, Mo.

W&M-410. Rev. Runkel was born in Ober Engelheim not far from Mainz, Germany.

W&M-420. Note that Prof. Luther Kuhlman's account of local Lutheran history is more accurate than those of some other Lutheran pastors.

W&M-421. Pastor Jacob Goering (1755-1807) born in York County was pastor at Hagerstown and Middletown (1791). Rev. Bernard Michael Hausihl (Houseal) (1727-1794) born at Heilbronn, Germany was pastor at Frederick and Antietam. As a Tory, he later became an Episcopal pastor in Halifax, Nova Scotia.

W&M-427. All Saints Parish (1742-1908) must not imply a church building that early. A fund of 100 pounds to complete a church building became available in 1750.

W&M-434. For the Episcopal graveyard on East All Saints St. and prominent leaders buried there, see Holdcraft Vol. I, page 22.

W&M-443. The father of Charles Carroll of Carrollton was Charles Carroll of Annapolis not Daniel Carroll. The land acquired by Daniel, et al, was near later Emmitsburg. John Cary printer from Philadelphia started a Catholic school in his print shop on North Market St., Frederick about 1756. Early Jesuit priests included Fathers John Williams 1765, James Walton, also James Framback and James Pellentz of Conewago Chapel. Father John Dubois served 1792-1806 and Father Frances Maleve, 1811-1822. The latter from Russia was the first priest recorded on Carroll's Manor. The earliest Catholic settlement in Frederick County was led by Elder and Livers families near Mt. St. Marys beginning about 1734. See W&M-324.

W&M-445 (top): McTavishes.

W&M-448. There is no basis for the statement "Somewhere about this time a band of several hundred Tories, Hessians and Indian adherents of the British cause had been publicly hanged here". Four men were executed brutally as recorded in W&M-96. For the Catholic Cemetery of Frederick at Third and East St. and prominent leaders buried there see Holdcraft Vol. I page 22.

W&M-453. United Brethren and Methodist Churches have become the United Methodist Church. Rev. Philipp Wilhelm Otterbein (1726-1813) was born at Dillenburg, south of Marburg, Germany. He served the Reformed Congregation in Frederick and later was a leader in founding the United Brethren Church. See Glatfelter.

W&M-455. Jacob Weller BS (blacksmith), a founder of the United Brethren Church of Mechanicstown (later Thurmont) was a grandson of emigrant Jacob Weller (from Westphalia and Berks County, Pennsylvania) who became the first Moravian leader. See M&C-II.

The Lineage of Harbaughs near the end of the page follows: Jost Herbach (d. 1792), emigrant from Germany in 1736, had a grandson George (1774-1853) who married Anne Snyder (1779-1837). They were parents of Rev. Henry Harbaugh (1817-1867), the author. Jost, Jr. (1741-1832) had no son Daniel. Jost's son Leonard Harbaugh (1749-1822), the noted builder of Baltimore, and wife Rebecca (Reinbeck) did have a son Daniel. See W&M-995.

W&M-457. Rev. Robert Strawbridge from County Leitrim, Ireland, settled near Sam's Creek in later Carroll County by 1766. See *The Story of American Methodism* by Frederick A. Norwood, Nashville TN. (1974) (GS).

W&M-459. Schwarzenau village is near Berleburg, northwest of Marburg, Germany.

W&M-460. Bishop Daniel Leatherman came to upper Middletown Valley about 1756 from Little Conewago Settlement near later Hanover, Pennsylvania. The Dunkards (later Church of the Brethren) were active in Frederick County as early as 1748 (M&C-I-170). (Cf *Brethren Encyclopedia* edited by Donald Durnbaugh (1983) (GS). Bottom of page: Jacob Danner.

W&M-466. Tom's Creek Lutheran Church was in the Tom's Creek area south east of Emmitsburg but not on the banks of the stream.

Union Chapel near Mt. Pleasant and Daysville was used originally by Dunkards. Numerous early Albaughs are buried there.

W&M-475. A communion set of pewter inscribed 1747 was found at the Glade Schoolhouse and is believed to have been used at the Glade Reformed Church near Walkersville and perhaps at the earlier Union Monocacy Log Church south of Thurmont. It is displayed at the Schaff Library of the UCC Theology Seminary at Lancaster.

W&M-476. The early more direct successors to the Monocacy Congregations were the Apples Union Church, the Glade Valley Reformed Church and the Lutheran Church at Frederick. The later Lutheran Church at Creagerstown has falsified its history to make it appear that they are the direct and only successor to the church in German Monocacy Settlement. Pages 477 to 478 are too full of untruths for correction. For example, Rev. John Casper Stover emigrated with his father Rev. J. C. S. Sr. as stated on page 480. The church at Creagerstown was not built until about 1790. Before that, Lutherans worshipped at Monocacy, Apples and Frederick.

W&M-479. Bottom: In 1747 Muhlenberg preached in the new German Reformed Church in Frederick. The Lutherans had no suitable church for his use.

W&M-480. There is no support for the location of Monocacy Church near Creagerstown. It was south of Thurmont (see W&M-3). Rev. Valentine Kraft; Rev. Bernard Hausihl.

W&M-482. Bethel Church. German settlers did not fill up the Monocacy Valley. English speaking settlers, usually owning slaves, were especially numerous east of Monocacy River and south of Frederick.

W&M-486. The Union Church at Toms Creek was begun closer to 1758. This is a rare case of Lutherans not claiming the earliest possible founding date. Rev. John George Bager (Baugher) was first pastor. Rev. Jacob Weimer (1724-1790) emigrated in 1751 from Hunspach in northern Alsace (B3).

W&M-478. Middle of right column: Daniel Swomley.

W&M-490. St. Mark's Episcopal Church is at Petersville in southern Middletown Valley.

W&M-494 bottom. This refers again to the Monocacy log church which was near the German Monocacy Road which did indeed run from Double Pipe Creek (later called Detour) to Lewistown. The church was not on the west bank of Monocacy River, but near upper Hunting Creek which lay far west of Monocacy River. See on map on cover of M&C-I. The location east of Monocacy on the road to Woodsboro advocated by Rev. George A. Whitmore is incorrect. The false stone monument remains in a nearby front yard.

The home of Jacob Weller where first Moravian services were held is about 1/4 mile north of the Monocacy Church site. The Jacob Weller farm with the first Moravian graveyard became the Firor farm and now belongs to George Moser on Moser Road south of Thurmont. Near the Moser barn is the one remaining gravestone from the Weller Moravian graveyard that of Johannes Henge (John Hankey). See Hankey in W&M-810.

W&M-495. Herrnhut is in Saxony, eastern middle Germany.

Contrary to the common mistake of column 2, Daniel Dulany the Younger was neutral in the revolution and his property was not confiscated.

W&M-496. Notice that the Lutheran and Reformed Churches of Church Hill on Ballenger Creek Road were built near where the Moravian Meeting House was built in 1768. After most Moravians on the Manor had moved to North Carolina. the Moravian church there was abandoned. See booklet *Moravian Families of Carroll's Manor* by George E. Russell (Middletown, 1989). A Reformed and Lutheran Church was built on the site.

W&M-497. Note that the Brethren Congregations met in homes for many years before they built meeting houses such as those of Pleasant View and Grossnickle's in Middletown Valley.

W&M-498. Right Column: Rev. Father Francis Maleve was a native of Russia.

The first Swedish Lutherans in America settled near Wilmington, Delaware, where Gloria Dei Church was built about 1698 with support from Hans Steelman. See M&C-I.

There was no settlement at Jerusalem near Myersville as early as 1711 as claimed here and as marked on a monument still at Jerusalem Cemetery. Jerusalem Church served Lutherans briefly in the 1780's before St. John's Lutheran Church was built at nearby Church Hill. Later a Lutheran church was built in Myersville.

Augustine Herman did not make a boundary between Maryland and Pennsylvania.

Among the false claims here is one correct statement, that Monocacy Settlement was near Catoctin Furnace (called Johnson's Furnace at that time).

W&M-500. The true date of building the Jerusalem Church is revealed by the deed of 1786 from Philip Rodenpiller. When I visited St. Johns Church with my father Calvin Ezra S. about 1925, a few old people claimed to recall the Jerusalem Lutheran Church.

The first Lutheran settlement in the upper valley was not at Jerusalem but around Middletown with the first Lutheran Church on what later became the Ahalt farm southwest of Middletown. A few gravestones mark the church site.

Millard Rice pointed out that Scharf and W&M are wrong in stating that Smithfield, the earlier name for Middletown, was from the smithshop of Frederick Lauber. It was named for Richard Smith who was in court records of 1749 to 1755 as keeper of Middletown Valley roads. He operated a tavern on the "Great Road to Conococheague".

W&M-501. For the early Lutheran Pastor in Middletown Valley, John Valentine Nicodemus, see Glatfelter.

St. Johns Lutheran Church at Church Hill built about 1790 has a remarkable cemetery second only in interest to that of Apples Church north of Thurmont. The gravestone of Mrs. Hehl (1763-1792) wife of the pastor, has one of the finest examples of German folk art in Frederick County, a geometric styled lily.

W&M-501. Pastor Abraham Reck, Jr. (1791-1869) who served St. John's Lutheran Church at Church Hill north of Myersville 1829-1836 had an interesting career. He was a grandson of Christian Sr. born in Germany (before 1754-1791). His parents Abraham and wife Margaret lived near Littlestown, Pennsylvania. Abraham, Jr. was in the catechetical class of Rev. John Grubb of Taneytown. He studied theology with Rev. F. V. Melsheimer of Hanover and was licensed to preach by the Lutheran Church in 1812. He succeeded Rev. Christian Street at Winchester, Virginia. His revival methods in evangelism encountered opposition and attempts were made to murder him. (See Evangelical Review, July 1870 (GC)). He was also accused of being a Methodist fanatic. When Rev. Reck came to the Middletown and Myersville congregations in 1829, he could preach in both German and English. He guided the early career of Rev. Ezra Keller who founded Wittenberg College (M&C-I).

Pastor Reck preached at Indianapolis, IN (1836-1841) and later in Ohio at Cincinnati and Germantown. In 1820 he married Louisa Motter of

Shepherdstown, WV. In 1870 his widow was still living and eight of their 11 children. He is buried at Lancaster, Ohio. Rev. Reck has been credited with founding Gettysburg village in Darke County, Ohio. The Reck family has been studied by Ted Houk of Seattle, WA. (1976), by Paul A. Reck, Sarasota, FL (1975), by Nancy Morrison of Historical Society of California and by Mrs. Nancy Walz of Carmel, IN. The latter has given information on children of Abraham and Louisa in files of CES.

W&M-503. St. Luke's Lutheran Church is at Feagaville between Frederick and Jefferson. Mt. Zion Lutheran Church is about a mile northeast of Feagaville.

W&M-507. Woman's College, later Hood College, history is given in a booklet *Hood College Through the Years (1893-1968)* and in *A History of the Joseph Henry Apple Library, Hood College (1893-1965)* by Mary F. S. Drye (Washington D.C. 1969). In 1892 when the Potomac Synod of the Reformed Church decided to discontinue Mercersburg College it established a men's college, Franklin and Marshall at Lancaster, Pennsylvania, and resolved to found a college for women south of the Mason and Dixon Line. Properties were offered at Manchester and Westminster, Maryland, at Lexington, Virginia and at Martinsburg, West Virginia. However, only at Frederick was the possibility of taking over an existing educational institution with buildings.

Professor Hiram Winchester had begun his school, the Frederick Female Seminary in a rented building on North Market Street which had been occupied by the Bartgis Hotel. In 1843, the cornerstone was laid of East Hall on East Church Street. Winchester Hall consisting of two brick, three-story buildings joined by a two-story passage-way was built in 1843-1844 financed by a lottery for the Frederick Female Seminary of Professor Winchester chartered in 1840. The Greek Revival styled buildings have six impressive Ionic Columns.

In 1865, Rev. Thomas became principal until 1873 and was followed until 1885 by professor and Mrs. Hackleton. Dr. William Purnell began as principal of the school in 1885 but financial difficulties developed between him and the trustees so that in 1893 he resigned and the trustees of the Frederick Female Seminary offered to lease the ground, buildings and equipment to the Potomac Synod of the Reformed Church to establish a college for women. Later the Potomac Synod was joined by the Pittsburgh Synod.

Professor Joseph H. Apple was president of Woman's College beginning in 1893 and served for 41 years. See W&M-1000 and 40th Anniversary booklet (FH). Beginning in 1897, Mrs. Margaret E. (Scholl) Hood (1833-1913) made substantial gifts to the college in memory of her husband John Mifflin Hood (1821-1894). Prof. Apple had first met Margaret when he was a student at F and M and she founded the Daniel Scholl Astronomical observatory on the campus at Lancaster. For an account of the Scholl family of Margaret Hood see M&C-I. In 1913 the name of the college was made Hood College. New buildings were erected on Scheutzen-Groff Park on the northwest edge of Frederick where the college moved in 1915. A news article stated that the college could be reached from town by trolley (7 cents) or by taxi (20 cents). (FH). Renovated Brodbeck Hall was the first building utilized. Bequests of Mrs. Hood in detail are shown in an article in the *Frederick News* in 1913 (FH).

Prof. Apple, was succeeded as president in July 1934 by Dr. Henry Irvin Stahr who had been on the Board of Christian Education of the Reformed Church. During his tenure, Hood College received recognition by the Association of American Universities. In July 1948, Dr. Andrew Gehr Truxal became president, coming from the Department of Sociology of Dartmouth College. In July 1961 Dr. Randle Elliott began ten years as president, resigning in May 1971.

Since 1975, the president of Hood College has been Dr. Martha E. Church, a geographer and experienced educational administrator, also an international mountain climber and photographer. Her degrees include Wellesley College AB, University of Pittsburgh, MA, University of Chicago PhD. and many honorary degrees. Dr. Church has served on Boards of the National Geographical Society and Carnegie Foundation and has been Chairwoman of the American Association for Higher Education. Before coming to Hood, Dr. Church served from 1965-1971 as Dean and Professor of Geography at Wilson College, Chambersburg, Pennsylvania Among major advances at Hood College during the Presidency of Dr. Church have been new graduate study programs and the new library dedicated in 1992. A special supplement of the Frederick News on February 28, 1986 celebrated the selection of Hood College as first in the group of 74 small Eastern colleges surveyed by U. S. News and World Report. (FH). In 1993, Hood celebrated 100 years as one of the most successful enterprises of Frederick.

W&M-511. Saint Elizabeth Ann Seton. The following additions to the account of her life came largely from the book *Elizabeth Bayley Seton* by Annabelle M. Melville (1951) and from *Notable American Women* edited by Edward T. James et al, (Harvard Univ. Press, Cambridge MA., 1971).

Elizabeth Ann was born August 28, 1774 to Dr. Richard Bayley M.D. and first wife Catherine (Charlton). Dr. Bayley was a pioneer in the study of diphtheria and in surgery. He lectured at Columbia College in New York City and is said to have been the city's first health officer. His father emigrated from Hoddeston, Hertfordshire, England. Dr. Bayley's mother was Susanne Le Compte of New Rochelle, N.Y. of French Huguenot lineage. Elizabeth Anne's maternal grandfather was Rev. Richard Charlton an emigrant from Ireland to Staten Island.

In 1794, at age 20, Elizabeth Ann married the young New York merchant William Magee Seton of Anglo-Scottish origin. They had children born as follows: Anna Maria 1795; William 1796; Richard 1798; Catherine Josephine 1800; Rebecca 1802. They were members of an Episcopal Church in New York City. In 1800 William's importing business became bankrupt resulting from an undeclared war between France and the U. S.

In 1803 with her sick husband and her oldest daughter, Elizabeth Ann sailed to Italy hoping for improvement in her husband's health. He died in Pisa on December 27, 1803. She was befriended by her husband's former business associates Antonio and Filippo Filicchi and their wives of Leghorn, Italy, who introduced her to the teachings of the Roman Catholic Church. Elizabeth Ann Seton became Catholic on March 14, 1805 and was confirmed by Archbishop John Carroll of Baltimore in 1806. She attempted to establish a school for girls in New York City without success. Rev. William Valentine Dubourg, President of St. Mary's College in Baltimore, invited her to open a boarding school for girls near the college. However, at Baltimore, she was persuaded by Samuel Sutherland Cooper, a wealthy Philadelphia convert studying for the priesthood, that she should establish a school in Emmitsburg instead. Her husband's sisters, Cecilia and Harriet Seton, also converts to the Catholic faith, joined her in the venture at Emmitsburg where they served for the rest of their lives. The group which arrived at Emmitsburg on June 21, 1809 included Elizabeth's children and two pupils. The site for the school was provided by Rev. Cooper.

The progress of Mother Seton with her school and her organization The Sisters of Charity is well described in W&M-513-518. Before her death from tuberculosis on January 4, 1821, branches of the Sisters of Charity had been established in Philadelphia in 1814 and in New York City in 1817. Capable followers carried her work forward. Her grandson, Rev. Robert Seton (1839-1927), became an Archbishop.

Melville gives the following steps in Mother Seton's attaining Sainthood. In 1907, an Ecclesiastical Court of Investigation was formed. Twelve volumes of her writings were sent to Rome in 1914 for examination which was completed January 15, 1936. A Decree of the Congregation of Rites formally introduced her cause on February 28, 1940. Her virtues were declared heroic and the title "Venerable" was bestowed in 1959. The remains of Elizabeth Ann then were removed from the community graveyard and placed at the altar of St. Joseph's Central House at Emmitsburg. On March 17, 1963 she was Beatified and the title "Blessed" conferred. On September 14, 1975, by Pope Paul VI, she was canonized as Saint Elizabeth Ann, the first native-born American to be canonized.

W&M-521. Mt. St. Mary College and its early history receive much less space in W&M than Mt. St. Joseph's. John DuBois (1764-1842) was born in Paris. After graduating from the College, Louis-le-Grand, he studied at the theological Seminary of St. Magloire in Paris and was ordained to the priesthood on September 22, 1787. He served in Paris as assistant curate of St. Sulpice and as chaplain to a community of Sisters of Charity of St. Vincent dePaul until his work was interrupted by the French Revolution. In May 1791, Rev. John Du Bois made his escape from France, arriving in Norfolk, VA in August 1791, with letters of introduction from Lafayette to prominent Virginians. For a time, he was a house guest of James Monroe. He was allowed to celebrate Mass in the State House at Richmond.

Rev. Du Bois became an American citizen and was assigned missionary work by Bishop John Carroll of Baltimore. He built the first Catholic Church in Frederick, MD, and used it as a base for missionary travels in Maryland, Virginia, and Pennsylvania. In 1807, he established a preparatory seminary at Emmitsburg. In 1808 he joined the Society of St. Sulpice and affiliated the Society with his log college which became Mt. St. Marys College and Seminary. In the first years when the college consisted of a single log building, Rev. Du Bois served as President, Treasurer and Professor. The year 1824, brought major difficulties to the college. A disastrous fire destroyed a building which had just been completed. In that year, the college separated from the Sulpician leaders of Baltimore who desired to reduce the college to its original function as a minor seminary. Meanwhile, Father Du Bois had assisted Elizabeth Seton (later Saint Elizabeth Ann) in founding her first convent of Sisters of Charity in 1809.

In 1828, Father Du Bois left Emmitsburg to become Bishop of the Diocese of NY and to live on Manhattan. In the latter part of his service there he was assisted by his former student at Emmitsburg, Father John Hughes. Bishop Du Bois traveled in Europe in 1829 and retired in 1839. He died December 20, 1842 and was buried at Old St. Patrick's Cathedral in New York.

After Father Du Bois left Emmitsburg the college was led briefly by Father Simon Gabriel Bruté who had been a scientist and physician in Paris. He laid out the hillside gardens of the Grotto which continue today. In 1834 he left to be Bishop of Vincennes, IN (New Catholic Encyclopedia (N.Y.C., 1967) and Who Was Who).

Patrick and Margaret (McKenna) Hughes of the village of Annaloghan in County Tyrone, Ireland had 7 children of whom two born before they settled at Chambersburg, Pennsylvania, became prominent leaders of the Catholic Church at New York City. Ellen Hughes (1806-1866) attended St. Joseph's College at Emmitsburg and entered the Sisters of Charity in 1825. In 1849 she founded New York City's Catholic Mission and first Catholic Hospital, St. Vincents, of which she served as Superior. Surprisingly, Ellen Hughes is buried in the Catholic Cemetery at Frederick (dates below ground).

Bishop John Joseph Hughes (1797-1864) the third of the children of Patrick and Margaret, was born on a small farm in County Tyrone. In 1816, Patrick and an older son had emigrated and in 1818 the rest of the family followed to Chambersburg. There John worked in quarries, repairing roads and as a gardener. Several of his applications for admission to Mt. St. Mary's Seminary were not successful because there was no more room. However, Rev. Du Bois offered to take him as a gardener until a vacancy occurred. In 1820, Rev. John Hughes was ordained in St. Joseph's Church, Philadelphia. Publication of his controversial sermons and writings where Anti-Catholicism was strong in Philadelphia and elsewhere brought him national attention.

Father John Hughes was consecrated Bishop of New York City and State in 1838. Bishop Hughes went to Europe in 1839 seeking aid in Paris, Rome, Munich, Vienna and Dublin. On his return he engaged in his greatest contest over the question of religion and the public schools. He became Archbishop of New York in 1850.

In 1861-1862, Archbishop Hughes undertook a trip to Europe in support of the Union at the request of President Lincoln and Secretary Seward. Lincoln's government recommended Hughes to the Pope as a Cardinal. In July 1863 Archbishop Hughes made his last public appearance at the request of Gov. Horatio Seymour of NY who was attempting to stop draft riots in New York City. He was succeeded by Archbishop John McCloskey (1810-1885) another graduate of Mt. St. Mary's College and Seminary. (New Catholic Encyclopedia, (N.Y.C. 1967)).

W&M-536 (2nd. column). Mr. Frew should be Abraham Faw (See M&C-589).

W&M-563. The contemporary early physicians in Frederick, Dr. Philip Thomas and Dr. Adam Fischer, must not be forgotten. *The Archives of Maryland,*

Volumes 12 and 16, show that during the Revolution the name of Fischer occurs more frequently representing the local Committee of Correspondence than that of Dr. Thomas. On November 25, 1776 the colleagues of Dr. Fischer on the Committee of Correspondence of the Middle District of Frederick County at Frederick were recorded as Baker Johnson, Christopher Edelin, John Adlum and Conrad Grosch. On January 10, 1777 Adam Fischer was appointed Surgeon of the Battalion of Militia led by Col. Charles Beatty.

Adam and Margaret Fischer lived in the first block of North Market St. Their deed is dated 1768. The Reformed Church at Frederick recorded the birth of Adam Fischer, Jr. on February 4, 1765. At the time of his death in 1785 Dr. Fischer was serving as Collector of Taxes of Frederick County. Widow Margaret, as executrix of the estate, was ordered in June 1788 to pay glassmaker John Frederick Amelung 500 pounds which had been granted by the Maryland Assembly in April.

W&M-563. McKinsey could have named several outstanding early physicians of Frederick who also were civic leaders. According to Scharf, in 1769 Dr. Philip Thomas was succeeded by Dr. John Fischer, and Dr. John N. A. Bogen. The latter was a German mercenary surgeon who had been confined to the Barrack. He married a daughter of Henry Koontz and located on West Patrick Street. John Fischer was the first grave inspector of Fredericktown, a member of the Revolutionary Committee of Observation and a member of the first Masonic Lodge organized in 1799. Dr. John Tyler (1763-1841) returned in 1786 from studies in Europe to practice surgery in Frederick. Dr. Tyler was a student of the great John Hunter in London. He also was an author of articles in the Maryland Chronicle and Universal Advertiser, a State Senator and member of the Committee to greet Lafayette in 1824.

W&M-585. For families of a number of the Frederick County physicians see index, also the following: Morris A. Birely (M&C-II); Goldsborough (M&C-I); C.N. Schildknecht (M&C-II); Fairfax Schley (Schley Genealogy by CES, 1993 at F and FH); James A. Shorb (NC).

W&M-597. The following lawyers and justices are in the records of the Frederick County Court who are not included on W&M-597. They first appeared in court records on the dates given:

Daniel Dulany, the Elder 1749	Thomas Beatty 1749
William Cummings 1749	Thomas Cresap 1749
Nathaniel Wickham Jr. 1749	Joseph Chapline 1749
Henry Munday 1749	George Gordon 1749
William Griffith 1749	Hugh Parker 1749
John Rawlins 1749	Dr. James Doull 1750
Capt. Thomas Prather 1749	Josiah Beall 1750
Nathan Magruder 1750	John Clagett 1750
Nathaniel Alexander 1750	Alexander Beall 1751
John Needham 1751	Henry Wright Crabb 1751
James Smith 1753	Joseph Wood 1753
Joseph Smith 1753	William Webb 1753
John Smith Prather 1754	David Lynn 1754
William Luckett 1758	Charles Jones 1754

Andrew Heugh 1758
Thomas Norris 1758
Thomas Price 1763
Kensey Gittings 1763
Evan Shelby 1763
Samuel Postlethwaite 1763
Enoch Innis 1764
Joseph Warford 1764
Thomas Stone 1765
Benjamin Nicholson 1765

Moses Chapline 1758
Peter Bainbridge 1758
Jacob Ducket 1758
James Dickson 1763
William Blair 1763
Samuel Chase 1763
Edmond Key 1764
William Paca 1764
Arthur Bordley 1765
Samuel Beall 1765

Early court records of Frederick County (1748-1765) have been abstracted in the book *This Was the Life* by Millard Milburn Rice, (Baltimore 1984).

Note that in this period Fredericktown was the county seat of all of Western Maryland extending from the limits of Baltimore and Prince Georges Counties westward. No Frederick County Court Records survive from March 1756 through March 1758 when Western Maryland settlements were disrupted by Indian attacks during and after the French and Indian War.

W&M-597. Thomas Stone, the Signer. The fame of Charles Carroll of Carrollton who never lived in Fredericktown has eclipsed that of a second Maryland Signer of the Declaration of Independence who lived in Frederick from 1764 until 1771, namely Thomas Stone (1743-1787). In August 1765 on the recommendation of Edmund Key, Esquire, he was admitted as a lawyer to practice before the Court of Frederick County. Thomas's father was David Stone (1709-1773) a landowner of Charles County (son of Thomas) (1677-1727) who married first Sarah or Mary Hanson (b. 1714) (daughter of Samuel (1685-1740)). Thomas' mother was Elizabeth (Jenifer) (d. by 1778) (daughter of Dr. Daniel (d. c1729) and Elizabeth M. R. J. T. (Whythill). Other relatives are given in *A Biographical Dictionary of the Maryland Legislature* (1635-1789) by Edward C. Papenfuse, et al (Johns Hopkins Univ. Press, 1985). Thomas Stone married Margaret Brown (1751-1787) daughter of Dr. Gustavus Brown (1689-1762) and second wife Margaret (Block) (of Frederick County). Dr. Brown emigrated from Scotland in 1708. Signer Thomas Stone and Margaret had a son Frederick, born in Frederick in 1768 who died in Princeton N.J. in 1793 of yellow fever. Their daughters were Margaret (1771-1809) who married Dr. John Moncure Daniel of Stafford County, VA and twin Mildred (1771-1836) who married Travers Daniel, Jr.

Thomas Stone was educated in a private school in Charles County and studied law under Thomas Johnson (1732-1819). He attained the status of Esquire in 1778. Stone was a leader in the State Conventions preceding the Revolution and in the State Assembly thereafter. He was elected to the Continental Congress 1774-1784 and to the Federal Convention that formed the Constitution.

After leaving Frederick lawyer Stone practiced at Port Tobacco and then bought a house in Annapolis in 1783. When his wife died suddenly in 1787, his physician recommended a sea voyage to cure him of despondency. He died in Alexandria while awaiting the ship.

W&M-614. The Peaks of Otter near Lynchburg, VA are not visible from Braddock Heights. High Knob of Gambrill Park is a better observation point from which one can see under best conditions the mountains at the beginning of the Skyline Drive near Front Royal, VA, also Signal Knob near Strasburg and the Bull Run Mountains southward.

W&M-623. The census of 1790 of Frederick County unfortunately is in no order and without separation into geographic districts (in contrast with the 1800 census). Some of the German family names recorded in 1790 are in hardly recognizable forms. A number of these listed below have genealogies in the Library of Congress and alternate spellings are given in the Directory of the Library of Congress (LC). For example 27 different spellings of Schmucker are listed. In the list below the first form of the name is that of the 1790 census which is followed by a later, more common local spelling:

Averhart, Everhart
Boalus, Bowlus
Bookey, Brookey
Cocklenberg, Kohlenberg
Coplintz, Coblentz
Craybill, Grable
Culsell, Cutsail
Delander, Delauter
Devendall, Diffendahl
Dull, Doll
Feuerhacke, Fearhake
Fisor, Feiser
Fluke, Flook
Fundebaugh, Fundenberg
Harine, Horine
Heckathon, Heckathorn
Heldebright, Hildebridle
Holsoffle, Holtzapple
Kulp, Kolb
Lengenfelter, Lingenfelter
Licklider, Lichtleider
Lookenpeale, Luckingbill
McLocklin, McGlaughlin
Nexendurf, Nixdorff
Nuse, Nusz
Peckenbaugh, Beckenbaugh
Pettinger, Pittinger
Romer, Roemer, Raymer
Roar, Rohrer
Routsong, Routzahn
Simmerman, Zimmerman
Sommers, Summers
Stonecypher, Stonesifer
Titlo, Ditlo
Tuttero, Dutrow
Upcraft, Updegraff
Vesterbaker, Wertenbaker
Wilyard, Willard

Bizer, Biser
Bontz, Bantz
Bumbgardner, Baumgardner
Colour, Culler
Coon, Kuhn
Creglo, Kregelo
Dahoof, Dayhoff etc.
Deloyder, Delauter
Dickenstreet, Dickensheets
Englebright, Engelbrecht
Fivecoat, Finefrock
Fralick, Fraley
Getsingtanner, Getzendanner
Hawn, Hahn
Heichew, Hiteshew
Holler, Haller
Ikenbread, Eigenbrodt
Kiefover, Kefauver
Koon, Kuhn
Lemmon, Lehman, Layman
Lescalute, Lescalleet
Lambrick, Lambrecht
Macelfish, McElfresh
Merring, Mehring
Nashbaum, Nusbaum
Osterday, Easterday
Pentz, Bentz
Prangle, Brengle
Ransburg, Ramsburg
Roop, Rupp
Shilkinack, Schildknecht
Snouk, Snook
Stimble, Stemple
Tarr, Darr, Derr
Tofler, Dofler
Uler, Uhler
Vanfenson, Van Fossen
Willer, Weller

        Woolhide, Wilhide   Winbegler, Winpigler
        Yengling, Yingling   Yesterday, Easterday

See M&C-II for a discussion of German family names.

W&M-648. Geology. The western Appalachian Regions in origin are later than most of the Piedmont. Especially west of the Cumberland Valley periods later than the Ordovician are represented. The oldest rocks in general are in the eastern Piedmont and in southern Middletown Valley. They are Pre-Cambrian, before life occurred. The limestones are Cambrian and Ordovician in age. The outstanding Monadnock of Frederick County is Sugar Loaf Mt. which is one of the few natural areas preserved locally. See CES in Frederick News and Post, June 18, 1992, with notes on its protectors Louise and Gordon Strong of Iowa and Chicago.

Schooley Mt. is not in Pennsylvania but near Long Valley in northern New Jersey.

W&M-649 and 652. The red sandstones and shales were formed in the Triassic Period about 200 million years ago. Dinosaur tracks were found in these rocks near Bridgeport on the Monocacy River east of Emmitsburg. In the late Triassic and early Jurassic Periods cracks miles long formed through which lava flowed usually cooling to solid rock beneath the surface.

After removal of much of the overlying red sandstone by erosion ridges of durable diabase remained, generally trending north-south in Frederick County. Diabase locally has been called trap rock, ironstone or "Gettysburg granite". Freshly broken surfaces of diabase are bluish grey to dark blue. On weathering it turns yellow and later dark brown. Besides ridges of diabase a few large masses (sills) occur such as Big Roundtop and Harper's Hill in the Pennsylvania part of Monocacy Watershed and smaller sills near Rocky Ridge.

W&M-652. The basic volcanic rock most abundant in our mountains is Catoctin Meta-basalt or Catoctin Greenstone. In contrast to diabase, basalts are very finely crystalline because of rapid cooling of surface lava of real volcanoes. Catoctin greenstone and white quartzite are the commonest rocks of Catoctin and South Mountain, also of hills in northern Middletown Valley. The acidic rocks are quartz and meta-rhyolite (blueish gray). Rhyolite has a similar chemical composition to granite, but has much finer crystals resulting from rapid cooling of lava erupted from true volcanoes. Our rhyolite is more correctly called meta-rhyolite since over many millions of years changes in crystallinity have occurred to make it exceeding strong and durable in spear points and other artifacts of prehistoric Americans (especially those of the Archaic Period 9,000 to 1,000 B.C.). The best meta-rhyolite for tools was from prehistoric quarries and pits of South Mountain in PA, but smaller deposits extend southward nearly to the Potomac. Catoctin Greenstone continues in the mountains of VA, but not meta-rhyolite. No local true flint was available so the meta-rhyolite was utilized by prehistoric Indians even at distances of several hundred miles. Rhyolite spear points often are incorrectly called arrowheads. Tiny triangular true arrowheads (after about 600 A.D.) are much less abundant.

W&M-653 (Top right column). The very deep rocks exposed in southern Middletown Valley no longer are called granite. These rocks, the oldest visible in Frederick County (except stony meteorites) are now called Grenville Schists.

They decompose to soil so fast that good specimens are hard to find. Parts of lower Catoctin Creek have few rocks showing. Great expanses of Grenville rocks occur from the Adirondacks to northern Quebec. Deep erosion along the Potomac has opened a window of these early rocks in Frederick and Loudon Counties. These basement formations were brought nearer to the earth's surface by the folding, which produced the ancient super mountain of which Catoctin Mountain and South Mountain are remnants.

In spite of many new theories such as plate tectonic processes, most of the book *The Physical Features of Carroll and Frederick Counties* by Anna J. and George N. Stose (Baltimore 1946) hold true today. Road building and city growth have exposed more geology. Limestone, lime, crushed stone and water are among geologic products. Local Calico, or Potomac Marble has had little further use as an ornamental material since the beautiful pillars which still can be seen in the U. S. Capitol. Differences in hardness of the different pieces in the conglomerate rock make it hard to polish. Pebbles may come loose during working or on weathering. The recent commercial development south of West Patrick St. extended has left some large attractive masses of calico rock in view.

Triassic Red sandstone ("Seneca Red Sandstone") has had little recent use in building but can be seen in old structures such as the first buildings of the Smithsonian Institution and old residences in Washington. Catoctin Mountain sandstone or quartzite is much more durable and attractive as in buildings of Mt. St. Mary's College.

After the formation of the red Triassic rock strata, with associated diabase lava, the Frederick County area was no longer under water and no more sedimentary or volcanic rocks formed. The predominant opinion of Maryland Geologists seems to be that glaciation of the Ice Ages did not reach as far south as our state. However, I believe that glacial conditions of the Wisconsin and/or earlier Illinois glaciations extended southward along the Appalachian Mountains. The huge worn quartzite boulders remaining near Yellow Springs suggest this. Thurmont is largely built on quartzite gravels which came down the mountain through nearby gaps.

W&M-656. The John Digges Road mentioned here ran through later Marston and Linwood in later Carroll County westward to the copper mine of John Digges. In 1748 assignments of road care the John Digges Road was said to cross the road from Frederick to York at Great Pipe Creek. The Digges copper mine has been misplaced in recent publications even over the Mason-Dixon Line in Pennsylvania. I and Prof. Basil L. Crapster of Gettysburg visited what we are certain is the correct site near where the road south of Middleburg crosses Little Pipe Creek, the county boundary. On the north side (Carroll County), upstream about 1/4 mile on the steep slope, are evidences of excavation and rocks showing blue azurite. Local residents confirmed that Maryland state geologists had studied the site. John Digges is said to have worked this so called mine as early as 1742. About 1750 English miners opened copper mines near Finksburg and between Johnsville and Liberty. In 1765, Stephen Richards and Dr. John Stevenson of Baltimore operated the Liberty mine with James Smith as manager. Ore from the Liberty mine was shipped to England before the Revolution. During the closing years of the Revolution, the Liberty mine was claimed to be the largest single producer of copper in North America. (C.M.

Abbott in William and Mary Quarterly, April 1970). Before the Civil War the mine near Liberty had been operated by Evan T. Ellicott and Isaac Tyson, Jr. (See W&M-276).

W&M-657. The definition of the Carroll County-Pennsylvania line begins with Rock Creek crossing the Mason-Dixon Line. There is no Rocky Creek in the area.

W&M-658. Mechanicsburg should read Mechanicstown which later became Thurmont. Eight lines later should be Sabillasville.

W&M-660. Maryland Troops in the French and Indian War 1757-1759. Note that there are a very few German family names such as Bumgardner, Grimes, Heinzman and Teater (Tieter).

ADDITIONS TO VOLUME II (BIOGRAPHICAL)

W&M-693. Judge James McSherry (1842-1907) and wife Clara Louise McAleer (b. c.1844) (d/o Hugh of Ireland and Harriet of Maryland) are buried in the Catholic Cemetery at Frederick.

Patrick McSherry (1725-1795) born in Lurgan County, Armagh, Ulster, Ireland, emigrated in 1750 with wife Catherine Gartland (1741-1813) of Armagh to later eastern Adams County, Pennsylvania. There are incomplete genealogies by Thomas C. McSherry and by Margaret Fitzgerald (G) (N) (WB). Patrick and Catherine lived near Littlestown and are buried at Conewago Chapel. He founded McSherrystown and was a leader of the Irish and German Catholic settlers.

Ann Ridgely (Sappington) wife of James McSherry lived 1794-1864. Author and historian, James McSherry (1819-1869) and wife Eliza (Spurrier) (1817-1883) are buried in Frederick Catholic Cemetery. In the census of 1800, the only Spurrier was Thomas in eastern Frederick County. He and wife between 26 and 45 years of age had two sons and 7 daughters. Many Spurriers have lived near Mt. Airy. See genealogy in (MS1359) and CES files.

W&M-696. Gen. Louis Victor Baughman (1845-1906) and wife Helen (Abell) (1856-1940) are buried in Frederick Catholic Cemetery. He was a son of John William (d. 1872) and Mary Louise Jane (Jamison)(d. 1917) both buried in the Catholic Cemetery of Frederick. John William, Jr. also buried there, lived 1846-1914. The family name is derived from Bachmann, a dweller near the brook, a name abundant in southwestern Germany and German Switzerland.

W&M-700. Admiral Winfield Scott Schley (1839-1911) was born on the farm Richfields north of Harmony Grove and Frederick on the west side of Monocacy River. In 1863 he married Ann Rebecca Franklin, daughter of George Edward and Maria Caroline (Johnson) of Annapolis. They are buried at Arlington Cemetery.

Children of W. S. and Ann Schley were Lt. Thomas Franklin (b. 1864), who married Lila Mercer Langhorne and served in U. S. Army; Maria Virginia (b. 1867) who married Hon. Ralph Montague Stuart Worthley of England and lived at Mt. Kisco NY in 1911; and Dr. Winfield Scott Schley Jr. (b. 1873) who practiced medicine in New York City.

The lineage of W. S. Schley is taken from the Schley genealogy by CES, (1993) (FH). John Thomas Schley (1712-1790) born in Moerzheim south of Landau in the south Pfalz, Germany, married in 1737 (Maria) Margaret Wintz (1712-1787). He was a son of Eva Brigitta and Nicholas; she was a daughter of Johan Georg and Anna Barbara. Thomas Schley, schoolmaster at Appenhofen near Moerzheim, led a group of emigrant families by ship directly to Maryland about 1744. Formerly it was believed that they left Moerzheim earlier. However, Dr. Fritz Braun of (K) pointed out that they must have left Germany after their daughter Maria Margaret was baptized there on May 22, 1743. Thomas Schley by tradition built the first house in Frederick in 1745 or 1746. He was an outstanding leader of the early German settlers at Fredericktown founded by Daniel Dulany in 1745. He was leader of the Reformed Congregation including its music director and schoolmaster and also a tavern keeper. The following ancestors of Admiral Schley lived in Frederick or farmed nearby:

(2) (George) Jacob (1735-1811) m. 1761 at Lancaster, PA Margaret Fortney (c. 1743-1821). He was a gunsmith & served in the Revolution.

(3) John George (1767-1835) m. 1792 Mary Ferree Shriver (1773-1855), daughter of David and descendant of Andreas Schreiber of Alsenborn near Kaiserslautern. See W&M-710.

(4) (John) Thomas (1806-1876) m. 1831 Georgiana Virginia McClure (1814-1846) (daughter of John of Baltimore). Their third child was Admiral W. S. Schley.

The career of Admiral Schley eclipsed that of Gen. Elwell Stephen Otis, born in Frederick in 1838 who led U. S. troops in the Philippines in 1896-1900. (Frederick News January 18, 1991).

W&M-702. William C. Birely (1850-1936) and wife Laura V. (Sinn) (1853-1936) lived at 218 N. Market St., Frederick. His parents were J. William (1816-1896) and Mary Rosanna (Cramer) (1823-1896), both buried at Mt. Olivet. The paper mill of Wilhelm Beyerle is shown on the Bond Map of 1858 west of Myersville on Grindstone Creek. Birely and Byerly families of Frederick County have been discussed in M&C-II, see also W&M-976.

Descendant William Cramer Birely of Olney, MD calls attention to William C. Birely (1779-1821) in records of Rocky Hill Church who had children; Margaret, Rebecca, Charlotte, Mary, Elizabeth, and John William.

In the 1800 census of Frederick County, Frederick Byerly lived in Frederick District; Jacob and George Byerly (both 26-45 years of age) lived in Emmitsburg District. A Joseph Byerly served in the Maryland Militia in the Revolutionary War.

W&M-703. William G. Zimmerman (1859-1943) and wife Georgie F. (Whaley) (1863-1945) are buried at Mt. Olivet. Their lineage follows:

(1) Emigrant Hans Michael (1706-1741) of Meckesheim, Germany, m. Elisabeth Dodderer (1709-1799).

(2) (John) Michael, (1732-1762) m. Elisabeth ----.

(3) George (1755-1820) m. Elisabeth Weiss (1760-1823) both buried at Woodsboro Reformed Cemetery.

(4) Solomon (1793-1846) m. Susannah Shank (1812-1888). He is buried at Woodsboro Reformed Church; she at Woodsboro Mt. Hope Cemetery.

(5) Henry Otho (1837-1910) m. Martha Ellen Albaugh (1840-1917): both buried at Woodsboro Mt. Hope Cemetery; parents of William G. See W&M-979 and (Z).

A Zimmerman family, sometimes using the translated name Carpenter, and separate from those studied by Myers, settled in southern Adams County, and in Maryland near the Mason-Dixon Line. According to Beryl McPherson in files of the Emmitsburg Public Library two daughters of Madame Marie Ferree married Carpenters. A grandson of Marie was Peter Zimmerman who settled about 1765 on Carroll's Tract in later Liberty Township, Adams County. The nearby Mennonite Cemetery was sometimes called the Zimmerman Graveyard. (See M&C-I). Peter Zimmerman and wife Mary Shriver had 11 children. With the account of these Zimmermans in the files at Emmitsburg is the story of young Mary Zimmerman stolen about 1765 by Indians and returned 10 years later with her son. Other early families who came along with the Zimmermans to the area of Flat Run and bought land from the Cochran tract near the state border, were Martins, Overholtzers and Weavers.

W&M-703. George William Smith (1832-1915) and wife Susan Virginia (Howard) (1831-1892) are buried at Mt. Olivet at Frederick. The lineage follows:

Johan Schmidt (c. 1710-1785) the emigrant of 1730 was naturalized in 1761 with Frederick Reformed Communion. By tradition he was from the area of Darmstadt, Germany. In 1744 he was granted the tract called New Germany west of Ballenger Creek Road on a northern branch of Ballenger Creek. The farm is marked G. W. Smith on the Titus Atlas of 1873.

The lineage on page W&M-704 omits a generation; the son of emigrant Johan was John Smith (c. 1753-1802). He was a Revolutionary soldier and on the local Committee of Observation in 1775. John married Elizabeth Keiser as disclosed in the typed genealogy by Dorothy Foreman Still (after 1958) in files of CES.

The wife of George John Smith (1776-1832) was Rebecca Getzendanner (1786-1854). Both are buried in Mt. Olivet. Judge George Smith (1807-1871) and wife Lydia (Baugher) (1809-1834) are buried in Mt. Olivet; also his second wife Mary E. (Nixdorff) (1814-1859). Lydia was the mother of George William (1832-1915). Notes from the diary of George William Smith were recorded by descendant Virginia Pearl (Smith) Weidman (FH).

Howard Luther Smith (1867-1951) the youngest son of George William and Susan Virginia (Howard) married (Nellie) Leona Thomas (1873-1951) the daughter of David D. and Harriet (Trundle) Thomas. Their first child born January 22, 1894 was Helen Leona Smith, renowned artist who still paints in her studio at Old Braddock at age 100. She studied art at Maryland Institute and at Columbia University. Helen has taught at Hood College and is recorded in Who's Who of American Artists.

Susan Virginia Howard was a daughter of Edward H. (1798-1877) and Anne (Buckey) (1804-1878) granddaughter of Peter Buckey (1775-1848) and wife Mary Salmon (1778-1864) and great granddaughter of Mathias Buckey (1728-1794) and wife Anna Maria Hoffman (1737-1800) emigrants from Minfeld, South Germany, near the border with Alsace. A genealogy of local Howard families is by Elizabeth H. Howard in 1977.

About 240 local Smith names are in the index of the Zimmerman Genealogy by Margaret E. Myers (F) (FH). Records of some of the 40 Smiths in the Frederick County Militia of the War of 1812 include family data. (LC)

W&M-706. Daniel W. Zentz (1862-1935) married in 1889 Effie G. Lohr (1867-1954). Both are buried at Thurmont U. B. Cemetery. He was a son of Abraham S. Zentz (1828-1898) and Sarah D. (Biggs) (1834-1905) both buried at Thurmont. Abraham S. was a son of Abraham Zentz of near Taneytown. Abraham had a brother Daniel whose son Newton M. Zentz bought Zentz's Mill in

Frederick in 1895. The lineage of Sarah D. Biggs from various sources may be as follows:

    (1) John Biggs of Worcestershire, England m. Mary Hall.

    (2) John Biggs, Jr. (1687-1761) m. Eva Brink (b. 1690 NY State); moved to Monocacy Manor.

    (3) William Biggs (1725-1803) m. Amy (1729-1798).

    (4) Benjamin Biggs (1761-1819) m. Elizabeth Ohler (1766-1856).

    (5) Benjamin Biggs, Jr. (1798-1870) m. Delilah Groff (1801-1836) daughter of Henry.

In the 1850 census Benjamin Jr. lived in Emmitsburg District with his mother Elizabeth, and children including Sarah who married Abraham Zentz.

W&M-707. David D. Zentz is not in JMH. His wife Laura M. (Colliflower) (1868-1954) is buried at Graceham. His parents were Abraham S. and Sarah above. For Colliflower ancestors see W&M-1238.

W&M-707. Judge William Randolph Young (1836-1912) and wife Cornelia A. E. (Brown) (1842-1930) are buried at Myersville U.B. Cemetery. Jacob Young of D. (1799-1876) and wife Mary A. (Rhoads) (1796-1881) (d/o Jacob) are also buried at Myersville. A David Young and 16 other Youngs served in the War of 1812. For earlier Young families in Middletown Valley see W&M-931.

W&M-708. Peter Winebrenner was an early settler at Hanover. Winebrenner dates from JMH follow:

    Philip (1759-1844) m. Eve C. (1757-1834) buried at Glade Reformed Cemetery.

    Christian (1799-1891) m. Harriet (1805-1837) buried ditto. Christian 2nd m. Phoebe Cramer (1815-1893) buried ditto.

    Col. David C. (1834-1903) s/o Phoebe m. Rebecca Bentz Markey (1841-1902) buried at Mt. Olivet.

    D. Charles (1871-1939) m. 1896 Eleanor Nelson Ritchie. 2nd m. Heloise Denegre (1869-1956) buried at Mt. Olivet.

        Sons of Eleanor were David C. III (1897-1940) who became Maryland Sec. of State and Philip, a manufacturer of Philadelphia.

A prominent Winebrenner from near Walkersville was Rev. John Winebrenner (1797-1860) founder of the Church of God. He was educated at Glades School and Dickinson College and studied for the Reformed ministry with Rev. Helfenstein in Philadelphia. He was ordained at Hagerstown by the Potomac Synod of the Reformed Church in 1820. He served at Salem Reformed Church in Harrisburg from 1820 to 1823. The congregation reacted against his religious views on revivals, Sunday schools, anti-slavery, and temperance. Rev. Winebrenner then devoted his energies to founding a new denomination called the Church of God, but known in earlier years as Winebrennarians. He was an opponent of slavery and during his lifetime the Church of God, like the Church of the Brethren, was a "peace church", conscientiously objecting to war. In 1980 the Church of God had about 36,000 members. Rev. Winebrenner died in Harrisburg where he is buried. The book *John Winebrenner: 19th Century*

Reformer was written by Richard Kern (1974); *History of the Churches of God* is by C. H. Forney (1914).

W&M-709. James Edward Walker (1849-1905) and wife Annie Markell (1853-1934) are buried at Mt. Olivet. A Robert Walker is in the court records of Frederick County of 1752. In the census of 1800, in the area of Fredericktown a John Walker and wife lived with ages above 45 years. The parents of James Edward were William W. (1818-1899) and Elizabeth (Smith) (1825-1899) both buried at New London Methodist Cemetery.

In Frederick County Militia of 1812 are Andrew, Jonathan, Stephen and William Walker. George Walker (1790-1851) moved to Champaign County Ohio (LC).

W&M-710. Henry Williams (1837-1918) and wife Henrietta Marian (Stokes) (1838-1926) are buried at Mt. Olivet. Williams families were early in Frederick County. A Richard Williams applied to the new Frederick Court for bounty for killing 9 wolves in the county in 1749. Henry Williams (1742-1820), native of Pennsylvania, married Jeanette Witherow (1779-1854) of an early family in southern Adams County. They are buried at Emmitsburg Presbyterian Cemetery. Their son John H. Williams (1814-1896) married Eleanor Shriver, daughter of Judge Abraham (1771-1848). They are buried at Mt. Olivet. Abraham was a son of David and Rebecca Shriver of Union Mills in Carroll County.

Both Eleanor (Shriver) Williams and Admiral Winfield S. Schley of W&M-700 are descendants of the Andrew Schreiber family of south Germany and the Huguenot Ferree family as traced in the Genealogy of the Shriver Family by Samuel S. Shriver (1885) (FH). Andreas Schreiber and family including Andreas Jr. emigrated from Alsenborn, a village near Kaiserslautern, Pfalz, in 1721. Andreas Sr. (son of Jost) was born in 1673 and in 1706 married Anna Margaretha Hess, widow of Johan Jung or Young. The Schreibers settled first at Goshenhoppen in Berks County, PA where Andreas Sr. died. In the spring of 1734 Andreas Schreiber Jr., later Andrew Schriver Jr., (1712-1797) and his bride Anna Maria Keyser settled westward in the frontier woods of the Little Conewago area north of later Littlestown. Their son David (1735-1826) spelled the name Shriver as continued in Maryland while most of their descendants in Pennsylvania use the spelling Schriver. David (1735-1826) married Rebecca Ferree (c.1741-1812) granddaughter of renowned Marie Ferree. At first they farmed on Little Pipe Creek in what became Carroll Co., Maryland and later settled at Union Mills on Big Pipe Creek, a farm preserved as an historic site today. Many prominent people were descendants including recent Sargent Shriver of the Peace Corps. W&M index contains 54 page references to Shrivers. Some Schriver descendants in Adams County are traced by Harold Ditzler in newspaper articles filed at (G). For Union Mills see Thomas W. Kemp MHM 35, 382 (1940).

A different Shriver family settled at Greenmount, Pennsylvania, south of Gettysburg and spread southward around Emmitsburg. According to a booklet *History of The Shriver Family*, by Mr. Pearl J. Shriver, of Mantua, NJ (about 1927) Ludwig Schreiber or Lewis Shriver (1750-1815) from Beirach (probably Biberach) south Germany emigrated about 1790 via Baltimore and built a stone house at Greenmount south of Gettysburg. His son George Lewis (1792-1852) married Sarah Krise (1796-1822), daughter of Peter and Elizabeth, who was buried at Emmitsburg Lutheran Church. George L. Shriver married a second time to Mrs. Mary (Fisher) Rife. Christian Krise Shriver (b. 1818) married Alice Jane Fisher a granddaughter of Thomas Jr. and Catherine (Warner) Fisher. (See M&C-II).

W&M-711. Joseph Dill Baker (1854-1938) and wives Emma N. (Cunningham) (1854-1883) and Virginia (Markell) (1863-1941) (daughter of Charles) are buried at Mt. Olivet. Joseph D. Baker, banker of Frederick, was a son of Daniel Baker (1811-1888) and Ann Catherine (Finger) (1813-1888) who are buried at Mt. Olivet. Baker Park in Frederick is named for Joseph D. Baker, a prominent banker.

W&M-715. George W. Wertenbaker (1842-1904) and wife Catherine Virginia (Cartzendafner) (1846-1916) are buried at Sabillasville in Otterbein Cemetery. They had 5 children to die as infants. George's great grandfather probably was Jacob Wortenbecker, over 45 years, in the census of 1800 in Middletown Valley. He and his wife, under 45 years, then had 5 daughters and 3 sons living with them. George's grandfather John Wertenbaker (1768-1865) and wife Betsy (Derr) (1773-1854) are buried also at Sabillasville as are George's parents, Lewis Wertenbaker (1816-1866) and wife Catherine (Dutrow) (1813-1897).

W&M-716. The Wood families of the New Market to Unionville area have been descendants of very early settlers Charles Sr, and Joseph who arrived in the Linganore area coming westward by the Annapolis Road before 1748. (M&C-II). This family must be distinguished from that of Judge Joseph Wood and son Col. Wood who lived at Woodsboro. In 1749 Joseph Wood was Constable of Pipe Creek Hundred. In 1750 Joseph Wood (wife Mary) sold 584 acres on Linganore Creek to Edward Dorsey of Annapolis. Joseph Wood of Linganore was on the Grand Jury of the Frederick County Court in 1750. In 1751, he was overseer of the middle portion of the road from Thomas Beatty's plantation to Baltimore. In a deed of 1756, Charles Wood, farmer sold to John Seagar, 100 acres of the Resurvey on Charles' Choice which lay on the south side of the main branch of Linganore Creek. Charles Wood had other early deeds. In a deed of 1753 Charity, Judith and Janet Wood, daughters of Jacob Wood deceased, were each given a negro girl by George Read, planter. Several from Linganore Wood families served in the Maryland Militia in the Revolution.

Charles Wood (1827-1910) and wife Kate (Worthington) (1837-1932) are buried at New Market ME Church. Some generations may be missing between the emigrants and brothers Henry and John. In the 1800 census in eastern Frederick County lived families of William Wood and wife over 45 years; William Wood and wife under 45 years with 4 young sons and 2 daughters; Joseph over 45 years with 5 sons and 10 slaves and Bennet Wood (26-45) with wife under 26 and a daughter under 10 years (LC).

W&M-717. David A. Wagaman (1851-1942) and wife Susan C. (Harbaugh) (1857-1917) are buried at the Reformed Church in Sabillasville. His grandfather David Wagaman (1793-1863), also his parents Richard (1823-1904) and Anna M. (Miller) Wagaman (1827-1899) are buried at the Reformed Church at Sabillasville.

W&M-718. John M. Watson (1854-1923) and wife Alice (Crawford) (1862-1919) are buried at Thurmont U.B. Cemetery. Emigrant James Watson (1768-1870) married widow Mary (Gibson) Hindman. It is stated in (WB) that James lived more than 101 years and is buried at the Presbyterian Cemetery of Lower Marsh Creek. (LC).

W&M-720. Ancestors of Trail families of Maryland were traced to Blebo, County, Fife, Scotland, with coat of arms before 1418, (*Men of Mark in Maryland* by B.C. Steiner et al, Baltimore 1907 vol. 3). *The Genealogy of Trail Families of Scotland and Maryland* by Robert Trail of Riverton, IL (1979) begins with Rev. Robert Trail (1603-1676) (FH). The families of Mathias and Markell are included. Trails were early in the Montgomery County area. A Charles Trail lived near Middle Ford of Seneca Creek in 1752. A number of Trails are recorded in the *History of Montgomery County*, by T.H.S. Boyd (Clarksburg 1870). For example, Charles Trail left his wife Susannah the tracts of Trail's Choice and Buxton's Delight. Several Trails are listed in the Maryland Militia in the Revolution.

An early Trail in the Frederick area was Hannah (1772-1868), wife of James of William, who has a gravestone in Mt. Olivet. Edward Trail (1798-1876) a native of Montgomery County married Lydia Christine Ramsburg (1802-1884). They were farmers and prominent citizens of Frederick County. In the 1850 census they lived with the following children: Charles E., lawyer; Charlotte A. age 22; Lewis R, a saddler, 20; Susan E., 18; Anna E. 15; Allen 10; Fanny L, 8; Mary V. 6. In 1854 living in Buckeystown District were Ann Trail age 70, together with farmer William T. Trail age 37 and Evan Trail age 32, all born in Maryland.

Edward Trail bought lots in Frederick from Elias Brunner Jr. in 1823 and from Richard Potts in 1826. Edward also bought part of lot 24 in Frederick on the road to McPherson Mill at the eastern edge of Frederick on Love Lane in 1830. Articles about Edward and son Charles Trail are in Vol. III of *Men of Mark*. Col. Charles Edward Trail (1825-1909) and wife Ariana McElfresh (1828-1892) are buried at Mt. Olivet. Some of their descendants follow:

(1) Ariana Theresa (1852-1923) m. Dr. Alfred McGill Belt, (1847-1918) (Mt. Olivet); dau. Ariana T. m. Alan Arnold (Children: Alan, Jr.; Ariana Trail m. William Kenety).

(2) Florence (1854-1944) (Mt. Olivet), author and scholar; unm.

(3) Charles Bayard (1857-1914) diplomat, banker m. Grace Winebrenner (1869-1941) (Mt. Olivet). See W&M-1336 for descendants.

(4) Anna M. m. Rev. John B. Harding, Episcopal pastor in Baltimore and Philadelphia. Children: Anna (d. 1967); Constance (d. 1969).

(5) Henry (1862-1923) (Mt. Olivet); No issue.

(6) Bertha (1864-1940) (Mt Olivet); No issue.

(7) Arthur (1867-1921) (Mt. Olivet); No issue.

Florence Trail has 10 publications listed in N.U.C. She wrote a *Memorial of Arianna McElfresh Trail*, her mother, published in Boston and a *History of Italian Literature* printed in New York City in 1903. Other works by Florence Trail are at (FH). (LC)

W&M-722. Thomas McCleary Wiles (1851-1931) and wives Jennette L. (Zimmerman) (1854-1893) and Callie V. Renn (1858-1924) are buried at Middletown Lutheran Church. The early settlers in the Valley had the German name Weil which was anglicized and acquired an s. In the 1800 census Thomas Weil or Wiles was over 45 years living with wife under 45, 3 daughters and 7 sons. In Middletown Reformed records of 1770-1775, George and Elizabeth Weil were sponsors of baptisms. In Lutheran records at Middletown Peter and Maria Magdalena Weil had children baptized in 1784 to 1799. In 1765 George Wiles bought part of tract Chevy Chase from George Yeast (wife Catherine). Witnesses were Thomas Beatty and Peter Bainbridge.

Peter Wiles (1795-1869) is buried at Middletown Lutheran Church. Son Thomas Wiles (1824-1912) is buried also at the Middletown Lutheran Church but his wife Barbara's stone has not survived. Other Wiles families farmed east of Catoctin Mt.; see W&M-1387. See also *Wiles Families of Frederick County Maryland* by Marie D. Wiles and Earl H. Davis, Plattsmouth, NB 1976. According to descendant Carl Wells of Lucas, Ohio, Thomas Wiles and family moved from Virginia to Middletown Valley by 1780. He and his wife had sons George, William, Samuel and James. George Weil and wife Marta Elisabeth are in the records of the Reformed Church first in 1771. A Peter Weil and wife Maria Magdalene are the earliest Weil or Wiles in Lutheran records at Middletown in 1784. James and Thomas Wiles served in the Maryland Milita in the Revolutionary War.

W&M-723. Frederick W. Welty (1849-1910) and wife Catherine (McIntire) (1853-1929) are buried at Emmitsburg Catholic Cemetery. In the census of 1800 Casper Welty, over 45 years was the only Welty in northern Frederick County. He lived with one son 26-45. Andrew (1814-1877) and wife Rebecca (Black) (1819-1910) are buried at Emmitsburg Catholic Church.

W&M-723. Vernon T. Watkins (1871-1943) and wife Edith P. (Mount) (1878-1941) are buried at Browningsville Methodist Church near Kemptown. At the same place are buried his parents William Thomas Watkins (1837-1891) and Sarah E. (Williams) (1844-1928). The 1800 census of eastern Frederick County shows the family of Jeremiah Watkins 26-45 years and wife under 26 years. They had a daughter and two sons.

John Watkins or Wadkins served in the Frederick County Militia in 1812. At least 7 from Watkins families served in the Maryland Militia in the Revolution.

W&M-724. The census of 1800 confirms Michael Wachter living not far from Frederick at age over 45, but it is doubtful that he was born in Germany. Michael's gravestone in Mt. Olivet shows death in 1844 at 75 years. S&H records the following Wachters arriving at Philadelphia: Jacob and Martin 1749, Gabriel 1751, Hans Georg 1752 and Georg 1767 (from Memmingen, Germany).

John H. Wachter (1859-1946) and Emma F. (Zimmerman) (1867-1935) are buried at Utica as is his grandfather Jacob Wachter (1782-1861). The parents of John H. were Michael Wachter (1821-1910) and Ann Rebecca (1823-1917) also buried at Utica who had another son Jacob William whose gravestone there records that he died in 1956 at age 101.

A typed genealogy of Wachter families by Wesley N. Wachter is in the files of J. M. Holdcraft in Frederick.

W&M-724. Dr. Charles L. Wachter's grandfather Rev. Michael Wachter (1799-1850) and wife Maria M. (Wiest) (1800-1856) are buried at Mt. Olivet. Their son Dr. Leander Wachter (1826-1902) and wife Elizabeth (Anders) (1823-1902) are buried at Ellerton St. John's Lutheran Church. About 120 local Wachter names are in the index of the Zimmerman genealogy by Margaret E. Myers (F) (FH).

Emma F. (Zimmerman) Wachter was a daughter of John A. J. and Mary M. (Firestone) Zimmerman. Nicholas Feuerstein a carpenter, age 40 and Nicholas Jr., age 21, emigrated in 1753 from Thal near Drulingen in northern Alsace. Nicholas Sr. and wife Ana Catharina (Nunnemacher) had 9 children most of whom are recorded by Frederick Lutheran Church (B3).

A number of emigrant Feuersteins have been researched by George Ely Russell in (N) 52, #4 (Dec 1964) and later in WMG 9, 1 and 2. Of these Nicholas Jr. and Mathias sons of Nicholas and Catharina (Nunnemacher) came to Frederick County from northern Alsace.

Nicholas Feuerstein, Jr. arrived at Philadelphia in 1753 and in 1761 married Eva Catharina Schwab. After living in Bedford County, Pennsylvania and serving in the Revolutionary War, they settled in 1786 on a farm near Trapp (later Jefferson) in southern Middletown Valley. In 1796, they sold their Maryland farm and purchased a farm three miles from Natural Bridge, VA. Of their 8 children, none apparently remained in Frederick County but moved to Virginia, Ohio, Tennessee, and Pennsylvania.

Mathias Feuerstein (1744-1829) married about 1774 Mary Ann Beaver (Bieber). During the Revolution he served in the Militia of York County, Pennsylvania. They settled on a farm in Frederick before 1787. In 1790 Mathias and Mary Ann were living in Frederick County with the following of their 14 children. Later the family except for Jacob moved to southwestern Pennsylvania and Ohio:

(1) Jacob (1775-1830) m. Mary Hohl (1780-1832); both buried at Mt. Olivet Cemetery at Frederick.

(2) Sarah (b. 1778) m. Daniel Perky (d. 1854) lived in Holmes County, OH.

(3) John F. (b. 1782 Frederick Lutheran Church) m. Rachel Rowler (d. 1848); lived in Columbiana County, OH.

(4) George (b. 1784) m. Rebecca Karl (d. 1851); lived in Wayne County, OH.

(5) Solomon (b. 1786) m. Elizabeth Baird (d. 1841); lived in Stark County, OH.

(6) Mary Firestone (b. 1788) m. Richard Karl; lived in Columbiana County, OH.

(7) Daniel F. (b. 1796)

The descendants of Jacob Firestone made notable contributions to Frederick, but now the name has almost disappeared from the county. In the census of 1850, Joshua Firestone (1802-1883) a millwright and wife Christianna (1807-1887) lived near Frederick with children Margaret (b. c.1832) and Luther (b.

c.1833). Frederick K. Firestone (1819-1856) a tailor and wife Rebecca (b. c.1826) lived in Frederick without children. In Frederick in 1886 were Byon H. Firestone, Prof. of Music, Charles Frederick, clerk and Oscar F., machinist.

W&M-725. Nathaniel J. Wilson (1836-1902) and wife Ann S. (1838-1921) are buried in Frederick Catholic Cemetery. Their son George I. (1866-1910) and wife Clara K. (1868-1937) are buried at Mt. Olivet. Edward J. Wilson and 11 other Wilsons were in the Frederick County Militia in 1812. See also W&M-1243 (LC).

W&M-726. John G. Warrenfeltz (or John C. as JMH recorded) lived 1844-1918 and wife Margaret E. 1852-1886. Daniel Warrenfeltz (1814-1909) and wife Susan (Ludy) (1823-1898) are buried at Wolfsville Reformed Church.

Usually Germanic family names became shorter in America, but the Swiss name Werenfels was an exception. The early generations of Warrenfeltz families in America were disclosed by Leah Leatherman Spade in the Frederick News of July 27, 1983. (Johan) Jacob Werenfels (1731-1807) from Canton of Basel emigrated in 1749 and lived for about 25 years in Lancaster and York Counties, Pennsylvania. The family moved to the Hagerstown area briefly then to upper Middletown Valley. Jacob Warrenfeltz had the following children:

(1) Jacob Jr. m. 1803 Mary Ann Measell (at least nine children).

(2) Catherine (Caty) m. 1811 Conrad Green.

(3) Hannah m. 1808 Daniel Garnand (seven children).

(4) John m. 1809 Mary Leatherman (10 children); son Daniel lived 1814-1909.

(5) Philip m. 1812 Catherine Leatherman (both died 1850), At least six children. Sons Joshua, Philip and Ezra (to Utica).

(6) Maria (Polly) m. 1813 Christian Weller; lived near Thurmont.

(7) Peter m. 1817 Sophia Rouzer. Son Uriah (1825-1917) to farm north of Thurmont. Peter 2 m. 1838 Sarah Valentine.

(8) Elisabeth m. 1816 Paul Marker (6 children), moved to Ellerton, Ohio near Dayton.

(9) Christina, twin, m. 1818 Daniel Leatherman (9 children).

(10) Susannah, twin of the above, m. 1818 William Patton, moved to near Dayton, Ohio.

(11) Magdalena m. 1819 John Jacob Firor (at least 5 children); lived in Thurmont area.

Mary Warrenfeltz (1809-1879) and husband Peter Marker (1797-1881) had 16 children according to researcher Samuel M. Andruska of Silver Spring, Maryland. Jacob Warrenfeltz, Jr. (1824-1903) from Frederick County settled on a farm near Chewsville in Washington County. Descendants are given by Williams (1906).

W&M-727. Leonard Randolph Waesche (1846-1934) and wife Mary Martha (Foreman) are buried at Blue Ridge Cemetery at Thurmont. His mother Catherine (Castle) (1811-1891) is buried at the United Brethren Cemetery in Thurmont. Leonard and Mary's son Admiral Russell Randolph Waesche (1886-1946) was Commander of the U. S. Coast Guard. He was born in Thurmont and

Thurmont. Leonard and Mary's son Admiral Russell Randolph Waesche (1886-1946) was Commander of the U. S. Coast Guard. He was born in Thurmont and is buried in Arlington Cemetery. Russell attended Purdue Univ. and graduated from the Coast Guard Academy in 1906. In 1911 he married Dorothy Luke; they had sons Russell R. Jr., Harry Lee (in CO) and James Mountford. In 1933 Russell married Agnes Rizzuto and they had one child, William Alexander. The Waesches lived in Chevy Chase, the Coast Guard Headquarters being in D.C. See also W&M-1437.

W&M-728. Judge Glenn Howard Worthington (1858-1934) and wife Julia (Alvey) (1867-1951) are buried at Mt. Olivet. His grandparents John H. Worthington (1783-1858) and Ann H. (1791-1866) also are buried at Mt. Olivet. Their son John T. (1826-1905) married Mary R. Simmons (1832-1902); both are buried at Mt. Olivet.

Early Worthington families are included in the book *Side-Lights of Maryland History* by H. D. Richardson. (Cambridge, Maryland 1967). (W) (BF); See also *Worthington Families 1741-1854* in (MS 1406).

John Daniel Worthington bought land in Frederick County in 1765 from Lawrence Creager. John Worthington sold a property to William Worthington in 1768. A John Worthington served in the Maryland Militia in the Revolution.

Thomas Contee Worthington (1782-1847) a Commander in the War of 1812 moved from Anne Arundel County to Frederick to practice law and was elected to Congress in 1824. He was unmarried. (LC)

W&M-729. Charles E. Wilhide (1862-1916) and wife Martha A. (Harbaugh) (1868-1934) are buried at the United Brethren Cemetery on the hill in Thurmont.

That three Wilhide brothers came together to America is not supported by records. Friedrich Wilheit and wife Lucretia and children set out for America from the village of Schwaigern or Schweigern near Sinsheim, not far from the Neckar River and southeast of Heidelberg. (M&C-II-170). Apparently the father perished en route, since only the children and mother were recorded by S & H arriving in 1731 in Philadelphia as follows: Frederick Jr., Melchior, Barbara and Lucretia over 16 years; Frederick III, and Elisabeth under 16 years.

There are early land records of emigrant Friedrich Jr. For example in deed of 1752 Frederick Woolhide sold to Jacob Peck, carpenter, for 157 pounds about 100 acres which had been "taken up" in 1738 by Barnet Weymer (wife Barbara). In 1752 Frederick Woolhide, farmer, bought 74 acres of the tract Jerusalem. It lay on the northeast side of Little Hunting Creek, next to the tract Bonnett's Resolution. Wilhide records are in the Moravian Archives. See also (WP).

From Der Kurier September 1992 comes the following lineage:

(1) Samuel Wilheit of Baden-Wuertemberg

(2) Friedrich Wilheit Sr. baptized 1687, ditto.

(3) Frederick Wilhide, Jr. (1723-1792) emigrated to near what later became Thurmont.

(4) Anna Margaret Wilhide (1760-1822).

Descendant Frederick Wilhide (b. c.1777) married Catherine Peitzell (1787-1936). Their son Benjamin (1802-1871) and wife Mary Barbara (Knouff or Knauff) (1798-1882) are buried at Thurmont U. B. Cemetery. Mary was a daughter of Henry and Mary Ann (Weil) Knauff of Middletown Valley. Arnold Randolph Wilhide (1839-1923) and wife Isabella M. (Wilhide) (1842-1882) also are buried at the Thurmont U. B. Cemetery.

Another emigrant Johann Michael Willheit (1671-1746) born in Schwaigern, settled in Orange County, Va. Ten generations in Germany and U. S. were listed with dates and locations (Der Kurier, March 1991).

Henry, George and Jacob Willhide served in the Frederick County Militia in the War of 1812. (LC)

W&M-730. Charles Monroe Utz (1869-1927) and wife Rosa E. (Shriver) (1871-1856) are buried at Monrovia Brethren Cemetery as are his parents, Bishop Samuel H. (1840-1915) and Lucinda (Kelley) (1845-1941). It is very doubtful that the ancestor Rev. Daniel (1728-1818) was born at a place called Amsterdam in Germany. The grandparents of Charles M. were John Utz (1801-1871) and Elisabeth Hohf or Hoff (1810-1852) buried at Johnsville Beaver Dam Cemetery. *The Utz Family of Piney Creek Church of the Brethren near Taneytown, Maryland* was written by Norman Utz about 1978. In the 1800 census Jacob Utz and wife both (26-45 years) lived in Westminster District.

W&M-732. Henry Unverzagt (1833-1920) and wife Magdalene E. (Ropp) (1836-1928) are buried in Middletown Lutheran Cemetery. (LC). In 1886 Henry Unverzaght farmed near Harmony.

W&M-732. Samuel Amos Urner (1855-1921) and wife Annie M. (McKinstry) (1856-1921) are buried at Unionville Methodist Church. His parents Jonas Urner (1822-1895) and Tabitha R. (Norris) (1823-1892) also are buried at Unionville. Samuel's grandfather Samuel Urner (1797-1872) is buried at Unionville, but his wife Elisabeth who died young (1800-1828) is buried at Uniontown Pipe Creek Cemetery.

W&M-733. George Thomas Marshall Martin (1841-1884) and wife Mary Ellen (Whitmore) as well as his parents Abiah Martin (1809-1883) and Anne Sophia (Currens) (1820-1889) are buried at Emmitsburg Mt. View Cemetery. The grandparents of George T. M. namely John Martin (1771-1860) and wife Mary (1775-1856) are buried at Emmitsburg Lutheran Cemetery.

There were Martins of British origin early in Frederick County. A John Martin was Constable of Monocacy Hundred in 1749 and a John Martin, Jr. was on the Grand Jury of Frederick County in 1750. At that time, German speaking settlers did not hold such positions. Martins of German Mennonite origin in the Graceham to Emmitsburg area have been studied by Edward V. Duggan in *Pennsylvania Mennonite Heritage*, October, 1991. Related Martin families of Washington County, Maryland have been traced in *Biographical Annals of Franklin County* (1905, reprinted) (G) and by Williams (1906).

The Whitmores of Frederick County derive in part from Mennonite Widmyers of Lancaster County. See *Pennsylvania Mennonite Heritage*, April 1991 and W&M-891. Frederick and James Whitmore are listed in Frederick County

Militia of 1812. In 1800 in Emmitsburg District lived Abraham, Benjamin, John and Henry Whitmore, all over 45 years of age and younger Jacob.

W&M-734. James W. Troxell (1831-1904) and wife Mary E. (Zacharias) (1841-1915) are buried at Mt. View Cemetery, Emmitsburg, as are his parents Joseph (1803-1888) and Amy (Haff) (1808-1888).

The emigrant Troxell or Drachsel ancestor of those of Emmitsburg was not Frederick but Johannes Sr. and son (John) Peter according to the book *Troxell Trails* by Richard M. Troxel (Gateway Press, Baltimore 1977) and a lineage received from J. Richard and Dorothy Hershey of Gettysburg. In this remarkable case two brothers of known birth in Switzerland who emigrating from northern Alsace (B3) left many descendants in Frederick County.

Jakob and Margaret (Brengel) Trachsel had the following children born at Lenk, a village near Adelboden, in Canton Berne, Switzerland:

(1) Elisabeth (c. 1684-1721).

(2) Johannes (1690-1751) m. Anna Maria Hunsecker (?); emigrated 1737 and settled at Egypt, Lehigh County, Pennsylvania. Descendants near Emmitsburg including James W. Troxell.

(3) Peter (1691-1766) m. Juliana Catharina (1703-1795) emigrated 1733; will at Frederick; their 7th child was George Frederick (1741-1796) ancestor of Troxells of Apples Church.

(4) Benedikt Trachsel m. Katharina ---.

Jacob and Margaret died at Wolfersheim in the Saar area of southwest Germany in 1721.

Johannes and Anna Maria Troxell above had the following children born at Wolfersheim:

(1) (John) Peter (1719-1799) m. Barbara Saeger (b. 1723); emigrated in 1737 to Egypt village near Bethlehem, Pennsylvania; in 1776 to Tom's Creek. Peter and second wife (Catherine) Maria Magdalena (Schreiber) are buried at Tom's Creek Church.

(2) Michael (b. 1721);

(3) Nicholas (b. 1721) twin.

(4) Catrina (b. 1728).

The eleventh child of emigrant (John) Peter Troxell (born when he was 60 years old) was Frederick Troxell (1779-1853). Frederick's mothers was second wife Maria Magdalena, daughter of John Jacob Schreiber and wife Anna Maria (Roth). Frederick and wife Catherine (Wilson) (1784-1815) who are buried at Emmitsburg Lutheran Church, were parents of Joseph Troxell (1803-1888).

A related lineage of Troxells of the Emmitsburg area progressed: (1) (John) Peter (1719-1799) buried Tom's Creek; (2) George Frederick (1741-1796); (3) John (1773-1857); (4) David (1805-1886), buried at Apples Church; (5) Samuel Joseph (1850-1923) buried at Graceham; (6) Robert (1871-1951) buried Emmitsburg Lutheran Church; (7) Elias; (8) Dorothy m. J. Richard Hershey of Gettysburg.

Abraham and George Troxell of Washington County, Maryland served in the Revolution. For Troxells at Gettysburg see (WB) and (G). See also the Troxell Reunion Genealogy (Rocky Ridge, 1936) by Ethel Close Buckey. (CES file)

Being placed at the Historical Society of Frederick County is a Troxell genealogy received in 1993 from Mary Walters of Las Vegas, NV, based largely on *Troxell Trails* and a similar study in 1969 by Jack D. Salmon of Royal Oak, MI.

W&M-735. William Howard Smith (1862-1914) and wife Ida M. (1868-1938) are buried at Mt. Olivet. A Joseph Smith (1801-1891) is buried at Charlesville Reformed Church where are buried the parents of William Howard, namely Perry Green Smith (1820-1892) and wife Susannah Rebecca (Geesey) (1823-1907). The latter's name was earlier spelled as Giese. In Emmitsburg District in 1850 lived Adam Giese, 60 years and wife Elizabeth, 50, also John Giese, 26, all born in Germany.

W&M-736. Leading lawyer of Frederick, Jacob Rohrback (1863-1945) and wife Ida Rebecca (Ramsburg((1867-1942) are buried at Mt. Olivet. His parents, Martin N. Rohrback (1832-1900) and wife Ellen Catherine (Brunner) are also buried at Mt. Olivet.

Jacob Rohrback was a leader of the Young Men's Bible Society of Frederick County to whom I as its colporteur reported gifts and sales of Bibles in summers around 1930. I was fortunate to obtain this stimulating employment, wandering around rural areas of Frederick County, through the recommendation of my cousin Charles W. Lough.

Henry and Noah Rohrback and descendants are discussed in Williams (1906). The original name Rohrbach means roaring brook. A book on *Rohrbach and Related Families* was published by Lewis H. Rohrbaugh in 3 volumes, (F), (FP) and (H).

W&M-737. Josiah F. Smith and wife Ellen A. (Fox) (1843-1919) are buried at Wolfsville Lutheran Church where his parents also are buried, namely John Smith (1804-1877) and wife Catherine (1809-1896). In the 1800 census the only Fox family of Middletown Valley was that of Frederick (over 45 years). John, Peter and Samuel Fox served in the Frederick County Militia of 1812.

Serving in the War of 1812 were 50 Smiths. Most information was recorded for Gaspar BS (d. 1858 at Hiltons, TN); George (d. 1855) of Woodsboro; Henry (d. 1816 at Frederick); Jacob (c.1796-1880 of Myersville); John of John (1792-1845); Joseph (d. 1849); Dr. Samuel Price (b. 1795) practiced in Taneytown, then in Cumberland; Solomon (d. 1823) m. Sarah Ann Fogle (b. c.1790); William (b. c.1798) to Sullivan County TN then Talapoosa, AL.

W&M-739. Joshua Summers (1845-1922) and wife Mary E. (Leatherman) (1848-1928) are buried at Middletown Reformed Church. His parents George (1802-1884) and Catherine (1805-1876) are buried in the same cemetery. Joshua had grandparents Jacob Summers (c.1767-1850) and wife Elisabeth (c.1769-1849) buried at St. John's Church near Ellerton.

Many from Summers families served in the Maryland Militia in the Revolution. A few non-German Summers were in early Frederick County since William Summers was on the Grand Jury in 1750.

W&M-740. Harry F. Shipley (1874-1942) and wife Fannie S. (Easterday) (1873-1915) are buried at Mt. Olivet where also his parents Frederick Shipley (1819-1883) and Margaret (Bear) (1828-1895) are buried. For ancestors see *Shipley Families of Maryland* by L. Parks Shipley (Baltimore 1971 and Summit, NJ 1980). (FH) (WL). The Shipley Reunion Committee had a publication at Baltimore in 1937 (WL) (LC).

W&M-740. George W. Shryock (1836-1921) and wife Mary E. (Bell) (1846-1918) are buried at Utica. His grandparents, Valentine (1787-1843) and Ann Christine (1763-1842) also are buried at Utica; also Henry Shryock (1795-1875) and wife Catherine M. (Geisburt) (1810-1885). Henry served in the Militia in 1812 under Capt. Joseph Wood. A genealogy of Shryock Families has been written by Joseph G. Shryock (Philadelphia 1930).

Johannes Schreyack signed the Lutheran Articles of Muhlenburg in 1747 at Monocacy Church south of later Thurmont. In 1760 John Shriock (wife Jane) bought 4 pieces of land northwest of later Lewistown.

Early Shryock families have been clarified by Christine (Moose) Shryock of Gettysburg. Johan Georg Schreyack (b. c.1702) and wife Barbara (b. c.1705) with his two younger brothers Michael and Jacob emigrated via Philadelphia in 1733. After living briefly in York County they settled in the German Monocacy area. Their daughter Susanna Elisabeth married Francis Albert; only son Christian (1735-1822) married Eva Marie (1739-1793) and secondly in 1794 Magdalena Shingle.

Children of Christian Shryock of near Creagerstown follow: (George) Valentine (1760-1794) m. Ann Christina Derr (Lutheran, Utica); Daniel (1761-1814) (probably to KY) married Ann Cassel; Frederick (1763-1856) m. Frances Troutman (to Fayette County, KY); Adam (1766-1829) m. Rosannah Wood (to Woodward County KY in 1807); Matthias (1774-1833) m. Mary Elizabeth Gaugh (to Lexington, KY); Elizabeth (1776-1794) m. John Harmon; John (1777-1851) (to Spencer County, IN); Maria Catherine (b. 1779) m. John Casper Schaffner (to KY).

Children of (George) Valentin Schryock and Anna Christina (Derr) of near Utica follow: Jacob Daniel (1784-1836) m. Ann Baltzell; Anna Maria (1785-after 1861) m. Walker; Valentine, Jr. (1787-1843) m. Elizabeth Stimmel (no children); Catherine (1789-1813); George (1791-1861) m. Elizabeth Flore (lived at Gettysburg, no children); Henry (1795-1875) m. Catherine Margaret Geisbert; lived in Creagerstown-Utica area.

Children of Henry Shryock and Catherine Margaret (daughter of Jonathan Geisbert) follow: Mary Ann Elizabeth (1829-1901) m. John J. Valentine; Rebecca Catherine (1831-1903); (Henry) Valentine (1833-1914) (buried in Mt. Joy Luth., Adams County, Pennsylvania) m. Juliann A. Grimes; George Washington (1836-1921) m. Mary E. Bell; Sarah Ann Dorcas (1840-1922); James William (1843-1857); John J. (1846-1910); Florence Violetta (1852-1862). Most of the above are buried at St. Paul's Lutheran Church at Utica. Henry was a manufacturer of woolens at a mill near the mouth of Hunting Creek south of Creagerstown.

Lt. John and Lt. Leonard Shryock of Washington County served in the Revolution.

W&M-741. Nicholas Cronon Stansbury (1843-1910) and wives Mary Frances (1842-1872) and Mary Agnes (1851-1915) were buried at the Thurmont U. B. Church. His grandfather Abraham Stansbury (1769-1855) and wife Rebecca I. (1794-1859) were buried at Tom's Creek Methodist Church. The parents of Nicholas were Nicholas (1810-1887) and Amelia (Phillips) (1814-1873) buried at Thurmont U. B.

In the 1800 census were a William Stansbury and wife over 45 years of age in the area of Westminster, Maryland (LC).

W&M-742. Noah Phillips Stansbury (1845-1928) and wife Sarah J. (Barton) (1849-1935) were buried at Keysville, Carroll County. He was a son of Nicholas and Amelia (Phillips) above. Nathaniel Phillips lived in Emmitsburg District in 1800.

W&M-742. The Stoner families of Union Bridge and Johnsville areas, most of whom have belonged to the Church of the Brethren, are descendants of Johannes Steiner emigrant by 1728. See the book *Stoner Brethren* by Richard R. Weber, Columbia, Maryland 1993. They were not related to the early Steiners or Stoners of the Reformed Church in Frederick. Emigrant John acquired in 1764 Spring Garden tract about 3 miles west of later Union Bridge. He died near Antietam Creek in Washington County in 1769. John Stoner Jr. died in 1774 and is buried at Wolfe's Cemetery near Union Bridge. The book includes related families of Albaugh, Arnold, Crumpacker, Long, Miller, Pfoutz, Rinehart, Rupp and Royer.

John R. Stoner (1825-1908) and wife Martha R. (Stansbury) (1847-1918) are buried at Thurmont U. B. Cemetery. His parents Daniel (1787-1878) and Nancy (Roop) (1797-1852) are buried at Beaver Dam Brethren Cemetery near Johnsville as is David Stoner (1758-1843) and wife Elisabeth Stoner (1758-1839). At a nearby Stoner family graveyard are stones of Elisabeth (1744-1813), Jacob (1752-1804) and his wife Atrian Stoner (1745-1831). Notes on Stoner families by Naomi R. Hett are in the files of CES.

A Jacob Stoner estate of 1750 is in court records of Frederick County showing heirs; Benjamin, Henry, John, Ann and Magdalena. In the Frederick County Militia in 1812 were Christian, David, Ezra and Jacob Stoner. See W&M-742.

W&M-743. Trenton C. Schroyer (1864-1947) and wife Lola E. (Gaver) (1869-1947) are buried at Wolfsville Lutheran Church in northern Middletown Valley. Buried at Jerusalem are his grandparents, John (1801-1866) and Sarah (Wertenbaker) (1804-1861). His parents Lawson Schroyer (1831-1866) and Willamina Witmer (1834-1915) also are buried at Wolfsville.

Schroyer is the dialect form of Schreyer. Before coming to Middletown Valley the earlier settlers in Heidelberg Twp. in eastern Adams County, Pennsylvania, used the High German spelling as did George Schreyer, who was taxed there in 1750.

Jonathan David English, Jr. (1859-1930) to whom T. C. Schroyer sold his store in Wolfsville married Emma Leatherman (1862-1942) (daughter of Isaiah and Sarah Ann (Schildknecht)). Both are buried at Mt. Olivet. Jonathan Jr. and Emma had one child, Grace Leatherman English (1896-1973) who married in 1940 Reid Nicodemus.

W&M-744. McClintock Young, Frederick's outstanding inventor, lived 1836-1913. He and wife Louisa (Moberly) who died in 1886 are buried at Mt. Olivet. See Moberlys W&M-1117.

W&M-745. Thomas Schley (1851-1909) and wife Mary Martin (Claggett) (1859-1923) are buried in Mt. Olivet. For emigrants John Thomas and Margaret Schley see W&M-1354. John Schley (1767-1835) and wife Mary (1773-1855) are buried at Mt. Olivet as are their son Edward (1804-1857) and wife Margaret Eve (Brengle) (1808-1890), the parents of John.

W&M-745. Daniel J. Snook (1827-1900) and wife Mary Ann (Harmon) (1829-1912) are buried at Mt. Olivet. His parents Daniel (1799-1886) and Anna Margaret (Hill) (1799-1848) are buried at Utica. The Snooks were early in Frederick County. A Henry Snuke, farmer of Frederick County left here to settle near Lebanon, NJ in 1762. Descendants of John Adam Schnock are traced in the genealogy *The Snook Families* by R. Maurice E. Snook of Athens Ga. 1980 (F) (H). John Adam Schnug was born at Nordhofen in middle Germany and was given permission to migrate from Vilbach in 1744. See *Westerwald to America* by Annette K. Burgert and Henry Z Jones (Camden ME., 1989). (LC) (G).

W&M-746. George C. Shafer (1848-1916) and wife Laura V. (Toms) (1853-1925) are buried at Mt. Olivet. His grandparents George Shafer or Schaefer (1787-1859) and Elisabeth (Ramsberg) (1792-1868) are buried at Middletown Reformed Church. Their son Joseph (1812-1886) and wife Elizabeth Ellen (1820-1886) are also buried at Middletown Reformed Church. The Shafer spelling was used already in 1800 in Middletown Valley where there were the following: John, George, Jacob, Lewis and Nicholas, between age 26 and 45 years, all with households.

The family of John Shafer, (1748-1835?) was contributed by Dorothy Grayble Bentz. About 1775 he married Anna Maria Darner in York County, Pennsylvania. She died in 1837 and he married Elizabeth Linebaugh in Frederick County. Children of Anna Maria included:

(1) Catherine (b. 1776-1839) m. Daniel or David Schroyer (1776-1826); children to IN.

(2) Elizabeth (1779-1834) m. Peter Kepler (1783-1847); to Wayne County, IN

(3) Mary (1781-1867) m. John Willard (1777-1831); buried at Burkittsville.

(4) John (1784-1835) m. Eva Biser (1792-1823); buried Middletown Reformed Cemetery.

(5) George (1787-1857) m. Elizabeth Remsberg (1792-1868); buried Middletown Reformed Cemetery.

(6) Maria Magdalene (1791-1799).

(7) Henry (1793-1871) m. Mary Magdalena Willard (1800-1864); buried at Burkittsville..

(8) Margaret (1795-1874) m. William Jarboe (1795-1836); gravestone in Middletown Reformed Cemetery.

Helen H. Ramsburg gives the father of the above children as John Shafer, Jr. (1753-1823) who married Anna Maria Darner in Middletown in 1775. Nancy Kiddoo of Whippany, NJ, has suggested that John Jr. may have been a son of Johannes Schaefer (1709-1795) and wife Margaret (1725-1795) whose burials are in the Reformed records at Frederick and who were reported from Alsace. An additional son Jacob (1777-1790) may have been named after grandfather Jacob Darner.

An Alexander Shafer (b. 1711) who emigrated from the Palatinate in 1732 was said to have founded Schaeferstown in Lebanon county, PA in 1745. His son John had two children, John Jr. and a daughter who settled near the Antietam Creek about 6 miles from Hagerstown. (Williams, 1906).

W&M-747. Nicholas G. Schaffer (1857-1925) and wife Ella M. (Grove) (1862-1837) are buried at Mt. Olivet. The German Schaefer settlers south of Frederick are distinct from those in Middletown Valley above. Jacob Schaffer (1801-1839) and wife Ann Catherine (Uttz) lived near Ballinger Creek Church where his gravestone is found. Their son Peter (1798-1883) and wife Elizabeth (Brunner) (1803-1853) are buried at Mt. Olivet. The Brunner Family and their relatives emigrated from Switzerland to Klein Schifferstadt near Manheim in the German Pfalz and later to Schifferstadt House in Frederick. They are discussed in the recent book *Joseph Brunner of Rothenstein, Schifferstadt and Frederick* by Donald Lewis Osborn (Lee's Summit, MO, 1991) (FH).

Jonathan A. Schaffer (1828-1898) and wife Anna Rebecca (Whitmore) (1830-1873) buried at Mt. Olivet were parents of Nicholas G. Schaffer. Jonathan married for a second time to Martha E. Garrott whose gravestone at Mt. Olivet lacks dates. (LC)

W&M-748. Clarence B. Stottlemyer (1856-1900) and wife Lydia A. (Warrenfeltz) are buried at Grossnickle Brethren Church near Ellerton in Middletown Valley.

Early settler David Stadelmayer (c. 1725-1789) and wife Mary Magdalena, who emigrated in 1750, are said to have operated a mill at the site of Spoolsville on Catoctin or Middle Creek west of Middletown (north of the National Pike). If David came in fact from Munich, Germany, that is remarkable, since it is so far from the Rhine River, the usual route of emigration for early settlers to Pennsylvania, and Western Maryland. David Stottlemire bought land from Nicholas Fink in Middletown Valley in 1761. The census of 1800 shows the following Stottlemyer households in Middletown Valley, all with children: Dewalt over 45 years; Magdalena over 45; David, George and Jacob 26-45; John 16-26.

The will of David Stottlemyer gives children: Dewalt, David, Jr., George, Jacob, John, Mary Ann Alexander, Eve Magdalena, Catherine and Elisabeth. Jacob Alexander of Henry and wife Mary were executors. David Stadelmeyer and wife Anna Magdalena had daughter Anna Maria baptized at Frederick Reformed Church in 1758. Records of Zion Lutheran Church, Middletown, include baptism of Anna Maria in 1782, daughter of George and Catherine Statelmeier and the burial of Peter Stattmeyer in 1804. Jacob Stottlemyer married Hedwig Schumacher in a Frederick Reformed Church record.

Stottlemyers in the Frederick County Militia in the War of 1812 included David, George, Jacob, John and Joseph.

William Hamilton Stottlemyer (1836-1905) and wife Susannah (Hoover) (1836-1913) parents of Clarence B., were buried at the Brethren Church north of Ellerton. William H. may have been a son of one of the following buried at Brethren Cemetery: John (1791-1867); John P. (1796-1879).

The parents of Henry F. C. Stottlemyer, namely Daniel (1796-1874) and Joanna (Recher) (1798-1895) are buried at Wolfsville Reformed Church. The names of four generations from David Stottlemyer are given in (BL).

W&M-749. William I. Renner (1874-1936) and wife Minnie E. (Long) (b. 1875) are buried at the Rocky Ridge Mt. Tabor Church. His parents George I. Renner (1849-1907) and Margaret E. (Derr) (1851-1913) are buried at the Rocky Ridge Brethren Church nearby.

Their ancestor William Renner (1742-1793) is buried at Rocky Hill Church near Woodsboro. His grandson, Elder Isaac Renner (1811-1880) married Sophia Wolf (1813-1899). The former tavern in New Midway where George Washington stopped could not have been built as early as 1717 as claimed.

A Phillip Renner served in the Maryland Militia in the Revolutionary War. (LC)

W&M-750. John Rouzer (1815-1894) and wives Phoebe Key (Landers) (1816-1846) and Emma K. (Parrish) (1840-1918) are all buried at Apples Church near Thurmont as are his father Daniel (1767-1850) and wives Sophia (Schover or Schober) (1772-1810) and Juliana (Matthews)(1779-1854).

A genealogy of *Rouzer Families of Frederick and Washington Counties* has been written by Larry E. Rouzer of Fallston, Maryland (BM). A large *Rouzer Genealogy* was produced by descendant Edward J. Hogan of North Canton, Ohio in 1990 (FH). The latter states that Hans Rauscher of Duehren near Sinsheim married Elisabetha Meyer. Their son Leonard born at Tannheim, Tyrol, married Gertraut Freyhoffen of Euchtersheim, Germany. They had a son Martin born 1686 who in 1709 married Maria Salome Hoffman. Their son Gideon Rauscher (1715-1783) settled in Amwell Twp., NJ, where he was Elder of the Dunkard Church. His son Martin Rouzer (1734-1777) moved to near Rocky Ridge with wife Sarah (1737-1815). They are buried at Apples Church. Their children follow:

(1) Henry (b. 1763, NJ; d. 1794) m. Eva Greta Shutaire (b. 1763).

(2) Daniel, see above and below.

(3) Abraham (1769 Rocky Ridge-1819) m. Mary Berger.

(4) Catherine (1775-1822) m. Ludwig Protzman.

Daniel Rouzer and Sophia (Shover) of Thurmont had children:

(1) Peter (1792-1877) m. Rachel Hope Martin. Peter 2nd m. (Gettysburg) Mary Jane Geiselman. Peter had about 18 children and descendants in Virginia, Pennsylvania, Tennessee, and Texas.

(2) Catherine (1794-1818) m. William Hiteshew; lived in Frederick.

(3) Jacob (1795-1824) m. Rebecca Miller; lived in Thurmont, later to Henry, Kentucky.

(4) Sophia (1796-1834) m. Hezekiah Peter Warrenfeltz at Thurmont.

(5) Sarah (1799-1847).

(6) Daniel Jr. (1801-1828).

(7) Lydia (b.1802) m .George Kallenberger at Frederick, moved to Ohio.

(8) Martin (1804-1847) m. Rosanna Gernand; lived near Thurmont; seven children in Frederick County

(9) Henry (1806-1887) m. Catherine Schlosser; buried at Thurmont.

Daniel and second wife had one son John Rouzer (1815-1894) who married Phoebe T. Landers. Later descendants are detailed by Hogan (FH).

W&M-752. The name Riemensperger in Germany underwent many changes in America, but most descendants of Stephen (1711-1789) living early north of Frederick adopted Ramsburg. Related settlers south of Frederick and in Middletown Valley more often have used Remsburg or Remsberg. J. M. Holdcraft stated that Stephen Riemensperger came to the Monocacy Valley from Pennsylvania about 1732, also that all those of related names in Pennsylvania and Maryland are descended from Stephen or from his two nephews Jacob and George who came to America a few years later and settled in western Buckeystown district.

Emigrant Stephen married in 1739 Anna Catharine Brunner (1718 to before 1789). She was a daughter of Joseph and Catherine (Thomas) Brunner. Stephen's family lived just north of the village of Harmony Grove, north of Frederick. Stephen Riemensperger was a leader of the German settlers of early Frederick County, second only to Thomas Schley. He was the first German who served on the Frederick County Grand Jury (1752-1753). Genealogies of the numerous Ramsburgs and Remsburgs have been written by Rev. Wilson L. Remsburg, (Funkstown, Maryland 1912 and revised 1936) (FH) (NY) and by Bertha A. B. Fleming (Williamsport, IN, 1966 and additions) (F) (NY). Early Ramsburgs are recorded by the Reformed Church of Frederick.

In the records of Frederick County Militia of 1812 are Frederick, Joseph and Lewis Ramsburg.

Some descendants of Stephen Reimensperger (1711-1789) and wife Anna Catherine Brunner follow (largely from the genealogy of Rev. Wilson L. Remsburg (b. 1848):

(1) John (b. c.1741-1807) m. Anna Maria Brunner (c.1741-1825), children: Jacob, John, Stephen, Catherine, Elizabeth.

(2) Christian (b. c.1743) m. Susanna; son Stephen m. Elizabeth Eickhofe (only son Stephen, Jr. died unmarried). Daughter, Catherine.

(3) Catherine (b. c.1745) m. John Steiner. Children: Henry, Catherine m. John Derr, Stephen, Christian, Frederick, Mary m. Brent Wilson, Elizabeth, John.

(4) Jacob (b. c.1747) m. Anna Elizabeth Devilbiss. Children: Elizabeth, John George, Susanna, John, Jacob, Christian, Casper, Frederick, Henry, Catherine, Uriah D. m. Anna Staley.

(5) Elias (b. 1748) m. Catherine; to Somerset County, Pennsylvania, sons John George (b. 1777) and John Jacob (b. 1779).

(6) Eve Margaret (b. c.1750) m. Henry Myers (d. 1779). Children: Henry and Anna Margaret.

(7) (Philip) Henry (c. 1752-1807) m. Susanna Devilbiss; to Strasburg, Virginia. Children: Stephen, John, Henry, Christian, Casper, Susanna, Philip second m. Catherine Stickley of Virginia, returned to Middletown, Maryland area. (Children: Elizabeth, Israel, Joseph, Anna, Samuel).

Burials of the above generally were in Reformed Church cemeteries especially at Frederick. About 180 local Remsburg and Ramsburg names are in the index of (Z).

Recent research indicated that emigrant Stephen R. was a native of Buch, Switzerland, near Winterthur, not Alsace. His Riemensperger relatives who lived at Walldorf, near Heidelberg, Germany, later emigrated to south of Frederick.

John Remsburg (c. 1767-1821) and wife Ann Rebecca Stilley (1784-1863) were buried at the Reformed Church at Frederick. Their son Elias (1804-1869) married Catherine Houck (b. c.1804) and the latter's son John Stephen Ramsburg married Drusilla Hellen Beeson.

John Adam Remsperger, probably a relative slightly older than immigrant Stephen, apparently lived also north of Frederick. It is believed that he married Catherine Ubinger. Their children in the Frederick Reformed records included Stephen (b. 1754), John (b. 1759), and Catherine (b. 1761). John married Elisabeth Miller whose children born in Frederick County included Elizabeth (b. 1788), John (b. 1791) and Magdalena (b. 1795). The family lived briefly near Redstone, Pennsylvania and then moved to Carroll County, OH and a son George settled in Hardin County, Iowa. Around Carrollton, OH, live descendants, the Rainsbergers, who hold reunions.

W&M-752. Jonas A. Ramsburg (1849-1930) and wife America V. (Boller) (1861-1942) are buried at Thurmont's Blue Ridge Cemetery. David J. Ramsburg (1823-1899) (son of John) and wife Catherine (Geasy) (1820-1886) are buried at Utica.

A Philip Wilhelm Boller (1766-1848) was born in Appenheim, Germany (M&C-II).

W&M-754. Col. John R. Rouzer (1839-1914) and wives Harriet E. (Wilhide) (1845-1868) and Julia (Wilhide) (1839-1902) (widow of E. Willman) are buried at Thurmont United Brethren Cemetery. Col. John was a son of Peter Rouzer (1792-1877) and wife Rachel Hope (Martin) (1799-1840) who are buried at Apple's Church.

Daniel (1767-1850) was not the first Rouzer to settle in Frederick County. See W&M-750.

Children of Peter Rouzer and Rachel Hope (Martin) who survived infancy were:

(1) Mary Elizabeth (1820-1899) born Augusta County, Va. and buried Thurmont U. B. Church, m. Joseph Freeze and had 10 children.

(2) James Madison (1822-1885) born Augusta County Va. and buried at Gettysburg, m. Mary Jane Geiselman and had eight children. Served Company K, 1st Pennsylvania Reserve Inf. 1861-1865.

(3) Daniel Riley (1824-1860) born Augusta County, Va. and killed near Apple's Church, m. Elizabeth Meals and had seven children.

(4) Catherine Jane (1827-1898) born Augusta County, Va. buried at Congressional Cemetery, D.C., m. Joel Weller and had four children.

(5) (Barbara) Anna (1830-1890) born at Jacob's Creek, Frederick County, buried Elmwood Cemetery, Shepherdstown, WV, m. Washington A. Bennett and had two children.

(6) Uriah Alphonso (1833-1899); birth in Apple's Church Records. Buried Knoxville Tennessee, m. Mary Emily Murphy and had 10 children. He changed spelling to Rouzer.

(7) Eliza Adeline (1836-1910) Apples Church records, m. James Howell, second m. Joshua Smith.

(8) John Robert (1839-1914) buried Thurmont U. B. Church, m. Julia Wilhide Willman whose husband had been killed in Battle of Gettysburg. Children were Mary Catherine (1872-1949) m. Harry N. Brown, Margaret C. (b. 1876) m. Lester Armacost, Clifford S. (1879-1884), Horace C. (b. 1885) m. Dorothy Barker Munroe of RI.

W&M-756. Although the Routzahn family was not very early in Middletown Valley they multiplied rapidly with numerous sons to spread the name. Ludwig was said to have been born in 1767 in Germany Twp., later Adams County, near Littlestown. He emigrated to north of Myersville. If it is true that John Ludwig moved to Frederick County in 1756, I have found no evidence of this. The Routsons or Routzahns who settled around Uniontown in Carroll County have no relation to those of Middletown Valley to my knowledge. A John Routsong from New Windsor was in the Frederick County Militia in 1812.

Routzahn genealogy in the Middletown Valley is extremely complex. In the period of 1790 to 1827 at least 11 different Routzahn couples had babies baptized. However, the Routzahn families discussed in W&M seem to be in three lines descending from Ludwig II as shown:

(Johan) Ludwig Rauenzahner, wife and two sons emigrated in 1750. Their older son Adam Routzahn (1736-1827) and wife Catherine (1736-1831) had son Ludwig II (1767-1856) who married Esther Sheffer (1767-1815). They are buried in Middletown Lutheran Cemetery. Among their descendants were the following.

(1) Benjamin (1790-1839) m. Elizabeth and 2 m. Catherine; Middletown Lutheran Church.

(a) John (1811-1888) m. Sarah Coblentz (1810-1886); both buried at Middletown Lutheran Church.

(2) Jacob (1792-1876) m. Catherine Floyd (1800-1873); both buried at St. John's Lutheran Church near Ellerton.
    (a) Ludwig III (1824-1900) m. Mary Marker (1832-1890); both buried at St. John's Lutheran Church.
(3) Adam (1796-1840) m. Elizabeth Floyd, buried 1888 at Springfield, OH.
    (a) Elias (1825-1900) m. Malinda Bittle (1829-1902); both buried Middletown Lutheran Cemetery.

Many related Routzahns are shown in published records of Zion Lutheran Church, Middletown, in *Names in Stone* and in files of JMH.

Adam Roughsong was in Frederick County by 1787 when he acquired 25 acres of a tract called Shoemaker's Tricks. For the career of Dr. Ezra Keller and wife Caroline (Routzahn), daughter of Adam and Elizabeth, see M&C-I.

There were many other early Routzahns besides those above. In the Frederick County census of 1800 there were additional households of Susanna, over 45 years; Henry; Adam of Adam, Adam of George and their wives 26-45.

In the lineage of Elias S. Routzahn who married Sarah E. Grossnickle we have no evidence of an emigrant Frederick. The emigrant was John Ludwig as disclosed in the genealogy *Hans Rauenzahner Family* by Doris Suresch, genealogist (Glen Burnie, Maryland 1988). Ludwig and wife emigrated from Beerfelden, Germany. See also (R).

Among Routzahns who remained in Pennsylvania were John Rauenzahn, who was taxed for 158 acres in Manheim Twp., York County, in 1782-83 (13 members of household) and John Routzahn who was taxed for 158 acres in Germany Twp. near Littlestown in 1799. Routzahns have been numerous around Bendersville in northern Adams County, Pennsylvania.

W&M-757. In the lineage of Jacob L. Routzahn (1864-1950) the parents of Ludwig II have been omitted, namely Adam (1736-1827) and Catharine. Mary E. (Kesselring) wife of Jacob L. lived 1867-1948. Both are buried in Myersville United Brethren Cemetery.

W&M-758. Howard P. Ramsburg (1855-1932) and wife Mary E. (Leatherman) (1859-1942) are buried at Utica. Although Henry was born in West Virginia near Shepherdstown he was a son of John Ramsburg of Frederick County. His son Jacob (1808-1877) and wife Annie Elizabeth Snook (1798-1889) are buried at Utica. Lewis P. Remsburg (1830-1908) and wife Julia Catherine (Putman) are buried at the Glade Reformed Cemetery near Walkersville. See early Ramsburgs in W&M-752.

W&M-758. Dr. Benjamin C. Perry (b. 1881) and wife Minnie Lucille (Nash) probably are buried outside of Frederick County. Perrys were early in Maryland. Benjamin and James Perry in 1749 were on the first Grand Jury of Frederick County then including present Montgomery County and all of western Maryland (LC).

W&M-759. George F. Poffenberger (1870-1918) married Elizabeth Routzahn. He is buried at Myersville U. B. Church. There is no known gravestone for Adam who was born about 1729 according to his age of 4 on reaching Philadelphia in 1733. His wife may have been Gertrut (1730-1812) buried at Church Hill Cemetery of St. John's Lutheran church north of Myersville.

Daniel Poffenberger of the next generation lived approximately from 1750 to 1845 according to his stone in the cemetery at Church Hill. John Poffenberger, grandfather of George F., lived 1788 to 1830. He and wife Mary Ann Bogner (1786-1873) are buried at Church Hill. Their son Hezekiah (1828-1908) and wife Rebecca Ann (Gaver) (1831-1908), the parents of George F. Poffenbeger, also are buried at Church Hill.

For descendants of John Poffenberger (1797-1874) and Daniel of Sharpsburg, see Williams (1906). In this *History of Washington County* are articles on 12 Poffenberger families.

Annette K. Burgert in her book of 1985 has given some descendants of Johan Georg Pfoffenberger of Ulmet, near Lichtenberg and the Saar River. It does not include son Adam and Christianna, children who were recorded in S&H. In the following I have made additions from an article by Mrs. Frank Seubold in Palatine Immigrant magazine, Spring 1978. Tax records were taken from *Pennsylvania Archives* series 3 (GC) (GL). Many people of Western Maryland are descendants of Poffenbergers.

Johann Georg Pfaffenberger (d. 1765 Berks County, Pennsylvania) was naturalized in 1744, married c1716 Anna Martha and emigrated in 1733 from Ulmet.

(1) John George (bef. 1717 at Bosenbach Luth. Church - 1758 in Augusta County, Virginia); Children:

(a) John George (1745-1829) m. Elizabeth Gally.

(b) Peter (1747-1817) m. Mary ----.

(c) Catherine m. John Homan; taxed in Robeson Twp. Berks County 1780.

(d) Mary (1752-1840) m. James Stell Coberly; to Ohio.

(2) Elizabeth Catherine (b. 1719 at Ulmet) m. Johan George Sherman. Taxed in Tulpehocken Twp. Berks County 1784.

(3) (Johan) Christian (1722-1784) m. Gerdraut Stupp (1730-1812). Taxed in Bethel Township, Berks County, 1779; she bur. St. Johns Luth. near Ellerton; eight children given later.

(4) Susanna Johannet (1724-25) (Ulmet Ref. Church).

(5) Adelheid Elisabeth (b. 1726) (Ulmet) m. Rev. Dominicus Bartholomaei.

(6) Johan Peter (1729-1790) m. Ottilia Marguerite Boetzel. A John P. was taxed in Tulpehocken Twp. Berks County 1779. A John Pafanberger was taxed in Mt. Pleasant Township in later Adams County in 1781; seven children named by Burgert.

(7) Michael m. Anna Catherine Lieb. Taxed in Tulpehocken Township, Berks County, 1779.

Children of Christian Poffenberger and Gerdraut above:

(1) George, taxed single, Bethel Twp. Berks County 1779.

(2) Nicholas.

(3) Christian (or Christopher?) Poffenberger (1754-1837) bur. St. John's Luth. near Ellerton.

(4) Daniel (c.1758-1845) m. ----, 1831; 7 children in W&M; bur. St. John's.

(5) Michael (b. 1767) m. Catherine ----.

(6) Jacob (1769-1846) m. Magdalena 1777-1820; bur. St. John's.

(7) Peter (b. 1772).

(8) Eva Catherine (b. 1776).

Compare lineage suggested by Margaret Westfield (M&C-II-563.)

W&M-761. Calvin L. Putman (1873-1929) married Effie M. Fisher in M&C-II. Calvin's parents John J. Putman (1856-1931) and wife Rose B. (1866-1953) are buried at Mt. Olivet. Calvin's grandparents John J. Putman, Sr. (1826-1907) and wife Rebecca (b. 1833) are buried at Utica. W&M gives his wife as Annie Summers perhaps an earlier marriage yielding Calvin L.

The census of 1800 shows a household of John Putman (over 45 years) in Middletown Valley with 3 sons and 2 daughters. Another John Putman (c. 1793-1872) is buried at St. John's Lutheran Church near Ellerton along with wife Ann E. (1795-1883).

W&M-762. George W. Peters (1858-1944) and wife Lucy Minnie (Dixon) (1861-1944) are buried at Mt. Olivet as are his parents Thomas (1818-1906) and Olivia (Burnside) (1820-1903). In the Frederick County Militia of 1812 were Charles, John, Michael and Samuel Peters.

W&M-763. Horace Peters born in 1850 was a son of John (1818-1903) and Cassandra (Nicholson) (1822-1864) who are buried at Hyattstown. (LC)

W&M-763. Albert Lindsay Pearre (1866-1944) and wife Nannie E. (Dixon) (1871-1942) are buried at Mt. Olivet. His parents were James W. (1839-1916) and Marian (Lindsay) (1840-1870) daughter of Benjamin and Sarah. They are buried at Unionville Methodist Church. His parents James Pearre (1809-1882) and Eliza (Duderar) (1814-1898) are buried at Unionville where the earlier James Pearre Sr. (1760-1825) and wife Sarah 1768-1857 are buried. A genealogy of Pearre and Lugenbeel Families is discussed in *Maryland and Delaware Genealogist*, Winter, 1984 (WP). A James Pearre Collection (1831-1880) (Unionville) is (MS 1038).

James Pearre surveyed the tract Stoney Hive in 1743 on the later Frederick-Montgomery County line east of Sugar Loaf Mountain.

W&M-764. Grayson E. Palmer (1875-1951) and wife Bessie Cramer (Birely) (1883-1973) are buried at Thurmont Blue Ridge Cemetery. Her lineage is given in M&C-II. Their son Edgar married Anna Levy and his brother Victor S. married Helen Tabler. Grayson's parents Jacob E. Palmer (1832-1905) and Matilda (Miller) (1847-1915) are buried at Utica.

There were unrelated early Palmers in Monocacy Valley. In 1741 Thomas Palmer surveyed Palmer's Choice adjoining on the south tract Metre of John van Metre, west of Monocacy river and southeast of later Frederick. There were several Palmer families in Middletown Valley, notably Peter born 1795 and Jacob born about 1801; both lived in Catoctin District. Christian Balmer ancestor of Peter had emigrated via Philadelphia in 1732.

W&M-764. Lewis M. Nixdorff (1827-1909) and wife Eliza P. (Miller) (d. 1908) are buried at Mt. Olivet as are his parents Henry (1780-1839) and Susan (Medtart) (1788-1870). Henry was a son of Samuel Nixdorff and wife Barbara who had other children: Samuel, Susanna, Magdalena, Elizabeth, George and Tobias (Frederick Lutheran Church).

W&M-765. McPherson Families. The lineage of Dr. William Smith McPherson and continued follows:

> (1) Robert McPherson (c.1689-1749)and wife Janet (c. 1689-1767) were emigrants from North Ireland to Marsh Creek Settlement, west of later what later became Gettysburg, arriving in the 1730's.
>
> (2) Son Robert McPherson Jr. (1730-1789) m. 1751 Agnes Miller (1732-1802). He was a leader in the Revolution in York County, Pennsylvania, while living west of Gettysburg. Robert and Agnes had six daughters and three sons (WB).
>
> (3) Son Col. John McPherson (1760-1829) m. Sarah Smith (1767-1821) of Frederick Maryland. They became leading citizens of Frederick and led in entertaining Lafayette and son in 1824. It is believed that he built Prospect Hall Mansion on the southwest edge of Frederick (deed WR39-657 (1811)). By family tradition Sarah was a daughter of a Tory General.
>
> (4) Son Dr. William Smith McPherson (1792-1879) m. Catherine Cornog Davis, daughter of John N. of Philadelphia. They lived in Frederick and Baltimore.
>
> (5) Dr. William S. McPherson, Jr. (1824-1917) m. Harriet Anderson McPherson (1825-1896) (cousin). They lived in Frederick and after about 1855 in the Auburn mansion at Catoctin Furnace.
>
> (6) Son Thomas Buchanan McPherson (1850-1922) m. Louise Niven (1858-1943) of Roselle, NJ. They lived in Omaha but returned to Auburn in 1915. Their children were: Louise (1878-1975) who lived at Auburn; Thomas B. Jr. (1888-1951); William S. III (1888-1953) and Margaret (1892-1977) who married Clement E. Gardiner, Jr. (1888-1930).

Sources of the above were Clement E. Gardiner III and a genealogy by William Lindsay McPherson of Blacksburg, VA. For McPhersons in Adams County, see (WB). For J.H.T. McPherson (b. 1865) see NC Vol. 13. A McPherson Family Museum is at Newtonmore, south of Inverness, Scotland.

The approximate date of 1805 for building of Auburn mansion at Catoctin Furnace by Baker Johnson is confirmed by the deed to the site of 1803, also by the names Blackford and Thornburgh on 7 iron firebacks built into fireplaces of the mansion. Benjamin Blackford and Thomas Thornburgh operated the Furnace from 1801 to 1812. Auburn which has 20 rooms has been preserved remarkably while the ironmaster's mansion near Little Hunting Creek became a ruin long ago. For the history of Episcopal Harriet Chapel and Catoctin Furnace see the book *Faith in the Furnace* by Elizabeth Y. Anderson (1984). (LC)

W&M-766. Descendants of Col. John McPherson and Sarah included Robert Grier (1788-1824) m. Maria Davis. Children were Catherine Davis Grier (1818-1880) and Robert Grier (1819-1899) m. Melissent Fowler Washington (1824-1893) of Frederick; Horatio m. Mary Sophia Buchanan (children: John Smith and Harriet Anderson m. William Smith McPherson); Edward Brien m. Ann Talbot (children: Edward Brien m. Mary Diller, Cornelia m. John Thomson Douglass); Harriet Smith m. John Brien (son Robert Coleman m. Ann Elizabeth Tiernan); Alexander m. Matilda Chase Johnson.

W&M-767. Mosheim M. Metzger (1845-1919) unmarried and his parents William (1809-1868) and Lydia (Toms) (1815-1899) are buried at Myersville Lutheran Church. Long before William moved from York County to Middletown Valley there were Metzgers in our area. The records of Monocacy Lutheran Church show that Georg Valentin Metzger had a son baptized in 1753.

W&M-767. William R. Murphy (1856-1944) and wife Susan Ann Bussard (1861-1890) were buried at Mt. Olivet. His parents Horace L. (1824-1908) and Charlotte D. (Thompson) (1836-1919) are buried at Urbana Catholic Church. William's grandfather William Murphy married Annie V. Elder (1817-1899) of Emmitsburg. James and Thomas Murphy enrolled in the Frederick County Militia of 1812. (LC)

W&M-768. John William Molesworth (1848-1912) and wife Margaret M. (Reinhart) are buried at Mt. Olivet. His parents Thomas (1815-1895) and Mary Ann Darby (Kane) (1819-1892) are buried at New Market M.E. Church. Mary Ann may have been a daughter of Catherine Cain (bc 1788) of New Market District (census of 1850).

W&M-769. William H. McClaine (1849-1930) and wife Laura E. (Wagaman) (1852-1926) as well as his father Joseph (1817-1882) are buried at the Reformed Church of Sabillasville. The 1800 census of Emmitsburg lists the family of John McClean and wife (26-45 years of age) with three sons.

George and James McClain served in the Frederick County Militia of 1812. Early McClains or McCleans were in the south of the county and in Adams County (WB).

W&M-770. Jacob L. Moser (1837-1911) and wife Catherine (Grossnickle) (1835-1909) are buried at Grossnickle Meeting House north of Ellerton. His parents, Elias Moser (1809-1862) and wife Lydia A. Harp (1814-1880) are buried at Thurmont U. B. Church.

The unrelated Moser who settled in northern Monocacy area was Leonard who arrived on the ship *Adventure* at Philadelphia in September, 1732 along with a group of other Mosers. The ages of adults Leonard, Christian, Mattlena and Paulus were not given. Other Mosers on the ship were Tobias, (30 years), Eva (40), Eva Barbara (16), Basion (6), George (48), Hans George (8), Hannah Margaret (12), Michel (38), Simon (11), Susanna Barbara (40), Ann Maria (10), and Margaretta (8). I have found only records of Leonard in Frederick County.

In 1735 the youth Leonard Moser was with leader Thomas Cresap supporting Maryland in the so-called "War between Maryland and Pennsylvania" over the boundary dispute. At Conojohela, south of later Wrightsville, Pennsylvania, where Cresap and others from Maryland had settled west of the Susquehannah River in defiance of Pennsylvania authorities, Moser was captured by the Lancaster County sheriff and about 30 Pennsylvania supporters, and he was in prison briefly. Along with several other followers of Cresap who retreated from Pennsylvania territory about 1736, Leonard Moser came to the German Monocacy Settlement. He was a sponsor of two baptisms in records of Monocacy Lutheran Church in 1743. In 1744 Leonard Moser was a sponsor of the baptism there of Elisa Julyana, daughter of Jacob Weller, who later became the leader of the Moravian congregation. In 1744 Leonard married Maria Kochher. Several records indicate that Leonard was a weaver. In Frederick County Court records of 1751, the apparent relative by marriage, Michael Coker, age 11, was apprenticed to Leonard Moser, weaver. In 1758, when the Moravian Congregation of Graceham was formally organized Leonard and second wife (Maria) Sarah were members.

Emigrant Leonard Moser had tracts of land surveyed in 1754. In 1764, he sold to Mark Harman, farmer, 30 acres of the tract Nolin Mountain near Great Hunting Creek. In 1765, Leonard with permission of wife Sarah sold to surveyor Thomas Brooke of Prince George's county two tracts on Hunting Creek as follows:

> (1) Part of tract Germantown, starting at the south side of a branch running into Hunting Creek.
>
> (2) 20 acres of Stoney Ridge (opposite) on the north side of Hunting Creek. The Germantown tract is believed to have been the site of the Old Monocacy Log church south of later Thurmont, indicated from my research described in M&C-I. The last recorded deed of Leonard and wife Sarah was their sale in 1771 of 20 acres of the tract Paradise on a branch of Hunting Creek to Charles Beatty.

Rev. Jacob Lischy recorded baptisms of Samuel Moser (1751) and Elizabeth Moser (1755) children of Leonard by his first wife. The following children of Leonard and Sarah are recorded in the Moravian Archives of Graceham:

> (1) John Michael (b. 1759); first son John (b. 1784).
>
> (2) Samuel (b. 1761).
>
> (3) Frances (b. 1763).
>
> (4) Christian (b. 1765).
>
> (5) Ann Elizabeth (b. 1767).
>
> (6) Henry (b. 1769).
>
> (7) Joseph (1772-1773).

Numerous Moser descendants were named after Leonard the immigrant including the grandfather of present George L. Moser who now owns Stoney Ridge and lives on Moser Road south of Thurmont.

Most of the Mosers of upper Middletown Valley are from a different line, apparently unrelated to Leonard of Monocacy Valley. They initially belonged to the Church of the Brethren and descendants are buried at Grossnickle Meeting House, Myersville and Burkittsville. According to descendant Harold E. Moser their emigrant ancestor from the Palatinate was John Jacob Moser who with four sons and two daughters was among those settled first by the British in the Hudson Valley around 1710. They were among the Germans who fled the harsh conditions there and settled in southeastern Pennsylvania. John Moser, the youngest of the four sons, married in Pennsylvania and died young in 1744. His sons Conrad and Valentine settled in Middletown Valley about 1745 and became ancestors of many Mosers there.

W&M-770. See also W&M-1441. Francis H. Markell (1860-1925) and wife Mary Louise (Keller) (1863-1944) also his parents Francis (1821-1883) and Caroline (Delaplaine) (1833-1905) are buried at Mt. Olivet. Mary Louise Markell was one of the most active members of the Historical Society of Frederick County of her time in research, but her handwriting is difficult to decipher.

Conrad Markell emigrated about 1748 from Alsace and settled at Frederick. His son William Markell and wife Mary (Boyer) had son John (1781-1860) who married Catherine (Mantz) (1788-1857). They are buried in Mt. Olivet. A great grandson of William was Charles Frederick Markell (1855-1941), a lawyer and author who lived in D. C., Baltimore and Birmingham, AL). (NC Vol. 31). A Markell genealogy has been written by Norton W. Merkel, Bucks Co, Pennsylvania about 1977 (Y). Jacob and John Markell served in the Frederick County Militia in the War of 1812.

W&M-771. Thomas J. Mohler (1839-1891) and wife Laura V. (Tucker) (1847-1935) are buried at Mt. Olivet. Other Mohler families have lived around Utica and Frederick.

W&M-771. Josiah G. Messner (1841-1922) and wife Elizabeth (Domer) (1831-1911) are buried at Thurmont U. B. Cemetery. In the 1800 census of Emmitsburg George Mesner, age between 26 and 45 lived alone.

W&M-772. Col. D. John Markey (1882-1982) married M. Edna Mullinix, a daughter of Lorenzo E. Mullinix (1855-1930) and Annie E. (1860-1942). Col. John and Edna are buried in Arlington Cemetery, VA; her parents in Mt. Olivet. Col. John's parents John Hanshew Markey (1835-1899) and Ida Maria (Willard) (1853-1941) are buried at Mt. Olivet where also are buried Col. Markey's grandparents David J. Markey (1809-1885) and wife Susan (Bentz) (1810-1887). Ida was a daughter of Ezra and Laura (Biser) Willard of Merryland Tract. David Markey was Constable of Frederick Town Hundred in 1813.

Col. D. John Markey and wife Edna (Mullinix) had two children: D. John (1909-1959) generally known as Jack and Mary Elizabeth who married Harold Hooper (d. 1992) and lived in Walkersville. Harold was Vice Pres. of Hood College. Jack and wife Mary Alice (Mobley) had sons: David John III, Richard Edward, Jay Atlee, Peter Byron and Robert William. Some earlier Mobleys are given in M&C-II.

Col. David John Markey served at the shoe store in Frederick of his father at 7 N. Market St. He coached football at Western Maryland College and at Maryland Agricultural College (later U. of Maryland). During World War I Markey rose to be a Brig. General on the General Staff of the U. S. Army, but continued to be known in Frederick as Col. Markey. From 1924 to 1963, he was on the American Battle Monuments Commission. He accompanied General John J. Pershing on trips in Europe for the Commission. Col. Markey married secondly Carlotta Kinnamon (c.1904-1982) of Talbot County. When Col. Markey died in 1963, he was survived by sisters Mrs. Susan J. Fickling (Mrs. Thomas J.) of Frederick and Mrs. Eleanor Hughes of Braddock Heights.

Another son of John H. Markey and wife Ida M. Willard was Willard Markey (1878-1916) who married Bertha LaRue Zimmerman (1880-1937) daughter of George H. and Florence Zimmerman. Willard and Bertha have two children: Nancy Virginia Ackler, family historian, of 702 Walker Ave. Baltimore and Willard Hanshew Markey who married Leona Palmer. Willard Markey is known internationally as a manufacturer of hand bells. His firm Malmark, Inc. is located in Bell Crest Park, Plumsteadville, near Doylestown, Pennsylvania.

W&M-773. Henry F. Maxell (1850-1916) and wife Jemima (Stansbury) (1850-1927) are buried at Mt. View Cemetery at Emmitsburg. He was a son of Samuel Maxell (1809-1882) and Jane M. (Furgueson) (1811-1886) who are buried at Emmitsburg Lutheran Church. Maxells were early in Pennsylvania. In 1742 David Maxel was granted a warrant for 250 acres in Lancaster County, Pennsylvania. (LC)

Julia M. Maxell married Robert Hockensmith of the prominent family of Emmitsburg of whom the first settler was Conrad Hockenschmidt whose will discloses sons George, Jacob, Michael and Conrad, Jr. For later generations, see Beryl McPherson in History of St. Elias Lutheran Church by Rev. Ronald Fearer.

W&M-774. William E. Mercer (1840-1905) and wife Ida S. (Webster) (1843-1927) and his parents William (1808-1857) and Susan (Smith) (1799-1868) are buried at Middletown Lutheran Church. In 1800 there were already 14 Smith families in Middletown Valley.

W&M-775. Samuel B. Martz (1866-1933) and wife Rosie (Stottlemyer) (1871-1933) also his parents Lewis J. Martz (1836-1905) and Margaret (Staley) (1844-1922) are buried at Mt. Olivet. Martz or Merz families were early in Frederick County. In 1756, Dewald and wife Catherine Merz were sponsors at Monocacy Church. *Martz Families of Maryland* (Frederick, 1973) was written by Ralph F. Martz. See also W&M-1591. In the 1800 census of Frederick Town District was the household of George Martz and wife, both over 45 years of age. In the Frederick County Militia of 1812 Capt. George Martz (c.1786-1868) is recorded with wife Catherine (1778-1858); they lived near Frederick.

W&M-776. Emory L. Coblentz (1869-1941) and wife Amy A. (Doub) (1871-1904) also his parents Edward L. (1840-1902) and Lucinda (Bechtol) (1847-1935) are buried at Middletown Reformed Church.

Hans Nicholas Coblentz or Koblenz (born at Friedelsheim, Germany in 1698) and wife Anna Catharina emigrated via Philadelphia in 1743. They settled in Germany Township of later Adams County, Pennsylvania and attended St. John's Lutheran Church near Littlestown. Herman Coplance paid taxes in Germany Township in 1767. One of their sons was John Jacob. They intermarried with the Hesson Family (M&C-II).

W&M-777. Lewis W. Mehrling (1861-1933) and wife Estella (Whitmore) (1867-1932) also his parents John Lewis (1815-1893) and wife Ann Elizabeth (1819-1890) are buried in Mt. Olivet. Ostheim, Germany, where John Lewis was born is near Hanau, northeast of Frankfurt am Rhein. Mehrling families several generations earlier had fled northward from Catholic Salzburg. See files of descendant Jacob Mehrling Holdcraft at Frederick and M&C-II. Of the three brothers George, Lewis and Nicholas Mehrling who emigrated about 1855, Nicholas settled in Indiana.

W&M-778. Irving R. Morgan (1860-1933) and wife Ida M. (Fox) (1866-1852) and his parents James W. (1833-1902) and Delilah B. (Recher) (1838-1885) are buried at Wolfsville Lutheran Church. By tradition, the Morgan family (earlier Maugan) originated in Wales. David Morgan, grandfather of Irving operated grist and paper mills in Middletown Valley. Irving and Ida were grandparents of Leah Leatherman Spade of Wolfsville.

Five generations of the Recher family at Ziefen, Switzerland are disclosed (BL). Peter Recher (1724-1791) emigrated in 1751. His parents had been lacemakers and he was a weaver. Peter and wife Mary Anna (b. 1730) had at least six children including John (1765-1803) who married Anna Rosina Protzman (1772-1852) (daughter of Jacob and Joanna (Linebaugh)). Their daughter Joanna (1798-1895) married Daniel Stottlemyer (1796-1874) (son of David and Margaret Ann (Magruder). Their daughter Roseanna married Daniel A. Biser.

W&M-780. George Washington Miller (1847-1923) and wife Emma J. (Harbaugh) (1859-1920) are buried at Mt. View Cemetery at Emmitsburg. His parents John A. Miller (d. at 51 years) and wife Amelia Ann (Eyler) (1822-1884) are buried at Sabillasville Reformed Church. (LC)

Henry Eyler (1770-1857) and John Eyler (1783-1866) were in the Frederick County Militia in the War of 1812. The former died in Westmoreland County, Pennsylvania. Children of John and Rebecca (Harbaugh) are given.

W&M-781. Joseph A. Ludy (1868-1918) and wife Lillie (Leatherman) (b. 1860), and also his parents William (1820-1899) and wife Susan (Dutrow) (1829-1908), are buried at Myersville U. B. Church. Joseph's grandparents Nicholas, Sr. (1776-1863) and Eve Ann Ludy (1779-1847) are buried at St. John's Lutheran Church at Church Hill near Ellerton and north of Myersville. In the census of 1800 in Middletown Valley were four households of John and Philip over 45 years of age and Jacob and Nicholas Ludy not yet 45 years old.

W&M 781. Frank Nathan Maynard (1857-1935) and wife Eliza D. (Downey) (1867-1956) and his parents Nathan (1824-1888) and (Jemima) Eleanor (Chiswell)(1834-1916) were all buried at Mt. Olivet. The grandparents of Frank N. were Thomas Maynard (1775-1830) and Ruth (Griffith) (1784-1855) also buried at Mt. Olivet.

Maynards were early in Frederick Co. Thomas Maynard was Deputy Ranger of Frederick Co. in 1749. After Frederick Co. was formed he became Constable of Linganore Hundred. E. R. Goldsborough of the Historical Society of Frederick Co. wrote that the Maynard families were most confusing of all early local families in their genealogy. Descendants of Henry Maynard of London and Anne Arundel Co. and wife Mrs. Sarah (Hopkins) (m. 1704) are discussed by John F. Dorman. (N)

W&M-783. (Joseph) Thomas Maynard (1860-1952) and wife Elsie (Barnes) (1872-1945) are buried at New London Methodist Church (Central Chapel). His parents Judge Howard Griffith Maynard (1817-1899) and Sarah Newton (Chiswell) (1836-1892) as well as his grandparents Thomas Maynard (1775-1830) and wife Ruth (Griffith) (1789-1855) are buried at Mt. Olivet. (LC)

W&M-784. Thomas H. Haller (1855-1935) and wife Cora Elizabeth (Bowers) (1859-1946), also his parents Thomas (1816-1882) and wives Lydia (Shearer) (1820-1845) (daughter of Lewis) and Caroline Rebecca (Fessler) (1828-1901) are all buried at Mt. Olivet. The grandfather of Thomas H. was Tobias Haller, Sr., who married Elisabeth Hechler in 1792.

The early Hallers flourished around Jefferson in southern Middletown Valley. In the 1800 census, Peter Haller over 45 years lived with his wife, another female over 45, a male 10-16 and a male 26-45. George Haller and wife 26-45 with 2 sons and a daughter under 10 years lived in western Frederick Co. in 1800. There are numerous Hallers in the records of Frederick Lutheran Church. Among the early ones are George Michael and wife Dorothea who had Catherine born in 1763; Gottfried Haller married in 1777 Elisabeth Abel with witnesses Christopher and Catherine Haller. Christopher Haller in 1783 married Barbara Lutz with witnesses Michael and Dorothea Haller; Michael Haller married in 1787 Catherine Dorff with witnesses George Michael Haller and sons Gottfried and Christopher. The Middletown Lutheran Church has records of Hallers beginning in 1796 when Peter Jr. and wife Magdalena had Johannes baptized and in 1800 when they baptized Peter III with Peter, Sr. as a sponsor. Daniel and Catherine had children baptized there in 1803 to 1808.

There are many gravestones of Hallers in Frederick Co. but only a few old ones such as Elisabeth (1772-1863) wife of an early Tobias, Jacob (1794-1873) and wife Mary (1797-1845), and Joshua (1777-1850) with wife Catherine (1787-1866), all of whom were buried at Mt. Olivet.

In the Frederick Co. Militia of 1812 were Elisha, George, George William, Henry, Jacob, Philip, Tobias and William Haller. (LC)

W&M-785. Dr. Sabritt Sollers Maynard M.D. (1835-1913) and wife Clayonia (Thomas) (1844-1921) are buried at Mt. Olivet. See also 781.

Sabritt Sollers Maynard (1772-1834) son of Thomas and Ariana (Dorsey) was named a Major of 1st. Battalion 20th Regt. of Frederick Co. Militia in 1812. His grandparents were Sabritt Sollers and wife Mary (Heighe) daughter of James of Calvert Co. His great grandfather John Sollers Maynard died in Calvert Co. in 1699. Maj. Sabritt in 1806 married Mary Dorsey (d. 1820).

W&M-786. Charles Perry Levy (1873-1912) and wife Roberta H. (Dixon) (1878-1949) are buried at Mt. Olivet. His grandfather Perry J. Levy (1813-1897) and wife Elizabeth D. (van Swearingen) (1819-1890) are buried at Middletown Lutheran Church. Son Charles V. S. Levy (1844-1895) and wife Mary Grace (Strobel) (1844-1899) are buried at Mt. Olivet.

Levy families lived earlier in the area of Frederick. In 1800 census David Levy, Sr. and wife were over 45 years, apparently living with 8 children and 5 slaves. David Jr. and wife, 26-45 had 3 children under 10 years. Jacob Levy, 26-45 apparently a widower had 4 children under 16 years.

David T. Levy was in the Frederick Co. Militia in 1812. He married in 1820 Elizabeth Myers (b. c.1797) in Frederick. After 19 years at Middletown they moved to Carrollton, Ohio.

W&M-787. John S. Long (1856-1949) and wife Emma I. (Philips) (1854-1935) are buried at Mt. Tabor Church at Rocky Ridge. His parents Abraham (1828-1894) and Amanda (Mengis) (1835-1915) also are buried at Mt. Tabor Church.

A John Long paid taxes on 50 acres in Germany Township, Adams Co., PA in 1789. Also in Germany Township were Philip Long taxed in 1784-1809. See W&M-1599.

W&M-788. Simon Lohr (1830-1919) and wife Fransanna B. (Mort) (1840-1931) are buried at Thurmont United Brethren Church. His parents John (1794-1863) and Christina (Overholtzer) (1801-1879) are buried at Apples Church near Thurmont. His parents were Joseph Lohr (1755-1837) and wife Mary (1756-1822) who are buried at Emmitsburg Lutheran Church.

Joseph and Balzer Lohr paid taxes in Germany Township, Adams Co., PA near Littlestown in 1782 (PA Archives, 3rd. series 21-561). (LC)

W&M-789. Amos Lease (1838-1924) and wife Mary (Houck) (1850-1929), daughter of John, are buried at Mt. Olivet.

The Lease name is of Germanic origin. Lorentz and Anna Felicitas Lies emigrated from Essenheim in 1741 (M&C II-72). Jacob and Maria Dorothea Lies had Philip born April 2, 1772 with sponsor Wilhelm Lies in records of Frederick Reformed Church. They also had offspring Elisabeth in 1774 and Henry in 1777. Wilhelm and wife Elisabetha had daughter Margaret baptized in 1796 in Frederick Reformed records. In the census of District 7 of Eastern Frederick Co. in 1800 Jacob Lease (over 45 years) and wife were living with 4 children, while Jacob, Jr. (26-45) had 3 children. William Lease and wife (both over 45) apparently had 6 children. (LC)

W&M-789. Harvey B. Lease (1866-1926) and wife Alma P. (Sanner) (1869-1951) are buried at Mt. Olivet. His parents Robert (1832-1885) and Mary (Sheetenhelm) (1843-1885) are also buried at Mt. Olivet at Frederick. (LC). In 1800 in Liberty Township lived Frederick Shittenhelm and wife, over 45 years, also Jacob S. and wife, between 16 and 26.

W&M-790. H. Melvin Keller (1853-1910) and wife Hellen (Schildknecht) (1856-1939) are buried at the United Brethren Church in Myersville. Hellen was pronounced Healen according to daughters Josie and Naomi. See M&C-II. Melvin's parents Henry (1820-1901) and Sarah (Biser) (1828-1901) are buried at Middletown Reformed Church. Living nearby in 1850 were Jacob Biser (b. c.1793) and wife Catherine (b. c.1800).

There were several Kellers in early Frederick Co. Conrad Keller of Taskers Chance was naturalized in 1740 (T&D). Jacob Keller is in court records in 1750 and 1764. In 1754 he was about 67 years old. His estate was settled by wife Elisabeth and Jacob, Jr. John Jacob, Sr. (1743-1824) purchased part of Ramshorn Tract near Myersville in 1750. Jacob, Jr. had a will probated in 1825 showing sons Jacob III, David and Abraham (deceased) and Andrew Keller, who bought 100 acres of Ramshorn in 1768. John Keller (wife Magdalena) sold 250 acres of Ramshorn in 1789.

No Daniel Keller of suitable dates as grandfather of Melvin appears in census and gravestone records. Could Daniel be in fact David (1784-1863) a son of John Jacob Keller (1743-1824) and Anna Maria (Humbert) (1747-1809)?

John Jacob and wife Anna Maria (Humbert) (1747-1809) (daughter of William and Mary Humbert of Germany had children:

(1) Barbara (1769-1826) m. Mathias Brandenberg (1763-1818); dau Catherine m. Jacob Biser; son Henry m. Mary Biser.
(2) John (b. 1771).
(3) Anna Mary (1773-1859); unm; buried Middletown Ref.
(4) Jacob, Jr. (1775-1841) m. Rosanna Doub (1786-1854) d/o Jacob and Louisa; farmed part of Ramshorn; 6 ch.
(5) Abraham (1779-1822); bap. Middletown Ref. Church.
(6) Catherine (1782-1805) m. George Routzahn (1774-1867).
(7) David (1784-1865); miller near Little Catoctin Cr. west of Middletown; son Henry m. Sarah Biser.
(8) Magdalena, bap. 1789 Middletown Ref. Church.

Keller baptisms occur in early records of Monocacy Lutheran Church. For example Rudolph had a daughter Elisabeth in 1755 with sponsors John and wife Elisabeth Margaret Stoll (Stull). Casper Keller and wife Anna Margaret (Trautman) (daughter of Leonard) had an infant baptized in 1758. Rudolph Keller's will probated in 1769 shows wife Juliana. Rudolph's tract Devalt's Forest went to his children: Frederick, Jacob, Conrad, Elisabeth, Maria, and Ann. Executors were Frederick Whitman and Caspar Keller. Another important ancestor was Casper Keller. Noted great granddaughter, Helen Keller, in her book *The Story of My Life* wrote that he was born in Bern, Switzerland. However, Kathleen Rizer of Dayton, Ohio, believes that he was John Casper born 1736, son of Conrad of the Reformed Church, Lancaster, PA. Conrad, a native of Germany was naturalized in 1740. Casper was confirmed at the Frederick Reformed Church in 1754. He was a millwright and built a mill on Linganore Creek. In 1803 a Casper was taxed in Hagerstown and in 1809 was the keeper of the Workhouse of Washington Co.

The book on Maryland Militia in the War of 1812 gives information about Conrad, Frederick and Jacob Keller. (LC)

W&M-791. Henry Milton Kefauver (1837-1925) is buried in Middletown Reformed Cemetery. His wife Elizabeth (Young) died in 1898. His parents Henry Kefauver (1810-1786) and Maria (Biser) (1811-1891) also are buried in Middletown at the Reformed Church.

Philip Kiefhaber and wife Anna Maria lived briefly in the Little Conewago Settlement near later Littlestown, PA, before they bought land in Middletown Valley from Caleb Touchstone in 1750. Philip was naturalized as a communing member of the Brethren Church of Bishop Daniel Leatherman in 1760. Philip appears in Frederick Co. court records in 1752. Nicholas (1756-1817) was a son of Philip and Anna Maria (Beckenbach) (Beckenbaugh). Nicholas had a sister Susanna. Philip Jr. (born 1747) and wife Magdalena (1750-1807) sponsored a baptism at Middletown Reformed Church in 1803. In Middletown Lutheran records Jacob Kiefhaber and wife Anna Maria had son John George baptized in 1786. In Lutheran records of Frederick Anna Maria Kiefhaber in 1773 married George Meyer. See *Kefauver Families*, a genealogy by Viola Holter Shue (Middletown 1976) (F) (H), also W&M-1362.

Jacob Kefauver who married Lenora Coblentz was a son of George and great grandson of immigrant Philip. Jacob and Lenora had son Oliver Henry who married Lillie May Neikirk and farmed in Middletown Valley. Their son Grayson Neikirk Kefauver (1900-1946) was author of books on high school teaching and was Fellow of American Association for Advancement of Science. In 1922 he married Anna Elizabeth Skinner of Tucson, AZ. (NC vol 35).

Col. Lloyd A. Kefauver M.D. (1882-1976) of St. Louis, MO served in U.S. Army Medical Corp. worldwide and is buried at Arlington Cemetery. His children included Admiral Russell Kefauver of NC, Mrs. Miriam Campbell of St. Louis, Mrs. Jean Cole of SC; his brother George W. Kefauver lived at Middletown.

An early Kiefhaber settler in the Little Conewago area of Heidelberg Township of later eastern Adams Co., was Conrad, (d. 1798) who was naturalized in 1764 and by tradition was a brother of Philip who settled in Middletown Valley. Conrad's son Nicholas (1751-1817) married Mary Catherine Forney (1752-1798). They were taxed in 1800 for 150 acres and distilling equipment in Conewago Twp. The will of Nicholas discloses sons Philip; Peter, wife Catherine (son Frederick); Jacob (c. 1780-1863); and Conrad. Nicholas, Peter and Jacob Keefauver were taxed in Cumberland Twp. near Gettysburg. Franklin S. Keefauver, son of Jacob and Maria (Sell) born in Adams Co., in 1826, settled in Darke Co., OH. From Conrad a lineage of 8 generations has been traced to Senator Estes Keefauver born in 1903 at Madisonville, TN. (G).

W&M-791. Conrad Kaempf (1685-1764), wife Maria (1695-1758) and children in 1733 emigrated from Unter Gimbern, east of Sinsheim in the Baden area of Germany (southeast of Heidelberg). After spending some time around New Holland, PA where a daughter was born they moved to the area of Rocky Springs west of Frederick (not to Kemptown). However, the oldest son was settled soon where Ballenger Creek crosses Ballenger Creek Road. Conrad was naturalized based on Communion in 1743 in the Reformed Congregation of Monocacy.

The children of Conrad and Maria follow (more information is in M&C-I):

(1) Christian (1715-1790) m. Elizabeth Ferree; 2m Gertrude ----.

(2) (John) Gilbert (1717-1794) m. (Susannah) Margaret Getzendanner (1724-1814).

(3) (John) Frederick (1725-1844) m. Regina ----.

(4) (John) Peter (1727-1808) m. Catherine ----; son Solomon and wife Barbara Hershberger settled about 1800 at Kemptown south of New Market.

(5) (Anna) Catherine (b. 1731) m. Enos Hedges.

(6) Maria Sophia (b. 1734) (record at New Holland, PA).

(7) Elizabeth (b. 1744) m. Adam Getzendanner (1724-1783).

From Gilbert and Margaret Kemp were descended son Frederick (1747-1814) m. Dorothea Hershberger (1753-1831), both buried at Rocky Springs; grandson David (1791-1869) m. Ruth Serine Lakin (1800-1872) buried at Jefferson and great grandson David Columbus 1841-1920, m. Anna Serena (Slyh) Walcutt (1844-1931) of Columbus, Ohio.

About 150 Kemp names are indexed in the Zimmerman genealogy. (Z)

W&M-792. Rhodes R. Kemp (1866-1930) and wife Charlotte V. Eby (1870-1944), as well as his parents Charles Wesley (1830-1876) and Columbia A. Rhodes (1831-1899), are all buried at Mt. Olivet.

Immigrant Frederick Kemp (1725-1804) and wife Regina had son Rev. Peter (1749-1811) a founder of the Church of the Brethren who married Mary Lehman or Leaman (1758-1845). The latter had son Peter Kemp (1803-1885) who it is believed married Elizabeth Myers, 1804-1836) and lived near Walkersville. Their son Charles Wesley Kemp married Columbia A. Rhodes.

Rhodes, Rhoads and related families prominent in Frederick Co. history are believed to be descendants of Germanic Roth families (pronounced in Continental Europe Roat). The rapid change to Rhodes and other spellings may be accounted for by the old hizzing pronunciation of TH by the English and by confusion with the English word rot. W&M contains 18 references to Rhodes.

Henry Rothes (wife Catherine) sold part of Tasker's Chance back to Daniel Dulany in 1749. Henry Rode sold land to Jacob Baney (Beny) in 1760. Henry Roads bought from John George Arnold the tract Rhod's Purchase, a portion of Ramshorn with deed of 1749. Henry Rhodes (wife Catherine) sold the tract Cuckhold's Horns next to Ramshorn to Samuel Bussard in 1763. Henry Rhodes signed a petition led by Stephen Ramsburg against unjust taxation of German settlers. Henry Rhode Jr. bought land from Solomon Vickory in 1805. Henry Rott bought land from Barton Philpot in 1783. These are various ways that English officials wrote down what they heard Germans enunciate. There may have been a Rhodes family of English origin in Western Maryland. A John Rhodes had an estate settlement in Prince George's Co., in 1735; kin were Nicholas Roads and George Williams.

W&M-795. Rev. George F. Kindley (1830-1913) and wife Elizabeth (Boyer) (1837-1925) as well as his parents George F., Sr. (1806-1887) and wife Hepsabah (Etchison) (1809-1879) are buried at Kemptown Methodist Church. The second wife of George Sr. was Sallie, (1817-1891).

Maria Barbara Kindle (1700-1775) wife of David Kindle (1686-1772) was buried at the Lutheran Church in Frederick. (M&C II-70). A genealogy of *Descendants of William Kindley* born 1740 was written by Bessie J. M. Wimberley, (Arlington, VA 1967) (FH). (LC)

W&M-796. William H. Krantz (1844-1931) and wife Alice E. (Boyer) (1845-1922) are buried at Mt. Olivet. His parents were Frederick J. and Catherine (Stup (1823-1879) (daughter of Daniel and Elizabeth (Wedrick)). Frederick Krantz's second wife was Laura V. (Mealey) (1842-1896); his grandmother Catherine (Arter) Krantz (1820-1890) is buried at Mt. Olivet.

Arrivals from Germany at Philadelphia were Michael and Valentine Krantz, age 32 years, in Sept. 1738.

W&M-797. E. Frederick Klein, Jr. (1836-1905) and wife Mary M. are buried at Linganore Brethren Church along with three daughters Lizzie R. (1861-1950),

Anna M. (1864-1953) and Ida M. (1872-1946). At the same church are buried their brothers: David E. (1862-1951) and wife Maggie V. (1865-1923); George L. (1866-1938) and wife Amanda E. (1865-1947).

Descendants of earlier Kleins have been abundant locally as Klines and Clines especially in upper Middletown Valley and around Frederick. In the 1800 census of Middletown Valley were families of George Klein and wife, both over 45 years, and Daniel Klein and wife, both between 26 and 45 years of age. Frederick Cline, over 45 years, apparently lived with a son. In 1800 in Frederick District lived families of Jacob and Stephen Kline and their wives, all between 26 and 45 years.

In records of the Frederick Co. Militia in 1812 are Peter Klein, also Charles, George, Henry John, and Philip Kline, as well as Casper, Frederick and Philip Cline. (LC) Many Klines and Littles have lived in eastern Adams Co., PA (WB).

W&M-798. George W. Stocksdale (1831-1922) and wives Amanda (Buckingham) (1843-1916) and Mary C. (Crooks) (1843-1916) are buried at Thurmont United Brethren Church. Robert Crooks (b. c.1801), a teacher in Emmitsburg, was born in Pennsylvania in 1850.

W&M-799. Walker Neill Jolliffe (1876-1931) married Lulla Vinton (Burkhold). According to a gravestone at Mt. Olivet W. N. Jolliffe and wife Louise had a baby Mary Louise who died in 1907. Jollifes were early in Frederick County, VA, where wills were probated for William 1770; James 1771 and John 1777. (LC).

W&M-799. George M. Isanogle (1849-1908) and wife Ann Matilda (Bowers) (1844-1920) are buried at Thurmont United Brethren Church. His parents Michael M. (1811-1888) and Ann Elizabeth (Jackson) (1815-1896) are buried at Utica. Michael Isanogle enlisted under Capt. Joseph Ward in the Frederick County Militia of 1812.

W&M-800. Dr. Samuel T. Haffner M.D. (1848-1910) and wife Susan (Whitmore) (1860-1936) are buried at Mt. Olivet. In the Frederick area in the census of 1800 are four Haffner households. Frederick and Michael were over 45 years old. Frederick Jr. and Michael Haffner were between 26 and 45 years old. Haffner is a dialect form of Hoefner and Heffner. In the Frederick Co. Militia of the War of 1812 were Daniel, Jacob, John, Lawrence and Michael Heffner.

W&M-801. Prof. Charles Henry Jourdan (1830-1913) and wife Adelaide (Dielman) (1852-1911) are buried at St. Anthony Catholic Cemetery beside the Grotto at Mt. St. Mary's. Adelaide's father was Dr. Henry Dielman, composer and musician (1811-1882) born at Frankfurt am Rhein and wife Emily (Dawson) (1815-1870) of Baltimore. (LC)

Emily's father was Capt. Philoman Dawson. Henry and Emily's son Lawrence or Larry Dielman is remembered as a flute player at Mt. St. Mary's. He lived from 1847-1923 and is buried at St. Anthony's.

W&M-803. Dr. John Oliver Hendrix M.D. (1869-1927) and wife Cora May (Whipp) (1863-1934) are buried at Mt. Olivet. He was the early family physician of C.E.S. and parents in Frederick. (LC)

W&M-806. William H. Hogarth (1863-1930) and wife Anna M. (Shawbaker) are buried at the M.E. Church at New Market. The "Gettysburg Granite" which he sold was not granite but the lava rock diabase (much darker and higher in iron content than granites).

W&M-806. Abraham Hemp Jr. (1869-1943) married wife Maud S. (Doty) (b. c.1878). He is buried in Jefferson Union Cemetery. In the 1800 census near Frederick lived Henry Hemp (between 26 and 45 years). Frederick Hemp (1789-1845) and wife Julia (Keller) (1792-1871) are buried at Jefferson as are their son Abraham Sr. (1825-1910) and wife Hannah (Slifer) (1822-1910).

W&M-807. Philip Merle Hiteshew (1860-1931) and wife Margaret (Keller) (1863-1925) and his parents Philip (1800-1872) and Matilda J. (Retgering) (1819-1883) are buried at Mt. Olivet. Jacob Hiteshew (1760-1838) and Mary D. Hiteshew (1769-1850) were buried in the Reformed Church Cemetery in Frederick. Other Hiteshew families have lived near Thurmont and Taneytown. See also W&M-1116.

W&M-808. Col. George Robertson Dennis (1831-1902) and wives Fanny (McPherson) (1836-1930) and Alice (McPherson) (1830-1861) are buried at Mt. Olivet. Son George R. Jr. (1870-1957) stated on his gravestone at Mt. Olivet that he was a great great grandson of Gov. Thomas Johnson. The latter was never a Justice of the Supreme court as stated in W&M-809. George R. Dennis Jr. married Mary Worthington McGill (1877-1943). John McPherson Dennis (1866-1936), son of Col. George and Fanny, was Treasurer of the State of Maryland. His wife was Mary (Chiles) (1870-1957) daughter of Cornelius Carr and Annie (Haller) Chiles of Independence, MO.

According to a file at (FH) Edward and Joseph Dennis, both about 21 years, emigrated to Maryland from London about 1775. (LC)

W&M-809. Ephraim D. Hauver (1844-1923) and wife Martha Ellan (Gordan) (1849-1903), also his parents Christian (1801-1869) and wife Mary (Brown) (1803-1883) are buried at Foxville Lutheran Church. Ephraim's grandfather Peter Hauver or Haber II, (1754-1837) was born in Pennsylvania.

Early Hauvers are shown in the following lineage of Anna Maria (Hauver) Willard. Compare W&M-1093.
(1) Georg Haber and wife Susanna emigrants 1752.
(2) Peter Hauver Sr. (1754 PA - 1837) m. Hannah Casebier.
(3) (Joseph) Christian Hauver (1801-1869) m. Mary Ann Brown (1803-1883).
(4) Peter Hauver II (1823-1907) m. Susan Anna Maria Fox (1826-1876).
(5) Anna Marie Hauver (1866-1959) m. George Allen Willard (1884-1974).

Hauvers are buried at Foxville Lutheran Church also at Myersville and Middletown. A George and wife Susanna (1783-1856) are buried at Apple's Church near Thurmont.

W&M-810. Frederick W. Hankey (1847-1916) and wife Sarah E. C. (Domer), also his parents Frederick (1811-1883) and Mary A. Gernand (1820-1862), are buried at Apples Church near Thurmont. The earlier generation of Isaac Hankey and Susan M. (Apple) (1773-1851) are also buried there. Apparently the great great grandfather of Frederick W. was the emigrant from Germany in

1749 Johanne Henge (1736-1775) whose interesting and crudely inscribed gravestone was in the first graveyard of local Moravians in the orchard of church leader Jacob Weller (on the present George Moser farm). Most of the gravestones were broken up for road material early in this century, but I was told by George Moser that the Henge stone was saved by having fallen into the hole of a groundhog. In 1993 the stone is against a tree near the barn of the Moser farm, near the intersection of Moser Road and Hessong Bridge Road, south of Thurmont. It was John Hankey Jr. who married Barbara Gall and has a deed of 1783. (Ancestors of Maj. Susan Hankey Weber).

W&M-811. Edwin Stone Houck (1867-1915) and wife Susan Brunner (Hammett) are buried at Mt. Olivet but her stone has no dates. His father Dr. Henry J. Houck (b. c.1842) married Mary Eugenia Stone (1846-1907). Edwin's grandparents Henry Houck (1806-1888) and wife Mary G. (1815-1843) are buried at Mt. Olivet. John Houck (1793-1855) married Eleanor McCann at New Market. He served in Militia of 1812.

Johannes Adam Hauck emigrated from Lambsheim, Germany. This and other Houcks or Haug origins are given in M&C II-63. Peter Houck (1735-1798) married (Anna) Margaret Baltzell (c. 1750-1828). Their son Peter Jr. (d. c.1836) or possibly Josiah, was the father of Henry (1806-1888). (LC)

W&M-813. Worthington C. Glaze (1859-1936) and wife Anna M. (Myers) (1863-1941), as well as his parents Joseph (1823-1906) and Margaret Ann (Cramer) (1830-1892) are buried at Mt. Olivet. Joseph's father was David Glaze (died at 78 years) and wife Elizabeth (1799-1884) who also are buried at Mt. Olivet. Margaret Ann's parents Amos (1799-1884) and Barbara (Cramer) (b. c.1798) farmed near Walkersville.

W&M-813. Roy Ingles Hyndman (1874-1954) and wife Laura Jane (Brown) (1869-1940) are buried at Mt. Olivet.

W&M-814. Dr. Bradley H. Hoke M.D. (1871-1948) and wife Alice M. (LaMar) (1873-1942), also his parents Samuel Jr. (1848-1902) and Sarah E. (Hartman) (1850-1940), are buried at Mt. Olivet. Samuel Hoke Sr. (1810-1893) and wife Catherine (1814-1883) also are buried in Mt. Olivet. The father of Samuel Sr. may have been Henry or David Hoch who were taxed in Heidelberg Twp. of later Adams Co., Pennsylvania in 1778.

W&M-815. James H. Harris (1852-1923) husband of Laura V. (Heinlein) has a gravestone in Mt. Olivet Cemetery. His parents were Thomas (1815-1889) and Mary (Blamey) (1820-1893) who are buried at Fairmount Cemetery at Libertytown. Daniel, George, John and Michael Harris served in the Militia of 1812.

An outstanding teacher, band leader and churchman was S. Fenton Harris (c. 1883-1979) who with wife Alberta (Staley) (d. 1950) are buried in Mt. Olivet. He was born at Yellow Springs to George W. (1835-1883) and wife Mary E. (1848-1903) who are buried at nearby Indian Springs Reformed Church. Fenton was the youngest of 9 children. His grandfather was Sgt. George W. Harris (d. 1883), a Union veteran.

W&M-815. Judge John Columbus Motter (1845-1915) and wife Effie Buhrman (Marken) (1853-1911) are buried at Mt. Olivet. He was the second son of Jacob Motter (1814-1872) and Jemima (Troxell) (1810-1881) who are buried at Mountain View Cemetery at Emmitsburg. Lewis Motter (1779-1837) and wife Mary M. (d. 1858) are buried at Emmitsburg Lutheran Church. A son of Lewis and Mary was Isaac who moved to Washington Co., and some of whose descendants are given by Williams in 1906. See also Beryl McPherson in Emmitsburg Chronicle newspaper, April 27 and May 11, 1972.

A John Motter was taxed in the city of Lancaster in 1772 and a George Motter had land in Lancaster Co., in 1782. The German name is spelled Matter. (PA Archives Series 3, Vol 17).

Valentine Motter and wife Catherine who settled in Middletown Valley by 1760 had children: Elizabeth (b. c.1753 in PA) m. Frederick Birely (c. 1753-1806); Ludwig (b. 1763); John (c. 1767-1833) of Shepherdstown had 3 marriages; Valentine m. Susanna Engle, to Washington Co.; Henry d. c.1830) m. Catherine Schmid, lived in Middletown; Catherine (b. 1769); Magdalena; Anna (b. 1775). See Donna V. Russell, *Western Maryland Genealogy* Jan. and April 1987. A Georg Motter (1724-1796) was said to have settled in Manheim Twp, York Co. and some of his descendants came to Frederick Co. in late 1700s. A relation to Valentine is unproved.

According to Beryl McPherson (alias Samuel Carrick) in Emmitsburg Chronicle, May 18, 1972, Lewis Motter, settler at Emmitsburg, was a son of Valentine Motter born in York Co. PA in 1752. Wampler believes that the Motter families emigrated from Alsace.

W&M-817. William H. Hinks (1844-1912) married Ruth Griffith Welsh (d. 1889) and secondly Alice Chase Auld. William was a son of Samuel (1815-1887) and Susan (Nixdorff) (1816-1909) who are buried in Mt. Olivet.

W&M-818. Henry A. Hahn (1852-1933) and wife Anna Mary (Zimmerman) (1851-1932) also his parents Adolph (1832-1910) and Caroline (1827-1906) are all buried at Mt. Olivet.

W&M-819. John E. Harshman married Vallie A. Easterday. He was a son of Elias (1831-1902) and Susan (Warner) (1836-1887). They are buried at Grossnickle Meeting House of the Church of the Brethren, north of Ellerton. *The Harshman (Hirschmann) Families* in two volumes by Clarence and Malvourneen Harshman was published at Berkeley CA in 1976 (F). See also W&M-1346. Christian Sr. and Jr. also John Hershman are in the census of 1800 in Middletown Valley.

W&M-820. John W. Humm (1857-1930) and wife Clara A. (Mainhart) (1858-1911) are buried at Mt. Olivet. His parents Edward (1831-1879) and Jane R. (Renner) (1838-1884) are buried at Utica. In Liberty District in 1800 were households of Mary Renner (over 45 years) and younger Abraham Renner.

W&M-820. George M. Hett (1877-1927) and wife Amy E. (Gonso) (1877-1933) as well as his parents Henry (1846-1920) and Mary E. (Fout), are buried at Mt. Olivet. A brother of George M. was Clarence H. who married Naomi Reifsnider (M&C-II). Jacob Gonso (d. 1862) was in the Frederick Co. Militia in 1812. He married in 1819 Margaret Keller and their children were given.

W&M-822. Dr. Harvey F. Getzendanner was born in 1865 according to his stone in Mt. Olivet. He married Almetta E. (Stein) (1868-1941).

When Christian Getzendanner arrived in later Frederick Co. the area was not "filled with hostile Indians". For Indians of early 18th century see M&C-I. The Getzendanner family originated with Giezendanners near Ebnat, Switzerland. See W&M-1456. Christian's son John (b. 1764) and wife Catherine (Tabler) (1770-1851) had son Jonathan (1798-1859) who married Anna Elizabeth (1801-1883). The latter buried at Mt. Olivet had son John D. Getzendanner (1823-1879) who in turn had son Dr. John W. who married Isadora V. Fout and were parents of Dr. Harvey. Adam, George, Jacob and Solomon Getzendanner enlisted in Frederick Co. Militia of 1812 (LC).

W&M-823. (Charles) Albert Gilson (1875-1950) (unmarried) with parents Charles A. (1840-1892) and Harriet E. (Morrison) (1844-1908) are buried at Mt. Olivet. Albert's grandparents were Richard Gilson (1795-1874) and wife, the widow, Martha Hoff (Biggs) (1799-1873) who are buried at Tom's Creek Methodist Church site. Richard's first wife Mary (1795-1825) is buried at the same location. (LC)

W&M-823. Charles M. Gilpin (1854-1926) and parents George F. (1817-1891) and wife Maria L. (McCulloh) (1820-1899) are buried at Mt. Olivet.

W&M-824. Col. Luke Tiernan Brien (1827-1912) and wife Mary Virginia (Wilson) (1829-1907) are buried at Urbana Catholic Cemetery. His parents were Robert Coleman Brien (1805-1834) and Ann, the daughter of Luke Tiernan.

W&M-826. John T. Gaver (1842-1930) and wife Eliza Jane (Spitler) (1846-1917) are buried at the Grossnickle Brethren Church north of Ellerton. His parents John P. Gaver (1817-1875) and Elizabeth (Cline) (1822-1897) are buried at the same place.

Early Gavers or Gebers in Pennsylvania were Henry taxed in Bucks Co. in 1739 and in Northampton Co. in 1758. Adam Geber had land surveyed in Berks Co. in 1785. Christian Geber was taxed in Philadelphia Co. in 1783. In 1773 Daniel Gaver received a deed for a tract north of Myersville. In the 1800 census of Middletown Valley Peter Gaber and wife were over 45 years while Samuel Gaber and wife were between 26 and 45. Henry Gaver, possibly grandson of the emigrant, had Maria Catherine born 1815 in Middletown Lutheran records. In Middletown Reformed records John and Mary Gaver baptized Elisabeth in 1814 and Sarah in 1825. John T. Gaber's grandparents George (1791-1837) and Mary (Raymer or Roemer) (1796-1865) are buried at Grossnickle Meeting House. A Geber family arriving in Philadelphia in Sept. 1731 consisted of Henrick Sr. age 50; Katharina, 48; Johannes, 20; Henrick Jr, 18; Sarah, 16; Maria, 9; and Daniel, 3.

In the Frederick Co. Militia of 1812 were George, Henry, John and Peter Gaver.

W&M-827. Adolphus Fearhake, Jr. (1840-1913) and wife Agnes (Elliott) (1847-1913) are buried at Mt. Olivet. His grandfather Georg Feuerhacke, son of Martin was schoolmaster at the glassworks village of Gruenenplan near Hanover in North Germany before emigrating with John F. Amelung to New Bremen (later Park Mills). See M&C-II. Glassworks in New Jersey and Pennsylvania were earlier than that of Amelung, but did not produce handsome presentation, engraved goblets to compare with the best from New Bremen. A son of emigrant Georg was Adolphus Fearhake, Sr, (1795-1882) who married Elisabeth Lease (1803-1869). They are buried at Mt. Olivet.

W&M-828. John Michael Fisher (1827-1920) and wife Mary E. (Valentine) (1833-1898) are buried at Creagertown Lutheran Church. His parents were Isaac (1797-1872) and Sarah (Rowe) (1796-1867) who are buried at Emmitsburg Lutheran Church.

Thomas Fisher, Sr. (d. 1793) emigrated from southern Germany in 1751. He married Eva King daughter of Abraham and Anna Maria Koenig all of whom farmed near Littlestown in eastern Adams Co. PA Thomas Fisher Jr. (1763-1845) and wife Catherine Warner (1770-1844) farmed in southern Adams Co. near the Mason-Dixon line and attended church in Emmitsburg where they are buried at the Lutheran Church. Their children included twins Abraham (1796-1885) ancestor of C.E.S. and Isaac (1796-1872). More details can be found in M&C-II. W&M omitted a generation, giving only one Thomas Fisher.

W&M-829. Archibald Everett Fisher (1884-1952) and wife Vallie E. (Ramsburg) (1885-1952) lived on East Second St. in Frederick and are buried at Mt. Olivet. His parents Willis Everett Fisher (1855-1922) and wife Mary E. J. (Reifsnider) (1858-1945) farmed southeast of Emmitsburg and later on Ballinger Creek Road near Frederick. Their children were Edith Julia (1882-1972) the mother of C.E.S., Archibald Everett and (Mary) Ruth (1891-1918).

Abraham Fisher (1796-1885), a twin noted above, married Elizabeth Benner (1797-1829) daughter of Christian of near Gettysburg. They farmed and operated Fisher's Mill near where Possum Creek empties into Great Conewago Creek. Abraham and Elizabeth had twin sons Abraham Jr. (1826-1915) who married Julia Ann Diehl (1829-1910) and Isaac Newton who married Elizabeth S. Everett (1835-1927). Abraham Jr. and Julia Ann moved about 1859 from north of Gettysburg to the farm east of Frederick on Old Annapolis Road owned in 1993 by his great grandson C.E.S. and wife Althea J. The children of Julia Ann except for Willis Everett, migrated to NE, OK, and AZ and were joined later by their mother.

The children of A. E. and Vallie Fisher are given in M&C-II.

W&M-829. John P. Flook (1859-1928) and wife Martha (Young) (1864-1946) as well as his parents Dawson F. Flook (1838-1912) and Elizabeth (Harp) (1837-1929) are buried at the United Brethren Church in Myersville.

Jacob Pflug emigrated in 1750 from Oberseebach near the Rhine River in Alsace. Jacob and wife Anna Margaretha had sons including (John) Jacob (1698-1777), (John) Martin (b. 1701) and (John) Peter (b. 1704). The Flook family came to Middletown Valley about 1752. See *Jacob Fluck of Middletown and Descendants* by Patricia A. Anderson (N) 72, (3), 163 (1984). Jacob above had a son John who was the father of Jacob Flook (1786-1853) who married in 1818 Esther Biser (b. 1788). In W&M-1032 one generation is omitted.

W&M-830. William H. Fuss (1848-1909) and wife Louisa Maria (Overholtzer) (1853-1940) are buried at Mountain View Cemetery, Emmitsburg. His parents were John (1825-1890) and wife Hettie (1828-1887) buried at Tom's Creek Methodist Church. Another John Fuss (1754-1836) and wife Mary (1760-1840) are buried at Taneytown Reformed Church. Other Fuss families buried at

Taneytown are given by Scharf. In the 1800 census of the Emmitsburg area were Conrad Fuss and wife 26-45 years and William Fuss, 16-26. In the Frederick Co. Militia of 1812 Conrad Fuss was a Private under Capt. John Galt.

W&M-831. Walter Alexander England (b. 1864) and wife Fannie Temple (Hood) (1868-1915) are buried at Mt. Olivet, as are his parents John W. England (1824-1873) and Mary Ellen (Hendry) (1839-1883). Fannie's parents were George A. Hood (1822-1908) and Mary J. (Baer) (1828-1910) who are buried at Mt. Olivet.

The grandparents of Walter A. were Nathan England (1787-1859) and wife Harriet (1805-1857) who are buried near Lover's Rock south of Libertytown.

W&M-832. Dr. Franklin Buchanan Smith M.D. (1856-1912) and wife Charlotte Patterson (Dennis) (d. 1889) are buried at Mt. Olivet. For emigrant Johan Schmidt and their early ancestors see W&M-704. Henry Nixdorff who lived 1780-1839 and his wife Susan 1788-1870 have gravestones at Mt. Olivet. Dr. Smith's parents George Smith (1807-1871) and second wife Mary E. (Nixdorff) (c. 1815-1859) are buried in Mt. Olivet. Also there is George Smith's first wife Lydia (Baugher) (1809-1834).

W&M-834. James B. Elder (1856-1924) and wife widow Sarah B. Hess (Smith) (1854-1938) are buried in Emmitsburg Catholic Church as are his parents James A. (1831-1898) and wife Mary F. (1834-1893). Grandparents of James B. were Joachim Elder (1785-1863) and wife Mary (c. 1799-1850) also buried at Emmitsburg Catholic church. Great grandparents of James B. were Aloysius Elder (1757-1827) and wife Mary J. (1774-1842) buried at the Elder family graveyard near Mt. St. Mary's.

W&M-835. The account of the Elder family in W&M contains several errors corrected in the book *Descendants of William Elder* (1707-1775) by Sister Mary Louise Donnelly (1986) (E) (EM). William Elder was born in Maryland; his father William (wife Elizabeth Finch) emigrated from London. William Elder and his friend Arnold Livers moved to the frontier in what later became Frederick Co. from Mt. Calvert in eastern Prince Georges Co., east of the area that became Washington, D.C., about 1734. (LC)

William and wife Ann (Wheeler) (1709-1739), who first settled near Paynes's Hill between what later was Mt. St. Mary's and Thurmont, had children as follows:

(1) William III (1729-1804) m. 1752 Sabina Wickham (d. 1786).
(2) Charles (1730-1804) m. 1760 Julia Ward (1737-1814).
(3) Guy (1731-1805) m. c 1756 Eleanor Wickham (d. 1759), 2m Eleanor Ogle Beall (widow of Ninean Magruder Beall).
(4) Richard (1734-1790) m. 1764 Phoebe Delozier.
(5) Mary (1735-1798) m. Richard Lilly (1728-1793) born in Bristol, England.

William Elder and second wife Jacoba Clementina (Livers) (1717-1807) had the following children:

(6) Elizabeth (1743-1820) m. 1760 Edward Brawner (1736-1783).
(7) Arnold (1745-1812) m. Clotilda Phoebe Green (1752-1833) no children.

(8) Ann (1746-1806) m. 1771 Henry Spalding (d. 1816). Buried at St. Joseph's Church, Taneytown.
(9) Thomas (1748-1832) m. 1771 Elizabeth Spalding (1750-1848); to Bardstown KY; 12 children.
(10) Ignatius (1749-c. 1800) m. Elizabeth ----; to Washington Co., KY, by 1792; one dau. Mary.
(11) Francis (1755-1816) m. Catherine Spalding (1766-1809).
(12) Aloysius (1757-1827) m. Elizabeth Mills (1757-1802), 2m Mary Josephine Green Hayden (1775-1842).

Clementina raised all twelve children and lived 90 years on the frontier. According to the *Archives of Maryland*, Arnold Livers, father of the heroic Clementina, was born in Holland. By tradition he was a son of King James II who was driven from England in the Revolution of 1688 which ended freedom of religion for Catholics in Maryland until 1776.

W&M-836. David Eyler (1813-1863) and Mary (Doub) (1819-1892) are buried at Thurmont United Brethren Church. His parents were George (1782-1871) and Elsie Ann (Kauffman) (1784-1878) who were buried at the same place.

Apparently in America the German family name Euler became Eyler, Eiler and Oyler. In the Conewago area of eastern later Adams Co., PA Jacob Eyler had an infant baptized in 1743 and Valentine Eyler one in 1748. In District 4 of Frederick Co., including Eyler's Valley near Mechanicstown (later Thurmont) in 1800 were two households of Frederick and Jonas Eyler both over 45 years of age. Conrad Eyler from Manheim Twp, York Co., PA died in 1751 near Friend's Mountain (near Emmitsburg). Jonas Eyler (1752-1825) from PA married Anna Regina Harbaugh (daughter of George and Catherine (Williar) Harbaugh (1759-1844) buried at Graceham. Frederick Eyler (1741-1821) and wife Barbara (c. 1746-1841) are buried at Apples Church near Thurmont. Frederick Eyler (1776-1859) and wife Margaret (Williar) (1783-1861) are buried at Graceham. The following includes additions to their children:

(1) Caroline (b. 1812) m. Robert Clugston.
(2) Horatio died in infancy in 1814.
(3) John Frederick (1814-1900) buried at Thurmont U. B. Church.
(4) Maria Catherine m. John Benchoff.
(5) Lizzie E. (1822-1864) m. Samuel M. Diffendal. Children: Mary Jane (1847-1864), and Margaret Ann (1852-1861), buried at Thurmont U. B. Church.
(6) William (b. 1817)
(7) Charles A. (1818-1901) m. Charlotte (1835-1879), buried at Thurmont U. B. Church.
(8) Rebecca Ann b. 1820.
(9) Mary Jane (1826-1854) m. Cyrus C. Kuhn; lived in Thurmont.

A genealogy of Eyler Families has been written by John Eiler (Albuquerque NM, 1973). Three Henry Eylers and John (1783-1866) served in the War of 1812.

W&M-838. William Warren Doub (1865-1927) and wife Harriet E. (Remsburg) (1873-1949) are buried at Middletown Lutheran Church. His parents Jonas A. (1840-1907) and wife Ann Frances (Waters) (1842-1916) are buried at the same cemetery. The grandparents of William W. were Enos Doub (1808-1896) (son of Abraham) and wife Mary Elizabeth (Sheffer) (1809-1878) buried at Myersville U. B. Church.

Pastors of the early Lutheran Church spelled the German name Daub and Taub meaning dove. Daniel W. Daub of German descent was said to have settled in Frederick Co. area in 1744 (Williams 1906). In Frederick Co. Court Records of 1754 Jacob Doup (Daub), a servant aged 18 years was given a value of 8 pounds and one shilling in the estate of Henry Cameron, locksmith. Jacob had 3 more years to serve. Jacob Doub who died about 1771 had sons George, John, and Frederick (will). A descendant John Doub married Catherine Routzahn at Beaver Creek, Washington Co., in 1831; some descendants are given by Williams (1906). A Georg Taub or Doub married Catherina Lang; they emigrated in 1764 from Berwangen near Sinsheim, southeast of Heidelberg, Germany in 1764 (Burgert 1983). A Heinrich Taub and wife Margaretha had son John George born in 1761 in records of Monocacy Lutheran Church. Early land records include sales of property by Nicholas Daub to Samuel Grabill in 1763 and in the same year to Abraham King (of near Littlestown). In 1796 Jacob Doup was granted a resurvey of 713 acres called Menfelt. George Doub died about 1798 leaving wife Catharine and children: George, Margaretha, Catherine, Jacob and Polly McClain. William McClain was executor.

In the census of 1800 in Middletown Valley lived Jacob Toup Sr. and wife both over 45 years with 4 sons and 2 daughters. The following are in records of Zion Lutheran Church of Middletown:

> Jacob and Louise Doub, sponsors 1798
> Heinrich and Tese Ann Doub, baptized Louisa 1819
> John and Catherine Taub baptized Catherine 1819
> John Doub m. Sophia Flight 1820
> Henry and Margaret Doub baptized Anna Maria Carolina 1826

Abraham Doub (1777-1853) (great grandfather of William Warren) and wife Catherine (1783-1853) are buried at Myersville United Brethren Church. Their daughter Lydia (1810-1863) also is buried there.

Daniel R. and Catherine (Funk) Doub and descendants lived in Washington Co. (Williams 1906). Jonathan Doub (1811-1863) born in Frederick Co. came as a young man to Washington Co. where he married Catherine Rinehart and farmed near Beaver Creek. Descendants are given by Williams. (1906). (LC)

W&M-839. Among the forebears of Robert Lee Davis (b. 1867) who married Cora Layton of Hyattstown, were his grandparents, Eli Davis (1809-1887) and wife Rachel (Morsell) (1809-1886) who had son Isaac T. (1841-1913). The latter and wife Sarah F. (Spalding) (1842-1905) buried at Urbana Catholic Church, were parents of Robert Lee Davis.

The Henckel Genealogy by William S. and Minnie W. Jenkin gives the early generations of the Davis family. Jenkin Davis (c. 1695-1747) emigrated from Parish Kilkomin Co. Cardigan in South Wales before 1700. Before coming to Western Maryland he lived in Radnor Twp. of Chester Co., PA. John Davis (1706-1774) married Elizabeth Anderson. Their son Richard (1751-1791) married Catherine Hinkle and they moved to a farm near New Market with 7 children. Their son George Davis (1775-1850) married Elizabeth Hyatt.

Elizabeth's son Eli (1809-1887) married Rachel Morsell (1809-1886), daughter of William Morsell Jr. John Davis (1706-1774) was a signer of the Muhlenberg Lutheran Articles at Monocacy Church in 1747. He became an early Methodist pastor.

An entirely different line of early Quaker Davis families started with emigrant Meredith Davis and wife Ursula (Burgess) who milled and farmed near Buckeystown. His estate was settled in 1754 with executor Meredith Jr. The latter had an inventory in 1765 with executor his widow Sarah D. (Claggett) Davis. Some descendants are shown in the book *Buckey's Town* by Nancy Willmann Bodner (1984). (LC) Serving in the 1812 War were 22 from local Davis families.

Ephraim Davis of Wales was the first of the name in Washington Co. according to Williams (1906).

W&M-840. William Schnauffer (1866-1933) born in Baltimore and wife Mary (West) (1862-1954) are buried at the Episcopal Church at Petersville. In Frederick County the German name has become Snouffer; see W&M-1322.

W&M-841. Elmer E. Dixon (1876-1958) and wife Amy C. (Kump) (1879-1954) of Abilene, Kansas, are buried at Mt. Olivet. His parents were Thomas O. (1840-1895) and Julia (Hiteshew) (1846-1896), also buried in Mt. Olivet. An earlier Dixon at Frederick was John H. (1772-1854) buried at Mt. Olivet. James and Hezekiah served in the Frederick Co. Militia in 1812.

W&M-842. George William Dean (1836-1908) and wife Laura (Gonso) (1848-1919) are buried at Mt. Olivet. He was a son of John Dean (1808-1888) and wife Margaret E. (Barrick) (1814-1852), also buried at Mt. Olivet. In Frederick District in 1800 lived Robert Dean (over 45 years) and family. (LC)

W&M-843. Cornelius E. Derr (1845-1916) and wife Mary E. (Metzger) (1852-1905) are buried at Zion Lutheran Church at Middletown as are his parents, Samuel Derr (1822-1896) and wife Mary M. (Yaste) (1824-1905). Cornelius' second marriage in 1908 to Annie E. (Putman) Warner (1859-1941) produced no children. The grandparents of Cornelius were Jacob Derr (1782-1848) and Margaret (Long) (1784-1868), also buried at the Lutheran Cemetery in Middletown. Jacob was a son of Philip Derr (1756-1821) who in 1777 married Barbara Koogle (1755-1815). Philip was a son of emigrant John Derr who died in Frederick Co. in 1785. See Wampler. There are nearly 50 references to Koogle families in W&M. According to Williams (1906) five Kugel brothers from the Darmstadt area settled after 1765 near Bolivar west of Middletown. One was Henry Adam whose descendant George Koogle (1829-1892) studied at Wittenberg college in Springfield Ohio and became a Judge of the Orphan's Court of Frederick Co. He married Mary Jane Kailor (1835-1915). Their children and other descendants of Henry Adam are given by Williams (1906). Minor corrections of W&M-843 and 844 are Lydia Toms, Morris Derr and Beula I. Derr.

W&M-844. James E. Doll (1867-1949) and wife Gertrude B. (Spalding) (1877-1948) are buried in the Catholic Cemetery at Frederick. His parents Lewis H. Doll (1831-1890) and wife Annie F. (Ogle) (1837-1916) are buried at Mt. Olivet. Grandparents of James E. Doll were Ezra Doll (1800-1842) and wife Harriet (1802-1886) who are buried at Mt. Olivet.

Settler Conrad Doll emigrated from Barbelroth between Landau and Karlsruhe. The census of 1800 in Fredericktown District spelled the name Dull close to the pronunciation of Doll in German. Conrad and Joseph were over 45 years old. Conrad apparently lived with a son and 2 daughters under 26 years. Joseph had 3 sons and 4 daughters under 16 years. Joseph Jr. and wife, 26-45, had 3 children under 10 years. George Dull and wife were 16-26 in age and had a daughter under 10 years.

The Reformed Church records at Frederick and gravestones disclose the following early Dolls:

> Conrad m. 1761 Anne Maria Schisler.
> Conrad and Anna Maria (1745-1798) had daughter Maria in 1762.
> Joseph and Charlotta had Joseph in 1769.
> Joseph and Catherine (d. 1822) had Ezra in 1800.
> John m. 1800 Susan Kortz; witnesses were Joseph Doll Sr. and Jr.
> George (1777-1846) son of John m. 1799 Catherine Schmitt; (d. 1822); witnesses were Mathew Schmitt and Joseph Doll.

Doll families also have lived in Adams Co., PA (WB).

W&M-844. Joseph W. L. Carty Jr. (b. 1867) who married Minnie Rebecca Dixon (1866-1939) was a son of J. W. L. Carty (1823-1867) and Mary (Lugenbeel) (1834-1924) who are buried at Mt. Olivet. Joseph Sr. had an earlier marriage to Margaret C. (1825-1850) also buried at Mt. Olivet. The parents of Joseph Sr. were William Proctor Carty (1789-1822) and Henrietta (Haller) (1797-1863) who also are buried at Mt. Olivet. In the Frederick Co. Militia of 1812 were James Carty and John Carty who married Margaret Holtz.

W&M-845. Dr. George Henry Riggs, M.D. (1870-1957) and wife Cordelia (Duvall) (1873-1940) are buried at Mt. Olivet as are his parents Hon. Christopher M. (1825-1900) and wife Angeline (LaBarre) (1835-1923). His ancestors Henry Riggs (1796-1861) and Rebecca (Musseter) (1802-1887) are also buried at Frederick. Capt. Henry Riggs (dc 1849) of the War of 1812 and of New Market married in 1821 Mary Hobbs (b. c.1792).

W&M-846. Jacob M. Birely (1844-1914) and wife Martha Ellen (Feeser) (1848-1920) are buried at Mt. Olivet. His parents William (1816-1852) and Anna Elizabeth (1814-1862) are buried at Haugh's Church near Ladiesburg north of Woodsboro. The Beyerle emigrant ancestors are believed to have come from near Sinsheim southeast of Heidelberg, Germany. See M&C-II. (LC)

W&M-846. Col. Anthony Zaarr Kimmel (1836-1897) and wife Mary (Morgan) (1838-1913) are buried in the James-Kimmel graveyard (with a stone wall on the Kimmel farm on Old Annapolis Road 2 miles east of Linganore High School). The oldest gravestone inscription found there by Holdcraft is that of John James "the original proprietor" July, 1700 - August 1, 1750. Col. Anthony's father (1798-1871) is called Major General Anthony Kimmel in W&M-846 but on the gravestone of his wife Sydney Ann (James) (1806-1848) he is called Col. Anthony. The Col. abandoned a legal career in Baltimore and married Sydney Ann James who grew up at the old James stone house on present Lime Kiln Road east of New London. Major Sir Pratby James an unmarried uncle of Anthony died about 1850 leaving Anthony about 1400 acres in the Linganore area. Sir was a given name of the Major. Col. Kimmel was said to own about 100 slaves of which 42 left the Linganore farm on the day that news of the Emancipation was learned. It is said that General Anthony built the stone house on the northern part of the James farm and showed his prestige by moving a section of Old Annapolis Road to pass his house instead of that of his father-in-law. The three fine old stone houses on the old Annapolis Road are shown on the 1808 map of Frederick Co. by Charles Varlé. Apparently Sydney Ann's father Major Daniel (wife Margaret) was a son of settler John James. Perhaps the fame and style of the James and Kimmel families encouraged jealousy of the local rumors that the James families were related to notorious Jesse James of St. Joseph, MO.

W&M-848. Pratby James Kimmel (b. 1860), son of Col. Anthony, married Annie Gibson (1869-1955) who is buried at the Methodist Church at New London. They had two young sons Pratby J. Jr. and Gibson who were buried on the farm graveyard in 1884 and 1899. Other descendants are given by B. F. McPherson in the Gettysburg Times, March 26, 1963. (G)

Another Kimmel family settled near Feagaville and left records at Zion Lutheran Church. Frederick Kimmel (1820-1891) and wife Agnes (Kreh or Gray) (1822-1891) emigrated from Saxe-Weimar, Germany. Their first five children were born in Carroll Co.:

    (1) Mary C. (1847-1908) m. George Mehrling (1847-1920) (Mt. Olivet).
    (2) John (b. 1849) m. Emma Whipp.
    (3) George F. (d. c.1880).
    (4) William Harmon (1853-1921) m. Catherine M. (1853-1939) (Mt. Olivet).
    (5) Elton G.
    (6) Annie Mahala Charlotte (1861-1916) m. Nathaniel Cephus Stockman (1856-1944) (Feagaville Zion Church).
    (7) Charles Theodore (b. 1864) m. Irene Elizabeth Baker.
    (8) Amanda Alice (1868-1939) m. John H. G. Stride (1869-1923) (Jefferson Union Cemetery).

W&M-849. John McCleary Culler (1880-1935) and wife Mary Ada (Biggs) (1884-1971) are buried at Mt. Olivet. His parents William L. (1851-1944) and Jane R. (Wiles) (1853-1936) are buried at Middletown Lutheran Church. Grandparents of John M. were William Culler and wife Alice (Brandenburg).

The only child of John M. and Mary Ada Culler is Dr. John M. Jr. surgeon who married Mary Ruth (Fisher) Harner (b. 1918); they have lived in Frederick. Mary Ruth's lineage is given in Monocacy and Catoctin II.

The only Culler in the 1800 census of Middletown Valley was Michael Koller who had daughter Susan baptized in 1781. Michael and wife Eleanora had Michael Jr. in 1789. Jacob and Elizabeth Koller had son George baptized in 1799 and son Michael in 1803. These records are from Lutheran Church of Middletown. A booklet on Culler Descendants was written by Millard Rice in 1969 (JMH). (LC)

Over 140 Culler names are indexed in (Z).

W&M-850. Hon. Lewis David Crawford (1868-1936), buried at Thurmont's Blue Ridge Cemetery, married Edna M. Sheffer of Fairfield, PA. He was a son of George W. (b. c.1834) and Laura E. (Birely) (b. c.1845) daughter of John and Susan of Hauvers District.

George W. was a son of James H. Crawford (b. c.1813) and wife Caroline (b. c.1813). In the 1800 census of Emmitsburg District were households of David Crawford over 45 years in age and of David Jr. between 16 and 45. Evan L., Jonas, Robert, Samuel and William Crawford enrolled in the Frederick Co. Militia in 1812.

W&M-850. Charles A. Castle (1851-1935) and wife Annie (Phillips) (1851-1901) are buried in Mt. Olivet as is his father Daniel Castle of T. (1817-1898) who married Susan Routzahn. Grandparents of Charles A. were Thomas Castle (1783-1845) and Barbara (Long) (1787-1879) who are buried at Zion Lutheran Church at Middletown. In the 1800 census of Middletown Valley Thomas Cassell and wife were over 45 years with 4 sons and 2 daughters. George Cassell was over 45 years with wife between 26 and 45.

A genealogy of *Descendants of Henry Cassell* (Henry Cassell died 1756) was written by Jane W. Stafford (Lexington, KY 1984) (WP). A Henry Cassell is in records of Conewago Lutheran Church near Hanover, PA in 1743. John Henry Cassell and wife Anna Margaret (Bencker) lived in Mt. Joy Twp. (an area that later became Adams Co.) in 1730s. They settled in Frederick Co. about 1750. The only Cassell reported as arriving early at Philadelphia was Christian in September of 1738. Joseph Cassell and wife Charity had Elijah baptized in 1796 in Middletown Reformed records.

W&M-851. The parents of Rev. Commodore I. B. Brane were Henry (1808-1867) and wife Margaret (1800-1893) buried at Mt. Olivet Cemetery in Frederick.

W&M-853. John Baumgardner (1840-1915) native of Germany and wife Frannie E. Sinn (1843-1914) are buried at Mt. Olivet as are his parents Thomas (1811-1873) and Margaret (1807-1883). Son Harry D. Baumgardner was known not only for his butcher shop on N. Market St. near 5th. St., but in his later years for his alleged gold mine near Braddock Heights. Harry's daughter Estelle, a civic leader of exceedingly rapid speech, and husband Donald Leatherman, are noted in M&C-I.

W&M-854. Princeton Buckey (1875-1953) and wife Louisa Rothermel (Griesemer) (b. 1880) are buried at Mt. Olivet. His parents were Daniel E. and Louisa C. (Duttera) (1838-1914). Princeton was a descendant of Peter Bucke, emigrant from Minfeld and not from better known Mathias.

The Buckey families of Frederick were not related to Col. Henri Bouquet, of Switzerland, as often supposed. Col. Henri was born 1719 at Rolle on the north shore of Lake Geneva. He owned land in Western Maryland but did not live here for any length of time.

Mathias Bucke (1727-1794) was born to Abraham and Elisabeth at Muenfelden Germany (which has since become Minfeld), near Kandel, in the far south of the Pfalz near the border with Alsace. My wife and I visited Minfeld and found a Bucke family still living there. They stated that some of their relatives use the French spelling of Bouquet. Mathias with brother-in-law Hans Georg Hoffmann emigrated to Maryland before 1762. Mathias had married Anna

Maria Hoffman (1737-1800). His second wife was Christine (1752-1808) who was buried at the Lutheran Church in Frederick. Mathias and family settled near Little Tuscarora Creek, north of Frederick. Mathias Buckey and Mary had the following children:

(1) John (1756-1800) m. 1777 Elizabeth Koontz (sons George (c. 1779-1834), John and Henry).

(2) Mathias Jr. m. 1780 widow Christina (Roemer) Grosch (1752-1808), (d/o of Michael Roemer); their sons were Michael and Jacob.

(3) Rosina.

(4) George (c. 1762-1825) m. 1787 Christina Haas (d. 1814). Children: David (saddler in Buckeystown), Daniel, Rebecca Charlotte m. Lewis Kemp, Henrietta Lydia.

(5) Valentine (d. 1826) m. 1793 Charlotte Remsberg; no children.

(6) Margaret m. 1792 Peter Sawyer (d. 1793); 2m 1799 Zachariah Danner; children: Cassandra, Evelina, Joel B., Juliana, Zacharas Jr.

(7) Catherine (b. 1772) m. 1804 Andrew England. Children: Caroline, Sarah, Mary Ann, Juliann, and Catherine.

(8) Peter (1775-1848) m. 1796 Mary Salmon (1778-1864). Children: Edward, Ann, Catherine, Mary Elizabeth, Eliza, Eleanor.

Mathias' son John established a tavern in Buckeystown in the 1780s and son George started a tannery there about the same time. The limestone tavern buildings remains. See book *Buckey's Town* by Nancy Willmann Bodmer (1984). Buckeystown was named for the Buckey brothers. (John) Peter Buckey (b. 1736 at Minfeld) purchased a lot in Frederick in 1767. Two of the children of Peter and wife Anna Maria (Schaefer) were baptized in the Reformed Church records at Frederick: George (1771-1862) and Magdalena (b. 1774).

These and later Buckey records were compiled by M. E. Rogers and available from John R. Buckey of Fairview Park, Ohio.

George P. Buckey (1771-1862) and wife Susanna (1775-1835) are buried at the Glade Reformed Cemetery near Walkersville. Their son Ezra (1803-1858) is buried at Beaver Dam Cemetery near Johnsville. He was a grandfather of D. Princeton Buckey. Peter Buckey and wife Mary lived at Libertytown where son Edwin (1797-1881) was born. Four of their daughters married prominent local families of Getzendanner, Howard and Smith. See J.M.H.

Ethel Close Buckey was a collector of genealogical data relating to Frederick Co. See Biggs and Troxell families.

W&M-854. Rev. Guy P. Bready (b. 1882) and wife Bessie (Schuler) (1881-1941) are buried at Mt. Olivet. His grandparents George A. (1811-1894) and wife Annie (1814-1892) also are buried at Mt. Olivet as are his parents E. Tobias Bready (1853-1924) and Mary T. (Hayes) (1853-1912).

After his service at Walkersville Pastor Guy Bready was the Reformed minister and teacher for many years at Taneytown. Among those who praised Guy's teaching was my deceased colleague Dr. Basil T. Crapster, Prof. of History at Gettysburg College who received degrees at Princeton and Harvard.

W&M-855. Jonathan J. Bielfeld (1857-1918) and parents Rev. Herman Bielfeld (1815-1895) and wife Friedaricke A. H. (1825-1908) are buried at Mt. Olivet.

The Marken and Bielfeld Printing Company after many years was still in operation near Fort Detrick in 1994.

W&M-855. William A. Black (b. 1869) was a son of Joseph H. (1836-1885) and Matilda C. (Norris) (1837-1902) buried at Mt. Tabor Church at Rocky Ridge, as are his grandparents William Black (1808-1880) and wife Barbara (Martin) (1808-1887). In the 1800 census of northern Frederick Co. were families of Henry Black and wife over 45 years with 4 sons and 3 daughters also the family of Joseph Black (26-45) and 3 daughters.

W&M-856. John S. Newman (1870-1940) and wife Amy R. (Parsons) (1871-1929) are buried at Mt. Olivet as are his parents Jacob M. (1843-1927) and Catherine E. (Shaw) (1844-1902). A Jacob Parson (26-45 years) with 4 young children lived in Frederick District in 1800. (LC)

W&M-857. Harvey D. Beachley (b. 1867) was a son of John W. (1844-1920) and Marietta Susan (Smith) (1848-1909) who are buried at Middletown Reformed Church. Also buried there are Harvey's grandparents Daniel Beachley (1802-1874) and wife Esther (Shoemaker) (1807-1845). The original German family name was Biechle (final e pronounced). In 1779 a Henry Biegle was taxed for 200 acres in Alsace Twp., Berks Co, PA. In the 1800 census of Middletown Valley, Henry Beagley was over 45 years and his wife between 26 and 45. They had 8 children. Henry Beachley (1758-1831) and wife Anna Barbara (1763-1852) have gravestones at Middletown Reformed Cemetery. They were parents of Daniel. Beachley families of Boonsboro and Hagerstown are given in Williams (1906).

W&M-858. Albert W. Bartgis (1854-1936) and wives Salome (Smith) (1861-1899) and L. Fanny (Koogle) (1861-1928) are buried at Myersville Lutheran Church. His parents Titus V. Bartgis (1816-1886) and wife Mary J. (Hedges) (1828-1863) are buried at Middletown Lutheran Church.

Contrary to W&M, brothers (Johan) Georg and Michael Bartgis or Baertges (sons of Mathias of Kleinich near Bernkastel, Germany) emigrated in 1748. This was long after William Penn visited America. Emigrant Michael (1719-1791) was the father of printer Mathias Bartges (1751-1825) of Frederick who with his mother had middle name Echternach after a town near the border of Luxemburg. Mathias the printer was born in Lancaster, PA and married Susanna Schreiner. He learned printing in Philadelphia from William Bradford and fought in some early battles of the Revolution. Mathias printed his first almanac in German at Frederick in 1777 and his newspaper in English in 1786. About 1811 he made his son Mathias E. Jr. (wife Margaret Dertzbaugh) a partner in the printing business. Grandson Mathias E. III lived 1789 to 1861 and is buried at Middletown. In 1824 at the tavern of Mathias E. Bartgis were displayed an elephant, lion, lama and lynx. Rev. (Benjamin) Franklin Bartgis (farmer) a brother of Mathias E. Jr. married Anna Heffner. They had Franklin Jr., the father of Titus Bartgis (1816-1880).

W&M-859. Rev. M. L. Beard (1849-1915) and wife Katherine Sophia (Bowers) (1860-1910) are buried at Middletown Lutheran Church. Among the ancestors of Rev. Beard may be the Beard of Beard's Church built about 1756 near Leitersburg, one of the oldest churches in the Antietam area. See Wentz, *History of the Evangelical Synod of Maryland (1920)* and Williams (1906).

W&M-860. Joseph Byers (1824-1898) and wife Eleanor (1828-1912) are buried at Emmitsburg Lutheran Church. The 1800 census of Westminster District gives three Byers families headed by Gabriel (26-45); Catherine (over 45); Mary Byers with female companion both 26-45 and four slaves.

Contrary to W&M the German family name is Beyer from which came dialect form Boyer and perhaps Bayer. Many German names acquired a final s in America. (see M&C-I).

Ellen's mother Catherine "Diffenball" Gilbert may have been a Diffenbaugh. Christoph Diefenbach was confirmed at Rott and emigrated from Oberseebach near Wissenbourg in northern Alsace to Westminster, MD. He was naturalized in 1767. Names of four children are given (B3).

The husband of Mrs. Frances Wampler of Westminster probably was a descendant of Johan Christian Wampffler who emigrated in 1747 from Herbitzheim, north Alsace (B3).

W&M-860. David Franklin Bussard (1855-1896) and wife Susan E. (Blessing) (1857-1931) are buried at Myersville Lutheran Church. His father John Wesley Jr. (1820-1893) was buried at Middletown Reformed Church and his mother Catherine (Poffenberger) (1812-1889) at St. John's Church near Ellerton.

Settler Daniel Bussard or Bossert married Sophia Renner. Best known was their son Peter (1761-1802) who married Margaret or Becky Householder (1762-1839). They were neighbors of Bishop Daniel Leatherman near Bussard Flats west of Catoctin Furnace. John Wesley Bussard, son of Peter Jr. (1792-1864) and Sarah (1800-1872), is buried at Thurmont United Brethren Church. He and wife Susan (Delauter) had son John Wesley Jr. (1820-1893).

David Buzzard married in 1816 Mary Shank at Middletown. In 1323 they moved to Montgomery County, OH, and later to Carroll County, IN. David as well as Daniel Bussard (1771-1830) of New Market and Peter (1792-1864) of Thurmont served in the War of 1812.

Bussard Families from Peter (1761-1802) is a genealogy by Ruthella Bussard (Frederick 1974, with supplement 1978).

W&M-861. Blessing Families of Middletown Valley in 1800 were headed by Jacob Sr. (over 45 years); Jacob Jr. (26-45) had three children under 10 years; Phillip (26-45) and wife under 26 had six children under 10 years; and George and wife (26-45) had seven children under 10 years. There was also Conrad Blessing who with wife Catherine had a son Philipp born 1794 (Middletown Lutheran).

George Blessing (1794-1873) buried at Ellerton St. John's Lutheran Church married Susan Easterday (1802-1884). George's farm is marked as the "Highland Battlefield" on a map of the Titus Atlas of 1872. George Blessing and son drove off a Confederate group of horsemen who tried to steal horses.

Benjamin L. Blessing (1826-1886) (a son of Susan and hero George) and wife Sarah (Blessing) (1857-1931) were parents of Susan E. Blessing who married David F. Bussard.

W&M-862. Cyrus W. Blickenstaff (1863-1935) and wife Flora M. (Palmer) (1863-1941) as well as his parents Jacob (1831-1904) and wife Margaret

(Grossnickle) (1839-1891) are buried at St. John's Lutheran Church near Ellerton.

Ulrich and Jost Blickensdoerfer whose family originated at Hedinger, Canton Zurich, first fled to Germany. They emigrated from Speyer in the Rhine Valley in 1749. Yost bought land in Middletown Valley in 1762 and 1772. Yost wrote to Annapolis complaining against treatment by Magistrate Capt. Peter Bainbridge in 1766. In the Middletown Valley of the census of 1800 were three Blickenstaff families. Joseph and Yost and their wives were over 45 years old. Yost with a child under 10 years probably was Yost Jr. David Blickenstaff was between 26 and 45 years with wife under 26 years. Contrary to W&M-862 John Blickenstaff (1804-1884) buried at Ellerton Brethren Church may have been a son of Yost Jr. John's wife Mary (Fair) (1786-1876) was buried at St. John's Church. Her dates are confirmed in the 1850 census. Jacob (1831-1904) was their son. See *History of the Blickensderfer Family* (BE).

Another source records immigrant (Hans) Jakob Blickensdoerfer whose wife was Veronica Magdalena (Burkholder). Their son Joseph or "Yose" Blickenstaff (1735-1826) married in 1799 secondly Margaret Faller (1778-1830). Their son Daniel (1800-1843) married Margaret Rebecca Custer (1800-1830), daughter of John Custer (1774-1843) and wife Susannah Grossnickel (1775-1839), and granddaughter of George Custer with first wife Susanna (Long).

Susannah (Grossnickle) Custer was a daughter of (Bernard) Peter Grossnickel (1750-1822) and wife Christina (Studebaker) (1754-1836). Peter Grossnickel was a son of Peter Jr. and wife Margaretha (Becker) and grandson of 1746 emigrant Grossnickel. Christina was a daughter of Clement Stutenbecker and wife (Anna) Catharina (Melchers). Clement's father emigrated in 1736 on ship Harle.

Numerous Blickenstaff descendants are buried at Grossnickle Meetinghouse of the Church of the Brethren and at the United Brethren Church at Wolfsville, both in northern Middletown Valley.

W&M-863. Isaiah H. Buhrman (b. 1858) was a son of Henry of J. (1819-1901) and Charlotte (Fahs) (1818-1897). All were buried at Foxville Lutheran Church. An earlier Isaiah L. Buhrman (1759-1815) is buried at Foxville. The grandparents of Isaiah H. were Jacob Buhrman (1783-1854) and wife Maria C. (1792-1862).

W&M-864. (John) Steward Annan (1874-1932) married Elizabeth A. Morrison. He and parents James Cochran Annan (1837-1894) and wife Rosa J. (Stewart) (1841-1922) are buried at the Emmitsburg Presbyterian Cemetery. Grandparents of Stewart Annan were Dr. Andrew Annan (1805-1896) and wife Ann Elizabeth Motter (1810-1884) who are buried in the same cemetery near Emmitsburg. In the 1800 census of the Emmitsburg area the only Annan household was that of Robert and wife both between 26 and 45 years of age. They had 2 daughters and 2 sons under 10 years of age, also 5 slaves.

W&M-864. Jesse C. Clagett (1851-1911) married Mary S. Price (daughter of Thomas Price of Philadelphia). Jesse is buried at Mt. Olivet as are his parents Thomas (1813-1887) and Cynthia (Norwood) (1815-1895). Also using the spelling Clagett were Henry Clagett (1770-1841) and wife Julia (1773-1830) who are buried in the family graveyard near Catoctin Creek in Middletown Valley (off

Boss Arnold Road on a farm owned in 1958 by Ralph Virts). See also W&M-344. Clagett or Calggett families were prominent in early Maryland Seven were officers in the Revolutionary War and at least 20 served in the ranks. Most lived in Prince Georges Co., (LC) (M&C-II). George Price was enrolled in the Frederick Co. Militia of 1812. He married Catherine Coale.

W&M-865. Dr. Ralph Browning M.D. (1869-1925) is buried at Myersville Lutheran Church. He and wife Addie (Harris) were parents of Maud and R. Avery Browning (1898-1953) (buried Myersville Lutheran). Avery was my teacher of chemistry at Frederick High School in 1926-27. He promoted our interest in science by allowing us to do some experiments of our own designing. My attempts to make matches led to an explosion and a scar remaining on my wrist after 66 years.

M&W-866. Alvey R. Brandenburg (1863-1949) and wife Estelle E. Fox (1866-1957) are buried at Foxville Lutheran Church. His parents Samuel (1824-1888) and Juliann (Grossnickle) (1829-1916) are buried at the Brethren Church (Grossnickle's) north of Ellerton. Mathias Brandenburg was early in Middletown Valley. He bought land from Michael Jesserang in 1769.

In the 1800 census of Middletown Valley there were already 4 Brandenburg households: Samuel was over 45 years of age. David, Mathias and William were 26-45 in age. Samuel (1756-1833) who was a soldier in the Revolution married Mary Bear (1760-1817). Their son Henry (1792-1869) married Mary (Kemp) (1801-1859). They are buried in the Brandenburg family graveyard near Wolfsville. They were parents of Samuel.

A genealogy of Brandenburg Families was written by Bertha Ann Fleming of Lafayette, IN in 1965. Solomon Brandenburg, a north German nobleman, whose lands were confiscated emigrated before his sons: John Anthony emigrated via Philadelphia in 1740; son William Henry (1728-1796) emigrated in 1752, and was buried at Lutheran Church in Frederick; and Jacob emigrated in 1766 (BL,FH).

William Henry had 8 sons: Aaron, Samuel, Jacob, William, Mathias, Israel, Conrad and Frederick. Mathias (1763-1818) married Barbara Keller and had children in will: Henry, David, Frederick, Isaac, Abraham, Daniel and Catherine.

In the Frederick Co. Militia of 1812 Jesse Brandenburgh (b. c.1795) son of Jacob and Elisabeth, served as a substitute for his brother Jacob. In 1818 he married Matilda Turner near Flushing in Belmont Co., Ohio. (LC)

W&M-869. John C. Ambrose (1857-1924) and wife Amanda (Smith) (1852-1925) are buried at the United Brethren Church of Thurmont. His parents George H. (1828-1880) and Matilda (Marker) (1829-1903) are buried at Sabillasville Reformed Church. The parents of George H. were John (b. c.1799) and Mary (b. c.1797) who farmed in Catoctin District.

The early Ambrose was Matthias (1695-1784) who emigrated via Philadelphia in 1732 and first settled in the Conestoga area of Lancaster Co. He and wife Catherine had 4 sons born in Pennsylvania. Matthias and family arrived in the Monocacy area about 1738 and built Ambrose Mill on Owens Creek just north of later Thurmont. The gravestone at Apples Church believed to be that of

Matthias is marked 1690-1784. The prominence of Matthias Ambrose in the early German Monocacy Settlement is shown by many references in T and D. Matthias' daughter Catherine Salome (1725-1804) married John Weller Sr. and it was she who led most of her children to the Bardstown area of KY. See M&C-II. Capt. Jacob Ambrose served in the Revolution.

By 1800 the Ambrose family had spread to Middletown Valley where Henry and wife were 26-45 years in age with 4 sons and 4 daughters. In 1800 Henry of Peter and wife also 26-45 had 6 daughters and 2 sons. In 1800 in the Emmitsburg area Catherine Ambrosius over 45 years was living with her daughter and 2 grandsons under 10 years; also Henry Ambrosius and wife (both 26-45) with only one daughter (under 10 years).

Katherine Ambrose (1855-1929) married Washington Ridenour (1859-1921), a farmer of Mechanicstown District. The Ridenour name occurs frequently in W&M. Ridenour lineage beginning with Jacob (1779-1825) and wife Maria (Schmidt) (1779-1815) of Graceham is being studied by Sylvia Olson of Springfield, Ohio.

Johan Henrich Reitenauer emigrated in 1738 from Rexingen near Drulingen in northern Alsace (B3). He was born in 1713 and married in 1737 (Anna) Catharina Fuehrer, daughter of Benedict. Their son Matthew was baptized in 1749 at Monocacy Lutheran Church. Also emigrating in 1738 was Peter Reitenauer born 1723 to Hans Nicolaus and Anna Magdalena (Arnet). Peter's daughter Elisabeth was baptized at Monocacy Church in 1748. Eight other children were named (B3). A third Reitenauer emigrating in 1738 was Hans Balthasar from the same town in northern Alsace. He was born in 1696 and in 1718 married Maria Elisabeth Zenss, daughter of Johan Jacob (B3). Their son Adam (b. 1731) and wife Wilhelmina had daughter Christina born 1763 as recorded by the Frederick Lutheran Church. For the baptism Valentine and Christina Creager were sponsors.

At least 6 Ridenours served in the Maryland Militia in the Revolutionary War, namely David, Henry, Jacob, Ludwig, Martin and Nicholas.

W&M-869. John H. Abbott III (1835-1918) married Julia M. (Hanshew) (1839-1923) grand-niece of Barbara Fritchie. His parents were John H. Abbott Jr. and Julia A. (Dorff) (1809-1897). All except John H. Jr. have gravestones in Mt. Olivet at Frederick.

Children of John H. Abbott III and Julia were Eleanor B. (1870-1955) and Henry H. (1875-1931) who married Jane E. Staley. Eleanor Abbott was well known for her collection of memorabilia of Barbara Fritchie. (LC)

W&M-870. Rev. Charles F. Ausherman (1865-1926) and his wife Caroline (Grossnickle) (1864-1895) also his parents John Ausherman Jr. (1828-1873) and wife Elizabeth (Leatherman) (1834-1908) are buried at Grossnickle Meeting House near Ellerton. The grandparents of Rev. Charles were John Ausherman Sr. (1791-1864) and wife Lydia (Arnold) (1798-1885) who are buried at Pleasant View Brethren Cemetery near Burkittsville.

In the 1800 census of Middletown Valley there was only one Asherman family: Henry and wife were over 45 years with three young daughters and three young sons, also five slaves.

W&M-871. Dr. S. Philip Appleman (b. 1849) (physician and artist) had grandparents Philip (1754-1830) and wife Maria (Brunch) (1761-1852) who are buried at Middletown Lutheran Cemetery. Their son John (1783-1864) married N. Agnes Sadler (d. 1884); they are buried at Rose Hill Cemetery in Hagerstown. If this lineage given in W&M is correct Dr. Philip's father was quite old when his son was born.

W&M-872. Dr. Levin West M.D. (1864-1944) unmarried and his parents Patrick McGill West (1825-1904) and wife Eleanor (McGill) (1827-1903) are buried at Petersville Episcopal Church. Patrick was a son of Levin West (1789-1863) and wife Elizabeth H. (1801-1872) and grandson of Joseph West.

A John West along with Joseph Wood of Israel Creek was press-master for the first court of Frederick Co. in 1749. A Samuel West was on the Frederick Co. Grand jury in 1750. Also in the early court records at Frederick were John West Jr. who used Monocacy Ferry in 1753 and Joseph Jr. recorded in 1762. A Thomas West and wife of 16-26 years lived in Liberty district in 1800. The census of 1800 shows in Middletown Valley three West families headed by Benjamin, Erasmus and Thomas, all between 26 and 45 years. (LC)

W&M-872. Clement Ausherman or earlier Aschermann (b. c.1868) was a son of Elder David (1838-1907) and wife Amanda L. (Remsburg) (1841-1923) who are buried at Pleasant View Church of the Brethren near Burkittsville. Amanda was a daughter of Samuel (b. c.1807) and Maria (b. c.1809) of Locust Valley. See also W&M-870.

W&M-873. Charles H. Brown (1859-1937) and wife Nettie J. (Addison) (1866-1947) are buried at Blue Ridge Cemetery of Thurmont. His parents Joseph B. Brown (1830-1910) and wife Diana (Buhrman) (1830-1923) are buried at the Lutheran Church at Foxville.

The many Browns of northwestern Frederick Co. are more completely documented by Williams (1906) where 17 Brown families are recorded, many of whom moved from Frederick Co. to Washington Co. W&M record Browns on 154 pages, almost as many references as to Zimmermans. Williams gives the following children of Ignatias Brown Sr. and wife Elizabeth (McAfee) of Hauver's District (most were deceased in 1906) who married:

> William B. (1808-1879) m. Elizabeth Fox (1806-1886).
> Jeremiah (1808-1835) m. Mary Ann Flaut (1806-1898).
> Susan (1809-1860) m. David Harbaugh (1808-1880).
> Elizabeth m. George Gardenour (1806-1898).
> Ignatius m. Catherine Schriver (d. 1843).
> Thomas A. (1815-1912) m. Catherine Oswald (b. 1819).
> Joseph (1819-1904) m. Mary Doub, 2m Lenah C. Schildknecht, 3m Virginia Routsang.
> John (1823-1912) m. Margaret Fox.

From this family descended a great number of Browns in the area including Thurmont, Foxville, Wolfsville, and Smithsburg as disclosed in a printed genealogy by Andree W. W. Taylor of Huntsville, AL in 1992 (with assistance of

Donald J. Wolf of Frederick). Marriages with Hauver, Pryor, Harbaugh and Buhrman families are recorded.

Taylor traces the Brown name to William Browne (1620-1665) of England who came at age 13 as a servant and shoemaker with the first settlers of Maryland in 1634. He found many references to William in St. Mary's Co. and a few to his wife Margaret and their children. The first descendant in Frederick Co. was William Browne, who signed the petition in 1742 to form Frederick Co. He settled in the Toms Creek area near Emmitsburg and was appointed Constable of Upper Monocacy Hundred. Son Thomas Browne Sr. (c. 1738-1787) married Hannah Pittinger (b. 1746) daughter of Daniel Pittinger and Elizabeth (Biggs). They farmed on the north edge of Monocacy Manor but Hannah died at Foxville. Hannah had children: Susannah, Mary, Joseph, John, Ignatius Sr. (1781-1830), Rebecca and Catherine (and possibly older William Sr. and Thomas Jr.). The dates of the children of Ignatius Sr. above are given by Taylor.

A genealogy of Brown and Baltzell families was written by Thomas Baltzell Brown of Lincoln NB (1964) (FH). There are nearly 7 pages of Brown gravestones in J. M. H. but very few early ones. Unrelated other Browns lived in southern Frederick Co., some from Virginia.

W&M-875. George W. Bittle (1866-1946) and wife Mary E. (Routzahn) (1865-1936) are buried at Myersville Lutheran Church. His parents Thomas F. Bittle (1838-1917) and wife Mary E. (Waters) (1840-1893) as well as his grandparents Jonathan (1798-1855) and wife Rachel (Bogner) Bittle (1803-1885) are buried at St. John's Lutheran Church north of Myersville. Andreas and Johanna Georg Buettel emigrated in 1752 and Christoff in 1753.

George Michael Bittle moved from near Littlestown, PA to Turkey Hill near Myersville in 1789 and can hardly be called an early settler of Middletown Valley. See M&C-II. Thomas Bittle was taxed for 25 acres in Germany Twp. east of Littlestown in 1780 and George Bittle, single, was taxed without land in the same twp. in 1781. A Frederick Bittle was taxed for livestock in Radnor Twp. of Chester Co., PA in 1765 (*PA Archives*, Series 3, vol. 11, page 64). See also W&M-1390.

Several recent genealogies of Bittles have been written. Among these are *Bittle Ancestors* by Robert D. Bittle (LaVale, MD 1991) and a large work by Frank L. Bittle of Florida. (FH)

Bittle families have included leaders in education and the Protestant ministry. Dr. David Frederick Bittle (1811-1876) son of Thomas and Mary (Baer) of Myersville was President of Roanoke College, Virginia (1853-1876). He married Louisa C. Krauth of Gettysburg. Rev. Daniel Howard Bittle was first President of North Carolina College. Rev. Jonathan Elmer Bittle (1864-1939) son of Thomas F. and Mary E. (Waters) of Myersville was Lutheran pastor and author. He married in 1888 Mollie May Buhrman. Children are Helen E., Mabel A. and Frank B. (Wentz).

W&M-876. Thomas F. Bittle. See W&M-875.

W&M-877. William Metzger Bittle (1841-1928) and wife Catherine (Routzahn) (1840-1931) are buried at Myersville Lutheran Church. His parents Jonathan

(1798-1855) and Catherine (Bogner) (1803-1885) are buried at St. John's Lutheran Church near Ellerton. See also W&M-875.

W&M-877. Luther Henry Harrison Brown (1840-1908) and wife Sarah Louisa (Brandenburg) (1843-1917) of Montgomery Co., MD are buried at Browningsville Methodist Church south of New Market. From the area Benjamin and Frederick Brown enrolled in the Frederick Co. Militia of 1812.

W&M-878. Garrison M. Brandenburg (1845-1927) and wife Mary E. (Norwood) (1844-1928) are buried at Kemptown Methodist Church south of New Market. Also buried there are his parents Lemuel (1810-1826) and wife Charlotte (Kindley) (1805-1887).

In the census of 1800 in Middletown Valley were households headed by Samuel Brandenburgh, over 45 years; also David, Mathias and William, 26-45 years. with young children.

W&M-879. Thomas Souder Thrasher (1849-1911) and wife Charlotte B. (Lakin) (1851-1903) and his parents Robert K. (1820-1879) and second wife Margaret (Souder) (1819-1904) are buried at Jefferson Union Cemetery. Also buried there are the grandparents of Thomas namely Thomas Thrasher (1774-1842) and Martha (Johnstone) (1790-1876).

In 1800 census there were 4 Thrasher households in Middletown Valley as follows:

> Benjamin and wife were both over 45 years and living with 2 sons and 3 daughters under 26 years, also 8 slaves.
>
> Eli (26-45) and wife (16-26) had 4 daughters and a son under 10 years, also 3 slaves.
>
> Elias and wife both 26-45 had 5 sons under 10 years, one daughter 10-16 years and 4 slaves.
>
> Thomas Thrasher and wife both over 45 years lived without children with 9 slaves. (LC)

W&M-880. Clarence C. Carty (1847-1911) and wife Joanna (Fox) (1847-1884) as well as his parents Joseph W. L. (1823-1867) and wife Margaret C. (Hardt) (1825-1850) are buried at Mt. Olivet. Joseph had a second marriage to Mary M. Lugenbeel (1834-1924) also buried at Mt. Olivet. Joseph had grandparents with gravestones in Mt. Olivet, namely William Proctor Carty (1789-1822) and wife Henrietta (Haller) (1797-1863). (LC)

Ezra and Michael Hart were enrolled in the Frederick Co. Militia in 1812. Ezra from the Middletown area moved westward in Pennsylvania, dying in 1853 near Altoona.

W&M-881. (John) Nicholas Zimmerman (b. 1832) married Julia Ann Measell (d. 1894). The early lineage here is inaccurate. See W&M-979. The parents of Nicholas, wagon-maker, were J. Nicholas Sr. (b. c.1809) and wife Elizabeth (b. c.1812) who lived near Frederick.

W&M-882. Levi C. Leatherman (1846-1917) and wife Lizzie Ann (Derr) (1856-1926) are buried at Utica Lutheran Cemetery. See Wampler for her lineage. Levi was a son of Daniel Jr. (1821-1909) and Caroline (Michael) (1823-1871) also buried at Utica.

Godfrey Leatherman Jr. married in 1818 Mary Anna Recher. Their son Daniel (1797-1859) married Christine Warrenfeltz (1795-1857) buried at St. John's Lutheran Church near Ellerton. Christine's son Daniel Jr. married Caroline above. Christine's first child Jacob Warrenfeltz (1819-1891) married Susannah Grossnickle, (1825-1857). Daniel with second wife Emeline Margaret (Gross) moved to Washington Co. Another son of Godfrey Jr. was Jacob Leatherman (1799-1900) who married in 1824 Sarah Wolfe (1808-1887). They lived in Wolfsville and are buried in the Reformed Cemetery. Leah Leathermans Spade is a descendant.

Early arriving at Philadelphia from Germany were Hans Dewalt Ledermann with 5 other family members in Sept. 1727 and Hans Peter who arrived in Sept. 1731. Dewalt was taxed for 100 acres in Philadelphia Co. in 1735.

W&M-885. Rev. George K. Sappington (1855-1916) and wife Elizabeth C. (Frazier) (1855-1913) are buried at Beaver Dam Brethren Cemetery near Johnsville. His parents were Thomas Sappington (1792-1857) and second wife Louisa (Klein) (1827-1912) who are buried at Mt. Olivet. The first wife of Thomas was Sarah R. (Cole) (1795-1841) who is buried at Liberty Catholic Church. James and John Sappington served in the Maryland Militia during the Revolutionary War.

W&M-886. Wilson L. Pryor (1854-1930) and wife Ida T. (Stottlemyer) (1858-1920) are buried at Thurmont United Brethren Church. His father Samuel H. (1822-1903) and wife Dorothy (Wolf) (1826-1915) are buried at Foxville Lutheran Church. (LC)

W&M-887. Charles Wertheimer (1861-1948) and wife Annie May (Hiteshew) (1867-1931), as well as his parents Frederick (1823-1893) and wife Clotilda (Karley) (1834-1923) are buried at Frederick's Mt. Olivet Cemetery. (LC)

W&M-889. John H. Lighter (1834-1918) and wife Mary M. (Kepler) (1833-1879) are buried at Middletown Reformed Church as are his parents Peter (1795-1863) and wife Elizabeth (Everhart) (dates hidden). The Lighter grandparents of John H. were Henry (1754-1823) and Catherine (Staley) (1757-1823). They left 5 sons and 5 daughters according to the gravestone at the Reformed Cemetery in Middletown. Emigrant from Germany, Jacob Leiter or Leuter purchased land near Leitersburg, later Washington Co. in 1762 (Bell). Besides (John) Henry the census of 1800 shows a Lewis Lighter, age 26-45, in Middletown Valley with 4 children under 10 years. For Leiter and Lighter Families see Williams 1906 and *Leiter Families* by John A. Leiter (Portland, OR 1971).

W&M-889. Judge Russell E. Lighter (1875-1951) and ancestors are buried in the Reformed Church Cemetery at Middletown. Daniel J. Lighter (1842-1918) son of Peter and Elizabeth given above, and wife Mary A. (Vananda) (1851-1925) also are buried at Middletown Reformed Cemetery. They were parents of Judge Russell Lighter.

The emigrant was Jacob whose eldest son John Leiter (c. 1734-before 1790) was in Dauphin Co., PA. Jacob Jr. and other children went to far Western Maryland.

W&M-890. Edward F. Fry (1854-1935) and wife Sarah E. (Shafer) (1856-1936) are buried at Point of Rocks Episcopal Church. He was a son of Samuel F. and

Christina (Stoneburner) (Fry). Christina's ancestors used the German spelling of Steinbrenner. (LC)

W&M-891. George H. Whitmore (1844-1922) and wives Henrietta F. (Gittings) (1847-1904) and Isabella (Carr) (1846-1931) are buried at Fairmont Cemetery at Libertytown where also are buried his parents William Whitmore (1818-1898) and wife Mary E. (Will) (1815-1893). William was a son of George Whitmore (1778-1848) and wife Sarah (Cover) (1780-1847) who are buried at Haugh's Church near Ladiesburg.

Emigrant Benjamin Witmer from Barbelroth, Pfalz, settled in Lancaster Co., Pennsylvania. Benjamin Jr. (1705-1769) moved to Tom's Creek Settlement southeast of Emmitsburg as did his son Henry. See article by Phillip E. Bedient in Pennsylvania Mennonite Heritage, April 1991.

An article about Rev. George A. Whitmore is in the 6th. Congressional Biography book at (FH). It was he who publicized the wrong location of Monocacy Log Church. (M&C-I) (LC).

W&M-893. John Mason Grove (1842-1925) and wife Sarah Alice (Willard) (1846-1920) are buried at Middletown Reformed Church. His parents were Jacob (1793-1878) buried at Mt. Olivet and Elizabeth (1802-1854) buried at Middletown Reformed Church. John Mason's grandfather was Jacob Grove Sr. (1759-1834) who married Christina (Doyle) (1764-1830). They are buried at Middletown Reformed Church. According to the census of 1800 Jacob and Christina Graf or Grove then had 5 sons and one daughter, also 4 slaves.

In 1800 Charles Grove and wife in Middletown Valley were over 45 years; they had 3 sons and 3 daughters living at home. In Middletown Reformed records Peter and Barbara Graf had John born 1794. In the church records the Grove spelling was adopted in 1817.

For Grove families in Washington Co. see Williams 1906. Local Grove families are believed to descend from Graff or Graf families of Lancaster Co., PA (*The Groff Book* by Clyde L. Groff et al (Groff History Associates, Ronks, PA)).

Jacob Graff (1737-1819) and wife Catherine (1742-1823) settled before 1765 at Sharpsburg where they were buried at the Reformed Church. Jacob was said to have been a son of John of Lancaster Co. and grandson of emigrant Hans Graf. (Wms 1906).

W&M-895. Judge William H. Pearre (1836-1917) and wives Julia (Lindsay) (1836-1862) and Ruth Ann (Buckingham) (1833-1915) are all buried at Unionville M.E. Church. The Judge's parents were Rev. James Pearre (1808-1882) and Eliza (Dudderar) (1814-1898). His grandparents were James Pearre Sr. (1760-1825) and wife Sarah (1768-1857) who are buried at Unionville M. E. Church.

W&M-896. Charles C. Waters (1867-1926) and wife Rosa L. R. (Jones) as well as his parents Dr. James K. (1838-1916) and Annie M. (Hill) (1840-1884) were buried in Thurmont United Brethren Cemetery. Grandparents of Charles C. were Somerset R. Waters (1796-1860) and wife Rachel (1801-1875) who are buried at Mt. Airy Methodist Church.

In the 1800 census in the Mt. Airy area lived widow Lucretia Waters, over 45 years of age, with 3 grown daughters. In the Fredericktown area lived Jacob Waters and wife (26-45) with 2 young sons and 3 young daughters.

A Waters family was prominent early in the southern part of later Montgomery Co. In 1749 William Waters was Constable of Newfoundland Hundred. In 1760 John Waters was Constable of the district near the Potomac. In 1753 Richard Waters, Planter, bought 30 acres of Williams' Lot on Seneca Creek from Basil Wiliams, a carpenter and tavern keeper, whose wife was Mary. In the same year Richard Waters bought from Joseph Williams the tract Collinger Folly beginning at the head of a glade draining into Seneca Creek.

At least 20 members of Waters families served in the Militia in the Revolutionary War. (LC)

W&M-896. Charles W. Johnson (1857-1918) and wife Amanda (Wiseman) (1860-1934) are buried at St. Johns Lutheran Church near Ellerton as are his parents John W. Johnson (b. c.1834) and Caroline (Routzahn) (1838-1928). Grandparents of Charles W. were Jacob Johnson (1795-1867) and wife Catherine (Bittle) (1800-1876) (daughter of George). In the 1800 census there were 7 Johnson families in Middletown Valley. Three were headed by Joseph, Mathias and Thomas Sr. who were over 45 years old. The Frederick Co. Militia of 1812 had at least 17 Johnsons. (LC)

W&M-897. Samuel Miller (1809-1894) and wife Sarah A. C. (Easterday) (1819-1913) are buried at Mt. Olivet. His parents Adam (c. 1770-1866) and wife Elisabeth (Baer) (1782-1857) are buried at the Miller graveyard at Highland on Catoctin Mt. northeast of Myersville.

The great numbers of Millers in our area have been but little resolved. For example, 27 Millers were enrolled in the Frederick Co. Militia of 1812. Some of these records include marriages and other family data.

W&M-898. Peter J. Carpenter (1851-1919) born near Lancaster, PA married Hattie Hall (1869-1935) daughter of B. Franklin Hall and wife Sidney Ann (Sheetenhelm) of New Market District. They are buried at Mt. Olivet as are his parents John C. Carpenter (1808-1880) and wife Margaret (Davis) (1818-1894). The ancestors in Lancaster Co., Pennsylvania may have been Zimmerman families.

The Hall family was early in the area of New Market, having a survey before 1746. In 1800 in the area were Benjamin Sr. and households of possible sons Benjamin, Henry and Lewis. According to Scharf the village of New Market was laid out about 1793 by Nicholas Hall whose ancestors came from New Market, England. In 1794 the tract New Market Plains of over 1500 acres was surveyed by Nicholas Hall.

W&M-899. Thomas C. Fox (1841-1928) and wife Ruth A. (Buhrman) (1845-1892) are buried at Foxville Lutheran Church, as are his parents George P. Fox (1795-1878) and Sophia (Bussard) (1800-1875). A grandfather of Thomas C. was George Fox (1771-1842) whose wives were Elizabeth (1773-1816) and Mary M. (1792-1861). In the 1800 census of Middletown Valley the only Fox household was headed by Frederick who was over 45 years old. His wife was under 45 years. They had 3 sons and 4 daughters.

Philip Jacob Fuchs (later Fox) emigrated in 1767. His son George married Anna Elizabeth Hartman (daughter of Phillip Jr. and Margaretha). Their son (George) Philip Fox (1795-1878) married Sophia Bussard (1800-1875). Sophia's parents were Peter Bussard Sr. (1761-1802) and Margaretha Rebecca (Householder) daughter of (Johan) Adam and wife Elisabetha. Peter Bussard's parents were Daniel Bussard Sr. (1736-1814) and wife Sophia (Renner) (1740-1826).

The Fox or Fuchs families in Frederick Lutheran records may not be related. The earliest there to baptize offspring were Christopher and wife Magdalena Fuchs 1765; Peter and Margaretha 1769; Mathias and Magdalena 1769; George and Maria 1773; Henry and Anna Eva 1775; Michael and Anna Maria 1778; and Balthasar and Juliana 1779.

Christopher, Edward, Elijah, Frederick and Michael Fox served in the Maryland Militia during the Revolution.

W&M-899. John T. Best Jr. (1874-1947) and parents John T. (1839-1902) and Margaret Joanna (Dorsey) (1841-1895) are buried at Mt. Olivet. John T. Sr. had a second marriage to Emily C. Ford (1856-1946) who is buried at Mt. Olivet also. David Best grandfather of John T. Jr. lived 1804-1880. He and wife Anna Mary (1802-1871) are buried at Mt. Olivet. The great grandfather of John T. was buried near Littlestown Pennsylvania

Best descendants held a reunion in Frederick in July 1992 which included a talk about early Littlestown Pennsylvania (LC)

W&M-901. Frederick Clayton Miller (1854-1916) and wife Julia D. (Sheffer) (1860-1935), also his parents Frederick (1822-1904) and wife Lydia Ann (Dorner) (1823-1894) are buried in Jefferson Union Cemetery.

Local Millers contributed to the Revolution by officers Abraham, Isaac, Jacob, Philip and William Miller.

W&M-901. William Steiner Ramsburg (1860-1922) and wife Clara A. Jeannette (Stup) (1860-1950) are buried at Mt. Olivet. His parents Urias D. (c. 1825-1903) and wife Ann S. (Staley) (1837-1921) are buried at Charlesville Reformed Church. The parents of Urias D. were Frederick Ramsburg and wife Lydia A. (Snook). He was buried at Bethel Lutheran Church but the dates are no longer legible.

The emigrant ancestor Stephen Riemensperger settled just north of Harmony Grove rather than at Charlesville. See W&M-752.

W&M-902. Capt. Daniel Rinehart (1823-1886) and wives Margaret (Hyder) (1830-1860) and Rebecca (Norris) (1839-1920) are buried at Beaver Dam Brethren Cemetery near Johnsville. His parents were Israel (1792-1871) (buried at Pipe Creek Cemetery near Uniontown) and Mary (Snader) (Rinehart) of Union Bridge.

A daughter of Capt. Daniel and Margaret Rinehart was Olivia Rinehart who studied in Paris and taught art at Western Maryland College. Distantly related William Henry Rinehart (1825-1874) was a nationally known sculptor who grew up near Union Bridge. Rinehart genealogies are listed in M&C-II-174. (LC)

W&M-903. Reno Sheffer Harp (1866-1946) had wives Annie E. (Brightbill) (d. 1896) and Bessie D. (Zentz). (See lineage W&M-705). His parents were Daniel V. (1835-1913) and wife Lugenia Frances (Sheffer) (c. 1843-1896) who are buried at Myersville United Brethren Church.

It is extremely unlikely that Reno's emigrant Harp ancestor arrived in Pennsylvania as early as 1707. It was Reno Harp who erected the monument at Jerusalem Cemetery near Myersville stating falsely that settlers arrived in the area as early as 1710. The nearest German settlers at that time were in Conestoga area of Lancaster Co., PA. This untruth probably comes from the book *Thirty Thousand Names of Immigrants in Pennsylvania* by I. D. Rupp (1875, reprint 1927) page 12 or from stories that refugees from Bohemia Manor in Cecil Co., MD moved westward very early.

In the 1800 census in Middletown Valley were households probably of widow Mary Harp over 45 years; also George Harp and wife 26-45 with a son and two daughters.

In baptisms of Middletown Reformed Church records in 1772 was a sponsor Joerg Peter Herge (Harp?). George Harp Jr? (1765-1844) and wife Catherine (Toms) (1774-1849) are buried at St. John's Lutheran Church north of Myersville. Reno's grandfather John Harp (1798-1877) and wife Elizabeth (Doub) (1804-1857) are buried at Myersville United Brethren Church. There is no evidence that the Doubs were of French origin; they were German Daubs. (Reno probably guessed wrong from the Doub River in France, pronounced very differently).

Abraham Toms is believed to have been a son of William who died in 1823. Roy Wampler after much research has concluded that the Toms family was German in origin. A Henry Thom native of Germany was naturalized in Maryland in 1765.

A different account of Harp families was given in an article about John H. Harp (Williams 1906, page 738). Michael Harp emigrated via Philadelphia in 1740. John Harp "doubtless a relative of Michael" came to Middletown Valley from Reading, PA in 1750 along with several brothers. John died in 1796 leaving sons George and Jacob. George married a Miss Toms and farmed near Myersville. Descendant Jacob Harp married Lydia Kline and they moved to Washington Co. in 1839.

Gravestone records show that early Harp families belonged to the Church of the Brethren at Grossnickle Meeting House in upper Middletown Valley where George (1765-1844) and wife Catherine (1774-1849) were the earliest recorded. Harp families also were around Monocacy Brethren Church at Rocky Ridge, east of Thurmont, where Daniel Harp (1805-1874) and wife Mary A. (1816-1894) have gravestones. (LC)

W&M-906. Rev. Thomas Scott Bacon (1825-1904) and second wife Sophia T. Graff (1846-1914) are buried at Mt. Olivet in Frederick.

W&M-907. (John) Henry Lampe (1841-1910) and wife Elizabeth M. (Ross) (1842-1912) are buried in Mt. Olivet as were his parents from Germany, Julius (1801-1881) and Christine (1810-1882). A son of Henry and Elizabeth was Allen Lampe (1879-1934) who married Ada E. Lough (1879-1957). See M&C-II. A descendant of Julius and Christine was Dr. J. Harold Lampe (d. 1896) of Baltimore who was Professor of Electrical Engineering at John's Hopkins and at North Carolina State College. (LC)

W&M-908. Cornelius A. Staley (1834-1883) and second wife Mary A. C. Measell (1838-1913) are buried at Mt. Olivet. His parents were Frederick (d. 1858) and Elizabeth (Shaffer) (d. 1864) who were buried in Frederick Reformed Church Cemetery. Frederick was a son of Jacob (1751-1815) and first wife Anna Barbara (1753-1793). Jacob was a son of emigrant Melchior (1719-1791) and wife Anna Barbara (1726-1790).(S)

The abundant Staley families are among the most challenging of Frederick Co. Henry Stehli and three sons Jacob, Johan Jacob and Melchoir emigrated from Switzerland to the vicinity of Rocky Springs northwest of Frederick and had many sons few of whom moved westward. Later Staleys spread to Middletown Valley and to north of Frederick. Few of the early Staleys have left gravestones (not one of the many Jacob Staleys). The following tentative, incomplete outline of the first three generations largely follows Burch (S) with my additions from Church and Courthouse records.

Heinrich Stehli and wife Maria Steinbruchel of Switzerland emigrated in 1751 after sons Melchior in 1743 and Jacob in 1749 who also were born in Switzerland. (S&H). They all settled in Frederick Co.

I. Jacob Stehli (1698-1760) m. Anna Margaret Rebstock, born in Switzerland and died 1761. They farmed near Rocky Springs. In 1754 Jacob was overseer of the road from Frederick to the Fulling Mill of Jacob Peck. Their known children:

(1) Anna Maria m. c.1756 Hans Georg Schorb; 2m 1761 Adam Hildebrand.
(2) Philippina m. 1761 Christoph Stull (d. before 1794) Ch: Adam (son John 1792-1863) bur. Bethel Lutheran Church), John, Catherine, Elizabeth, Magdalene, Jacob. 2m 1794 Balthasar Getzendanner.
(3) Jacob m. Catherine Barbara (1759-1793), see later.
(4) Henry (b. 1747-1800) m. Catherine; see later.
(5) Joseph m. Juliana Schaffer?
(6) Philip
(7) Catherine m. Funk.

II. Johan Jacob Stehli (1703-1764) m. Elisabeth (1718-1795); records in Frederick Reformed Church, later to Middletown Valley.

(1) Elizabeth (1750-1823) m. 1773 Daniel Biser.
(2) Jacob m. Ann Castle, see later.
(3) Henry (d. 1806) m. (Anna) Mary; sponsors at Middletown Reformed Church; no ch. recorded.
(4) Catherine (b. 1758-1823) m. 1780 Henry Leiter (1754-1823); dau. Hannah (1799-1858).
(5) Ann (d. 1825).
(6) Daniel in will.

III. Melchoir Staley (1719-1791) m. (Anna) Barbara (1726-1790). He was born in Maschwanden, Switzerland; farmed near Rocky Springs; 6 ch. (unnamed) in will.

(1) Susanna Barbara (1747-1800) m. John Engel.
(2) Jacob (1751-1815) m. Mary Elizabeth (d/o Jacob Staley who died 1814). Lived near Rocky Springs, see later.

III. Melchoir 2m 1794 Eva Margaret Winter, see later.

THIRD GENERATION OF STALEYS

I. (3) Jacob Staley of Jacob m. (Catharine) Barbara (1759-1793) Rocky Springs and Frederick Reformed Church.

- (a) Joseph m. Elizabeth Staley?
- (b) George Peter (b. 1773) m. Elizabeth; son Peter (b. 1798)
- (c) John (1777-1850) m. Margaret E. (1781-1854) buried Mt. Olivet; son Cornelius (1808-1883) m. Rhuanna Snively (1809-1889) d/o Adam and Catherine of Washington Co.
- (d) Jacob (b. 1789) m. Elizabeth Way?
- (e) Susannah (b. 1792)

I.(4) Henry Staley of Jacob (1747-1800) m. Catherine; (Frederick Reformed Records) Children:

- (a) Henry (1778-1829) m. Margaret
- (b) Daniel (b. 1783) m. Elizabeth House?
- (c) Esther (b. before 1784)
- (d-f) David, Samuel and Mathias all born after 1784
- (g) Catherine (b. 1786)
- (h) Sophia (b. 1788)
- (i) Elias (b. 1790)

I.(5) Joseph Staley of Jacob (d. 1808) m. Maria Juliana Heffner (Hoefner) (1755-after 1818); Frederick Reformed Church.

- (a) Joseph (1775-before 1808) m. 1800 Catherine Guthman (Goodman)
- (b) Anna Maria (b. 1776) m. 1796 Henry Schmit
- (c) John Jacob (b. 1778) m. Elizabeth Kemp (1783-1813) daughter of Frederick and Dorothy
- (d) Elizabeth (d. 1864)
- (e) Catherine (1781-1816) m. 1802 Samuel Wachter
- (f) George (b. 1783) m. 1805 Catherine Staley
- (g) Solomon (b. 1786) m. 1807 Margaret Butler
- (h) Magdalena (Molley)
- (i) Margaret (1790-1815) m. 1814 Michael Brunner
- (j) Moses (1792-1840) m. Ann Elizabeth Stull; sons: Frederick (b. 1827) to Champaign Co., OH; Lewis Edward; Josiah Oliver
- (k) Susanna (b. 1794) m. 1814 George Brunner
- (l) Maria Julianan (b. 1800)

II. (2) Jacob Staley of Johan Jacob (1756-1822) m. 1780 Ann Castle; Middletown Reformed Church; order of children uncertain.

- (a) John (b. 1785); m. 1817 Elizabeth Geasy?
- (b) Jacob (b. 1787)
- (c) Lydia (b. 1791) m. 1810 John Stille

II. (2) Jacob 2m Nancy
- (d) Joseph (b. c.1793) m. Rebecca; ch including Margaret (b. 1830); Ann Rebecca (b. 1832); Joseph Henry (b. 1838)
- (e) John Henry (b. 1794)
- (f) Malinda (b. 1800)
- (g) Conrad m. 1828 Margaret Smith; son Josiah Edward (b. 1833)

III. (2) Jacob Staley of Melchoir (1751-1815) m. Anna Barbara (1753-1793); ch from (S) and his will:
- (a) Jacob (1773-1814) m. Catherine d. c.1815); lived near Lewistown, blacksmith. Ch: Joseph, John, Mary Elizabeth
- (b) John Peter m. 1797 Elizabeth Schaefer; buried Frederick Reformed Church; son Peter S. (b. 1798) m. Margaret Albaugh (1797-1873); Frederick Reformed Church
- (c) Charlotte (1777-1815)
- (d) Anna Maria (1779-1815)
- (e) Barbara (1781-1830) m. 1802 Isaac Hedges, buried Mt. Olivet
- (f) Jacob H. (b. 1783)
- (g) Frederick (1785-1858) m. 1811 Elizabeth Schaffer
- (h) John (b. 1789); prisoner of British (1812)
- (i) Susanna (1791-1858) m. John Reese (1789-1862); buried Mt. Olivet.

III. (2) Jacob of Melchoir 2m 1794 Mary Elizabeth Staley (1766-before 1811).
- (j) Jonathan (1795-before 1811) (Frederick Ref. Church)
- (k) Catherine (b. 1797)
- (l) Samuel (b. 1799) (Frederick Ref. Church)
- (m) George (1801-1870) m. 1825 Hestor Ann Bopst (b. 1805); buried at Rocky Springs
- (n) Tobias (1804-1877) m. 1827 Susannah Miller (1809-1891); children including Cornelius (b. 1844) in 1850 census.

Of Staleys in the 1850 census north of Frederick were Solomon born in 1805 in Pennsylvania, wife Julia Ann and 10 children. More than 100 later Staleys were recorded as related to Zimmerman families (Z). A study of *Descendants of Lewis Mahlon Staley* (1853-1923) by Margaret E. Myers is with files of JMH. Many later Staley descendants are given by Burch (S) and on gravestones of three pages of JMH.

W&M-908. Mahlon C. Kefauver (1841-1933) is buried in Middletown Reformed Cemetery. Nicholas, his ancestor, was a son of Philip Kiefhaber the early settler in the valley. George (1785-1861) son of Nicholas, married Mary Castle (1782-1851) and their son Henry (1810-1876) and wife Mary (Biser) (1811-1891) were parents of Mahlon. See also W&M-791 and 921.

W&M-911. Dr. Elmer C. Kefauver M.D. (b. 1868) married Mary Alice Atlee (1867-1957) of Virginia. His parents were Richard Calvin Kefauver (1843-1925) and Laura V. (Toms) (1847-1936) daughter of Ezra and Sophia (Doub). Richard's parents were Daniel Kefauver (1808-1876) and second wife Catherine (Bechtol) (1813-1895) (daughter of Lewis and Catherine (Stemple)) who are buried at Middletown Reformed Cemetery. Daniel was a son of George

Kefauver (1785-1861) and Mary (Castle) (Cassel) (1782-1851). George's grandfather Philip who settled in Middletown Valley had will of 1778 showing surviving sons Philip Jr., Peter, Nicholas and Jacob. See also W&M-791.

Dr. Elmer and Mary Alice Kefauver had only one child, Lillian S. born March 10, 1898, who married Sherman Philip Bowers (1889-1962) a prominent lawyer of Frederick. Lillian celebrated her 94th birthday in Spokane, WA. She taught music at Church St. School in Frederick in 1923.

W&M-911. George W. Crum Jr. (1857-1921) and wife Mary V. (Etchison) (1857-1926) are buried at Jefferson Union Cemetery. His parents were George W. (1811-1896) and Susan S. Remsburg (1830-1911) who also are buried at Jefferson Union. Grandparents of George W. Jr. were Henry Crum (1776-1848) and Barbara Ann (Hoffman) (1779-1837) also buried at Jefferson.

These Crum families around Jefferson, who descend from Henry and Barbara Ann, who came from Virginia about 1800, must not be confused with other Crums near Frederick and in the Walkersville to Liberty area who descend from Crom families of Holland (W&M-1145), nor with descendants of the later emigrants from Germany, Casper Crum Sr, and wife Christina (W&M-1574). (LC)

W&M-913. James K. Waters (1853-1936) and wife Laura F. (Leatherman) (1854-1907) are buried at St. Johns Lutheran Church near Ellerton. His parents also buried there are James H. (1816-1876) and wife Anna (Schlosser) (c. 1819-1893). See also W&M-896.

W&M-913. Harry Eugene Chapline born 1869 was a son of Isaac Thomas Chapline (1837-1876) and wife Laura (Schley) (1842-1922) who are buried at Mt. Olivet. Laura's lineage from John Thomas and Margaret Schley, emigrants from Appenhofen near Landau south Germany, is given in a *Schley Genealogy* by C.E.S. (FH). Joseph Chapline (1707-1769), who in 1763 founded Sharpsburg in Washington Co. is discussed by Williams (1906). The Chapline ancestor emigrated to Virginia in 1610; William C. came to Maryland in 1682 and had son William Jr. Moses Chapline's inventory in 1765 had executors Joseph and Jennett Chapline. Joseph's inventory in 1769 had executors William Joseph Jr. and James. James and Joseph Chapline were officers in the Revolution.

W&M-914. Thomas Augustus Chapline (1871-1947) and wife Mary C. (Byerly) (1871-1937) are buried at Mt. Olivet. The dates of his parents Isaac and Laura are above.

W&M-915. George Elijah House Jr. (1824-1902) and wife Ann (Rice) (1822-1915) are buried at Mt. Olivet. Numerous House families have lived in Frederick and in southern Middletown Valley. Among the early ones with gravestones were William (1733-1822) said to have emigrated from Alsace in 1750 (LW); Stephen T. (1776-1842) (Middletown Lutheran); John (1768-1865) (Burkittsville Union Cemetery and Caleb (c. 1760-1824) (stone at Braddock Heights).

In the census of 1800 in Middletown Valley were Caleb, George and William, Sr. House all over age 45; two other households were headed by Daniel and John House in the 26-45 age range. In 1800 in Frederick were William, over 45, and Jacob, 26-45. (LC)

W&M-916. Valentine Stickle Brunner (1818-1889) and wife Margaret M.(Pyfer) (1817-1910) are buried at Mt. Olivet. The following is from the book *Joseph Brunner of Rothenstein, Klein Schifferstadt and Frederick* by Donald L. Osborn. (Lee's Summit, MO., 1991)

Joseph Brunner (1676-1752+) was a son of Heinrich and Maria (Braun) Brunner of Rothenstein a village between Memmingen and Kempten in the Allgaeu area of southern German Swabia. By 1693 Joseph had gone northwestward to the Odenwald area where he was confirmed in the Reformed Church at Lindenfels. Joseph was in Klein Schifferstadt near Manheim at the time of his marriage to Catherine Elisabeth Thomas in 1700. The Brunner house remains in Klein Schifferstadt today. Joseph, Catherine and the following children emigrated via Philadelphia in 1729.

(1) Anna Barbara (1701-1767) m. 1723 Christian Getzendanner (d. 1766). See descendants (GZ).
(2) (Johan) Jakob (1703-after 1775) m. Maria Barbara Storm (dau. of Christian Sturm of Klein Schifferstadt).
(3) Gabriel (b. 1706).
(4) Johannes (1708-1776) m. Anna Maria Deladre? (dau. of David of Klein Schifferstadt).
(5) (Johan) Valentin (b. 1711).
(6) (Johan) Heinrich (1715-c.1775) m. Magdalena.
(7) Maria Catherina (1718- after 1765) m. Stephen Riemensperger later Ramsburg (c. 1712-1789).
(8) Elias (b. 1723) m. Albertina.

The Brunner family arrived in the Monocacy area by 1736.

Jacob and Maria Barbara had son John (1745-1819) who married Christina Storm. The latter had Jacob (d. 1760-1822) who married in 1786 Magdalena Schneider (c. 1768-1816) and became parents of John Brunner (1792-1844) who married (Anna) Maria Stickle (1794-1829). The latter were parents of Valentine S. Brunner. John had a second marriage in 1830 to Sophia Doll, daughter of Joseph and sister Ezra Doll. Joseph Brunner gave Schifferstadt House in Frederick to son Elias in 1753.

W&M-917. W&M includes no article on descendants of early Snyder (Schneider) families who lived around Mt. Airy, Frederick and Middletown Valley. In the 1800 census of eastern Frederick were families of John Snider (over 45 years) and wife under 45; John Snider between 26 and 45 years; and Christian Snider between 16 and 26 years of age. In Frederick District was George Schnider over 45 years who lived alone. In 1800 census in Frederick District lived Abraham Snyder and wife between 26 and 45 in age, also Elizabeth Snyder, between 26 and 45 years with young children. The Snyders have proliferated in Washington Co. where 22 families have articles in Williams (1906).

W&M-918. Whendell L. H. Zentz (1869-1949) buried at Thurmont United Brethren Cemetery was a son of Abraham S. (1828-1898) and Sarah D. (Biggs) (1834-1905) buried at the same cemetery. See W&M-706.

W&M-918. Dr. C. M. Benner M.D. born in 1877 was a son of Alonzo (1846-1912) and wife Virginia (Miller) (1849-1921) buried at Liberty Chapel.

Christian Benner Sr. apparently was born in Germany, by tradition near Manheim, Pfalz and emigrated as a child. After he died suddenly in 1767 his widow Anne Margaret had her second son Christian Jr. in 1768. Then she attended Falckner Swamp Church near later Pottstown, PA. In 1790 census Christian Benner Jr. appears in York Co. (later Gettysburg area of Adams Co.). He married Anna Maria Biesecker and they farmed in Adams Co. Benner's Hill on the Gettysburg Battlefield is named for the family. The Christian Benners of near Gettysburg were my ancestors through marriage of Christian Jr's. daughter Elizabeth with Abraham Fisher. (M&C-II).

Christian Jr. and Anna Maria (1765-1853) had son John (1793-1850) who married Esther Plank (d. 1855). The latter had son George (1819-1911) who lived in Taneytown and was the grandfather of Dr. C. M. Benner. (LC)

W&M-919. McGill Belt (1856-1937) and wife Anne R. (Barnard) (1859-1923) are buried at Point of Rocks Episcopal Church as were his parents John Lloyd (1819-1889) and wife Sarah Eleanor (McGill) (1818-1903). John Lloyd Belt's parents were Alfred (1788-1872) and wife Charlotte (Trundle) (1787-1824) also buried at Point of Rocks.

At least 9 Belts are recorded in the Maryland Militia of the Revolution. Lloyd Belt was enrolled in the Frederick County Militia in 1812. His wife was Elizabeth Causlet Metcalfe (Thomas).

W&M-920. Peter N. Hammaker (1857-1925) and wife Ida C. (Miller) (1859-1916) are buried at Mt. Olivet Cemetery in Frederick. For his ancestors see Williams (1906).

W&M-921. Harry Joshua Kefauver (1878-1946) and wife Miriam (Evans) (b. 1881) have gravestones at Mt. Olivet. He is a son of Mahlon C. (1841-1933) buried at Middletown Reformed Church. See W&M-908.

W&M-922. Charles Abraham Ogle (1872-1948) and wife Carrie G. (Barnes) (1872-1936) are buried at Unionville Methodist Cemetery. His parents were Ephraim (1829-1911) and Mary A. (Fillinger) (1832-1914) buried at Beaver Dam Brethren Cemetery near Johnsville. Grandparents of Charles A. were Thomas A. Ogle (1784-1850) born in New Jersey and wife Sarah or Annie (Webb) (b. c.1801). See W&M-1584.

The 1800 census of Liberty District had only the household of Peter Ogle and wife, both over 45 years with 5 daughters and 2 sons. In 1800 in Emmitsburg District were three Ogle households headed by Joseph over 45 with 2 daughters and one son; Mary Ogle over 45 with 5 sons and 10 slaves; and Sybilla (Schley) Ogle (widow of Thomas) 45 years with 2 daughters, 2 sons and 4 slaves. In 1800 in Fredericktown District lived only Benjamin Ogle and wife over 45 years with one daughter and 5 sons, also 6 slaves. Many Ogles had moved to the Middle West.

Almeda Heckathorn who married George Ogle in 1856 probably was a descendant of Jacob Heckendorn who emigrated in 1750 from Retschwiller, northern Alsace. He married Anna Barbara Jung and had Jacob Jr. in 1744. They attended church at Tom's Creek around 1761. (LC)

W&M-923. Maurice C. Brandenburg (1859-1952) and wife Martha A. (Bussard) (1869-1949) are buried at Middletown Reformed Church as are his parents Daniel (1823-1902) and wife Lydia A. R. (Remsburg) (1829-1914). Isaac Brandenburg (1797-1876) and Catherine (1793-1868) also buried at Middletown Reformed Church were parents of Daniel. In 1800 in Middletown Valley were four Brandenburg households as follows: Samuel and wife, over 45 years, with six daughters and four sons; David (26-45); Matthias and wife 26-45 with six sons and a daughter; and William and wife 26-45 with a daughter and two sons.

W&M-923. Calvin Brown Anders (1850-1910) and wife Anna Mary (Repp) (1855-1895) are buried at Mt. View Cemetery, Union Bridge. His parents Aaron (1817-1875) and Mary Ann (Stoner) (1827-1856) are buried at Mt. Olivet.

A Jacob Anders (c. 1789-1834) and wife Elizabeth Shrier (b. 1789) are buried in Beaver Dam Cemetery near Johnsville. They had three sons including Moses (1816-1848) and two daughters. (See *Anders Root Directory* by Norman C. Anders, (Lehigh Acres, FL). (FH)

Scharf page 617 gives children of Moses Anders and wife Eliza Ellen (Harlan) (1815-1892) (daughter of Joshua and (Sarah Wood)). See also W&M-1514.

W&M-924. Hon. Aaron Repp Anders (1879-1923) apparently unmarried is buried at Mt. Olivet. See his parents Calvin and Mary above. The mill of Anders and Reifsnider later was known as Glissan's Mill on Linganore Creek about a mile east of the New Market-Liberty Road; and far up-stream from Linganore Hills Inn.

W&M-926. John P. T. Mathias (1848-1927) and wife Elizabeth Agnes (McCurdy) (1858-1928) are buried in Mt. Olivet Cemetery. His parents farmers Philip Mathias (1811-1892) and Eleanor Carmack (Stimmel) (1820-1907) are buried at Creagerstown. Philip's parents were Griffith Mathias (1787-1851) born in PA and wife Susan (Huffer) (c. 1780-1875).

Mrs. Theresa M. Trail Michel calls attention to a genealogy of Mathias families by Rev. Joseph Mathias which states that emigrant John Mathias, after the death of his first wife, sailed from Newport, Wales, with bride Elizabeth (Morgan). They settled among other Welsh near later Doylestown, PA. Among the children of emigrant John were sons John, Rev. Joseph (Baptist), Griffith who fought in the Revolution and the youngest, David, who married Hannah Pugh (daughter of Daniel) and settled near Taneytown. They had several daughters and one son Griffith who married Susanna Huffer.

The census of 1850 shows that Griffith Mathias was born in Pennsylvania. This confirms what I was told by relative Ruth Webster Rogers of Thurmont, that the Mathias ancestors of Senator Charles Mathias came later to Frederick Co. than the very early settlers Jacob Mathias (1704-1782) from Northern Alsace (B3) and wife Margaret (1709-1788). Some of the numerous descendants of the latter have used the name Matthews. The beautiful gravestone of Margaret at Apples Church apparently was made by the same artist who made the stone of Mrs. Hehl at St. John's Church, Church Hill north of Myersville.

Charles McCurdy Mathias (1886-1967), son of John P. T. and Elizabeth Agnes married in 1921 Theresa McElfresh Trail (c. 1896-1988) daughter of Bayard.

Charles was a lawyer in Frederick and Thurmont. He and my father Calvin Ezra had business ventures together. Charles and Theresa Mathias had children as follows:

(1) U. S. Senator Charles McCurdy Jr. (b. 1922) married 1958 Ann Hickling Bradford of Cambridge, MA. Their children are Charles Bradford (b. 1959) and Robert Fiske (b. 1961).

(2) (Edward) Trail m. Elizabeth Royer, divorced; 2m Natasha Zavoiko; they live in Baltimore; Children: Edward Northcroft Trail and Steven Philip McCurdy.

(3) Theresa McElfresh (b. 1926) m. 1955 Glenn Carlyle Michel (1922-1987). He was a lawyer in Frederick. Children: Theresa Trail (b. 1957) and Frederick Mathias (b. 1959) m. Kathryn J. Strodel (1959-1984).

Charles McCurdy Mathias, Jr. born in Frederick in 1922 received a B.A. degree from Haverford College, studied at Yale University and received a law degree from the University of Maryland. He served in the U.S. Navy (1942-1946) including liberation of the Philippines and occupation of Japan. He practiced law with his father in Frederick and became Assistant Attorney General of Maryland (1953-1954), City Attorney of Frederick (1954-1959), member of the Maryland House of Delegates (1959-1960) and was reelected 3 terms to the U. S. House of Representatives. Charles was first elected to the U. S. Senate in 1968 and served continuously until retirement in Jan. 1987.

W&M-927. Charles Byerly (1874-1944) and wife Regina (Eisenhauer) are buried in Mt. Olivet. The grandfather of Charles was pioneer photographer Jacob Byerly (1804-1883) of Newville, Cumberland Co., PA, whose first marriage was to Catherine Bear (1809-1841) daughter of David and Esther. From this union came John Davis Byerly (1839-1914) who at Frederick married in 1869 Mary Markell (1849-1922). The Byerlys are buried at Mt. Olivet. The grandson of John Davis was John Francis Byerly whose second marriage was to Virginia James (b. 1899) who lived in Frederick until 1992 with family heirlooms. See M&C-II. Jacob Byerly was honored recently as a pioneer photographer by the Museum of Eastman Kodak Co., (LC)

W&M-928. Melville E. Doll (1839-1903) who married Hannah M. Danner is buried at Mt. Olivet as are his parents Ezra (1800-1842) and Harriet (Zeiler) (1802-1886). See W&M-844 for earlier Doll families. Conrad and Joseph Doll were officers in the Revolution.

W&M-928. Frederick Worman Cramer (1883-1945) and his parents George (1851-1924) and wife Mary O. (Worman) (1850-1890) are buried at Mt. Olivet. Mary's parents were William (1826-1868) and Mary Elizabeth (1828-1909) and grandparents Moses Worman (1777-1861) and wife Margaret (1777-1858) all buried at Mt. Olivet.

In Frederick Reformed Church records (Johan) Jacob and Anna Catharina Kraemer baptized son John in 1751 with sponsors Johan and Juliana Catherine Berg (later Barrick). They leased land on Monocacy Manor. George Kraemer (c. 1738-1796) married Maria Magdalena Holtz and had Adam (1766-1803) and John (1769-1842) (buried at Utica). John and wife E. Catherine (1780-1858) are buried at Utica. Adam married Appollonia Devilbiss in 1792. A George

Kraemer married Maria Hammond in 1797 with witnesses John and Peter Kraemer. In Frederick Lutheran records a William Kraemer married Anna Bayer in 1769.

Early Kraemers leased on Monocacy Manor and had few deeds. In 1765 George Creamer, farmer, bought 45 acres from Valentine Creager, blacksmith. In 1771 a George Kramer (son of Jacob) sold to William Berg, farmer, 15 acres on the west side of Little Monocacy Creek near Sugar Loaf Mt. In 1778 Casper Cramer bought from Benjamin Cornell 1 1/2 acres of Brooke's Discovery on Rich Land near later Taneytown. (These are the only Cramer deeds until 1778). A genealogy of *Descendants of Hans Adam Kraemer of Kreutz Creek, York Co.* has been written by Edgar S. Creamer. (Y)

In the census of 1800 in Creagerstown area lived Jacob and John Cramer (26-45 years). Jacob (1767-1849) and wife Magdalena (1744-1856) are buried at Utica as are John (1769-1842) and wife E. Catherine (1780-1858). In Liberty District in 1800 were households of John, Peter and William Cramer all over 45 years. Adam, Catherine and George (26-45) were also heads of families there. In the Taneytown area were Casper Creamer, over 45 years, and family and also Philip in range of 16-26 years. In 1800 in southern Frederick Co. lived Adam Cramer (26-45) and family.

(Johan) Baltzer Kramer and relatives with Conrad Voltz emigrated in 1773 from near Saarbruecken in southern Germany to Manheim, PA near Lancaster where they worked briefly as glassblowers for Stiegel before founding south of Frederick after 1775 the glass works which they sold to John Friedrick Amelung after Conrad's death in 1784. The Kramers worked for Amelung until his business failed and then Baltzer, Christian and George with their families moved westward to New Geneva, PA. See book *Johann Baltsar Kramer, Pioneer American Glass Blower*, by LeRoy Kramer (Chicago 1939). (Y) (LC)

W&M-929. John Sebastian Lakin was a son of Capt. William (1794-1850) and Susan (Remsberg) (1807-1877) who are buried in the Lakin family graveyard in southern Middletown Valley (about midway between Jefferson and Point of Rocks). John S. and wife Bertha Ellen (Cochran) (1865-1940) are buried at Jefferson Union Cemetery. Buried in the family graveyard are early settlers Abraham Lakin Jr. (1713-1796) and wife Sarah (1715-1797).

Early settler Abraham Lakin in 1743 surveyed a tract called Two Brothers which he divided to his sons Abraham Jr. and Joseph. Abraham and wife Martha (Lee) had 10 children including sons Benjamin, Joseph and Abraham Jr. Joseph married Elizabeth Fee and they moved west to Ohio. Abraham Jr. and wife Sarah had 7 children including John, Abraham Jr. (1756-1799) and Daniel.

Also buried in this remarkable family graveyard are Abraham Lakin IV (1792-1854) and wife Elizabeth (1812-1861); Benjamin (1795-1814); Eleanor (1799-1836); John (1790-1821); Sarah (1789-1821); William (c. 1794-1850) and wife Susan (1807-1877).

The census of 1800 in Middletown Valley records widow Mary Leakins, over 45 years, living with three daughters and four sons. Daniel Leakins and wife (26-45) had six daughters and one son.

A genealogy of Lakin and Leakin Families was written by Rev. William I. Fee (Markell File at (FH)).

W&M-929. Allen D. Hoover (1861-1932) and wife Clara I. (Fisher) (1863-1930) are buried at Thurmont United Brethren Cemetery. His parents Elder George A. (1835-1887) and Susan E. (Shearer) (1833-1917) are buried at the Rocky Ridge Church of the Brethren. Allen's grandfather Daniel Hoover also is buried there. The lineage of Clara I. is traced to emigrant Thomas Fisher Sr. and wife Eva King in M&C-II.

Early Hoovers in land records of Frederick Co. include: Andrew (b. 1762) (ancestor of Pres. Herbert Hoover, see M&C-II); Adam (1767) bought land from Jonathan Hager; Hance V. in 1772 bought land from John Shroyer; John in 1763 bought lot from Raphael Taney; Jacob in 1765 bought land from John Evey; Leonard in 1761 bought land from Henry Brunner; Michael in 1773 bought land from Abraham Hull; and Ulrich in 1763 bought a lot in Taneytown from Raphael Taney.

W&M-930. Marion S. Michael (1852-1937) and wife Alice W. (Copeland) (1851-1927) are buried at Mt. Olivet. His parents Ezra (1826-1896) and Sophia J. (Thomas) (1842-1908) are buried at Utica. Ezra's second wife was Elizabeth Ann (Dudderar) (1832-1881) buried at Utica. Ezra's father Andrew Michael (1773-1851) and mother Jennie or Jane (1781-1840) have stones in Mt. Olivet. Two daughters of Andrew and Jennie married Delashmutts of Buckeystown District, a family discussed by George Ely Russell in *Western Maryland Genealogy*, Jan. 1989.

A Daniel Michael is in Frederick Co. Court records of 1759. In 1762 Andrew Michael, blacksmith, bought two lots on the road from Frederick toward Conococheague from Casper Myer, farmer. They were part of the old grants Long Acre and Tasker's Chance. Other Michaels are shown before the Revolution in deeds. Christopher Michael bought from Luke Barnard 250 acres of the tract The Sun is Down and The Moon is Up. Christopher deeded a property to Peter Michael in 1771. Nicholas Michael bought 46 acres of Stony Hall from Ulrich Erb and wife Margaret in 1758. In 1768 Lodowich Michael bought a property from Joseph Smith. In 1773 Jacob Michael bought a property from Ann Dickson. William Michael bought a property from Daniel Dulany Jr. in 1764 and from Conrad Shawn in 1766.

Fredrich Jacob Michael (born in 1750 at Albersweiler near Bad Bergzabern in southern Pfalz) was buried in 1783 at the Frederick Lutheran Church (LW).

A typed report *The Michael Family* was written by James Parker and Mildred Michael Crewe (Mrs. Jerome J. of Buckeystown). They give the following emigrant brothers from Germany via Annapolis:

(1) Christopher (1708-1783) emigrated in 1753, naturalized 1763.

(2) William (b. 1715 Onantzbach, Franconia); naturalized 1761; Lutheran; bought lot 279 in Frederick 1764.

(3) Andrew (1720-1800) emigrant 1757, m. Barbara Maria Sinn; bought part of Taskers's Chance; blacksmith; 10 children; most south of Frederick. (LC)

W&M-931. Ira Young (b. 1870) and wife Virdie F. (Baker) (1872-1939) have markers in Frederick Memorial Park. His parents were Jacob (1824-1906) and Charlotte E. (Ahalt) (1832-1923) who are buried at Middletown Lutheran Church. From the 1850 census Jacob was a son of Daniel (b. c.1796) and wife Mary M. (b. c.1799). Charlotte was a daughter of Mathias and Phoebe who farmed near Middletown.

A generation seems to be lost in the early Young lineage given here by W&M. In the Reformed and Lutheran Records after Conrad Jung (1728-1825) and wife Mary Magdalene (1731-1824) no sons John and Daniel are shown. Apparently sons Conrad Jr. (wife Elizabeth), Henry (wife Anna Maria), Peter (wife Magdalena) and Jacob (wife Veronica) had children born in the 1780s and 1790s. Only in the following generation recorded at the Middletown Lutheran Church were there a John and a Daniel (wife Elizabeth) who had children around 1800-1820; Compare W&M-1120.

Conrad Young is said to have lived west of Middletown in 1762. Besides Conrad who was an elder in Lutheran Congregation at Middletown in 1788-89, there was Johan Jakob Young, elder in the church in 1779. Conrad Young Jr. was elder in Zion Lutheran Church in 1797 and 1799, a later Jacob in 1801, John in 1820-1822 and Henry Young in 1826.

A great number of Young families is characteristic of Frederick Co. In the 1850 census there were more than 200 individual Youngs, even more than Jones. In a recent directory the Frederick area had 164 telephones of Youngs, to 40 Yinglings and 250 Jones. Yingling or Jungling also means a young person.

David Young from Alsenborn came to Little Conewago with Andrew Schreiber about 1734. An early Young record is the birth of Johannes Jung in 1756 to Ludwig and Magdalena recorded by Monocacy Lutheran Church. Jacob Jung was a sponsor there in 1755. Other early Young settlers are shown in area gravestones as follows:

Frederick Catholic Cemetery: Andrew (1779-1828); Ann (1788-1818), wife of Thomas; Winney (b. 1784), wife of Andrew.

Apples Church near Thurmont: Casper (1746-1813), David (d. 1823) and wife Elizabeth (1768-1823), Catherine (1783-1838), John (1775-1841), Maria (1780-1850).

Frederick Reformed Church: Anna Margaret (1779-1850); Catherine (1780-1863), wife of Gideon Young.

Locust Valley west of Middletown: Conrad (1766-1813), Elizabeth (1774-1843).

McKinstry M.P. Church, south of Union Bridge: Mary Young (1787-1865).

Dewalt or Devault Young was known as a maker of bricks both in Frederick and Washington Counties. Descendants of Dewalt and wife Catherine lived in Washington Co. (Wms 1906). (LC)

W&M-932. Rev. John Snader Weybright (1863-1948) and wife Annie Elsworth (Saylor) (1862-1948) are buried at the Church of the Brethren at Rocky Ridge east of Thurmont. His parents were Samuel (1837-1915) and Mary A. (Snader) (1837-1918) who also are buried at Rocky Ridge. A grandfather of Rev. John was John Weybright (1819-1891) born in Ohio, a descendant of emigrant (Johan) Martin II (1715-1774) of Lancaster Co. See M&C-II. (LC)

W&M-933. James G. Stevens (1869-1944) and wife Nannie (Staup or Staub) (1874-1948) are buried at Creagerstown as were his parents Charles (1818-1896) and second wife Eliza Adaline (Crouse) (1827-1852). See also W&M-1491. In the Frederick Co. Militia of 1812 were Joseph Stevens also Renzin Stevens who married Polly Durbin.

W&M-933. Benjamin Franklin Norwood (1861-1935) and wife Mary Agnes (Cecil) (1862-1914) are buried near Hyattstown at Sugar Loaf Chapel. The census of 1800 of southern Frederick Co. gives two Norwood families of Jeremiah and wife both over 45 years of age and Belt Norwood and wife also over 45 years. The latter couple had four daughters and five sons. (LC)

W&M-934. George H. Zimmerman (b. 1850) married Florence Frazier (1851-1911). His parents William H. (1826-1907) and Sarah A. (Donsife) (1829-1912) are buried at Mt. Olivet. To the latter's children in W&M should be added Ella who married Joseph A. Ridenour.

Emigrant from Germany, Michael Zimmerman had son George who with wife Elizabeth had son George (1776-1850) who married Rosanna Barrick (1796-1876). Rosanna was the mother of William H. above, See W&M-979 for a more complete Zimmerman genealogy. (LC)

W&M-935. Eli G. Haugh (1866-1936) and wife Molly (Strausburg) (1868-1914) are buried in Mt. Olivet Cemetery. His parents William Jr. (1811-1899) and second wife Elizabeth (Cramer) (1824-1914) are buried at Haugh's Church near Ladiesburg north of Woodsboro. The first wife of William Jr. was Isabel (Hardman) (1807-1861) also buried at Haugh's Church. Eli G. Haugh had grandparents William Haugh Sr. (1774-1845) and wife Catherine (1777-1824) also buried at Haugh's Church. Haugh is pronounced as the bird Hawk and must not be confused with Houck families (German Hauck) pronounced Howk). In the 1800 census of eastern Frederick Co. were two Hauk families, Paul over 45 years of age and wife had 9 children under 26 years and William Hauk (26-45) and wife (16-26) had one child. The emigrant ancestor is said to have been Hezekiah. Daniel Haugh enrolled in the Frederick Co. Militia of 1812.

W&M-936. Dr. Jesse W. Downey M.D. (1848-1910) and wife Mary W. (Hammond) (1849-1925) are buried at New Market Methodist Church as are his parents William Jr. (1825-1902) and wife Margaret J. (Wright) (1824-1907). Dr. Jesse's grandfather William Sr. (1788-1825) married Cordelia (Dorsey). William Sr. is buried also at New Market M.E. Church. A John Downey who married Lydia Evans enlisted in Capt. Flautt's Rifle Company of the Frederick Co. Militia of 1812.

W&M-937. Frank Downey (1859-1932) and wife Frances (Lawrence) (1858-1915) are buried at New Market M.E. Church. His father was William Jr. (1825-1902) above. (LC)

William Jr. and Margaret were grandparents of Maj. Frederick Louis Detrick, MD in whose honor Fort Detrick was named. (See Frederick News June 10, 1993.)

W&M-941. John Joseph Molesworth (1847-1919) and wife Annie Mary (Wolfe) (1851-1922) are buried at Prospect Cemetery near Mt. Airy as are his parents, Mathias (1818-1888) and Catherine (Condon) (1821-1896). Mathias was a son of Samuel Molesworth (b. c.1782). Catherine probably was a daughter of Catherine Condon (b. c.1796).

W&M-942. John W. Bowers (1843-1925) of Washington Co. and wife Mary E. (Barker) (1853-1940) are buried at Mt. Olivet. For Bowers in Washington Co. see Wms. (1906).

W&M-943. Joseph E. Staley (1847-1924) and wife Clara (Angleberger) (1852-1919) are buried at Mt. Olivet. His parents Daniel (1805-1849) and Amelia (Hedges) (1818-1849) are buried at Rocky Springs northwest of Frederick. See W&M-908. and (S).

W&M-943. John Hershberger (1860-1938) and wife Mary Katherine (Hooper) (1869-1918) are buried at Mt. Olivet. For their ancestors in Washington Co., MD see Williams (1906). In the 1850 census the only Hershberger family in the county was that in Frederick District of James W. (b. c.1824) and wife Sara A. (b. c.1829) with infants Amanda E. and Laura V. See W&M-1959.

W&M-944. Charles Wright Eby (1839-1912) and wife Mary G. (Darling) are buried at Mt. Olivet. He was superintendent of the Maryland School for the Deaf at Frederick for nearly 40 years.

W&M-944. George A. Pearre (1874-1948), his wife Jean B. (1880-1947) also his parents James A. Pearre (1823-1912) and wife Ann Rebecca (Delashmutt) (1830-1909) are buried at Mt. Olivet. The earliest survey in present Frederick Co. by a Pearre was that by James in 1743 of Stoney Hive on the Montgomery Co. line east of Sugar Loaf Mt. For Pearre families in the area of Unionville in northeastern Frederick Co. see W&M-763.

W&M-946. Thomas M. A. Stoner (1847-1928) and wife Laura V. E. (Bowman) (1849-1947) are buried at Beaver Dam Brethren Cemetery near Johnsville. Also buried there are his parents Augustus (1816-1897) and second wife Ann (Hammond) (d. 1852). Grandparents of Thomas were Abraham and Rebecca (Ream) (1796-1857) also buried at Beaver Dam. In 1800 in the Libertytown district there were 6 different Stoner households. Jacob and John were over 45 years in age, David, Isaac and Samuel 26-45 had children under 10 years, while Benedict and wife (16-26) had one young son. In Taneytown District in 1800 were households of Jacob and John Stoner and wives (all 26-45). Jacob owned two slaves. For Church of the Brethren Stoners see (ST).

Stoners who enrolled in the Frederick Co. Militia in 1812 were Christian; David m. Catherine Bell; Ezra (d. 1828) m. Mary Fogler (b. c.1794); Jacob and James.

W&M-947. John Lambert Michael (1836-1925) and wife Mary C. (Custard) (1844-1912) are buried at Mt. Olivet as are his parents Harry S. (1807-1875) and Mary E. (Crown) (1811-1892). Henry's parents were Andrew Jr. (1773-1851) and wife Jane (1781-1840) also buried at Mt. Olivet. Andrew Sr. and William Michael are in the 1800 census in southern Frederick Co. along with households of Andrus (16-26), Jacob (26-45) and Rebecca Michael (over 45).

See also W&M-930. Andrew, Charles W., Conrad, Henry, John and Lewis Michael enrolled in the Frederick Co. Militia in 1812.

W&M-947. John Wachter Hyder (1833-1913) married Sophia E. Stull (1842-1865) and secondly Susan Elizabeth Snook (1858-1942), all buried at Haugh's Church. John W. was a son of Jacob Hyder (1790-1860) and Sarah (Lightner) (1796-1869) both buried at Rocky Hill Church near Woodsboro. Some Hyders of Carroll Co. are in M&C-I.

W&M-948. Henry Claggett Duvall Jr. (1845-1915) son of Henry Claggett and Sarah M. (Claggett) (1821-1883) is buried at Petersville Episcopal Church. The Duvall pioneer Mareen (c. 1630-1694) emigrated from France to Ann Arundle Co. Grandparents of Henry C. Duvall were Dr. Grafton Duvall (1780-1841) and wife Elizabeth (Whittaker) (1785-1813) also buried at Petersville Episcopal Church.

Samuel Duvall living in the south of Frederick Co. was one of those who petitioned in 1749 for a road to be built from Nelson's Ferry (later Point of Rocks) to Fredericktown. Children of Samuel (1708-1752) included Mary Cassandra, Samuel Jr. and Jeremiah (d. 1774). Very early records of Duvalls in land records of Frederick Co. include Samuel, Elias and Alexander in 1750, Acquilla in 1754 and Lewis in 1756. William Duvall son of Benjamin bought land between branches of Bush Creek in 1755. Duvalls who are recorded in the Maryland Militia in the Revolution included Aquilla, Gabriel, Jacob, Levi, Lewis, Marsh M., Samuel, Sennit, Capt. William and Zadok. In the Frederick Co. Militia of 1812 were Daniel (1786-1846), Elisha, John (to Detroit), Samuel and Thomas (1787-1869). For Duvall genealogies see also (LC), (WP) and Scharf.

W&M-949. Uriah A. Lough (1853-1928) and wife Margaret A. E. (Reifsnider) (1846-1925) are buried at Mt. Olivet. His parents George Jr. (1808-1876) and Christina (Flickinger) (1821-1905) are buried at New Oxford, PA. Lineage of Loughs of New Oxford and Frederick is given in M&C-II.

Charles W. Lough (1874-1965) son of Uriah and Margaret married Eleanor May Fisher (1874-1963) of Philadelphia. They lived on Upper College Terrace in Frederick. My cousin Charlie Lough continued on S. Market St. the monument business begun by his father. Their daughters living in 1994 are Margaret E. Lough of Frederick and Grace E. (Lough) Zweizig (widow of Rev. Charles R.) living in Allentown, PA (LC)

W&M-950. Harry C. Stull (b. 1879) and wife Lottie A. (Remsburg) (1881-1918) are buried in Mt. Olivet. His parents were Frederick (1835-1905) and Ann R. (Holtz) (1835-1907) also buried in Mt. Olivet. Frederick's parents were Jacob (c. 1799-1865) and Mary (c. 1795-1860) who are buried at Apples Church near Thurmont.

The earliest Stulls in Western Maryland were English in origin. John Stull Mill was at the later site of Hagerstown. The children of John Stull, miller, and wife Martha are given in his will of 1757. Peter Stull on the Frederick Co. Grand Jury in 1749 probably was English speaking, not a German Stoll.

The German settlers, such as Adam Stoll who emigrated in 1727, became Stulls, pronounced similar to the German family name. When Adam Stull Sr. and wife Barbara sold 75 acres to John Stull, the farmer signed as Adam Stoll. Children of German Adam Stull Sr. (wife Barbara) in his will of 1772 are Christoph who married Philippina Staley; Adam Jr. deceased who had son Peter and daughter

Catherine Devilbiss; and John Jr. The Stull's Ford of Monocacy was just above the mouth of Owens Creek. Christopher Stull in will of 1790 disclosed sons, Adam, John and Jacob (boy) and daughters Catherine, Elizabeth and Magdalena (under 17 years). Frederick Stoll's will of 1815 in the Frederick Courthouse is written in German script. Peter Little was a witness. The first Stull in records of Rocky Hill Church was the birth of Susannah to Johannes and Catherine April 3, 1778. Over 400 local Stull names are in the index of (Z).

W&M-951. Melvin A. E. Biser (1853-1915) and second wife Esta M. (Neikirk) (1871-1943) are buried at Middletown Reformed Cemetery as are his parents Daniel (1828-1899) and Rosanna (Stottlemyer) (1827-1911). Daniel's parents were Jacob (1793-1830) and Catherine (Brandenburg) (1795-1863) who are buried at Middletown Reformed Church. German Jacob Biser, (c. 1725-1804) emigrated via Philadelphia in 1746 to Montgomery Co., PA (BL). The death of his wife Catherine is recorded by the Reformed Church at Frederick. Son Jacob Biser Jr. and his father moved on to Hampshire Co., WV about 1795. Frederick (1763-1823) was the youngest of the 7 children of Jacob Sr. and Catherine. He bought land east of Wolfsville in 1768. Frederick married Mary Margaret Coblentz, daughter of Peter Coblentz and wife Elisabeth (Hessong). Their children were Daniel, Elisabeth, John, Peter, Jacob, Catherine, Mary and Margaret. Descendants of Frederick and Mary Margaret married into families of Ridgeway, Dinterman, Haugh, Brown, Wills, Warrenfeltz, Jordan, Mummert, Keller, Krantz, Flook, Stottlemyer, Dawson, Zimmerman, Grove and Brandenburg. Mrs. Lebherz published a supplement in 1989 giving more descendants of Daniel, Jacob and Frederick, the sons of emigrant Jacob and wife Catherine.

W&M-952. Irving S. Biser (1869-1951) and wife Celeste Grace (Stone) (1876-1947) are buried at Mt. Olivet. For the lineage of this brother of Melvin see above.

W&M-952. Daniel Stottlemyer married Joanna Recher, daughter of John and Rosanna (Protzman) Recher. Emigrant Daniel Protzman (b. 1749) married Gertrude Baumgardner at Graceham. Daniel was a son of Lorenz Protzman of Wittgenborn near Wachtersbach in Hesse according to Mrs. Marion Bale of New Providence, NJ.

In the Frederick Co. Militia of 1812 was Jacob Protzman drafted at Creagertown. He served near D.C., at the Battle of North Point and at Baltimore. He married Elisabeth Ringer (b. c.1787). Jacob died in 1832 at Hagerstown.

W&M-952. Oscar B. Coblentz (1878-1948) married in 1903 Margaret E. Pontius (b. 1880). He and his parents Edward L. (1840-1902) and wife Lucinda F. (Bechtol) (1847-1935) are buried at Middletown Reformed Cemetery. The parents of Edward were Philip Coblentz (1812-1899) and wife Mary Ann (1818-1870) also buried at the Middletown Reformed Church as were John Philip Coblentz (1776-1853) and wife Elizabeth (1778-1857). See W&M-776 for earlier Coblentz families.

About 1940 I met Oscar Coblentz on a Pennsylvania R.R. train bound for New York City from Baltimore. It stands out in memory that he, as an engineering scientist, appreciated the pioneering researches in physical chemistry at Johns

Hopkins by Professor Harry Clary Jones who grew up on a farm near New London north of New Market. See W&M-1247.

W&M-953. Andrew C. McBride (1860-1910) and wife Annie E. Routzahn (1861-1927) are buried at Mt. Olivet where also are buried his parents William (1822-1908) and wife Elizabeth M. (House) (1824-1888).

The only McBride family recorded in Middletown Valley in the census of 1800 was that of James and wife who had only one son (under 10 years of age). An Edward McBride (16-26 years) lived alone in Emmitsburg District in 1800. (LC)

W&M-954. John T. Martin (1845-1932) and wife Margaret C. (Conway) (1849-1919) are buried at Petersville Episcopal Church. (LC)

Martins have been abundant around Thurmont (See Edward V. Duggan in PA Mennonite Heritage Oct. 1991) and also in Adams Co., PA (WB).

W&M-955. Charles V. C. Sanner (1848-1932) and wife Anzonette or Nettie Toms (1852-1928) are buried at Mt. Olivet. The parents of Charles were John (1825-1900) and Sarah Ann (Schildknecht) (1830-1900) who are buried at Middletown Lutheran Church. The lineage of Sarah Ann from emigrant Wilhelm Schildknecht and wife Barbara is given in M&C-II. Grandparents of Charles were Vincent Sanner (1794-1869) and wife Susan (Hutzell) (1787-1866) also buried at Middletown Lutheran Church.

A son of Charles and Nettie Sanner was Emmons Chauncey (1889-1981) who married Ava Myrtle Ramsburg daughter of William S. and Clara A. J. (Stup) Ramsburg. Their son Charles Steiner Vincent (1917-1978) married (Jean) Patricia Feiser (b. 1917). The latter has been a leader in Frederick Co. historical activities especially at Rose Hill Manor.

W&M-955. Vernon W. Nicodemus (1870-1950) married Emma Elizabeth Shawbaker. He and his parents Peter (1846-1929) and Emma (Zumbrun) (1849-1945) are buried at Mt. Olivet. Grandparents of Vernon were Isaac C. Nicodemus (1816-1877) and Susanna (Dudderar) (1816-1888) who are buried at Unionville Methodist Church.

One emigrant Nicodemus in 1763 was Rev. Valentine Erasmus (1730-1812) from Mendenbach near Herborn in Hesse. He was an early German Reformed pastor in the Monocacy area (Glatfelter).

In the 1800 census of old Frederick Co. the Westminster District had families of Henry Nicodemus and wife both over 45 years, living with 4 grown daughters; John Nicodemus and wife both 26-45, with 4 daughters, 2 sons and one slave; and Philip and wife, both 26-45, with 2 daughters, 2 sons and one slave. See also W&M-970. In the Frederick Co. Militia of 1812 were Henry who married Catherine Cassell and Andrew (1787-1853) who married Rachel Cassell.

W&M-956. Joshua A. L. Rice (1864-1898) and wife Frances E. (Moser) (1862-1949) are buried at the Brethren Church at Mountaindale. His parents Samuel (1816-1900) and Mary Ann (Shaffer) (1822-1907) are buried at Lewistown Methodist Church. His father was Henry of Middletown Valley who married Elizabeth Wachter, both of whom were born about 1788 according to the census of 1850.

Early Rices in Middletown Valley in the census of 1800 were Peregrin and Benjamin, both between 26 and 45 years and each with a single slave.

The Rice families further south in Middletown Valley around Jefferson were believed by Millard M. Rice, to have been English in origin. Millard wrote a report 1979 entitled *William Rice and Descendants of Frederick Co.* which is with files of J.M.H. After the death of Benjamin Rice in 1820 his two sons John Clifford and James migrated to Ohio. See book by Millard M. Rice (b. c.1894) entitled *New Facts and Old Families* (Redwood City, CA. 1976) and booklet William Rice (b. c.1788) and Descendants by M. M. Rice (1979)

Frederick Reformed Church records show the marriage of John Rice in 1788 to Elizabeth Melvin with Benjamin Rice as witness. Michael and Elisabeth Reiss had son Jacob in 1791. In Lutheran records at Middletown Michael and Anna Margaretha Reis had son Jacob in 1784. In Frederick Court records John Rice sued Martin Wetsel in 1753.

Lewis Albert Rice (1861-1941) believed that he was a descendant of Edmund Rice of Plymouth England who emigrated to MA in the 17th century. He was a son of Albert Thomas (1823-1901) and Ann Sabina (Mantz) (1818-1872) buried at Mt. Olivet; and grandson of George (1774-1829) and Elizabeth (Dofler) (1781-1856) who also are buried at Mt. Olivet. Lewis A. Rice married Susan Addie Blumenauer (1858-1926). He was one of the original incorporators of the Great Southern Manufacturing Co., publishers of the Frederick News, and was President of the SAR of Maryland (1937-1939). Lewis A. Rice was widely known through the wholesale grocery company Rice and Haller. In 1931 his two sons Lewis Albert and Rieger Rollins became partners.

W&M-957. Alpheus Douglas Thomas (1846-1925) and wife Mary Catherine (Crum) (1852-1932), as well as his parents Ezra Michael (1824-1895) and Amanda (Stockman) (1824-1904), are buried at Frederick in Mt. Olivet. Ezra and Amanda farmed in Jefferson District in 1850. Earlier near Jefferson were George Thomas (1782-1855) and Michael Thomas (1793-1839).

Of the many Thomas families in Middletown Valley in the census of 1800 Jacob and William A. and their wives were over 45 years. Jacob of Jacob, Jacob of Michael, William and John were 26-45 years. Only John had slaves (8). John Thomas (1763-1849) and wife Eleanor (McGill) (1768-1822) are buried at Petersville Episcopal Church where also is Gov. Francis Thomas (1799-1876). Also at Petersville are buried Lloyd Thomas (1790-1867) (son of John and Eleanor) and wife Mary (Rutherford) (1801-1838) (daughter of James and Eleanor (Brown)). Catherine Thomas (1732-1806) is buried at the Reformed Church at Middletown.

W&M-958. George D. Toms (1859-1945) and wife Annie C. (Bittle) (1864-1950) and his parents Ezra (1826-1894) and Sophia (Doub) (1829-1903) are buried at Myersville United Brethren Church. Parents of Ezra were Jacob Toms Jr. (1796-1887) and wife Mary (Floyd) (1805-1878) who also are buried at Myersville U. B. Church. The gravestone of Jacob Toms Sr. (c. 1767-1854) at Jerusalem graveyard northwest of Myersville states that he was born in Germany. His wife Magdalene (c. 1768-1852) also is buried at Jerusalem where the church briefly was Lutheran followed by United Brethren.

Samuel Toms (b. 1744) the father of Jacob Toms Sr. may have been in Middletown Valley since a Catherine Toms (d. 1770), mother of Samuel, bought a tract called Humbert's Delight there in 1759. A tract called Tom's Bottom, the western part of later Middletown, was bought in 1763 by Philip Kefauver (T&D). A John Toms died about 1753 and his wife Catherine died in 1770. A Henrich Thom born in Germany received communion at the Lutheran Church in Frederick in 1765.

Resurveys of land were acquired in Frederick Co. by Samuel Toms in 1788, by John Toms in 1794, also by William Tom in 1794.

Serving in the Revolution from Washington Co. are recorded Adam, George, Mathias and Michael Tom (without s). (LC)

W&M-959. Harry Rhoderick Flautt (1878-1920) and wife Ella C. (Brengle) (1877-1957) are buried at Mt. Olivet as are his parents Louis Calvin (1856-1928) and wife Jennie Catherine (Rhoderick) (1853-1931).

In 1800 census of Emmitsburg District were households of Joseph Flautt over 45 years with 2 slaves; Paul Flaut aged between 26 and 45; and Bostian Flautt and wife 26-45 who had a daughter and a son under 10 years. A Peter Flatt (Flautt?) emigrated in 1764 from the town of Holscht in the Odenwald area of southern Germany (M&C-II). Flautt (Flaht) genealogies have been written by Rachel S. Schwartz (Dixie Press 1971) (H) and by Mrs. Frank S. Schwartz and Harry D. Bowman (Hagerstown, MD 1972). (H), (W)

W&M-959. George W. Wachtel (1846-1931) and wife Louisa C. (Metzger) (1846-1922) are buried at Myersville Lutheran Church. His parents were Solomon (1819-1851), buried at St. John's Lutheran Church near Ellerton, and Catherine (Smith) daughter of Jacob. Louisa's parents were William Metzger (1809-1868) and wife Lydia (1815-1899) farmers in Middletown District.

W&M-961. George D. Dinterman (1857-1932) and wives Susan A. M. (Bussard) (1857-1886) and Phoebe E. (Sheffer) (1858-1938) are buried at Zion Lutheran Church at Middletown. His parents John P. (1822-1868) and wife Charlotte C. (Derr) (1835-1912) also are buried at Middletown Lutheran Church. Charlotte's parents were Daniel Derr (1812-1902) and wife Elizabeth (1812-1893) farmers in Middletown district. See Wampler.

W&M-963. Ernest Helfenstein (1869-1938) and wife Mary Grace (Levy) (1871-1952) as well as his parents Cyrus G. (1828-1895) and Annie E. (Trail) (1835-1915) are buried at Mt. Olivet.

Emigrant Rev. John C. Albert Helfenstein (1748-1790) was born at Mosbach near Sinsheim southeast of Heidelberg. Rev. Helfenstein married Catherine Karcher of Philadelphia (Glatfelder). Generations earlier the American Helfensteins may have had a connection with Helfenstein Castle ruin at Geislingen northwest of Ulm Germany (M&C-II). Rev. Jonathan Helfenstein (1784-1829) son of the emigrant was buried at the graveyard of the Reformed Church in Frederick where he served as pastor for 17 years. Jonathan's son Cyrus G. and Annie's children included Rev. Edward Trail Helfenstein who became Episcopal Bishop of Maryland and Ernest (1869-1938) who wrote a history of the Episcopal Church at Frederick. Ernest and wife Mary Grace (Levy) had children: Ernest Jr., Anna Trail and Mary G. The first Ernest Jr. and wife

Maurine (Thurmons) of Tennessee had son Edward T. Helfenstein who retired recently from insurance business in Frederick. In the Frederick area Helfenstein often has been pronounced Heffenstein.

W&M-964. William H. Summers (1851-1916) and wife Mary L. (1871-1953) are buried at Myersville U. B. Church. His parents Henry W. (1826-1902) and wife Easter C. (Derr) (1832-1876) are buried at Middletown Lutheran Church. Henry's parents were George W. Summers (1802-1884) and Catherine (Michael). The parents of George were Jacob (1767-1850) and wife Elisabeth (Horine) (1769-1849) who are buried at St. John's Church near Ellerton.

In the census of 1800 there were 3 Summer or Sommer households in Middletown Valley headed by Jacob, Christopher (Stofle) (1760-1849) and Valentine, all of whom had sons under 10 years. The Summers biographies in W&M give largely descendants of Jacob. Valentine Summers was granted a resurvey of tract Christina's Good Will in 1764 (Scharf).

In the Frederick Co. Militia of 1812 were Jacob Summer (1791-1868) of Middletown Valley and William Summers a coppersmith born in Frederick.

W&M-965. Charles G. Walter (1846-1897) and wife Caroline S. (d. 1906) are buried at Mt. Olivet. His father may have been John Walter (1790-1872) buried at St. Anthony's Cemetery near the Grotto at Mt. St. Mary's. Also buried in the Emmitsburg area are John W. Walter (1813-1879) and John W. Walter born in 1891. Walters have flourished in Adams Co., PA (WB)

Jacob, Joseph and William Walter from the Carroll Co. area served in the Frederick Co. Militia in 1812.

W&M-966. John Thomas Barnes (1835-1914) and wife Eliza Jane (Ecker) (1842-1918) are buried at Unionville Methodist Church. His grandfather Zadock (1768-1849) and wife Elizabeth (Polsen) (1773-1855) are buried at Taylorsville Methodist Church. The father of John Thomas was Levi Zadock Barnes (1802-1862) and wife Susannah (Lindsay) (1805-1881) who are buried at Unionville Methodist Church.

In the 1800 census of Libertytown District lived 6 Barnes families. Edward and Philomel and their wives were over 45 years of age. David, Zacharias and Zaddock were 26-45 years. Only Zaddock owned a slave.

W&M-967. D. Rupley Keller (1862-1940) and wife Jennette E. (Routzahn) (1863-1951) are buried at Middletown Reformed Church as are his parents Henry (1820-1901) and Sarah (Biser) (1828-1901). Henry's parents were David Keller (1784-1863) and Hannah (1788-1865) also buried at Middletown Reformed Church. David was the seventh child of Johan Jacob (1743-1824) and Anna Maria (Humbert) (1747-1908) who farmed part of the tract Ramshorn near Myersville.

W&M-968. Vincent Sebold who died in 1925 is buried at St. Anthony's Cemetery at Mt. St. Mary's. Also buried there are his grandparents Peter Sebold (1783-1875) and wife Elizabeth (1799-1859). His parents were Samuel and wife Ann (Miller) (1818-1889) who moved from Sabillasville to near Mt. St. Mary's. See also W&M-790.

W&M-969. Wm. T. Brown (1858-1939) and wife Hannah A. (Compher) (1862-1954) are buried at Mt. Olivet. Their immediate ancestors lived in Loudon Co., VA.

W&M-970. Judge Augustus W. Nicodemus (1833-1917) and wife Barbara A. (Fulton) (1836-1909) are buried at Mt. Olivet. His parents were John (c. 1802-1870) and Hannah (Englar)(b. 1805) who farmed near Frederick. Grandparents of Augustus were John L. Nicodemus and Anna March (Neff). Henry Nicodemus (c. 1728-1801) settled in the Carroll Co. area and married Ann Mary who died in 1814 at age 77. They are buried in the Nicodemus Family Cemetery at Marston near New Windsor. Henry's arrival at Philadelphia in Sept. 1751 has been recorded (S and H).

Adam Nicodemus was born about 1710 at Koblentz or Heidelberg, Germany according to German Archivist Emil Thomas in a letter to George Leicester Thomas. His sons were believed to have included emigrants Conrad, Friedrich, born Feb. 26, 1733 and Rev. Valentine Nicodemus also born about 1733 who emigrated via Philadelphia in 1761. The latter preached at Sharpsburg and Shepherdstown according to Williams (1906). Two sons of one of the emigrant Nicodemus brothers were Valentine and Conrad who settled near Boonsboro, in Washington Co. Other early Nicodemus settlers in Frederick Co. land records were Frederick (1765 and 1772) and Valentine (1771). See also W&M-955. A (John) Adam Nicodemus age 30 emigrated in Oct. 1753 and a John Henry in Sept. 1751 both via Philadelphia.

One of the sons of Augustus W. Nicodemus Sr. and Barbara was Edgar R. Nicodemus (1871-1957) who with wife Mary Bertha (Thomas) (1874-1955) lived in Buckeystown and is buried at Mt. Olivet. Their daughter Dorothy Adelaide Nicodemus, a retired librarian born in 1904, lives in Frederick. She is a descendant of both German and English Thomas families of Frederick Co.

A. W. Nicodemus Inc. began making and selling ice cream in Buckeystown in 1878. Edgar R. Nicodemus began ice cream business in Frederick in 1921. Conrad and Frederick Nicodemus of Washington Co. served in the Revolution.

W&M-971. Charles R. Hildebrand (1867-1928) and wife Esta L. (Fink) (1871-1918) are buried at Middletown Lutheran Church. His parents Lewis A. (1831-1900) and Amanda L. (Windpigler) (1836-1915) are buried at Mt. Olivet. The parents of Lewis were John Hildebrand (1798-1875) and wife Lydia (1800-1876) who are buried at Rocky Springs.

The 1800 census of the Fredericktown area shows households of Jacob and Joseph Hildebrand, both of ages between 26 and 45 years. In Buckeystown area lived John Hildebrand (1776-1862) and wife Margaret (Myers) (1773-1858) who are buried at Ballinger Creek Church Hill. In the 1800 census of Buckeystown area lived Henry, over 45 years and John between 16 and 26. (LC)

W&M-972. Clinton B. G. Harwood (1851-1931) and wife Dollie C. (Moore) (1874-1958) are buried at Mt. Olivet as are his parents Dr. Thomas Noble Harwood M.D. (1816-1902) and wife (Anne) Jane (Claggett) (1841-1932). Jane's parents were Thomas (1813-1873) and Cynthia (b. c.1815) who farmed near New Market.

W&M-973. J. Marshall Miller (1857-1956) and wife Fannie (Harling) (1862-1896) are buried at Mt. Olivet. His parents George W. (1834-1906) and Caroline (Hill) (1836-1915) are buried at Utica. George W. was a son of George Miller (1791-1861) and wife Catherine (Harbaugh) (1806-1875) buried at Creagerstown. The father of George was John who died in 1793 and whose probable wife was Eve (Miller), age 26-45, in the 1800 census of Creagerstown area.

I remember seeing Marshall Miller walking to his work at the Fredericktown Savings Institution from his home at 800 N. Market St, Frederick. The daughters of Marshall and Fannie were Edith Marshall (1892-1938) and Virginia H. Miller (1903-1956) buried at Mt. Olivet. They were interested in local history and genealogy.

For the many Millers in Adams Co. see (WB) and (G).

W&M-974. Edward S. Eichelberger (1856-1914) married Miriam Gray of Worcester, MA and they lived on Court Square in Frederick. His parents were Grayson (1821-1870) and Amanda (Baugher) (1822-1885) buried at Mt. Olivet. Grayson's parents were George M. Eichelberger (1784-1854) and Jane (Grayson) (1795-1870). The father of George M. was Leonard Eichelberger (1750-1811) who settled in Manheim Twp. near York, PA and was a son of emigrant Philip Friedrich (c. 1693-1776) born at Ittlingen near Sinsheim. The latter emigrated with his brother George in 1728. A Hans Georg, 29 years and Juliann, 29, emigrated via Philadelphia in 1733.

Eichelbergers settled in Adams Co. and at Hanover, PA. Ludwig (d. 1807) and wife Elisabeth attended St. John's Lutheran Church near Littlestown. Adam and wife Mary (Adams) Eichelberger moved to Frederick Co. (F). Eichelbergers of Frederick and Emmitsburg were outlined by McPherson and Gilliland at (E).

W&M-975. Henry Percival Mussetter born 1859 married Mary L. Dreyer. His parents were John (1801-1879) and Martha E. (Hyatt) (1819-1892) who are buried at New Market Methodist Episcopal Church. Henry's grandparents Christopher Mussetter (1772-1851) and wife Ruth (Ijams) (1783-1874) are buried at Mt. Olivet. Christopher's father was Christian Mussetter who settled near New Market. Ruth was a daughter of Plummer and Jemima Ijams.

The 1800 census of Liberty to New Market area gives 5 Mussetter households. Christian Sr. and Michael Sr. were over 45 years of age; Christian Jr., Alexander and Michael Jr. were 26-45 years old.

The only Hyatt farmer in southern Frederick Co., in the 1800 census was Ely (over 45 years) and wife (under 45 years). They had 5 daughters, 4 sons and 16 slaves. Asa Hyatt (1787-1848) and wife Mary Ann (Phillips) (1796-1859) are buried at Hyattstown Methodist Church. (LC)

W&M-976. Samuel M. Birely (1859-1904) and wife Belva A. E (Cramer) are buried at Thurmont U. B. Church. His parents Samuel (1794-1879) and Barbara A. (Kemp) (1833-1899) are buried at Haugh's Church near Ladiesburg, where Samuel's first wife Margaret (1795-1856) also is buried. See W&M-846 for earlier Birely (Beyerle) ancestors, also M&C-II.

W&M-977. Jacob T. Huffer (1857-1933) and wife Emma E. (Shaffer) (1858-1937) as well as his parents David (1823-1903) and Ann C. (Ahalt) (1832-1898) are buried at Middletown Lutheran church. Jacob had grandparents Joseph L. Huffer born about 1800 and wife Catherine born about 1802. Ann C. was a daughter of Jacob Ahalt (b. c.1806) and wife Mary (b. c.1813) who farmed in Middletown District.

In the census of 1800 in Emmitsburg District lived an Adam Hufferd and wife of age between 26 and 45. They had 3 children under 10 years of age. In 1800 in Middletown Valley were the households of Elizabeth Ehalt (over 45 years) also Jacob "Ehartt" and wife (26-45).

W&M-977. William Lynch Gross (1857-1930) and wife Anna C. (Householder) (1866-1951) are buried at Petersville Episcopal Church. His parents were Charles (1815-1892) and Elizabeth (Boteler). Henry (1778-1846) and Elizabeth (Cost) (1780-1852) buried at Jefferson Union Cemetery were parents of Charles. Henry Gross was a son of Jonathan alleged to have been born in Germany. A Henry Gross over 45 years of age with wife 26-45 and 6 children lived in Emmitsburg District in 1800.

W&M-978. Henry M. Gittinger (1853-1923) and wife Susan Fessler (Simmons) (1862-1941) are buried at Mt. Olivet. His parents George (1798-1886) and wife Catherine (Young) (1819-1898) also were buried at Mt. Olivet. The first wife of George was Charlotte (Scholl) born in 1801. See M&C-I for Scholls.

In 1800 there were three Gittinger or Gettinger households in the area of Fredericktown, namely John Sr. and wife over 45 years.; John Jr. and wife of ages between 26 to 45; and Jacob (26 to 45) with wife under 26 and 3 children under 10 years.

Henry B. Fessler (1814-1873) and wife Ann Eliza (1814-1883) also John Fessler (1787-1869) and wife Susan (1790-1862) are buried at Mt. Olivet at Frederick. Earlier Johannes and Barbara Fessler are in records of Frederick Reformed Church.

W&M-979. Charles H. Heffner (1865-1918) and wife Minnie G. 1862-1937) are buried at Mt. Olivet. His parents Frederick D. (1831-1919) and wife Julia Ann (Eyler) (1828-1904) are buried at Feagaville Zion Church. Grandparents of Charles were Daniel Heffner and wife Susan (Eyler).

A Friedrich Heifner was on the Grand Jury of Frederick Co. in 1760. The south German dialect pronunciation of Heifner is Heffner. Six Heffners served in the War of 1812.

W&M-979. Isaac C. Zimmerman (1851-1933) and wife Laura M. (Mull) (1852-1938) are buried at Mt. Olivet, as are his parents Peter Thomas Zimmerman (1819-1891) and wife Anna Maria (Cronise) (1823-1910). Peter's parents were Henry Zimmerman (1791-1875) and wife Charlotte (1790-1864) buried at the Ballinger Creek Zimmerman graveyard. Henry's parents were Michael Zimmerman (1750-1821) and Eva (Cronise). Michael was a son of emigrant John George (1714-1795) and wife Anna Catherine (Seidel) (1724-1804). The Zimmerman family was already settled in the area of Carrolton Manor by 1762.

Below is given an outline of early Zimmerman families from research of Margaret E. Myers (Z):

Hans Georg Zimmerman had son Andreas who married Mrs. Anna Elisabeth (----) Freyberger in records at the Reformed Church of Meckesheim near Sinsheim, southeast of Heidelberg. Two of their sons (Hans) Michael and (Johan) Georg with wives and children emigrated in 1730 to Pennsylvania and many of their descendants have lived in Frederick Co. (Children who did not emigrate are omitted here):

II. Second child (Hans) Michael (1706-1741) married Anna Elisabeth Dodderer (1709-1799) (d/o George Philip and Veronica); left records at Goshenhoppen Reformed Church, Montgomery Co., PA

    (c) (John) Michael (1732-1762) m. Elisabeth ----; most children went to NC but son George (1755-1820) married 1784 Elisabeth Weiss (1760-1825); both are buried at the Reformed Cemetery at Woodsboro.
    (d) George (1738-1793) married 1763 Maria Catherine Christ (1745-1828) (d/o Jacob and Catherine); both buried in Lichtleider graveyard north of Lewistown. (Stone removed to Utica). By deed of 1768 George bought from Handel Barrick (wife Judith) the Mill Place tract on Little Hunting Creek.

VII. Seventh child (Johan) Georg (1714-1795) m. 1742 in PA Ann Catharina Seidel (1724-1804) (d/o John and Anna Elisabeth); both were buried at Frederick Lutheran Church. By deed 1762 George acquired Huffenhardt tract west of Carrollton Manor, south of Frederick.

Children of George and Catherine Zimmerman:

    (a) Anna Elisabeth (b. 1744) m. Philip Sinn (Frederick Reformed Church).
    (b) (John) George Jr. (b. 1745) m. Margaret ----, to N.Y. City.
    (c) Michael (1750-1821) m. Eve Cronise (b. 1751) (d/o George and Anna Maria).
        Son George (1782-1865) m. Charlotte Young (1784-1755); to near Feagaville.
        Son Henry (1791-1875) m. Charlotte Thomas (1793-1864); buried at Ballinger Creek Zimmerman graveyard.
    (d) Anna Catherine (b. 1752) m. Henry Brunner (d. 1776) (Frederick Lutheran Church), 2m Peter Wolfe.
    (e) Andrew (1754-1826); paper maker; buried at Frederick Reformed Cemetery.
    (f) (George) John (1755-1813) m. Eleanora Holtz (b. 1756) (d/o Jacob and Catherine); Frederick Reformed Church.
    (g) Anna Mary (b.1757) m. Peter Burkhart; Frederick Lutheran Church.
    (h) Mary Ann Elisabeth (b. 1759).
    (i) John Nicholas (1756-1826) m. Elisabeth Troxell (b. 1769); Rocky Hill Church near Woodsboro; ran paper mill.
    (j) Maria Elisabeth (b. 1761) m. Elias Brunner Jr. (1756-1826); Frederick Reformed Church.
    (k) Benjamin (1764-1808) m. Catherine Ebbert.
    (l) Susanna (1765-1840) m. John Nicholas Holtz (1762-1849); both buried Frederick Reformed Cemetery.
    (m) John Henry (b. 1767); Frederick Reformed Church.

W&M-981. William H. Shipley (1843-1917) and wife Mary E. (Ketler) (1844-1914) are buried at Mt. Olivet. William's parents were William G. Shipley (1811-1883) and Maria (b. c.1817) of the Brethren Church at Monrovia. The many Shipleys of Maryland are descendants of Adam Shipley (born 1688) of Yorkshire according to genealogy by L. Parks Shipley Sr. (Baltimore 1971 and Summit N.J. 1980). Other Shipley genealogies are given in M&C-II. Shipleys served in the Maryland Militia in the Revolution and in the Frederick Co. Militia of 1812.

W&M-981. John Walter (1825-1905) of Germany and Frederick and wife Elizabeth (Pampel) (1827-1902) are buried at Mt. Olivet. Pampel relatives of Mrs. Walter are buried at Emmitsburg Catholic Church and at Frederick Catholic Cemetery. See also W&M-965.

W&M-982. R. Claude Dutrow (1857-1919) and wife Ida E. (Beck) (1856-1933) are buried at Mt. Olivet, as are his parents Richard P. T. (1828-1877) and Lucretia (Lakin) (1832-1897). Richard's parents Samuel (1796-1873) and Elizabeth Ann (Geisbert) (1801-1863) also are buried at Mt. Olivet. Samuel may have been a son of Conrad Duttero in the census of 1800. A Conrad Dotter paid taxes in Germany Twp. near Littlestown, PA in 1767-1783.

A John Tutterah is in the Frederick Court records of 1760. Johannes Doderer sponsored a baptism in 1758. Michael Dotterer and wife Elisabeth had daughter Margaret in 1773. In Frederick Reformed Records Balthasar Dotterer and wife Elisabeth had daughter Maria Barbara in 1779.

The German pastors more often spelled the name Dodderer or Dotterer. The ending may be a double diminutive, eg son of son of Dodd. (see M&C-II. chapter on family names). See spellings in Frederick Co. Districts 2, 3, 5 and 6 of 1800 census.

Georg Philip Dodderer from Sinsheim emigrated in 1724 to Pennsylvania (B1). J. M. Holdcraft stated that the Dodderers, Dutrows (& about 40 other spellings) are descended from Georg Philip Duddra of Frederick Twp, Montgomery Co., PA. His grandsons Jacob and Conrad settled in Frederick Co.

Published genealogies include *Dotterer, Dudderar, Dutrow, etc, Families* by Henry S. Dotterer (Philadelphia 1903 (L) (G); ditto of Maryland and Pennsylvania by Albert Dudrear Jr. (1976) (G); *George Philip Dotterer (d. 1741) and Descendants* by Ralph B. Strassburger, (Guynedd Valley, PA 1922); ditto by Rev. William B. Duttera (Dushore, PA 1928) (F) (H) (GC).

W&M-983. Sida S. Buhrman (1854-1941) and wife Mary J. (Buhrman) (distant relative) are buried at Mt. Bethel Church at Garfield northeast of Myersville, as are his parents Silas (1828-1892) and wife Leah (Stottlemyer) (1832-1875). Silas had a second marriage to Rohanna (1843-1910) buried also at Garfield. The grandparents of Sida were Henry Buhrman Jr. (1796-1872) and Ann (Barnes) (c. 1799-1883) both buried at Mt. Bethel Church, Garfield.

Earlier Henry Buhrman Sr. and father John are not in the 1800 census under those names. There is a tradition that they changed their family names. See also W&M-863.

W&M-984. Charles C. Coblentz (1857-1945) and wife Emma F. (Ropp) (1857-1945) are buried at Middletown Reformed Church. His parents were Oliver P.

(1824-1878) and Rebecca (Menchy). The grandfather of Charles was Peter Coblentz (1802-1847) buried at Middletown Reformed Church. The Peter Coblentz (1732-1808 and wife Elizabeth (1745-1824) buried at Middletown Reformed Church probably were grandparents of Peter born in 1802. See also W&M-776.

W&M-985. David W. Summers (1840-1920) and wife Annie M. (Rothenhoefer) are buried at Middletown Reformed Church as were his parents George W. (1802-1884) and Catherine (Michael) (1804-1875). Grandparents of David were Jacob Summers (c. 1767-1850) and wife Elizabeth (Horine) (c. 1769-1849) who are buried at St. Johns Lutheran Church on Church Hill north of Myersville. (LC)

See W&M-764 for Summers in 1800 census. A John Somer bought land in Middletown Valley from Henry Hessing (Hessong) in 1768. The German family name Somer is pronounced similar to English Summer. A final s often was acquired by family names in America as in Bowers, Myers and Hedges.

W&M-986. Millard F. McBride (b. 1867) has gravestones without date of death both at the Church of God at Locust Valley and at Mt. Olivet. His first wife Minnie J. (Hargett) (1865-1896) also has stones at both cemeteries. The second wife of Millard was Viola J. (Wilson) who has a stone at Mt. Olivet without dates. Millard's parents were Lewis McBride (1834-1916) and wife Sarah (Sigler) (1839-1900) buried at Locust Valley. A great grandfather of Millard was probably James McBride whose age was in the range of 26-45 years in the census of 1800 of Middletown Valley.

W&M-987. Jacob D. Rice (1849-1933) and wife Catherine E. (Wachter) (1844-1918) are buried at Lewistown Methodist Church as are his parents Samuel (1816-1900) and Mary Ann (Shaffer) (1822-1907). Jacob's grandfather Henry Rice (1824-1910) and wife A. M. Catherine (Wastler) (1836-1919) are buried at St. John's Lutheran Church near Ellerton. See also W&M-956. Catherine was a daughter of Philip Wachter Jr. (1812-1886) and Susannah (1813-1899) of Frederick District. (LC)

W&M-988. Maurice Foster Ahalt (1871-1953) and wife Sarah V. (1878-1932) are buried at Middletown Lutheran Church. Foster's parents were Matthias S. (1838-1921) and wife Martha J. (Sheffer) (1842-1927) who are buried at the same cemetery. Martha's parents were Daniel Sheffer (1807-1863) and wife Mary (1815-1907) buried at Middletown Lutheran Church.

Matthias Ehehalt and wife Elisabeth emigrated from Germany via Philadelphia in 1753. He had 2 sons and 5 daughters. Matthias Ehehalt died before 1775 when Jacob Flook and Andrew Beck were his executors in Frederick Co. Jacob Ahalt and wife Eva had infant John 1792, Jacob 1795 and Elizabeth 1799 baptized at Middletown Lutheran Church. Matthias Jr. and Elisabeth had Anna Maria in 1771 baptized in the Reformed Church at Middletown. In the 1800 census widow Elisabeth Ahalt was living with a son Mathias Jr. or Jacob who had married Eve Margaret Young, daughter of emigrant Conrad Young of Locust Valley.

W&M-989. David P. Oland (1857-1905) with wife Elizabeth C. (1856-1926) and second wife Nannie C. (1860-1886) are buried at Mt. Olivet. David's parents were Frederick Oland (1821-1908) born in Hanover, Germany and wife Mary

A. E. (Shaffer) (1825-1869) also buried at Mt. Olivet. The spelling Shaffer was used by George Jacob and John in the Frederick Co. Militia of 1812.

W&M-990. John R. Wright (1840-1916) and wife Loretta (Knodle) (1847-1909) are buried at Libertytown Catholic Church as are his parents John A. Wright (1810-1853) and wife Julia Ann (Danner). John Wright (1781-1850) the grandfather of John R., is buried at Frederick Catholic Cemetery along with wife Sophia (1788-1848). In 1800 the only Wrights in Frederick District were Mary and Sophia both between 26 and 45 years. Other early Wrights in the south of the county were Quakers. (LC)

W&M-990. Milton George Urner (1839-1926) and wife Laura A. (Hammond) (1845-1923) are buried at Mt. Olivet as are his parents Samuel (1799-1872) and wife Susanna (Norris) (1802-1853).

A Martin Urner of Chester Co. PA bought two tracts of land on Sam's Creek area in 1761 from Allen Farquhar. One of these was called Chance; it began next to the Ovill tract of James McCollom.

W&M-991. Hammond Urner (1868-1947) and wife Mary Lavinia (Floyd) (1872-1956) are buried at Mt. Olivet Cemetery as are his parents above. Floyd families lived at Middletown where John (1766-1826) is buried at Zion Lutheran Church. The sculptor Joseph Walker Urner (1989-1987), son of Hammond and Mary, married Irma A. Bradshaw. He was in Naval Air Service in World War I before studying art. Urner made the bust of Thomas Johnson and of R. B. Taney in front of Frederick's old courthouse, also the Alabama Monument on the Gettysburg Battlefield. Children of Joseph and Irma are given in Frederick News 7/7/1987 at (FH).

W&M-992. John T. Shafer (1858-1936) and wife Mary M. (Ranneberger) (1873-1942) are buried at Mt. Olivet. His parents were Hamilton J. (born 1832) and wife Lydia (Koontz) who lived at Burkittsville. John T. had grandparents Henry Shafer (1793-1871) and wife Mary Magdalena (1800-1864) both buried at Burkittsville Union Cemetery. One of the earliest Shafers in Middletown Valley was John Jr. (1753-1823) who married Anna Maria Darner (1754-1837). Henry was their son.

The 1800 census of Middletown Valley shows two Shaffer households. Esther, over 45 years, apparently a widow, lived with 3 grown children. John over 45 years in age lived with wife under 45, 3 daughters and 3 sons. See also W&M-746.

W&M-993. John W. Leatherman (1858-1916) and wife Flora F. (Gaver) (1860-1928) are buried at Middletown Lutheran Church. His parents Peter (1831-1905) and Julia M. (Bowlus) (1833-1915) are buried at Grossnickle Brethren Meeting House in upper Middletown Valley. Peter's parents were Rev. Jacob Leatherman (1787-1863) and second wife Catherine (Harp). His first wife was Susanna Harp (1795-1836) sister of Catherine. Rev. Jacob's father Elder Peter (1757-1845) and wife Mary Ann (Swigart) (1764-1835) are buried at the Swigart-Ambrose family graveyard near Ellerton. Rev. Jacob and Susan (Swigart) had 6 children. Bishop Daniel Leatherman (1697-1755) father of Peter, according to recent research was born at Saalstadt, southern Pfalz, Germany, about 15 miles from Trippstadt, and near the former Air Force Base at Ramstein. In the 1500s Leatherman ancestors were said to have come from Niedertripp near Solothurn, Switzerland. After leading a Brethren Congregation at Little Conewago Settlement near Hanover, PA, Daniel and wife Catherine came to Frederick Co. about 1758.

W&M-994. Charles C. Maught (1854-1943) and wife Julia K. (Remsburg) (1857-1922) are buried at Jefferson Union Cemetery as are his parents Andrew C. H. (1818-1892) and wife Mary A. R. (Long) (1823-1902). Grandparents of Charles C. were John Maught (1787-1848) and Molly (Easterday). John was buried at Petersville Episcopal Church. It was his father Andrew Macht (1758-1840) later Maught, who was confined in the so-called Hessian Barracks at Frederick as a member of a Bayreuth German Regiment captured at Yorktown. In 1784 Andreas Heinrich Macht married Maria Barbara Reichert. They settled on the Merryland tract and belonged to the Petersville Episcopal Church. Maria Barbara had the following children (GM):

(1) Catherine (1785-1853) m. George Rhodes.

(2) Mary Ann (died 1851).

(3) John (c. 1789-1848) m. Polly Easterday.

(4) Samuel m. Sarah House.

(5) William (1798-1853) m. Elizabeth Schaff.

(6) Daniel m. Phoebe Blessing.

(7) Henry (1804-1877).

Andrew Macht was naturalized in 1814.

W&M-995. John H. Whitmore (1855-1941) and wife Sarah E. (Smith) (1859-1916) are buried at Monocacy Brethren Church at Rocky Ridge east of Thurmont as are his parents David Whitmore (1812-1877) and wife Martha M. (Hospilhorn) (1828-1897). David's parents were Henry (1780-1861) and wife Solomo (Fundenburg). For earlier Whitmore ancestors see W&M-891 and PA Mennonite Heritage 14 # 2 (April 1991). Bible records of Benjamin Whitmore (d. 1818) of Toms Creek Church were published in June 1964. Frederick Co. deed N-68 of 1770 shows that heirs of Abraham Witmer or Whitmore were Abraham Jr., Benjamin, David and Henry who were granted 100 acres of Benjamin's Good Luck by Benjamin Biggs.

A Johannes Wittmer and wife Maria Elisabeth emigrated from Barbelroth, Germany, about 1755 to Fredericktown where they appear in Reformed Church records. Barbelroth in southern Pfalz is between Landau and Karlsruhe. About 1785 they moved to Rockingham Co., VA. More information has been collected by Linda Stofflebean of Alta Loma CA. (FH).

W&M-995. Thomas Chalmers Harbaugh (b. 1849), unmarried, moved to Casstown, Ohio, but still wrote poetry and prose about Middletown Valley. His father Morgan Clark M. Harbaugh was born about 1809 and mother Caroline (Routzahn) was born about 1808.

Jost Herbach or Yost Harbaugh with family including George Harbaugh (1726-1787) emigrated from Kirschweiler Hof near Kaiserslautern in southern Pfalz. Publications about the Harbaugh families include *Yost Harbaugh and Descendants* (1736-1856) by Rev. Henry Harbaugh (Chambersburg 1856); Rev. Henry, the famous pioneer in Pennsylvania German studies, was born just beyond Hauver's District Frederick Co., near Rouzersville, PA. See Richard E. Wantz in *Pennsylvania Folklife* (Autumn 1991). A Harbaugh genealogy was written by

Howard L. Spessard (Hagerstown 1971) (H). An outline of the early Harbaughs is in the book *Biographical Records of Franklin Co., Pennsyvania* (reprinted 1992), (G) from which the following in large part was abstracted. HV indicates they lived in Harbaugh Valley (northwest of Thurmont). See also Scharf.

Jost Herbach born in Switzerland emigrated 1736 from Germany to Berks Co., PA and in 1743 moved to Kreutz Creek Settlement near present Hellam in York Co. where he died in 1792. Children by his first wife follow:

(1) George (1726-1787) born in Switzerland m. Catherine Willard (1721-1791) from Erlenbach near Kaiserslautern, Pfalz. To HV about 1761. Ch: George, John, Anna, Regina, Elizabeth.

(2) Ludwig (1729-1809) m. Christiana (1727-1797) (HV) Ch: Christian, Jacob, Henry, Peter, Yost, John, Elizabeth, Mary, Christiana, Margaret.

(3) Jacob (Switz. 1730-1818) m. Anna Margaretta Smith (1740-1803) (d/o George) (HV); gp of Dr. Henry Harbaugh. Ch: Anna Margaretha, Jacob, John, Susanna, Catherine, Barbara, Juliann, Anna Maria m. John Shriver, Henry, George (son Rev. Dr. Henry), Yost, Elias. Many descendants in Franklin Co., PA

(4) John (1735-1803) m. ----; lived in Springarden Twp. York Co. Ch: George, Jacob, John, Margaretta, Mary, Elizabeth, Julia.

(5) Henry (d. 1779); unsound mind.

(6) Yost (1741-1832) born Kreutz Creek m. ----; Braddock Exp.; Rev. War; PA Legislature. Ch: Eve, Anna Margaret, John (Adams Co. PA), Jacob (Adams Co., PA), dau m. Benjamin Emmert.

Jost Herbach by 2m to Mary Elizabeth ---- had children:

(7) Leonard (1749-1822) m. Rebecca Rinebeck (d. 1833 in Balto.) He was renowned builder in Baltimore and D.C. See paperback *Leonard Harbaugh* by Leroy Graham (Lanham, MD 1982). Ch: William, Leonard, Thomas, Joseph, Samuel, George, Jesse, David, Charles, Daniel, Benjamin, Frederick, John, Rebecca.

(8) Mary Elizabeth (1753-1835) m. Godfrey Lenhart (1754-1819). Ch: Margaret, Elizabeth, Henry, William, Catherine, two other daughters.

(9) Anna Margaret.

(10) Anna Catherine.

See also Harbaugh studies at (WP).

W&M-996. R. Scott Derr (1852-1928) and wife Sarah C. (Leatherman) (1856-1946) are buried at St. Lukes Church at Feagaville. His parents David (1817-1884) and Sarah A. (Smith) (1821-1892) are buried at Mt. Olivet. Scott's grandparents John Derr (1780-1845) and wife Elizabeth (Haupt) (1792-1846) are buried at Middletown Lutheran Church. John was born in Maryland, not in Pennsylvania. For earlier ancestors see W&M-843 and Wampler.

W&M-997. S. Elmer Brown (1862-1945) and wife Clara Wilcoxon (1863-1957) are buried at Mt. Olivet as are his parents Samuel H. (d. 1901) and wife Sarah Jane (Horner) (1826-1899). Clara's ancestors William Wilcoxon (1782-1862) and wife Ruth (1788-1864) are buried at Mt. Olivet. Five Wilcoxons served in the Maryland Militia in the Revolution.

W&M-997. Marshall L. Zimmerman (1869-1931) and wife Emma V. (Easterday) (1869-1936) are buried at Charlesville Reformed Church north of Frederick. He was a son of Edward Joshua (1830-1907) and Mary Ann (Wachter). Marshall's grandparents were Jacob E. Zimmerman (1801-1883) and Barbara (Stull) (1807-1884) who also are buried at Charlesville. Grandparents of Marshall were John Nicholas Zimmerman (1759-1826) and wife Elizabeth Troxell. See earlier ancestors in W&M-979.

W&M-998. B. Frank Doll (1882-1940) as well as his parents Alexander H. (1851-1915) and Emma E. (Duvall) (1856-1908) are buried at Mt. Olivet. Frank's paternal grandparents were Joshua Doll (1824-1863) and Ellen (Hood) (1829-1894). See also W&M-844 and 928.

W&M-999. J. Frederick Putman (1863-1950) and wife Martha N. (Zimmerman) (1868-1952) are buried at Mt. Olivet. His parents were John J. Jr. (1826-1907) and Rebecca (Shriver) (b. 1833). Frederick's grandparents John J. Putman Sr. (1793-1872) and wife Annie E. (Summers) (1795-1883) are buried at St. John's Lutheran Church near Ellerton. See also W&M-1060 and 1446.

W&M-1000. Professor Joseph Henry Apple, Jr. (1865-1948) was a descendant of Johan Peter Appel and wife Elisabetha Catharina who emigrated from the Palatinate in 1732 to Lehigh County, Pennsylvania (NC 32 and 46). Their son, John Apple, married Anna Maria Bogert whose son Andrew married Catherine Neuspiegel. Judge Andrew Apple, Jr., who married Elizabeth Gilmore, lived in Lancaster and was honored with an LLD degree by Franklin and Marshall College. Their son, Rev. Dr. Thomas Gilmore Apple, born in Easton, Pennsylvania, who married Emma Miller, was President of Mercersburg College and later of Franklin and Marshall College. Their son, Dr. Henry Harbaugh Apple (1869-1943) also became President of Franklin and Marshall. Joseph Henry Apple, Jr. (1865-1948) was born at Rimersburg, Pennsylvania, a son of Rev. J. H. Apple and Elizabeth Ann (Geiger). He was educated at F & M. while his relative was President. His degrees were AB 1885, AM 1888 and Honorary Ph.D. 1919. Professor Apple was the first President of Woman's College, later Hood College. See W&M-507, also, Tercentenary History of Maryland, Vol. 2 (Baltimore 1925).

Professor Joseph Henry Apple, Jr. in 1892 married Mary E. Rankin (d. 1896) of Clarion, Pennsylvania. Their daughter Miriam Rankin (1893-1950) was librarian of Hood College (1914-1950). Daughters Charlotte and Mary Rankin died young. Professor Apple and second wife Gertrude Harner (1868-1953) are buried at Mt. Olivet Cemetery. Their children are Elizabeth Harner, who married Russell McCain and lived at Frederick, Emily Gertrude, who married Paul Payne, and Joseph Henry III, who married Mattie Medora West and lived at Berkeley Springs, WV. The latter's son, Joseph H. Apple IV, is an electrical engineer in the Washington, D. C. area.

Gertrude Apple taught English at Hood College and started the Herald, the college magazine. Professor Apple, during his 41 years as President of Hood, taught in nine departments, but principally philosophy. Hood grew to 500 students, with 57 on the faculty and using 14 buildings. Nearly 1,600 were awarded degrees. Through programs open to the public, Professor Apple brought more culture to Frederick than did any other person I know about. He was a leader in Frederick community organizations, including the YMCA, Reformed Church, Historical Society and Sons of the American Revolution. Dr. Apple wrote a booklet, *Frederick in Song and Story* (Frederick News-Post, 1932).

Another Apfel or Apple, namely Johan Peter, arrived in Philadelphia in 1932. In 1740 he married Maria Catherine Henckel (1711-1785), youngest daughter of famous Rev. Anthony Jacob Henckel. They first lived south of Frederick, but later moved to a farm adjoining Apple's Church near Thurmont. They had the following children:

    Eva Rosina (b. 1742) m. Haus or House
    Johan Peter, Jr. (1744-1775) m. Elizabeth (1 daughter only)
    Maria Charlotta (1746-1820) m. Sebastian Moyer (Myer)
    Maria Catherine (1747-1829) m. Matthias (Mathews)
    Anna Magdalena (b. 1750) m. Michael Birely
    Johan Martin (b. 1751) died young

This Apple family name has lived on in Apple's Church. (LC)

W&M-1002. Joseph S. Grinder (1855-1925) is buried at St. Joseph Catholic Church west of Buckeystown, as are his parents, Samuel (1813-1874) and Harriet A. (Null) (1819-1906). Joseph's ancestor Michael (1758-1839) married Sevilla (1771-1833). They are buried at Glade Reformed Cemetery near Walkersville. According to Holdcraft, soldier Michael Grinder came to American with French troops under Lafayette.

W&M-1002. Cephas H. Zimmerman (1860-1948) and wife Ella C. Derr (1862-1928), as well as his parents Peter T. (1819-1891) and wife Ann M. (Cronise) (1823-1910), are buried at Mt. Olivet at Frederick.

Michael Zimmerman (1750-1821) was the son of early settler George (1714-1795). See W&M-979. Henry (1791-1875) and wife Charlotte (Thomas) are buried at the Zimmerman graveyard near Ballinger Creek. Their son Peter T. (1819-1891) and wife Ann Maria (Cronise) (1823-1910) are buried at Mt. Olivet.

Early deeds of settler George Zimmerman near Ballinger Creek south of Frederick include 750 acres of the tract Huffenhart for 950 pounds in 1762 from George Gumpf (wife Rosannah). In 1766 George bought 154 acres of a resurvey on DeLashmutt's Folly for 130 pounds from Thomas DeLashmutt, Jr. (wife Margaret) of Carolina and Mary Ray of Frederick County.

W&M-1003. John E. Hargett (1838-1924) and his wife Ellen L. (Zimmerman), also his parents Samuel (1811-1893) and wife Eleanor (Waters Burns) (1811-1880), are buried at Mt. Olivet. John's grandparents, John Hargett (1787-1859) and Barbara C. (Schaeffer) (1780-1856) are buried at Church Hill on Ballinger Creek Road.

In the census of 1800 two Hargett households were in Buckeystown District. Peter Hargett and wife were over 45 years of age, Abraham (1753-1824) and wife Mary (1753-1831) had eight children. They are buried at Church Hill on Ballinger Creek Road.

W&M-1004. Joseph Dawson Huffer (1834-1921) and wives Elizabeth A. S. (Remsburg) (1839-1870) and Margaret Ellen (1847-1937) are buried at Middletown Lutheran Church. His parents Joseph L. Huffer (1800-1880) and Catherine (Mullindore) (1802-1889) are buried at the Reformed Church in Middletown. See also W&M-812 and 977. (LC)

W&M-1005. Charles Singleton Huffer (1866-1947) and wife Jennie C. (Heightman) (1868-1932) are buried at Middletown Lutheran Church. He was a son of Joseph Dawson Huffer and Elizabeth (Huffer) above.

W&M-1005. Charles H. Derr (1841-1912) and wife Mary (Nikirk) (1845-1921) are buried at Middletown Lutheran Church, as are his parents Daniel (1812-1902) and Elizabeth (Coblentz) (1812-1893).

Philip Derr (1750-1821) and wife (Barbara Koogle) (1755-1815) were early settlers in Middletown Valley. Their son Jacob (c.1782-1848) and wife Margaret (Long) (1783-1868) are buried at Middletown Lutheran Church. Daniel, above, was their son. See also W&M-843 and Wampler. Wampler points out that Jacob Derr died too early to have joined the Republican party founded in 1854.

W&M-106. George Washington Stitely (1833-1911) and wife Esther C. (Pfoutz) (1838-1918) are buried at Beaver Dam Brethren Cemetery near Johnsville. His parents Samuel M. (1802-1890) and wife Elizabeth (Eberly) (1804-1891) are buried at Rocky Hill Church near Woodsboro. Grandparents of George W. were Jacob (1789-1852) and wife Mary.

In the 1800 census of the Taneytown area a Frederick Stitely and wife of ages between 26 and 45 years were living with four sons and three daughters.

W&M-1007. Samuel A. Stitely (1849-1917) and wife Missouri Victoria (Hahn) (1851-1940) are buried at Rocky Hill Church. He was a brother of George W. Stitely above.

W&M-1008. Hon. Melvin P. Wood (1848-1915) and wife Annie M. (Griffith) (1854-1927) are buried at New Market Methodist Episcopal Church. His parents were Joseph (1822-1896) and Eva R. (Burgess) (1824-1875) who are buried in the same cemetery. See W&M-716 for earlier Wood families of the Linganore area.

W&M-1009. Warner T. Grimes (1806-1896) and wife Sarah E. (Hesson) (1846-1935) are buried at Thurmont United Brethren Cemetery. His parents were Samuel (1763-1842) and second wife Catherine (c.1786-1866) who are buried at Creagerstown. Five genealogies of Grimes families are given in *Maryland Magazine of Genealogy* (Spring 1979). See also W&M-1070 and 1520.

The Hesson family is discussed in M&C-II. In the census of 1800 William Grimes and wife were over 45 years old, living with three daughters and one son. In 1800 another Grimes household in the Creagerstown to Emmitsburg area was that of Joshua (26-45) and wife (16-26) who had four sons under 10 years of age. (LC)

W&M-1009. Luther A. T. Horine (1830-1896) and wife Susan Rebecca (Shafer) (1840-1925) are buried at Burkittsville Union Cemetery, where also are buried his parents Tobias (1800-1880) and wife Magdalena (Routzahn) (1802-1873).

The emigrant to Middletown Valley was (Johan) Tobias Horein (1725-1773) who married at Falckner's Swamp in 1751 Elizabeth Boussert. Tobias and Adam Horein, Jr. emigrated from Hein or Hyne near Heilbronn, southern Germany. Tobias emigrated in 1749 and Leonhart Horein in 1747. See genealogies by Darle Horine Jones (Rialto, CA, 1970) and by Donna V. Russell in W. MD Gen. (July 1985).

W&M-1009. Emory C. Remsberg (1867-1932) and wife Viola I. (Thomas) (1874-1950) are buried at Middletown Reformed Church, where also are his parents Henry C. (1834-1922) and wife Mehala M. (Kefauver) (c.1845-1893). See W&M-752. (LC)

W&M-1010. George S. Martz (1855-1937) and wife Clara R. (Warner) (1867-1945) as well as his parents David (1813-1860) and wife Harriet S. (Wachter) (1821-1906) are buried at Mt. Olivet Cemetery. There also are buried Maj. George Martz (1786-1868) and wife Catherine (Reese) (1787-1858). The census of 1800 gives an earlier George Martz, Sr. and wife who were over 45 years in age living in the area of Fredericktown.

Earlier John H. Mertz, native of Wuerttemburg, southern Germany, settled in Lancaster County, Pennsylvania and later was a miller in the Middletown Valley (M&C-II). Son George settled on Tuscarora Creek northwest of Frederick and was buried at the Lutheran Church in Frederick. His widow Anna Christina (1728-1804), a daughter of Wilhelm and Justina Heime, of Germany, was buried there also. (LW)

Ralph F. Martz wrote *Martz Families of Maryland* (Frederick, 1973) but his documentary research was limited. See also W&M-1591. (LC)

W&M-1011. Mahlon Luther Rice (1854-1950) and wife Anna Melissa (Grove) (1869-1930) are buried at Myersville U. B. Church. His parents Henry, Jr. (1825-1910) and Catherine (Ambrose) (1836-1919) are buried at St. John's Lutheran Church north of Myersville. See W&M-956 for earlier Rice families.

A Jacob Reis is in Frederick County land records in 1755; his wife's name was Mollie. Possibly he was a son of Jacob (d. 1804) whose wife was Barbara.

W&M-1011. Francis T. Lakin (1840-1912) and wife Mary F. (Gerry) (1851-1928) are buried at Mt. Olivet. He was a son of William (1794-1850) and Susanna (Remsberg) (1807-1877) who are buried at the Lakin family graveyard.

The date of 1683 is that of the conditions for granting land by the English government and must not be mistaken for the date of the Frederick County deed of settler Joseph Lakin.

The stones at the family graveyard in southeastern Middletown Valley as read by Holdcraft are Abraham Lakin (1713-1796) "one of the first settlers of Frederick County, Maryland." In the same remarkable graveyard are Abraham II (1756-1799), the father of William above, and Abraham III (1792-1854) with wife Elizabeth (1812-1861). In the Frederick County Militia of 1812 were John, Benjamin and William Lakin.

W&M-1012. Hiram T. Smith (1847-1936) and wife Laura (Dutrow) (1851-1935) are buried at Myersville U. B. Church. He was born near Rohrersville in Washington County. In 1800 the only Dutrow in Middletown Valley was John Duttro (over 45 years) and wife. They had three daughters and five sons.

W&M-1013. Daniel Francis Roddy (1855-1940) and wife Catherine (White) (1872-1944) are buried at St. Anthony's Cemetery at Mt. St. Mary's. His parents were Abraham (1809-1893) and wife Hannah (Rife) (1819-1894) who also are buried at St. Anthony's; also buried there are Daniel's grandparents Hugh Roddy (1763-1847) and wife Margaret (Philips) (1780-1857).

Abraham Rife of near Taneytown and Daniel Rife of later Thurmont were in the Frederick County Militia of 1812. Daniel married Elizabeth Sumbrun.

W&M-1013. James O. Harne (1847-1907) and wife Annie M. (Burrier) (1849-1927) are buried at Garfield United Brethren Church in northern Middletown Valley. His parents were Henry R. L. Harne (1818-1903) buried at Lewistown M. E. Church and Elisabeth (Blickenstaff). See also W&M-1557. In Frederick District in 1800 was the family of Henry Harne and wife both between 26 and 45 years of age. They had three daughters and three sons.

W&M-1014. Daisey A. Dudderar was born in 1867 at Oak Orchard in the northern Linganore area; he married Myra L. Ecker. His parents were Peter Dudderar (1825-1910) and Josephine (Brightwell) (1822-1889) who are buried at Unionville Methodist Church. Also buried at Unionville are Benjamin Dudderar (1777-1854) and wife Rebecca (1779-1857); also David Dudderar (1782-1859) and wife Margaret (1794-1863) of Oak Orchard. See also W&M-982 and 1222.

Duddra/Dodderer families have been studied at (WP). Emigrant Michael Duttera settled near Littlestown, Pennsylvania and had sons Conrad, John, Philip and Michael. Children of Conrad were given (WB).

W&M-1015. Cephas M. Thomas (1851-1929) and wife Laura V. (Schaeffer) (1856-1921) are buried at Mt. Olivet as are his parents Josiah (1826-1906) and wife Susan Rebecca (Thomas) (1827-1907).

The gravestone of Gabriel Thomas (1721-1894), grandfather of Cephas, states that he was born at Klein Schifferstadt in the Pfaltz. This stone and others from the German Thomas family graveyard near Mountville (on the west edge of Buckeystown District) have been removed to Church Hill on Ballinger Creek Road. John Thomas (1757-1796) (a son of Gabriel and wife Anna Margaret) married Elizabeth Remsburg (1764-1825). Their son Peter Thomas (1792-1846) married Susanna Whipp (1798-1875). He was buried in the German Thomas family graveyard. Susannah's gravestone is in Mt. Olivet. They were parents of Josiah above.

For this and other Thomas families in W&M an outline is given below of the German Thomas families from the book *Genealogy of the Thomas Family (German)* published in 1954 by Frederick County's pioneer in genealogical research, George Leicester Thomas (with assistance from distant relative Emil Thomas of Germany). Six sons of Michael and Anna Thomas settled in Frederick County about 1742.

Michael Thomas (b. 1688) married, at Klein Schifferstadt near Manheim, Anna Veronika Lang (b. 1690) daughter of Peter and Barbara of Flanders. They emigrated with children in 1732 via Philadelphia. Their children follow:

    (1) Christian (b. 1714) m. 1745 Magdalena **
        Settled on Tasker's Chance near Frederick site by 1742
        Children baptized in Reformed records 1751 and 1753
    (2) Michael (b. 1718) m. 1744 Barbara **
        Settled near Frederick, moved to near Keedysville
        Will (Hagerstown) gives children, including Jacob and Michael
* (3) Gabriel (1721-1794) m. 1744 Anna Margaret **
        Farm west of Adamstown, deed 1754
        Child baptized 1748 Reformed at Frederick
* (4) Valentine (1724-1796) m. 1751 Margaret **
        Farm west of Adamstown
        Children baptized at Frederick Reformed Church

Most living local descendants are from grandsons George and Jacob, also Charlotte

    (5) Anna Catherine (b. 1726)
* (6) John (b. 1728) m. 1753 Catherine Getzendanner
        Farm near Adamstown
        Received 1/3 of Poplar Thicket from Gabriel 1754
        Children included Henry, Catharine, Barbara, Mary
    (7) Christopher (b. 1729) m. 1756 Mary Weiss
        Lived near Frederick; (G. L. T. lost their records)

* Lived on tract Poplar Thicket and next to George Remsburg family, also from Schifferstadt, with whom children married. According to Dr. Fritz Braun of Kaiserslautern the Thomas family arrived in the Monocacy area by 1742.

** A number of early Thomas sons are believed to have married Remsburg (Riemensperger) daughters. See W&M-1037. Others married local Zimmermans. Over 180 Thomas names are in the index of (Z).

W&M-1016. Aquilla Reese Yeakle (1848-1915) and wife Fannie B. (Hane) (1848-1917) also her parents William (1822-1869) and wife Mary L. (Cline) (1827-1905) are buried at Mt. Olivet Cemetery at Frederick. The grandfather of Aquilla was Henry Yeakle of Hagerstown.

W&M-1017. The parents of Lewis R. Dertzbaugh (b. 1882) were William Henry (1850-1923) and wife Emma (Bennett) (1851-1930) who are buried at Mt. Olivet. The great grandparents of Lewis were John Dertzbaugh (1755-1815) and wife Catherine (Metz) who were buried in the Reformed Cemetery at Frederick, as were his grandparents John, Jr. who in 1799 married Christina Knauff. The emigrant ancestor is said to have been Georg Adam Dertzbach (1724-1780) who immigrated in 1748. He married Maria Magdalene Wolf and was father of Peter who married Margaretha.

George Dertzbaugh (1790-1856) served in the Frederick County Militia of 1812 under Capt. Henry Steiner. In 1813 he married Catherine Kregloe (1793-1863). They had children: Catherine m. Daniel Derr, Margaret m. Henry L. Fiegler, Mary m. Joshua Young.

Another son of William Henry and Emma Dertzbaugh was Frank, the father of Frank, Jr., born about 1910, who married Jane, a daughter of Howard L. Metzger of Myersville. Frank and Jane are retired in Frederick in 1994.

W&M-1018. Samuel D. Thomas (1861-1919) and wife Annie W. (Worman) are buried at Mt. Olivet as are his parents David (1815-1877) and wife Elizabeth (Hildebrand) (1820-1908).

W&M-1019. Parents of (Henry) Abraham Schildknecht were not natives of Germany. His grandfather, the emigrant from south Germany, was Wilhelm Schildknecht (d. 1807) who signed his name correctly after arrived at Philadelphia in 1768. In 1779 he was taxed near Kutztown in Berks County, Pennsylvania. In 1782 farmer William and wife Barbara moved from Washington County across South Mountain to the present farm area of Robert Hotz, southwest of Myersville. They gradually acquired adjoining land including the 25 acres of William's Home where the ruin of their tiny stone house remains today. Long after William's death the house was marked on the 1873 atlas of Frederick County as William's house. Their son Henry (1774-1808) married neighbor Mary Smith (1775-1827), daughter of Michael. Her gravestone at St. John's Lutheran Church near Ellerton is the earliest S. family stone in our area. (See M&C-II).

Mary's son Jacob (1798-1882) married Maria Routzahn (1806-1882). They farmed north of the home farm of William and Barbara on the eastern slope of South Mountain south of new highway I-70. Their son (Henry) Abraham (1830-1909) married in 1853 Sarah Ellen (Marken) (1829-1859). Abe Schildknecht, a prosperous farmer and banker, married a second time to Esther (Flook) (1831-1909). Their children and some grandchildren are given in M&C-II.

W&M-1019. Howard M. Huffer (1859-1948) and wife Emma (Schildknecht) (1864-1956), daughter of Abraham, are buried at Frederick Memorial Park. His parents, David (1823-1903) and wife Annie C. (Ahalt) (1832-1898) are buried at Middletown Lutheran Cemetery. Howard's grandfather, Joseph Huffer (1800-1882) and wife Catherine (1802-1889) are buried at Middletown Reformed Church. For Huffers in Washington County see Williams (1906). See also W&M-812.

W&M-1020. Lewis A. Hildebrand (1832-1900) and wife Amanda Winpigler (1836-1915) are buried at Mt. Olivet. Lewis' parents were John (c.1798-1875) and Lydia (Albaugh) (1800-1876) who are buried at Rocky Springs. See also W&M-971.

W&M-1021. Lewis J. Martz (1836-1905) and wife Margaret C. (1844-1922) are buried at Mt. Olivet. His parents David S. (1814-1860) and Harriet S. (Wachter) (1821-1906) were buried at Mt. Olivet also. Cf. W&M-775.

W&M-1022. John D. Storr (1864-1937) and wife Addie C. (McDevitt) (1872-1940) are buried at Charlesville Reformed Church north of Frederick. His father Henry C. Storr (1830-1895) born at Liverpool, England, married Elizabeth Glaze (1837-1917); they are buried at Mt. Olivet. A Valentine Glass (26-45 years) lived in Emmitsburg District in 1800.

W&M-1022. Bradley E. Clem (1877-1953) married Bertha M. Storr, daughter of Henry and Elizabeth (Glaze) above.

Philip Clem (1725-1871) emigrated from Adersbach near Sinsheim, southeast of Heidelberg, Germany. See early generations in America in M&C-I. Jacob Clem (1791-1847) is buried at Utica. Jacob W. Clem (1819-1899) and Mary M. Hiteshew (1824-1863) who are buried at Utica were parents of John H. Clem (1850-1928) who married Wilhelmina S. Stull (1855-1947). They also are buried at Utica. John H. and Wilhelmina were parents of Bradley E. Clem. (LC)

W&M-1023. Jacob Hoke (1848-1930) and wife Mary Elizabeth (Keilholtz) (d. 1899) are buried at Mountain View Cemetery at Emmitsburg. His parents were Jacob (b. 1808) and Mary (Link) (b. c.1810) of Emmitsburg District whose gravestones were not reported. The census of 1850 called Jacob a mechanic born in Pennsylvania.

Kramer J. Hoke, son of Jacob and Mary Elizabeth above, had an outstanding career as an educator, including a professorship at William and Mary College in VA.

A genealogy entitled *Hoke Families* was written by George W. Hoke (Covington, Ohio, 1953). Hokes have lived in Adams County, Pennsylvania. (WB)

W&M-1025. Lorenzo E. Mullinix (1855-1930) and wife Annie E. (1860-1942) are buried at Mt. Olivet. Lorenzo's parents Leonard C. Mullinix (1828-1891) and Elizabeth Simpson (Etchison) (1828-1889) also are buried at Mt. Olivet.

In the 1800 census of Liberty District was the household of Robert Mulleniux and wife who were between 26 and 45 years of age. A Robert T. Mullinix (1836-1908) is buried at Browningsville Methodist Church. In 1760 John Mullinix, Jr., planter, of Ann Arundel County, bought land in the Linganore area and sold a portion to Abraham Moore in 1766. In 1776 Thomas Mullineux (and wife Elizabeth) sold land to John Lawrence on a branch of Linganore Creek.

W&M-1026. John C. Lamar (1856-1923) and wife Hattie A. (Hays) are buried at Mt. Olivet Cemetery in Frederick. His parents Benoni Lamar (1819-1889) and wife Mary C. (Thomas) (1819-1889) are buried at the Episcopal Church near Point of Rocks. See W&M-1183.

W&M-1027. Lloyd C. Culler (1869-1960), a mayor of Frederick, and wife Anna Mary (Murray) (1875-1936) are buried at Feagaville. His parents were Thomas W. (1834-1888) and Jane Turner (Anderson). The paternal grandfather of Lloyd C. Culler was Philip Culler (1811-1884) who married Ann Rebecca (1825-1908). They are buried at Jefferson Union Cemetery. Capt. Henry Culler (1786-1861) and wife Anna (Fister) (1789-1856), buried at Jefferson, were great grandparents of Lloyd C. In the census of 1800 of Middletown Valley the only Culler family was that of Michael and wife who were over 45 years of age. They had two daughters (between 16 and 26 years) and four sons in age between 10 and 26 years.

W&M-1028. Edward A. Toms (1868-1933) and wife Estie O. (Gaver) (1871-1940) are buried at Zion Lutheran Church, Middletown, as are his parents Isaiah J. (1839-1914) and wife Mary C. (Schindler) (1891-1924). Grandparents of Edward were Jacob Toms, Jr. (1796-1887) and Mary (Floyd) (1805-1878) who are buried at Myersville U. B. Church. Jacob Toms, Sr. (1767-1854) and wife Magdalena (c.1768-1852) are buried at Jerusalem Cemetery northwest of Myersville. The stone of Jacob, Sr. states that he was born in Germany. The census of 1800 in Middletown Valley gives a Jacob Thomas over 45 years and another head of household David Toms between 26 and 45 years. See also W&M-1521.

W&M-1028. William Anderson (1834-1888) and wife Zoe Lee (Hunter) (1869-1949) are buried at Mt. Olivet, as are his parents Thomas William (1834-1888) and wife Jane (Turner) (1831-1888). William's grandparents were Samuel B. Anderson and Elizabeth (Hall) of Prince George's County (LC)

W&M-1030. Millard F. Flook (1855-1933) and wife Melissa E. (Bowlus) (1860-1930) are buried at Middletown Reformed Church, as are his parents Daniel (1826-1870) and wife Elizabeth Susan (Mumma) (1822-1897). Grandparents of Millard were Jacob Flook (1794-1859) and wife Mary A. (1809-1855) who are buried at Jefferson Union Cemetery. Jacob Flook, Sr. (1760-1840) and wife Elizabeth (1767-1842) have gravestones in the Reformed Cemetery at Middletown. See also W&M-829.

W&M-1030. George C. Huffer (1848-1917) and wife Mary M. (DeLauder) (1855-1922) as well as his parents Joseph L. (1800-1882) and wife Catherine (Mullendore) (c.1802-1889) are buried at the Reformed Cemetery in Middletown. See also W&M-812.

W&M-1031. Harry B. Funk (1872-1930) and wife Annie B. C. (Demory) (b. 1885) are buried at Mt. Olivet as are his parents Venniah B. (1846-1914) and Georgianna (Dixon) (1847-1931). Harry's grandparents William Funk (1822-1889) and wife Catherine (1821-1910) are buried at Mt. Olivet. Harry and Rudolph Funk, both over 45 years, had families in northern Frederick County in 1800 census. (LC)

W&M-1031. George H. Hogan (1870-1926) married Bessie L. Magalis, daughter of Richard. George and his mother Mary (Hymes) (1847-1930) are buried at Park Heights Cemetery, Brunswick. His father, Michael Hogan (1848-1900), is buried at Petersville Episcopal Church. Michael Hogan, born about 1816 in Ireland, was a lay brother at the Jesuit Novitiate of Frederick in the census of 1850. (LC)

W&M-1032. Cyrus F. Flook (1866-1932) and wife Elizabeth (Eby) (b. 1870) have stones in Myersville U. B. Cemetery. In the same cemetery are buried the parents of Cyrus, namely Dawson F. (1838-1912) and wife Elizabeth (Harp) 1837-1926). Perry C. Flook (1816-1842), grandfather of Cyrus, was a son of Jacob (1786-1853) and Esther (Biser) (b. 1788).

W&M has omitted a generation here. Jacob Flook (1786-1853) was a son of John and grandson of German emigrant Jacob who died about 1777.

No evidence of five emigrating brothers has been found or of Huguenot origin of the German Flook or Fluck families. See also W&M-829. Wampler cites some evidence that the emigrants came from Alsace where German dialects are spoken.

W&M-1033. A Galt genealogy of unknown authors was abstracted by Beryl McPherson in the Emmitsburg Chronicle of July 17, 1970. Galts were said to have originated in Dreghorn Parish, Scotland. Robert Galt emigrated from north Ireland via New Castle, DE, in 1710 to near Pequea Creek in Lancaster County. His son James married Miss Alison and had sons Robert, John, William, James and Thomas. Descendant Matthew Galt (1746-1828) (son of a James, d. 1773) and wife Mary (1757-1844), who farmed near Taneytown, had sons James, Peter and Moses (c.1785-1845). James had a son Sterling (1796-1885) who married Margaret Grayson (1798-1851) (daughter of Nathaniel). Margaret's son Mathew William and wife Mary J. lived in the DC area where they founded a jewelry store and had the following children:

(1) Charles Ernest, lived in DC, unmarried

(2) Annie E. m. Reginald Fendall

(3) Walter Allen

(4) Norman (1864-1896) m. Edith Bolling (1872-1961) of southwest, VA; Edith's 2nd m. in 1915 to President Woodrow Wilson (1856-1924)

(5) Sterling (1865-c.1925) m. in 1892 Harriet Virginia Wingerd (1870-1897), lived in Emmitsburg, children:

    (a) Sterling, Jr. (1893-1936) m. Dorothy Hawks, lived in N.Y. City, no children

    (b) Harriet Virginia (1896-1943), unmarried, pianist.

Sterling's 2nd m. to (Harriet) Lucy Higbee (1870-1959); no children but raised Harriet's two.

Most dates above are from Piney Creek Presbyterian Church between Taneytown and Harney.

The Emmitsburg Chronicle newspaper of October 15, 1915 recorded the visit of President Wilson, widow Edith Galt and the President's daughter Margaret to the home of Sterling and Lucy Galt. The President's auto party arrived at 12:15, had luncheon and left Emmitsburg at 3:15 p.m. Soon thereafter Edith (Bolling) Galt became the second wife of Woodrow Wilson, during whose later illness she assumed political influence without precedent among previous presidential wives.

The two wives of Sterling Galt, community leader of Emmitsburg, were cousins, granddaughters of Joshua Motter (1801-1875), the oldest son of Lewis Motter (1779-1837) and wife Mary (Martin). See W&M-1446. Joshua's second child Virginia Catherine (1828-1913) married Adam B. Wingerd (1821-1883) Joshua's third child Lucinda Motter (1833-1929) married Dr. Elnathan Elisha Higbee (1830-1889). They were parents of Lucy Galt and Rev. E. L. Higbee, also grandparents of Mary Higbee Hoke (Mrs. Harold M.) of Emmitsburg.

Sterling Galt was called "a pillar of Emmitsburg" for his long operation of the *Emmitsburg Chronicle* and leadership in civic enterprises. Around 1909 he organized a great Emmitsburg Homecoming with a parade, bands and floats. The town continues to have outstanding spirit. The obituary of Sterling Galt is in the *New York Times* of December 30, 1922. His funeral service was held at an Episcopal Church in DC.

W&M-1034. Brook Buxton II (b. 1839) married Emma J. Spurrier (1837-1913) who is buried at Prospect Church near Mt. Airy. Also buried there are Brook's parents Brook Buxton, Sr. (1801-1869) and wife Kitty (Mullinix) (1806-1866). For Mullinix see W&M-1025. Spurriers lived near Westminster from where came Lancelot (b. c.1791) and Green (b. c.1794) who are recorded in the Frederick County Militia of 1812.

W&M-1034. Thomas Randolph Jarboe (1828-1894) and wife Lauretta (Eagle) are buried at Mt. Olivet. His parents William Jarboe (1795-1836) and wife Margaret (Schaffer) (1796-1874) are buried in the Reformed Cemetery of Middletown. William has the earliest Jarboe stone in Middletown Valley.

Emigrant John or Jean Jarboe (b. 1619) of Dijon, Burgundy, France, was naturalized in southern Maryland in 1666. His descendant John Raphael Jarboe farmed on Carrollton Manor and belonged to St. Joseph's Church west of Buckeystown (Archives of Maryland and Grove). In the Maryland Militia of the Revolution were Charles, Joshua, Peter, Richard, Robert, Stephen and Thomas Jarboe, most of southern Maryland.

In the 1800 census of the Buckeystown area Raphael Jarboe and wife Catherine (1766-1834), with three sons and a daughter all under ten years, were the only Jarboes. Catherine was buried at the Catholic Cemetery in Frederick. A Stephen Jarboe is recorded in the Frederick County court records in 1761. Stephan, a bricklayer, gave a bill-of-sale in 1764 to Msgr. Thomas Hartly for three pounds and two shillings. Samuel Jarboe (1804-1883) and wife Margaret (1819-1857) are buried at St. Joseph Catholic Church near Buckeystown.

W&M-1035. Robert Edmonston Delaplaine (1885-1955) and wife Ruth (Mullinix) (1885-1964) were buried at Mt. Olivet Cemetery, as were his parents William Theodore (1860-1895) and wife Fannie (Birely) (1862-1954). Grandparents of Robert were Theodore Crist Delaplaine (1810-1900) and Mrs. Hannah A. (Wilcoxon) (1818-1886), daughter of Capt. Eden Edmonston and the widow of Jesse Wilcoxon. Great grandparents of Robert were Joseph Delaplaine (1785-1875) and wife Rosanna Crist (1790-1858). The ancestors of Joseph have been traced from emigrant Nicholas Delaplaine (M&C-I).

W&M-1037. Charles Thomas Ramsburg (1841-1918) married Margaret Claggett (b. c.1846). He is buried at Middletown Reformed Church. His parents were Henry (1796-1865) and Elizabeth (Coblentz) (1795-1881) buried at the same place.

In the outline below the ancestry of Henry's father John (1760-1844) from Riemenspergers of Walldorf, Germany, is shown. John and Catherine, who moved northwestward from near Adamstown across Catoctin Mountain, first appear in records of Middletown Lutheran Church in 1791.

One of the children of Charles and Margaret (Ramsburg) was Vallie E. (1885-1958) who married Archie E. Fisher (1884-1952) and lived on East Second Street in Frederick. My aunt Vallie gave me the Bible of my great grandfather Abraham Fisher, Jr. (1826-1915) with family records. Thus, she stimulated my interest in family history.

W&M-1037. Johan Georg Riemensperger (later Remsburg) son of Christian and Eva Dorothea (Frey), born at Walldorf near Heidelberg, emigrated in 1754. He is said to have been a nephew of Stephen who settled north of Frederick. Descendants of (Johan) Georg Riemensperger (1736-1820) and wife Maria Elisabetha (Brunner) (1739-1787) are given below largely from the genealogy by Rev. Wilson L. Remsberg (b. 1848) of Sharpsburg:

(1) Anna Maria (1758-1824) m. Gabriel Thomas (1753-1808). Children: John, Henry, George, Charlotte, Gabriel Jr., Margaret, Peter, Mary, Elias.

(2) John (1760-1844) m. Catherine Thomas (1776-1866), to Middletown about 1790. Children: George, Mary, Elizabeth, Henry, Catherine, John, Sarah.

(3) Catherine (b. 1762) m. Henry Hershberger; to Jefferson. Children: John B., Mary, Henry, Elizabeth, Catherine, Thomas, Susan.

(4) Elizabeth (1764-1835) m. John Thomas (1757-1796). Five children.

(5) Anna Margaret (1767-1811) m. Henry Thomas. Children: Mary, Michael, Stephen, George, Susan.

(6) George Peter (1770-1847) m. Catherine Culler (1777-1866). Children: Sebastian., Jacob, Susan, Anna, Catherine, Elizabeth.

(7) Charlotte (1772-1853) m. Valentine Buckey (d. 1826). No children.

(8) Stephen (b. 1774) m. Catherine Whipp, moved to Montgomery County near Dickerson in 1797. Daughter Caroline m. Jacob Hefner. Daughter Eliza m. Robert T. Cooley.

(9) Barbara (b. 1777) m. Stephen Steiner. No children.

(10) Sebastian, Sr. (1779-1841) m. Elizabeth Steiner (d. 1868), lived near Jefferson. Children: Elias, William, Mary, Catherine, Sophia, Elizabeth, Susanna, Daniel Thomas, John Henry.

(11) Susannah (b. 1782) m. Christian Steiner.

Most used the family name Remsburg.

W&M-1038. Alexander Ramsburg (1838-1922) and wife Hannah Sophia (Cronise) (1835-1923) are buried at Mt. Olivet. Her parents were Frederick (1804-1866) and Anna (1799-1896) who are buried at Lewistown Methodist Church. Alexander's parents were Jacob Ramsburg (1808-1877) and Elizabeth (Snook) (1798-1889) who are buried at Utica. For Snook families see W&M-745.

From the outline of descendants of Stephen Riemensperger (1711-1789) with W&M-752, Henry was a son of Philip Henry and wife Susanna (Devilbiss) who moved to VA, but after his second marriage Philip returned to Middletown Valley. Some authors have falsely stated that a separate Ramsburg family emigrated via VA.

W&M-1039. William H. Ashbaugh (1837-1912) married Martha J. Dyer. He is buried at Mt. View Cemetery at Emmitsburg. His parents John (1808-1862) and Margaret (Hann) (1798-1866) are buried at Mt. Olivet.

W&M-1040. Samuel U. Gregg (1866-1950) and wife Fannie E. Shaff (1864-1895) are buried at Jefferson Union Cemetery where also is buried his father

James W. (1840-1884) who married Mary C. Fawley. (LC). In Middletown Valley in 1800 lived George Shaff and wife, both over 45 years in age.

W&M-1042. John H. Zimmerman (b. 1850) was a son of Gideon M. (1823-1896) and Christiana (Wolfe) (1820-1871) who are buried at Church Hill on Ballenger Creek Road. John's grandparents were Henry Zimmerman (1791-1875) and Charlotte (Thomas) (1790-1860) who also are buried at St. Matthew's Cemetery on Church Hill. The outline with W&M-979 shows that Henry was a son of Michael Zimmerman (1750-1821) and grandson of (John) George (1714-1795) who settled next to Carrollton Manor in Buckeystown District around 1762.

W&M-1043. Dr. Walter Ralph Steiner (b. 1870) was a son of famous Dr. Lewis Henry Steiner (1822-1882) and wife Sarah Spencer (Smyth) (1838-1914) who are buried at Mt. Olivet. Also buried there are the parents of Dr. Lewis Henry, namely Christian Steiner (1797-1862) and wife Rebecca (1802-1862).

A genealogy of the Steiner Family was written by Drs. Lewis H. and Bernard C. Steiner (1867-1926) published at Baltimore in 1896. This shows the lineage to Christian as follows:

(1) Jacob Steiner or Stoner (1713-1748) emigrated from Germany in 1731; wife unknown; had sons John, Henry and Benedict.
(2) Capt. John Steiner (d. 1798) m. Catherine Elizabeth Remsberg (1739-1792)
(3) Henry Steiner (1764-1831) m. Elizabeth Brengel (1767-1833)
(4) Christian Steiner m. Rebecca Weltzheimer (1802-1862), daughter of Dr. Lewis and Margaret (Meyer).

The gravestone of first settler Jacob Stoner (1713-1748), moved from the Reformed Church to Mt. Olivet, is the oldest stone in Mt. Olivet. Its long, interesting inscription is no longer legible, but has been recorded by Scharf. The ruin of Jacob Steiner or Stoner's Mill Pond house, of German medieval construction, remains in a field near Ceresville, north of Frederick (M&C-I.)

Capt. Henry Steiner (1775-1825), born in Frederick, married in 1806 Rachel Rebecca Murray (1784-1856), daughter of John and Rebecca. Rachel died in Cincinnati. Their daughter Henrietta Steiner (b. 1809) married Rev. T. P. C. Shelman (1811-1882), son of Michael and Sarah Maria. Some descendants are given in (CF), Vol. 1, 503.

Papers of Lewis H. and Bernard C. Steiner, MS 785, MS 791, MS 1430, are at (BM).

John Steiner, the oldest son of emigrant Jacob, married Catherine Elizabeth Ramsburg (1739-1792) and they had 11 children. Their fifth child was Stephen (1767-1829) who married first Barbara Ramsburg (1777-1820) and they had children George, Charlotte and Daniel. Stephen's second wife was widow Elizabeth (Birely) (Bausman) (1788-1866). She was a daughter of Frederick Ludwick Birely (1752-1806) and Elizabeth (Motter). More descendants are given in a booklet about the Steiner House in "Battletown" (near top of hill on West Patrick Street) (files of FH).

W&M gives little about leading Maryland citizens Dr. Lewis H. Steiner, M.D. and his son Dr. Bernard C. Steiner of Frederick, both of whom became Chief

Librarians of Enoch Pratt Library in Baltimore. The career of Dr. Lewis included medicine, education, military service, and politics. Son Bernard was historian, author and successor to his father at Enoch Pratt.

Lewis Steiner was educated in Frederick, graduated in 1846 from Marshall College and received the M.D. from University of Pennsylvania. He was awarded an honorary LLD from Delaware College and Litt. D. from Franklin and Marshall. Dr. Lewis, M.D. began practice in Frederick, but moved to Baltimore in 1852. From about 1855 he became more interested in teaching chemistry, botany and medicine at National Medical College in D.C. and the Maryland Institute. He became the first Professor of Chemistry of the College of Pharmacy of the University of Maryland. During the Civil War he was Chief Inspector of the U.S. Sanitary Commission which was a forerunner of the American Red Cross. After the war, Lewis, with bride Sarah Spencer (Smyth) of Guilford, CT, returned to Frederick where he became President of the County School Board with a special interest in education of negro children. His publications included articles in medical and scientific journals and translations of German fiction for Sunday school books of the Reformed Church Publication House. Dr. Steiner served as Maryland State Senator (1871-1883) and was political editor of the *Frederick Examiner Newspaper*. He continued active in medicine and became President of the American Academy of Medicine, which he helped to found. In 1886 Enoch Pratt Free Library opened in Baltimore, with Dr. Lewis Steiner as librarian. In 1892 Lewis Steiner died and his son Bernard C. succeeded him as Librarian of Enoch Pratt.

Dr. Walter Ralph Steiner, son of Lewis and Sarah, graduated in the second class at the Johns Hopkins Medical School, where he studied with noted Drs. Asher and Welch. He practiced medicine in Hartford, CT and became the President of the American Medical Library Association. Walter's brother Bernard Christian Steiner (1867-1926) grew up in Frederick. He graduated with honors from Yale university in 1888 and earned the Ph.D. in history from Johns Hopkins in 1891, where he studied with professors Daniel Gilman and Woodrow Wilson. He was called from teaching at Williams College in 1892 to succeed his father at Enoch Pratt Library. The tremendous productivity of Dr. Bernard Steiner as educator, lawyer, historian and librarian has been accounted for in part by his retentive memory, his prodigious energy and his remaining a bachelor until age 45. He taught history at Johns Hopkins part time and in 1897 became Dean and Professor of Constitutional Law in the Law School of University of Baltimore. He was the first editor of the Maryland Law Review. Bernard wrote more than 100 articles, including many on Maryland history in MHM. His major books were *the Life and Correspondence of James McHenry, (Washington's Secretary of War)*, and his *Life of Chief Justice Roger B. Taney*. He was editor of the *Archives of Maryland*, volumes 36 to 45. For 34 years until his death in 1926 Dr. Steiner served as Librarian of Enoch Pratt and he was a national leader in the Presbyterian Church. More details are in the booklet *First 40 Years of Enoch Pratt Library* (1986) by Richard L. Steiner (FH).

W&M-1044. David F. Mayne (1851-1941) and wife Hannie May (Bopst) (1859-1950) are buried at Mt. Olivet. They had no children. David's parents were David Main (1821-1910) and Annie C. (Engle) (1830-1903) who are buried at Rocky Springs.

Family historian William E. Main of Frederick believes that all local Mains are descendants of George Mehn (1722-1773) and wife Elisabeth who settled near High Knob (Gambrill Park). Their children were Frederick (b. 1754), John (1756-1832), Rosina (b. 1759, George (d. 1822), Magdalena (1740-1744) and Adam (1746-1822). W. E. Main has traced six generations descending from Adam.

John Jacob Main (1793-1872) was enrolled in the Frederick County Militia of 1812. In 1819 he married Sarah Bopst (1801-1882) and they farmed near Rocky Springs west of Frederick, where they are buried.

W&M-1044. Edward Nichols (1834-1910), born in Barnesville, Montgomery County, and wife Anna Virginia (Trundle) (1833-1916) are buried at Mt. Olivet. Other Trundles have been buried at Frederick, Point of Rocks and Liberty. Walter Trunnel (1746-1818) is buried at Urbana Episcopal Church. Among those enrolled in the Maryland Militia of 1812 were Jacob Nichols (b. 1788), son of Johan and Philippina, who married Sarah Rawlins in 1818, also Raphael Nichols who married Sarah Grimes, and John Nichols who married Rebecca Paggett.

W&M-1044. Charles William Ahalt (1866-1936) and wife Pearl M. (Boyer) (1871-1927) are buried at Middletown Lutheran Church. His parents were Benjamin S. (1834-1923) and Sarah E. (Derr) (1837-1922) also buried at Middletown Lutheran Church. The parents of Benjamin were Mathias Ahalt (1803-1881) and wife Phoebe (1809-1893) who are buried at Middletown Lutheran Church. See also W&M-988.

W&M-1046. Walter C. Doty (1871-1924) and wife Madora Shaff (1873-1951) are buried at Jefferson Union Cemetery where also are buried his parents Abner (1842-1915) and Emily Jane (Porter) (1846-1924). Emily's parents were Philip Porter (1812-1882) a blacksmith and wife Mary J. (1817-1888) who are buried at Jefferson Union Cemetery. Among those in the Frederick County Militia of 1812 were John A. Porter (c.1792-1855), who married Mary Ann Watt (second marriage to Catherine Baer), and James Porter, born in Frederick County (LC).

W&M-1047. Nicholas D. Hauer (1817-1912) and wife Ann C. (Meyer) (1823-1885) are buried at Mt. Olivet Cemetery. His grandfather Nicholas Hauer (1747-1831), ancestor of Barbara Fritschie, was a native of Dildendorf, Alsace, near Saarbruecken. His son Daniel (1768-1841) and wife Margaret (Mantz) (1785-1846) are buried at Mt. Olivet. In the Frederick County Militia of 1812 besides Daniel there were Adam, who married Catharine Lambert, George, who married Catherine Schellman, and Henry Hauer (b. 1777), who married Catherine.

W&M-1048. Morris Alleman Birely, M.D. (1872-1947) and wife Bertha (Bushey) (d. 1957) are buried at Blue Ridge Cemetery at Thurmont. His parents were Samuel (1794-1877) and second wife Barbara Ann (Kemp) (1833-1899) who are buried at Haugh's Church near Ladiesburg, north of Woodsboro. Earlier ancestors are given in MC-II.

W&M-1049. Charles F. Oland (1854-1929) and wife Clara V. (Craver) (1855-1945) are buried at Mt. Olivet, where also are buried his parents Frederick (1821-1908) and wife Mary Anna E. V. (Schaffer).

W&M-1049. John Hamilton Saylor (1854-1892) and wife Sarah E. (Diehl) (1849-1932) are buried at Beaver Dam Brethren Cemetery near Johnsville, where also are buried his parents John Saylor (1820-1906) and wife Margaret (Hoffman). Grandparents of John H. were Solomon Saylor (1797-1863) and Catharine (Hoffman). An early Saylor was Jacob who wrote to Annapolis in 1766 complaining of treatment by Magistrate Capt. Peter Bainbridge. In the census of 1800 in eastern Frederick County lived Daniel Sailor and wife, both over 45 years of age. They had three sons.

The spellings Saylor and Sailor derive from the dialect pronunciation of the German family name Seiler.

W&M-1050. Charles C. Biser (1862-1931) and wife Carrie M. (Miller) (1863-1937) are buried at Middletown Reformed Church, where also are buried his parents Henry (1821-1900) and wife Sophia (Routzahn) (1826-1912).

Frederick Biser (1763-1823) was born in America, but Frederick's father Jacob, Jr. and grandfather Jacob, Sr. were born abroad. See W&M-951.

W&M-1051. Dr. Charles A. Norwood, D.D.S. (1843-1934) and wife Pauline B. (Mills) (1851-1919) are buried at Fairmount Cemetery at Libertytown, as were his parents R. Nelson Norwood (1813-1891) and wife Rachel (Wagner) (1815-1919). In the Frederick County Militia of 1812 John Waggoner served under Capt. Joseph Wood of Woodsboro.

W&M-1052. John W. A. Haugh (1854-1913) and wife Louisa E. (Flickinger) (1858-1953) are buried at Haugh's Church near Ladiesburg. A Paul Haugh, Sr. (1780-1847) is buried at Taneytown Reformed Cemetery. William Haugh (1774-1845) and wife Catherine (1777-1824) are buried at Haugh's Church, as are William's son John (1801-1862) and his wife Catherine (Smith) (1805-1872). The parents of John W. A. Haugh were William M. Haugh (1826-1892) and wife Henrietta L. (Leather) (1828-1905), also buried at Haugh's Church. Paul and William Hauk are in the census of 1800 in Libertytown District.

W&M-1053. John H. Bohn (b. 1865) married Susannah R. Alexander (1869-1934) who is buried at Unionville Methodist Church. His grandparents were Michael Bohn (1809-1877) and wife Annie (Saylor) (1813-1883), who are buried at Beaver Dam Brethren Cemetery near Johnsville.

Johanes Nicholas Bohn (b. 1734) emigrated in 1750 from Postorff in northern Alsace. His parents were Johannes Bon and wife Anna Margaret (Fus), daughter of Hans Peter, of Postorff. John Nicholas and wife Anna Maria had daughter Catherine, born in 1763 and recorded by Frederick Lutheran Church. Nicholas was naturalized in 1765 (B3).

W&M-1054. Americus C. Cronise (1850-1937) and wife Alice E. (Bream) (1854-1899) are buried at Lewistown Methodist Church. The grandparents of Americus were Frederick Cronise (1804-1866) and wife Annie (Nicodemus) (1799-1896). Their son Jacob (1827-1906) married Annie M. Ramsburg and they had 15 children, one of whom was Americus.

A Croneis (Kroneis) Genealogy was written by William G. Harman (Plainfield, NJ, 1955). A very large file of Cronise family data is at (FH).

Johan Georg Kroneiss was born near Strasbourg, Alsace. His widow, Anna Maria, married George Dorne (later Dern). Children of Georg and Anna Maria follow:

(1) Johannes (1748-1803) m. Anna Maria Fay (1754-1823) of Frederick; three of their children went to Wayne County, NY.
(2) Susanna (b. 1755) m. Adam Sensbauer.
(3) Eva m. Michael Zimmerman (1744-1821) of Frederick County
(4) Heinrich (1758-1815) m. Barbara Wort (1761-1804). Heinrich's second marriage to Elisabeth Knouff (Knauff), (Middletown, Maryland, Reformed Church).
(5) Johan George, Jr.

In the 1800 census John Cronys, in age between 26 and 45, with wife and two children under 10, lived in Emmitsburg District. In Fredericktown District lived John Kroneis, over 45; also Henry Kroneis, age between 24 and 45.

The Cronise families of Lewistown were ancestors of Maj. Frederick Louis Detrick in whose honor Fort Detrick was named. John Henry Detrick (1806-1848), son of Philip, married in 1825 Elizabeth Cronise (1807-1844), daughter of John Jacob Cronise and wife Catherine (Fundenberg). Their son Louis Frederick Detrick (1831-1986) married Katherine Umstead (1838-1898) of Montgomery County, Pennsylvania, and they lived at New Market, later Baltimore, Maryland. Their son John Umstead Detrick (1864-1916) married Lillie Downey (1867-1902), daughter of William and Margaret. They are buried at New Market M.E. Church as is their son Major Frederick L. Detrick, M.D. (1889-1931) who graduated from the Medical School of University of Maryland in 1913, served the U.S. Army Air Force in France in World War I and later the 104th Aero Squadron of the Maryland National Guard. The latter had summer camp on Frederick's abandoned early airport which later became the nucleus of Fort Detrick.

W&M-1054. Marion R. Brandenburg (1858-1936) and wife Laura C. (Routzahn) (1858-1936) are buried at the Reformed Cemetery in Middletown, as are his parents Eli (1830-1911) and Susanna (Main) (1835-1917). Marion's grandparents were Henry Brandenburg (1792-1869) and wife Mary (Biser) (1801-1859). See also W&M-866 and 1470.

W&M-1056. James H. Gambrill, Jr. (1866-1951) and wife Susan May (Winebrenner) (1866-1902), daughter of Col. D. C., are buried at Mt. Olivet Cemetery. His parents James Henry Gambrill, Sr. (1830-1932) and wife Antoinette Frances (1838-1894) also are buried at Mt. Olivet.

Although born in Baltimore, James H., Jr. was educated in Frederick public schools and Frederick City College. His leadership in milling industries, banking and as Vice President of Hood College (1942-1951) are detailed in the Hood College Magazine of Winter 1991. He and Susan had daughter Susan May and son James H. Gambrill III.

A Gambrill Genealogy (300 years) was written by Mary A. M. Bowerman (Dubuque, Iowa, 1973). Richard Gambrill of England was an ancestor of Richard Gambrill (1804-1888) born near Annapolis. (Wms. 1906).

W&M-1057. Peter G. Sauble (1858-1925) and wife Emma Amanda (Willier) (1860-1941) are buried at Beaver Dam Brethren Cemetery near Johnsville. According to a gravestone at Beaver Dam Cemetery, Peter's father William Sauble (1831-1894) married Mary A. Blizzard (1837-1915).

Rev. Jacob Lischy in York County, Pennsylvania, in 1761 baptized John Adam, infant son of Leonard and Catherine Sabel. For Sauble families of Taneytown see M&C-II.

W&M-1058. Adam Taylor Etzler (1849-1927) and wives Laura E. (Blume) (1854-1879) and Emma F. (1858-1936) are buried at Liberty Fairmount Cemetery. Adam apparently descended from three generations of Daniel Etzlers, all with gravestones at Liberty Chapel as follows:

(1) Daniel (1766-1819).
(2) Daniel II (1793-1873) m. Mary (b. c.1820).
(3) Daniel III (1821-1897) m. Mary Angeline Nusbaum.

In *Pennsylvania Archives* Third Series, Volume 21 is Andrew Etzler who paid taxes on 160 acres, three horses and five cows in 1779 in Heidelberg Township in later eastern Adams County, Pennsylvania. In the same township, George Etzler in 1779 to 1783 paid taxes on 150 acres. His household had 10 members. A third alleged Etzler brother may be John Etzler and wife over 45 years in age with five slaves in the 1800 census of Liberty District of Frederick County.

Dr. D. Wilbur Devilbiss, retired in Frederick, has written three volumes of genealogy of Etzler families as follows (F):

Volume I, John and John George Etzlers and Descendants.
Volume II, Andrew Etzler and Descendants.
Volume III, Descendants of Daniel Etzler, Jr. (grandson of Andrew).

According to Martha Davidson of Greenville, Illinois, (FH) 1925, the brothers John, Michael and Andrew Etzler arrived in Philadelphia in 1751 from Tarlogle (?), Germany. Michael had children George, Michael Jr., Elizabeth and Polly. Children of George were Mary, Magdalena, John (her grandfather), Catherine, George, Hannah who probably lived in York County before moving to Western Maryland. Her John married Mary M. Peters, daughter of Jacob, of Hagerstown. They moved to Virginia and her descendants further west.

W&M-1059. Cyrus T. Biser (1849-1915) and wife Sarah A. R. (Derr) (1849-1935) are buried at the Reformed Cemetery in Middletown. Frederick (1763-1823) born in America was the youngest son of emigrant of 1746 Jacob Beyser. See W&M-951 and (BL). The three brothers are doubted. Henry Biser (1821-1900) and wife Sophia (Routzahn) (1826-1912) are buried at Middletown Reformed Church.

W&M-1060. Howard Luther Smith (1867-1951) and wife Nellie Leona (Thomas) (1873-1951) were parents of Helen Leona Smith, born January 21, 1894, who remains active in 1994 as artist of local scenes at her studio at Old Braddock, west of Frederick. Her 100th birthday was celebrated on January 21, 1994 by a gala luncheon which filled the dining room of Hood College with relatives and friends from throughout the U.S.A. Helen's paternal grandparents were George William Smith (1832-1915) and Susan Virginia (1831-1892) who are buried at Mt. Olivet. See W&M-703 for earlier ancestors.

W&M-1060. Greenberry H. Putman (1858-1913) and wife Ida B. (Joy) (1860-1936) are buried at the Catholic Cemetery at Frederick. His parents John J. (1826-1907) and Rebecca (Shriver) (b. 1833) have gravestones in Utica Cemetery. Grandparents of Greenberry were John Putman (1793-1872) and Ann E. (1795-1883) who are buried in the northern Middletown Valley at St. John's Lutheran Church.

In the 1800 census of Middletown Valley John Putman and wife were over 45 years of age, with four sons and two daughters. A second Putman household there consisted of Jacob and wife (26-45 years) with three daughters.

W&M-1061. Joseph H. Hedges (1838-1923) and wife Ann Sophia (Kefauver) (1844-1922) are buried at Middletown Lutheran Church. His ancestor Charles Hedge (1712-1795 and wife Mary (Stille) (b. 1715) moved from north of Frederick to northwestern Middletown Valley. Many more records in the Valley are of Charles' son Shedrick or Shadrack Hedges (1753-1846) who married in 1782 Mary Dickson. Unfortunately we have no gravestones from most of the early Hedges. It is doubted that Middletown Valley was full of Indians at the time of settlement. However, a few Indian attacks are believed to have occurred near Foxville in the 1760s at the end of the French and Indian War. It was Shadrack, Jr. who married Mary M. Miller (c.1797-1869), daughter of Abraham and had sons Joseph H. and the well known Rev. Shadrack Abraham Hedges (1835-1925) who married Mary Elizabeth Hill of Shepherdstown, WV. Shadrack, Sr. and Jr. were leaders in Zion Lutheran Church of Middletown.

Among the earliest settlers in the upper Monocacy Valley were Joseph Hedges (d. 1732), and second wife Catherine Stalcop (d. 1749) with their children born in southeastern Pennsylvania. An outline is given below of their children most of whom moved to WV and further west. See my articles in the *Frederick News*, November 10 and December 1, 1990 and (FH):

(1) Solomon Hedges (1710-1801) m. Rebecca van Meter (1711-1770); to near Keyser, WV by 1740.

(2) Charles (1712-1795) m. Mary Stille or Stilley (b. 1715); Charles second m. to Isabella Wirk; many descendants in Middletown Valley.

(3) Joshua (1714-1790) m. Elizabeth Chapline; to Hedgesville, WV.

(4) Jonas (1716-1804) m. Agnes Powelson; to Berkeley County, later WV near Hedgesville.

(5) Joseph, Jr. (1718-1753) m. Mary Beckenbaugh; ancestors of Josiah Hedges founder of Tiffin, Ohio; Mary Beckenbaugh second m. to John Wilson.

(6) Samuel (b. 1720); unmarried.

(7) Ruth (b. 1722) m. Bentley in Berkeley County, WV; Ruth's second m. to Abraham van Meter (son of John); lived near Keyser, WV.

(8) Catherine (b. 1724 in Chester County, Pennsylvania) m. Thomas Shepherd; 2m Jacob Julien (d. 1747); 3m in 1747 Col. Joseph Wood (1743-1793), founder of Woodsboro (See M&C-II.)

(9) Dorcas (b. 1726 in Chester County, Pennsylvania); unmarried.

(10) (?) Peter m. Elizabeth; not in Joseph's will, but in newspaper article of Keyser, WV (FH).

Widow Catherine (Stalcop) Hedges married Isaac Bloomfield, from whom Bloomfield north of Frederick received its name. Peter above may have been a son of an unclarified other Joseph Hedges who also lived early in the Monocacy Valley.

In the Maryland Militia in the Revolutionary War were officers Lieut. William Hedge and Ensign Joseph Hedge.

W&M-1061. Thomas Arnold (1841-1923) and wife Annie L. (Ray) (1842-1880) are buried at Pleasant View Brethren Cemetery near Burkittsville. His parents were John (1795-1860) and Sarah (Karn) (1798-1878) who are shown in the 1850 census of Middletown District and also are buried at Pleasant Valley.

The grandfather of Thomas, namely Rev. David Arnold (1753-1844) of Pleasant View Church, was born in America. See W&M-1188. David's brothers and sisters moved westward. (LC)

W&M-1062. William H. Naylor (1848-1927) and wife Edith A. (Wagaman) (1855-1943) are buried at Sabillasville Reformed Church. His parents were William (1812-1882) and Rebecca Housman (c.1808-1898) also buried at Sabillasville. (LC)

W&M-1063. David T. Stup (1861-1934) and wife Hester C. (Thomas) (1863-1942) are buried at Church Hill on Ballenger Creek Road. His parents Emanuel D. (1836-1916) and wife S. Harriet P. (Webster) (1840-1910) are buried at Mt. Olivet. David's grandfather, David Stup (1801-1869) and wife Susan (Bast) (1810-1895) are buried also at Mt. Olivet at Frederick. In the 1800 census of Frederick County were two Stoup households; both Adam and Peter were in age between 26 and 45.

W&M-1064. William Hilleary Lakin (1830-1910) and wife Ellen Catherine (Kemp) (1835-1916) are buried at Jefferson Union Cemetery. His parents William (1794-1850) and wife Susan (Remsburg) (1807-1877) are buried at the Lakin family graveyard in southeastern Middletown Valley. Earlier Lakins are given in W&M-929.

W&M-1065. August W. Nicodemus, Jr. (1870-1950) and wife Annie M. (Thomas) (1874-1940) are buried at Mt. Olivet. His parents were Augustus W., Sr. (1833-1917) and Barbara A. (Fulton) (1836-1909). Buried with them at Mt. Olivet are numerous children who died in infancy. John Nicodemus married Hannah Englar (1804-1852) daughter of David Englar (c.1771-1839) and wife Elizabeth (1777-1849) who are buried at Pipe Creek Brethren Cemetery near Uniontown. For earlier generations see W&M-955 and 970 and the Englar genealogy booklet. According to descendant Kent C. Nicodemus of Walkersville the family descended from Johann Henrich born in Mendenbach, Pfalz who married Anna Maria Baile and lived later in Carroll County. Descent is through their oldest son John. See also W&M-970.

W&M-1066. Arthur A. Peddicord (1856-1921) and wife Mary Louise (Jamison) (1859-1935) are buried at the Catholic Cemetery at Libertytown, where are buried also his parents Henry Adolphus (1831-1905) and wife Mary

(Mercer) (1832-1898). A Nathan Peddycord is in the Frederick County court records of 1750.

W&M-1067. Raymond G. Ford (1868-1922) and wife Mattie J. B. (Keller) (1868-1943) are buried at Mt. Olivet. He was born in St. Mary's County. (LC)

W&M-1068. George P. Buckey (b. 1829) married Elizabeth R. Shriner (1830-1906) of Carroll County. He was a son of Ezra (1803-1858) and first wife Susan (Root) (1789-1841). Ezra is buried at the Brethren Beaver Dam Cemetery near Johnsville. Susan is buried at the Buckey family graveyard near New London.

Col. Henry Bouquet had no known descendants in Frederick County. See W&M-854.

The grandparents of George P. were George P. Buckey (1771-1862) and wife Susanna (1775-1838) who are buried at Glade Reformed Church near Walkersville. The great grandfather of George P. was Peter, emigrant from Minfield (earlier Muenfelden) in southern Pfalz. This village where Bucki families still live is not near the Rhine River as some authors have claimed. See also W&M-854.

W&M-1069. Joab W. Davis (1832-1912) and wife Elvira W. (Kindley) (1839-1890) are buried at Kemptown Methodist Church south of New Market. J. M. H. did not find gravestones of his parents, Ephraim and Elinor (Burgee). See also W&M-839.

W&M-1069. (Daniel) Oliver Sayler (1852-1912) and wife C. Bernella (1856-1922) are buried at Beaver Dam Brethren Cemetery near Johnsville, as are his parents Solomon (1823-1903) and Harriet (Albaugh) (1829-1905). Solomon Sayler, Sr. (c.1797-1863) and wife Christina also have stones in Beaver Dam Cemetery. See also W&M-1049.

W&M-1070. William B. Grimes (1838-1913) and wife Ann Louisa (Garber) (1849-1919) are buried at Haugh's Church near Ladiesburg at the northeast edge of Frederick County. In the 1850 census of the Woodsboro area lived William C. Grimes (b. c.1813), wife Elizabeth Ann (Baer) (b. c.1814) and seven children. Next to them lived Mary Grimes (b. c.1785) who may have been his mother. In Emmitsburg District in the 1800 census were households of William Grimes and wife over 45 years, with three daughters and one son; also Joshua Grimes (26-45) and wife under 26 years, who had four sons under 10 years.

W&M-1072. Charles Carnon Ridgely (1858-1934), born in Howard County, married Rachel Thomas Maynard. He was buried at Mt. Olivet. A genealogy of Ridgely, Dorsey and Greenberry families was written by Henry R. Evans (Washington, D.C., 1935) (Y). Many Ridgley papers are at Maryland Historical Society (MS 692, etc.) Five local Ridgelys served in the War of 1812.

Rachel's parents Benjamin Maynard (1819-1868) and Eliza M. P. (Claggett) (1823-1886) are buried at Mt. Olivet. See other Claggetts in W&M-864, 1281, 1344.

The Hampton Mansion built by Charles Ridgely (1733-1790) is a National Historic Site at Towson, Maryland.

W&M-1073. Charles Edgar Poole (1854-1926) and wife Harriet D. (Downey) are buried at the New London Methodist Church. His grandfather Henry Poole

(1764-1922) married Margaret James, daughter of Daniel. Their son Thornton Poole (1810-1886 and wife Rachel Ruth (Owings) (1812-1886) were buried at Liberty Catholic Church. They were parents of Charles Edgar.

There were eight Poole households in Libertytown District in the 1800 census. Of these the heads Henry, Sr. and William, and their wives were over 45 years of age. Brice, Dennis, George, Henry, Jr., Luke and Samuel were aged between 26-45 years.

A genealogy of descendants of John and Priscilla Poole of Montgomery County, Maryland was written by Martha S. Poole in 1973. Charles E. Poole from Montgomery County, Maryland, married Laura Hays of Frederick County and opened a store at Gapland on South Mountain, west of Burkittsville in 1891. (Williams 1906).

W&M-1074. Joseph M. Dronenburg (b. 1873) married Eva Horn. Jacob Dronenburg (1805-1890), grandfather of Joseph, and wife Mary M. (Madery) (1818-1883) are buried at Urbana Methodist Church. Joseph's parents were John T. Dronenburg (1842-1928) and Mary (Dixon). John T. is buried at New Market M. E. Church with a later wife Katie L. (1870-1939). Dronenburg families were discussed by George E. Russell in W. MD Genealogy, 2, 49 (1986).

Jacob Dronenburg, Sr. in 1801 married Mary Madera at the home of widow Rachel Madera near the Amelung Glass Furnace. Because some of the Amelung descendants on the Pacific coast called their mansion Madera I have considered that it might have been a Madera who engraved the art on Amelung goblets and thus made J. F. Amelung famous. Madera is said to be both a Spanish and Portuguese family name.

W&M-1075. John Henry Witter (1837-1919) and wife Annie E. (Baker) (1838-1928) are buried at Mt. Olivet as are his parents Emmanuel and wife Sarah (Baker) who lived near Boonsboro. See Williams, 1906.

W&M-1075. A. Henry Norris (1842-1916) and wife Julia Elizabeth (Gaither) (1855-1940) are buried at Unionville Methodist Church. His parents Nicholas Norris (1804-1866) and Mary Ann (McKinstry) (1816-1892) also are buried at Unionville. An earlier Henry Norris was in the Frederick County Militia of 1812.

A William Norris is in the court records of Frederick County in 1751. Thomas Norris was appointed to a committee to lay out an improved road from Frederick toward York, Pennsylvania, in 1755. There were three Norris households in Liberty District in the 1800 census. Benjamin (over 45 years) and wife (26-45) lived with six daughters and three sons. Amos and John and their wives were 26-45 years in age.

In 1800 a John Norris (over 45 years) lived in Westminster District. In 1800 in Taneytown District lived families of Nathaniel Norris (over 45) and Thomas Norris (26-45). In 1800 in Fredericktown District was the family of Samuel Norris (over 45 years) and in the Buckeystown area lived a John Norris and wife (26-45) (LC)

W&M-1077. William J. Kepler (1871-1952) and wife Mary Lizzie (Summers) (1873-1947) are buried at Middletown Lutheran Church, as were his parents William J., Sr. (1831-1894) and wife Annie M. (Beachley) (1833-1884). The grandparents of William J. were John Kepler (1804-1879) and Elisabeth (b. c.1807). In the 1800 census of Middletown District Mathias Kepler and wife were over 45 years of age. (LC)

W&M-1077. George P. Sheffer (1845-1909) and wife Amanda D. (Shank) (1845-1931) are buried at Middletown Lutheran Church, as are his parents Daniel (1807-1863) and Mary C. (Bowles) (1815-1907). A grandfather of George P. was Philip Sheffer (1776-1844).

W&M-1078. Charles Joseph Arnold (1872-1933) and wife Mary (Orrison) (1876-1928) are buried at Mt. Olivet. His parents David (1821-1899) and Mary Ann (Wiener) (1836-1921) are buried at Burkittsville Union Cemetery. For earlier Arnolds, see W&M-1188.

W&M-1078. Daniel Calvin Bready (1842-1929) and wife Maggie E. (Padgett) (1842-1911) are buried at Mt. Olivet. The Padgett family earlier lived on Carrollton Manor. Also buried at Mt. Olivet were Daniel's parents George A. Bready (1811-1894) and wife Annie E. (Boutler) (1814-1892). See W&M-854. Solomon Paggett, under 26, was head of a household in southern Frederick County in 1800.

W&M-1079. Grayson H. Staley (1881-1965) and wife Bertha Frances (Coblentz) (1883-1935) are buried at Mt. Olivet. He was the fifth child of Joseph Edward (1847-1924) and wife Clara A. C. (Angleberger) (1848-1931) of near Rocky Springs. Joseph E. was a son of Joseph and grandson of Jacob, Jr. and wife Catherine Barbara. Jacob Stehli (1698-1760), one of three emigrating brothers, married Margaretha Rebstock (d. 1761). (S) See W&M-901.

W&M-1080. Charles J. Doll (1859-1930) and wife Mary (Cramer) (1867-1931) are buried at Mt. Olivet as are Roger Allen Doll (1872-1958) and wife Eva (Sanders) (b. 1872). The parents of Charles were George C. Doll (1829-1895) and wife A. Elizabeth B. (Wisong) (1834-1909) who are buried at Mt. Olivet also.

The German name is Doll, but in Germany it is pronounced close to Dull. In the 1800 census of Fredericktown District were Joseph and wife over 45 years in age living with four daughters and three sons. Joseph, Jr. and wife were between 26-45 years old, living with three children under 10 years. See also W&M-844. A genealogy of Doll families (1672-1972) was written by Charles E. Doll III of Mt. Clement, MI in 1972. (F)

W&M-1080. William L. Boteler (1859-1934) and wife Lily S. (Stewart) (1864-1953) are buried at Mt. Olivet. His parents Benjamin A. (1825-1906) and Ellen (Thomas) (1823-1903) are buried at Urbana Methodist Church. Probable great grandparents of William L. were Henry A. Boteler (1766-1943) and wife Mary (1776-1858) who are buried at Jefferson Union Cemetery. Boteler families of western Maryland are discussed by Williams (1906).

An ancestor of Boteler and Butler families was claimed to be Simon de Bouteller, a Norman Captain of Cavalry, serving William the Conqueror in 1066. Descendants Henry, Charles and Rupert Boteler early received grants of land near Upper Marlboro in Prince George's County. An Edward Boteler who married Priscilla Lingan was progenitor of Botelers in Frederick County. A

Henry Boteler married Ellen Elsby and settled at Browningsville in Washington County. (Wms. 1906).

W&M-1081. David M. Warner (1848-1898) and wife Jane E. (Martz) (1854-1939) are buried at Woodsboro Mt. Hope Cemetery. His parents Emanuel (1820-1881) and Margaret (1818-1882) are buried at Haugh's Church north of Woodsboro.

It is improbable that German Martz ancestors emigrated to America in 1700. See W&M-775 and 1591. The name Warner is a dialect form of German family name Werner or Woerner. It is probable that some early Warners of English origin were in western Maryland. A John Warner of Prince George's County was in the Frederick County court records of 1751.

Four Warner families are in the 1800 census of Westminster District of which John and wife were over 45 years in age. Warner family records without author and date are at Westminster (W). (LC)

W&M-1082. Thomas William Fogle (1839-1921) and wife Lydia Ann (Fox) (1835-1931) are buried at Woodsboro Mt. Hope Cemetery. His parents apparently were William and Margaret (Strine) (1820-1878). Margaret is buried at Rocky Hill Cemetery near Woodsboro. The grandparents of Thomas W. were John (b. c.1786) and wife Catherine (Eyler) (b. c.1791).

Andrew Vogel (Fogle) (1727-1786) from Hettenhausen near Fulda, Germany about 1747 settled near Rocky Hill Church. He married Susannah Catherine Bager (Baugher). (B1)

Andreas and Susanna Catherine Fogle had children baptized at Rocky Hill Church: Mattheis, 1768; Johan Baltzer, 1771; Elisabeth, 1773. Seven other children are given in *Anders Root Directory* by Norman C. Anders. (FH)

The *Genealogy of Fogle and Strine Families* by Alma Thomas Fogle (1976) (F) begins with Baltzer Vogel (1800-1862) and wife Margaret (Wetzel) (1804-1884) who are buried at Haugh's Church. From them six generations of Fogles are given. Paul E. Fogle of Middletown is studying Fogle families. Descendants of Balser Fogle (1816-1891) have been studied by Kenneth E. Fogle of Frederick (1971).

W&M-1083. Andrew D. Arnold (1866-1939) and wife Amanda Catherine (Young) (1866-1956) are buried at Burkittsville Union Cemetery. His parents were David (1821-1899) and wife Mary Ann (Wiener) (1836-1921) who are also buried at Burkittsville. See W&M-1188 for descent from emigrant Georg Arnold.

W&M-1083. Chester M. Hauver (1867-1920) and wife Effie V. (Eccord) (1872-1953) are buried at Mt. Olivet. His parents were Melancthon (1841-1924) and Rebecca (Buhrman) (1842-1924) who are buried at Foxville Lutheran Church. Chester's grandparents were Christian Hauver (1801-1869) and wife Mary (Brown) (1803-1883) who also are buried at Foxville. Names of Chester's great grandfather Peter and some other early Hauvers were written as Haber, a well known German family name.

W&M-1084. Nathan Addison Englar (1849-1909) and wife Leanna (Wolfe) (1856-1913) are buried at Mt. View Cemetery at Union Bridge. The parents of

Nathan A. were Nathan (1806-1883) and wife Margaret (Kinzer) (1810-1885) who are buried at the Brethren Cemetery at Beaver Dam near Johnsville.

A booklet *The Englar Family* was written by Philip Englar. It is believed that emigrant Philip (1736-1817) and brother Jacob came from Switzerland, perhaps from Appenzell. Philip married Margaret Holverstot (1742-1819); both are buried at Wolfe's Cemetery south of Union Bridge. Philip was a Minister of the Pipe Creek Brethren Church. Their fourth child was Elder David Englar (1773-1839) who married Elizabeth Stem (1777-1849) and also preached at Pipe Creek. Both are buried at Pipe Creek Cemetery. Their third child Hannah Englar (1804-1852) married John Nicodemus (1801-1871). Hannah and John Nicodemus, who farmed near Frederick, had children: Nathan; John Lewis (1828-1904) m. Nancy Cassell (Castle) (1831-1902), daughter of David; Augustus W. (W&M-970) and Eli (1840-1919). John and Nancy were parents of Dr. John David Nicodemus (1854-1938) who married Rebecca Nelson (1858-1927). Their children are given in W&M-1509.

W&M-1085. Millard Fillmore Culler (1855-1924) and wife Annie C. (Remsburg) (1855-1912) are buried at Jefferson Union Cemetery. His parents, Daniel (1810-1894) and wife Anna Mary (Hargett) (1815-1891), also are buried at Jefferson Union Cemetery.

The claim that three Culler brothers emigrated together is unsubstantiated. Jacob Koller (d. 1765) emigrated in 1749. He is believed to have had three sons, Michael, Jacob, Jr. and Andrew. A Jacob Koller surveyed 30 acres in Bucks County, Pennsylvania in 1745 (Pennsylvania Archives, Third Series 24, 139). A John Koller was taxed for 100 acres, two horses and two cattle in Greenwich Township, Berks County in 1767. A Jacob Koller was taxed in Richmond Township, Berks County in 1785. In the Monocacy Lutheran records Jacob Koller and wife Magdalena had son Johannes Heinrich, born in October 1755.

Emigrant Jakob Koller (d. 1765) by his second wife Elisabeth had Jacob, Jr. and Andrew whose wife was Charlotte. Jacob, Jr. and wife Mary Magdalena had sons as follow:

(1) John (c.1742-1796) m. Anna Maria Miller.

(2) Michael (1745-1818) m. 1772 Eleanor Schmidt (1747-1806), (d/o Jacob and Catherine).

(3) Jacob III (c.1749-1773) m. Elisabeth Miller (d/o Jacob of Hunting Creek).

Michael Culler (1745-1796) settled about 1768 on tract Den of Wolves, north of Frederick. He sold this in 1774 and moved to Middletown Valley.

Millard Rice in his book *New Facts and Old Families* (1976) gives dates of eight children of Michael and Eleanor, also of two later generations. Three of Michael's sons, namely Jacob, Philip and Michael, Jr. migrated to Ohio.

The census of 1800 shows that Michael Koller, over 45 years, had moved to Middletown Valley while Jacob, also over 45 years, was still living north of Frederick with five daughters. Records of Zion Lutheran Church of Middletown record that Michael was a church official in 1789. Michael and wife Eleanor had a daughter Susannah baptized there in 1781. A Jacob Koller was a deacon at Zion Church in 1806 and in 1822. A Jacob and wife Elisabeth had son Michael born in 1803. John Koller (1774-1847) and wife Anna Mary had son Jacob born in 1808. Capt. Henry (1786-1861) and wife Anna (1789-1856) had Col. Henry, Jr. (1817-1873) and Jacob (b. 1822).

W&M-1086. John W. O. Ahalt (1852-1925) and wife Amanda Jennie (McDuell) (1855-1930) are buried at Middletown Lutheran Church, where also are buried his parents Jacob B. (1811-1863) and wife Mary A. (Smith) (1813-1887). See also W&M-988.

W&M-1087. Nicholas O. Cline (1834-1910) and wife Anna A. (Michael) (1842-1922) are buried at Mt. Olivet, as are his parents Casper (1795-1871), born at Abbottstown, Pennsylvania, and wife Catherine (Evans) (1798-1854), who also are buried at Mt. Olivet. Casper married secondly Corilla Evans (1801-1882), sister of his first wife. The grandfather of Nicholas was Alexander Cline, born at Waterford, Ireland. Casper served in the Frederick County Militia of 1812. (LC)

W&M-1089. Rufus R. Zimmerman married Anna Maria (Blessing) (c.1842-1899) who is buried at Mt. Olivet Cemetery. Also buried there are his parents Elias Zimmerman (1819-1902) and wife Anna Maria (Greenwald) (1819-1901).

Early settlers near Carrollton Manor were (Johan) George Zimmerman (1714-1795) and wife Catherine (Seidel) (1724-1804). Grandson George Zimmerman (1784-1865) was buried at Zion Church, Feagaville. He married Charlotte Young (1784-1855) who was a grandmother of Rufus. See W&M-979.

W&M-1091. Luther Adolphus Horine (1857-1895) and wife Anna V. (Culler) (1861-1941) are buried at Jefferson Union Cemetery, where also are buried his parents Joel (1823-1943) and Catherine (Koontz) (1829-1909). See W&M-1009 for earlier Horines. In 1800 in Middletown Valley lived Jacob Coontz and wife, both between 26 and 45 years of age.

W&M-1091. David Michael Barrack (1841-1914) and wife Lillie A. (Mayne) (1843-1914) are buried at Glade Reformed Cemetery near Walkersville, where also are buried his parents Jacob (1805-1878) and wife Catherine (Smith) (1811-1852). David's grandfather was Peter Barrick (1763-1841).

The emigrant was Johan Wilhelm Berg (Barrack) born in Nordhofen in Westerwald, Germany, in 1683 (son of Johan Peter) (T&D). He married Johanata Maria Andreas. The dialect word for Berg in High German meaning hill or mountain is Barrack, but Barrick has been used.

William Berg leased a farm on Monocacy Manor in 1742; Christian Berg and John Berg leased farms there in 1743. The 1800 census of the Fredericktown District shows George and William Barrach and their wives (all 26-45 years of age) with children under 10 years. In 1800 in Emmitsburg District lived John Barrack and wife, both over 45 years. In 1800 in Taneytown District lived John Barrack, Sr. and wife over 45; also John Barrack, Jr. and wife 26-45 years. In 1800 in Libertytown District lived seven Barrack families. The heads of households who were over 45 years were Catherine, Christian and Jacob. Only Christian and Jacob had slaves. In the same District was Henry Barrick and wife, both 26-45. J. M. H. has three pages of local Barricks with gravestones. A genealogy of Barrick (Berg) families has been written by Vincent P. Barrick of D.C. (F) (GC). In the War of 1812 at least nine Barricks served. See also

Barrick (Berg) Families of Frederick County by Eloise Barrick Weller (Evansville, IN, 1989) (F).

Susan Catherine (Barrick) (1840-1916) and husband John Lincoln McMaster (b. 1852) have gravestones in Glade Reformed Cemetery near Walkersville. Their son LeRoy McMaster (1879-1946) was a chemist and educator in St. Louis, MO (NC, Vol. 34). His ancestor William McMaster, a native of Ayrshire, Scotland, was brought to the U.S. as a British prisoner in 1777 and settled in Gettysburg.

W&M-1092. Richard Schaffer Hargett (b. 1881) married Laura Maud Riggs. He has a gravestone at Mt. Olivet Cemetery which lacks dates. His parents were John E. (1838-1924) and wife Ellen (Zimmerman). Riggs families were early in Montgomery County, where near Brookeville John and Samuel Riggs owned large tracts in early 1700s.

W&M-1092. (Ransom) Rush Lewis (1864-1953) and wife Laura (Yerkes) (1860-1924) are buried at Mt. Olivet, as are his parents Jacob (1813-1853) and Elizabeth (Winger) (1832-1913). Rush Lewis had a second marriage to Margaret Duvall (1870-1947) (Mt. Olivet). Jacob had an earlier marriage to Delia (1813-1853) (Mt. Olivet). Descendant Elizabeth Lewis Peters taught English in China and was a supporter of the Historical Society of Frederick County. She died in 1989 at 90 years. (LC).

W&M-1093. Dr. Edgar Howard Willard, (b. 1887) was a son of Charles Francis (1857-1915) and wife Ann Rebecca (Hoskinson) (1859-1915) who are buried at Burkittsville Union Cemetery. Grandparents of Dr. Edgar were Ezra Willard (b. c.1821) and wife Laurette. In 1850 Ezra lived with his mother Mary Willard (b. c.1781). This gives a bridge to the Willard lineage outlined in my article of August 21, 1991 in the *Frederick News*. Dr. Edgar can be traced from Europe as follows:

(1) Nicolaus Vieilliard (b. c.1635) m. Katharina Grosjean. They fled from France to Erlenbach near Kaiserslautern in southwest Germany.

(2) Jacob (1667-1717) m. Maria Elisabeth Gordier (1682-1770); she is buried at Graceham.

(3) Dewalt Williard (1711-1782) m. Anna Katherine Kirch (d. 1813) (Reformed Church Middletown Records).

(4) Elias Williard (1734-1819) m. Rosina Gumpf (1743-1819).

(5) John Willard (1777-1831) m. Mary Schaefer (1781-1869); buried Burkittsville Union Cemetery; parents of Ezra.

As late as the 1850 census more descendants were using the spelling Williard than Willard. It is believed that the French form of the family name was derived from a village in France.

While early Dewalt Willard moved westward to Middletown, his brother Peter and mother settled in the Moravian colony at Graceham and were ancestors of many Willards around Thurmont and adjacent Catoctin Mountain, including "mountain man" George A. Willard, who was reputed to have discouraged President Herbert Hoover from fishing in Little Hunting Creek.

(1) Peter Williar (1714-1794) m. Elizabeth Schlim (1722-1792).

(2) Andrew Williar (1758-1827) m. Margaret Harbaugh (1761-1819).
(3) Charles Williard (b. 1795) m. Elizabeth Ricksecker (1798-1834).
(4) Hiram Alexander Willard (1824?-1901) m. Mary Jane Roberson (?) (1833-1887).
(5) William Kelly Willard (1860-1952) m. Anna Maria Hauver (1866-1959).
(6) George Allen Willard (1884-1974) m. Mae Harne (b. 1907). The former farm of George on Catoctin Mountain west of Catoctin furnace adjoined Mink Farm Road at the head of Catoctin Hollow Road. Children of George and Mae are Harold Ralph m. Ruth M. Lewis; Herbert Eugene m. Mary E. Anders; Roy Milton m. Mary C. Eckenrode; (George) Arthur m. Mary P. Green. The brother of George Allen, still living at Foxville, is Clifford D. Willard, Sr.

Margaret (Harbaugh) Williar was a daughter of George Harbaugh and Catherine (Williar) and a granddaughter of (Johan) Peter Herbach of Harbaugh Valley, whose emigrant father Jost Herbach died at Kreutz Creek Settlement near Hellam, Pennsylvania. (LC)

W&M-1093. John T. Norwood (b. 1872) married Carrie Miller. His parents were Lorenzo B. Norwood (1848-1926) buried at Kemptown Methodist Church and Jennie (Fleming) (according to W&M). Buried beside Lorenzo is wife Elizabeth W. (1850-1929). See W&M-1216.

W&M-1094. Cornelius William Virts (1865-1941) and wife Mary S. (Grimm) (1866-1958) are buried at Middletown Reformed Cemetery, where also are buried his parents Cornelius (1825-1906) and Catherine (Ellen) (1834-1892). Virts ancestry in Washington County is given by Williams (1906).

W&M-1094. Edward M. L. Lighter (1858-1939) and wife Jennie G. (Sanner) (1868-1947) are buried in Middletown Reformed Cemetery as are his parents, Charles H. Lighter (1834-1917) and wife Virginia E. (Grove) (1834-1880). Edward's grandparents were Lawson Lighter (1810-1855) and Catherine (Bowlus) (1812-1895). In the 1800 census of Middletown Valley John Henry Lighter was over 45 years of age and his wife between 26 and 45. They had four daughters and five sons. See also W&M-889.

W&M-1095. John R. Roelke (1866-1943) and wife Vernie V. (Karn) (1867-1937) are buried at Mt. Olivet. His parents were C. L. Peter Roelke (1824-1892) and Mary Ellen (Anderson) (1828-1917) daughter of Robert and Mary Ann. They are buried at Mt. Olivet also. Grandparents of John R. were John Roelke (1782-1855) and Dorothea Justina (1791-1859) who are buried at the Reformed Church of Frederick. Dates of emigration from Hesse of a number of Roelkes are given in M&C-II. The spelling Roelkey is used by some families. Cf. W&M-1541. (LC)

W&M-1096. Christian H. Eckstein (b. 1845) married Mary K. (Feinour) (1846-1922) who is buried at Mt. Olivet. His parents, Christian, Sr. (1822-1843) and wife Elizabeth (Kepple) (1823-1892), also are buried at Mt. Olivet.

W&M-1098. John Emmert Price (1840-1909) and wife Mary C. (Ordeman) (1851-1932) are buried at Mt. Olivet. German Preis or Price families are discussed (BE).

Prices of English origin were in Frederick County early. A Thomas Price was Constable of Fredericktown Hundred in 1753. A Benjamin Price is in the court records of Frederick County in 1754 and was a Justice in 1763-1765. Joseph Price in 1763 was one of the Constables paid 400 pounds of tobacco for suppressing "tumultuous meetings of negroes."

Price families of Frederick County were discussed in Maryland-DE Genealogy, Winter/Spring 1990. Col. Thomas Price, son of Capt. John and Rebecca (King) was born in Philadelphia in 1732 and died in Frederick County in 1795. Thirteen names of children were given. (LC)

W&M-1098. Harry C. Hickman (1870-1948) married Mary E. Ritchie. He, and parents George H. C. (1844-1911) and wife Mary E. (Ritchie) (1852-1936), are buried at Point of Rocks Episcopal Church. William Hickman, a grandfather of Harry, was married to Eliza Everhart, a daughter of Philip and Laura, and a niece of Lawrence Everhart. In 1800 Christopher Hickman, over 45 years, and wife under 45 lived in Frederick District. (LC)

W&M-1100. Morris R. Holter (1865-1950) married Cora E. R. (Main). His parents were George B. (1829-1908) and wife Ann Mary E. (Coblentz) (1837-1910) who are buried in the Reformed Cemetery at Middletown. Grandparents of Morris were William Holter (1795-1868) and Margaret (Beard) (1800-1860). Great grandparents of Morris were George Holter and wife Margaret (Arnold) (1755-1830) (Zion Church near Feagaville).

A genealogy of Holter families has been written by David S. Shue (Middletown, 1978). (LC). The only Holter recorded as emigrating via Philadelphia was Hans Adam, arriving in September 1751.

W&M-1101. Otis O. Arnold (1870-1952) and wife Mary S. (Herring) (1868-1925) are buried at Mt. Olivet. His parents Mahlon S. C. (c.1835-1898) and Mary Ellen (1848-1894) are buried at Pleasant View Church near Burkittsville. Mahlon's parents were John Arnold (b. c.1794), son of Rev. David, and Sarah (b. c.1800). See W&M-1188. In the 1800 census of Middletown Valley Casper Herring and wife (both between 26 and 45 years) had three daughters and two sons.

W&M-1101. John Howard Allnutt (1865-1915) is buried at St. Joseph's Church on Manor. His grandparents were Robert D. and wife Mary M. (Danson) (1788-1855), also buried at St. Joseph's Church. John's parents were William P. (1810-1888) and wife Helen S. (Jewell) (1833-1879), buried at the same place. (LC)

W&M-1102. Daniel Vincent Beachley (1868-1948) married Mary L. Rudy and they attended Zion Lutheran Church at Middletown. His parents were Ezra (1832-1909) and Sarah E. (Sanner) (1837-1913) buried at Middletown Reformed Church. Daniel's grandparents were Daniel Beachley (1802-1874) and Esther (1807-1845), buried at the same place.

In the 1800 census of Middletown Valley was the household of Henry Beagly who was over 45 years in age; his wife was under 45. they had four daughters and four sons. (LC)

W&M-1104. Dr. Thomas S. Eader, D.D.S. (1860-1952) and wife Catherine R. (Ebert) (1860-1928) are buried at Mt. Olivet, as are his parents Augustus L. (1819-1907) and wife Ann M. (Mann) (1838-1919). Also buried at Mt. Olivet are grandparents of Dr. Thomas, namely Thomas Eader (1790-1847) and wife Margaret (Weaver) (1793-1860).

In the 1800 census there were two Weaver households in Frederick District. Christian and Michael and their wives were all above 45 years of age. Each had sons and daughters.

Besides Thomas and Margaret Eader others in records of the Frederick County Militia of 1812 were Lazarus Eader (d. 1858) and wife Catherine (Carnes) (1800-1880), also William M. Eader (1791-1865) and wife Ann (Stalling).

W&M-1105. Newton R. Schaeffer and second wife Elizabeth C. (Stone) (1855-1920) are buried at Mt. Olivet. His first wife Fannie A. (Fulmer) (1862-1881), who died soon after marriage, is buried at Feagaville Zion Cemetery. Newton's parents John H. Schaeffer (1807-1887) and wife Sarah (Shann) are buried at Church Hill on Ballinger Creek Road.

In 1800 in Buckeystown District lived widow Susanna Shaffer with one daughter. There were two other Shaffer households, of Peter, John and their wives, all between 26 and 45 years of age.

W&M-1106. Dr. T. Clyde Routson, M.D. (1873-1947) and wife Margaret M. (Millard) (1878-1944) are buried at Mt. Olivet. This spelling of the family name is prevalent around Uniontown in Carroll County. Some of their gravestones were recorded in J. M. H., Vol. III. John Routsong from New Windsor, who married Catherine Biser in 1816, was enrolled in the Frederick County Militia of 1812. See W&M-756 and (R).

W&M-1108. John Lewis Green (1872-1917) and wife Carrie May (Barrick) (1874-1950) are buried at Mt. Olivet. Joseph D. (1842-1906) and wife Sarah I. (1849-1915) also are buried at Mt. Olivet. Douglas Green (1811-1915) and wife Lydia E. (Wiles) are buried at Lewistown Methodist Church. In 1800 Samuel Green (over 45 years) and Luke Green (26-45 years) lived in Middletown District.

Greens were early in southern Frederick County. In 1747 Abraham bought a tract called William and Elizabeth near later Urbana from William Mears, whose wife was Elizabeth. Near later Emmitsburg, Arnold Elder, son of pioneer settler William Elder, married Clotilda Green. After his death, she married Roger Brooke.

Many Greens enrolled in the Frederick County Militia of 1812. These included Francis of Middletown; George of Woodsboro; Henry of Washington County; John; Joseph of Emmitsburg; Joshua (to Ohio); Lawrence of Catoctin District; Lewis, married Eliza Cary at Frederick; Lewis of Libertytown; and Samuel.

W&M-1109. Raymond C. Reich (1834-1903) and wife Phoebe (Delashmutt) (1840-1915) are buried at Mt. Olivet, as were also his parents Philip (1797-1892) and wife Rebecca D. H. (Ayers) (1807-1870). In Fredericktown District in the 1800 census John Reich and wife (26-45 years) lived with nine children.

W&M-1109. George D. Lease (1866-1936) and wife Ida Elizabeth (Dinterman) (1865-1945) are buried at Glade Reformed Cemetery near Walkersville, where are buried also his parents Oliver Daniel (1839-1917) and wife Minerva (Zimmerman) (1835-1911). The grandparents of George D. were Daniel Lease and wife Catherine (Sheetenhelm) (1802-1887), buried at McKaig east of Frederick. See also W&M-789. In the 1800 census of Liberty District were households of Frederick Sheetenhelm and wife (both over 45 years) and Jacob Sheetenhelm, under 26 years.

W&M-1110. Harry W. Bowers (1864-1918) and wife Anna I. (Fox) (1868-1935) are buried at Mt. Olivet at Frederick, as are his parents William D. (1828-1888) and Charlotte E. (Routzahn) (1835-1907). The grandparents of Harry W. were Daniel Bowers (1795-1872) and wife Margaret (1794-1854), buried at Beaver Dam Brethren Cemetery near Johnsville. Their son William D. and wife Charlotte who lived in Frederick had children as follows:

(1) Joseph Edmund (1857-1924) m. Emma Kate ---- (1857-1925).

(2) Cora E. (1859-1946) m. Thomas M. Haller (1855-1935).

(3) D. Jerney (1862-1879).

(4) Harry W. m. Anna I. Fox (daughter of Charles). Lumber business and later Clerk of the Court. Children: Clara, Elizabeth, Viola R., William D., and Harry Hubert.

(5) Ralph R. (c.1867-1938) m. Harriet M. Quynn (1866-1942).

(6) Grayson E. (1871-1951) m. Chrysse Byrd Dell Firestone (c.1870-1966) (daughter of Martin Luther Firestone and Katherine Virginia (Gall) of Martinsburg, WV).

William D. Bowers (1826-1888) with Joseph Routzahn started the Bowers Lumber County of Frederick in 1868. Descendants of William D. and Charlotte have continued to operate the company, now at Walkersville (operated by G. Hunter Bowers at 95 years and one of his grandsons).

Children of Grayson and Chrysse Bowers follow:

(1) G. Hunter (b. 1897) m. Isabel Houck (c.1900-1961) (daughter of Charles and Virginia (Cromwell)). Children: G. Hunter, Jr.; Dr. Charles R. of Anderson, IN; Mrs. Robert G. Butler of Utah.
G. Hunter's second marriage to Frances Good; live in Frederick.

(2) Dr. Ralph F. (b. c.1899, deceased) m. Ruth Worman (1901-1978) (daughter of William J. and Mary); lived in Memphis, TN. Children: Ralph F., Jr. of Columbia, MO; Mrs. Betsy Dolan of Asheville, NC.

(3) Charles F. (Fritz) (c.1901-1980) m. Catherine Dean (d. 1980); architect of Frederick. Children: Charles F., Jr. at Hagerstown; Virginia Dean m. Jack T. Wood.

(4) Martin L. (1905-1971) m. Helen Potter of New York City (1905-1986); with Lumber Company. Children (triplets): Martin L., Jr. m. Natalie Colbert; Grayson R. of Emmitsburg; Sally m. Landon M. Proffitt, live in Frederick.

An article about the career of survivor Hunter Bowers appeared in the Sons of American Revolution Magazine of Spring 1992. Lt. Hunter was an early ROTC graduate who served in the 24th U.S. Cavalry Division against Pancho Villa on the Mexican Border. At 95 years he was first in seniority of SAR members in Maryland and fifth of the 27,000 members of SAR in the U.S. (LC)

W&M-1111. David Kemp Cramer (1855-1909) and wife Fannie (Mercer) (1860-1946) are buried at New London. His parents Ezra Lewis Cramer (1825-1900) and Henrietta (Kemp) (1835-1896) are buried at Mt. Olivet.

The John George Cramer (c.1738-1796) claimed here as first in Frederick County married Maria Magdalena Holtz. They settled on "Dulany Manor" probably meaning Dulany's Lot next to Monocacy Manor. There is no stone of his son John who died about 1820 and had a brother Henry. John's son Ezra Cramer (1797-1859) and wife Mary (Winebrenner) (1792-1872) are buried in Glade Reformed Cemetery near Walkersville. They were parents of Ezra Lewis Cramer.

The only Cramer deed at Frederick Courthouse before 1778 is that of Casper, who bought land near later Taneytown in 1774. It was on a branch of Alloway Creek and near Brooke's Discovery on Rich Lands.

W&M-1113. (Henry) Dorsey Etchison (1867-1939) and second wife Mary Helen (Ward) (1885-1935) are buried in Mt. Olivet Cemetery, where also are buried his parents Henry Nelson Etchison (1827-1903) born in Jefferson and wife Mary E. (Louthan) (1840-1873). The only child of lawyer Dorsey and Mary Helen to reach maturity is James Milton (b. 1908) of Frederick who in 1936 married Helen m. Delaplane (1910-1990) daughter of Frank Delaplane (1872-1945) and Alice (Cash) (1871-1957). The maternal grandparents of Jim Etchison were John H. and Claudia Hillard (Ward) of Montgomery County. Dorsey Etchison's first wife Sarah A. (1831-1862) is buried at Mt. Olivet.

Frederick Etchison (1785-1832), saddler, and wife Christiana (Day) (1780-1865) lived in Jefferson. Their son Henry Nelson, a carpenter and undertaker who moved to Frederick, was married three times. With first wife Sarah Lingan (Boteler) were born sons Marshall Lingan Etchison (1851-1919) and William Hezekiah Boteler Etchison (1857-1914); with second wife Mary E. (Louthan) was born (Henry) Dorsey; there were no children from Henry Nelson's marriage to Mrs. Hepzabah Etchison Davis (Smith) who is buried at Kemptown.

Marshall L. Etchison of Frederick will be long remembered as a musician, historian and collector of books, paintings and furniture most precious in local history. His Marshall Etchison Collection presented to the Historical Society of Frederick County is the only one of its kind. The collection includes three music books written by John Thomas Schley and the following books printed by Matthias Bartgis at Pleasant Dale, northwest of Frederick: *History of the American Revolution in Scripture Style* (in English, 1823) (probably written by Richard Snowden); *History of the American Revolution* (in German, 1809); *Maryland Pocket Companion* by a Gentleman of the Bar (1819); *New Guide to the English Tongue* by Thomas Dilworth (no date); *New German ABC* (1795); *Pious County Parishioner* (1808). Marshall Etchison married Sybelle M. Mullinix (1852-1933). They are buried at Mt. Olivet Cemetery.

William H. B. Etchison (1857-1914) operated a furniture store at 18 South Market Street, Frederick. He married Josephine Pearre (1861-1947) of Unionville. They were parents of Josephine P. Etchison who, beginning in 1938, administered the C. Burr Artz Public Library of Frederick for 30 years. Her brother William P. died in 1929. Her brother Carol Lee Etchison (1899-1977) managed electroplating of chromium and nickel for the Everedy Company in Frederick. Carol encouraged this writer in industrial chemistry by giving him brief employment before he joined DuPont. Carol married Emma Taylor (d 1966) and secondly Mary Brewer.

John G. Etchison (c.1823-1880) was a carpenter and undertaker (beginning 1848) in Jefferson; probably he was a son of Frederick and Christiana. John married Julia Ann Cochran (c.1827-1903). Their son McKendree Reiley Etchison (1864-1952) married Anne Jeanette Kessler and they lived in Frederick. Their oldest son was Rev. Dr. Page McKendree Etchison (1892-1952) who was a leader in religion in D.C. for 35 years. He was President of the American Bible Society. Page married Lucille Shannon (b. 1894). His brother Bruce lived in Hagerstown. Anne and McKendree had daughter Julia who after an outstanding career as teacher at Frederick High School married John H. Hanna, Jr. Julia's sister married Harry M. McDonald, Professor at Towson State University. Anne and McKendree's son (Arthur) Hart Etchison (c.1899-1982) married Marjorie Lantz and continued the family traditional vocation as an undertaker in Frederick.

Other Etchison families have lived around Monrovia and New Market. Thomas H. (1817-1893) and wife Mary E. (1822-1881) are buried at the M. E. Church at New Market; also there were Byron (1847-1921) and wife Mary F. (1853-1919).

Etchison families have been numerous and prominent further east in Maryland. A genealogy titled *The Etchison Family from Scotland to Montgomery County, Maryland* in two volumes has been published in Georgia. James Day of Montgomery County has a genealogy of Etchisons of Maryland in progress. (LC)

W&M-1115. Russell Paxton Hilleary (1875-1953) and wife Edith Baldwin (McKown) (1877-1949) are buried at Petersville Episcopal Church, where are also his parents Thomas (1827-1917) and wife Mary Elizabeth (1836-1922). Russell's grandparents Henry Hilleary (1791-1834) and wife Cornelia (Williams) (d 1838) also are buried at Petersville. Henry's gravestone states that he was a son of Thomas II and Anne (Perry). Cornelia's stone records that she was a daughter of Walter II and Anne (McGill) Williams.

The 1800 census of Buckeystown District records two Hillary households, those of Ozburn, age 26-45 years, and Thomas, over 45 years, wife 26-45 years, six sons, three daughters and two slaves. In 1800 in Middletown District were heads of families John Hillery, over 45 years with 24 slaves, and Thomas Hillery, (26-45) living alone.

W&M-1116. Capt. Philip L. Hiteshew (1840-1910) and wife Frances A. (Wilcoxon) (1848-1904) are buried at Mt. Olivet. His parents in the 1850 census were Daniel (1804-1853) and wife Susan (Grinder) (b. c.1809). In the 1800 census of Taneytown District of old Frederick County were five Hiteshew heads of families. Jacob was over 45 years of age, Nicolas, Peter, Philip and William were under 45.

W&M-1117. Mehrl F. Moberly (1870-1944) and wife Mamie E. (Neidhart) (1869-1896) are buried at Mt. Olivet, where also are buried his parents Charles E. (1839-1911) and Frances E. (Reynolds) (1843-1922). Farming in New Market District in 1850 were Thomas Mobberly (b. c.1784) and wife Elizabeth (b. c.1790). (LC)

W&M-1118. Preston Sweadner Devilbiss (1858-1887) and wife Mary L. (Buckey) (1859-1951) are buried at Glade Reformed Cemetery. His parents John Hanson Devilbiss (1824-1871) and Jane R. (Walker) (1822-1899) are buried at New London Methodist Church. Ancestors of John Hanson were George Devilbiss (1715-1785), emigrant at 16 years who married Anna Catherine Stull. Their son Adam (1750-1784) married Catherine Barrick (b. 1760). Their son David (1788-1856) married Elizabeth Campbell (1794-1866) and had son John H. Devilbiss.

George, 16 years, and Casper Devilbiss, 10 years, apparently brothers emigrated from Germany in 1731. On the same ship were Hans Michel, 22, another Hans Michel, 18, and Magdalena Develbesin, 18. A large two volume genealogy of descendants of George (1715-1785) was prepared by Dr. (David) Wilbur Devilbiss of Frederick in 1976 (F). A small booklet entitled *Devilbiss Family in U.S., 200 Years*, by Thomas D. DeVilbiss (Fort Wayne, IN, 1927) treats some descendants of Casper in Frederick Co. and the Middle West (F). The Devilbiss Camp Meeting site near Lewistown at the foot of Catoctin Mountain is mentioned. Raiders from the mountain interrupted services by "letting down the ropes" of the tent. However, old Elder Grub tarred the ropes, leading to a popular song. Rev. John Wesley Devilbiss who went to Texas as a missionary started the use, in the Mid-west, of the capital V in the family name with change of accent to make it sound like a French name.

Educator and genealogist Dr. D. Wilbur Devilbiss, President Em. of Salisbury State University on Eastern Shore, is retired and living in Frederick in 1994. His descent is from emigrant George Adam (1750-1784); Adam Jr. (1794-1883); Basil Pinkney (1831-1899) and Susan Ann (Naill) (1839-1879) of near Johnsville; David McClellan and Ida Belle (Etzler) of Johnsville. Dr. (David) Wilbur (b. 1904) married Bernice Barbara Ryan (b. 1905) who shares his interest in family history.

W&M-1118. Dr. Charles H. Diller, M.D. (1851-1919) and wife Anna Virginia (Saylor) (1850-1922) are buried at Woodsboro Mt. Hope Cemetery. His parents John (1822-1890) and Margaret Ellen (Cramer) (1830-1911) are also buried there. Martin Diller settled near Johnsville. Martin (1792-1861) and wife Rachel (Wolf) (1791-1849) are buried at Rocky Hill Church near Woodsboro. They were parents of John above.

Diller genealogies available include *Diller Genealogy* by Lynn M. Diller (1975) (WN); *Caspar Diller and Descendants of Lancaster County* by J. L. Ringwalt, et al (Philadelphia, 1877, continued 1942) (L); *Descendants of Martin Diller* (who moved from New Holland, Pennsylvania to Johnsville in 1828) by C. H. Diller (New Holland, Pennsylvania, 1910).

John Hanson Diller of Liberty District married Ida Kreglo. John Kregelo (1784-1871) is buried at Taneytown Lutheran Church. Germanic word endings in "o" are very old in Gothic language. Kregelo families have been found in Bad Marienburg, middle Germany (*Westerwald to America* by Annette K. Burgert and H. Z. Jones, Camden, Maine, 1989). Johan Henry Kreglo (1734-1787) emigrated from Germany in 1753 and was in Weisenberg Township, Lehigh County in 1759. He married Barbara Schopp and they had sons Henry (1761), John (1763), and David (1779). A different John Kregelo from the village Daaden in Westerwald also emigrated in 1753 (S&H).

W&M-1119. Thaddeus Meade Felton (1871-1934) and wife Florence (Hanks) (1872-1916) are buried in Mt. Olivet Cemetery. Holden S. Felton and wife Mary H. lived in Frederick where he had a law office on North Court Street. Their daughter, Ruth N., married Col. Mark L. Hoke who was appointed Commander of Fort Detrick in 1983.

W&M-1120. Charles T. K. Young (1866-1914) and wife Alice I. (Sencil) (1863-1922) are buried at Middletown Lutheran Church. The lineage of his father Daniel is given below.

Conrad Jung (1728-1825) and wife Mary Magdalene (1731-1824) are buried at Middletown Lutheran Church. Their son Henry Young (1779-1859) and wife Hannah (1779-1862) also are buried there. A son of Henry and Hannah was Hezekiah Young (1806-1885) who married Malinda (1808-1884). They were parents of Daniel Young (1832-1902) who married Lucretia (Koogle) (1851-1902). All dates are from Middletown Lutheran Cemetery.

In a deed of 1756, Conrad Young bought 125 acres of a tract called Exchange from Casper Shoaf whose wife was Anne.

Land records of Frederick County show a number of other Young families. Ludwig, joiner or cabinet maker, bought lot 117 in Frederick from Daniel Dulany in 1753. William Young in 1753 bought part of Duke's Woods near later Libertytown from Samuel Collard of Prince George's County, whose wife was Eleanor. Collard's executor was Arnold Livers.

Andrew Young, farmer, in 1754 bought Ross' Range from John Ross, Esquire, of Annapolis. Dewalt Young of Little Conewago near Hanover, Pennsylvania bought in 1756 part of Pleasant Meadow tract on a branch of Patapsco River. A John Young bought land from Peter Apple in 1760.

W&M-1121. Henry M. Wiener (1840-1913) married Frances A. Miller of Howard County. He and his parents John Michael (1804-1891) and Ann Margaret (Goetz) (1802-1872) are buried at Petersville Catholic Church. (LC)

W&M-1122. Henry Nelson (1840-1912) and wife Mrs. Sidney A. (Hall) (1850-1906) are buried at New London Methodist Church. His parents Nathan (1798-1875) and wife Matilda (Poole) are buried on the Nelson farm graveyard near New London. These Nelsons who came from Virginia are not related to the Nelsons who were early around Point of Rocks. Family data of Nelsons beginning with John Henry born 1821 are given in the Adams Family Bible at Hood College Library. Lucia Linganore Nelson died in 1865 at age 23 months.

Brothers Benjamin, Henry (1896-1873) and Nathan Nelson and their brother-in-law George Devilbiss were among the first Board of Trustees of Central

Chapel (M. E. Church) at New London in 1830. Another brother, Robert Nelson, may have been the father of Dr. Robert Nelson of Walkersville. A descendant of Henry is Jack Shreve of Cumberland, Maryland who is collecting family data.

The unrelated Nelson families of the Point of Rocks area descend from among the very earliest settlers in Frederick County. In 1696 Arthur Nelson was granted 45 acres of Broken Island in the Potomac, a short distance upstream from the mouth of Monocacy River. In 1724 a tract on Conoy (later Heater's) Island near later Point of Rocks Village, was surveyed for Arthur Nelson. It has been suggested that these Nelsons were Nielsons of Swedish origin because one of their properties was called Sweeds Folly. However, an article about descendant J. Arthur Nelson (b. 1876) of Baltimore claims English origin by way of Virginia. (See the Tercentenary History of Maryland, Vol. 2, 1925). Descendants included Gen. Roger Nelson (1758-1815). See also *Who Was Who* and C.E.S. in *Frederick News*, July 7, 1990. (LC)

W&M-1123. Dr. Joseph W. Long, M.D. (1879-1937) and wife Daisie (Hinea) (1882-1954) are buried at Woodsboro Mt. Hope Cemetery. His grandparents Christopher Long (1790-1867) and wife Elizabeth (1794-1861) are buried at Jefferson Union Cemetery. Dr. Joseph's parents John W. Long (1828-1889) and Charlotte E. (Culler) (1835-1885) also are buried there. (LC)

W&M-1123. Rev. Thomas J. Kolb (1844-1914), Elder of Rocky Ridge Brethren Church, married Margaret Saylor, born in 1837. Elder Thomas' parents were David R. Kolb (1818-1894) and wife Amelia (1815-1883) who are buried at Creagerstown.

Kolbs were early in the Monocacy Valley. John Michael Kolb, Sr. was in Frederick County in 1745 and names of his 10 children are in Lutheran records (LW). Christopher Kolb and wife Anna Maria were sponsors of a baptism at Monocacy Lutheran Church in 1755. In Lutheran records at Frederick, George Michael Kolb, Sr. (1723-1806) had eight sons and three daughters. In 1800 census in Fredericktown District were six Culp households. Jacob, Sr., Michael and their wives were over 45 years of age. Younger were George, Henry, Jacob, Jr., and William, all of whom were heads of families. In 1800 in Emmitsburg lived Isaac Culp, over 45, and family, and in Libertytown District was the family of Philip Culp.

A History of the Kolb, Kulp or Culp Family from 1707 was written by Daniel Kolb Cassel (Norristown, Pennsylvania, 1895). Other genealogies are given in M&C-II.

S. Denmead Kolb of Box 155, Salisbury, Maryland is working on a genealogy. He is a descendant of Johannes Michael Kolb, Sr., emigrant, son John William (1776-1835), his son Frederick William, his son who was William Augustus, and his son David Denmead, the father of S. Denmead Kolb. John William Kolb was 1st Lieut. guarding British prisoners at the Frederick Barracks in October 1814. (LC)

W&M-1125. Charles R. Holter (1870-1956) and wife Ura Viola Lucretia (Ahalt) (1879-1910) are buried at Middletown Reformed Church, where are buried also his parents William (1831-1899) and Elizabeth J. (Coblentz) (1836-1924). See also W&M-1100. William Holter (c.1796-1868) served in the

Frederick County Militia of 1812. He married Magdalena Beard and had son William.

W&M-1126. Albert L. Hauver (1853-1950) and wife Minnie E. (Williar) (1853-1921) are buried at the Lutheran Church at Foxville, west of Thurmont, where also are buried his parents Peter Hauver (1823-1907) and wife Susan M. (Fox) (1828-1876). Also buried there is Peter's second wife Joanna (1836-1906). The grandparents of Albert were Christian (1801-1869) and wife Mary (Brown) (1803-1883) who also are buried at Foxville Lutheran Church. See also W&M-809.

W&M-1127. Glenn O. Garber (1881-1931) married Margaret C. Zeigler; they are buried at Mt. Olivet. Glenn's parents were (John) David (1855-1913) and Florence O. (Roderick) (1860-1944) who are buried at Liberty Chapel. His Garber grandparents were William (1816-1901) and wife Mary (1822-1890) who are buried at Beaver Dam Brethren Cemetery near Johnsville.

Garber or Gerber families of Dunkard faith were early in the Monocacy area but Dunkard records, except for gravestones, are few. A Johannes Gerber baptized his daughter Anna in Monocacy Lutheran records in 1756.

John Garber moved to Shenandoah County, Virginia from Maryland in 1775. His son Elder Abraham (1760-1846) organized a Brethren congregation on Middle River in Augusta County, VA. Another son, Daniel Garber, moved further south to near Harrisonburg, VA.

Gerber families originated in Langnau village in Canton Bern, Switzerland. Michael Gerber arrived at Philadelphia in 1734 and settled in York County, Pennsylvania. Johannes H. Gerber (1717-1787) emigrated in 1750. After a short time with his brother in York County, he settled in Frederick County, becoming an Elder at Beaver Dam Brethren Church before moving on into the Shenandoah Valley. Six of his seven sons became Elders of Brethren Churches.

A Samuel Garber born in 1822 near Union Bridge married Elizabeth Keller of Hanover. Their children and some grandchildren are given by Williams (1906). In the 1800 census of old Frederick County there were seven Garber families in Libertytown District. The oldest heads of families were Christian, Martin of Samuel, Samuel, and Martin, Sr. A Garber Genealogy was written by Clarke M. Garber (Mansfield, OH, 1937 and 1964) (Y); another by Dean K. Garber (Goshen, IN, 1970) (WP). (LC)

W&M-1128. Dr. James K. Waters, M.D.(1838-1916) married Annie Mary (Hill) (1840-1884) who is buried at Utica. Dr. Waters and his second wife Sarah E. (Bowman) (1844-1926) are buried at Thurmont U. B. Church. His parents Somerset R. Waters (1796-1860) and wife Rachel (McElfresh) (1801-1875) are buried at Mt. Airy Methodist Church. See also W&M-896.

W&M-1129. Samuel E. McBride (b. 1870) and wife Annie M. (Grove) (1868-1939) have stones in the Middletown Reformed Cemetery. His parents Lewis (1834-1916) and Sarah (Sigler) (1839-1900) are buried at Locust Valley Church of God. In the 1800 census James McBride and family lived in Middletown Valley.

W&M-1129. Herman Augustus Buckey (1849-1938) and wife Margaret E. (Nusbaum) (1848-1932) are buried at Glade Reformed Cemetery. In the same cemetery are buried Herman's ancestors beginning with George Peter Buckey (1771-1862) and wife Susan (Creager) (1775-1838); their son George William Buckey (1814-1890) and wife Elizabeth (Rhoderick) (1822-1865) were parents of Herman.

The Buckey emigrants to Frederick County who came from Minfeld, southwest Germany, have no relation to Col. Henry Bouquet who came from Switzerland. Herman was a descendant of Peter Bucki and wife Anna Maria (Schaefer) of Minfeld, not from better known Mathias (after whose sons John and George, Buckeystown was named). See W&M-854.

W&M-1131. Hanson Boyer (1835-1906) and wife Susan M. (Koogle) (1843-1915) are buried at Middletown Lutheran Church. His parents Michael (1802-1882) and wife Elizabeth (Jacobs) (1805-1877) are buried at Jefferson Methodist Church.

Boyer, pronounced very differently, is a common French family name, but the Boyers of Western Maryland are believed to have descended from immigrants from Germany, Switzerland or Alsace with earlier names Beyer or Bayer. The book *American Boyers, 7th Edition*, by Donald A. Boyer (York, Pennsylvania, 1984) included descendants of Samuel Beyer of Germany and Gabriel Beyer of Philadelphia County.

In Middletown Lutheran records are Philip Beyer and wife Catherine in 1794; Salmon Beyer and wife Maria who had twins Susan and Hannah in 1811; Jonathan Beyers and wife Anna Maria had son George in 1823. Michael Byers of near Westminster served in the Frederick County Militia of 1814 and married Margaret Duttero (cf. W&M-860).

In 1762 Philip Boyer bought 200 acres on Little Pipe Creek from John Chrissman (wife Mary). A Philip Boyer in 1768 bought part of the tract Chittam Castle from William Dickensheets whose wife was Catherine. It started at a spring draining into Linganore Creek. In 1769 Henry Boyer bought land from Daniel Vale. Also in 1769 Michael Bayer purchased land from Rosena Beighler. In the 1800 census of Middletown Valley were Jonathan Boyer and wife, both 26-45 in age.

A Donald A. Boyer states that most American Boyers descend from Johan Philip Beyer (1701-1758) who was born in Flomersheim in the Palatinate. In 1721 Philip married Maria Elisabeth Beck (b. 1701). Other Boyers are said to be descendants of Johan Christopher Bayer (b. 1677) from Gruenstadt in the Palatinate. More Boyer genealogies are cited in M&C-II, also (WP). (LC)

W&M-1131. Ezra C. Wachter (1838-1920) and wife Juliann B. (Stull) (1840-1926) are buried at Charlesville Reformed Church north of Frederick. Gravestones at nearby Bethel Lutheran Church give Philip Wachter, Sr. (1786-1875), the alleged son of the immigrant who married Ammareliss (Widerick) (1788-1863). Philip Wachter, Jr. (1812-1886) and wife Susannah (1814-1899) also are buried at Bethel. They were parents of Ezra. See also W&M-724.

W&M-1132. George Marshall Wachter (b. 1881) and wife Hattie Anne Estelle (Schaeffer) (1882-1935) have gravestones in Glade Reformed Cemetery near Walkersville. His father was Thomas M. Wachter (1839-1920) who is buried at Mt. Olivet at Frederick. George's grandparents were Joshua Wachter (1814-

1883) and wife Ann Maria (1813-1885) buried at Charlesville Reformed Church. They were parents of Thomas M. who married Cynthia A. C. Measell. See also W&M-724.

W&M-1132. Benjamin F. Reich (1861-1942) who was unmarried is buried at Mt. Olivet. His parents were William (1815-1901) and Lucy (Brown) (1828-1911). Ben Reich's grandparents were John Reich (1765-1835) and Phebe (Steiner) (1773-1842). All of these are buried at Mt. Olivet.

W&M-1133. John William Cramer (b. 1848) married Rebecca Elizabeth Spahr. She was a daughter of Abraham (1820-1909) and Elizabeth (Bush) (Spahr) (1827-1899) who are buried at Woodsboro Mt. Hope Cemetery. John William's parents were Samuel Cramer (1809-1858) and wife Susan (Buckey) (1812-1887) who are buried at Glade Reformed Cemetery near Walkersville. John William's Cramer grandparents were Henry (1778-1845) and wife Elizabeth (Barrack) by W&M; by gravestones at Glade Cemetery his second wife was Barbara (1786-1862). See also W&M-1301 and 1506.

W&M-1134. John H. Grove (1862-1939) and wife Cora E. (Huff) (1871-1950) are buried at Mt. Olivet. His parents were Elias (1838-1896) and F. Henrietta (Kehne) (1837-1929). John had grandparents Reuben Daniel Grove (1795-1878), born near Hanover, Pennsylvania, and Maria (Lantz) (1801-1874) who are buried at Mt. Olivet. See W&M-1188 for ancestry of Reuben.

Numerous genealogies have been written of Graf, Groff and Grove families of Pennsylvania and Maryland (M&C-II, 152). Mrs. Katherine Grove Bradshaw of Frederick has written genealogy showing her descent from Reuben and Maria.

W&M-1135. Daniel Josiah Gernand (b. 1848) married Annie M. Garber. They belonged to Beaver Dam Brethren Church, but J.M.H. did not find their gravestones. Daniel's parents were Andrew Augustus (1821-1879) and Julia Ann (Snook) (1823-1893) who are buried at Johnsville M. P. Church. Daniel's grandfather Jacob Gernand (1797-1871), buried at Graceham, was a son of John Adam and Anna Catherine (Weller). Jacob's first marriage was to Elizabeth Williar (1787-1822), daughter of Andrew and Margaret (Harbaugh). Jacob's second marriage was to Anna Theodora Becker (1803-1830), (daughter of John Frederick and Anna Elisabeth (Schneider)). Jacob's third marriage was to Sybilla Wilhide (1804-1886), (daughter of Frederick and Catherine (Peitzell)). Children by all three marriages are recorded in the Moravian Archives. Andrew Augustus Gernand's mother was Elizabeth (Williar) Gernand.

Another son of (John) Adam and Anna Catherine (Weller) Gernand was William (1792-1825), a shoemaker of Mechanicstown and member of the Frederick County Militia of 1812. He married Anna Elisabeth Johnson. Names of their children are given.

In the 1800 census of Middletown Valley was the household of George Gernant over 45 years and wife under 45. They had five daughters and three sons. In Emmitsburg District in 1800 was the family headed by Adam Garnand and wife, both 26-45 years of age. They had five young sons.

W&M-1136. John T. Tabler (1844-1919) and wife Frances E. (Knott) (1872-1933) are buried at Mt. Olivet. His parents William Tabler (1808-1888) and wife Harriet (Smith) (1817-1861) are buried at Hyattstown Methodist Church. John's grandparents Lewis Tabler (1781-1847) and wife Mary Catherine (Leather)(1789-1867) also are buried at Hyattstown.

W&M-1137. Clarence Worthington Hilleary (1842-1912) and wife Charlotte Oram (Wheeler) (1848-1937) are buried at Petersville Episcopal Church. His parents were Tilghman Hilleary (1796-1869) and wife Ann (Worthington) (1801-1964) who are buried at Petersville also.

A Thomas Hilleary surveyed land near later Park Mills and Sugar Loaf Mountain in 1741. See also W&M-1115. Henry and John Hilleary served in the Maryland Militia in the Revolution.

W&M-1138. No other records of recent immigrant Lewis Otte were found, but attention is called to early Ott families. John Jacob Ott (c.1754-1822) and wife Anna Mary (1767-1812) are buried near Miller's Bridge east of Thurmont. (*Fogle and Strine Genealogy* by Alma T. Fogle, 1976) (F).

Bernhardt Ott of the Frederick Reformed Church had son Michael (1760-1827) who in 1786 married Elisabeth Wertenbacher. Their son John (c.1799-1878), a potter in Frederick, and wife Ann M. (b. c.1804) are buried at Mt. Olivet. Their son George M. (b. c.1839) and wife Jennie (1849-1936) had daughters of Frederick City, Mary Castle Ott, educator, (W&M-562) and sister Hal Ott, who was first grade teacher of the writer at North Market Street school, Frederick. Serving in the War of 1812 were Frederick, George, Michael (1794-1872) and Peter Ott (1785-1858).

W&M-1138. Ira McDuell Staley (1869-1954) married Myrtle Ruch of Pittsburgh. He and his parents Daniel O. (1838-1913) and wife Anna Elizabeth (McDuell) (1835-1907) are buried at Petersville Episcopal Church. Daniel was a son of Cornelius (1808-1883) and wife Ruanna (1809-1889) who farmed near Rocky Springs. Cornelius was a son of Jacob of Jacob. (W&M-908 and (S)).

W&M-1139. Thomas R. Saylor (1879-1949) married Daisy F. Eyler (b. c.1877). He and his parents Ezra James Saylor (1844-1910) and wife Tillie or Tilitha A. (Anders) (1834-1912) are buried at Woodsboro Mt. Hope Cemetery. Grandparents of Thomas were Henry Saylor (1807-1854) and Catherine Mary Donsife (1817-1894) who are also buried at Mt. Hope. See also W&M-1049.

A John Frederick Saylor of Creagerstown area was drafted into Capt. Creager's Company of the Frederick County Militia of 1812. He was a drummer at Bladensburg and at North Point. He married Susan Thumb and secondly Susan Frantz. They lived at Fairfield, Pennsylvania and had 13 children. (LC)

W&M-1141. John D. Hendrickson (1855-1921) and wife Louis A. (Hunt) (1858-1945) are buried at Mt. Olivet, where are buried also his parents Daniel (1826-1898) and Mary C. (Haugh) (1833-1909). Grandparents of John D. were John Hendrickson (1801-1892) and wife Anna (1798-1959) who are buried at Beaver Dam Brethren Cemetery north of Johnsville.

In the 1800 census of Frederick District there were no Hendricksons, but in the Taneytown area were households of Israel Hendricks and wife, both in range of ages 16-26; also Amaria Hendricks and wife, 16-26 years with five children. Carroll H. Hendrickson II of Frederick is studying his ancestors. (LC)

W&M-1142. William Henry Lease (1827-1893) and wife Anna Martha (McAllister) are buried at Mt. Olivet. His parents William, Jr. (1774-1845) and wife Mary (Riner) (1793-1882) are buried on the Lease farm graveyard near McKaig (east of Frederick). In the 1800 census of the Liberty area were three Lease households. Jacob, Sr. and William and their wives were over 45 years. Jacob, Jr. and wife were under 45 with three sons under 10 years.

W&M-1143. Harry M. Howard (1878-1954) and wife Fannie I. (Oland) (1880-1959) are buried at Mt. Olivet, as are his parents William H. (1836-1885) and Ellen R. (Culler) (1843-1891). Grandparents of Harry were Edward Howard (1798-1877) and Annie H. (Buckey) (died at 74) daughter of Peter and Mary (Salmon) who also are buried at Mt. Olivet.

John Howard of Gideon was a member of the Frederick County Grand Jury in 1750. In the 1800 census of Liberty District were households of Ephraim Howard (over 45 years) who owned 15 slaves and Joseph Howard (over 45 years) who owned 16 slaves. Widow Barther Howard (over 45 years) had three slaves. Charles Howard (age 26-45) had eight slaves.

Four Howard genealogies are noted in M&C-II, 157. According to Elizabeth Holter Howard in *Genealogy of Howard Families (1977)*, Mathias Howard, Sr. emigrated to Virginia about 1630. Joshua Howard of Manchester, England was born about 1665. Col. John Eager Howard, whose name occurs in the song "Maryland My Maryland", was his grandson.

Maryland Historical Society has many boxes of papers of Howard families (MS 469). More than 50 Howards served in the Maryland Militia in the War of 1812. Elisha, Joseph, Richard and Thomas Howard were enrolled in the Frederick County Militia of 1812. (LC). See also Scharf.

W&M-1143. Edward C. Shafer (1863-1924) married Eva S. E. Nicodemus. He is buried at Mt. Olivet. His parents Martin T. (c.1826-1898) and wife Mary Catherine (Grove) (1826-1863) are buried at Burkittsville Union Cemetery. See also W&M-746 and 992.

W&M-1144. Contrary to W&M, Henry Shafer's wife was Mary Magdalena (Williard) (1800-1864), daughter of John and Frances (Kepler). Henry's father John Shafer (1753-1823) was born in America. Henry and Mary had 12 children studied by Helen Ramsburg. See W&M-1621.

W&M-1145. Emory C. Crum (1894-1930) married Ethel M. Myers. He is buried at Mt. Olivet. His grandparents were John W. Crum (1823-1905) and Mary Elizabeth (Browning) (1827-1888) who are buried at Liberty Chapel. Emory's parents were Henry H. Crum (1868-1923 and Mary A. (Cramer) (1864-1920) who are buried at Mt. Olivet Cemetery. Emory must be a descendant of Gilbert Crum and Martha (Jansen) who early settled on Monocacy Manor. In 1850 John and wife lived in Liberty District with Sarah Crum (b. c.1793) apparently his widowed mother. Henry and Sarah Crum baptized at Rocky Hill Church daughter Mary, born October 28, 1824.

The following lineage of Crum families of Dutch origin includes research of Linda Bischoff of Enterprise, AL and Dr. Robert Crum Frey, Jr. of Wilmington, Delaware. Numbers to left are successive generations. From New Jersey the Gilbert Crums settled on Monocacy Manor and Abraham Crums on Reich's

Ford Road southeast of Frederick (near tracts surveyed earlier by John van Meter).

(1) William Crom (d. before 1662 in Holland) m. Maycke Hendricks. Children: Lysbeth (b. c.1647); Gysbert (b. c.1650); Geertje (b. c.1653). Maycke second m. to Jan Joosten van Meter, born in Theil area of Holland, d before 1705) at Burlington, NJ. children: John, Rebecca, Lysbeth, Isaac, Hendrix.

(2) John van Meter Crom (c.1656-1745) m. 1682 in NY Sara Dubois; he surveyed tracts southeast of later Frederick.

(2) Gysbert Crom (c.1650-1724) m. Geertje van Vliet; Holland to Marbletown near Kingston, NY. children: Willem (b. c.1675) first and eight others recorded in Dutch Church at Kingston.

(3) William Crum (c.1675-after 1741) m. 1699 in NY Wyntje Roosa (c.1680-after 1643) daughter of Heyman Aldertse and Ann Margariet (Roosevelt); lived near Kingston, NY. Children included Gilbert and Abraham, who moved from near Burlington, NJ to Frederick County about 1754 or earlier.

(4) Gilbert Crum (1700-1762) m. Martha Jansen (d. c.1789). From Kingston, NY to Harlingen, NJ to Monocacy Manor by 1756. In 1759 cared for road from Ogle's Ford to Biggs Ford. Children from wills; all born in NJ:

    (a) Wiyntje (1727-before 1762).

    (b) Cornelius (b. 1729).

    (c) William (1731-1790) m. Mary Ann Barrick (c.1747-1798).

    (d) Hannah m. Vought or Fout.

    (e) Gilbert m. Elizabeth.

    (f) Martha.

    (g) John m. Elizabeth (c.1735-1793) (Frederick Ref. Church).

        (1) John, Jr. (b. 1761) m. in 1785 Mary Crum (cousin) (b. 1765, Glade Ref. Church).

        (2) Ephraim (b. 1771) m. Hannah Creager (Glade Church).

    (h) Elizabeth m. John Barrick.

    (i) Peter to Huntingdon County, Pennsylvania (?).

    (j) Mary (b. 1750) m. William Barrick.

    (k) Abraham Crum (b. 1753), born Readington, NJ.

Children (a) to (e) above may be from an earlier marriage from their positions in will of 1762.

(4) Abraham Crum (1708-1787) m. Aeltje Pieterse (d. 1754). From NJ to southeast of Frederick on Reich's Ford Road. Both buried near Reich's Ford Road.

    (a) William (1741-1810) m. Catherine; John (b. 1777), Isaac (b. 1779). William second m. in 1792 to Amelia Wise or Weiss.

    (b) Antie (b. 1746 at Harlingen, NJ).

    (c) Aelte (Alice) (b. 1751) m. Wilson.

      (d) Weintje (b. 1753, Readington, NJ, Dutch Ref. Church).

      (e) Nina m. Beckwith (in will).

(4) Abraham Crum second m. to Elizabeth Plummer, Quaker, widow of Philoman, Sr. (d. 1747).

(5) William Crum (c.1731-1790) m. Mary Ann Barrick (c.1747-1798); lived in Monocacy Manor area; Frederick Ref. Church; will 1793.

      (a) Mary (b. 1765).

      (b) Sarah (b. 1767).

      (c) Abraham m. 1796 in Hagerstown Susanna Ringer; lived in Washington County.

      (d) William, Jr. m. 1793 Anna Margaret (Sponsors 1800). Lost Monocacy Manor land 1781; bought 319 acres in 1796.

      (e) Christopher (1774-1846) m. Ann (1777-1841) both buried at Glade Ref. Church.

      (f) John, an ex. of father, lost Monocacy Manor lease 1781.

(5) William Crum (1741-1810) second marriage in 1792 to Amelia Wise. Lived on Reich's Ford Road; will at Frederick.

      (a) William, Jr. m. 1793 Elizabeth Levy; second m. to Rebecca. Children in Frederick Ref.: Maria (b. 1794); Abraham (b. 1796); William (b. 1798); David (b. 1800).

      (b) John in 1800 census; ex. of William, Jr.; land east of Monocacy River.

      (c) Abraham (1771-1796); buried on Reich's Ford Road; ex. of William, Jr.

      (d) Isaac; will 1823, received land west of Monocacy River.

      (e) Margaret m. Razor or Raser; she witnessed Frederick Ref. wedding in 1787. Children from Amelia's will: Catherine, Elizabeth, Margaret, Jacob, Christiana and Mary.

      (f) Daughter m. Joseph Hardman. Children from Amelia's will: Henry, Joseph, Jacob, George, Nancy, Elizabeth, Margaret.

Other Crums are shown in records of Rocky Hill Church and Frederick County Equity Records. See W&M-911 and W&M-1574 for Crum families not of Dutch origin.

W&M-1146. Melancthon Gaver (1851-1934) and wife Clara F. (Kefauver) (1853-1927) are buried at Middletown Lutheran Cemetery, where also are buried his parents Joseph (1816-1877) and Ann Catherine (Remsburg) (1821-1895). See W&M-826.

W&M-1146. Josephus W. Shafer (1861-1951) and wife Ida M. (Kefauver) (1860-1944) are buried at the Reformed Cemetery in Middletown, where also are buried his parents Samuel (1828-1911) and Louisa (Kephart) (1828-1905). Grandparents of Josephus were George Shafer (1787-1857) and wife Elizabeth (Ramsburg)(1792-1868) also buried at Middletown Reformed Church. George's parents were John Shafer, Jr. (1753-1825) and Anna Maria (Darner)

(1754-1837). Helen H. Ramsburg, Dublin Road, Walkersville, has the Bible of her great grandparents Samuel and Louisa Shafer.

W&M-1147. John C. Leatherman (1852-1952) and wife Susan Rebecca (Grossnickle) (1852-1909) are buried at Grossnickle's Meeting House of the Brethren Church north of Ellerton. Peter Leatherman (1757-1845), son of Bishop Daniel, and wife Annie (Swigart) were buried on the Leatherman farm. Their son Jacob Leatherman (1798-1880) and wife Susanna or Sally (Harp) (1806-1887) are buried at Wolfsville Reformed Church. Their son Elder George Leatherman (1827-1907) and wife Rebecca E. (Johnson) (1827-1908) are buried at Grossnickle Meeting House. They were parents of John C. See also W&M-993.

W&M-1148. George Carlton Leatherman (1858-1955) and wife Mary Ellen (Leatherman) (1863-1930) are buried at the Brethren Meeting House north of Ellerton. His parents were Elder George (1827-1907) and wife Rebecca E. (Johnson) (1827-1908) who also are buried at the Cemetery at the Brethren Meeting House. See W&M-1147.

W&M-1149. Jacob M. Huffer (1836-1910) and wife Sarah E. (DeLauder) (1852-1918) are buried at Middletown Reformed Church. His first wife Phebe Ellen (Ahalt) is buried at Zion Lutheran Church, Middletown. The parents of Jacob were Joseph L. (c.1800-1882) and Catherine (Mullendore) (1802-1889) who are buried at Middletown Reformed Church. See also W&M-1030. For Mullendore families see Wms. (1906).

W&M-1149. Lewis H. Fraley (1863-1922) and wife Christiana (Burke) (1862-1949) are buried at Mt. Olivet. Lewis was a descendant of Hessian mercenary Johan Heinrich Froelich (1756-1830), born at Wichmannshausen in northeastern Hesse, who was interned at the Barracks in Frederick during the Revolution. Henry and wife with six children were living in Emmitsburg District in 1800. Lewis' grandfather Dr. Henry Fraley (1815-1893) and wife Elizabeth (Fagan) (1815-1895) are buried at Mt. Olivet. Their son Dr. M. Augustus Fraley (1837-1906) and wife Adaline A. (Young) (1838-1871) also are buried at Mt. Olivet. They were parents of Lewis H. Solomon Fraley (1802-1882) of Frederick County had daughter Mary Ellen Fraley (1840-1917) who died at Cumberland, Maryland (Der Kurrier, September 1992).

More about Revolutionary soldier Heinrich Froelich, who deserted from the Barracks in 1783, was published by Nancy Kiddoo. (GM). With wife Anna Margaret (Wilhide) he had 14 children whom she listed from records of Apples Church and Graceham Moravian Archives. For example, Barbara (b. 1784) married John Shupp. William S. Cramer wrote about Henry's ancestors in Germany in the *Johannes Schwalm Historical Magazine*, Vol. 3, #1 (1985). About 180 Fraley names are indexed in (Z).

W&M-1150. Joshua Arnold (1833-1897) and wife Annie H. (Heffelbower) (1842-1917) are buried at Pleasant View Brethren Cemetery near Burkittsville, where are buried also his parents John Arnold, Sr. (1795-1860) and wife Sarah (Karn) (1798-1878). See also W&M-1061 and 1188.

W&M-1151. Rev. George Washington Garber (1860-1939) and wife Mary Catherine (Smith) (1849-1912) are buried at Beaver Dam Cemetery north of Johnsville. See W&M-1127.

W&M-1152. Daniel Swomley (1830-1915) and wife Eliza Catherine (Trayer) (1835-1908) are buried at New Market Methodist Church. His parents Mahlon (1799-1845) and Sarah (Miles) (1800-1891) are buried at the Quaker Cemetery at Monrovia, south of New Market. In the 1800 census of eastern Frederick County Daniel Swomly and wife both between 26 and 45 years of age lived with a daughter and two sons.

W&M-1152. John McElfresh Griffith (1827-1908) and wife Rachel Ann (Norris) (1834-1911) are buried at McKaig Methodist Church east of Frederick. His parents were Capt. Nace or Nacy and wife Ruth (McElfresh) (1789-1869) (buried at New Market M. E. Church).

Richard Griffith (over 45 years) was in the Linganore area in the 1800 census. *The Griffith Family* is by R. R. Griffith (Baltimore, 1892) (FH) and *Griffith Family* by Frances M. Smith is in J. Am. Gen. 2, 280, (Y) (W). (LC)

W&M-1153. C. Edward Derr (1850-1912) and wife Annie M. (Zimmerman) (1850-1923) are buried at Mt. Olivet where also are his parents David (1817-1884) and wife Sarah A. (Smith) (1821-1892).

John Derr (1780-1845) married Maria Esther Smith (1784-1813) and secondly married Elizabeth Haupt (d. 1846). They are buried at the Lutheran Church at Middletown. Elizabeth was the mother of David above. See Wampler.

W&M-1154. Dr. Lloyd T. MacGill (1829-1908) and wives Marie O. (Riggs) (1834-1863) and Rachel E. (Edwards) (1840-1927) are buried at Mt. Olivet, as are his parents Basil (1794-1850) and wife Elizabeth (Dorsey) (1794-1850).

W&M-1155. William Ecker (1842-1908) and wife Augusta Ann (Barnes) (1840-1899) are buried at Unionville Methodist Church, where also are buried father Jacob (1816-1849) and grandparents John Ecker, Jr. (1783-1836) and wife Rachel (Crumpacker) (1781-1833), also his great grandparents John Ecker, Sr. (1747-1821) and wife Elizabeth (1753-1811). (LC)

W&M-1156. Christian Railing (1842-1927) and wife Margaret (Mehrling) (1843-1905) are buried at Mt. Olivet, as are his parents Henry (1810-1885) and Catherine B. (Smith)(1812-1877). For descendants of Adam Rehling of Hesse-Darmstadt see M&C-II.

W&M-1157. Lewis Edward Derr (1837-1885) and wife Ann R. C. (Mentzer) (1844-1915) are buried at Middletown Lutheran Cemetery, as are his parents Philip (1807-1867) and Elizabeth (Crone) (1811-1889). Philip was a son of John and grandson of Philip. See W&M-843 and Wampler. In the 1800 census of Middletown Valley are noted the households of Conrad Crone, Sr. and Jr. The latter and wife (both between 26 and 45 years) had two sons under 10 years.

W&M-1157. Charles S. Miller (1865-1916) and wife Sarah A. E. (Derr) (1866-1918) are buried at Middletown Lutheran Cemetery, as are his parents John D. (1842-1905) and wife Mary M. (Stephens) (1845-1925). A John Miller (1777-1823) and wife Ann Catherine (1776-1839) are buried at Middletown Lutheran Cemetery. They possibly are ancestors of Charles and of the Millers, who were keepers of South Mountain Tavern.

W&M-1158. Daniel Octavius Staley (1838-1913) and wife Ann Elizabeth (McDuell) (1835-1907) are buried at Petersville Episcopal Church. His parents

Daniel (1805-1849) and wife Amelia (Hedges) (1818-1849) are buried at Rocky Springs. See W&M-908, 943 and (S). Serving in the Frederick County Militia of 1812 were Abraham Staley (b. c.1783) who married Elizabeth Shaffer; Moses Staley (d. 1840) married Ann Elizabeth Stull; and Peter, Jr. (b. c.1798) married Margaret Albaugh (1797-1873). They attended Frederick Reformed Church.

W&M-1158. Jacob H. Diehl (1856-1940) and wife Ella (Snook) (1855-1929) are buried at the Brethren Cemetery at Beaver Dam near Johnsville, as are his parents Moses Diehl (1819-1890) and wife Catherine (Hyder) (1823-1909). A grandfather of Jacob was Martin Diehl (1786-1844) who also is buried at Beaver Dam. (LC). Many Diehls have lived in Adams County, Pennsylvania (WB).

W&M-1160. John H. Frazier (or Frazer) (1874-1916) married Mary A. Fineman. He is buried at Mt. Olivet. His parents George W. Frazier (1829-1887) and Rebecca (Donaldson) are buried at Knoxville Reformed Church.

In the 1800 census of Middletown Valley were six Frazier families. William and Thomas Frazier, Sr. were 26 to 45 years in age. Apparently there were two families headed by widows: Sarah over 45 years had one slave and Rebecca who was under 45. Thomas, Sr. had 26 slaves and William had two slaves. Heads of families also were young Jonathan and Levy Frazier.

In the Frederick County Militia of 1812-1814 served Fielder Frazier who married Sarah Ann Phillips at Frederick Catholic Church in 1829; Jeremiah (1785-1883) who married Catherine Pickings at Frederick (later in D. C.); and Josiah (d. 1875) who married Eveline (b. c.1798). (LC)

W&M-1160. Charles E. Keller (1851-1917) and wife Vallietta S. (Weagley) (1858-1898) are buried at Mt. Olivet Cemetery. His parents were Jonathan (b. c.1815) and wife Jane Louisa (Springer) (b. c.1818). A grandfather of Charles was Michael Keller (1770-1847) who laid out "Keller's Addition" to Middletown. Michael was buried in the Middletown Reformed Cemetery. Michael Keller, Sr. and wife Maria had (John) Michael born 1770, in Middletown Reformed records. Sponsors of his baptism were Johannes and Magdalena Keller.

There have been numerous different Keller families in Frederick County with some outstanding individuals (M&C-I and II), but few genealogies are available. In the 1800 census of Middletown Valley are five families. Philip Keller and wife were over 45 years. The heads of four families were under 45 years, namely Jacob, John, Philip, John and Michael.

A John Keller mentioned in Frederick court records in 1754 was 67 years old. In records of Zion Lutheran Church in Middletown, earliest Kellers were Jacob and wife Anna Maria (1783), John and Magdalena (1781), and John and Barbara (1786). See also W&M-790 and 967.

W&M-1161. Charles W. Wright (1857-1920) and wife Mary J. (Brown) (1856-1930) are buried at Point of Rocks Episcopal Church where are also buried his parents John P. (1828-1904) and wife Sarah E. (Divine) (1827-1909).

W&M-1162. George Henry Gilbert (1853-1929) and wife Amanda (Selman) (1855-1917) are buried at Prospect Cemetery west of Mt. Airy. In the census of 1800 Frances Gilbert, over 45 years, had a family in southern Frederick County. In 1850 census in New Market District, Henry Gilbert (b. c.1792), farmer, lived with John W. Gilbert (b. c.1820), shoemaker, and wife Rachel (b. c.1821).

In 1800 in Middletown Valley Christian Gilbert and wife were over 45 years old. Jeremiah Gilbert and his wife were under 45. They had two daughters and five sons. In 1800 in Westminster District George Gilbert and wife were between 26 and 46 years old living with three daughters and four sons. In Libertytown District in 1800 Raymond Gilbert and wife, both under 45 years, lived with four daughters and three sons. They had two slaves.

Christian Gilbert was granted 308 acres of Resurvey of Tract Good Hope in 1797. Thomas Gilbert was granted an enlargement of 392 acres of his tract Gilbert's Inheritance in 1786 (Scharf). Gilberts also have lived in Adams County, Pennsylvania (WB).

Research by Audrey Gilbert of West Alexandria, Ohio, found that Thomas Gilbert (d. 1793) acquired land northwest of Harmony in Middletown Valley in 1752. He and wife Elizabeth had children Rebecca, Elizabeth, Susanna and Jeremiah (c.1751-1822), who by wives Magdalena Catherine (Weaver) and Zepporah (Powell) had 23 children born in Frederick County. Most of the children and grandchildren lived in Montgomery County, Ohio, or in Indiana. (LC)

A George Gilbert (b. c.1779) living in Woodsboro District in 1850 was born in Pennsylvania according to the 1850 census. An early settler in Adams County was emigrant Barnabas Gilbert (d. 1802) who was a founder of Benders Church in Menallen, later Butler Township, in 1781. Barnabas married Catherine Bender, daughter of Jacob, who sold the land for the church.

W&M-1163. William Rinehart (c.1804-1864) and wife Rebecca (Barrack) (c.1804-1869) are buried at Glade Reformed Cemetery near Walkersville. William's parents George and Susanna (Smith) lack gravestone records, but the 1800 census shows a George Rinehart and wife over 45 years in the Fredericktown area and a George Rinehard over 45 with wife, 26-45 years, living in the Westminster District. A prominent early Rinehart was David (1755-1818) who, in 1800, had five children in the Taneytown area. He is buried in the Wolf Cemetery near Union Bridge. A John Jacob Reinhard had his daughter Anna Margaret baptized near Taneytown in 1753.

W&M-1163. Harry E. Zimmerman (1871-1952) married Fanny L. Hoke (b. 1880). They are buried at Mt. Olivet Cemetery. His parents were John David (1855-1906) and Martha Ellen (Valentine) (1849-1922) buried at Mt. Hope Cemetery, Woodsboro. Harry's grandfather Solomon Zimmerman (1793-1846) and second wife Susannah (Shank) (1812-1888) are buried at Woodsboro Reformed Church. His great grandparents were George Zimmerman (1755-1820) and Elisabeth (Weiss) (1760-1823) who were early settlers. (See (Z) and W&M-797.)

W&M-1164. Carlton P. Ahalt (1839-1918) and wife Manzella (Willard) (1841-1907) are buried at Burkittsville Union Cemetery. His parents, Samuel (1806-1889) and Mary Ann (Schlosser) (1815-1863) are buried at Middletown Lutheran Cemetery. For earlier Ahalts see W&M-988.

W&M-1165. Charles E. Victor Myers (1871-1941) and wife Ella B. (Howard) (1872-1956) are buried at Mt. Olivet. His parents were George W. (1828-1907) and Ann M. (Thomas) (1828-1905) also buried at Mt. Olivet. The following lineage was traced by Margaret E. Myers:

Peter Myers (1795-1870) married in 1820 Rebecca Fortney (1804-1865), daughter of David (1780-1851) and Elizabeth (Lewis) (1777-1847). They lived in Buckeystown district. Some descendants follow:

(1) Ann E. Myers (b. 1821) m. John Thomas.

(2) David L. (b. 1823) m. Susan Elizabeth Specht.

(3) Mary Catherine (1825-1892) m. William H. Hargate.

(4) George Washington* (1828-1907), born near Adamstown, m. Ann Margaret Thomas* (1828-1905), daughter of George Jacob Thomas and Charlotte (Thomas), who had children:

(a) Thomas Franklin* (1861-1939) m. Carrie G. Hopkins* (1865-1939) of Frederick, had children:

(1) Ethel Marion Myers (b. 1886) m. Emory C. Crum* (1884-1930).

(2) Mary Edna (b. 1889) m. Joseph H. Keene.

(3) George Washington (b. 1891) m. Sally Pearl Delphey.

(4) (Franklin) Ross* (1893-1986), prominent banker in Frederick, m. Emma Louise James*, no children.

(5) Arthur "Tim" Vinton (b. 1899) m. Anna Margaret Diffendall.

(b) Anna M.* (1863-1941) m. Worthington Glaze* (1859-1936).

(c) Mary Isabelle (b. 1864); unmarried.

(d) George C. F.* (1867-1930) m. Mary Etta ----* (1861-1917), second m. to Carrie Hubbard.

(e) Charles E. Victor (b. 1871) m. Ellen Howard.

(5) Tilghman Peter (1830-1860) m. Lucinda V. Ramsburg (1832-1921), buried Ballenger Creek Church Hill.

(6) Francis M.* (1833-1891) m. Margaret L. Minor* (1838-1924).

(7) Rebecca Ellen (b. 1836) m. James William Copeland.

(8) Andrew L. (b. c.1837).

(9) Mahlon L. (b. c.1838)

(10) George R. (b. c.1841).

(11) Iseter A. Myers (b. c.1843).

* Buried in Mt. Olivet at Frederick.

W&M-1165. Thomas F. Myers (1861-1939) and wife Carrie G. (Hopkins) (1865-1939) are buried at Mt. Olivet. His parents and grandparents are given in the preceding article.

W&M-1166. Isaac L. Hankey (1840-1926) and wives Mary Elizabeth (Geesey) (1860-1890) and Edna (Hull) (1874-1951) are buried in Mt. Hope Cemetery, Woodsboro. His parents Peter Hankey (1805-1890) and wife Mary A. (Krise) (1811-1882) are buried at Mt. Tabor Church, Rocky Ridge, east of Thurmont. For earlier Henge and Hankey ancestors, see W&M-810.

W&M-1167. Daniel Peter Zimmerman (1842-1911) and wife Catherine L. (Stitely) (1843-1907) are buried in Woodsboro Mt. Hope Cemetery. His parents were Solomon (1793-1846) and wife Catherine (Cramer) (1788-1833), (not Solomon and Susannah Shank). The grandparents of Daniel were George Zimmerman (1755-1820) and wife Elizabeth (Weiss) (1760-1823). Their children included Solomon and Mary (1790-1872) who married George Shank (not Cramer). (Z) gives six other children of George and Elisabeth. See also W&M-979. Stitely families are shown in W&M-1006 and 1499.

W&M-1168. Francis V. Staub was married to Frances Murphy (1872-1921); they are buried at the Catholic Cemetery in Frederick, where also are buried his parents Andrew J. (1828-1873) and Mary E. (Stone) (1834-1900). A Jacob Staub, Sr. (d. 1821) is buried at Conewago Chapel at the eastern edge of Adams County, near McSherrystown, Pennsylvania. Another Jacob Staub (1811-1872) is buried at the Catholic Cemetery at Petersville in southern Middletown Valley. For early Staub and Little families, see (WB) and (G). In the Frederick County Militia of 1812 were Jacob Staub (c.1791-1872) whose wife was Catherine (b. c.1791); and John Staub (1788-1852) m. Margaret Hawman and died at Littlestown. Note also the Staup families who lived around Woodsboro and Creagerstown. (JMH).

W&M-1169. William H. Renn (1871-1955) and wife Edith G. (Smith) (1873-1949) are buried at Mt. Olivet, as are his parents George Calvin (1843-1920) and Mary C. (Zimmerman) (1843-1911). William's grandparents were John H. Renn (1811-1884) and Sarah Ann (House) (1819-1890).

Renn families were said to move into western Maryland in 1794 when a small tract was acquired near Ballenger Creek. George and Catherine Renn were great grandparents of William Hanson Renn, who married Edith G. Smith, (daughter of Henry and Mary A. (Heller). Names of 11 children born to them at Adamstown are given in Tercentenary History of Maryland. (LC)

W&M-1170. G.S. Clinton Bopst (1865-1959) and wife Nettie J. Sponseller)(1869-1931) are buried at Mt. Olivet as are his parents William (1819-1874) and Sarah (Lease) (1827-1895). Earlier ancestors were in Washington Co. (Wms 1906). Sponseller ancestors of Pennsylvania are in M&C-II.

W&M-1170. George H. Davis (b. 1863) was a son of Aaron Davis and Elizabeth Eve (Degrange) (1826-1889). Only she has a gravestone at Mt. Olivet. See W&M-839.

W&M-1171. Charles J. Ramsburg (1861-1938) and wife Mayme E. (Pitzer) are buried at Utica Church as are his parents Nelson D. (1836-1924) and wife Eliza (Harmon) (1838-1912).

The Ramsburgs were not early settlers of Virginia as stated by W&M. Descendants of Stephen Riemensperger, later Ramsburg, north of Frederick, had gone to farm in nearby WV near Shepherdstown, but later Jacob came back to Frederick County. Jacob (1808-1877) and wife Annie Elizabeth (Snook) (1798-1889) are buried at Utica. See W&M-752.

W&M-1172. Harry G. Tritapoe (1881-1936) married Mary M. Boyer (b. c.1895). He is buried at Jefferson Union Cemetery where also are buried his parents Samuel E. (1845-1930) and Sarah E. (Vincel) (1847-1919).

A Paul Tritt and wife, both over 45 years, and a younger Peter Tritt lived in Middletown Valley in the census of 1800.

W&M-1173. Oscar Daniel Culler (1868-1924) and wife Ella V. (Feaster) (1864-1942) are buried in Jefferson Union Cemetery, as are his parents John Henry (1838-1911) and Amanda L. (Derr) (1839-1914). See also W&M-1085.

W&M-1174. Singleton E. Remsburg (1843-1921) and wife Frances (Shafer) (1844-1925) are buried at Middletown Lutheran Church. His father Samuel (1807-1880) and wife Maria (Bowlus) (1809-1873) are buried also at Middletown Lutheran Cemetery. Apparent ancestors were John Remsburg (1760-1844) and wife Catherine (Thomas) (1776-1866) who moved from Buckeystown District to Middletown Valley about 1790. See W&M-1037.

W&M-1174. William E. Bittle (b. 1868) and wife Fannie May (Toms) (1868-1957) have stones in Myersville Lutheran Cemetery. His parents William M. (1841-1928) and Catherine (Floyd) (1840-1931) are buried in Myersville Lutheran Cemetery. For earlier ancestors wee W&M-875.

W&M-1176. William Beckley Cutshall (1865-1939) and wives Myrtle E. (Lough) (1869-1898) and Cora E. (Shaw) (1869-1931) are buried at Woodsboro Mt. Hope Cemetery, as are his parents William (1831-1912) and Henrietta J. (Hull). William's grandfather, Philip Cutshall (1791-1864), is buried at Woodsboro Reformed Church.

Cutshall in Frederick County has often been pronounced "Cutsale". Peter Cutsail and wife, both over 45 years of age, lived in Liberty District in the 1800 census.

In the Frederick County Militia of 1812 was a Samuel Cutshall (b. c.1790). In 1812 he married Mary Darner in Frederick County.

W&M-1177. Clinton Oscar Remsburg (1852-1940) and wife Amanda C. (Wiles) (1858-1937) are buried at Middletown Lutheran Church, where also are buried his parents Josephus (1796-1873) and Catherine (Crone) (1829-1918). Clinton's grandparents were Joseph Remsburg (1796-1873) and Madeline (Bowlus) (1798-1883) who also are buried at the same place. John Remsburg (1760-1844) and wife Catherine (Thomas) (1776-1866) moved from Buckeystown District to Middletown Valley about 1790. See W&M-1037.

W&M-1178. Lewis C. Harbaugh (1852-1924) and wife Alverta (Brown) (1850-1924) are buried at St. Jacob's Lutheran Church in Upper Harbaugh Valley, over the Mason-Dixon Line in Adams County, Pennsylvania. His parents Hiram Harbaugh (1829-1899) and Anna Maria (Williard) (1827-1879) are buried at Sabillasville Reformed Church. The grandparents of Lewis were Elias (1782-1854) and Anna Catherine (Pentzer) (1793-1849) who are buried at the Harbaugh family graveyard near Sabillasville. Great grandparents were Jacob (1763-1842) and Mary M. (1771-1824) buried at St. Jacob's Church. For earlier Harbaughs see W&M-995.

W&M-1179. Samuel D. Harbaugh (1870-1951) and wife Daisy (Williard) (1873-1950) are buried at Thurmont's U. B. Church. The gravestones of Hamilton Harbaugh and wife Cornelia (Pryor) were not found. Samuel's grandparents David Harbaugh (1809-1880) and wife Susan (Brown) (1809-1860) are buried at Foxville Lutheran Church. Samuel's great grandparents were John Harbaugh (1764-1834) and wife Elizabeth (Winters) (1763-1827) buried at the family graveyard near Sabillasvile. For ancestors Jacob and father Jost, see W&M-995.

W&M-1180. Richard Cornelius Mercier (b. 1842) and wife Emma D. (Oxley) (of Montgomery County) have left no known gravestones. However, Cornelius Mercier (c.1824-1907) and wife Annie (1840-1905) are buried at Mt. Olivet Cemetery. Richard may have been a son by an earlier marriage of Cornelius to Sarah (Gaither). Cornelius (b. 1794), son of Richard, was enrolled in the Frederick County Militia of 1812. He married in 1829 Sarah Gaither who was a daughter of Maj. Samuel and Ruth (Shipley) Gaither.

W&M-1181. Richard Simpson Bohn (1851-1928) and wife Amy Virginia (Saylor) (1849-1923) are buried at Beaver Dam Brethren Cemetery near Johnsville, where also are buried his parents Emanuel (1811-1882) and wife Elizabeth (Smith) (1808-1890). (LC)

W&M-1182. Frank G. House (b. 1853) and wife Emma (Ahalt) left no gravestones found by J. M. H. His parents, buried at Burkittsville Union Cemetery, were Greenberry House (1825-1919) and Mary M. (Grove) (1828-1916). Frank's grandparents Eli P. House (1785-1868) and second wife Ruth A. (Ridgely) (1783-1863) are buried at Jefferson Methodist Church.

In the 1800 census in Middletown Valley were five House households. Caleb, George and William, Sr. House, over 45 years in age, owned four, four and eight slaves respectively. Daniel and wife (26-45) lived with two daughters and five sons. John House and wife (26-45) had only one daughter (under 10) and no slaves. Jacob and William House had families in Fredericktown District in 1800. House family members are buried at Mt. Olivet, Middletown and Brunswick.

W&M-1183. The Lamar family, as recorded here, apparently was from research of Dr. Lewis Lamar, whose gravestone has not been found in our area. Thomas Lamar (1777-1864) and wife Mary (Willard) (1782-1840) are buried in Jefferson Union Cemetery.

John Lamar served on the first Grand Jury of Frederick County in 1749. Also in the court records of 1749 is Alexander Lamar. Seven other Lamars are in the Frederick County court records before 1766. A genealogy of the Lemar and Lamar families has been written by Harold D. LeMar (Omaha, NB, 1941).

Peter and Thomas Lamore of French descent were naturalized about 1661 (NA). John Lemaire born in Anjou, France, was naturalized in 1674 in Maryland.

William B. Lamar (1800-1872), son of Thomas of near Jefferson, married Elizabeth Harley, daughter of Joshua. Their descendants moved to the area of Boonsboro, Washington County. See Wms. 1906.

In the 1800 census there were four Lamar households in Middletown Valley: William B. and wife were over 45 years of age, living with seven children and 14 slaves; John, over 45, was alone except for five slaves; Peter and wife (26-45) had 10 children and no slaves; Thomas (16-26) lived alone.

Sergt. Richard Lamar (c.1795-1815) of the Frederick County Militia of 1812 married Mary Johnson and soon died in Middletown.

W&M-1185. Dr. Austin A. Lamar (1876-1932) is buried at Middletown Reformed Church. Gravestones of his wife Lena E. (Newcomer) and parents Dr. Lewis Lamar and wife Susan C. (Snyder) were not reported. Buried also at Middletown Reformed Church is Lewis H. Lamar (1911-1930) For other Lamars see W&M-1183. (LC)

W&M-1186. William Jarboe Grove (1854-1937) and wife (Annie) May (Hardey) (1857-1933) were buried at St. Joseph's Catholic Church near Buckeystown. She was a daughter of Dr. Thomas E. and Cora (Wiener) Hardey. William's parents were M. J. Grove (1824-1907) and wife Susan (Jarboe) (1829-1889). She was buried at the Catholic Church west of Buckeystown. He is buried at Burkittsville Union Cemetery along with a number of children who died young.

William J. Grove's gravestone states that he was a descendant of Col. John Jarboe of St. Mary's County and Hans Graef, Lancaster County, Pennsylvania.

The earliest Groves in Pennsylvania and Maryland have been outlined by Mrs. Katherine Grove Bradshaw of Frederick. Hans Graf (1661-1746), born in Switzerland, fled to Alsace and reached Philadelphia in 1695. After several years in Germantown, Pennsylvania, where his first wife died, he settled in Lancaster County at Groffdale. Hans had one son Jacob by his first wife. Hans and second wife Susanna had nine children: Peter; Samuel; Mark; Daniel; John or Hans, Jr.; David; Hannah; Fronich; Mary. John, Jr.'s descendants became Groves and many of the others changed to Groff.

John Grove, Jr. (1697-1780) married Elizabeth Carpenter or Zimmerman (daughter of Henry). They moved from Pennsylvania to near Keedysville in Washington County, Maryland. They had children: Elizabeth m. Baltzer Henkel; Jacob m. Catherine Staley; George m. Mary Ferree; Henry (1741-1787) who lived near Hanover, Pennsylvania; and his grandson Reuben Daniel (1795-1878) who moved to Frederick County before 1814.

The early Groves to live in Middletown Valley are identified in the 1800 census as Charles and wife, over 45 years of age. In 1800 Jacob Grove and wife were 26-45 years, living with five young sons and one daughter. George and wife, both aged 16-26, were the only Groves with a slave.

Leonard Calvert led the colonists to Maryland. Page 1187: Neither the first, George, or second Lord Baltimore, Cecil, reached America.

George Washington Grove (1800-1888) and Elizabeth (Biser)(1804-1881), grandparents of William J., are buried at the Catholic Church near Buckeystown. William's father Manasses Jacob Grove (1824-1907) was famous locally as founder of M. J. Grove Lime Company at Lime Kiln north of Buckeystown and elsewhere. William Jarboe Grove succeeded his father as head of the Lime Company and recorded history and genealogy of the Buckeystown area in his book *History of Carrollton Manor*. (FH)(HC). See also Tercentenary History of Maryland, Vol. IV, 616, and page 773 for Edward Dawson Grove (b. 1861 to M. J. and Susan (Jarboe)).

W&M-1188. James H. Grove (1869-1930) and wife Anna C. (Forsyth) are buried at Mt. Olivet Cemetery at Frederick. He was a son of M. J. Grove and

Susan (Jarboe) noted above. Children of James H. and Anna were James H., Jr., William Jarboe, and Manasses Jacob.

A number of related Groves are in BL and in *History of Carrollton Manor*. See also W&M-894.

Leonard Grove had sons Martin and Daniel R. They moved from Middletown Valley to the area of Rohrersville in Washington County in 1865. See Wms. 1906. (LC)

W&M-1188. David Arnold (1821-1899) and wife Mary Ann (Wiener) (1836-1921) are buried at Burkittsville Union Cemetery. His parents John (1795-1860) and wife Sarah (Karn) (1798-1878) are buried at Pleasant View Brethren Cemetery near Burkittsville.

It was the grandfather of Rev. David Arnold (1759-1844) who was the Arnold settler in Frederick County from Germany. Johan Georg Arnold (1702-1769) was born in Eppenbach according to records of nearby Reformed Church of Zuzenhausen (B1). These villages near Sinsheim, southeast of Heidelberg, have been visited by this writer. Johan Georg was a son of Wendel and Anna Catherine (Schneider) Arnold. Johan Georg married Anna Maria Barth, born in 1702 at Zuzenhausen, to Nicholas Barth (1673-1714) and wife Regina (Wacker). In 1738 John George, wife and children emigrated via Philadelphia and quickly settled in Frederick County. By survey of 1739 John George bought from Daniel Dulany, the Elder, the well known tract Rams Horn, 494 acres southwest of Myersville. Most of the children and grandchildren of John George and Anna Maria migrated westward from Frederick County, but son Andrew (1740-1821) and wife Catherine (Stoner) (daughter of John) had son Rev. David Arnold, born in Middletown Valley, who in 1785 married Elisabeth Slifer (1768-1851) (daughter of John). They remained in southern Middletown Valley, farming near Burkittsville. They were leaders of the Pleasant View Church of the Brethren and were ancestors of most local Arnolds. David was grandfather of David Arnold (1821-1899) above.

Related other Arnolds are given in the genealogy, *The German Baptist Arnolds*, by Lester H. Binnie (Manchester, IN, 1990). *A History of the Arnolds* was written by Emra T. Fike. An article about a son of emigrant John George, namely Samuel Arnold (c.1734-1805) was written by H. Minot of Somerset County, Pennsylvania, and by descendant Pitman Arnold in Pennsylvania Gen. Mag. 19, 125 (Sept. 1953). For Arnolds in Adams County, Pennsylvania, see (WB).

W&M-1189. Hiram E. Remsburg (1867-1947) and wife Emma M. (Young) (1867-1945) are buried in Middletown Lutheran Cemetery, where also are buried his parents Singleton E. (1843-1921) and wife Frances Ellen (Shafer) (1844-1925). See W&M-1174 and 1377.

W&M-1190. Calvin C. Zimmerman (1848-1924) was buried at Mt. Olivet Cemetery. His parents, Rev. William H. (1817-1873) and Mary E. (Cronise) (1818-1887) also are buried at Mt. Olivet.

(Johan) Georg Zimmerman(1714-1795) and wife Anna Catherine (Seidel) (1724-1804) settled west of Carrollton Manor in southern Frederick County about 1762. Calvin's great grandparents Michael Zimmerman (1750-1821) and wife Eva (Cronise) (b. 1751) were parents of Henry (1791-1875) who married Charlotte Thomas (1790-1864). They are buried at the Zimmerman farm graveyard near Ballinger Creek Road and they were parents of Rev. William. See also W&M-979 and (Z).

W&M-1191. George C. Rhoderick (1861-1924) was a son of G. Carlton Rhoderick, Sr. (1835-1906) and Mary Ellen (Koogle) (1835-1914) who are buried at Middletown Lutheran church. George C. and wife Clemma B. (Gross) (1861-1944) are buried at the same place.

Great grandparents of George C. were Benjamin Rhoderick (1778-1867) and Susanna (Fink) (1791-1852) who are buried at Burkittsville Schoolhouse. Grandparents of George C. were Mahlon Rhoderick (1810-1880) and wife Mary Ann (Flook) (1811-1899) who are buried at Mt. Olivet.

A genealogy of *Rhoderick and Related Families* (1684-1978) has been written by Henry S. Rothrock (Wilmington, DE, 1979 and 1984). The German name Rothrock means red coat. Philip Rothrock (b. 1714 at Leiseilheim, near Worms) emigrated in 1733. Children by two marriages are in the book *Genealogies of Pennsylvania Families* (Baltimore, 1981). Philip Jacob and wife Katharina are recorded as Moravians at York, Pennsylvania. Their oldest son, Jacob Rhoderick (1741-1817), married Barbara Weller (1747-1802) of York and they moved to Baltimore in 1782, where he was an innkeeper and merchant. Their younger son, Philip (1746-1825), married Eva Elizabeth Weller (1749-1839) and had 10 children. Philip is buried at the Moravian Church, Friedburg, NC. The sons of Philip Jacob of York, Ludwig and Andrew, settled in Frederick County. (BE). (LC). Andrew and Ludwig Roderick settled in the Washington County area before 1761. Andrew's son David (b. 1770) in 1801 married Elsie Landis in Hardy County, VA (FH). Descendants have spread to Carolinas, Ohio, Indiana, Illinois, Kansas, Colorado and California.

W&M-1193. Reuben Saylor (1851-1931) and wife Margaret A. (Wright) (1851-1917) are buried at Mt. View Cemetery, Union Bridge. His parents were Reuben Saylor, Sr. (1818-1888) and wife Hannah (Smith) (1819-1899) who are buried at the Brethren Beaver Dam Cemetery. The grandparents of Reuben, Jr. were Jacob Saylor (1790-1865) and wife Hannah (Garber) (1799-1875) who also are buried at Beaver Dam.

In Emmitsburg District of the 1800 census Frederick Sailer and wife were over 45 years in age. Sayler and Saylor families are prominent in histories of Dunkard, later Brethren, Churches in America (BE). The family name derives from the dialect pronunciation of German Seiler.

W&M-1195. Charles J. Barrick (1846-1928) and wife Emma J. (Eichelberger) (1847-1908) are buried at Mt. Tabor Cemetery at Rocky Ridge east of Thurmont. There also are buried his parents George W. Barrick (1816-1895) and wife Susan (Crise) (1824-1893). Michael Barrick (1779-1863) and wife Mary (1784-1854), grandparents of Charles, are buried at Rocky Springs. See W&M-1091 for earlier Barrick or Berg ancestors.

John, Peter and Philip Barrick were officers in the Maryland Militia in the Revolutionary War from Frederick County. Nine from Barrick families served in the Frederick County Militia of 1812 as follow: Cornelius (b. c.1792), a carpenter who joined at Woodsboro, is in Creagerstown District in the census of 1850; Ezra (c.1794-1864) died at Carlinville, IL; Capt. Frederick; George of Peter (1779-1863) buried at Glade Reformed Cemetery; Henry (d. 1834 at Ridgeville); John (d. 1844 at Woodsboro) m. Esther Kurtz (b. c.1783); Lewis; Samuel (b. c.1790), 10 children by two wives, in Tippacanoe County, IN; Samuel to New Philadelphia, OH m. 1832 Hetty Crum of Frederick County; William (b. c.1789).

W&M-1196. Samuel W. Lewis (1833-1914) and wife Catherine (Toms) (1840-1918) are buried at Mt. Bethel church at Garfield, north of Myersville. His parents were William and Sarah (Wolf) (1804-1880), also buried at Garfield.

A Benedict Lewis in the 1800 census who had 26 slaves probably lived in southern Middletown Valley. A Jacob Lewis, over 45 years of age, lived in the Fredericktown District in 1800. A Thomas Lewis, over 45, and a younger Thomas Lewis lived in the Buckeystown District in 1800.

W&M-1197. George A. Dean (1841-1922) and wife Emma C. (Gorton) (1841-1901) are buried at Mt. Olivet. A Robert Dean, over 45 years of age, and family lived in Fredericktown District in 1800.

W&M-1198. Clayton M. Zimmerman (1867-1956) and wife Myra Beaty (Heberlig) (1870-1957) are buried at Mt. Olivet, as were his parents Ephraim I. (1830-1894) and wife Maria E. (Thomas) (1834-1926).

Contrary to W&M, it was the father of his grandfather, Henry Zimmerman (1791-1875), who came from Germany. There were only two emigrant brothers. See W&M-979 and (Z).

W&M-1199. Charles H. Trout (1862-1945) and wife Cora (Anders) (1867-1954) are buried at Mt. Hope Cemetery, Woodsboro, where also are buried his parents John Trout (1812-1898) and Catherine (Dorcas) (1820-1882).

Most of the Trout families of Frederick County are believed to be descendants of Hans Leonard Traut (1620-1692) who was Buergermeister of Impflingen, south of Landau in the Pfalz. A grandson, Hans Martin (b. 1677) from nearby Offenbach and wife Judith, emigrated in 1733. Their children are given in M&C-II. Martin's son Henry (1711-1746), grandson Henry, Jr. (1732-1775), and the latter's son Jacob, were ancestors of John, who married Catherine Dorcas. Troutville, located northwest of Woodsboro where Broad Run crosses the road from Woodsboro to Creagerstown, was named for John Trout (1812-1898)

Michael Trout (1734-1798), a brother of Henry (1732-1775), was an ancestor of George E. Trout now living at Buena Park, CA. The latter has written a *Trout Genealogy* emphasizing western descendants (1990). Other Trout genealogies have been written by Patricia Anderson of Frederick, Maryland and by Margie M. Trout of McClean, VA. Trout families of York County, Pennsylvania have been studied by V. Kyle Trout of Airville, Pennsylvania. (LC)

W&M-1200. George L. Kaufman (1865-1924) and wife Fannie May (Houck) (1870-1902) are buried at Mt. Olivet, where also are buried his parents John C. (1822-1891) and Marie M. (Dutrow) (1825-1885). George's grandfather Conrad Kaufmann, who died in 1820's at 56 years, and wife Barbara (1779-1849) are buried also at Mt. Olivet.

Earlier Kaufman families, believed unrelated to the above, have been in Frederick County. Johan Kaufmann, born in Minfeld, southern Pfalz, to Johan and Maria Elisabeth, emigrated to Pennsylvania in 1754. He died in Frederick in 1793. (M&C-II). Mathias Buckey also came from Minfeld. In records of the Reformed Church of Frederick, Johannes and wife Johanna Kaufman baptized their Margaretha in 1775. Henry and Elizabeth Kauffman baptized their daughter Maria in 1799. Henry Kaufman was enrolled under Capt. John Brengle in the Frederick County Militia in 1814. (LC)

W&M-1203. Albert Levi Haines (1854-1929) and his parents, Francis W. (1829-1898) and wife Elizabeth Ann (Lambert) (1829-1904), are buried at Unionville Methodist Church. Albert's grandparents John Haines (1782-1859) and wife Susan (Shults) (1794-1859) are buried at Sam's Creek Methodist Church. John settled at the village of Weldon near the Linganore Creek.

In the Frederick County Militia of 1812 were enrolled Eli, Henry, Isaac and John Haines. John married Susanna Deberry in 1820.

The 1800 census of Liberytown District gives three Haines families: George and wife were over 45 years in age; Aaron and Nathan and wives were in the 26-45 age range. In 1800 there were seven Haines households in Westminster District, of which Jacob, Michael and Nathaniel were over 45 years of age. In Taneytown District in 1800 were families of Samuel and William Haines in age 26-45 years.

A genealogy, *Haines Family of Carroll County, Maryland* was written by John Milton Reifsnider (W). *Haines Families*, by Betty E. Haines of Felton, Pennsylvania, was written in 1979 (L). Other Haines genealogies are listed in M&C-II.

W&M-1204. Herbert Augustus Runkles (1883-1948) married Elsie Snyder. He is buried at Prospect Cemetery near Mt. Airy. According to the census of 1850 his father, Joseph Henry (b. c.1841), was a son of Basil Runkles (1809-1906) and Rebecca (b. c.1825). Basil's second marriage was to Mary E. (1836-1910). In the census of 1800 Jacob Runkles and wife were over 45 years of age; Joseph and wife were between 26 and 45.

Rev. John William Runkel (1749-1832), born at Ober Ingelheim near Mainz, Germany, emigrated with his family in 1764. He was Reformed Pastor at Frederick from 1784 to 1802. Rev. Runkel died at Gettysburg and was buried at Emmitsburg Lutheran Cemetery. (Glatfelter, 1979). His wife Catherine lived 1749 to 1820.

Runkel and Runkels families continue to live in Frederick County.

W&M-1025. George W. Stauffer (1849-1921) and wife Clara A. (Neidig) (1855-1893) are buried at Mt. Olivet, as is his father Simon Wesley (1821-1887), who married Ann Rebecca Cramer. Grandparents of George were Joseph Stauffer (1799-1858) and wife Catherine (Cronise) (1780-1868), who are buried at Israel Creek Cemetery south of Woodsboro. About 1796 Daniel Stauffer bought land near present Stauffer Road north of Ceresville from Bernard Lingenfelter. In the 1800 census were Yellis Stowfer and wife over 45 years of age also Christian Stowfer and wife 26-45 years.

Enrolled in the Frederick County Militia of 1812 were George Stauffer (b. 1788) (son of Daniel and Christina), and John Stauffer, drummer. Both came from "Upper Frederick County".

According to Williams (1906), emigrant Peter Stauffer and son Jacob came from Canton Schaffhausen, Switzerland, and settled in Earl Township, Lancaster County, Pennsylvania. In AD 1100 Stauffers had been chalice bearers to the Duke of Swabia. Another account states that Veronica Stauffer arrived in Philadelphia in 1729 with Swiss Mennonites, along with her four sons Henry, John, Samuel and Christian. They came from Muckenheiser, about six miles below Worms near the Rhine, where Mennonites fleeing Switzerland settled in 1680.

Numerous genealogies of Stauffer families are available, but few with emphasis upon our area (M&C-II) (Y) (L) (WN). In Williams (1906) are articles on 24 Stouffer and Stauffer families of Washington County (LC)

W&M-1206. John J. Culler (1858-1929) and wife Annie E. (Thomas) (1858-1936) are buried at Church Hill on Ballenger Creek Road. His parents Philip (1812-1884) and Ann Rebecca (Dixon) (1825-1908) are buried at Jefferson Union Cemetery. Grandparents of John J. were Capt. Henry Culler (1786-1861) and wife Anna (Feaster) (1786-1856) also buried at Jefferson. Michael Culler and wife, the great grandparents of John J., were over 45 years of age in the 1800 census of Middletown Valley. This was the only Culler household recorded in the Valley at that time. See also W&M-1085.

Lieut. Henry Culler served in the Frederick County Militia of 1812. In 1809 he married Anna Feaster. He was a farmer and miller near Jefferson and member of the State Legislature.

W&M-1027. Samuel G. Haugh (1847-1927) and wife Ella S. (Birely) (1852-1928) are buried at Haugh's Church north of Woodsboro, as are his parents John Haugh (1801-1862) and wife Catherine (Smith) (1805-1872). See also W&M-935 and 1052.

W&M-1028. Dr. Thomas Brashears Johnson, M.D. (1868-1925) and his parents Dr. William H. (1827-1901) and wife Laura (Brashear) (1837-1895) are buried at Mt. Olivet. Dr. William H. was a grandson of Maj. Roger Johnson and a great-nephew of Gov. Thomas Johnson (1732-1819). Thomas Johnson, the grandfather of the Governor, emigrated about 1660 from Great Yarmouth, Norfolk, England to Calvert County. See *The Life of Thomas Johnson* by Edward Schley Delaplaine (N.Y.C., 1927), also CF Vol. 2, and NC Vol. 9.

Other Johnson families were in Frederick County early besides the family of the first governor. John Johnson of Catoctin was on the Grand Jury in 1749 and 1752. An early Johnson graveyard is near High Knob in eastern Middletown Valley. A Johnson with the German Lutherans in upper Middletown Valley was an ancestor of the writer (M&C-II). In records of the Frederick County Militia of 1812 are Erasmus, Jacob, John, Joseph, Nathaniel, Robert, Thomas and William Johnson. Nathaniel or "Uncle Nat" (colored) died at 104 years on Carroll's Manor. He was brought to America in 1820 and was sold by heirs of Alexander H. Brown to Christian Thomas, who was his 18th master.

W&M-1210. Prospect Hall. With Mrs. Isabelle Nash is given a fictional account of Prospect Hall where it is incorrectly claimed that the property was confiscated. The true history of Prospect Hall from documentary sources also is fascinating as I summarized in the *Frederick News* of September 24, 1992. Most of the sources are in the files of the Historical Society of Frederick County. A house was built early on or near the site of Prospect Hall by James Dickson on the 229 acres of the tract Dickson's Struggle, which had been granted to Dixon in 1748 by Basil Warring. After the choice hill property on the southwestern edge of Frederick passed through a number of owners, it was acquired by Daniel Dulany II (1722-1797) who presented it to his son Benjamin Tasker Dulany (1752-1816), who in 1773 married Elizabeth French, a ward and neighbor in Virginia of George Washington. Benjamin moved to Prospect Hill because he had succeeded, with his father's help, to be appointed Clerk of the Frederick County Court. Benjamin and Elizabeth must have lived in an earlier house on Prospect Hill, since research by Anne F. Effland indicated that the present mansion, Prospect Hall, was most likely built by Col. John McPherson, who owned the property from 1811-1844.

A tradition that may be true is that Benjamin T. Dulany and wife Elizabeth presented to George Washington the horse Blueskin from their pasture at Prospect Hill. Washington rode Blueskin on ceremonial occasions as depicted on entering New York City by Currier and Ives. Since Blueskin was gun-shy and light in color, George used his other, dark horse, Nelson, more often in battle. The tradition that Blueskin was buried on Prospect Hill may be doubted, since when the old horse was returned to the Dulanys after 1785, they lived in Alexandria, VA.

Numerous writers have stated falsely that all Dulanys were Royalists, or Tories, whose lands were confiscated after the Revolution. Daniel Dulany, the Elder, who founded Fredericktown, died in 1753. His son Daniel II, or the Younger, was neutral and his lands were not confiscated. His son Benjamin Tasker was a patriot and close friend of George Washington. Some Dulany relatives who were Tories and returned to England are given in my *News* and *Post* articles of August 17 and September 24, 1992. The principal Tory land confiscated in Frederick County was Monocacy Manor (approximately Walkersville to Woodsboro east of Monocacy River). This Manor had been inherited by Frederick Calvert, the Last Lord Baltimore. (LC)

W&M-1212. Dr. Robert Lee Hammond, M.D. (1862-1934) and wife Fannie O. (Gilbert) (1869-1945) are buried at Mt. Olivet Cemetery, where also are buried his parents Dr. Richard T. (1815-1896) and wife Mary Agnes (Cramer) (1823-1894), daughter of Ezra L. and Mary (Winebrenner) Cramer. Dr. Robert had grandparents Walter C. Hammond (1786-1846) and wife Matilda Merriwether (Worthington) (1794-1852), who are buried at the Hammond family graveyard near New London.

Gen. John Hammond (1643-1707) from the Isle of Wight was present at the founding of Annapolis in 1695.

Local historian E. Ralston Goldsborough has written that the Hammond genealogy is the most complicated of all Frederick County families. In the 1800 census of eastern Frederick County there are eight Hammond households listed. Of over 45 years in age were two John Hammonds, each having 11 slaves. Also over 45 years were Lott, Ormond and Vachel Hammond. Nathaniel and Phillomon Hammond were between 26 and 45 years, while Upton and wife were under 26 years.

Hammond Families of Maryland and Indiana was written by Imogene H. Brown (1976). Hammond families are included in the *Linthicum Genealogy* by Matilda P. Badger (Baltimore, 1936) (Y). There are Hammond studies by H. Hanford Hopkins at (BM) and in Wms. (1906), also CF, Vol. 5, and (N).

Fifteen Hammonds were officers in the Maryland Militia of the Revolution. At least 14 other Hammonds served in the ranks. In the Frederick County Militia of 1812 were Denton and James Hammon; Carroll, James, Simpson, Thomas and William Hammond.

W&M-1214. David H. Hoke (1850-1895) and wife Clara Ann (Geiselman) (1855-1932) are buried at Glade Reformed Cemetery near Walkersville. Hoke families of York and Adams Counties are recorded at (Y) (G) (WB). In Adam County have been many Geiselman families, descendants of early Frederick who settled in York County (WB) (LC).

W&M-1214. Elias Fogle (1841-1919) and wife Anna Elizabeth (Eyler) (1846-1936) are buried at Glade Reformed Cemetery near Walkersville. His parents Balser (1800-1862) and Margaret (Wetzel) (1804-1884) also are buried at the same place. In northern Frederick County in the 1800 census lived Michael Fogle and wife over 45 years of age.

W&M-1215. John Francis Smith (1874-1916) married Emily Nelson (1879-1939) (daughter of William Pinkney, Jr. and Henrietta H. P. (Maulsby)). They are buried at Mt. Olivet Cemetery. His parents were Dr. Francis Fenwick Smith (1828-1900) and wife Maria Lee (Palmer) (1844-1931), who are buried at the Catholic Cemetery in Frederick.

Leonard Smith (1734-1794) married Elizabeth Neale and their son Capt. John (1754-1805) married Elizabeth Fenwick. Capt. John and Elizabeth were parents of Leonard Smith (1794-1849) who married Eliza (Jamison) (1795-1875). They are buried also in the Catholic Cemetery at Frederick. Their fifth child at Frederick was Dr. Francis Fenwick Smith above. Some relatives are in M&C-II, 515.

In the records of the Frederick County Militia of 1812 were 47 Smiths, some with genealogical data.

W&M-1216. Frank C. Norwood (1855-1934) and wife Anne E. (1869-1928) are buried at Mt. Olivet. His parents R. Nelson (1813-1891) and wife Rachel (Wagner) (1813-1891) are buried at Fairmount Cemetery at Libertytown.

Gravestones of Belt Norwood and second wife Sarah (Gaither) were not found. Their son Joshua Norwood (1789-1859) (grandfather of Frank), and wife Catherine (Kemp) (1792-1874) are buried at Kemptown Methodist Church. They were parents of R. Nelson Norwood above.

In the census of 1800 in southern Frederick County were two Norwood households. Both Jeremiah and Belt Norwood were over 45 years of age. Belt and wife had five daughters and five sons. Jeremiah and wife had only one daughter.

W&M-1217. J. Claude Arnold (1882-1918) and wife S. Grace (Flook) are buried at Middletown Reformed Cemetery. His parents Joshua (1833-1897) and wife Annie (Heffelbower) (1842-1917) are buried at Pleasant View Brethren Church near Burkittsville. For earlier Arnolds in Middletown Valley see W&M-1188.

W&M-1218. Charles Milton Brane (1857-1921) and wife Sarah E. (Fisher) (1856-1942) of Middletown are buried at Middletown Lutheran Church, where also are buried his parents Ezra (1824-1901) and wife Lydia (Wiseman) (1820-1899). In the 1800 census of Middletown Valley Conrad Wisman and wife, both between 26 and 45 years, had three daughters and two sons. John Wisman and wife, under 26 years, had a son under 10 years.

W&M-1218. John William Shank (1845-1928) married Catherine Rebecca Hardy (1843-1909). They are buried at Glade Reformed Cemetery. Peter Shank (1784-1864), grandfather of John William, is buried at Woodsboro Reformed Church.

Andreas Schenck (1709-1762) of Dinkelsbuehl and Weidelbach (Wuerttemberg) emigrated in 1723. He married Rosina Billmeyer of Ansbach, Germany and they lived in York County. Their sons John George (b. 1739) and John Michael (b. 1749) settled near Woodsboro. Eight children of John George Schank are given in *Anders Root Directory* by Norman C. Anders (Lehigh Acres, FL, 1992) (FH).

W&M-1219. Edward Garber (b. 1869) married Lela Repp of Clemsonville. His parents were John S. Garber (1827-1894) and Juliann (Haugh) (1832-1915), who are buried at the Brethren Cemetery at Beaver Dam near Johnsville. For earlier Garbers see W&M-1127.

Jacob Stambaugh, who married Abalonia, may have been a descendant of Hans Jacob Stambach, who emigrated in 1741 from Birlenbach, near Wissembourg in northern Alsace (B3).

W&M-1220. Luther Z. Derr (1861-1918) and wife Sophia K. Boileau (1868-1942) are buried at Middletown Lutheran Cemetery, where also are his parents Samuel (1822-1896) and wife Mary M. (Yaste) (1824-1905). Luther's grandparents were Jacob Derr (1782-1848) and Margaret (Long) (1783-1868), who also are buried at the Middletown Lutheran Church. A corrected list of their children is given by Wampler.

W&M-1220. John W. Smith (1853-1911) and wife Ida Missouri (Delphey) (1857-1937) are buried at the Methodist Church at Middleburg, Carroll County. His parents may be John C. (1827-1909) buried at Eyler's Valley U. B. Church and Hulda (Boyer) (1830-1886) buried at the Brethren Meeting House near Ellerton.

W&M-1222. George E. Wilcoxon (1871-1923) and wife Rebecca O. (Dixon) are buried at Mt. Olivet, where also are his parents Andrew J. (1829-1893) and Mary (Getzendanner) (1832-1909). Grandparents of George were William Wilcoxon (1782-1862) and wife Ruth (1788-1864), also buried at Mt. Olivet.

The estate of Roger Wilcoxon in 1753 in Frederick Co. was administered by his wife Elizabeth.

Relatives were John and John, Jr., Wilcoxon. Other Wilcoxons lived in Prince George's County, where Thomas, Sr. had an inventory in 1777 showing related Josiah and William Wilcoxon; that of Thomas, Jr. in 1776 showed John and Jesse Wilcoxon as kin. Executors were Thomas and Edward Wilcoxon. John Wilcoxon, Jr. was in Frederick court records in 1751 and 1754.

W&M-1222. Benjamin Filmore Dudderar (1852-1935) and wife Lucretia Clay (Barnes) (1848-1919) are buried at Unionville Methodist Church, where also are buried his parents Peter Dudderar (1825-1910) and Josephine (Brightwell) (1827-1889). Grandparents of Benjamin were William Dudderar (1781-1847) and Margaret (Shriner) (1783-1849) who are buried at Unionville also. See W&M-982 for earlier settlers. For Shriners see W&M-1352.

W&M-1223. Dr. Howard Hanford Hopkins, M.D. (1848-1906) and wife Margaret (Mantz) (1850-1938) are buried at New London Methodist Church, north of New Market, where also are buried their son Dr. Howard H. Hopkins III (1875-1918) and wife Alice E. (Wood) (1877-1921). Dr. Howard Hanford Hopkins IV practiced as a dermatologist in Baltimore and did research of the New Market area. See his map with Urner of early settlers there (F). (LC)

W&M-1224. John Grahame Johnson (b. 1860) and parents Worthington Ross Johnson (1824-1898) and Ann Rebecca (Johnson) (1825-1913) are buried at Mt. Olivet. Ann Rebecca was a daughter of Thomas J. and Caroline (Worthington) Johnson and granddaughter of the first governor of Maryland. Worthington Johnson (1802-1864) and wife Mary Jane (Fitzhugh) (1800-1835), also buried at Mt. Olivet, were grandparents of John Grahame. Worthington was a son of Baker Johnson (1746-1811) and wife Catherine (1759-1814), who also are buried at Mt. Olivet. See W&M-1208.

The Johnson families were leaders in the Revolution, including brothers Col. Baker, Col. Benjamin; Col. James and Maj. Roger Johnson. See Scharf.

W&M-1225. Luther H. Wachter (1857-1933) and wife Florence V. (Crum) (1865-1929) are buried at Mt. Hope Cemetery, Woodsboro. His parents Michael (1821-1910) and Rebecca (Reese) (1823-1917) are buried at Utica. Luther's grandparents Jacob Wachter (1782-1861) and wife Margaret (1790-1861) are also buried at Utica. See W&M-724.

W&M-1226. Martin L. Wachter (1869-1957) and wife Florence V. (Bell) (1872-1920) are buried at Mt. Olivet. His parents were Wesley A. (1843-1923) and Susanna S. (Smith) (1845-1927), who are buried at Charlesville Reformed Church north of Frederick.

Philip Wachter, Sr. (1786-1875), grandfather of Martin, is buried at Bethel Lutheran Church north of Frederick, along with wife Ammareliss (Widerick) (1788-1868). Also buried at Bethel are Philip Wachter, Jr. (1812-1886) and wife Susannah (Reese) (1814-1899). See also W&M-724.

W&M-1227. Charles H. Linthicum (b. 1868) married Osie D. (Burger) (1875-1910), who is buried at Pleasant Grove Methodist Church. His paternal grandparents were John H. S. Linthicum (1812-1896) and Julia Ann (Garrott) (1810-1887), who are buried at the McElfresh graveyard at Hyattstown. The parents of Charles were John W. Linthicum (b. 1836) and wife Sarah Amanda (Hendry).

A genealogy *The Linthicum and Allied Families* was written by Matilda P. Badger (Baltimore, 1934). In the Maryland Militia of the Revolution were several Nathan Linthicums and John Linthicum, officers, also Archibald, Nathaniel, Richard and Zachariah Linthicum, privates.

W&M-1228. George C. Alexander (1855-1934) and wife Fannie (McClaine) (1864-1933) are buried at Thurmont Blue Ridge Cemetery. His parents were Tilghman (1818-1906) and wife Maria (Palmer) (1826-1912), who are buried at Burkittsville Union Cemetery. In the 1800 census of Middletown Valley, Jacob Alexander and wife were over 45 years of age, George and Henry Alexander and their wives were between 26 and 45 years. Henry had three daughters and a son. In the Frederick County Militia of 1812 were George, Henry, Jacob, Jacob, Jr., Michael G., Robertson and Valentine Alexander. (LC)

W&M-1229. Anderson Hicks Etzler (1861-1935) and wife Ida M. (Ecker) (1862-1901) are buried at Brethren Beaver Dam Cemetery near Johnsville. His second wife Dessie (Saxten) (b. 1875) is buried at Mt. Hope Cemetery at Woodsboro.

Daniel Etzler (1766-1819), great grandfather of Anderson, is buried at Liberty Chapel. Daniel Etzler, Jr. (1793-1873) also is buried at Liberty Chapel. His son George W. (1833-1886) and wife Margaret Caroline (Albaugh) (1833-1905) are buried at the same place. Anderson was their son.

In the 1800 census of Libertytown District there are four Etzler households. John and wife were over 45 years in age and owned five slaves. Andrew and Daniel were 26-45 year in age; Joseph and wife were between 16-26 years of age. See also W&M-1058.

W&M-1230. Harry William Boone (b. 1875) and wife Della M. (Valentine) (1875-1930) have gravestones in Haugh's Church Cemetery near Ladiesburg. Ancestor Emanuel Bohn (1811-1882) and wife Elizabeth (Smith) (1808-1890) are buried at Beaver Dam Brethren Cemetery near Johnsville. His son Henry Boone (1835-1902) and second wife Louisa (Yingling) (1844-1917) also are buried at Beaver Dam. They were parents of Harry William. In the 1800 census of Libertytown District was the family of Nicholas Boon and wife, both were over 45 years in age.

Enrolled in the Frederick County Militia of 1812 was Robert Boone (1790-1861), who was appointed Judge of the Orphans Court at Frederick in 1857. He and wife Catherine were parents of Dr. Jerningham Boone of near Buckeystown. (LC)

W&M-1231. Milton Carter (1833-1899) and wife Elizabeth (Baker) (1840-1920) are buried at Unionville Methodist Church. His parents were Henry Carter (1796-1857) and Charity (Scheinflew) (1802-1895), who are buried also at Unionville. Elizabeth's parents were John Baker (1812-1865) and wife Mary (Baile) (1811-1875), who are buried at the Baker family graveyard at Oak Orchard near Unionville.

Enrolled in the Frederick County Militia of 1812 were William Carter and Joseph Carter (who in 1805 married Catherine Fisher).

W&M-1231. Noah E. Cramer (1860-1930) and wife Ella Kate (Houck) (1871-1944) are buried at Mt. Olivet. His parents were George (1819-1890) and Catherine A. (Reynolds) (1827-1895) (daughter of Samuel and Catherine), who are buried at the Glade Cemetery near Walkersville. The parents of George were David (1776-1845) and wife Elizabeth (Barrick) (1789-1834) (daughter of Peter), who are also buried at Glade Reformed Cemetery. See also W&M-928.

Two Cramers are notable for each living more than 100 years. Mary Elizabeth Cramer (daughter of James Henry (1825-1899) and wife Elizabeth (1824-1915)) married Nicholas Clemson (d. 1933). They lived at Clemsonville 4.5 miles south of Union Bridge. Mary Elizabeth celebrated her 100th birthday in 1948 and was the oldest alumna of Hood College (FH). She told of her youth on Israel's Creek south of Mt. Pleasant where Union soldiers camped. She had eight children.

Lillian Cramer was born August 19, 1888 in Thurmont to Charles M. (1867-1932) and wife M. Jane (Fleagle). She was married three times (Charles Titlow, William Brengle and E. Allen Grumbine). Lillian Grumbine's 104th birthday was noted on national TV (FH). I remember the Grumbine grocery store at Fifth and Market Streets.

W&M-1232. Rev. Dr. Osborne Ingle (1837-1909) and wives Mary (Mills) (1839-1883) and Mary (Addison) (1868-1955) are buried at Mt. Olivet. (LC)

W&M-1233. Charles L. Cronise (b. 1848) was a son of Joseph (1823-1896) (buried in Mt. Olivet) and wife Margaret Rebecca (Brunner) (d 1894). See W&M-1054.

W&M-1233. Wilbert E. Cronise (1866-1923) and wife Belle (Keller) (1871-1946) are buried at New London Methodist Church. Wilbert's parents were George Wesley Cronise (1833-1870) and Anna Mary L. (Sheets) (1835-1869), who are buried at Mt. Olivet Cemetery. See W&M-1054.

W&M-1234. Lycurgus Levi Flanagan (1870-1949) married Florence M. Powell. He is buried at Utica. His parents John F. (1828-1880) and Minerva (Snook) are buried at Creagerstown. In northern Frederick County in the 1800 census was the household of Hugh Flanigan, over 45 years, apparently a widower, with three daughters, five sons and one slave. Enrolled in the Frederick County Militia of 1812 was Joseph Flanagan.

W&M-1234. J. Harry Kling (1868-1940) and wife Annie M. (Lease) (1869-1930) are buried at Mt. Hope Cemetery, Woodsboro, where also are buried his paternal grandparents David (1800-1880) and wife Susan (Stitely) (1797-1876) and his parents John D. Kling (1831-1917) and wife Amelia (Grimes) (1836-1914). For Lease see W&M-789; for Stitely see W&M-1006.

W&M-1235. Vernon T. Smith (1873-1943) and wife Ida I. (Barrick) (1872-1919) are buried at Mt. Olivet. Vernon's great grandfather Adam Smith (1783-1834) is buried at Woodsboro Reformed Church. His grandparents Peter Smith (1813-1902) and Elizabeth (Cramer) (1818-1892) are buried at Mt. Hope Cemetery at Woodsboro. Vernon's parents James W. (1849-1916) and Alice G. (Barrick) (1849-1909) are buried also at Mt. Hope.

In northern Frederick County in the 1800 census were three Smith households whose heads were over 45 years of age, namely Daniel, George and John. Apparently Vernon's line of Smiths at Woodsboro was different from the prominent one of John Smith, Sr. (c.1790-1860) and his father Middleton. See W&M-1237.

W&M-1236. Ernest Powell (1880-1951) and wife Mary C. (Shook) (b. 1885) have gravestones in the U. B. Cemetery of Thurmont. His parents Lewis J. Powell (1831-1895) and wife Hannah E. (Gaugh) (1836-1922) are buried at Utica, where also are buried his grandparents William Powell (1792-1870) and Phoebe (Burkett) (1798-1863).

In the 1800 census of Libertytown District was the family of William Powel (over 45 years) and wife (26-45) with four daughters and three sons (under 10 years). In Lutheran records of Monocacy, Thomas Powell and wife appear in 1776; Rebecca Powell married John Mackaid (McKaig?) in 1776; and Thomas Powl married Hanna Templin in 1792 (apparently in Middletown Valley). In the Frederick County Militia of 1812 were enrolled George, Nathan, Jonathan and Samuel Powell. William Powell served on the Frederick County Grand Jury in 1759 and Thomas Powell in 1761. (LC)

W&M-1237. James M. Smith (1843-1920) and wife Tacie E. (Eyler) (1846-1916) are buried at Woodsboro Mt. Hope Cemetery. His father John (1792-1845) married Susannah Ebert (1800-1872) and secondly Elizabeth (Frock). John and Susannah are buried at Rocky Hill Church. James M. was a son of Elizabeth (Frock).

Early Middleton Smith about 1759 married widow Rebecca Ramsay. James M. and many prominent recent Smiths of the Woodsboro area are descendants of Middleton Smith II who, in 1785, married Juliana Keller. Middleton lived at first in the Ballenger Creek area and there may be a relationship to Johan Georg Schmidt, naturalized in 1761. See W&M-704. Middleton Smith II, in will probated 1836, discloses a second wife Martha. Middleton's son John Smith, Sr. (1792-1860) is the John Smith so often referred to as early farmer Smith near Woodsboro in biographies in W&M. Below are the children of John by wives Susannah and Elizabeth, largely as recorded in a hand written genealogy given to me by my friend the late Webster Cash Smith:

John Smith and wife Susanna (Ebert) had children:
(1) Ezra (1817-1882) m. Margaret Derr (daughter of Solomon and Elizabeth (Holbrunner)), three children.
Ezra's second m. Rebecca Feiser (1834-1904), eight children.
Grandparents of R. Paul, Robert L., Nevin E. and Harry B. Smith.
(2) Mary (b. 1820) m. Dr. John Leggett of Woodsboro and Middleburg.
(3) Margaret (1825-1897) m. William C. Carmack (1820-1899), buried at Woodsboro Mt. Hope.
(4) Elizabeth (b. 1825) m. Thomas Holbrunner.
(5) Solomon (1831-1906) m. Adelina (1830-1898), both buried at Rocky Hill Church.
(6) Susan Christina (1836?-1911) m. Capt. Joseph Groff (1822-1903), buried at Mt. Olivet.

John Smith and second wife Elizabeth (Frock) had children:
(7) John, Jr. (1837-1909) m. 1859 Mary Jane Gilbert (1836-1915) (daughter of Michael and Margaret (Koontz)), nine children; buried at Mt. Hope.
(8) Ann Matilda (1840-1888) m. Charles E. Dougherty (1835-1907), seven children; she is buried at Mt. Hope, he is buried at Thurmont Catholic Church.
(9) James Madison (1843-1920) m. 1863 Tacie E. Eyler (1846-1916), no children.
(10) Calvin P. (1845-1926) m. (Mary) Elizabeth Albaugh (1855-1940), three children and many descendants, including W. Cash Smith.
(11) Isabella Lavinia (1849-1904) m. John Edward Stambaugh (1839-1904); buried at Mt. Hope.
(12) William A. (1857-1901) m. Anna B. Cutshall (1860-1838) (daughter of William and Henrietta (Hull)), buried at Mt. Hope.

In the will of Middleton Smith, probated 1836, his children in order mentioned were: Mary m. Fulton; Mary m. Valentine (children Sevilla Margaret, Melanchton, and William); Joseph; Catherine m. Humerick; John (see above); Juliana (to receive special care).

W&M-1238. James F. Crampton (1853-1925) and wife Annie M. (Fraley) (1863-1935) are buried at Mt. Olivet. His parents Joshua (1815-1895) and Annie Maria (Feaster) (1829-1910) are buried at Jefferson Union Cemetery.

The Cramphin family, later Crampton, as in Crampton's Gap in South Mountain, were early in Frederick County. Basil and John Cramphin were among petitioners to divide Prince George's County in 1742. John Cramphin opened a tavern in Frederick County in 1749. The earliest gravestone surviving is that of Ann Crampton (1777-1858) at Petersville Episcopal Church. See W&M-1478 for John, the father of Joshua.

In earliest courthouse records of Frederick County, Cramphins are prominent, for example: Ann in deed of 1749; Henry, inventory of 1750 with John C. as administrator; Alice received gift of land from Mary in 1749; Thomas sold land to Thomas Luckett in 1751; Thomas sold land to John in 1749; Nehemiah Ogdon sold a tract in Monocase to his son-in-law Thomas Cramphin in 1749; Thomas was in several deeds of 1763 and 1764.

W&M-1238. John T. Colliflower (1840-1917) and wife Mary Isabella (Hesser) (1841-1918) are buried at the Moravian Cemetery at Graceham. Also buried at Graceham are his parents John (1799-1882) and Mary Matilda (Wilhide) (1805-1875). For Wilhide ancestors see W&M-729.

The Colliflaur or Gorenflo family is believed to have been of French Huguenot origin but came from Friedenthal or Friedrichstal, Baden, Germany to America (M&C-II). Georg Adam (d. 1801) emigrated in 1749 according to Pennsylvania Folklife Magazine, Spring 1973, and from a report in the files of J. M. H. He settled near Cavetown in later Washington County on the tract Stoney Run acquired in 1754.

George Colliflower left his plantation to eldest son George, Jr. Younger son Michael (1758-1838) married Susan Snyder at Graceham and in 1805 settled on

Greenspring Farm. They were members of the Moravian Congregation at Graceham. Their son John Colliflower (1799-1882) and wife Mary Matilda (Wilhide) farmed south of Graceham, where they had eight children. Their son Michael Joseph (b. 1826), a contractor, married Harriet Elizabeth Shuff and they had nine children. This and more in my files come from Howard E. Colliflower, Jr. of Baltimore.

Colliflowers of Graceham were related to the interesting Six families. In the 1800 census of Taneytown District there were three households of Elizabeth and Leonard Six, both over 45 years; and younger Philip, from whom five generations follow:

(1) Philip Six, Jr. (1806-1879) m. Margaret Barnhart (1812-1898), buried at Keysville.

(2) William Ferguson Six (1847-1907) m. Mary Catherine Stambaugh (1848-1928), buried at Keysville.

(3) Newton Elmer Six (1877-1954) m. Bertha May Colliflower (1876-1963) of Graceham, also buried at Keysville.

(4) William Jago Six (1911-1991) m. 1945 (Gladys) Helen McKinnon (b. 1916 at Haverhill, MA). Helen contributed to M&C-I and II and this work. A number of her studies of local genealogy are at (WP). She lives in Frederick.

(5) William J. Six, Jr. (b. 1952 in Frederick) m. 1976 Sue Elizabeth Harp (b. 1952 in Frederick).

W&M-1239. Jesse Edgar Clary(1866-1946) and wife Laura N. (Urner) (1866-1940) are buried at Unionville Methodist Church, as are his parents Jesse T. Clary (1824-1894) and Susan (Dudderar) (1827-1887). In the 1800 census of eastern Frederick County Benjamin Clary and wife were over 45 years of age with eight children. Younger heads of Clary families in 1800 were Daniel, David and Rachel.

A Clary genealogy has been written by Ralph Shearer and Star Wilson Rowland of Fairfax, VA (c.1980). (LC). Clarys who served in 1812 were Adin (d 1815); Daniel; Nathaniel (c.1786-1851), to Noble County, IN; Samuel; and Zacharias, to Springfield, OH.

W&M-1239. Marshall D. Boone (1858-1914) married Clara I. Flaught (1862-1928). He is buried at Mt. Hope, Woodsboro; she is buried at Monocacy Brethren Church at Rocky Ridge. His parents were Dennis Boone (1822-1882) and Sophia (Waltz) (1822-1872). Sophia's parents may have been Isaac S. Waltz (1796-1879) and wife Maranda (1796-1873) buried at Israel Creek Cemetery south of Woodsboro. See also W&M-1230. Dennis was said to have been a descendant of Daniel Boone. (LC)

W&M-1240. Howard Marvin Jones (1874-1955) and wife Mabel Clarke (Pierce) (1877-1955) are buried at Park Heights Cemetery, Brunswick. (LC)

W&M-1241. Maj. Edward Yerbury Goldsborough (1839-1915) married Amy Ralston Auld, daughter of Robert and Jane (Chase) Auld and the grand niece of Chief Justice Salmon P. Chase of Ohio. Nicholas Goldsborough in 1679 married Elizabeth Greenbury, the daughter of an Indian Chief. William

Goldsborough (1763-1826) and wife Sarah (1770-1854) of Dorchester County, Maryland are buried at Mt. Olivet, along with their son Nicholas (c.1795-1840). Son Dr. Edward Yerburg Goldsborough (1797-1850) and wife Margaret (Schley) (1802-1876) also are buried at Mt. Olivet.

Margaret Schley was a daughter of John George Schley (1769-1835) and wife Anna Mary (Shriver) (1773-1853) (daughter of David and Rebecca (Ferree)). David Shriver was a son of emigrant Andreas Schreiber from Alsenborn near Kaiserslautern in the Pfalz, who settled near Hanover, Pennsylvania about 1734. Margaret's grandparents, John Thomas and Margaret Schley, were emigrants to earliest Fredericktown and leaders in the early Reformed Congregation at Frederick. See my Schley genealogy at (FH) (F).

Margaret, at age 22, danced with Marquis de Lafayette when he visited Frederick in 1824 with his son George Washington Lafayette. The Historical Society of Frederick County treasures a portrait of Margaret Schley in her Lafayette dress and the slippers which she wore. Two years later Margaret married Dr. Edward Y. Goldsborough. Dorothy Mackay Quynn wrote an account of Lafayette's visit to Frederick in MHM 49, 270 (1954).

According to gravestone inscriptions at Mt. Olivet, additions can be made to the children of Dr. Edward and Margaret: Dr. John Schley Goldsborough (1835-1885) m. Julia A. W. (1843-1878); Robert Henry (1836-1882).

The only child of Major Edward Y. Goldsborough, Jr. and wife Amy was E. Ralston Goldsborough (c.1880-1949). He graduated from Mercersburg Academy and from Lehigh University in civil engineering which he practiced in Frederick. From the 1930s Ralston devoted much of his time in research into local American Indian archeology and in local genealogy. He left a store of letters and reports in the files of the Historical Society of Frederick County. Ralston's short obituary in the *Frederick News* shows the low value that was given his scholarship. It stated that he died on May 10, 1949 at the County Home where he had lived since 1947, and where he had been paralyzed. He belonged to the Episcopal Church and he had given part of his collection of Indian artifacts to the School for the Deaf. E. Ralston Goldsborough was buried in Mt. Olivet Cemetery, but Holdcraft found no gravestone.

The Goldsboroughs have been prominent in Maryland for a long time. Six of the family were officers in the Revolution and six others were privates. Most came from Talbot County. Nicholas (son of William of Dorchester County) served in the Frederick County Militia of 1812.

Some sources for Goldsborough genealogy are given in M&C-II. (LC). Dr. Charles Edward Goldsborough practiced in Hunterstown in Adams County (WB).

W&M-1242. G. Lloyd Palmer (1866-1931) and wife Maymie (Delaplane) (1877-1952) are buried at Mt. Olivet. The Delaplane ancestors are given in M&C-I. Lloyd's parents were Jacob Ezra (1832-1905) and Matilda C. (Miller) (1847-1915), who are buried at Utica. See also W&M-764. (LC)

W&M-1243. Harry Ellsworth Wilson (1870-1933) and wife Lula (Hearn) (1872-1926) are buried at Unionville Methodist Church. William G. Wilson (1819-1886) grandfather of Harry is buried also at Unionville along with wives

Josephine (1831-1860) and Lydia Isabelle (Brightwell). Lydia was the mother of William H. H. Wilson (1843-1917), who married Carrie V. Six (1851-1939), all of whom are buried at Unionville. Harry E. was the first child of Carrie.

Wilson families were early in Frederick County. Joseph Wilson was Constable of Lower Monocacy Hundred in 1749. Thomas Wilson lived near Tom's Creek in 1750. Wadsworth Wilson served on a Frederick County jury in 1751. Early Wilsons noted in T&D include Thomas on Carrollton Manor, Robert near later Emmitsburg and John Wilson on Monocacy Manor. Prominent Wilson families are discussed by Scharf.

W&M-1244. Rufus Flickinger (1852-1910) and wife Esther O. (Albaugh) (1850-1897) are buried at Woodsboro Mt. Hope Cemetery, where also are buried his parents George (1824-1908) and wife Maria (Wikard) (1828-1875). Andrew and Jacob Fleckener families lived in Westminster District in 1800.

W&M-1246. Eugene L. Derr (1844-1921) and his parents John (1798-1866) and wife Elizabeth (Lugenbeel) (1808-1883) are buried at Mt. Olivet. Eugene's grandfather John married Catherine Stoner. See below.

A more accurate account of emigrant Sebastian Derr (1727-1802) is given by Wampler. Sebastian Doerr, son of Jacob and Maria Catherine, emigrated about 1750 from Ilbesheim near Landau in southern Pfalz, (not in Bavaria). In 1755 Sebastian purchased the Tract Dearbought west of the Monocacy River near later Ceresville north of Frederick. He married Elisabeth Loy (Ley), daughter of Johan Georg. His second marriage was to Catherine Brengle (c.1740-1790), daughter of Kilian of Wolfersheim, Pfalz, and wife Juliana.

By Sebastian Derr's first marriage were children:

(1) Sebastian, Jr., to Kentucky.

(2) Rosina (b. 1758) m. John Bucher.

(3) Elizabeth (b. 1761) m. 1780 George Getz (1758-1801).

(4) (John) Jacob (1762-1836) m. 1787 Margaret Wintz (d. 1839) at Harrodsburg, Kentucky).

By second marriage:

(5) Susannah (1767-1830) m. Caspar Devilbiss (1761-1835).

(6) John (1774-1838) m. Catherine Stoner (Steiner) (1774-1812).

(7) George (1777-1793).

(8) Thomas (1780-1845) m. Anna Barbara Stoner (1783-1814), to Tiffin, Ohio.

Wampler gives short accounts of two other Derr settlers in Frederick County, namely John Martin (1737-1872) and Abraham (1767-1829).

W&M-1247. James G. Jones (1835-1925) and wife Sarah Virginia (Burgess) (1840-1931) are buried at New London Methodist Church, as are his parents William (1782-1869) and Mary (Galt) (1800-1881).

James G. Jones was an uncle of prominent chemist of Johns Hopkins University, Harry Clary Jones (1865-1916), about whom I wrote in the *Frederick News* on April 18, 1991. The proliferous Jones families have left 57 Jones names in the cemetery of Central Chapel Methodist Church north of New London. Jones land grants, 1742-1827, are collected at Maryland Historical Society (MS 1332).

A John Jones of Charles County and wife Elizabeth moved to Frederick County where his will was one of the first probated in the new county in 1749. A John Jones, planter, whose wife was Hannah, made a will probated in 1760. He left children John, Jesse, Priscilla, Nicholas, Mary and Margaret. John Jones died in 1824 according to his broken gravestone at Central Chapel. He was the father of William Jones (1782-1869), whose son William, Jr. (1825-1895) married Joanna Clary (daughter of Henry and Sarah Clary). Professor Harry Clary Jones was their only child.

Members of the Frederick County Militia of 1812 included David, George, James, Jeremiah, several Johns, Nathan, Thomas, William and Zachariah Jones.

W&M-1248. Adrian Ceolfrid McCardell (1845-1932) and wife Alforetta R. Stonebraker (1848-1912) are buried at Mt. Olivet. His parents Wilfrid D. (c.1814-1861) and wife Catherine Humrichouse (daughter of Frederick Post and Hannah) are buried in Washington County. The McCardell name and origin were Catholic Irish, not Scotch Irish. However, early in Washington County, Maryland, they began to marry Protestants of German origin. The following generations come from M&C-I:

(1) Patrick McCardell (c.1716-1786) m. Mary ----; tobacconist at Hagerstown.

(2) James (b. before 1755) m. Rebecca ---- (before 1755-1834); 2m. Christiana; farmed near Hagerstown.

(3) Thomas (1779-1843) m. Anna Maria Nogle (Nagel) (d. 1861), farm near Hagerstown.

(4) Wilfrid D. m. 1845 Catherine Humrichouse, farm near Williamsport; Maryland House of Delegates. She and children belonged to the German Reformed Church.

W&M-1249. Jesse Pfoutz (1883-1958) and wife Malla Dean (Pittinger) (1886-1932) are buried at Pipe Creek Brethren Cemetery near Uniontown. He was a son of Elder Isaac Pfoutz (1803-1901) and second wife Catherine E. (Doyle) (1799-1880), who are buried at Beaver Dam Brethren Church near Johnsville.

Hans Michael Pfoutz emigrated in 1727 from Rohrbach near Sinsheim, Baden, southeast of Heidelberg (B1). His son Jacob and wife Magdalena had eldest daughter Margaretha who, about 1744 in Pennsylvania, married Andreas Huber (1722-1794). These ancestors of President Herbert Hoover farmed in later Carroll County near Union Bridge and attended the Quaker Meeting House still there. About 1762 they moved south to near the Yadkin River in NC. (M&C-I).

Elder Isaac may have been a son of John Pfoutz (1769-1855) and wife Esther (1777-1848) or of the Jacob Pfoutz (26-45 years) who is in the 1800 census of Libertytown District. Another descendant of emigrant Michael Pfoutz is said to have been John Michael III (1734-1824) and wife Barbara (Crumpacker) (1734-1813). The Pfoutz family must not be confused with the Ffout, Pfout and Fout families of western Maryland. (LC). For Pfoutz families in Adams County see (WB).

The usual lineage of President Herbert Hoover given in (NC 56, 295) is that of M&C-I, involving Andreas Huber who emigrated from Ellerstadt, Pfalz, where a house is marked. Recently Annette K. Burgert has challenged this (B1). She has stated on page 181 "It seems more logical that the Andreas Huber who emigrated at the age of 15 in 1738 is the Andreas born May 13, 1724 in Ittlingen." The latter village is near Sinsheim southeast of Heidelberg.

W&M-1250. Marion F. Riddlemoser (1848-1911) and wife Margaret A. (Smith) (1851-1931) are buried at Mt. Olivet. His parents Ephraim (1806-1892) and wife Julia Ann (Smith) (1805-1884) are buried in the Catholic Cemetery in Frederick.

Jacob Riddlemoser (1784-1850) of Pennsylvania and wife Amelia (c.1798-1872) are buried in the same cemetery. Ephraim R. (1806-1892) was a son of Jacob by first wife Mary (Diffindall).

W&M-1251. (David) Chester Kemp (1873-1958) and wife Sophia Markell (Detrick) (1879-1964) are buried at Mt. Olivet. His parents D. Columbus (1841-1920) and wife Annie S. (Walcutt) (1849-1931) are also buried there.

This Kemp lineage is abstracted largely from M&C-I:

(1) John Conrad Kaempf (1685-1764) and wife Anna Maria (1695-1758) of Untergimbern near Sinsheim, Baden. See W&M-791.

(2) Gilbert Kemp (1717-1794) m. (Susannah) Margaret Getzendanner (1724-1814), farmed near Rocky Springs, west of Frederick.

(3) Frederick (1747-1814) m. Dorothea Hersperger (1763-1831), lived near Rocky Springs.

(4) David (1791-1869) m. Ruth S. Lakin (1800-1871).

(5) (David) Columbus and (6) David Chester, above.

(7) Stoll Detrick (b. 1904) m. Katherine Elizabeth Wright of Denton, Maryland; he has been the leader in antique business of New Market and family historian. Stoll and Katherine live retired in Denton in 1994.

W&M-1251. John D. Beard (1851-1931) and wife Barbara Burrier (1853-1929) are buried at Liberty Chapel. His parents John (1818-1851) and wife Sarah A. (Locke) (1817-1895) are buried at Rocky Hill near Woodsboro. Sarah and second husband Samuel Smith are buried also at Rocky Hill.

The census of 1800 of Libertytown District shows only one Beard household, that of Jacob and wife, both over 45 years in age. They had one daughter and one son, both under 10 years. The earlier German form of the name was Bard or Bart. Jacob served in the Frederick County Militia of 1812 as did Daniel Beard (b. c.1789). (LC)

W&M-1252. Adam David Birely (1839-1916) and wife Sarepta Jane (Anders) (1839-1919) are buried at Haugh's Church near Ladiesburg. His parents were Frederick (1805-1881) and Sabina (Harbaugh) (1805-1858), who also are buried at Haugh's Church. Earlier Birely generations follow:

(1) (Frederick) Ludwig Beyerle m. Eva Maria Heffner (daughter of Michael). He emigrated from Germany with father John Michael to Lancaster County, then to Monocacy area about 1762.

(2) George Ludwig (1755-1827) m. Elizabeth Inch (1754-1845); moved from near Apples Church to a farm near Ladiesburg, parents of Frederick above.

W&M-1253. Robert Augustus Kemp (1865-1942) and wife Daisy Alice (Birely) (1871-1947) are buried at Mt. Olivet, where also are buried his parents Charles Wesley (1830-1876) and wife Columbia A. (Rhodes).

See W&M-791 for emigrant Conrad Kaempf and family from Untergimbern near Sinsheim. (Not on the Rhine River, but further east.) They settled west and south of Frederick, not at Kemptown which came much later.

The following lineage is from M&C-I:

(1) (John) Conrad Kaempf (1685-1764) m. (Anna) Maria (1695-1758), he was naturalized in 1743.
(2) (John) Frederick (1725-1804) m. Regina, lived near Rocky Springs.
(3) Rev. Peter (1749-1811) m. Mary Lehman (Leaman); he was a founder of United Brethren Church, lived west of Frederick near Doub Cemetery.
(4) Peter (1803-1885) m. Elizabeth Myers (?) (1804-1836); carriage builder near Ceresville, later near Walkersville.
(5) Charles Wesley, above, carpenter at Walkersville, later to Frederick.

W&M-1254. (Charles) Edward Schaeffer (1844-1913) and wife Rebecca (Brane) (1842-1918) are buried at Mt. Olivet at Frederick, where also are buried his parents Peter (1798-1883) and Elizabeth (Brunner) (1803-1853).

If the ancestors of the Schaeffer family of southern Frederick County came from Berlin, this is very surprising. Very few of the early German settlers of Frederick County came from the Berlin area, which lay so far from available transportation via the Rhine River and Rotterdam. The name von Schaeffer suggested by the writer is also very unusual. The German preposition von, meaning of or from, has been used for locations, e.g. Kekulé von Stradonitz. To use it with a common vocational name such as Schaefer, meaning shepherd, is unlikely.

The Schaeffer households in the south of Frederick County in 1800 were headed by John and by Peter and their wives in age 26-45 years, who had young children. Susanna Schaeffer over 45, possibly a widow, lived with one female of 16-26 years. The Schaeffers of the Manor area may have attended Reformed Church in Frederick where their records begin in 1766. The widow of a Jacob Schaeffer was Elizabeth (1760-1795). Other Schaefer or Schaeffers in early Reformed records at Frederick were Peter (1732-1792), Adam (1732-1792), Adam (1740-1794), John's widow Margaret (1725-1795), Peter and wife Rosina (sponsors of baptism 1773). See also W&M-747.

W&M-1255. Lewis H. Bowlus (1846-1927) and wife Ann Sophia (Biser) (1847-1908) are buried at Burkittsville Union Cemetery. His parents Capt. Stephen R. (1822-1894) and Ann Caroline (Remsburg) (1824-1911) are buried at Middletown Lutheran Church. Nicholas Bowlus, Jr. (1786-1827) also is buried there.

The Bowlus name earlier was Baulus or Paulus, the Latin form of Paul. The earliest local records are in the Monocacy Lutheran Congregation book where

Andreas Paulus and wife Anna Maria had baptized children born as follows: Lukas, 1751; Rosina, 1753, and John George, 1756. Andrew (wife Anna Maria) acquired 30 acres of the tract Delight in Middletown Valley in 1753 from Mark Whittaker. Nicholas Bowlus, who was naturalized in 1765, married Catherine (1759-1829). Nicholas Paulas and wife Ann Margaretha baptized their infant in 1770 in Middletown Reformed records. A later Nicholas and Catherine had Charlotte Sarah baptized 1825.

The Paulus family was said to originate perhaps in Essenheim. The emigrant John, first in York County, Pennsylvania, had sons Daniel, Wenz, Killian, John, Jr. and Valentine, according to Karl Pfeiffer of Bradenton, FL. Andrew Bowlis' inventory in Frederick County in 1763 had administrators Mary Ann and Jacob Bowlis. Nicholas Baulus was noted as a relative.

In the census of 1800 the following Powlas households were in Middletown Valley: George and Nicholas with their wives were over 45 years of age; Henry and Jacob were younger heads of families.

W&M-1256. Douglas H. Hargett (1846-1908) and wife Emma M. (Whipp) (1852-1931) are buried at Mt. Olivet, as are his parents Samuel (1811-1893) and wife Eleanora (Burns) (1811-1880).

Abraham Hargett (1753-1824) and wife Mary (1753-1831), also their son John (1787-1859) and his wife Barbara C. (1780-1856), are buried at Church Hill on Ballenger Creek Road. The latter were parents of Samuel. In the census of 1800 Peter and Abraham Hargett, both over 45 years of age, had households in southern Frederick County.

Peter L. Hargett was said to have emigrated to the Frederick area in 1750 (*Men of Mark in Maryland*, by Bernard C. Steiner). The family name has a French diminutive ending but, like many of the Huguenots, the Hargetts may have lived later in Germany. (LC)

W&M-1258. Robert E. Clapp, Jr. (b. 1879) married Bessie M. Hargett (1882-1955) from Newton, NC and they moved to Frederick. In 1948 they purchased a home on Lindbergh Avenue, Frederick. Their son Judge Robert E. Clapp III and wife Josephine R. live on Araby farm south of Frederick where Gen. Grant met Gen. Sheridan after the Battle of Monocacy.

I was told by descendant Alma Fogle that Johan Ludwig and George Valentin Klopp, later Clapp, emigrated from near Bingen on the Rhine in 1727. Associated with the family is Klopp Castle. Baedeker's guidebook to the Rhineland of 1926 states that Klopp Castle above the town of Bingen is reached by Schloss-Strasse. It was destroyed by the French in 1689, but restored and extended in 1834 to accommodate the Bingen municipal offices. The castle was no longer so used when I climbed there in the 1960s.

W&M-1258. Abraham Webster Grabill's parents were Samuel (1829-1904) and Abbie (Repp) (1829-1899) who are buried at the M. P. Church at Johnsville. Abraham's grandfather was Abraham (1801-1877) who is buried in the Grabill family graveyard near Johnsville. In the 1800 census of Libertytown District were two Grabill households, namely John and wife over 45 years, and Moses Graybell and wife, 26-45 years. The early Grebuehl or Kraebuehl families were Anabaptists originating in Canton Zurich, Switzerland. Michael Greybuehl emigrated from Weierhof, a Swiss Mennonite Center in the northern Palatinate of Germany. See recent Pennsylvania Mennonite Heritage Magazines. A genealogy of Graybill families was written by Margaret G. Yingling (Baltimore, 1980). See also (WP) and (LC).

W&M-1259. Simon Theodore Stauffer (1845-1923) and wives Louisa (Claggett) (1848-1870) and Clara Courtnay (Offutt) (1853-1937) are buried at Mt. Olivet, where also are buried his parents Henry (1813-1893) and wife Matilda Noble (Magruder) (1814-1871). Simon's grandparents Joseph Stauffer (1779-1858) and wife Catherine (Cronise) (1780-1868) are buried at Israel Creek Cemetery on the road from Walkersville to Woodsboro. See also W&M-1205.

W&M-1260. George W. Burrier (1878-1914) has a gravestone at Liberty Chapel with birth date, which W&M give for George M. Gravestones are lacking for his wives Edna (Hesson) and Emma (Beard). The parents of George were Josiah (1844-1896) and Lavenia (Long) (1854-1938), who are also buried at Liberty Chapel. Grandparents of George were John Burrier (b. c.1807) and Barbara (Nusbaum) (b. c.1811), who appear in the census of 1850. Earlier Burriers of Liberty Chapel are discussed by Given Boyer Bjorkman in W. Maryland Gen., April 1990.

In the census of 1800 of Libertytown District were five Burrier households. Philip and wife were over 45 years in age; Adam, Jacob and John and their wives were 26-45 years in age; George and wife were between 16 and 26 years of age.

A book, *Leonard and Barbara Burrier and Their Descendants (1739-1988)* by Charles D. Burrier (New Market, Maryland, 1988) is with the files of J. M. H. About 140 Burrier names are indexed in (Z).

W&M-1261. Joshua Albaugh (1829-1900) and wife Susannah (Hawk) (1833-1918) are buried at Fairmount Cemetery at Liberty. His parents Valentine Adams Albaugh (1801-1867) and Rebecca (Brunner) (1806-1864) are buried at Frederick in Mt. Olivet Cemetery.

The Ahlbach family which arrived in Philadelphia in 1734 consisted of Zacharias, 36 years; Anna D., 37; John William, 26; Anna Elisabeth, 26; Johan Wilhelm, 11; Johan Gerard, 6; Anna Margaretha, 8; Gertrude Margaretha, 2; Johan Peter, 2.

After farming for a while in New Jersey, emigrant Zacharias Albach and son John William (1723-1794) settled near later Liberty Chapel. John William and wife Magdalena had son Abraham (1762-1830) who married Margaret Adams (1771-1848), the parents of Valentine. They are buried at Liberty Chapel. For early Albaughs see Anders Root Directory (FH).

Several genealogies of Albaugh families are given in M&C-II. A genealogy by an unknown author in my files gives the emigrant of Reformed faith as Johan Wilhelm (b. c.1690), emigrant 1734, who married a Gerhardt. Their sons were Zachariah, Johan William, Jr., John Gerhardt and John Peter.

W&M-1263. Richard Wallace Simpson (1833-1923) and wives Julia Ann (Hammond) (1834-1870) and Marian Livingston (McConkey) (1841-1917) are buried at Liberty Fairmount Cemetery. His first wife Tillie Root (c.1839-1957) is buried at Liberty Chapel. Richard's father Warfield Simpson and grandfather Joshua have not been found on gravestones. The early stone on the

Simpson family graveyard near Liberty is that of Richard Simpson, Jr. (1755-1798). Basil J. F. Simpson from Edinburgh, Scotland, emigrated in the 1730s and later settled near New London.

A Simpson family genealogy of eight pages was received from Mrs. Mildred Michael Crewe of Buckeystown in 1983. Francis Simpson (b. 1740) married Thomasin Worthington Warfield. Their son Basil J. F. (b. 1764) married Henrietta Worthington (d. 1799). Their son Basil (b. 1799) married Martha Howard. Their son Basil John Fletcher (1830-1900) born in Olney, Maryland, settled at New London, as a cabinet maker and blacksmith. Basil and wife Laura Jane (Nusbaum) (1841-1914) were members of Central Methodist Church. The children of the Simpsons follow:

(1) Minnie Worthington (1860-1949) m. Nelson Granville Jones (1853-1912).

(2) Effie Elizabeth Clarke (1862-1953) m. John Horace Albaugh (1857-1942).

(3) Basil Worthington (1864-1865), twin, drowned.

(4) Ridgely Delzell (1864-1946) m. Anna Florence Albaugh (1870-1948). Descendants in Frederick are given.

(5) James Clarke (1868-1895) m. Myra L. Cashaw (1872-1947).

(6) Allen Bowie (1872-1944) m. Mertie Beck.

Most of the dates above are from New London Methodist Cemetery. Wallace Warfield married a cousin of the Simpsons and later married Edward, Duke of Windsor. Richard and Jeremiah Simpson served on the Grand Jury of Frederick County in 1755. At least 20 Simpsons served in the Maryland Militia in the Revolution, most from southern Maryland. (LC)

W&M-1264. Dr. Thomas E. R. Miller, M.D. (1844-1915) and wife Margaret (Delaplaine) (1847-1916) are buried at Mt. Olivet Cemetery, as are his parents George (1791-1861) and wife Catharine (Harbaugh) (1806-1875). The latter was a grandmother of banker J. Marshall Miller (1857-1956). See W&M-973.

W&M-1265. Joshua D. Ahalt (1843-1922) and wife Laura Emily (Shafer) (1851-1932) are buried at Middletown Lutheran Cemetery, where also are buried his parents Mathias (1803-1881) and wife Phoebe (Rautzahn) (1809-1893). See also W&M-988.

W&M-1265. George Carlton Culler (1863-1915) and wife Rose L. (Lewis)(1864-1943) are buried at Jefferson Union Cemetery, where also are his parents John Harmon (1837-1898) and Lucinda C. (Kefauver) (1840-1922). See W&M-1085.

W&M-1266. Harry Emory Cramer (b. 1873) married Susan E. Kemp (1873-1897) and secondly Estella May Ramsburg (1877-1933), who are buried in Glade Reformed Cemetery near Walkersville. Harry's parents Ezra D. Cramer (1836-1911) and wife Amelia Catherine (Dudrear) (1849-1903) are buried at Mt. Olivet.

W&M-1267. Ezra Lewis Cramer, Jr. (1859-1921) and wife Ada Mary (Cramer) Cramer (1863-1944) are buried at Mt. Olivet, as are his parents Ezra Lewis, Sr. (1825-1900) and Henrietta (Kemp) (1835-1896).

It is very doubtful that a German Cramer arrived in America as early as 1705. See W&M-928 and 1111. Dulany's Manor is more often called Dulany's Lot (different from Monocacy Manor nearby).

Ezra Cramer (1797-1859) and wife C. Mary (Winebrenner) (1792-1872), buried at Glade Reformed Cemetery, were grandparents of Ezra Lewis, Jr. At the same place is buried the great grandfather of Ezra Lewis, Jr., namely John Cramer (c.1751-1825).

W&M-1269. Charles Henry Cramer (1852-1917) and his wife May (Devilbiss) (1861-1920) are buried at Glade Reformed Cemetery, where also are buried his parents Jeremiah (1825-1899) and Elizabeth C. (Stimmel) (1824-1915). Ezra and wife Mary (Winebrenner) in W&M-1267 above were grandparents of Charles Henry. See also W&M-928 and 1111. Magdalena Stimmell (b. 1774) married Col. Jacob Cramer (1774-1849) who commanded a regiment at D. C. in 1814. Their daughter Mary M. married David Coblentz of Middletown.

W&M-1270. (John) Luther Smith (1846-1917) and wife Ann Victoria (Ledwidge) (1848-1940) are buried at Mt. Hope Cemetery, Woodsboro. His parents Ezra (1804-1874) and wife Anna Margaret (Derr) (1804-1887) are buried at Rocky Hill Church near Woodsboro. Luther's grandfather was John, son of Middleton Smith of near Woodsboro discussed in W&M-928 and 1111.

W&M-1271. John Calvin Walker (1858-1915) married Clara V. Bartgis (d 1891), who is buried at Mt. Olivet. His stone is at Monrovia Brethren Cemetery south of New Market. John was a son of Jesse (1820-1869) and Jemima (Moxley), who are recorded at the same cemetery.

In addition to the early Walkers, given by W&M, a Nathaniel Walker lived in the Jefferson area in 1758. He was Constable of Lower Catoctin Hundred and overseer of a road across Middletown Valley in 1760. Nathaniel died about 1765. James Walker was a merchant in Frederick in 1753.

Besides English speaking Walkers, there is evidence of some German Walkers who had been Walchers. In 1762 Godlib (Gottlieb) Walker, a weaver, bought 100 acres of the tract Lamar's Generosity from Nathaniel Walker, shoemaker, whose wife was Elisabeth. The following Walcher immigrants arrived at Philadelphia: Jerg Michel (1751); Peter (1751); Johannes (1754).

W&M-1273. Marshall E. Waltz (1859-1936) and wife Laura E. (Harmis) (1860-1934) are buried at Liberty Chapel. His parents Enoch Joseph (1824-1899) and Caroline (Stitely) (1827-1868) are buried at Beaver Dam Brethren Cemetery. Marshall's grandparents Solomon Waltz (1793-1838) and wife Elizabeth (Etzler) (1798-1873) also are buried at Beaver Dam.

The emigrant Waltz may have embarked from Antwerp, Belgium, but Rotterdam, Holland, was the usual port. In the 1800 census of Libertytown District were three Wals households. Rinehart Wals and wife of 26-45 years; John and Jacob were between 16-26 years.

W&M-1275. William Sherman Devilbiss. See W&M-1297.

W&M-1275. Franklin L. Bowlus (1844-1918) and wife Sarah Ellen (Beachley) (1843-1932) are buried at Pleasant View Brethren Church near Burkittsville. He was a son of Capt. Stephen R. (1822-1894) and Ann Caroline (Remsburg)

(1824-1911), who are buried at Middletown Lutheran Church. Franklin's paternal grandparents were Nicholas (1786-1827) and Catherine (Orndorff) (1786-1848). See W&M-1255 for Franklin's brother Lewis. also, a genealogy *Bowlus (Baulus, Paulus) and Remsburg Families* by Charles D. Bowlus (Anderson, IN, 1901) (BM).

W&m-1276. Henry Baumgardner (1835-1917) and wife Caroline (Shawbaker) (1836-1904) are buried at Mt. Olivet. He was a son of Thomas (1811-1873) and Margaret (Sheffer) (1807-1883). W&M gives Thomas' birth in Germany as 1805. Caroline was a daughter of Jacob Shawbaker (1784-1864) and granddaughter of Adam Schabacker (c.1753-1823), a Hessian mercenary, and wife Maria Barbara (Schnautigel) (d. 1832). (GM). See other Baumgardners in W&M-853 and 1291.

W&M-1277. John W. Baker (1857-1942) and wife Cecelia A. (Devilbiss) are buried at Mt. Olivet. His parents were Joseph G. (1828-1899) and Hannah (Devilbiss) (1835-1907), who are buried at the Baker family graveyard near Unionville. There were six Baker families in the 1800 census of eastern Frederick County. Oldest were the heads Henry, Sr. and John and their wives over 45 years. Six Bakers were enrolled in the Frederick County Militia of 1812.

W&M-1278. George C. (Siedling (1828-1902) and wife Johanna Christina (Schade) (1829-1908) are buried at Mt. Olivet. In the Frederick County Militia of 1812, George Shade from "Upper Frederick County" was a musician.

W&M-1278. Marshall Naill Nusbaum (b. 1868) and wife Jennie A. (Buckey) (1869-1911) have records in stone at Sam's Creek Methodist Church. He was a son of Isaiah (1833-1901) and Maggie L. (Naill) (1835-1895), who also are buried at Sam's Creek. Marshall's paternal grandparents were Jacob Nusbaum (1807-1886) and Barbara (Hyde) (1808-1898) who are buried at Bethany Church at Covers Corners. An earlier Jacob Nusbaum served in the Frederick County Militia of 1812. (LC)

W&M-1280. Richard Bruce Murdoch (b. 1870) and wife Alice C. (Walker) (1864-1931) have gravestone records at Monrovia Church of the Brethren. He was a son of Richard Howard Murdoch (1826-1903) and wife Mary Ellen (Medairy) (Medare) (1848-1928) who are buried at Urbana Episcopal Church.

William Murdoch was on the first Grand Jury of Frederick County in 1749. Benjamin Murdoch and wife, both 26-45 years, are in the 1800 census of Buckeystown District with three daughters, three sons and 15 slaves. Genealogy of Murdock families has been recorded by William B. Marye, MHM 25, 262 (1930); also by Lewis D. Cook in magazine of Gen. Soc. of Pennsylvania 16, 39 (1948).

A John W. Murdock born in 1826 in Ayrshire, Scotland had descendants in Frederick and Washington Counties (Wms. 1906). Another John Murdock, a native of Ireland, married Harriet Barber of New Market, Maryland. Before the Civil War he was a supervisor of the National Turnpike. In the 1850s the couple moved to Boonsboro District of Washington County (Wms. 1906).

W&M-1281. Thomas John Claggett IV (1856-1911) and wife Mary Louise (Staley) (1859-1916) are buried at Petersville Episcopal Church, as are his parents Thomas J. III (1813-1873) and wife Ann P. (Hilleary) (1824-1897), also his grandparents Dr. Thomas J. II (1785-1835) and wife Sophia (1793-1862). The estate of Capt. Thomas Clagett (c.1684-1734) had Mary C. Clagett as executrix in Prince George's County. Another Thomas Clagett had inventory of 1738 in Prince George's County with Ann Clagett as executrix. John and Charles Clagett were relatives. See Tercentennial History of Maryland, Vol. 4, 643; Clagett and Hollingsworth Papers are in (MS). See also W&M-864. A genealogy of Clagett families was written by Brice C. Clagett in 1948.

W&M-1282. Albert E. Wallis (1844-1891) and wives Columbia F. (Dutrow) (1837-1883) and her sister Rebecca E. (Dutrow) (1833-1923) are buried at Mt. Olivet. See also W&M-948.

W&M-1283. Andrew J. Wachter (1840-1925) and wife Cornelia A. (Coblentz) (1840-1921) are buried at Utica. His parents were Philip, Jr. (1812-1886) and Susanna (Reese) (1814-1899) who are buried at Bethel Lutheran Church north of Frederick. Andrew's paternal grandparents Philip Wachter, Sr. (1786-1875) and wife Ammareliss (Widerick) (1788-1863) also are buried at Bethel. See also W&M-724 and *Wachter Families* by Wesley N. Wachter (1955) (with files of J. M. H.).

W&M-1283. George W. M. Albaugh (1867-1937) and wife Ella M. (Handly) (1864-1932) are buried at Mt. Hope Cemetery, Woodsboro. His parents Andrew H. (1840-1921) and wife Maranda (Clem) (1841-1924) are buried at Utica. George's paternal grandparents were John (1809-1891) and wife Elizabeth A. (1815-1897) who are buried at the Glade Reformed Cemetery near Walkersville. See also W&M-1261. In the 1800 census of northern Frederick County Stephen Hendly (over 45 years) and wife had eight children.

Ammareliss Widerick probably was a descendant of Martin Wieterich who emigrated from Hunspach, north Alsace, in 1752 (B3). He married in 1752 Dorothea Kauff of Seebach near Wissembourg, North Alsace.

W&M-1284. William A. Smith (1857-1901) and wife Anna B. (Cutshall) (1860-1938) are buried at Mt. Hope Cemetery, Woodsboro. He was a son of John (1792-1860) and Elizabeth (Frock) (1812-1886). See W&M-1237. William A. was the 12th and last child of John Smith (of Middleton).

W&M-1285. John D. Addison (b. 1830) is recorded on the gravestone of his wife Martha C. (Henry) (1840-1931) at Mt. Olivet. Addison families were prominent in early Maryland and Addison's Choice near Ceresville was one of the earliest tracts surveyed in Frederick County. See M&C-I. A genealogy of the Addison family was written by Elizabeth H. Murray (1895) and another by McHenry Howard in MHM 14, 387 (1919) (BF) (FH). (LC)

W&M-1286. Joseph Hamilton Hummer (b. 1857) was a son of Joseph (1815-1876) and Margaret (Eyler) (1825-1896) who are buried at Charlesville Reformed Church north of Frederick. In the 1800 census of Emmitsburg District were households of John Humer, over 45 years in age, and Jacob Humer between 26 and 45 years.

W&M-1287. George W. Webster (1845-1926) and wife Susan M. (Smith) (1852-1936) are buried at Mt. Olivet, but no stones were found for Thomas (b. 1815) and wife Leah A. (Jacobs). At Mt. Olivet are buried William Webster

(1806-1829), also George Webster (1782-1854), born in Birmingham, England, who emigrated in 1810, along with wife Thankful (Morgan) (1790-1876). Their daughter Juliana Johns (1821-1848) also is buried there. (LC). Websters of the Thurmont area are in M&C-II.

W&M-1288. Charles Henry Coblentz (1840-1927) and wife Frances Virginia (Routzahn) (1842-1897) are buried in Middletown Reformed Cemetery, as are his parents Henry (1807-1888) and wife Ann Magdalena (Routzahn) (1807-1868).

It is doubted that the Coblentz family lived at Coblentz where the Mosel River flows into the Rhine, far to the south of Prussia. See W&M-776. John Philip Coblentz (1776-1853) and wife Elizabeth (Culler) (1778-1857) also are buried at Middletown Reformed Church.

W&M-1289. Lewis Philip Coblentz (1835-1899) and wife Charlotte E. (Routzahn) (1844-1920) are buried at the Reformed Cemetery in Middletown, as are his parents Henry and Magdalena noted in the article above. A number of their children left our area, e.g. to D. C. and Kansas. See also W&M-776.

W&M-1289. John Calvin Coblentz (1845-1929) and wife Lucinda E. M. (Smith) (1847-1929) are buried at the Reformed Church in Middletown. His parents were John Coblentz of P. (c.1803-1878) and Sarah (Remsburg) (c.1807-1885). John's paternal grandparents were (John) Philip (1776-1853) and Elizabeth (Culler) (1778-1857), who also are buried at the Reformed Cemetery in Middletown. See W&M-776.

W&M-1290. George G. Coblentz (1858-1922) and wife Clara E. (Runkles) (1862-1949) are buried at the Reformed Cemetery in Middletown, where also are buried his parents Philip (1812-1899) and Mary Ann (Kefauver) (1818-1870). For earlier Coblentz families see W&M-776. For early Kefauvers see W&M-791.

W&M-1290. H. F. August Meier (1867-1923) and wife Charlotte (Schnebel) (1866-1913) are buried at Mt. Olivet. Note the modern German spelling Meier in contrast to older German Meyer and the prevalent local Myers.

W&M-1291. John McPherson Dennis (1866-1936) and wife Mary Carr (Chiles) (1870-1957) are buried at Mt. Olivet, as are his parents Col. George R. (1831-1902) and second wife Fanny (McPherson) (1836-1930). The first wife of Col. George was Alice (McPherson) (1830-1861) sister of Fanny, daughters of Col. John McPherson. See W&M-765.

W&M-1291. Jacob Baumgardner (1828-1901) and wife Mary (Leedy) (1827-1879) are buried at Keysville, south of Taneytown. In the 1800 census of Westminster District were three Baumgardner families, of which Jacob and Michael were over 45 years, while Henry was between 26 and 45 years.

W&M-1292. Parmalee Feiser (1855-1939) and wife Florence L. (Riggs) (1859-1922) are buried at Mt. Hope Cemetery at Woodsboro. His parents were Jacob, Jr. (1824-1871) and second wife Phoebe E. (Shank) (1823-1900) who are buried at Glade Reformed Cemetery near Walkersville. Jacob Feiser, Jr. and Sr. may have been descendants of Peter Feiser who was taxed for 95 acres in York Township, Pennsylvania in 1781 and Peter, Jr., taxed for 95 acres there in

1783 (Pennsylvania Archives, 3rd Series, Vol. 21). Baumgardners also were in Adams County, Pennsylvania (WB).

W&M-1292. Wallace W. D. Shipley (1853-1938) and wife Annie L. (Harn) (1865-1941) are buried at Unionville Methodist Church. The Shipley families who were prominent early further eastward in Maryland have been studied in *Shipleys of Maryland from Adam (Yorkshire to Annapolis, 1668)* by L. Parks Shipley, Sr. (Baltimore, 1971 and Summit, NJ, 1980) (FH) (WL); also in *Shipleys of Maryland* by Reunion Committee, College Park, Maryland (1937) (WL). See also W&M-980.

W&M-1293. William Philip Holter (1867-1953) married Fannie L. (Klein). He is buried at Mt. Olivet. His parents Peter Holter (1839-1892) and wife Mahala F. (Coblentz) (1845-1912) are buried at Middletown Reformed Cemetery. See W&M-1100 for early Holters.

W&M-1294. George Willis Zimmerman (1863-1944) and wife Lee Ella (Rhoderick) (1863-1934) are buried at Glade Reformed Cemetery near Walkersville, where also are buried his parents Wesley (1829-1865) and wife Rachel Ann (Lease) (1837-1877) (who later married Peter Feiser).

George Zimmerman who married Elisabeth Weiss was a grandson of emigrant Michael Zimmerman. George, Jr. (1796-1850) married Rosanna Barrick (1796-1876); they were parents of Wesley. See W&M-979.

W&M-1295. Harry Leslie Davis (1871-1946) and wife Florida Virginia (Molesworth) (b. 1876) have gravestones in the Catholic Cemetery at Libertytown. His parents John Franklin Davis (1844-1928) and wife Josephine (Spaulding) (1844-1897) are buried at Urbana Catholic Church. Harry's grandfather Eli Davis, who married Rachel (Morsell), was a son of George Davis and wife Elizabeth who are buried at Hyattstown. See W&M-839.

W&M-1296. Lewis F. Kefauver (1850-1949) and wife Joanna V. (Cookerly) (1851-1931) are buried in the Middletown Reformed Cemetery, where also are buried his parents Daniel (1808-1876) and second wife Catherine (Bechtel) (1813-1895), also his paternal grandparents George Kefauver (1785-1861) and wife Mary (1782-1851). See W&M-911 for earlier Kefauvers.

W&M-1297. Adam Francis Nusbaum (1841-1923) and wife Mary E. (Long) (1840-1922) are buried at Mt. Olivet. His parents Adam (1803-1877) and wife Rachel (Baumgardner) (1807-1885) are buried at Liberty Chapel, where also are buried his grandparents Abraham Nusbaum (1771-1839) and wife Anna Margaret (1771-1856). In the 1800 census of Libertytown District were households of John Nusbaum and wife, both over 45 years; David Nusbaum (26-45) with wife and five children; and John, Jr. (26-45) with wife and four children.

The Nusbaum name means "nut tree" in German. As in Baumgardner, the "au" is not pronounced with the High German sound as in how, but in a softer German dialect sound. Benedict Nusbaum, farmer of Ottweiler near Contwig, south Germany, emigrated with Johannes Nusbaum in 1743. In the 16th century Nusbaums lived at Ichertswil, Canton Solothurn, Switzerland.

W&M-1297. Adam Clark Devilbiss (b. 1878) married Jennie Blockson. His parents were Adam A. Devilbiss (1827-1908) and second wife Alberta

Josephine (Lookingbill). Adam's first wife was Anna Maria (Greenwood) (1828-1865). They are buried at Greenwood Cemetery at New Windsor. According to W&M, Adam A. was a son of Casper (1795-1868) and Ann Elinor (Barnett) (1807-1888) who were buried at Sam's Creek Methodist Church. This Casper may have been a grandson of emigrant Casper Devilbiss (c.1721-1777) and son of Casper (1761-1835) buried at Devilbiss family graveyard near Sam's Creek. More research is needed to complete the early genealogy of the Devilbiss families. A tentative outline follows:

The emigrant Devilbiss parents apparently died en route, since the following who arrived at Philadelphia in September 1731 were all young: (Johan) Michel, age 22 years; Johan, 18; Magdalena, 18; (Hans) Georg, 16; Casper, 10. From baptism records it may be concluded that they reached the Monocacy area about 1736. Children of three alleged brothers follow:

(a) (Hans) Michael Devilbiss (c.1705-1755) m. (Maria) Catherine Stull (daughter of John). They had daughters Margaret, Anna Maria and Anna Barbara (b. 1751 and sons John Jacob (b. 1743), and John Michael (b. 1748). From the latter are Divelbiss families of the West.

(b) (Hans) George Devilbiss (c.1715-1785) m. Anna Catherine Stull (Frederick Reformed Church). He leased lots on Monocacy Manor in 1743. Descendants have been studied by Dr. D. Wilbur Devilbiss of Frederick (F). The children mentioned in the will were the following:

(1) John (1743 Monocacy-1804) m. Margaret Cramer (d. 1816).

(2) George, Jr. (c.1745-1806) m. Barbara; 2m Rebecca Devilbiss.

(3) Catherine (1748-1800) m. 1771 George Creager, Sr. (1752-1815).

(4) Adam (1750-1794) m. 1778 Catherine Barrick (1760-1841).

(5) Barbara (1752-1836) m. John Brunner (1748-1829).

(6) Rosanna (1755-1832) m. Jacob Barrick (1755-1839).

(7) Frederick (b. 1760) m. 1784 Anna Maria (Polly) Schultz.

(c) Casper Devilbiss (c.1721-1777) m. Anna. He leased lots on Monocacy Manor in 1757 and 1761. Had many properties and descendants. Children from will, etc.:

(1) George (1747-1813) m. 1772 Elizabeth Ogle (1752-1803)?

(2) John (1750-1827) m. Rebecca Ogle (1755-1805) (daughter of Alexander), second m. Martha Devilbiss, widow of George, Jr.

(3) Ann Elizabeth (1752-1828) m. Jacob Ramsburg (1746-1826).

(4) Barbara (1757-1840) m. Samuel Fleming; 2m Arnold Hardy.

(5) Casper, Jr. (1761-1835) m. Maria Susannah Derr; to near Taylorsville.

(6) Susannah m. Henry Ramsburg (1752-1807) (son of Stephen).

John Devilbiss (1776-1822) buried in Glade Reformed Cemetery was a son of John and Margaret. John Devilbiss (1750-1827) buried on family graveyard was a son of Casper. (Some descendants are given in *Maryland and Delaware Genealogy Magazine*, Autumn, 1987.)

J. M. H. suggested that Teufelbiss was the original German name. Occasionally it was written as Devil and Teufel (German for devil). He believed that more present day local descendants were from emigrant Casper than from George. For many more descendants in Frederick Co. and the Mid-West see three volumes by Dr. D. Wilbur Devilbiss (F).

The Devilbiss families, largely descendants of George, who settled in Ohio and Indiana, several of whom became inventors and manufacturers, gave the name a French twist with change of accent to the second syllable making DeVilbiss. Allen DeVilbiss of Toledo, Ohio was the inventor of automatic scales for weighing.

W&M-1298. George H. Tritapoe (1841-1920) and wife Vandelia (Castle) (1847-1926) are buried at Burkittsville Union Cemetery. Descendants are buried there and at Jefferson Union Cemetery.

W&M-1299. George W. Gaver (1846-1919) and wife Susan R. (Bussard) (1853-1936) are buried at Middletown Lutheran Church. His parents Joseph (1821-1884) and Elizabeth (Wachtel) (1838-1882) are buried at Utica, where are buried also his grandparents George W. Gaver (1820-1896) and wife Elizabeth (1830-1882).

The German name as written by early pastors was Geber, but in the 1800 census of Middletown Valley there were two Gaber households listed. Peter Gaber and wife were over 45 years in age. Samuel Gaber and wife (26-45 years) had a daughter and three sons, all under 10 years.

W&M-1300. Melville Cromwell (b. 1844) and wife Abbie (Day) (1854-1915) have gravestones in Mt. Olivet. His grandparents Philemon Cromwell (1768-1851) and wife Mary (Fisher) (1779-1871) are buried at Israel Creek Cemetery near Walkersville.

Earlier Cromwells lived in the south of our area. Oliver Cromwell, Jr. had an estate settled in 1762 in which relatives Oliver and John G. Cromwell were disclosed. John Cromwell, son of Joshua, had an estate for which Comfort Cromwell was executrix. Kin were Oneal and Joshua Cromwell. In Buckeystown District in 1800 lived Joseph Cromwell and wife in age between 26 and 45 who owned seven slaves. For Cromwell and Worthington families (1741-1854) see MS 1406 at (BM). (LC)

W&M-1301. George H. Cramer (1845-1921) and wife Annie (Gernand) (1847-1921) are buried in Glade Reformed Cemetery near Walkersville, where also are buried his parents Samuel (1809-1858) and wife Susan (Buckey) (1812-1887). Samuel was a son of Henry (1778-1845) and Barbara (Barrick) (1786-1862) who are buried at the same place. See also W&M-1133.

W&M-1303. Oliver P. Devilbiss (1855-1935) and wife Alice E. (Oland) (1850-1929) are buried at Mt. Olivet Cemetery. He was a son of Solomon D. (1826-1902) and wife Susan Henrietta (Cronise) (1837-1926), who are buried at Glade Reformed Cemetery, where also are buried his grandparents David (1793-1859) and wife Catherine (Fulton) (1795-1855), daughter of Robert and Barbara.

George Devilbiss (emigrant at 16 years) m. Anna Catherine Stull; son John (b. 1743) m. Margaret Cramer (d. 1816); son George (1769-1815) m. Susan Berg (Barrick) (1769-1823) and had son David. See also W&M-1297

W&M-1304. Solomon David Devilbiss (1826-1902) is shown above with his ancestors. Susan's parents were Samuel Cronise (1800-1860) and wife Mary (Myers) (1808-1880) who are buried at Mt. Olivet. A large file on the Cronise families is at (FH).

W&M-1305. Samuel A. Eury (1841-1919) and wife Annie Elizabeth (Zumbrun) (1847-1903) are buried at Unionville Methodist Church. His parents Samuel, Jr. (1795-1864) and wife Mary (Lugenbeel), also his grandfather Samuel Eury (1765-1828), are buried at Unionville. In the census of 1800 in Liberty District lived Samuel Urrey and wife (16-26 years in age) with two daughters and two sons all under 10 years; also John Ury and wife (16-26 years).

W&M-1306. John S. Umberger (b. 1852) is recorded on the gravestone of his wife Sarah Catherine (Shipley) (1850-1906) in the Brethren Cemetery at Monrovia. J. M. H. recorded no gravestones of John's grandparents Michael Umberger (c.1815-1855) and wife, a daughter of Thomas and Elizabeth (Moberly). In the 1800 census of the south of Frederick County lived Nicholas Umbargher and wife (both between 26 and 45 years) and three children under 10 years.

W&M-1307. Horace M. Smith apparently is given by J. M. H. as Horace H. Smith (1853-1932) with wife Clara M. (1854-1931) who are buried at Mt. Olivet. His parents were William (1809-1887) and Ann Maria (Zimmerman) buried at Jefferson Methodist Church.

W&M-1307. Judge John E. Phleeger (1848-1924) and wife Amanda C. (Cline) are buried at Mt. Olivet. His paternal grandmother may have been Mary Phleeger (1764-1854) "widow of John" who is buried at Church Hill Cemetery on Ballenger Creek Road.

W&M-1309. Joseph Henry Runkles (b. 1841) is recorded on the gravestone of his wife Emily (Cashour) (1841-1905) at Prospect Methodist Church west of Mt. Airy. His father was Basil Runkles (1809-1906), also buried at Prospect Cemetery. See W&M-1204.

W&M-1310. Professor William H. Harry (1840-1918) and wife Mary C. (Hargett) (1841-1923) are buried at Mt. Olivet. There have been many Harry families in Washington County. See Wms. (1906). Mary C. was a daughter of John H. (b. c.1809) and Henrietta Hargett (b. c.1813) of Buckeystown District.

W&M-1311. Otho J. Gaver (1854-c.1911) and wife Sophia C. (Routzahn) (1854-1913) are buried at the Lutheran Church of Myersville, where also are buried his parents Joseph (1821-1884) and wife Mary (Dutrow) (1820-1890). See also W&M-826 and 1299.

W&M-1312. Peter Lilburn Hargett (1848-1927) is buried at Mt. Olivet as are his parents Samuel (1811-1893) and wife Eleanora (Burns) (1811-1880). See also W&M-1003. In the 1800 census of Fredericktown District were Dormack Burns and wife, both between 26 and 45 years of age.

W&M-1313. Lewis E. Shellman (1858-1940) and wife Mary E. (Summers) (1862-1942) are buried at Mt. Olivet. His lineage from records at (FH) follows:

(1) Emigrant Col. Johannes Mathias Schellmann (1724-1814) m. Maria Margaretha Fauth (Fout) (1732-1795), daughter of Balthasar and wife Susanna. Several sons moved to Georgia and descendants westward. Daughter Anna Maria (1754-1828) m. Jacob Schley (1751-1829).

(2) Jacob Shellman (1757-1840) m. Catherine Bentz (1759-1813), Frederick Lutheran records.

(3) Jacob Shellman, Jr. m. Charlotte Whipp, moved to Indiana after 1807.

(4) Daniel J. Shellman (1825-1894) m. Caroline S. (Zimmerman) (1827-1912), buried at Zion Lutheran Church near Feagaville. They were parents of Lewis E.

John Schellman who arrived here in 1743 helped to lay out Fredericktown and was a leading carpenter for the first buildings of the town. (*Frederick News*, March 4, 1992.)

W&M-1314. Charles Henry Hedges (1858-1941) and wife Alice C. (Erb) (1865-1953) are buried at Glade Reformed Cemetery near Walkersville, where also are buried his parents Daniel (1822-1894) and wife Catherine (Devilbiss) (1829-1894).

The Hedge, later Hedges, families are of English origin. See W&M-1139. The paternal grandparents of Charles were Enos or Eneas Hedges (1795-1873) and wife Catherine (Kemp) (c.1800-1878). Earlier Hedges are discussed with W&M-1061. (LC)

Charles Henry Hedges may be from a different line of Hedges from the better known pioneer settlers in the Monocacy Valley Joseph (d. 1732) and wife Catherine. Some possible ancestors of Charles Henry and Enos follows:

(1) William Hedge born in London m. Mary Caldwell. He died at New Castle, Delaware in 1678.

(2) William Hedge (1677-1702), possible brother of Joseph (d. 1732).

(3) William Hedges (d. 1742) m. Ann; Ann second m. Stephen Julien in Monocacy.

(4) Joseph Hedges (d. 1777) m. Mary (d. 1818).

(5) Andrew Hedges m. Christina (1775-1800), parents of Enos. Cf. C. E. S. *Frederick News*, February 16, 1991 and T&D. See also W&M-1061.

W&M-1315. John F. Kreh (b. 1861) and wife Julia (Buckey) were not found by J. M. H. on gravestones. His parents Peter (1825-1888) born at Schaafheim, Hesse-Darmstadt, and wife Elisabeth Hax (1825-1914) are buried at Mt. Olivet at Frederick. John's grandparents Theodore (1796-1865) and wife Elisabeth (1801-1880) also are buried at Mt. Olivet.

W&M-1316. William L. Rudy (1862-1945) and wives Mary E. (Cost) (1868-1898) and Rose C. (Coblentz) (1876-1953) are buried in Middletown Reformed Cemetery, where also are buried his parents T. Carlton Rudy (1837-1903) and wife Mary E. (Lighter) (1839-1917). Paternal grandparents of William were Hanson T. Rudy (1813-1883) and wife Ann Catherine (1815-1858), who are also buried at Middletown Reformed Cemetery along with Frederick Rudy (1785-1855) and wife Susannah (1788-1863). In the 1800 census of Middletown Valley Peter Rudy and wife were over 45 years of age living with three daughters and four sons.

In Middletown Reformed records Dieterich Rudy and Susannah Rudy had daughter Magdalena baptized in 1775 and John Jacob in 1777. The family name and early given names are Germanic.

W&M-1317. Elmer K. Ramsburg (b. 1870) and wife Sue I. (Smith) have stones in Mt. Olivet. He was a son of Urias D. (1825-1903) and Ann S. (Staley) (1837-1921) who are buried at Charlesville Reformed Church. His paternal grandparents Frederick and wife Lydia A. (Snook) are buried at Bethel Lutheran church (inscriptions obscured). For descent from immigrant Stephen see W&M-752. For Snook ancestors see W&M-745.

W&M-1317. John Albert Korrell (1853-1948) married Catherine C. Burger. He is buried at Rocky Springs. His father was immigrant John, who died in 1895.

W&M-1318. Emanuel Fogle (1827-1912) and his parents Andrew (1804-1863) and wife Elizabeth (Crumbaugh) (1803-1866) are buried in Beaver Dam Brethren Cemetery. See also W&M-1082 and 1214. In 1800 there were two Crumbaugh families in eastern Frederick Co., namely Conrad and wife both over 45 years of age, and Simon and wife who were between 26 and 45.

W&M-1318. Samuel Horning (1826-1898) and wife Mary (Hohf) (1832-1917) are buried at Beaver Dam Cemetery near Johnsville.

W&M-1319. Charles H. Fogle (1870-1952) and wife Elizabeth (Horning) (1865-1946) are buried at Beaver Dam. His parents were Nicholas, Jr. (1844-1878) and wife Mary (1840-1908) who are buried at Rocky Hill Church near Woodsboro. Also at Rocky Hill are buried his paternal grandparents Nicholas Fogle, Sr. (1810-1878) and Elizabeth (Wetzel) (b. c.1808). See also W&M-1082 and 1214.

Hans Martin Wetzel immigrated in 1731 at age 31 with wife Maria Barbara (Geist) age 33 and three children from Goesdorf near Woerth in north Alsace (B3).

W&M-1319. Hanson E. Crum (b. 1879) married Katie Dinterman. His parents were Jacob L. (1851-1920) and Nancy E. (Droneberg) (1859-1931) who are buried at Mt. Hope Cemetery, Woodsboro. His paternal grandparents were Solomon Crum (1826-1894) and wife Mary Catherine (Kanode) (1830-1911) buried in Mt. Hope Cemetery.

Note also Hanson Crum (1833-1901) and wife Matilda S. (1846-1909) buried at Mt. Olivet who might have been grandparents of Hanson E. The paternal great grandparents of Hanson E. was not Frederick Crum (b. c.1813) but Henry Crum of the Woodsboro area according to Dr. Robert Crum Frey, Jr., a descendant. Note that Henry and Sarah Crum baptized their daughter Mary at Rocky Hill Church in 1824. These Crum families are believed to have been descendants of Gilbert Crom (1700-1762) of Netherlands origin. See M&C-II-628 and W&M-1145. In the 1800 census of Libertytown District were three Crum households of Abraham, Ephraim and John Crum, all in age between 26 and 45. In 1800 in Fredericktown District were three households of William Crum, Sr. and wife (over 45 years), with four slaves, William, Jr. and wife, 26-45 years, and John Crum and wife, 26-45.

W&M-1320. John Emory Crum (b. 1881) was a younger son of Jacob L. and Nancy Elizabeth (Droneburg). See above.

W&M-1320. William G. Baker (1842-1922) and wife Ella (Jones) (1846-1919) are buried at Mt. Olivet as are his parents Daniel (1811-1888) and wife Ann Catherine (Finger) (1813-1888). William's younger brother Joseph D. Baker was discussed in W&M-711.

W&M-1322. David L. Hedges (1854-1934) and wife Florence C. (Zimmerman) (1858-1929) are buried at Glade Reformed Cemetery near Walkersville, where also are buried his parents Daniel A. (1822-1862) and Catherine M. (Devilbiss) (1829-1894). Hedges ancestors are discussed in W&M-1061.

W&M-1322. George A. T. Snouffer (1855-1926) and wife Josephine L. (Hinks) (d. 1918) are buried at Mt. Olivet where also are buried his parents Benjamin J. (1816-1876) and wife Eleanore E. (Moffett) (1816-1897). The paternal grandparents of George were George Snouffer (1792-1831) and wife Darkiss (Thomas) (1790-1821) (daughter of Benjamin) who are buried at the English Thomas graveyard near Point of Rocks.

In the 1800 census of Westminster area lived the family of John Snowfer and wife, both over 45 years of age. The German family name was Schnauffer. A Jacob Snouffer (1782-1852) is buried at Emmitsburg Lutheran Church. Hans Georg Schnauffer arrived in Philadelphia in September 1750 and Michael in September 1751.

Carl Henrich Schnauffer (1823-1854) born at Heimsheim near Stuttgart, Germany, was an author in Baltimore (BG).

W&M-1323. Dr. David Marshal Devilbiss, M.D. (1845-1911) and wife Lizzie M. (Clary) (1859-1925) are buried at Prospect Cemetery near Mt. Airy. He was a son of Adam W. (1812-1883) and Rosanna (Devilbiss) Devilbiss (1820-1875) who are buried at New London Methodist Church. Dr. David's paternal grandparents were David (1788-1856) and Elizabeth Campbell (1784-1866) who also are buried at Prospect Cemetery. See W&M-1118 for lineage of David.

W&M-1324. Abraham Fisher, Jr. (1826-1915) buried at Prospect Cemetery near Mt. Airy married Julia Ann Diehl (1829-1910) who is buried near Custer City, OK, where she followed her children. His parents of Adams County, PA were Abraham Fisher, Sr. (1796-1885) and Elizabeth (Benner) (1797-1829) who are buried in Adams County, PA. See M&C-II.

Contrary to W&M there were two Thomas Fishers, the emigrant in 1751 Thomas, Sr. (d. 1793) and wife Eva King (Koenig) (daughter of Abraham), and son Thomas, Jr. (1763-1845) and wife Catherine (Warner) (1770-1844). Thomas, Sr. lived near Littlestown, PA, and later at York where he was elected to the Committee of Observation during the Revolution and was an official of York County. Thomas, Jr. and family moved to a farm south of Gettysburg where Bullfrog Road crosses the Mason-Dixon Line.

Fanny (Royer) and husband John D. Fisher lived in Oklahoma and she later in Arizona. About 1930 Aunt Fanny showed my mother Edith Julia Schildknecht and myself the mill homeplace of Abraham, Sr. and Elizabeth east of Biglerville, PA. Fanny died at age 99 and was buried at Meadow Branch Brethren Cemetery near Westminster.

Willis Everett Fisher (1855-1922) was the only child of Abraham, Jr. and Julia Ann who did not move to the southwest. Willis and wife Mary Jane Esther (Mollie) Reifsnider (1858-1945) were grandparents of the writer. They farmed near Emmitsburg and later on Ballenger Creek Road near Frederick, before retiring on Clarke Place in Frederick.

Recent research by Annette K. Burgert has shown that (Maria) Eva (Koenig or King) wife of emigrant Thomas Fisher, Sr. was born in 1728 at Hoffen in northern Alsace. Her parents were Abraham Koenig of Bischweiler who married in 1724 Anna Maria Weimer, daughter of Hans Adam. Eight children are named (B3). The Kings were prominent early settlers near Littlestown, PA, after whom Kingsdale was named.

Early in Frederick's history is prominent unrelated Dr. Adam Fischer, surgeon in the Revolution and on the Committee of Correspondence. His son also was a physician.

W&M-1324. James Clay Darner (1860-1947) and wife Ada Koogle (Smith) (b. 1863) have stones in Middletown Reformed Cemetery, where also are buried his parents Henry J. (1831-1887) and wife Mary (Edmunds) (1832-1900). The paternal grandparents of James were John J. Darner (1789-1864) and wife Elizabeth (Routzahn) (1798-1890) who also are buried in the Middletown Reformed Cemetery.

In the records of Middletown Reformed Church Jacob and wife Barbara Derner or Doerner first appear in 1772. Andres and Anna Maria Doerner had their son John George baptized there in 1782. Darner is a dialect form of the family name Doerner.

W&M-1325. William Joshua Purdum (1851-1921) and wife Martha (Molesworth) (1856-1939) are buried at Prospect Cemetery near Mt. Airy. His parents were Josiah (1800-1884) and Sarah (Beall) (1817-1887) who also are buried at Prospect Cemetery. William's paternal grandparents were Joshua H. Purdum (1833-1874) and Martha (Browning) (1834-1929) who are buried at Browningsville Methodist Church. A John Purdom served on a Frederick County jury in 1750.

W&M-1326. Charles E. Kinna (1865-1934) and wives Ida F. (Suman) (1863-1895) and Florence V. (Stevens) (1872-1927) are buried at the Lutheran Church of Middletown. His parents were David Kinna (1835-1912) and wife Emeline (Fisher) (1834-1898) who were buried at Myersville United Brethren Church. David was a son of William Kinna (1812-1887) and wife Sarah Ellen (1814-1891) who are buried at Hyattstown.

Charles and Ida's daughter Annie E. married Floyd Schildknecht. They lived on old Route 40 west of Middletown.

W&M-1327. Charles May Anders (1847-1906) and wife Emma Almira (Eyler) (d. 1940) are buried at Mt. Hope Cemetery, Woodsboro, where also are buried his parents Moses (1816-1892) and wife Eliza Ellen (1815-1900).

Jacob Anders (c.1789-1834) and wife Elizabeth Shriner (1789-1838) (buried at Beaver Dam) had sons Moses (1816-1892) and David (1827-1848) as well as another son and three daughters (according to Norman C. Anders, Lehigh Acres, FL).

A Wilhelm Anders (1713-1783) was an original trustee of St. Peter's Church at Rocky Hill near Woodsboro. He married Elisabeth Rinehardt and had children including Adam who married Christina Schmidt at Rocky Hill, and William who is buried in Cabbage Run Valley Cemetery in Centerville. Peter Beard, who was executor of Wilhelm Anders, probably was related by marriage.

W&M-1328. Judge John Ritchie (1831-1887) and wife Betty (Harrison) (1839-1898) are buried at Mt. Olivet Cemetery. Betty was a daughter of William P. and Emily (Nelson) Maulsby. It is stated on Betty's gravestone that she was the mother of 18 children. Judge Ritchie was a son of Dr. Albert Ritchie (1803-1858) and wife Catherine Lackland (Davis) (1814-1842). Dr. Ritchie's second wife was Louisa (Packard) (1818-1857) of New York City who also is buried at Mt. Olivet. The grandparents of Judge Ritchie, Col. John Ritchie (1757-1826) and wife Ann (1769-1826), are also buried at Mt. Olivet. The second wife of Col. John Ritchie was Ann Barnhold (1769-1826). William Ritchie (1716-1765) married Mary Middaugh, daughter of Capt. John and Mary (Beatty).

In 1800 census there were five Ritchie families in Fredericktown District. William Ritchie was over 45 years in age. He and his wife had two daughters and two sons, also five slaves. Widow Mary Ritchie (over 45 years) apparently lived with four daughters and two sons, without slaves. John and Abner Ritchie were 26-45 years in age, the heads of small, young families. John Ritchie, whose age is not given, owned 12 slaves. The Frederick County inventory of Henry Ritchie's estate is dated 1767. The administrator was his brother Isaac Richey.

W&M-1331. Albert O. Young (1868-1890) married Rosetta Grace Frederick of Springfield, Ohio. He is buried at Monocacy Brethren Church at Rocky Ridge. Albert was a son of Lewis (1831-1892) and wife Elizabeth F. (Arnold) (1833-1902). Lewis was a son of Daniel Young (b. c.1796) and wife Mary M. (b. c.1799) of Middletown Valley. Elizabeth was a daughter of Peter Arnold (b. c.1806) and Mary (b. c.1807) farmers of Middletown Valley.

W&M-1332. Charles B. Darner (1866-1934) and wife Alta May (Zecher) (1869-1939) are buried at Middletown Reformed Church where also are buried his parents Henry (1831-1887) and Mary (Edmunds) (1832-1900). See also W&M-1324. Mary may have been a descendant of Nathan (b. c.1796) and Mary Edmunds (b. c.1769) of Virginia and later Middletown Valley.

W&M-1332. John H. Heffner (1862-1925) and wife Sarah J. (Staley) (1859-1934) are buried at Mt. Olivet Cemetery where also is buried his father Lewis C. (1828-1894) and his grandparents Samuel Heffner (1800-1880) and wife Sophia (Kizer) (1807-1882). In Fredericktown District in 1800 were families of Frederick, a younger Frederick, Michael (of Frederick) and Michael (of John) Haffner. Haffner is a dialect form of the name.

Heffners were early in records of Monocacy Lutheran Church. Friedrich Haffner had son Jacob Frederick in 1746 and Johan in 1753. A sponsor was Johan Haffner, but the mother's name was not recorded. Georg Friedrich was a sponsor for baptism in 1749 and Hans Michael in 1750. Laurentius or

Lawrence Haefner and wife Catherine Margaret had Friedrich born in 1760; sponsors to the baptism were Friedrich and wife Anna Maria Heffner. In 1763 Lawrence and Catherine baptized Maria Catherine with Johannes and Maria Catharina Stoll as sponsors.

W&M-1334. Eugene G. Smith (b. 1862) married Emma I. Measel. He was a son of Conrad, Jr. (1822-1903) and Elizabeth (Suman) (1819-1907) who are buried at Middletown Lutheran Church.

W&M-1335. Jacob H. Gorman (1878-1950) and wife Ida E. (Isanogle) (1834-1944) are buried at Mt. Olivet Cemetery. His parents lived in Dauphin County, PA. The only Isanogle family in Frederick County in 1850 was Michael (1811-1888) and wife Ann Eliza (1815-1896) who are buried at Utica.

W&M-1335. Charles H. Harbaugh (1876-1939) and wife Fanny Estelle (Angleberger) have stones in Mt. Hope Cemetery at Woodsboro. His parents George Martin Harbaugh (1846-1904) and wife Susan M. (Troxell) (1841-1917) are buried at Apple's Church near Thurmont, where also are buried the grandparents of Charles namely Henry Harbaugh (1800-1871) and wife Martha (Young) (1817-1888). See also W&M-995 and 1178.

W&M-1336. Charles Bayard Trail (1857-1914) and wife Grace (Winebrenner) (1869-1941) are buried at Mt. Olivet at Frederick as are his parents Col. Charles Edward (1825-1909) and wife Arianna (McElfresh) (1828-1892). See also W&M-720.

Children of Charles B. and Grace Trail follow:

(1) Grace Winbrenner m. Harry P. Babcock; no children.

(2) Florence m. Carl Seitz Davidson; sons Bayard Trail (1919-1979) and David McClellan (1923-c.1974).

(3) Theresa McElfresh (1896-1988) m. Charles McCurdy Mathias (1887-1967); children given in W&M-926.

(4) Beatrice (b. 1901) m. Matthew Clark Fenton, Jr.; lived in Baltimore, Maryland; children: Matthew III (b. 1925); Thomas Trail; Philip Schuyler (b. 1931).

(5) Charles Bayard, Jr.

W&M-1338. Henry R. Appleby (1861-1940) and wife Margaret E. (Carter) are buried at Unionville Methodist Church. His parents Rufus (1832-1902) and wife Martha A. (Bennett) (1836-1918) are buried at the Beaver Dam Brethren Cemetery near Johnsville. Margaret's parents were Henry Carter (1830-1894) and wife Margaret E. (Nicodemus) (1832-1874) who are buried at Unionville Methodist Church. Margaret was a daughter of Valentine Nicodemus (1794-1863) and second wife Barbara Ann (1807-1850) who are buried at Unionville M. E. Church.

W&M-1339. Clarence L. Ahalt (1873-1936) and wife Lola E. (Beachley) (d. 1874) are buried at Middletown Lutheran Church. He was a son of Matthias S. (1838-1921) and Martha J. (Sheffer) (1842-1927) who are buried at the same place, along with the paternal grandparents of Clarence, namely Matthias Ahalt (1803-1881) and wife Phoebe (1809-1893). See also W&M-988. Martha J. was a daughter of Daniel (1807-1863) and Mary Sheffer (1815-1907), farmers in Middletown Valley.

W&M-1340. John Calvin Castle (1850-1938) and wife Amelia Catherine (Stephens) (1851-1937) are buried at Middletown Lutheran Church. His parents were Daniel (1817-1898) and Sarah A. (Long) (1822-1910) who were buried at Mt. Olivet. John's paternal grandparents were Otho Castle (c.1792-1822) and wife Elizabeth (Baker) (1781-1852).

In the 1800 census of Middletown Valley were two Cassell households. Thomas and wife were over 45 years in age with two daughters and four sons. George Cassell was over 45 years but his wife under 45. They had three daughters and four sons.

W&M-1340. Samuel M. Summers (1837-1915) and wife Sarah A. (Michael) (1849-1914) are buried at Mt. Olivet. His parents George W. (1802-1884) and wife Catherine E. (Michael) (1804-1875) are buried at Middletown Reformed Church. The grandparents of Samuel were Jacob (c.1767-1850) and wife Elizabeth (1769-1849) who are buried at the Lutheran Church at Church Hill north of Myersville. See also W&M-964. Sarah A. was a daughter of Henry S. (1807-1875) and wife Mary A. (1811-1892), farmers in Buckeystown District, who are buried at Mt. Olivet.

W&M-1341. Reverdy J. Winebrenner (1844-1927) and wife Annie (Hill) (1847-1932) are buried at Mt. Olivet. His parents Christian (1789-1891) and second wife Phoebe (Cramer) (1805-1893) are buried at Glade Reformed Cemetery near Walkersville. Philip Winebrenner (1759-1844), grandfather of Reverdy, came from Pennsylvania. Christian's first wife was Harriet Rice (1805-1837) who is also buried at Glade Reformed Cemetery. See also W&M-708. Ann L. M. Hill was a daughter of William (1814-1892) and wife Nancy Ann (1821-1900) who are buried at Utica.

W&M-1342. Arthur Potts (1834-1914) and wife Helen (Mobberly) (d. 1925) are buried at Mt. Olivet Cemetery, as are his parents George Murdoch (1804-1893) and Cornelia (Ringgold) (1805-1868). Arthur's paternal grandparents were Judge Richard Potts (1753-1808) and Eleanor (Murdoch) (1744-1812). Richard's first wife was Elizabeth Hughes (1761-1793). Arthur's paternal great grandparents William Potts (c.1741-1817) and wife Elizabeth (Christian) (c.1754-1813) were moved to Mt. Olivet.

Arthur and Helen had one son Richard Potts, whose only son Arthur Potts and wife live near the family mansion at 106 North Court Street, Frederick in 1994. (LC)

W&M-1343. William H. Runkles (1839-1918) and wife Emily (Van Sant) (1841-1905) are buried at Prospect Cemetery near Mt. Airy, where also are buried his parents Samuel (c.1797-1887) and wife Elizabeth (Clary) (1809-1881). There is no Plary family in our area as given by W&M. In the 1800 census Joseph Runkles and wife were between 26 and 45 years of age, living with three sons under 10 years. Emily was a daughter of Moses Vansant, blacksmith, (1809-1858) and wife Susannah (1811-1899) who are buried at Fairmount Cemetery at Liberty.

W&M-1344. Dr. Thomas J. Claggett, M.D. (1785-1835) and wife Sophia (1793-1862) are buried at Petersville Episcopal Church. Their son Samuel (1831-1900) and wife Elizabeth (West) (1832-1910) also are buried at Petersville, as is their son Dr. Samuel Claggett, Jr. (1873-1914) who married Jeanette Benson Chew. See also W&M-864.

Col. Edward Clagett of London had son Thomas who died in Calvert County about 1701 (M&C-II). There were many Thomas Claggetts in Maryland thereafter. See Scharf. In the census of 1800 in Middletown Valley Thomas J. Claggett is listed as having 12 slaves but with no other information. Besides Dr. Thomas John (1785-1835) at Petersville Episcopal Church are buried Thomas J. Claggett (1813-1873) and wife Ann P. (1824-1897), also Thomas John, Jr. (1856-1911) (son of Thomas John and Ann (Perry)) and wife Mary Louise (Staley) (1859-1916) (daughter of George and Hannah Frances).

W&M-1345. Charles Silas Thomas (1858-1944) and wife Nora E. (Purcell) (1872-1933) are buried at Mt. Olivet where also are buried his parents Ezra Michael (1824-1895) and wife Amanda (Stockman) (1824-1904). Compare W&M-957.

W&M-1346. Charles E. Thomas, Jr. (1856-1888) and wife C. Kate (Yeakle) (1867-1932) are buried at Mt. Olivet. His parents were Charles E. (1826-1869) and wife Ella (Dutrow) who are buried in the Thomas graveyard near Point of Rocks. See *English Thomas Genealogy* by George L. Thomas and W&M-1412.

W&M-1346. Gravestones of Upton Harshman (b. 1866) and wife E. May (Rowe) were not recorded by J.M.H. but see the two volumes of *Harshman Families* by Clarence and Malvournean Harshman (Berkeley, CA, 1976) (F). See also W&M-819.

The paternal grandparents of Upton were John Harshman (1805-1871) and wife Elisabeth (Grossnickle) (1803-1873) who were buried at Grossnickle Meeting House north of Myersville, where also are buried Upton's parents John T. (1841-1908) and wife Nancy J. (Stottlemyer) (1846-1896).

The family name is derived from German Hirsch meaning deer or roebuck. The 1800 census of Middletown Valley shows three Hershman families. Christian, Sr. and wife were over 45 years of age, living with five daughters and three sons; Christian, Jr. and wife were 26-45 years of age without children at home; the same was true of John Hershman and wife.

W&M-1348. Alvey P. Harshman (b. 1878) who married Minnie A. Shuff was a son of John T. (1841-1908) and Nancy J. (Stottlemyer) (1846-1896). In the 1800 census of northern Frederick County was the family of George Shuff and wife, both over 45 years. They had five sons of ages between 10 and 26 years.

W&M-1348. Aquila A. Harshman (1873-1932) and wife Jennie C. (Cartee) (1876-1937) are buried at Grossnickle Brethren Meeting House north of Myersville. See his parents John T. and Nancy J. (Stottlemyer) above. In Middletown Valley in 1800 census lived families of apparent widow Susanna Carty over 45 years; John over 45 and wife younger; and Thomas Carty (16-26 years).

W&M-1348. William E. Harshman (1867-1933) and wife Margaret E. (Grossnickle) (1866-1921) are buried at Grossnickle Meeting House, where also are buried his parents Lawson P. (1839-1908) and wife Eva Ann (Warrenfeltz) (1845-1918). The latter was a daughter of Daniel (1814-1901) and wife

Susanna Warrenfeltz (1823-1898) who are buried at Wolfsville Reformed Church.

W&M-1349. Thomas L. Thomas (1848-1897) and wife Mary Catherine (Thomas) (1854-1918) are buried at Mt. Olivet. His parents Joseph Thomas (1810-1861) and wife Frances E. R. (Copelin) (1819-1854) are buried at St. Joseph's Catholic Church near Buckeystown.

W&M-1349. Frank L. Stoner (1863-1938) and wife Florence E. (Wilson) (1864-1928) are buried at Mt. Olivet. His parents Ephraim (1824-1904) and wife Margaret (Smith) (1832-1913) are buried at Johnsville Methodist Church.

Earlier Stoners buried in the Johnsville area include Jacob (1752-1804) and wife Atrian (1745-1831) in the Stoner family graveyard and Jacob (1799-1880) and wife Magdalene (1798-1882) buried at Beaver Dam Brethren Cemetery. In the census of 1800 of eastern Frederick County there were six Stoner households. John and Jacob and their wives were over 45 years of age. David, Isaac and Samuel were 26-45 years and Benedict Stoner, 16-26. In Taneytown District in 1800 were two Stoner families headed by Jacob and John, both between 26 and 45 years. See Brethren Stoners in (ST).

W&M-1351. Wheeler A. Smith (1887-1948) is buried at Myersville U. B. Church. Perhaps the great grandparents of Wheeler were John Smith (c.1805-1877) and wife Catherine (1809-1896) who are buried at Wolfsville Lutheran Church.

W&M-1352. Edward D. Shriner (1863-1930) and wife Nannie May (Getzendanner) (1867-1952) are buried at Mt. Olivet, where also are buried his parents Edward A. (1830-1901) and wife Margaret A. (Derr) (1832-1962) daughter of John Derr and Elizabeth (Luginbeel).

Johan Michael Schreiner of Gommersheim near Sinsheim southeast of Heidelberg had sons Michael (1749-1827) and Peter who emigrated in 1738 to Pennsylvania, and later settled near Uniontown in later Carroll County. Michael, Jr. (1774-1837) and Ann Elizabeth (Worman) (1776-1821) were great grandparents of Edward D. Shriner. They are buried at Unionville Methodist Church. Cornelius Shriner (1800-1854) and wife Rebecca (Scholl) (1806-1838) lived at Ceresville north of Frederick and are buried at Mt. Olivet. They were parents of Edward A. Shriner. Cornelius married for a second time to Phoebe Barrick (1819-1897) who also is buried at Mt. Olivet.

According to Rev. Dr. A. Pierce Middleton of Annapolis, Johan Michael Schreiner (b. 1710) emigrated with his parents Hans Adam (1686-1744) and Anna Margaretta in 1738. In 1739 Johan Michael married Anna Barbara Leonard of Lancaster, Pennsylvania and later moved near Unionville, Frederick County. Michael, Jr. (1774-1837) married Anna Elizabeth Worman (1776-1821) and they had children Cornelius, Basil and Abraham.

Valentine Shriner in 1751 married Anna Elizabeth Wolf of Lancaster and moved to Frederick about 1756. They had children born as follows: Eva Margaret 1757; Susanna 1759; Charlotte Amalia 1761; and John George 1771.

An article on the *Life and Times of Hans Adam Schreiner (1686-1744) of Gommersheim and His Descendants* by David L. Shreiner of Marietta, GA appeared in *Lancaster Connections 1 (4) 37* (1984). Son Michael (1708-1754) of

Lancaster County was a blacksmith and farmer. Descendants are around Chambersburg, PA, Elkhart, IN, Tucson, AZ and at least 20 other states.

W&M-1354. Gilmer Schley (1855-1939) and wife Emma Louisa (Wilson) (1862-1943) are buried at Mt. Olivet at Frederick where also are buried his parents Col. Edward (1804-1857) and Eve Margaret (Brengle) (1808-1890).

(John) Thomas Schley born at Moerzheim near Landau in southern Pfalz of Germany emigrated about 1744 with wife Margaret (Winz) and a party of German Reformed faith. See W&M-745. John Schley (1767-1835) and wife Mary (1773-1855) are buried at Mt. Olivet where also are buried his son Col. Edward and wife Eve Margaret. See also W&M-700.

W&M-1354. Edward C. Ensor (1832-1915) and wife Phoebe (Dance) (1838-1918) are buried at Sam's Creek Methodist Church.

W&M-1355. Raymond Lewis Frizzell (1880-1949) married Carrie Bankert. He is buried at New London Methodist Church, north of New Market, where also are buried his parents Bertha Oswald Frizzell (1851-1916) and wife M. Cora (Harding) (1857-1903). Other Frizzells have lived around Frizzellsburg on the old road from Taneytown to Westminster. In 1800 a Vachel Harding and wife had four daughters and four sons in eastern Frederick County.

W&M-1356. Joseph Hollin Kefauver (b. 1856) was a son of Daniel (1808-1876) and second wife Catharine (Bechtol) (1813-1895) who are buried at Middletown Reformed Cemetery. Paternal grandparents of Joseph were George Kefauver (1785-1861) and wife Mary (1782-1851) buried at the same place. There also is buried Nicholas Kefauver (1756-1817) son of early settler Philip. See W&M-911.

W&M-1357. Abram J. Eichelberger (1866-1928) and wife Minnie G. (Gittinger) (1869-1950) are buried at Mt. Olivet where also are buried his parents Adam L. (1824-1897) and Sarah E. (Hahn) (1826-1901). For earlier Eichelbergers see W&M-974. In 1800 John Gettinger, Sr. and Jr., also Jacob Gettinger, lived in Frederick District (LC).

W&M-1357. Frank E. Sheffield (1862-1935) and wife Annie C. (Welty) (1864-1942) are buried at Mt. Olivet. His parents Andrew Sheffield (1839-1890) and wife Crescent (1832-1905) from Saxony are buried at the Catholic Cemetery in Frederick. Many Weltys have lived around Emmitsburg.

W&M-1358. Henry K. C. Fox (1875-1950) and wife Lizzie E. (Hopwood) (b. 1876) have gravestones in Mt. Olivet Cemetery where also are buried his parents E. A. Fox (1850-1926) of Westphalia, Germany and second wife Caroline M. (Babel) native of Bavaria. Earlier Fox settlers are given in W&M-899 and 1491. James Hopwood (b. c.1811), a carpenter of Frederick, and wife Mary had a large family in 1850.

W&M-1358. J. Allen Grumbine (1853-1928) was a son of Daniel M. (1815-1895) and wife Mary A. R. (1825-1896). All are buried at Mt. Olivet. Daniel's parents Jacob and Margaret (Grumbine) were natives of Hanover, PA. Early Krumreins arriving at Philadelphia were Hans Michael in September 1732 and Georg Lenhart in 1748.

W&M-1359. George Hiram Bussard (1860-1938) and wife Margaret Adella (Miller) (1865-1923) are buried at Thurmont U. B. Cemetery. His parents Samuel Bussard (1813-1861) and Hannah (Toms) (1833-1876) are buried at Garfield Mt. Bethel Church in upper Middletown Valley. See W&M-860. Hannah was a daughter of William Tombs (1799-1868) and wife Mary (1806-1881), buried at Garfield.

W&M-1360. Otho J. Keller (1843-1899) and wife Margaret (Burnett) (1843-1881) are buried at Mt. Olivet Cemetery at Frederick as are his parents Jonathan (1814-1879) and Jane Louisa (Springer) (1818-1885). Otho's grandfather Michael Keller (1770-1847) is buried at Middletown Reformed Cemetery. See W&M-1160. Some descendants are given in the book *Buckey's Town* by Nancy Willmann Bodmer (1984).

W&M-1361. Oliver H. Kefauver (1851-1923) and wives Martha Ellen (Neikirk) (1852-1888) and her sister Lillie (Neikirk) (1859-1943) are buried at Middletown Reformed Cemetery. Oliver's parents also buried there were Jacob (1814-1882) (son of George) and wife Lenorah (Coblentz) (1819-1903). See W&M-791 and 911 for Kiefhaber ancestors.

W&M-1361. Howard D. Kefauver (b. 1879) married Mozell W. Karn. According to W&M-1297, Howard D. was a son of Lewis F. (1850-1949) and Jennie (Riddlemoser) (1851-1931) who are buried at Middletown Reformed Church. See W&M-791 and 911.

W&M-1362. Martin E. Kefauver (1876-1921) married Annie Lee DeLauder. He is buried at Mt. Olivet. His parents Daniel Edward Kefauver (1841-1922) and Amanda E. (Snyder) (1839-1903) are buried at Middletown Reformed Church.

A son of emigrant Philip was Nicholas Kiefhaber (1756-1817) who had son George (1785-1861); both are buried at Middletown Reformed Church. George Kefauver and wife Mary (1782-1851) had children Daniel, John, Jonathan, Henry, Jacob, Elizabeth, Mary Ann and Rebecca. Daniel (1808-1876) and second wife Catherina (Bechtol) (1813-1895) also are buried in Middletown Reformed Cemetery. They were parents of Daniel Edward. See also W&M-791 and 911.

W&M-1363. Charles H. Klipp (1869-1939) and wife Minnie M. (Putman) (1878-1942) are buried at Mt. Olivet, where also are buried his parents Henry (1846-1923) and Sarah E. (Miss) (1844-1913). The latter's parents were Lewis Miss (b. c.1807) and wife Elisabeth (b. c.1812) of Frederick who were born in Germany.

W&M-1364. J. Fenton Thomas (1849-1916) and wife Adelaide S. (Thomas) Thomas (1851-1895) are buried at Mt. Olivet, where also are buried his parents David (c.1815-1877) and Elizabeth (Hildebrand) (1820-1908).

Valentine Thomas (1724-1796) who was one of six German immigrant brothers married Margaret and farmed near Adamstown south of Frederick. See W&M-1015. Valentine's son Gabriel (1752-1795) married Ann Maria (1758-1821). They are buried at the German Thomas family graveyard. Their son George Thomas (1778-1845) (grandfather of J. Fenton) and wife Charlotte (Thomas)

(1787-1869) are buried at Church Hill on Ballenger Creek Road. They were parents of David.

W&M-1365. William H. Thomas (1869-1957) and wife Effie S. (b. 1872) have stones in Mt. Olivet. Also buried at Mt. Olivet are William's parents Zachariah G. Thomas (1839-1904) and wife Louisa E. (1840-1920).

John Thomas (b. 1728) son of Michael (b. 1688) and Anna Veronica (Lang) of Klein Schifferstadt, married Catherine Getzendanner and took land near later Adamstown in 1754. Their son Henry had son George Thomas of H. (1798-1883) whose third wife Julia Ann (Hargett) (1813-1878) was the mother of Zachariah G. above. See W&M-1015 and *German Thomas Genealogy* by George Leicester Thomas.

W&M-1366. Hiram Grove Thomas (1871-1951) and wife Sarah Ellen (Kefauver) (1875-1924) are buried at Mt. Olivet. He was a son of Zachariah G. and Louisa (Grove) (1840-1920) buried also at Mt. Olivet. See lineage of Zachariah above.

W&M-1367. George Washington Huffman (1859-1936) and wife Etta R. (Eyler) have gravestones in Mt. Hope Cemetery, Woodsboro. The grandparents of George W. were John (c.1764-1847) and Margaret (Barrick) (1783-1850) who are buried at Rocky Hill Church near Woodsboro. The parents of George W. were Henry Huffman (1819-1889) and wife Catherine (Greenwood) (1830-1864) who are buried at Rocky Hill Church.

In the 1800 census of Emmitsburg District was the family of Adam Hofman and wife, both over 45 years of age. In Fredericktown District in 1800 were four Hoffman families: John Hoffman was over 45 years with wife under 45. Three families of Conrad, Henry and Jacob, 26-45 years in age, had children under 10 years.

In early land records of Frederick County was Jacob Huffman in 1767-1773. Mary Hoffman bought land in 1762. Peter Huffman bought a lot in Taneytown from Raphael Taney in 1763. Eleven Hoffmans served in the War of 1812.

Many families of Frederick County retained the south German spelling Hoffmann except eliminating a final "n". One of the most outstanding of these was Dr. Charles Hoffman, Librarian of the Supreme Court in D.C. and a founder of the Historical Society of Frederick County. His emigrant grandfather John Hoffman came from Muehlheim. There are several German towns with this name meaning millhome. A prominent one is on the Mosel river. John called his farm west of Frederick by this name. According to descendant Charles E. Brengle of Baltimore in *Palatine Immigrant Vol. 8, 34* (Spring 1983), the parents of Dr. Charles were George H. (1772-1836) and Elizabeth (Creager) (1794-1869) who are buried at Creagerstown.

After serving 20 years as Librarian of the Supreme Court and Law Librarian of the Congressional Library, Dr. Hoffman, unmarried, retired in Frederick where he left some interesting historical articles in the Library of the Frederick County Historical Society. Dr. Charles left books, paintings and furniture to his brother John Henry Hoffman. To his friend the Director of Georgetown College he gave a locket containing hair of George Washington, also protraits in oil of Washington and Jefferson which had belonged to his grandfather John.

Another prominent Hoffman was settler Peter (d. 1809) who emigrated in 1742 from Frankfurt am Main. He lived at present Rose Hill Manor and later became a leading citizen of Baltimore (Y).

W&M-1368. For David Lowenstein (b. 1845 in Germany), merchant, and wife Clara (Stern) of Frederick see (J).

W&M-1369. Martin Grossnickle (1837-1919) and wife Celina (Warner) (1837-1900) are buried at Grossnickle Meeting House north of Myersville, where also are buried his parents Peter, Jr. (1806-1874) and wife Sophia (Brown) (1807-1891).

Johan Grossnickel at age 21 emigrated in 1738 from Wittenberg, Germany according to (BE). By tradition, the Grossnickel family emigrated from near Worms far south and west of Wittenberg. In 1800 the only Grossnickel family in Middletown Valley was that of Peter and wife, who were both over 45 years old. They had five daughters and two sons. A Peter Grossnickle arrived in Philadelphia in October 1746 (S&H).

The Grossnickle lineages are complex because of large families including many Johns and Peters. Many moved westward to Washington County, to Indiana and further. The following account comes in large part from articles in the *Frederick News* by Leah Leatherman Spade on July 24, 1991 and myself on July 13, 1991.

Johannes Grossnickel emigrated in 1738 to southern Pennsylvania where he and wife Susannah were joined by his brother Peter, emigrant in 1746 who had married Margaretha Becker in Philadelphia. Peter, Sr. died in 1755 and his widow married John Swomley; they then lived near New Market, MD. Peter, Jr. and brother John (sons of Peter and Margaret) went to live with their Uncle John and Aunt Susannah who had settled near Wolfsville. Young John (1754-1815) married Elisabeth Neff and had 12 children; they moved to near Johnstown, PA.

The first Grossnickel record in the courthouse at Frederick is in 1767 when John registered the mark used to identify his cattle, sheep and hogs. In 1770 John bought from Mathias Saylor the tracts Resurvey on Misery and Sugar Tree Bottom lying between Catoctin Creek and South Mountain. Like the Bittle, Hessong and Coblentz families in the same period, John Grossnickle is believed to have come to Middletown Valley from near Littlestown, PA, where he sold a property to my ancestor Abraham King of Kingsdale. Wills of John probated in 1782 and wife Susannah in 1803 show no direct descendants. Thus, the many Grossnickle descendants of our area are believed to come largely from Peter, Sr. and his son Peter II.

Peter Grossnickle III (1779-1859) married his first cousin Hannah Grossnickle and they lived at Highland on the northeast edge of Middletown Valley. In 1794 Peter bought the tract Rum Spring. The spring began at a branch of Catoctin Creek near the road from James Flemming's plantation to Catoctin Furnace. The will of Peter (wife Christina) probated in 1822 made executors his sons John (1783-1863) and Peter (b. 1785) (who were leaders in building Grossnickle Meetinghouse about 1845). Besides John and Peter their sons, Peter and Christina had the following daughters:

Susanna married John Custer.

Elisabeth married Jacob Harp.
Christina married Daniel Boyer.
Hanna married Peter Grossnickle of John.
Catherine, unmarried.
Mary married Jacob Hoover.

Peter Grossnickle of John was a son of John (1783-1863) and Mary (Hauver) (daughter of Christian) and a grandson of John and Catherine according to W&M.

Peter Grossnickle (b. 1783) and wife Rebecca Hauver had seven children of whom Rev. George (b. 1812) and wife Ann (Barnheiser) in 1865 led a migration from Middletown Valley to North Manchester, Wabash County, IN.

Jacob Grossnickle (1815-1882) (son of Peter (b. 1779) and Hannah (b. 1782)), married Catherine Durnbaugh (daughter of Jacob and Margaret) of Washington County, MD. They and descendants lived around Mapleville in the Beaver Creek area (Wms. 1906).

A Grossnickle Family genealogy was written by Warren Grossnickle (Manchester, IN, 1932), and another Grossnickle genealogy was published by Carol C. Boyer (Denver, CO, 1980).

W&M-1370. Peter Grossnickle of J. (1830-1911) and wives Maria E. (Bittle) (1834-1875) and Mary (Harshman) (1846-1922) are buried at Grossnickle Meeting House where also are buried his father John, Sr. (1783-1875) and mother Mary (Hauver) (1796-1875). John, son of emigrant Peter, Sr. was born in America.

W&M-1371. (Mahlon) Webster Grossnickle (1860-1923) and wife Alice H. (Gaver) (1861-1924) are buried at Mt. Olivet. He was a son of Peter of J. (1830-1911) and Maria E. (Bittle) (1834-1875) who are buried at the Grossnickle Meeting House. See Peter of J. above.

W&M-1372. William Harlan Grossnickle (1854-1922) and wife Martha Ellen (Routzahn) (1856-1929) are buried at the U. B. Church in Myersville. He was another son of Peter of John and Maria E. (Bittle). See W&M-1370.

W&M-1372. Charles C. Grossnickle (1858-1938) and wife Lizzie E. (Buhrman) (1850-1930) are buried at the Myersville U. B. Church. He was another son of Peter of John and Maria (Bittle). See W&M-1370.

W&M-1373. Tilghman F. Grossnickle (1852-1937) and wife Salome A. (Grossnickle) (1856-1918) are buried at Grossnickle Meeting House. According to W&M, Tilghman was a son of John Grossnickle, Jr. (1826-1858) and Mary (Leatherman) (1828-1898) who also are buried there.

W&M-1373. C. Upton Grossnickle (1856-1957) and wives Lizzie M. (1861-1884) and Ella M. (Leatherman) (1865-1945) are buried at Grossnickle Meeting House. W&M gives his first wife as Mary E. (Toms). His parents Elias and Nancy (Stottlemyer) (c.1829-1912) also are buried there. For early Grossnickles see W&M-1369.

W&M-1374. Richard C. Kefauver (1843-1925) and wife Laura V. (Toms) (1847-1936) are buried at Middletown Reformed Cemetery, where also are buried his parents Daniel (1808-1876) and second wife Catherine (Bechtel) (1813-1895). Daniel's first wife was sister Annie Virginia (Bechtel) (1846-1871). Richard's paternal grandparents were George Kefauver (1785-1861) and wife Mary (1782-1851) who also are buried at Middletown Reformed Church. For earlier Kefauvers see W&M-791 and 911.

W&M-1375. James Houck (1844-1931) and wife Alice (Cramer) (1850-1932) are buried at Mt. Olivet, where also are buried his parents Ezra (1802-1878) and Catherine (Bentz) (1806-1886), and his grandparents George Houck (1775-1867) and wife Catherine (1781-1838). George Houck was a son of Peter (1735-1798) and wife Margaret Catherine. For earlier Houcks see W&M-811.

W&M-1376. Rev. David Grossnickle (1828-1919) and wives Elizabeth (Michael) (1824-1882) and Sarah Catherine (Ashbaugh) (1845-1887) are buried at Beaver Dam Brethren Cemetery near Johnsville. His parents were Peter Grossnickle, Jr. (1806-1874) and Sophia (Brown) (1807-1891) who are buried at Grossnickle Meeting House. Rev. David's grandfather was Peter of John. See W&M-1369 and 1371.

W&M-1377. Henry C. Remsberg (1841-1922) and wives Mahala M. (Kefauver) (1845-1893) and Amelia W. (Grosh) (1859-1952) are buried in the Reformed Cemetery at Middletown, where also are buried his parents John Remsberg, Jr. (1800-1865) and Catherine (Coblentz) (1809-1850).

The gravestone of Georg Riemensperger (1736-1820) states that he was born at Walldorf near Heidelberg. This is one of the stones removed from the German Thomas family graveyard west of Adamstown to Church Hill on Ballenger Creek Road.

George Remsberg and wives Elizabeth (Brunner) (1739-1787) and Catherine (Sulser) (1776-1866) are buried on the German Thomas family graveyard near Mountville, west of Adamstown. John Remsberg (1760-1845), son of George and Elizabeth, married Catherine Thomas (1776-1866) and they are buried at Middletown Reformed Church. They were parents of John Remsberg, Jr. Related descendants of George of Walldorf are shown in W&M-1037.

The fifth child of Henry C. and Mahala was Prof. Charles H. Remsberg (1875-1946) who married Harriet A. Grosh (b. 1882). They have stones in Middletown Reformed Church. Prof. Remsberg was my teacher of trigonometry at Frederick High School in 1928. He helped convince me that scholarship could be enjoyable. Our class field trip to measure the distance from High Knob to White Rock sighting from a base line on the road near Harmony Grove was memorable.

W&M-1380. Foster C. Remsberg (1869-1944) and wife Amy A. (Kefauver) (1865-1956) are buried at Middletown Reformed Cemetery, as are his parents Henry C. and Mahala noted above.

W&M-1381. John W. Bussard (1850-1934) and wife Elizabeth (Summers) (1853-1909) are buried at Middletown Lutheran Church, where also are buried his parents Peter Hanson Bussard (1826-1905) and wife Charlotte M. (Curfman) (1829-1915). For earlier Bussards see W&M-860.

W&M-1382. Peter E. Bussard (1852-1936) and wife Alta Virginia (Culler) (1877-1953) are buried at Middletown Lutheran Cemetery. He was another son of Peter Hanson and Charlotte above.

W&M-1384. E. Austin Baughman (1882-1946) was a son of lawyer and Confederate Gen. Louis Victor (1845-1906) and wife Helen (Abell) (1856-1940). They are buried at the Catholic Cemetery in Frederick. See W&M-696.

W&M-1384. Noah E. Flanagan (1866-1938) and wife Martha E. (Green) (1873-1953) are buried at Mt. Hope Cemetery at Woodsboro. His parents John F. (1828-1880) and wife Minerva A. (Snook) (1837-1901) are buried at Creagerstown. Hugh Flannigan (over 45 years) was the head of a large family in northern Frederick County in the 1800 census.

W&M-1385. Charles Worthington Ross (1836-1905) and wife Cornelia (Ringgold) (1839-1927) are buried at Mt. Olivet, as are his parents William Johnson Ross (1806-1883) and wife Anna Maria (Davis) (1808-1838). William J. married later Eliza H. Stokes (d. 1842), daughter of William H. She also is buried at Mt. Olivet, as are the grandparents of Charles W., namely William Ross (1772-1852) and Catherine (Johnson) (1785-1864), daughter of Baker Johnson.

Ross Families by Blanche T. Hartman (Pittsburgh, 1929) is a genealogy. Another study of Ross families was written by Mary Ellen Emery in 1976. John Ross married Alicia Arnold in 1720 at St. James Church, Westminster, London and sailed for America soon after. They were ancestors of Francis Scott Key.

Charles Worthington Ross, Jr. (1869-1921) married Theresa (Kunkel) daughter of John J. (1848-1888). He is buried at Mt. Olivet. He was a son of Charles W. and Cornelia (Ringgold) shown above.

In the Maryland Militia in the Revolution were Lieut. Joseph Ross of Prince George's County and a dozen others of the name served as privates. In Frederick Court records Dr. David Ross in 1752 sued John Howard, merchant. (LC)

W&M-1386. Richard Potts Ross (1873-1944) and wife Blanche E. (Shriner) (1873-1951) are buried at Mt. Olivet as are their parents Charles W. and Cornelia noted above.

W&M-1387. Americus G. P. Wiles (1846-1904) and wife Sarah S. (Hummer) (1845-1912) are buried at Utica, where also are buried his parents Peter (1815-1848) and wife (Mary) Rebecca (Byerly) (1806-1879).

Americus and Sarah were parents of Dr. Charles P. Wiles, outstanding pastor and editor of the Lutheran Church and of Bradley Wiles who married Virgie Measle. The latter were parents of Helen and Americus. Dr. Americus G. D. or Mac Wiles was a college professor of English at the Citadel and President of Newberry College in SC. (See M&C-II.)

Early in Middletown Valley was George Weil or Wiles. In the 1800 census of the valley George Wyles and wife were over 45 years. Between 26 and 45 years of age were heads of households Jacob, Peter and Samuel Wyles. Peter and wife Rebecca were ancestors of the scholars Dr. Charles P. and Dr. Mac Wiles. A genealogy *Wiles Families of Frederick County* was written by Marie D. Wiles and Earl H. Davis of Plattsmouth, NB, in 1976.

W&M-1387. Dr. John James Liggett, M.D. (1846-1921) is buried at Haugh's Church and wife Julia Amanda (Harris) at Mt. Olivet. His parents Dr. John Enoch Hannah Liggett (1815-1869) and wife Mary Elizabeth (Smith) (1819-1876) are buried at Haugh's Church north of Woodsboro. The parents of Julia A. were Henry R. Harris (1820-1878) and wife Claracy (b. c.1822).

W&M-1390. Charles J. Bittle (1862-1946) and wife Effie Lenah (Brown) (1864-1928) are buried at the Lutheran Church at Myersville where also are buried his parents William Metzger Bittle (1841-1928) and Catherine (Routzahn) (1840-1931). Paternal grandparents of Charles were Jonathan Bittle (1798-1855) and wife Rachel (1804-1885) who are buried at Grossnickle Brethren Meeting House. Jonathan's father George Michael Bittle moved from near Littlestown, PA, to a farm near Fox Hill northeast of Myersville.

According to Robert D. Bittle of LaVale, MD, George Michael Bittle (b. 1759) married Anna Maria Elizabeth (b. 1759) daughter of David Bell (d. 1810). David Edgar Bittle (1889-1952) married Floy Miller Biser (b. 1889).

W&M-1391. Aaron Rosenstock (b. 1856) married Isabella Heidelberger of Baltimore. Rosenstock gravestones were not reported by J.M.H. Perhaps they are buried in the Baltimore area. In the 1850 census of Frederick were Philip Rosenstock, merchant, born in Germany about 1813, wife Henrietta born about 1819 and children: Levi (8 years), Belenda (6), Sarah (3) and Cornelia (1). See (J). In 1886 Joseph and Jacob Rosenstock lived at 3 East Patrick Street where their clothing store was located.

W&M-1392. Bernard Rosenour of Bavaria died in Baltimore in 1908. He and sons Abraham, Gerson and Benjamin were leading merchants in Frederick (J). In 1886 they, along with Miss Bella, Miss Celia and Mrs. Benjamin Rosenour, lived at 41 North Market Street. The "Double Store" of B. Rosenour at 39 and 43 North Market Street offered clothing, boots and shoes.

W&M-1393. George K. Birely (1820-1873) and wife Annie E. (Schley) (1827-1880) are buried at Mt. Olivet. His son Lewis (1860-1941), who did not marry, also is buried in Mt. Olivet. Earlier Birelys are given in M&C-II. See also (Schley).

W&M-1393. Maj. Charles A. Damuth (1841-1910) and wife Minerva (Arthur) (1841-1866) (daughter of John and Susan) are buried in Thurmont U. B. Cemetery and Apples Church respectively. Maj. Charles' second wife Henrietta (Root) (1845-1926) also is buried at the U. B. Church. The parents of Charles were David Damuth (1813-1901) and Catherine (Stauffer) (1813-1877) who also are buried there. Buried at Apples Church are Henry Damuth (1776-1840) and wife Anna M. (1769-1838).

Some early Damuths are in the Archives of the Moravian Church at Graceham including Johann and wife Catherine whose daughter Sophia Theresa was baptized in 1797. Possible European origins of Demuth families are given in M&C-II. Genealogical studies by recent Howard R. Demuth of Thurmont are in the Archives of Mt. St. Mary's College. (LC)

W&M-1394. James Clarke Kieffer (b. 1874) and related families of Washington County are discussed in Wms. (1906). *Kiefer Families* by Richard A. Keefer was published at DeKalb, IL in 1975. (LC)

W&M-1395. Oliver Cornelius Warehime (1859-1928) and wife Carrie E. (Whipp) (1865-1908) are buried at Mt. Olivet. Hanna Wareheim (1801-1873) and husband John (c.1799-1892) are buried at Pipe Creek Brethren Cemetery near Uniontown.

W&M-1396. Nelson D. Ramsburg (1836-1924) and wife Eliza A. (Harman) (1838-1912) are buried at Utica, where also are buried his parents Jacob (1808-1877) and Annie Elizabeth (Snook) (1798-1889). Jacob grew up in West Virginia near Shepherdstown. His descent from emigrant Stephen is outlined in W&M-752. Eliza was a daughter of George (1792-1862) and Elizabeth Harman (1815-1849) who are buried at Apples Church.

W&M-1397. Jacob Andrew Layman (1867-1932) and wife Mary Alberta (Miller) (1877-1945) are buried at Lewistown Methodist Church, where also are buried his parents George W. (1829-1902) and Sophia R. (Favorite) (1832-1905). An older brother of Jacob A. was christened Colonel Layman; his farm near Lewistown was visited by my father and myself about 1920 when I was impressed by a large white pine tree, a remnant of vanished forest.

Lehman (later Lemon and Layman) families were early in what became Carroll County. A John Lemon was appointed overseer in 1750 of the road from Great Pipe Creek to the temporary line with Pennsylvania. Some Lemon genealogies are cited in M&C-II. A Jacob Layman and wife, in age between 26 and 45 years, are in census of 1800.

A Philip Jacob Lehman emigrated in 1752 from Hunspach in northern Alsace (B3). He married in 1741 Anna Barbara Zimmerman, daughter of Bernhard. Jacob was naturalized in Maryland in 1762 and had four children baptized in Frederick Reformed Church. (LC).

W&M-1397. Albert Wilson Burkhart (1827-1910) and parents Charles Hedges Burkhart (1798-1879) and wife Elizabeth R. (Neighbors) (1804-1883) are buried at Mt. Olivet. The paternal grandfather of Albert was George who died in eastern Tennessee. In the census of 1800 George F. Burkhart and wife (both over 45 years) had the only Burkhart household in Fredericktown District. They lived without children but had one slave. In 1800 in Middletown Valley were households of Henry and of James Burckhart and wives, all in age 26 to 45. In Libertytown District in 1800 were families of Daniel Burket and of John Burket who, with their wives, were 26-45 years in age. Daniel had four slaves.

Some early Burkharts, Links and Smiths of near Woodsboro are of special interest as ancestors of President Dwight D. Eisenhower. Judith Burkhart (1769-1829) born in Frederick County to Captain Daniel and wife married Peter Link (1765-1825). Peter and Judith with their parents moved about 1780 to Augusta County, VA, where President Eisenhower's grandmother Elizabeth (Link) Stover was born in 1822.

Burckharts and Burkerts were early in York County, PA. Carl and wife Anna Margaret (of Flomborn, Palatinate) had son Paul who in 1740 married Eva Swope (d. 1756). Paul Burckhard had a child baptized at Conewago Lutheran Church in 1746. Records of Monocacy Lutheran Church include George Burkett naturalized in 1753 who bought a lot in Frederick in 1766. Michael Burkett was naturalized in 1765 with reference to Lutheran communion. George Burckhart and wife Mary Catherine had a son Christopher baptized in

1756 at Monocacy Lutheran Church. Also in 1756 Simon Burckhart had daughter Susannah Maria baptized at Monocacy Church. In records of Apples Church near Thurmont Peter Burckhart and wife Anna Mary (Ludwig?) had daughter Elizabeth baptized in 1778. Peter Burckhart, who was said to have emigrated in 1755 from Bergzabern, south Pfalz, married secondly Anna Margaret Zimmerman in 1773. They had daughter Elizabeth baptized at Apples Church in 1778. A John Burckhardt and wife Catherine had three infants to die in 1791 to 1794 (LW) (LC).

W&M-1398. Robert Lee Tyler (1862-1943) and wife Mrs. Eliza A. C. (Wachter) (1862-1941) (widow of Daniel H.) are buried at Mt. Olivet. His parents Dr. William, Jr. (1810-1871) and wife Jane DuVal (Robinson) (1826-1892) also are buried at Mt. Olivet.

The first Tylers at Frederick were Dr. John (1763-1841) and wife Catherine (1770-1831) who were buried at the old All Saints Church on East All Saints Street. His brother Dr. William Tyler (1784-1872) and wife Mary B. (Addison) (1790-1868) are buried at Mt. Olivet. Dr. William Tyler met Robert E. Lee at Harpers Ferry during the storming of the engine house. William served as surgeon of the 16th Reg. Maryland Militia. Descendant Jean Craver Gilbert says that Tylers also are related to Lechlider, Shankle, Buckingham, Wiles, Weddle, Reickert, McIntyre, Kaufman and Horne families. (LC)

W&M-1399. Lewis A. Snook (1836-1928) and wife Eliza A. (Pitzer) (1844-1911) are buried at Utica, as are his parents Daniel (1799-1886) and Ann Margaret (Hill) (1799-1848). Also buried at Utica are the grandparents of Lewis, namely Simon Snook (1812-1884) and wife Elizabeth (1815-1840).

In the census of 1800 in northern Monocacy Valley were five Snook families. John, Adam and Simon were over 45 years. Adam Snooke of Simon and wife were 26-45 years of age, with a daughter and three young sons. Jacob Snooke and wife were between 16 and 26 in age and had a daughter and a son under 10 years. John Adam Schnock was confirmed in the Frederick Reformed Church in 1768. A Snook family genealogy by Dr. Maurie E. Snook (Athens, GA, 1980) is available (F) (H).

W&M-1400. James Mifflin Hood (1821-1894) and wives Sarah Ann (Boggs) (1824-1869) and Margaret E. (Scholl) (1833-1913) are buried at Mt. Olivet. Margaret was a daughter of Daniel Scholl (1798-1873) and Maria Susan (Thomas). Her paternal grandparents were Christian Scholl (1768-1826) and wife Elizabeth Brunner (1775-1821). The Scholl family is discussed in M&C-I.

Margaret Scholl attended Frederick Female Seminary which by 1910 had become Women's College. With her financial support and the leadership of Prof. Joseph H. Apple, Hood College was founded in 1893. See W&M-507. *Margaret Scholl Hood's Diary (1851-1861)* has been published as a book by Picton Press, Camden, ME (1992) (FH). Mrs. Hood gave help to my father, Calvin Ezra Schildknecht, by a mortgage to provide the home where I was born at 714 North Market Street, Frederick.

For John Mifflin Hood (1843-1906), President of Western Maryland Railroad, see (NC-30). His paternal ancestor was Benjamin Hood, emigrant in 1668 from Dorset, England, to Hood's Haven estate on the Patapsco River. Son John married Elizabeth Shipley and John, Jr. married Rachel Howard.

W&M-1401. Charles E. Zimmerman (1854-1940) and wife Alverta E. (Fleming) (1867-1951) are buried at Mt. Olivet. He was a son of Edward D. (1822-1914) and Elizabeth Susan (Zimmerman) (1825-1908) who are buried at Church Hill on Ballenger Creek Road.

For early Zimmermans see W&M-978. Of the two brothers who emigrated in 1730 from Meckesheim, Michael lived in Pennsylvania and two of his sons settled north of Frederick. (Johan) Georg (1714-1795) the second brother settled by 1762 west of Carrollton Manor southwest of Frederick. He married Catherine Seidel (1724-1804) and their son John (1755-1813) married Eleanor Holtz (b. 1756). The latter's son John Zimmerman (1792-1863) married Catherine Lashorn. Edward D. was their son. See W&M-979.

W&M-1402. Frederick Stanley Stull (1873-1947) and second wife Dona E. (Wachter) (b. 1880) have gravestones at Charlesville Reformed Church. Frederick's first wife Illie E. (Wachter) died about 3-1/2 years after marriage. Frederick's parents were Frederick A. (1835-1905) and Ann R. (Holtz) (1834-1907) who are buried at Mt. Olivet at Frederick. The paternal grandparents of Frederick S. were Jacob Stull (1810-1864) and Eva (Staley) (1812-1877) who are buried at Bethel Church.

In the 1800 census of Fredericktown District, there were two Stull households. Adam and John Stull and their wives were between 26 and 45 years in age. Adam had four daughters and four sons. John had six daughters and two sons. Adam Stoll, Sr. was the earliest in Frederick

W&M-1403. *The Keedy Family* by Clayton C. Keedy seems to be one of the best articles in W&M. Note that the letters G and K were often interchanged in German names as in Getzendanner and Ketzendanner. It is well documented that Güting or Gueting, became Keedy. Henry Keedy patented his tract Mannheim in 1755, perhaps from his origin at Manheim on the Rhine. See also Wms. (1906).

W&M-1404. Clayton O. Keedy (1855-1924) and wife Irene (Ritter) (1859-1924) are buried at Mt. Olivet Cemetery at Frederick. His parents Dr. John D. and wife Mary A. (Zittle) are buried in Washington County. Zittles in Middletown Valley are noted in M&C-II. Zittlestown is in Washington County near Turner Gap of South Mountain and the Old National Pike. Nearby is the Washington Monument built by citizens of Boonsboro and recently restored.

W&M-1405. William C. Mercer (1874-1936) and wife Lavinia (Culler) (1873-1941) are buried at Mt. Olivet Cemetery. His parents William E. (1840-1905) and Ada S. (Webster) (1843-1927) are buried at Middletown Lutheran Church. William's paternal grandparents were William Mercer (1808-1857) and wife Susan (Smith) (1799-1868) who also are buried at Middletown.

W&M-1406. William N. Zimmerman (1852-1916) and wife Mary E. (Willard) (1852-1898) are buried at Mt. Olivet. His parents Gideon M. (1823-1896) and wife Christiana (Wolfe) (1820-1871) are buried at Church Hill on Ballenger Creek Road.

See W&M-979 for early Zimmerman families in the area northwest of Buckeystown. Settler George (1714-1795) had son Michael (1750-1829) who had son

Henry (1791-1875) who married Charlotte Thomas (1790-1864). The latter couple buried at Church Hill, were parents of Gideon M.

W&M-1407. Edward L. Willard (1850-1920) and wife Emma V. (Shafer) are buried at Middletown Reformed Church where also are buried his parents Dewalt (1808-1890) and wife Elizabeth (Flook) (1817-1881).

For immigrant Willards see W&M-1093. Dewalt J. Willard (1739-1808) married Elisabeth Brandenburg. Son Abraham (1776-1817) and wife Catherine (Biser) (1776-1843) are buried at Burkittsville Union Cemetery. They were parents of Dewalt.

W&M-1408. Judge Arthur D. Willard (1872-1959) and wife Mary E. Stoner (1876-1951) of Reading, PA are buried at Mt. Olivet. He was a son of Edward L. (1850-1920) and Emma V. (Shafer) (1856-1942) who are buried at Middletown Reformed Church. Arthur's paternal grandparents were Dewalt and Elizabeth (Flook) above. See W&M-1093 and 1407 for earlier Willards.

A second son of Judge Arthur and Mary is Henry Willard, a childhood playmate of the writer in northern Frederick. He and wife live in Catonsville, MD. His mother's playing of Chopin on their grand piano remains in my memory.

W&M-1408. Levi J. Wolfe (1835-1922) and wife Annie C. (Lutz) (1842-1928) are buried at Mt. Olivet, where also are buried his parents Samuel (1811-1893) and Barbara (Whitmore) (1811-1869). Levi's paternal grandparents were Jacob Wolfe (1788-1872) and wife Catherine (Main) (1772-1855) who are buried at the Reformed Church at Wolfsville. Contrary to W&M, this Jacob, veteran of the War of 1812, was born in Hagerstown to David Wolfe, Sr. and (Nancy) Matilda (Hauver), daughter of George and Susannah Hauver of Foxville. Descendant Donald Joseph Wolf of Frederick states that the last paragraph on page 1408 also is incorrect.

W&M-1409. Edward Joshua Zimmerman, Jr. (1858-1934) and wife Annie M. (Staley) (no dates) have gravestones in Mt. Olivet. His parents were Edward Joshua (1831-1907) and wife Mary Ann (Wachter) (1832-1907) who are buried at Charlesville Reformed Church.

See W&M-979 for the two emigrating Zimmerman brothers (Hans) Michael of Pennsylvania and (Johan) George (who settled southwest of Frederick). John Nicholas (1759-1826) the 9th son of George married Elisabeth Troxell (b. 1769) and they lived near Rocky Hill Church northeast of Woodsboro. Their son Jacob E. Zimmerman (1801-1883) married Barbara Stull (1807-1884); they were buried at Charlesville, north of Frederick. Edward was their son.

W&M-1411. Millard C. Zimmerman (1870-1941) and wife Annie R. (Sines) (1872-1956) are buried at Frederick Memorial Park. His parents Francis M. (1845-1906) and wife Martha A. C. (Coblentz) (1841-1884) are buried at Jefferson Union Cemetery. Millard's paternal grandparents were Daniel J. Zimmerman (1821-1879) and wife Charlotte (Snider) (1827-1895) who are buried at Jefferson Union Cemetery. Michael Zimmerman (1750-1829) and wife Eva (Cronise) probably were grandparents of Daniel. See W&M-979 and (Z).

W&M-1411. John P. Graff (1849-1933) and wife Clara A. (Simmons) (1859-1933) are buried at Mt. Olivet where also are buried his parents William (1804-1880) and wife Anna (Brown) (1809-1887). See W&M-893. (LC)

W&M-1412. Harry Lee Thomas (1882-1950) married Virgie M. Smith. He is buried at Mt. Olivet where also are buried his parents Amos Thomas (1846-1919) and wife Harriet E. (Snouffer) (1848-1912). Harry's great grandfather was Levin, not Levi.

The following lineage is largely from the *English Thomas Family* by George Leicester Thomas (Adamstown, MD, 1956). This genealogy has an introduction by artist Helen L. Smith who, at age 100 in 1994, still works at her studio at Old Braddock. The lineage includes information from Dorothy Nicodemus of Frederick who is a descendant of both the early English and German Thomas families.

(1) John Thomas of Wrotham, County Kent, England m. Margaret Reynes (d/o of John).

(2) Robert Thomas m. Margaret Goden.

(3) William Thomas m. Bridget Worley.

(4) Robert Thomas (b. 1599) emigrant and wife Abigail lived at Annapolis.

(5) Robert Thomas II m. Mary; lived in St. Mary's County.

(6) Luke Thomas (d. 1739) m. Winifred Taylor.

(7) Mark Thomas m. Winifred Abell (d/o Samuel, Sr.); lived in St. Mary's County.

(8) Mark Thomas II m. 1738 Elizabeth Winsett (d/o Richard of Wrotham, England); they moved before 1776 to near Point of Rocks.

(9) Benjamin Thomas (1741-1816) m. 1771 Eleanor Wells (1748-1812).

(10) (Robert) Levin Thomas (1786-1842) m. 1819 Margaret Duttera or Dutrow (1797-1832); son John B. (1819-1892) (Mt. Olivet) was grandfather of Harry Lee, above.

(11) Dr. Jacob Dutrow Thomas (1827-1894) m. 1848 Anna Mary Wolf (1820-1913).

(12) Adelaide S. Thomas (1851-1895) m. 1892 John Fenton Thomas (1844-1916).

(13) Mary Bertha Thomas (1874-1955) m. 1897 Edgar R. Nicodemus; lived at Buckeystown.

(14) Dorothy A. Nicodemus; lives retired in Frederick.

The children of Mark Thomas, Jr. and Elizabeth Winsett, settlers near Point of Rocks, were as follows:

(1) Edward (1740-1819) m. Mary Johnson.

(2) Benjamin (1741-1816) m. Eleanor Wells (1748-1812) (d/o William and Susannah of St. Mary's County).

   (a) Samuel H. (1777-1857) m. Elizabeth Kephart (d. 1857).

   (b) R. Levin (1786-1842) m. Margaret E. Duttera (1797-1832) (d/o John of Frederick County).

(3) Samuel S. (1749-1831) m. Elizabeth Palmer (1756-1833).

(4) Levin (d. 1853) m. Margaret McQuire (1797-1832); buried at English Thomas graveyard near Point of Rocks.
(5) John R. m. Elizabeth.

W&M-1413. William P. Morsell (1857-1943) and wife Annie V. (Howard) (1867-1946) are buried at Mt. Olivet, where also his mother Ann R. (Preston) Morsell (1815-1907) is buried. The Morsells came from western New York state.

W&M-1414. William V. Wolfe (1864-1940) and wife Annie B. (Kiser) (1869-1943) are buried at Mt. Olivet, where also are buried his parents Elihu R. Wolfe (1838-1889) and wife Margaret (McDevitt) (1842-1919). In the census of 1800 in Middletown Valley the only Wolfe household was that of David and wife, both between 26 and 45 years of age. They had three daughters and two sons. In the Frederick County Militia of 1812 were enrolled Jacob (1788-1872), Rev. John (1789-1855) Presbyterian and George Wolfe. (LC)

W&M-1414. Edward C. Krantz (1852-1928) and wife Mary C. (Biser) (1855-1901) are buried at Mt. Olivet where also are buried his father Frederick (1820-1890) and wives Catherine E. (Stup) (1823-1879) and Laura V. (Mealey) (1842-1896). Edward was a son of Catherine. See also W&M-796. Laura's parents were Isaiah (1801-1899), a miller near Middletown, and wife Elizabeth (1801-1861) who are buried at Mt. Olivet.

W&M-1415. Washington Z. Ramsberg (1834-1910) and wife Mary C. (Hargett) (1844-1921) are buried at Church Hill on Ballenger Creek Road. His parents Jacob (1802-1865) and wife Elizabeth (Willard) (1807-1848) are buried at Jefferson Union Cemetery. Washington's paternal grandparents George Peter Ramsberg (1770-1847) and wife Catherine (Culler) (1776-1866) are buried at the German Thomas graveyard, west of Adamstown. George Peter was the 6th child of (John)George Riemensperger (1736-1820) of Walldorf near Heidelberg and wife Maria Elisabeth (Brunner) (1739-1787). See W&M-1037.

W&M-1416. Rev. Isaac Martin Motter (1852-1927) married Ada Serene Kunkel. His gravestone is in Mt. Olivet. His parents were Lewis Martin (1815-1910) and Alice (Rudisel) (1818-1899) who are buried at Mountain View Cemetery, Emmitsburg. Rev. Isaac's paternal grandparents were Lewis Motter (1779-1837) and wife Mary (Martin) (d. 1858) who are buried at Emmitsburg Lutheran Church. Earlier Motters lived in York County, PA. See also W&M-815.

W&M-1417. Edward J. Utterback (1858-1937) and wife Lillie K. (Easterday) (1868-1932) are buried at Utica. In 1800 there were five Easterday households in Middletown Valley. Christian and wife, over 45 years, owned eight slaves.

W&M-1418. George A. Mort (1854-1931) and wife Caroline S. (Wachter) (1864-1942) are buried at Utica. His parents Samuel (1829-1892) and Margaretha A. (Waldeck) (1832-1915) are buried at Bethel Lutheran Church. A gravestone of George's grandfather John is lacking.

A George Mort (1794-1876) served in the Frederick County Militia in 1812. He married Mary Craig in Bedford County, PA, in 1820. He died in Allen County, OH.

It is surprising that a family has as its name the French word for death. Earlier forms of the name have special interest. In 1800 in Middletown Valley two households were headed by Henry and Valentine Mortar, both over 45 years of age. In Taneytown District Peter Mort (26-45) lived with his family. In Libertytown District in 1800 were three Mort families. John was over 45; Conrad and Mathias were between 26 and 45 in age. (LC). A Bartholomeus Morth (pronounced Mort in Continental Europe) emigrated via Philadelphia in September 1732.

A leading educator of Frederick County was a Mort descendant. Prof. James C. Biehl (c.1886-1960) was a son of James Addison Biehl and wife Sarah Catherine (Mort) (1856-1944), daughter of George W. and Rebecca (Geesey) Mort.

The only Biehl family in the Frederick County census of 1850 was that of George F. Biehl (b. c.1821), a miller, and wife Elliata (b. c.1828). Prof. J. C. Biehl was born near Lewistown. He attended school at Mountaindale and graduated at Boys' High School in Frederick in 1903. He described to me his discipline problems in beginning to teach at a one-room country school when some of the boys were larger that he. In 1918 J. C. became principal of Boys' High School where he had studied. In 1923 Biehl was my teacher and head of the middle school on East Church Street. In 1932-1934 Professor Biehl and I commuted from Frederick to teach at the Thurmont High School where he was the principal. Those were cold winters with temperatures reaching -15 degrees Fahrenheit one morning.

Prof. Biehl married Charlotte B. Whitmore (1878-1939), daughter of Jeremiah and Catherine (Fox) Whitmore of near Woodsboro. Their children are Katherine L., a former teacher at Frederick High School, and Dr. Harold P. Biehl, M.D. of Baltimore.

W&M-1419. James E. Bowers Myers (1862-1950), unmarried, is buried at Mt. Olivet where also are his parents Francis M. (1833-1891) and Margaret L. (Minor) (1838-1924). His grandparents Peter Myers (1795-1870) and Rebecca (Fortney) (1804-1865) are buried at Church Hill on Ballenger Creek Road. See W&M-1165.

W&M-1419. Walter B. Krantz (1856-1914) and wife Mary W. (Doll) (1857-1919) are buried at Mt. Olivet where also are buried his parents William H. (1825-1899) and wife Julia Ann (Beavers) (1835-1896) who came from Loudon County, VA. An earlier William Krantz (b. c.1785), a druggist in Frederick, and wife Theresa (b. c.1794) were born in Germany.

W&M-1419. Dr. Clifford Thomas Sappington, M.D. (1880-1925), unmarried, is buried at Liberty Catholic Cemetery with his parents Dr. Thomas Pearre Sappington (1847-1909) and wife Emma (Worman) (1854-1931). His grandparents were Dr. Greenberry R. Sappington, M.D. (1820-1885) and wife Sarah E. (1827-1888) who also are buried in the Catholic Cemetery at Liberty. The census of 1800 shows Dr. Francis B. Sappington, M.D. over 45, and wife under 45 years, to have the only Sappington household in Liberty District. They had four daughters and two sons, also eight slaves. It is doubted that "Frederick County was full of Indians" at that time!

W&M-1421. Dr. Thomas Pearre Sappington, M.D. (1847-1909) and wife Emma O. (Worman) (1854-1931) are buried at Liberty Catholic Church. For Sappington forebearers see W&M-1419. Henry Worman and wife, both over 45 years, lived in Liberty District in 1800 with a son and two daughters. In Frederick in 1850 lived John R. Worman (b. c.1816), wife Ruth A. (b. c.1821) and four young children.

W&M-1422. Dr. John J. Remsburg, M.D. (b. 1866) married Catherine C. Daugherty (d. 1906) of Baltimore. He was a son of Lewis P. (1830-1908) and wife Julia (Putman) (1831-1904) who are buried at Glade Reformed Cemetery. Dr. John's grandparents were Jacob (1802-1865) and wife Elizabeth (Snook) (1807-1848) who are buried at Jefferson Union Cemetery. Although Dr. John's great grandfather Henry was born in WV near Shepherdstown, he and his father John were of the Remsburg family of Frederick County. See W&M-758.

William P. Remsburg also was born in Jefferson County, WV in 1822. His son Lewis C., born 1846 near Middletown, was a farmer and politician in Tilghmanton District of Washington County (Wms. 1906).

Dr. Henry Ramsburg of Walkersville was a grandson of Henry Remsburg of WV who earlier lived in Middletown Valley.

W&M-1422. Emory Richard Remsburg (1858-1950) and wife Annie M. (Long) (1862-1921) are buried at Jefferson Union Cemetery. His parents John W. (1816-1898) and Adaline Virginia Remsburg (1824-1872) are buried at Middletown Reformed Church.

See W&M-752 for early descendants of Stephen Riemensperger. His son Henry (c.1752-1807) and wife Susan (Devilbiss) were parents of Christian (1785-1874) who with wife Catherine (1786-1854) are buried at Middletown Lutheran Church. Christian was the father of John W. Ramsburg. Morgan H. Ramsburg (1844-1920), a brother of Emory, and wife Martha A. (Pettingall) (1856-1912) are buried at Jefferson Union Cemetery.

W&M-1424. C. Thomas Kemp (1862-1930) and wife Mary Matilda (Schultz) (1861-1940) are buried at Mt. Olivet. The lineage of C. Thomas can be outlined (M&C-I):

(1) Conrad Kaempf (1685-1764) m. Maria of Untergimbern, southeast of Heidelberg, Germany.
(2) Christian Kemp (1715-1790) m. Elisabeth Ferree; farmed on Ballenger Creek Road.
(3) Col. Henry Kemp (1765-1833) 2m. Susan Miller (1772-1829); buried at Mt. Olivet.
(4) Ludwig or Lewis Kemp (1798-1854) m. Rebecca Charlotte Buckey (1798-1857); buried at Mt. Olivet.
(5) Lewis George Kemp (1824-1913) m. Sarah M. Miller (1821-1912); buried at Mt. Olivet; parents of C. Thomas.

David C. Kemp, son of Christian, had a grandson David C. Kemp born in Loudon County, VA, who moved to a farm a mile north of Williamsport (Wms. 1906).

W&M-1425. Albert S. Remsburg (1861-1939) and wife Clara E. (Routzahn) (1864-1948) are buried at Middletown Reformed Church, as are his parents John Harmon (1832-1898) and wife Mary E. (Lighter) (1837-1922). Albert's paternal grandparents were John, Jr. (1800-1865) and Catherine (Coblentz) (1809-1850) who are buried at the Reformed Cemetery in Middletown where also is his father John (1760-1844). The latter was a son of emigrant (John) George Riemensperger, settler in Buckeystown District around 1762. Thus Albert S. was not a descendant of emigrant Stephen, but of his alleged nephew George, emigrant from Walldorf near Heidelberg, Germany. See W&M-1037.

W&M-1426. Martin C. Kemp (1869-1952) married Annie H. Ramsburg, daughter of Washington Z. and Mary C. (Hargett) of near Jefferson. His lineage can be outlined as follows:

> (1) Conrad Kaemp (1685-1764) m. Anna Maria (1695-1758); emigrants with children from Untergimbern, southeast of Heidelberg.
>
> (2) (John) Peter Kemp (1727-1808) m. Catherine; lived near Indian Springs northwest of Frederick.
>
> (3) Solomon Kemp m. Barbara Hershberger.
>
> (4) William C. Kemp (b. 1825) m. Susan Stockman (b. 1830). He was a wagon maker near Jefferson.
>
> (5) Martin Kemp, 10th child.

W&M-1427. Marshall Orlando Ramsburg (1852-1937) and wife Mary E. (Ogle) (1858-1910) are buried at Glade Reformed Cemetery near Walkersville, as are his parents Lewis P. (1830-1908) and wife Julia Catherine (Putman) (1831-1904).

The Ramsburg family was not early in Virginia. Henry, the son of John from Frederick County, was born on a farm in WV near Shepherdstown. Jacob returned to relatives near Lewistown. See W&M-1037, 1377 and 1422.

W&M-1427. The Routzahn family emigrated from Beerfelden, Pfalz, Germany, according to genealogist Doris Suresch. Adam Rauenzaner (1736-1827) buried at Middletown Lutheran Church was married to Elisabeth. His son Ludwig (1767-1856) married Esther (1767-1815); they are buried at St. John's Lutheran Church north of Myersville. Their son (Peter) Benjamin (1790-1839) was the father of John (1811-1888) who married Sarah Coblentz (1810-1886); they are buried at Middletown Lutheran Church. Their son Herman L. Routzahn (1848-1935) and wife Martha E. (Kefauver) (1848-1915) also are buried at the same place. Their son John Lewis (1876-1952), musician and banker, married Lucille M. Thomas. See W&M-756 and (R).

W&M-1429. Charles M. Shank (b. 1863) who married Annie D. Keller was a son of George (1820-1896) and Mary A. (Routzahn) (1832-1912). They are buried at Myersville Lutheran Church. The paternal grandfather of Charles was Jacob Shank (1781-1867) who also is buried at Myersville Lutheran Church. Serving in the Frederick Militia in 1812 were Lieut. John Shank, Peter Shank (1793-1889) who moved to Dayton, OH, and Peter Shank (b. 1789) who married Barbara Beckenbaugh and moved to Montgomery County, OH.

W&M-1429. (Daniel) Edward Kefauver (1841-1912) and wife Mrs. Amanda E. Snyder (Lighter) (1839-1903) are buried at the Middletown Reformed Church. Edward first married Virginia Culler (1846-1871). His third wife was Mrs. Hattie H. Cundiff (Vosburg). Edward was a son of Daniel Kefauver (1808-1876) and Catherine (Bechtel) (1813-1895) who are buried at the Middletown

Reformed Cemetery. Edward's paternal grandparents were George Kefauver (1775-1861) and wife Mary (1782-1851) buried also at Middletown Reformed Cemetery. For earlier Kefauvers see W&M-791 and 1296.

W&M-1431. Curtis W. Thomas (1851-1922) and wife Abbie L. (Thomas) (1855-1930) are buried at Mt. Olivet. He was a son of George (of Henry) Thomas (1798-1883) and wife Julia Ann (Hargett) (1813-1879) who are buried at Church Hill on Ballenger Creek Road. The paternal grandparents of Curtis were Henry Thomas of John (b. 1765) and Ann Margaret (Ramsburg) (b. 1769). His great grandparents were John Thomas (b. 1728) and Catherine (Getzendanner). John was born two years before his parents emigrated from Klein Schifferstadt. See W&M-1015 for parents of John. According to Charles B. Thomas, present world expert on water-gardening, four early Thomas brothers married neighboring Remsberg daughters.

W&M-1432. Stephen A. Thomas (1853-1917) and wife Ella V. (Thomas) (1860-1956) are buried at Church Hill on Ballenger Creek Road along with his parents George of Henry (1798-1883) and wife Julia A. (Hargett) (1813-1879). See also W&M-1015.

W&M-1432. John William Thomas (1871-1951) married Addie M. Remsberg. He is buried at Mt. Olivet. His parents J. Franklin (1843-1921) and Mary Ellen (Zimmerman) (1847-1889) are buried at Church Hill on Ballenger Creek Road. John Thomas was born in 1728 before emigrating with his family in 1730. See W&M-1015.

W&M-1433. The oldest son of Curtis and Abbe (W&M-1431) was George Leicester Thomas, the local pioneer in genealogical research, whose studies in Frederick County and in southern Germany led to his two published works, *Genealogy of the German Thomas Families* and *Genealogy of the English Thomas Families*. Lester was born February 24, 1880. His first marriage was to Miss Bertz of Lancaster, who died soon after in 1903. The second wife of Lester was Pearl Brown, daughter of William A. and Helen K. (Kimber) Brown of Heart Lake, PA. Lester and Pearl had two children, George L., Jr. (1907-1977) who married Virginia L. Brosius, and Frances who married C. Lease Bussard.

When George Lester Thomas, Sr. was 10 years old his father Curtis bought 360 acres beside the Monocacy River south of Buckeystown. About 1917 George started raising goldfish and water plants as a hobby, but this gradually became a business on the 360 acres. A high point was the visit in June 1936 of Lily Pons (1904-1976) of the Metropolitan Opera and the establishment of Lilypons Post Office 21717 at Three Springs Fisheries. The Thomas family aquatic gardens with branches near Houston, TX and Palm Springs, CA, now called Lilypons Water Gardens, are leaders in the world. George Leicester Thomas, Jr. (1907-1977) retired from business in 1966 and it has been expanded by his sons Charles B. and G. L. II, with emphasis upon aquatic plants and water gardens rather than goldfish culture.

Virginia L. Brosius Thomas (Mrs. G. L. II) has continued the genealogical contacts and research with Germany initiated by her father-in-law. She brought Frederick people, including this writer, in touch with the late Dr. Fritz Braun of Kaiserslautern, with her distant cousin Emil Thomas of Schwegenheim and with the late Ernst Wagner of Schifferstadt. Virginia died March 24, 1994.

W&M-1434. Willie Clayton Cramer (1861-1922) and wife Susie Irene (Albaugh) (1865-1942) are buried at Mt. Olivet. His parents John David (1826-1899) and Annabel (Shull) (1842-1908) are buried at Glade Reformed Cemetery. Annabel's parents were Elias (1804-1856) and second wife Mary Scholl (1813-1894) who also are buried at Glade Cemetery.

W&M-1434. (George) William McGaha or Magaha (1855-1941) of Loudon County, VA, married Hannah Elizabeth Williams. He is buried at Burkittsville Union Cemetery. William's parents were Armistead U. Magaha (b. 1873) and wife Margaret E. (Wenner) (1876-1944) who have gravestones at the same place.

Luther Franklin Magaha (1879-1947) (buried at Mt. Olivet) married Julia (Bond). One of their sons, Luther, married Daisy Darr. They lived near Mt. Airy and were parents of Henry Magaha who with wife Florence live on Old Annapolis Road at Kimmel Road.

Another line of Magaha families from VA led to E. Paul Magaha, Sr., twice Mayor of Frederick. George William Magaha (1849-1936) of Virginia settled near Burkittsville and married Mary E. Sigler (1853-1923) They are buried in Burkittsville Union Cemetery. Their son George Ernest (c.1879-1946) married Esta Zecher (c.1880-1963) daughter of William Carlton and Margaret (Dean) Zecher of Middletown Valley. They lived at 708 North Market Street and George Ernest was in the garage and auto business. Their sons were Milburn (1903-1950), who married Helen Yinger and lived in Baltimore, and E. Paul Magaha (c.1909-1990) who married Alice Wilson (1906-1964) of Mt. Airy. Paul was Mayor of Frederick 1965-1966 and elected again in 1970. Their sons are E. Paul, Jr. and Douglas W.

W&M-1436. John Wesley Creager (1863-1910) and wife Effie D. (Williar) (1866-1948) are buried at Thurmont U. B. Church where also his parents are buried, namely James Creager (1817-1900) and Sophia (Firor) (1831-1904).

In the account of early Creagers W&M miss a generation. Johan Lorentz Krueger was born in 1715 at Bettelheim near Berleberg in the old Duchy of Wittgenstein (northwest of the city of Marburg in Westphalia). He married in 1742 Mary Elisabeth Hahn born 1715 in a neighboring village of Alertshausen. About 1738 Lawrence and party emigrated to Codorus Settlement in York County, PA and by 1747 they settled near Monocacy Church. The lineage from the Archives of the Moravian Congregation follows:

    (2) Lawrence Creager, Jr. (1754-1820) m. Anna Maria Harbaugh (1754-1837).

    (3) John Jacob (1779-1849) m. Maria Catherine Bush (1784-1847); he is buried at Graceham.

    (4) James (1817-1900) 2m 1859 Sophia Firor (1831-1904); children: John Wesley, and (Martin) Luther (1866-1948) m. Mary H. Wisotzkey (1867-1950) (Thurmont Blue Ridge Cem.).

The first marriage of James was to Elizabeth Weller (1819-1857).
Moravian Archives gives their children who matured as follows:

    (a) Sevilla Catherine (b. 1840) m. Wesley Delaplane.

    (b) Eleonora Adelaide (b. 1843)

(c) Jacob Frederick (b. 1848) m. Mary C. Clem.

(d) Anna Elizabeth (1853-1942) m. Mahlon J. Whitmore(1848-1915).

Creager Families of Frederick County (also of OH and IN) was written by Harriet F. Wright (Richmond, IN, 1958 and 1978). See also (WP).Peter and Michael Creager protested to Annapolis about ill treatment by Magistrate Capt. Peter Bainbridge in 1766. The Creager families (of those of German origin) led in the number of officers in the Maryland Militia in the Revolution: Capt. Daniel, Capt. Valentine, Ensign Lawrence, Ensign Michael and Ensign Adam Creager.

W&M-1436. David Franklin Davis (b. 1875) married Bertha Beckley of Frederick. He was a son of Franklin H. Davis (1844-1909) and wife of M. A. Rebecca (Coblentz) (1846-1931) who are buried at Middletown Reformed Cemetery. The parents of Franklin H. were William D. (1809-1877) and wife Ann E. (b. c.1820) of New Market District. See W&M-839 and 1069.

W&M-1437. James Theodore Waesche (1849-1934) and wife Cassandra (Cover) (1850-1931) are buried at the U. B. Cemetery at Thurmont. His parents George Henry Waesche (1807-1849) and wife Catherine (Cassell) (1811-1891) lived in Woodsboro District. James' brother (Leonard) Randolph (1846-1934) married Mary Margaret Foreman, daughter of George W. and Phoebe A. Foreman of Creagerstown District. Randolph and Mary of Thurmont were parents of Admiral Russell Randolph Waesche, who became the first full Admiral of the U. S. Coast Guard and an outstanding leader in World War II. Adm. Waesche was born January 6, 1886 in Thurmont and died October 18, 1946. The children of Randolph and Mary were Daisey, George, Edna C., Mary A., Phoebe Grace, Russell R., Donald M. and Clinton F. Adm. Russell and first wife Dorothy Luke had sons Russell R., Jr., a Commander in the Coast Guard, Lieut. Col. Harry Lee of the U. S. Air Force, and Ensign James H. of the Coast Guard. By second wife Agnes Rizzoto (Cronin) (d. 1947) a son William A. was born to the Admiral.

Adm. Waesche studied electrical engineering at Purdue University before attending the Coast Guard Academy. He was commissioned an Ensign in 1906, made head of Communications Division of the Coast Guard in 1916, Chief of Ordnance stationed in D.C. in 1928 and Commander of the Coast Guard in 1936. During his tenure, including World War II, the Coast Guard grew from 15,000 to 170,000 members. Waesche was named by President Truman to the Defense Board and was made a full Admiral in 1945. He received the Distinguished Service Medal in 1946. His obituary in the *New York Times* stated that he and Coast Guard played major roles in victory in World War II. The *Times* pointed out that the Coast Guard saved many seamen escaping from torpedoed ships, directed invasions by U. S. Marines in the South Pacific, seized a Nazi weather station in Greenland and foiled parties of Nazi saboteurs put ashore in 1942.

A portrait of Admiral Waesche is in a booklet *Historic Frederick* by Col. John R. Holt (Frederick 1949) (FH). In a genealogy by Margaret Belt Waesche (about 1930) the earliest Waesche in the U. S. was Frederick Waesche (1777-1825).

W&M-1438. J. Calvin Cronise (1843-1908) and wife Margaret (Baker) (1844-1922) are buried at Mt. Olivet where also are his parents Joseph (1823-1896) and wife Rebecca (Brunner) (1821-1894). See W&M-1054 and 1233.

W&M-1439. Daniel T. Ordeman (1848-1907) and wife Edith Best (1867-1931) are buried at Mt. Olivet as is his father Capt. Herman Ordeman (1812-1884). Edith's parents were David Best (1804-1880) and wife Anna Mary (1802-1871) who are buried at Mt. Olivet.

W&M-1439. George Edward Myers (1868-1941) and wife Mary Elizabeth (Steward) (1867-1944) are buried at Mt. Olivet, as are their son Edward Irvin (1896-1976) and wife Julia Susannah (Roelkey) (1895-1977).

Descendant genealogist Margaret Myers gives the following lineage: Charles George Meyer, Sr. (1822-1861) was born in Hildesheim Kingdom, northern Germany and died in Frederick. He married Augusta C. Stoffrigan (1817-1892). Their son Charles George, Jr. (1845-1922) born in Germany married Susan M. Wilhelmina Fox (1866-1914), daughter of Ernst August Christian Fox and first wife Catherine (Gladhill). Their son George Edward Myers married Mary Elizabeth Steward (daughter of William W. Steward and wife Mary Isadora Rebecca (Beall)). Their son Edward Irvin, Sr. married Julia Susannah Roelkey (daughter of Elroy Livingston Roelkey and wife Genevra "Jennie" Lucetta (Zimmerman)). Their children are Edward Irvin, Jr. and Margaret Elizabeth Myers of Frederick. The latter also has traced her lineage to the following in Pennsylvania and western Maryland:

Johan Georg Zimmerman (1714-1795), Meckesheim, Germany to Frederick Co., m. Anna Catharina Seidel (1744-1804). See W&M-979 and (Z).

Carl Wilhelm Ludwig Fuchs (1787-1857) m. Johanna Catharina Wildhagen (1787-1852); from Germany to Frederick. Son Ernst August Christian Fox (1820-1889), Westphalia to Frederick, m. Catherine Gladhill (1827-1863). Daughter Susan M. Wilhelmina (1846-1914) m. Charles George Meyer, Jr. (1845-1922), born in Germany.

Hans Philip Spannseiler (c.1676-1752) of Kirnbach near Sinsheim, Germany, m. Anna Barbara Mast; emigrated in 1732 to Lancaster County, PA. See M&C-II. Son Andrew Sponseller (1722-1779) m. Elisabeth Philipa Lease (Reformed Church, Frederick).

George Albright and wife Barbara had son Philip m. Anne Marie Ursula Dinckle. Their son John George Albright of Pennsylvania m. Susan Herman and had Charles Philip (c.1795-1864) (Mt. Olivet).

John Nicholas Herman m. Esther Schwenck. Their son Christian m. Susan Leitner. The latter's daughter Susan m. John George Albright of Pennsylvania and had son Charles Philip (c.1795-1864) (Mt. Olivet).

John Adam Leitner of York in 1779 and wife Maudlin had son John Adam, Jr., m. Anna Barbara Beard (daughter of George). Their daughter Susan Leitner m. Christian Herman of Pennsylvania They had grandson Charles Philip Albright (c.1795-1864) (Mt. Olivet).

George Frederick Measell, Sr. and wife Anna Maria had son George F., Jr., m. Rosanna Fry, daughter of Enoch. Their daughter Elizabeth

Rebecca m. Charles Philip Albright. Rosanna's son George Measell (1811-1874) m. Margaret Rebecca Martz. Both buried at Mt. Olivet.

Martin Adams and wife Anna Maria had son Valentine Adams, m. Eva Margaret Lingenfelter (dau. of Johan Georg and wife Eva Magdalena (Degen)). Eva's dau. Eve Margaret Adams (1771-1848) m. Abraham Albaugh (son of John William and Magdalena) (all near Liberty Chapel).

Jakob Trachsel and wife Margaretha (Brengel) of Lenk, Switzerland had grandson George Frederick Troxell (1741-1796), who settled near Apples Church, and married Appolina Loy (daughter of Johannes George Ley and Maria Elisabeth (Trout). Frederick's daughter Elizabeth m. John Nicholas Zimmerman. See W&M-734.

Balser Michell Martz and wife Anna had son Johan whose son John George and wife Anna Maria had son Maj. George Daniel Martz (1786-1868), m. Catherine E. Reese (1787-1858) (Mt. Olivet).

Johan Jost Reese or Riess had son Johan Adam who married Anna Catherine Margaret Seemahr. John Adam Reese, Jr. m. Susanna Barbara Margaret Neff (daughter of George Adam and Christina). Their daughter Catherine E. Reese (1787-1858) m. Maj. George Daniel Martz (Mt. Olivet).

Hans Graff had son Jacob, m. Catherine Staley. Jacob, Jr. m. Anna Maria Kuckerli or Cookerly (dau. of John, Sr.). Their dau. Catherine Grove m. John Adam Sponseller (1788-1870) (McKaig Cemetery).

John Daniel Dinckle m. Maria Ursula von Ernest. Dau. Anne Marie Ursula m. Philip Albright & had grandson Charles Philip Albright (c.1795-1864) of PA. 2m Elizabeth Rebecca Measell (both buried at Mt. Olivet).

Johannes Kreglo m. Elisabeth Sander (daughter of Elias). Their dau. Christina (1761-1807) m. John Jacob Sponseller; Son (John) Adam (b. c.1788) m. Catherine Grove (b. c.1788). Lived in New Market District. Early Kreglos were around Taneytown.

George Gladhill and wife Mary had son James, m. Mary Ann Ambrose (1804-1843), daughter of Henry and wife Sophia (Weaver). Mary Ann's daughter Catherine Gladhill m. Ernest August Christian Fox. James was buried at Sabillasville, Mary Ann at St. John's Lutheran Church north of Myersville. Matthias and Jacob Ambrose were early near Thurmont. (T&D)

W&M-1440. Charles F. Thomas (1848-1922) and wife Sarah C. (Baker) (1851-1929) are buried at Mt. Olivet at Frederick as are his parents William H. (1835-1917) and Mary A. R. (Harding) (1811-1865). George Thomas, the grandfather of Charles F., lived 1778-1845, and is buried with wife Charlotte at Church Hill on Ballenger Creek Road. His grandparents were Valentine Thomas (1724-1796) and wife Margaret. See also W&M-1015. In the 1800 census of Middletown Valley was the family of Adam Harding. In 1800 in southern Frederick County lived families of John and William Harding, both over 45 years of age.

W&M-1441. John Usher Markell (1862-1908) and wife Mary (Gambrill) (1867-1915) are buried at Mt. Olivet where also are his parents Francis (1821-1883) and wife Caroline (Delaplaine) (1833-1905).

Conrad Markell (1721-1782) was buried at the Frederick Lutheran Church. John Markell (1781-1860) and wife Catherine (1788-1859) are buried at Mt. Olivet. They were parents of Francis above. See also W&M-1015.

W&M-1442. James R. Ferrell (1821-1909) and wife Mary A. (Blessing) (1817-1895), widow of Simon, are buried at Jefferson Union Cemetery. His parents were Richard Ferrell and wife Margaret (Blessing) (1795-1862) who are buried at Petersville Episcopal Church. See Blessings in W&M-1513. Richard Ferrell was a stage driver during the War of 1812.

W&M-1443. John Frederick Stine (1841-1914) and wife Nannie Matilda (Brown) (1841-1906) are buried at Mt. Olivet. His parents Elias (1811-1881) and wife Elizabeth A. R. (Hessong) (1816-1892) are buried at Zion Church, Feagaville. Hessong ancestors are given in M&C-II. Living next to farmer Elias were farmers John Stein (b. c.1807), wife Mary C. (b. c.1807) and eight children in Frederick District of the 1850 census. (LC)

W&M-1443. Basil W. Lewis (1833-1910) and wife Cornelia A. (1834-1915) are buried at Jefferson Union Cemetery. Millard Rice said the Lewis Mill had been built before 1778 when it was in a deed of Jacob Cline. In the 1800 census of Middletown Valley the family of young Benedict Lewis had 26 slaves. George Jacob Benton Lewis (1859-1934) and wives Ida C. (Stockman) (1856-1883) and Rosa Virginia (Tucker) (1864-1940) are buried at Jefferson Union Cemetery.

W&M-1444. Joseph Jenkins Lee (b. 1870) was a son of Charles O'Donnell Lee (1841-1919) and wife Matilda Dale (Jenkins) (1849-1942) who are buried at Petersville Catholic Church.

Richard Lee born about 1590 in Shropshire, England emigrated with wife Anne to Virginia in 1651. Descendant, Governor of Maryland, Thomas Sim Lee (1745-1819), son of Thomas and Christiana, died at Needwood near Petersville (Who Was Who). Thomas S. owned 109 slaves according to the census of 1800. He and wife Mary (Digges) are buried at Upper Marlboro. Charles O. Lee was a son of Thomas S. Lee (b. c.1820) and wife Josephine (b. c.1826). Lee families are discussed in *Pillars of Maryland* by F. Sim McGrath (Richmond, VA, 1950) (FH) (LC), also in W&M-115.

W&M-1445. Walter R. Dorsey (b. 1871) married Harriet J. Welty. His parents were Charles A. (1845-1913) and Ann N. (Gaugh) buried at Graceham, where also are his grandparents Owen Dorsey (1817-1883) and wife Hetty (Hospelhorn) (1819-1904).

Dorseys, formerly D'Arcys, were early and numerous in western Maryland. Edward Dorsey qualified as a lawyer in the first court at Frederick in 1749. J. M. H. found three pages of Dorsey gravestones. In the 1800 census of Liberty District were 11 Dorsey households. Edward and John and wives were over 45 years of age. Eli Dorsey, over 45 years, had four daughters, four sons and 19 slaves. Other heads of families were Eli C., Arthur, Basil, Daniel, Elizabeth, Evan, Henry and Resaw Dorsey.

Dorseys of Maryland are said to be descendants of Thomas D'Arcy (d. 1605) of Hornsby Castle, Yorkshire, and London. In the Maryland Militia in the Revolutionary War 26 Dorseys served as officers and 19 Dorseys as privates.

Enrolled in the Frederick County Militia of 1812 were Abraham, Basil of Evan, Henry C., Michael and Otho Dorsey.

W&M-1446. Leonard C. Harbaugh (1845-1909) and wife Anna F. (Stem) (1846-1903) are buried at St. Jacob's Church in Pennsylvania north of Sabillasville in upper Harbaugh Valley. His second wife was Elsie (Working). Leonard's parents were Leonard (1818-1862) and Mary (Miller) (1819-1895) who are buried at Sabillasville Reformed Church. His paternal grandparents were Elias Harbaugh (1782-1854) and Anna Catherine (Pentzer) (1793-1849) buried at Harbaugh family graveyard near Sabillasville. Elias was a son of Jacob Harbaugh (1730-1818) and wife Margaret (Smith) (1730-1803) who also are buried at the family graveyard. See earlier Herbach family in W&M--995.

W&M-1446. Charles C. Putman (b. 1881) married Bessie N. Mort. His parents were Greenbury H. (1858-1913) and wife Ida B. (Joy) who are buried at the Catholic Cemetery in Frederick. The paternal grandparents of Charles were John J. Putman, Jr. (1826-1907) and wife Rebecca (Shriver) (b. 1833) who have gravestones at Utica. His paternal great grandparents were John J. Putman (1793-1872) and Ann E. (Summers) (1795-1883) who are buried at St. John Lutheran Church north of Myersville. In the 1800 census of Middletown Valley were two Putman households, of John over 45 years and Jacob 16 to 26. A genealogy of Putman and Wyant families was written by E. Clayton Wyand of Washington County, MD. See also W&M-1060.

W&M-1447. Dr. Edward Brook Sefton D.D.S. (1872-1953) and wife Mae G. (Slick) are buried at Blue Ridge Cemetery, Thurmont. His father Joseph W. was a guide of the Battlefield of Gettysburg and a grandson of Jacob Weller, B.S. (See M&C-II with descendants of Andrew Sefton (1807-1887)).

W&M-1448. Capt. Ignatius Dorsey (1834-1915) married Laura Hobbs. He is buried at Mt. Olivet. His parents Harry W. (1808-1872) and wife Sarah Ann (Waters) (1811-1840) are buried at the Dorsey graveyard near New Market. See W&M-1445.

W&M-1449. William Coale Sappington (1866-1945) and wife Ann Rosella (Stitely) (1870-1939) are buried at Liberty Catholic Church along with his parents Dr. Sidney (1827-1898) and wife Margaret E. (Wagner) (1831-1887). The paternal grandparents of William were Col. Thomas Sappington (1792-1857) (Mt. Olivet) and wife Sally (Coale) (c.1795-1841) (Liberty Catholic Cemetery). Col. Thomas married secondly Louise Klein (1827-1912) (Mt. Olivet). Earlier ancestors were Dr. Francis Brown Sappington who married Ann Ridgely. He was a son of Dr. Francis and wife Frances (Brown) Sappington of Wales.

W&M-1451. Sidney St. John Sappington (1871-1944) and wife Mary Simm (Boyle) (1883-1932) are buried at Liberty Catholic Cemetery, along with his parents Dr. Sidney (1827-1898) and wife Margaret E. (Wagner) (1831-1887). Dr. Augustus Sappington (1833-1889), younger brother of Dr. Sidney, and wife Irene (Mantz) (1839-1905) also are buried in Liberty Catholic Cemetery. Irene was a daughter of Casper Mantz (b. c.1814) and wife Elizabeth (1816-1880) of Frederick, and great granddaughter of Casper Mantz (1718-1791) (Mt. Olivet).

W&M-1453. Cornelius Franklin Harley (1842-1895) and wife Narcissa (Willard) (1852-1920) are buried in Middletown Reformed Cemetery. His parents

Otho F. (1795-1871) and wife Katherine (Willard) (1804-1874) are buried at Burkittsville Union Cemetery. In the 1800 census of Middletown Valley the only Harley household was that of Joshua and wife, both between 26 and 45 years of age. They had two daughters, four sons and two slaves. Narcissa's parents Abraham Willard (1806-1858) and wife Harriet (Hersperger) (1819-1885) are buried at Burkittsville Union Cemetery.

W&M-1454. George William Horman (1869-1951) and wife Mary (Zimmerman) (1869-1947) are buried at Mt. Olivet along with his parents William Henry (1844-1933) and Mary Elizabeth (Haller) (1853-1937). The census of 1850 gives no Horman, but only Harman families. George Harman (b. c.1793), a farmer in Creagerstown District, had son William Henry (b. c.1836). They apparently lived with William's grandmother Mary Harman (b. c.1775).

W&M-1455. Edward Ross Eyler (b. 1865) married Mary Wetzel. His parents Charles A. (1818-1901) and Charlotte L. (Gurley) (1835-1879) are buried at Thurmont U. B. Church. Edward's grandparents Frederick Eyler (1776-1859) and Margaret (Williar) (1783-1861) are buried at Graceham. An earlier Frederick Eyler (1741-1821) and wife Barbara are buried at Apples Church.

Eyler Families, a genealogy, has been written by John S. Eiler of Albuquerque, NM. In the Frederick County Militia of 1812 served Henry Eyler (b. 1770) who married Elizabeth Luckabaugh (b. 1800) and moved to Westmoreland County, PA.

W&M-1456. Edward T. Getzendanner (1825-1897) married Catherine E. Schaeffer. His parents Daniel, Sr. (1800-1873) and Mary Ann (Derr) (1803-1861) are buried at Mt. Olivet.

Dr. David C. Getzendanner, author of the Getzendanner/Giezendanner Family book of 1980, points out that the account of W&M-1456 and the gravestone of Christian Getzendanner contain errors. Both Christian and wife Anna Barbara Brunner were born in Klein Schifferstadt, Germany. They were married there in 1723 and there baptized their children Susanna and Gabriel in the Reformed Church before leaving for America in 1729.

Christian's father Johan Jacobus Getzendanner, born near Wattwil, Switzerland in 1659, was recorded first in Klein Schifferstadt in 1694. Earlier ancestors were Giezendanners in the Toggenburg Valley south of the villages of Ebnat-Kappel in St. Gall Canton, Switzerland. (GZ)

Christian's first land just west of later Frederick was Christian's Choice, surveyed in 1740. By 1752 his land holdings totaled over 1,200 acres. Christian (d.c. 1766) gave farms to sons Gabriel and Jacob in 1764, thus explaining why they are not mentioned in his will.

Christian and wife Anna (Brunner) had children born as follows: Susanna Margaret 1724; Gabriel 1727; Jacob 1729; Catherine 1734; Baltis 1735; Anna Maria 1739; Adam (1742-1783) m Elizabeth Kemp. Descendants, many from Jacob, Baltis and Adam, are given in (GZ).

Adam's sons were John (1764-1841), Christian (b. 1767) and Jacob (b. 1776). John by his second marriage to Catherine Tabler (1770-1851) had children: Elizabeth 1790; Mary 1792; Joseph 1794; Catherine 1796; Jonathan 1798-1859; Daniel, Sr. 1800-1873; Abraham (1811-1858) m. Mary Buckey (c.1813-1892).

Daniel married Mary Ann Derr (c.1803-1861) (daughter of John and sister of Elizabeth, wife of Jonathan). Their son Edward Tabler Getzendanner and wife Catherine E. (Schaeffer) had children: Anna Mary (1849-1864); Laura Virginia (1850-1930) m. Nelson Diehl (1839-1916); J. Winton (b. 1852); Daniel J. (1855-1899); William Reese (b. 1858); Addie E. (b. 1861) m. Dr. Barrick of Newark, OH; Nannie May (1867-1952) m. Edward Derr Shriner (1863-1930). Most of the above were buried in Mt. Olivet Cemetery. See also W&M-822 and (GZ).

David C. Getzendanner published in 1993 a genealogy of descendants of Jacob (b. 1729) and his son Thomas (1762-1844). Thomas moved to Union County, SC and there are many of his descendants living in southern states, including Getzen and Danner families.

W&M-1456. John Franklin Davis (1844-1928) and wife Josephine (Spalding) (1844-1897) are buried at Urbana Catholic Church. His parents were Eli (1809-1887) and Rachel (Morsell) (1809-1886). Spalding families occur in the Elder genealogy; see W&M-835. For ancestors of Eli Davis, see W&M-839.

W&M-1457. George C. Zentz (1874-1938) and wife Edna (Martin) (1876-1911) are buried at Thurmont U. B. Cemetery, as are his parents Abraham S. (1828-1898) and Sarah D. (Biggs) (1834-1905). See also W&M-706. George C. was grandfather of Carroll M. Zentz, born 1922 on his father's farm near Payne's Hill south of Mt. St. Mary's. He became a prominent auto and real estate dealer in Gettysburg.

W&M-1457. Arnold R. Wilhide (1839-1923) and wife Isabella (Wilhide) (1842-1890) are buried at the U. B. Cemetery in Thurmont, as are his parents Benjamin (1802-1871) and wife Mary B. (Knouff) (1798-1882). Arnold's grandparents were Frederick and wife Catherine (Peitzel) who moved to IN. See W&M-729 for earlier Wilhides. (LC)

W&M-1459. Frederick A. Ordeman (1857-1924) married (Sarah) Catherine Smeltzer of Springfield, OH. He is buried at Mt. Olivet along with his parents Capt. H. D. (1812-1884) of Bremen, Germany and wife Catherine (Schmaul) (1816-1889), native of Paris. Son Dr. (George) Frederick Ordeman (b. 1892) graduated from Washington and Lee College and from Johns Hopkins. He was a research chemist with the Standard Oil Company of Indiana and after 1946 Manager of the Wood River Refinery, living at Alton, IL. See W&M-1439.

W&M-1459. Eli A. Fry (1856-1946) and wife Anna Virginia (Stauffer) (1860-1913) are buried at Thurmont U. B. Cemetery along with his parents Joseph C. (1825-1899) and Mary J. (Ruse) (1829-1912). Eli's grandparents were John Fry and Elizabeth (Axline) who lived near Hillsboro, VA.

W&M-1460. William Keefer Burgee (1872-1933) married Sadie E. Davis. He is buried at Pleasant View Methodist Church where also are buried his parents Miel (1823-1903) and second wife Clara E. (Lawson) (1843-1888). Miel's first wife was Ellen (Linthicum) (b. c.1823) with whom he lived in New Market District in 1850.

Prof. Amon Burgee (1865-1945), (a brother of William), and his wife Mayme (Engleman) (1870-1962) are buried at Mt. Olivet. Amon was an outstanding educator of Frederick County. See also W&M-1462. The only Engleman in the census of 1850 was Mary (b. c.1828) living in Liberty District.

W&M-1461. Samuel B. Davis (1846-1902) and wife Rebecca M. (Ebert) (1850-1914) are buried at Mt. Olivet. According to the census of 1850 Samuel was a son of Eli Davis and wife Rachel (Morsell). See also W&M-839.

Rebecca's parents were Benjamin Ebert (1802-1868) and Caroline Maria (Birely) (1810-1875), daughter of John W. and Charlotte (Myers) Birely.

Ebert families lived around Walkersville, Woodsboro and Frederick. The earliest gravestone dates are those of Susannah (c1786-1860) at Glade Reformed Church. However, Adam and Margaretha Ebert had their daughters Elisabetha and Maria baptized at the Reformed Church at Frederick in 1757. Of the many Ebert families of Frederick, an early gravestone formerly at the Lutheran Church recorded John Ebert (1772-1851) and wife Rebecca (1776-1822).

W&M-1462. John Randolph Barnes (1833-1914) and wife Amanda (Baker) (1833-1900) are buried at Kemptown Methodist Church, south of New Market. Amanda was a daughter of Priscilla (b. c.1808) and Thomas Baker (b. c.1806).

In the census of 1800 were five Barnes households in Liberty District of Frederick County. Edward, Philomel and their wives were over 45 years of age. David, Zaddock and Zacharia were 26-45 years of age. Only Zacharia had a slave. Major Samuel Barnes (1788-1858) of the War of 1812 founded *The Political Examiner* newspaper of Frederick and was connected with newspapers in Baltimore.

Barnes families were early around Barnesville in Montgomery County. For example, John Barnes' estate of 1767 involved appraisers Henry Gaither and Ephraim Davis; kin were Weaver and John Barnes, and administrator widow Mary who had married Basil Mullican. Weaver Barnes was on the Grand Juries of Frederick County in 1754 and 1761. Thomas Barns of Prince George's County died about 1750 at the home of Daniel McCoy in Frederick County.

W&M-1466. William E. Hyatt (1848-1910) and wife Emma C. (Boyer) (1850-1918) are buried at New Market Methodist Church. He was a son of Henry M. Hyatt of Hyattstown and wife Rhoda (Walker) (1825-1909) (buried at the same church).

A number of other Hyatts are buried at Kemptown and Hyattstown, but the earliest stone found by J. M. H. is William Hyatt (1783-1848) at Middletown Reformed Church. In the census of 1800 in Buckeystown District was only one Hyatt household, that of Ely over 45 years and wife 26-45 years in age. They had five daughters, four sons and 16 slaves. In the Frederick Militia in 1812 were Asa, Jase, Joseph and William Hyatt. In 1814 William married Margaret Kiney (b. 1794); he died in Middletown in 1848.

W&M-1467. Daniel P. Warrenfeltz (1864-1936) and wife Rebecca D. (Cline) (1866-1939) are buried at the U. B. Church at Wolfsville. His parents Joshua P. (1819-1882) and wife Sarah A. (Easterday) (1829-1885) are buried at Wolfsville Reformed Church, where also are his grandparents Philip Warrenfeltz (1787-1858) and wife Catherine (Leatherman) (1791-1858). See W&M-726 for early Werenfels. Frederick Cline was early in the valley.

W&M-1467. Henry Oscar Burall (1870-1946) and wife Ida Mary (Angleberger) (b. 1873) have gravestones at New London Methodist Church, where also are buried his parents Samuel Burall (1821-1899) and wife Christiana (Fetterling).

Earlier Burials in our area were Nancy (1799-1841) buried at Mt. Olivet, also Solomon (1799-1871) and wife Elizabeth (1804-1873) buried at Prospect Cemetery near Mt. Airy.

Jacob Angleburgh (between 26 and 45 years) and family are in the 1800 census of Fredericktown District. In the 1850 census are families of David S. and Lydia; Joseph and Elizabeth; also George and Margaret. Jacob Angleberger (b. c.1773) was an ancestor.

W&M-1468. Charles L. Cline (1856-1924) and wife Alice C. (Brandenburg) (1864-1927) are buried at the Lutheran Cemetery in Middletown. His parents Thomas (1831-1909) and wife Catherine (Summers) (1834-1912) are buried at St. John's Lutheran Church north of Myersville. The paternal grandparents of Charles were Philip Cline (1787-1874) and wife Elizabeth (1791-1856) who also were buried at St. John's. The census of 1800 of Middletown Valley gives only one Cline household, that of Frederick Cline over 45 years who lived with a son aged 16-26 years. Also in the valley were two Klein families, namely Daniel and wife, both of 26-45 years with two children under 10 years; and George Klein and wife over 45 years with a daughter under 16 years and four sons, 16 to 26 years.

The earliest Kleins in Middletown Lutheran records were Peter and Anna Maria married in 1779 who had children born as follows: George 1781; Peter 1784; Catherine 1788.

In the Frederick county Militia of 1812 were several Klines and Kleins. Peter, unmarried, had brother Frederick, a hatter in Fredericktown; Lieut. Charles served under Capt. Daniel Marker; Frederick (b. c.1792) married Susanna Engle (b. 1803) (daughter of George and Susanna (Young)); George (d. 1846) who married secondly Sarah Elizabeth Poole (daughter of Frederick); Henry who served under Capt. Jacob Getzendanner; John (1795-1863) who died in Dayton, Ohio; and Philip Kline (b. c.1787) of Catoctin District, a musician under Capt. Daniel Marker.

W&M-1469. Edward E. Leather (1836-1914) is buried at Hyattstown Methodist Church. His parents were John Leather (1790-1865) and wife Mary (Leather) (d. 1839), daughter of George. Other members of Leather families are buried at the Methodist Church of Hyattstown.

W&M-1470. Henry L. Brandenburg (1853-1928) and wife Louise C. (Grossnickle) (1856-1914) are buried at Grossnickle Meeting House north of Myersville, along with his parents Samuel (1824-1888) and Juliann (Grossnickle) (1827-1916). Henry's paternal grandparents were Henry Brandenburg (1792-1869) and wife Mary (Kemp) (1801-1859) who are buried at Middletown Reformed Church. I have found no Jefferson Brandenburg. See W&M-866.

W&M-1471. Samuel T. Brandenburg (1858-1926) and wife Susan E. (Gaver) (1860-1945) are buried at Wolfsville Lutheran Church. His parents were farmers Samuel (1824-1888) and wife Juliann (Grossnickle) (1829-1916) who are buried at Grossnickle Meeting House. See W&M-866. Earlier Samuel Brandenburg (1796-1866) and wife Mary (b. c.1799) farmed in Middletown District, and Samuel Brandenburg (1756-1833) with wife Mary (1759-1817) are buried at Middletown Reformed Cemetery.

W&M-1471. William Joseph Seward (1861-1946) and wife Amanda C. (Babington) (1858-1937) are buried at Middletown Reformed Cemetery. Another daughter of William and Amanda was Annie (1887-1953) who was second wife of Edgar H. Koogle, a son of Sherman R. (1864-1930) and Fannie M. (1863-1923). Fred S. Palmer wrote to me in 1983: "I believe that I am the only one who has tried to unify the Koogle or Kuegel data, but with only marginal success." In the census of 1800 in Middletown Valley were households of Adam Cougle (26-45 years) and apparent widow Catherine Cougle (26-45), both with children under 10.

W&M-1473. David M. Whipp (1840-1929) and wife Marietta (Gaver) (1841-1928) are buried in Mt. Olivet. His father George T. (1818-1902) is buried at Jefferson Union Cemetery and his mother Lydia (Routzahn) (1820-1849) at Burkittsville Union Cemetery. The second marriage of George was to Mary A. B. (1822-1899). Lewis O. Whip (1841-1930) and wife Sarah E. (died at 48 years) are buried in Jefferson Union Cemetery.

The earliest Whip gravestones are those of George (1781-1823) and wife Mary (1782-1821) at Church Hill on Ballenger Creek Road, southwest of Frederick. In the 1800 census of southern Frederick County were Tobias Whip, over 45 years in age and his wife under 45, living with four daughters and four sons. A George Whipp (b. c.1792 in VA) married Mary Lashorn. He served in the Frederick County Militia of 1812 and in 1833 moved to Franklin County, OH.

W&M-1473. William H. Summers (1866-1940) and wife Mary L. (Brandenburg) (1871-1953) are buried at Myersville U. B. Cemetery. His parents Isaac J. (1838-1903) and wife Lucinda C. Brandenburg (1840-1922) are buried at Myersville Lutheran church. William's grandparents Samuel Summers (1798-1843) and wife Mary M. Bussard (1799-1883) are buried at St. John's Lutheran Church, north of Myersville.

In the census of 1800 of Middletown Valley there were three Somer or Summer families headed by Jacob, Stofle and Valentine who, with their wives, were between 26 and 45 years of age. They all had children under 16 years. In the Frederick County Militia in 1812 were Jacob Summer (1791-1868) who is buried with wife Catherine in the little Summers graveyard south of Church Hill near Ellerton; and William Summers, a coppersmith born in Frederick, who enlisted in 1808.

W&M-1474. Benjamin Singleton Ahalt (1834-1923) and wife Sarah Elizabeth (Keller) (1837-1922) are buried at Middletown Lutheran Cemetery along with his parents Mathias (1803-1881) and wife Phoebe (Routzahn) (1809-1893). For earlier Ahalts see W&M-988.

W&M-1475. Prof. Amon Burgee (1865-1945) and wife Mary Elizabeth (Engleman) (1870-1962) are buried at Mt. Olivet. His parents Miel (1824-1903) and Clara Elizabeth (Lawson) (1843-1888) are buried at Pleasant Grove Methodist Church. See also W&M-1462. (LC)

W&M-1476. George S. Beachley (1861-1912) and wife Cora A. (Hemp) (1837-1901) are buried at Middletown Lutheran Church. His parents John D. (1834-1917) and wife Edith (Vanfossen) (1836-1909) are buried at Pleasant View Brethren Church near Burkittsville. The paternal grandparents of George were Conrad Beachley (1804-1875) and wife Susan H. (Linebaugh) (1803-1888).

Before 1800 at Middletown Lutheran Church were Peter and wife Elisabeth Biechle; also Henry and Rosanna Biechle. See also W&M-857.

W&M-1477. Charles O. Easterday (1873-1944) and wife Effie J. (Koogle) (1871-1950) are buried at Myersville U. B. Church. His parents were Lawrence Easterday and wife Ellen (Herr) according to W&M. Note that J. M. H. found Laurence Easterday (1817-1895) and wife Sophia C. (1821-1870) buried at Wolfsville Reformed Cemetery. Christian Easterday, in German Ostertag, emigrated from the city of Noerdlingen, famous for its medieval walls, in the Franconia area of southern Germany (M&C-II). In 1762 Christian petitioned the Frederick County court for a license to open a tavern. His son Conrad, who may have been born in Germany, had a son Louis who married Eleanor Buxton. The latter's six children included Conrad, who in 1873 married Abbie Johnson. They had descendants around Sharpsburg (Wms. 1906).

In the census of 1800 there were five Easterday households in Middletown Valley: Christian and wife were over 45 years old as was their son Christian, Jr. A Conrad Easterday and wife (26-45 years) had four small children. Francis and wife were 26-45 years of age with four small chldren. Jacob Easterday (26-45) and wife had two daughters under 10 years. No Michael appears on a gravestone or in the census.

A genealogy of *Christian Ostertag and Descendants* has been written by Dr. H. G. Lanham of Westminster, MD (W), also *Easterday Families* by L. F. M. Easterday of Lincoln, NB (1908) (H).

W&M-1478. Joshua Crampton (1814-1898) and wife Anna Maria (Feaster) (1829-1910) are buried at Jefferson Union Cemetery. See also W&M-1238. In the 1800 census of Middletown Valley were families of Henry and Jacob Fister. Both had sons under 16 years of age.

W&M-1478. John W. Maught (1849-1880) and wife Florence M. (1856-1945) are buried at Burkittsville Union Cemetery. According to W&M John W. married Myra L. Young (1854-1941) who is buried at Middletown Lutheran church. See W&M-991 for Andrew, who was a German mercenary confined at the Hessian Barracks in Frederick. Frederick and Henry Muck of the Frederick County Militia of 1812 possibly may have been related.

W&M-1479. Emory Eugene Boyer (1866-1942) and wife Carrie Viola (Arnold) are buried at Jefferson Methodist Church along with his parents Oliver (1836-1907) and Martha M. (Rice) (1838-1916). Emory's paternal grandparents were Michael Boyer (1802-1882) and wife Elizabeth (1805-1877) who are buried also at Jefferson. See also W&M-1131. The one Boyer family in Middletown Valley in the 1800 census was that of Jonathan, 26-45 years.

W&M-1480. James W. Legore or LeGore (1854-1932) and wife Addie B. (Stull) (1861-1937) are buried at Mt. Hope Cemetery at Woodsboro. James and his older brother John, Jr. (1846-1877) were sons of John Legore (d. 1864) who farmed near New Oxford, PA. The lime company established north of Woodsboro by John, Jr. was continued by James, some of whose descendants are given in M&C-II.

Another LeGore family of Ezra (1819-1876) and wife Elizabeth (1821-1886) lived near Silver Run in Carroll County and descendants are buried there.

W&M-1481. Charles F. Main (1869-1945) and wife Della L. (Heffner) (1869-1943) are buried at Middletown Lutheran Cemetery along with his parents Frederick Tobias (1836-1916) and wife Mary (Shaffer) (1838-1910). The paternal grandparents of Charles were Capt. Daniel (1812-1894) and wife Malinda (Horine) (c.1814-1859) who also are buried at Middletown Lutheran Church.

In 1992 William E. Main of Frederick believed that most of the Mains of Frederick County have been descendants of George Moehn or Mehn (1722-1773) whose wife was Elizabeth. They lived near High Knob west of Frederick, where there is a Main family graveyard. Their children who matured were Adam (1746-1822); Frederick (b. 1754); John (1756-1832); Margaret Rosina (b. 1759); and George (d. 1822). Adam married Appolonia Weil in 1770 and in 1791 he married Anna Margaret Youtsey (1757-1844). Capt. Daniel Main was a farmer, miller and merchant near Hagerstown and a son of Adam of Middletown Valley according to Wms. (1906). His descendants included Martin Luther Main of Hagerstown and others in Texas and Missouri.

Many Mains are in records of the Middletown Reformed Church and in (Wampler). In the census of 1800 of Middletown Valley there were two Main households, of Adam (over 45 years old) and of Frederick (16-26) (LC).

W&M-1482. John H. Routzahn (1856-1934) and wife Ida Emma Jane (Remsburg) (1857-1917) are buried at Middletown Reformed Cemetery along with his parents Eli (1821-1880) and wife Mary Ann (Keller) (1813-1900). In the census of 1800 are recorded seven Routzahn households as follows: Adam Routsong, Sr. was over 45 years; Susannah, Henry, Adam of Adam, Adam of George and Christian Routzong were all between 26 and 45 in age; Benjamin Routsong and wife were between 16 and 26 years. See (R).

W&M-1482. Greenberry Dillard House, Jr. (1874-1954) and wife Bessie E. (Arnold) (1877-1923) are buried at Burkittsville Union Cemetery along with his parents Grove R. (1846-1931) and wife Melissa H. (Dillard) (1847-1929). His paternal grandparents were Greenberry J. R. House (1825-1919) and wife Mary M. (Grove) (1828-1916) who also are buried at Burkittsville. G. J. R. was a son of Eli P. House (1785-1868) and wife Lucinda (b. c.1786). In the 1800 census of Middletown Valley there were five House families. Caleb, George and William, Sr. were over 45 years of age. Daniel, John and their wives were between 26 and 45 years. All except John owned slaves.

W&M-1482. Charles William Miller (1847-1921) and wife Charlotte (Sheffer) (1848-1922) are buried at Jefferson Union Cemetery where also are his parents Frederick (1822-1904) and wife Lydia Ann (Dorner) (1823-1874). Charlotte's parents were John Philip Sheffer (1821-1901) and wife Lucinda (1831-1909) who farmed near Middletown.

W&M-1483. Frederick Miller above, born near Hanover, PA, first married Lydia Ann Dorner and later married Susan Charlton (1843-1925). They are all buried at Jefferson Union Cemetery. Susan's parents were John W. Charlton (b. c.1805), a miller of Jefferson District whose wife must have died before the 1850 census. The Charlton family was prominent in early Frederick.

W&M-1483. Daniel M. Miller (1876-1947) and wife California W. (Ahalt) (b. 1877) have stones in Burkittsville Union Cemetery. He was a son of Job M.

(1839-1907) and wife Sarah V. (Miller) (1842-1913) who are buried at Knoxville Reformed Church.

W&M-1484. Charles H. Butts (1868-1929) married Mollie V. Michael. On Charles' gravestone in Middletown Lutheran Cemetery were mounted his anvil and hammer used as a blacksmith. He was a son of Isaiah (1833-1898) and Amanda (Cramer) (1838-1915) who are buried at Myersville Lutheran Church. In the 1800 census of Middletown Valley were four Butts households headed by George, Sr., over 45 years, George, Jr., 26-45, and two Henrys, aged between 26 and 45.

W&M-1485. John C. Boyer (1842-1906) and wife Laura Etta (Slifer) (1846-1919) are buried at the Brethren Pleasant View Cemetery near Burkittsville. His parents Michael (1802-1882) and wife Elizabeth (Jacobs) (1805-1877) are buried at Jefferson Methodist Church. See W&M-1131. In 1800 in Middletown Valley were households of John, Jr. and wife (26-45) and Samuel Slyfer and wife (26-45).

W&M-1486. Robert A. Kefauver (1861-1934) and wife Alto Zero (Kepler) (1856-1897) are buried at Middletown Reformed Cemetery, along with his parents Jacob (1814-1882) and wife Lenorah (Coblentz) (1819-1903). Jacob was a son of George (1785-1861) and Mary (Cassel) (1782-1857). For settler Philip Kiefhaber, see W&M-791 and 911.

W&M-1487. Peter Slifer Hemp (1853-1928) and wife Mary C. (Arnold) (1856-1926) are buried at Mt. Olivet. His parents Abram (1825-1910) and wife Hannah (Slifer) (1822-1910) are buried at Jefferson Union Cemetery. Note the author's unusual appreciation of shade trees. See also W&M-806.

W&M-1487. George E. Cook, Jr. (1858-1926) and wife Elmira L. M. (Stockman) (1862-1950) are buried at Mt. Olivet. His parents, George E. (1827-1900) and wife Henrietta (Bast) (1824-1907), are buried at Jefferson Union Cemetery. Bast or Baust families have lived around Baust Church east of Taneytown.

W&M-1489. John Lewellyn Johnson (1856-1922) of Philadelphia and wife Rebecca Kay M. (Struble) (1861-1920) also of Philadelphia are buried at Mt. Olivet.

W&M-1489. Doctor Michael Wachter (1855-1928) and wives Victoria E. (Roberts) (1856-1898) and Fannie A. (Measell) (1867-1945) are buried at Utica. Doctor was his given name; he was a farmer near Utica north of Frederick. Doctor Michael's parents were Philip, Jr. (1812-1886) and wife Susanna (Reese) (1814-1899). His paternal grandparents were Philip Wachter (1786-1875) and Ammareliss (Widerick) (1788-1863), who are buried at Bethel Lutheran Church. See W&M-724. An Adam Reece and wife, over 45 years, lived near Frederick in 1800.

W&M-1490. Jacob A. Hankey (1845-1930) and wife Sarah Isabella (Graham) (1845-1936) are buried at Creagerstown. A James Graham (1781-1861) and wife Isabella A. (1783-1863) are buried at Harney. Jacob's parents were Frederick (1811-1883) and Mary A. (Gernand) (1820-1902) who are buried at Apples Church near Thurmont. See W&M-810 for early Hankey settlers. In the 1800 census of northern Frederick County were Adam Garnand and wife, both between 26 and 45 years of age. They had four sons.

W&M-1491. Jesse Fox (1867-1949) and wife Martha L. (Fogle) (1872-1916) are buried at Mt. Tabor Cemetery at Rocky Ridge east of Thurmont. His parents Hezakiah (1851-1945) and wife Mary M. (1855-1942) are buried at Mt. Hope Cemetery at Woodsboro. W&M gives Hezekiah's wife as Emily E. (Stambaugh). A Stambaugh genealogy is at (HN). Hezekiah's paternal grandparents were Balthasar Fox (1803-1895) and wife Nancy (1807-1887) who are buried at Rocky Hill Church.

In the 1800 census of Westminster District was the family of Henry Fox and wife, both over 45 years of age. In 1800 George Fox and wife, both 26-45 years, lived in Emmitsburg District. In Buckeystown District in 1800 lived Henry Fox and wife, both over 45 years, and also John G. Fox and wife, both 16 to 26 years. In Frederick District in 1800 were four Fox households headed by Henry and wife over 45 years, a younger Henry, Elizabeth (26-45 years) and John (16-26 years). See also W&M-899.

W&M-1491. Frank M. Stevens (1867-1937) and wife Elsie (Gaver) (1875-1952) are buried at Utica. His parents Charles (1818-1876) and Adaline (Grimes) (1827-1952) are buried at Creagerstown. The second wife of Frank was Eliza (Crouse) (1835-1908) who also is buried at Creagerstown.

Frank Stevens believed a tradition that an Indian trail which crossed Monocacy at Poe's Ford, and through his farm south of Creagerstown, was the Conestoga Trail which became the main Monocacy Road. With Rev. Harold Hann I investigated this, proving it could not be the Monocacy Road which, in fact, continued on the east side of the Monocacy River until reaching Hughes Ford east of Frederick.

In northern Frederick County in the 1800 census the only Stevens or Stephens household was that of Richard Stephens, over 45 years of age. (LC)

W&M-1492. Harry D. Baumgardner (1868-1944) and wife Margaret (Whisner) (1871-1927) are buried at Mt. Olivet. For his parents John F. and Fannie E. (Sinn) see W&M-853. Harry believed that he had a goldmine near Braddock Heights. Neighbors complained that their chickens fell into the hole. The Baumgardners lived at 429 N. Market St. next to their butcher shop.

W&M-1493. William D. Baker (1833-1917), unmarried, was a son of Aaron (1804-1887) and Sarah (Dixon) (1811-1855). They are buried at Glade Reformed Cemetery. William's paternal grandparents were Frederick Baker (1775-1864) and wife Susannah (1778-1847) who also are buried at Glade Reformed Cemetery.

In Fredericktown District in the census of 1800 were Baker households headed by Conrad and by Frederick, both over 45 years of age. In northern Frederick County in 1800 Baker families were headed by Christian and by Henry, both over 45 years, and by Samuel (16-26 years). In Middletown Valley in 1800 lived families of Conrad and Frederick Baker, both over 45 years. In the Frederick County Militia of 1812 were Basil Baker, under Capt. Joseph Wood; Henry from Taneytown; Henry, trumpeter; Jacob from near Hampstead; Jacob (d. 1833) who married Hannah Youtzey in 1824; Philip (b. c.1783 in Frederick County) enlisted 1814 at Harrisburg, PA.

W&M-1494. Adam A. Devilbiss (1825-1908) and wife Anne Maria (Greenwood) (1828-1865) are buried in Greenwood Cemetery near New Windsor. He was the eldest son of Casper (1795-1868) and wife Ann Ellender (Barnett) (1805-1888) who are buried at Sam's Creek Methodist Church. Note the important records of the children of Adam who moved west. An earlier Caspar Devilbiss (1761-1835) married in 1786 Maria Susanna Derr (1767-1830), daughter of Sebastian Derr and second wife Catherine. See also W&M-1297.

W&M-1495. Raymond P. Shank (1881-1938) married Ethel May Heaterale of Romney, WV. He has a gravestone at Mt. Olivet. He was a son of George D. (1851-1888) and Jennie (Bowers) (1851-1909) who are buried at Mt. Hope Cemetery, Woodsboro, along with Raymond's paternal grandparents Michael Shank (1804-1876) and wife Eva (1836-1919).

Shanks also have been in upper Middletown Valley. In the census of 1800 there were households of John and wife, over 45 years, and Mary, also over 45 years of age. The earliest Shanks in Christ Reformed Church records of Middletown were Christian and Juliana Schenk, whose son George was born in 1782. Adam Schenk and wife sponsored a baptism at the Lutheran Church of Middletown in 1811. See also W&M-1218.

Five Schenks arrived at Philadelphia between 1732 and 1752. In Maryland there have been a number of George and Jacob Shanks. A Hans Georg and a Hans Jacob arrived in 1732, aged 37 and 32 years respectively. John Shank from Lancaster County settled in Washington County, MD before 1800. Many descendants are given in Wms. (1906).

W&M-1495. Rev. Reese St. Clair Poffenberger (1880-1951) married Nannie F. McCoy (d. 1915). Rev. Poffenberger served Lutheran congregations in Maryland, Pennsylvania and Virginia as given by Wentz. His children by wife Nannie were Hypathia Hannah, Wilhelmina, and Nancy. By a second marriage in 1916 to Maude E. Albaugh he had two children, Reese and Jeanette.

Henry Poffenberger of Washington County and wife Elisabeth (Young) had a son Jacob (1803-1888) who married Amelia Stouffer (d. 1872). They are buried at the Lutheran Church at Bakersville. Some of their descendants are given by Williams (1906). Part of the Battle of Antietam was fought on farms of Poffenbergers. The Poffenbergers of Washington County may not be directly related to those of upper Middletown Valley. See W&M-759 and (H).

W&M-1497. Charles W. Zimmerman (1859-1950) and wife Fannie J. (Walker) (1860-1931) are buried at Mt. Olivet. He was a son of Isaiah Wesley (1829-1865) buried at Glade Reformed Cemetery and Rachel A. (Lease) (1837-1877). Isaiah's lineage follows:

(1) (Hans) Michael (1706-1741) emigrant m. Anna Elisabeth Dodderer; Montgomery County, PA.

(2) (John) Michael, Jr. (1732-1762) m. Elizabeth; Pennsylvania to Maryland to NC.

(3) George (1755-1820) m. Elisabeth Weiss (1760-1825); buried at Woodsboro Reformed Cemetery.

(4) George, Jr. (1796-1850) m. Rosanna Barrick (1796-1876) (d/o Jacob and Rosanna (Devilbiss)); buried at Glade Reformed Cemetery.

(5) Isaiah Wesley. See also W&M-979.

W&M-1497. Emery W. Saylor (1864-1932) and wife Addie O. (Brandenburg) (1870-1948) are buried at Mt. Hope Cemetery, Woodsboro. He was a son of John (1820-1906) and Margaret (Hoffman) (1822-1891) who are buried at the Brethren Beaver Dam Cemetery. See also W&M-1139 and 1193.

W&M-1497. Isaac Wallace Haugh (1836-1918) and wife Keziah (Strasburg) (1840-1910) are buried at Beaver Dam Brethren Cemetery. His parents were Henry Haugh (1797-1858) and wife Catherine (Linn) (1804-1886) who are buried at Haugh's Church north of Woodsboro. See also W&M-1052.

In the 1800 census of Libertytown District there were two Hauk households of Paul and wife who were over 45 years of age, and William (26-45) and wife (16-26). Trusting the durability of family name pronunciation, the Haughs are different from the Houcks (German Hauck). In family names of German immigrants landing at Philadelphia recorded by S&H, the nearest German names were Haag and Hauk. Of these a Hans Georg (age 41) entered in 1748; a Hans Michel in 1732; a Valentin in 1749, and Hans Dirk Hauk in 1728.

W&M-1498. Guy Oliver Repp (1882-1956) and wife Zola A. (Cramer) (1878-1958) are buried at Mt. Olivet. His parents Charles G. Repp (1850-1907) and wife Dora M. (Naille) (1862-1934) are buried at Mountain View Cemetery at Union Bridge.

The earlier Repp gravestones at Johnsville M. P. Church are those of Henry (1792-1874) and wife Mary (1792-1863). Henry, Jr. (1816-1895) and wife Lydia (Young) (1819-1896) were probable parents of Charles.

W&M-1499. Isaac P. Stitely (1854-1933) and wife Harriet L. (Belleson) (1853-1918) are buried at Beaver Dam Brethren Cemetery. His second wife was Phoebe A. (Haifleigh) (1862-1944) who also is buried at Beaver Dam. Isaac's parents were David R. (1831-1888) and wife Rachel (Pfoutz) (1834-1884) who also are buried at Beaver Dam. Isaac's paternal grandparents were Samuel (1802-1890) and Elizabeth (Eberly) (1804-1891) who are buried at Rocky Hill Church near Woodsboro. A Jacob Stitely (1789-1852) is buried at Rocky Hill.

W&M-1500. George Washington Belleson (1830-1925) and wife Margaret Ann (Eyler) (1832-1910) are buried at Beaver Dam Cemetery. They apparently were parents of Harriet Stitely above. The numerous Belleson families have lived in the areas of Mt. Airy and Kemptown.

W&M-1501. John Wesley Strausburg (b. c.1861) married Lizzie Harris. He was a son of Josiah (1831-1882) and wife Susan (Fogle) (1831-1912) who are buried at Beaver Dam Brethren Cemetery near Johnsville. In the 1800 census of Libertytown District were households of John Strasburgh (26-45 years) and wife (under 26 years), also Frederick Strasburgh and wife (both 16-26 years).

W&M-1501. Jacob A. Culler (1867-1947) and wife Grace A. (Keller) (1868-1942) are buried at Jefferson Union Cemetery, where also are buried his parents John Harmon Culler (1837-1898) and wife Lucinda C. (Kefauver) (1840-1922). For earlier Cullers see W&M-849 and 1265.

W&M-1502. Isaac Samuel Annan (1833-1909) and wife Julia L. (Landers) (1840-1913) are buried at Emmitsburg Presbyterian Church, along with his parents Dr. Andrew A. Annan (1805-1896) and wife Elizabeth (Motter)(1805-1896) and grandparents Dr. Robert L. Annan (1765-1827) and wife Mary (1769-1826). Isaac's great grandfather Rev. Robert Annan (1742-1819) of Cupar, Fife, Scotland, north of Edinburgh, married Margaret Cochran, daughter of William of the Carrollsburg Tract north of Emmitsburg (over the Mason-Dixon Line.)

W&M-1503. Edgar L. Annan (b. 1865) married Pauline McNair. His parents were Isaac and Julia whose dates are given above. The early McNair family lived across the Mason-Dixon line in Liberty Township of Adams County where Samuel and Alexander were taxed in 1801 (WB).

W&M-1504. Maj. Oliver Alexander Horner (1844-1897) and wives Ann Margaret (Grier) (1845-1872) and Anna E. (Annan) (1847-1935) are buried at Emmitsburg Presbyterian Church. He was the eldest son of David W. (1815-1887) and wife Susan (Robertson). David is buried at Piney Creek Presbyterian Church near Harney.

David Horner, an emigrant from Ireland, settled in later Adams County before 1760. In 1779 David Horner was taxed in Mt. Joy Township for 400 acres, four horses, six cows and three slaves. In the same year in Mt. Joy Township Robert Horner was taxed for 660 acres, four horses, three cows and one slave. (PA Arch., 3rd Series, 21, 65). In Gettysburg Dr. David Horner (b. 1797) was the father of Dr. Charles and Dr. Robert Horner. (LC)

W&M-1505. William A. Barton (1850-1915) and wife Clara L. (Ogle) (1852-1933) are buried at Mt. Hope Cemetery, Woodsboro. His parents were Henry and wife Sabina (Young). A gravestone at Apples Church records Sabina Barton (1823-1883), the wife of William H. His parents were Samuel Barton (1791-1878) and Amy (McWilliams) (c.1790-1857) who are buried at Thurmont U. B. Cemetery. (LC). In 1800 John McWilliams, between 26 and 45 years, lived in Emmitsburg District.

W&M-1506. Ezra D. Cramer (1836-1911) and wife Amelia Catherine (Dutrow) (1849-1903) are buried at Mt. Olivet. His parents Samuel (1809-1858) and wife Susan (Buckey) (1812-1887) are buried at Glade Reformed Cemetery. Ezra's grandparents were Henry (1778-1845) and wife Barbara (Barrack) (1786-1862).

In the 1800 census of eastern Frederick County were seven Creamer households of which the heads of three were over 45 years of age, namely John, Peter and William. In Emmitsburg District in 1800 were families of Jacob and John Creamer, both 26 to 45 years. See also W&M-928.

W&M-1507. Charles M. Pittinger (1857-1938) and wife S. Virginia (Bowers) (1857-1927) are buried at Mt. Hope Cemetery, Woodsboro. His parents were Andrew Levi (1816-1882) and wife Ann Elizabeth (Houx). Andrew is buried at Rocky Hill Church near Woodsboro.

In the 1800 census of eastern Frederick County the only Pittinger family was that of Adam and wife, both over 45 years of age. Pittingers were early in Frederick County. Martin Pittinger and wife Charlotte were sponsors at a baptism at Monocacy Lutheran Church in 1750. Daniel Pippenger in 1753 was appointed overseer of the road from Woodsboro to Great Pipe Creek.

Members of the Pittenger family of Puritans are said to have fled from Nottinghamshire, England, to Holland before 1610. Richard (d. 1715) emigrated from Holland to NJ in 1665 and married Syche Hendricksen. Their grandson Daniel Pittinger (1712-1796) married in 1731 Elizabeth Biggs (1713-1794), daughter of John Biggs, Jr. They moved to Monocacy area after 1737. About 1741 Daniel leased lot #2 on Monocacy Manor next to that of his father-in-law John Biggs, Jr.

W&M-1508. Edwin Devilbiss (b. 1862) was a son of Abner C. (1826-1892) and Lydia A. (Sweadner) (1825-1895) who are buried at New London Methodist Church. Edwin's paternal grandparents were David Devilbiss (1788-1856) and Elizabeth (Campbell) (1784-1866) who are buried at Linganore Devilbiss family graveyard. See W&M-1118 for lineage of David.

W&M-1509. Dr. John David Nicodemus, M.D. (1854-1938) and wife Rebecca (Nelson) (1858-1927), daughter of Dr. Robert, are buried at Mt. Olivet, where also are his parents John Lewis (1828-1904) and Nancy (Castle) (1831-1902). The paternal grandparents of Dr. John were John Nicodemus and wife Hannah (Englar) (1804-1852). She is buried at Brethren Pipe Creek Cemetery near Uniontown. For Castle or Cassell families see W&M-1340, and for Englar families see W&M-1084.

Children of John and Rebecca Nicodemus of Walkersville were as follows:

(1) John V. (1880-1951); Glade Valley Milling business.

(2) Kent Castle; Glade Valley Milling business.

(3) Ellen

(4) Edith (1886-1978); taught first grade at Walkersville for 35 years.

(5) Mary (b. c.1891); died at Homewood, Frederick, at over 100 years.

(6) Robert N.

(7) Elizabeth (1896-1947).

J. M. Holdcraft recorded in his files that there probably were four early Nicodemus brothers and a sister, Mrs. Baile (who had a son called Nicodemus Baile). The brothers may have been as follows:

(1) A settler in Franklin County, PA; (Johan) Adam? b. c.1723 emigrant Oct. 1753 (S&H); son Frederick (FC).

(2) A settler in Washington County, MD; Conrad had sons Valentine and Conrad, Jr. (Williams 1906).

(3) Rev. Valentine Erasmus Nicodemus, early pastor about 1795 at Zion Lutheran Church, Middletown.

(4) Henry Nicodemus (1728-1801) buried on homestead near Westminster, MD; emigrant 1751 (S&H).

    (a) Son John L. (1758-1825) m. Ann March Neff. A possible grandson was Valentine (1794-1863) m. Nancy Devilbiss (c.1800-1828), daughter of Casper; he is buried at Uniontown Methodist Church and she at Marston Nicodemus graveyard.

See Glatfelter for information about Rev. Valentine E. Nicodemus (1730-1812) who preached also at Shepherdstown, Silver Run, Toms Creek and Taneytown.

He, with father and three brothers, emigrated in 1763 from Medenbach near Herborn in Nassau-Dillenberg to settle first in Lebanon County, PA. By first wife Catherine Rev. Nicodemus had at least five daughters. By second wife Elizabeth, when he approached 70 years, he had at least one son John.

The only Nicodemus families in old Frederick County census of 1800 were those in Westminster District. Henry and wife were over 45 years of age. John and wife were between 26 and 45 years, with two sons and four daughters. Philip Nicodemus and wife also were between 26 and 45, with two sons and two daughters. See also W&M-970.

W&M-1510. H. Harwood Magruder apparently appears as R. Howard Magruder (1857-1925) on the gravestone in Mt. Olivet where also are his parents, Rufus K. (1816-1898) and America (Pritchard) (1826-1867). In the *History of Montgomery County, Maryland* by T.H.S. Boyd (Clarksburg, 1879) the Magruder name is one of the most abundant. There are 29 in the index, more than Smiths, Jones or Miller families. In 1728 the tract Magruder's Hazard was surveyed for Samuel and John Magruder. Many inventory summaries of Magruder estates have been published (IN) (FH).

Alexander Macgruether, the progenitor of Magruders of Maryland was a son of Alexander MacGregor of Perthshire, Scotland, alleged to have descended from Alpin, King of Scotland and Lady Margaret Drummond of Angus in Perthshire (CF).

A Magruder line beginning with Henry, Prince of Scotland around 1100 A.D. by an unknown genealogist is cited in (BL). Ninian Magruder Jr. was on Frederick County's first Grand Jury in 1749. Alexander Magruder was on the Grand Jury in 1752.

W&M-1511. Emily Hahn (1846-1880) first wife of Elisha Hahn is buried at Rocky Hill Church near Woodsboro. His parents Jacob (1824-1904) and Margaret (c.1829-1895) are buried at Utica. Elisha's grandfather is believed to have been Jacob Hahn.

Among early Hahn records are Sophia Hahn (1768-1773) buried at Graceham and Catherine Hahn who married Jacob Michael in 1772 (Frederick Lutheran Record). Rev. Galen Hahn of Sabillasville is collecting family data. Abraham, Bazil, Benjamin and Joseph Hahn of later Carroll Co. served in the War of 1812.

W&M-1511. Mahlon A. Bowers (1860-1932) and wife Louise V. (Perkey) (1862-1924) are buried at Mt. Hope Cemetery, Woodsboro. His father was Jonathan (1806-1866) buried at Lewistown Methodist Church.

In 1827 Jonathan Bowers married Rebecca Derr (b. 1803) a daughter of John Derr (1775-c.1823) and Elizabeth Brim (1781-1884). Jonathan lived at Lewistown and apparently worked at Catoctin Furnace. Jonathan had a second marriage to Catherine Rice (b. c.1818). His many heirs, given in deeds JLJ 16-255 and 448 of 1878, included Mahlon A. and Eli David Bowers. The latter of Lewistown married Lily Belle Weddle; they were parents of Sherman Philip Bowers (1889-1962) lawyer of Frederick who married Lillian S. Kefauver. See W&M-911.

Jonathan's parents were Frederick Bour and Elizabeth (Kurtz). They bought lot 164 in Lewistown in 1815 from Daniel Fundenberg.

W&M-1512. Lincoln Grant Dinterman (1856-1926) and wife Lettie M. (Seachrist) (1867-1954) are buried at Mt. Olivet. His parents George H. (1828-1896) and Susan (Smith) (1833-1897) are buried at Mt. Hope Cemetery, Woodsboro, where also are buried the paternal grandparents of Lincoln, namely George Dinterman (1800-1883) and wife Mary (1797-1882).

W&M-1512. William Henry Mort (1849-1931) and wife Seraphine Elizabeth (Cease) (1844-1919) are buried at Thurmont U. B. Church. His parents William (1811-1887) and wife Catherine (Oler) (1813-1888) are buried at Mt. Tabor Cemetery at Rocky Ridge.

In the 1800 census of Taneytown District are recorded Peter Mort and wife between 16 and 26 years of age. In the northern area of Frederick Co. in 1800 lived Lewis Morter and wife, but this may be a mistake for Motter. Ensign John Mort served in the Catoctin Battalion in the Revolution. See also W&M-1418.

W&M-1513. Tilghman H. Grossnickle (1860-1945) and wife Alice May (Carmack) (1859-1945) are buried at Haugh's Church near Ladiesburg. His parents were Daniel (1820-1884) and wife Ellen E. (Blessing) (1824-1908) who are buried at the Brethren Church at Rocky Ridge. Ellen's father was George Blessing (1794-1873) the Hero of Highlands who drove off a squad of Confederate Cavalry trying to steal horses. For earlier Grossnickles see W&M-1369.

The other famous Blessing descendant was Nellie Blessing Eyster (b. 1836) daughter of Abraham and Mary (Ent) Blessing in Frederick Co. Her paternal ancestors were said to have been Jacob and Eva (Easterday) Blessing, emigrants from Saxony (NC). Her early education was from Barleywood Seminary at Merryland Tract near Petersville and later with lawyer David A. S. Eyster of Harrisburg whom she married at age 16. Nellie was a leader in hospital work of the U. S. Sanitary Commission in the Civil War. After the death of her only son and mother in 1876 she moved to San Jose, CA. where she became a prominent author and leader in women's causes and temperance. After her husband's death Nellie moved to San Francisco where in 1890 she was elected President of the Pacific Coast Woman's Press Association. She wrote articles and books for young people. Her booklet appealing to Chinese to abandon opium and alcohol was printed in Shanghai in the Cantonese language. She published a book, *The Bright Side of Chinese Life* in 1900. See also Who Was Who vol. 4 and Frederick News, April 29, 1991.

W&M-1514. Joshua Carmack (1827-1892) and wife Amanda (Eyler) (1828-1894) are buried at Haugh's Church. In the 1850 census Joshua lived with his mother Ellen (b. c.1802) in Woodsboro District.

The prominent Carmack family of Frederick Co. has been studied by Norman C. Anders of Lehigh Acres, FL. Cornelius Carmack (1695-1748) and wife Guein (Corem) had sons John (1720-1812) and William (1716-1776) born in Cecil County. The latter and wife Jane (MacDonald) had second child Cornelius Jr. born in Monocacy area on June 18, 1736. Other children named in the will of Cornelius were Elizabeth Evans; Mary Richards, wife of Stephen; Catherine Richards wife of Daniel; Mary Beatty wife of William Sr. Before 1742 Cornelius and sons acquired the tract Duke's Woods at Liberty from Arnold Livers. Cornelius was on the first Grand Jury of Frederick Co. in 1749. William and Jane had sons Evan (1740-1830) who married Mary Wolf (1748-1805), daughter of Paul and John Cornelius (1742-1833) who married Mary's sister Sarah Wolf (1749-1822). Before 1779 John and Sarah moved to Hawkins Co., TN. The will of William showed children: Sarah Brightwell, wife of John; and sons William Jr., Evan, John, Levy who married Susannah Justice and Acquila who married Eunice Williams. John Cornelius and Sarah Carmack had daughter Sarah who married John Anders. Their son Jacob (1807-1877) married Sarah Shank. See Frederick News May 6, 1993.

W&M-1514. Joshua E. Mentzer (1862-1938) and wife Marcella (Hahn) (1861-1933) are buried at Haugh's Church north of Woodsboro as are his parents Amos (1806-1867) and wife Henrietta (Martin) (1831-1896). A Conrad Mantzer and a Samuel Manetzer are recorded in the 1800 census of Middletown Valley.

W&M-1515. John D. Kling (1831-1917) and wife Amelia (Grimes) (1836-1914) are buried at Mt. Hope Cemetery, Woodsboro. His parents David (1800-1880) and Susannah (Stitely) (1799-1876) are buried at Rocky Hill Church. In 1800 William Grimes and wife over 45 years and younger Joshua Grimes had families in northern Frederick Co.

W&M-1516. Isaiah W. Boller (1854-1926) and wife Susan C.(Smith) (1850-1936) are buried at the United Brethren Church at Thurmont along with his parents Henry A. (1827-1899) and Cassandra Matilda (Hahn) (1832-1920). Isaiah's paternal grandparents John R. Boller (1796-1880) and wife Mary (1806-1883) are buried at Graceham.

W&M-1517. George U. Koons (b. 1875) married Edna E. Otto (1879-1951) who is buried at Haugh's Church north of Woodsboro. Origins of different Kuntz families have been discussed (M&C-II). Several Kuntz settlers came from northern Alsace, eg Hans Georg Kuntz from Preuschdorf whose son Martin was apparently baptized 1749 in Monocacy Lutheran records (B3).

W&M-1517. Charles Edward Biddinger (1862-1933) and wife Alice Margaret (Fogle) (1870-1945) are buried at Haugh's Church. His parents David (1822-1901) and wife Mary Jane (Harmis) (1829-1913) are buried at the Brethren Cemetery at Beaver Dam. Possible grandparents of Charles were Adam Biddinger (1794-1875) and wife Elizabeth (1794-1860) who are buried at Beaver Dam. In the 1800 census of Liberty District were Adam Pittinger and wife both over 45 years of age. They had 4 daughters and 2 sons. (LC)

W&M-1518. William H. Smith (1860-1939) and wife Jennie (Shank) (1860-1930) are buried at Mt. Hope Cemetery, Woodsboro, along with his parents John Jr. (1837-1909) and Mary Jane (Gilbert) (1836-1915). William's paternal grandparents were John Smith Sr. (1797-1860) (son of Middleton) and second wife Elizabeth Frock (1812-1886). See W&M-1237. Mary Jane's parents were Michael Gilbert (b. c.1807), a shoemaker and wife Margaret (b. c.1810) of Woodsboro District.

W&M-1519. John Michael Smith (1873-1932) (buried at Mt. Hope) married Ada or Addie M. Wilhide (1870-1934) (Thurmont U.B.). He was a son of John and Mary Jane (Gilbert). See W&M-1237.

W&M-1519. Harry E. Albaugh (1873-1934) and wife Rosie E. (Measell) (1872-1962) are buried at Utica. His parents were Andrew H. (1840-1921) and wife

Maranda P. (Clem) (1841-1924) who also are buried at Utica. For earlier Albaughs see W&M-1263.

Albaugh Genealogies have been written by Noah H. Albaugh (Texas 1899); by Nancy Albaugh Leatherwood and C. J. Albaugh (1949) (WL); and by Frances C. Francis (1972) (G).

W&M-1520. William Grant Grimes (1869-1952) married Mabel (Fraley). Fraley is derived from the German family name Froehlich. See W&M-1149. William's parents were William B. Grimes (1838-1913) and wife Ann Louisa (Garber) (1849-1919) who are buried at Haugh's Church near Ladiesburg and north of Woodsboro.

In the census of 1800 in eastern Frederick Co. were 8 different Grimes households as follow: Joshua and wife and Catherine were over 45 years of age. Heads of families of age between 26 and 45 years were Basil, James, John, Samuel and William. A younger head was a second William Grimes. See W&M-1261.

In the Frederick Co. Militia in 1812 were Jacob Grimes, musician under Capt. Philip Smith; James Grimes (b. c.1790) who married Rebecca Ott in Frederick in 1811 and settled in Seneca Co., Ohio; Nicholas Grimes, born in Frederick Co., enlisted at Cumberland and was a prisoner of war in England.

W&M-1521. Claude E. Toms (1876-1952) and wife Annie C. (Grossnickle) (b. 1879) have stones in Myersville U.B. Cemetery as have his parents John H. (1829-1906) and wife Malinda A. (Sensenbaugh) (1838-1887). Claude's paternal grandparents were Jacob Toms Jr. (1796-1887) and Mary (Floyd) (1805-1878) who also are buried at Myersville U.B. Church. Jacob Toms Sr. (c.1765-1854) and wife Magdalena (1768-1852) are buried at Jerusalem Cemetery northwest of Myersville.

The census of 1800 of Middletown Valley records only one Toms household, that of David between 26 and 45 years. A pastor of the Middletown Reformed Church recorded Toms families as Thomas. Jacob Toms first appears here in 1774. Jacob and wife Susannah baptized daughter Charlotte in 1785. Jacob Jr. and wife Sophia had daughter Josephine Sophia baptized in 1838.

W&M-1522. Grayson H. Mercer (1879-1945) and wife Grace H. (Grove) (1882-1946) are buried at Mt. Olivet. His parents William E. (1840-1905) and Ada S. (Webster) (1869-1943) are buried at McKaig Methodist Church east of Frederick. Grayson's paternal grandparents were William (1806-1859) and Susan (Smith) (1799-1868) who are buried at Middletown Lutheran Church. In the 1800 census of Middletown Valley are 14 Smith families of which the heads over 45 years of age were Andrew, John Jr., John of Jacob and Michael. (LC)

W&M-1523. Millard F. Toms (b. 1873) and wife Lizzie E. (Leatherman) (1873-1946) have stones at Myersville U. B. Church, where also are buried his parents Ezra (1826-1894) and wife Sophia (Doub) (1829-1903). Sophia's mother was Catherine (b. c.1808) apparently a widow in the 1850 census of Catoctin District.

W&M-1524. John Albert Geesey or Geasey (1854-1911) and wife Ida Etta (Oland) (1859-1947) are buried at Mt. Olivet where also are his parents Theodore (1829-1899) and wife Martha (Wickham) (1828-1905). Buried at

Graceham is Rosina (Gladt) Geesey (1760-1804) (wife of Henry) who was born at Heidelberg, Berks Co., PA. Elias Giesey, grandfather of John A. was born to Henry and Rosina in 1803; he was not born in Switzerland. Moravian Archives reveals that Elias Giese had a brother Joseph born in 1802.

Frederick Henry Augustus Oland (1821-1909) and wife Mary A. E. (1825-1869) are buried at Mt. Olivet. Martha J. Wickham was a daughter of Lucinda (b. c.1802) and John B. Wickham (b. c.1797) a miller in Woodsboro District.

W&M-1525. Solomon C. Crum (1867-1913) and wife Alice V. (Hahn) (1877-1954) are buried at Mt. Olivet at Frederick. His parents Solomon (1825-1894) and wife Mary Catherine (Knode) (1830-1911) are buried at Mt. Hope Cemetery, Woodsboro. Solomon may have been a son of Henry and Sarah Crum who baptized daughter Mary in 1824 at Rocky Hill Church. Henry is believed to have been a descendant of Gilbert Crom of Dutch origin who settled early on Monocacy Manor. See W&M-1145.

W&M-1526. Joseph H. Engle (1862-1945) and wife Mary S. (Albaugh) (1869-1931) are buried at Mt. Hope Cemetery, Woodsboro. His parents were Nicholas (1816-1901) and Anna E. (Gall) (1826-1903) who are buried at Graceham. The 11 children of Nicholas and Anna Engel are recorded in the Archives of the Moravian Church of Graceham. (LC)

W&M-1527. John D. Baugher (1839-1911) and wife Sarah (Shankel) (1840-1920) are buried at Glade Reformed Cemetery along with his parents John (1823-1879) and wife Annie (Grinder) (1803-1890). John's paternal grandparents were Samuel Baugher (1764-1822) (Glade Cemetery) and wife Savilla (Bussard) who moved from Pennsylvania

Most of the Baughers of southern Pennsylvania and western Maryland are believed to be descendants of emigrants Rev. John George Bager (1725-1791) and wife Elisabeth (Schwab) or (Swope) (b. 1728). His long preaching career under adverse conditions included Little Conewago (1754-1757 and 1762-1763). Names and birth dates of 9 children of Rev. George and Elisabeth are given in records of St. Matthews Lutheran Church of Hanover, PA. (G). More about Rev. Bager is given by Glatfelter. He was born at Ottweiler, Pfalz and preached at Simmern in the Hundsrueck area of Germany before emigrating to Pennsylvania

W&M-1528. Samuel Cornelius Thomas (1848-1924) and wife Clara E. (Buckey) (1857-1917) are buried at Mt. Olivet. He was a son of George (of Henry) (1798-1883) and Julia Ann (Hargett) (1813-1879) who are buried at Church Hill on Ballenger Creek Road.

Samuel's grandparents were Henry Thomas (of John) and wife Anna Margaret (Ramsburg) (1767-1811). W&M has errors about great grandfather John (b. 1728) who emigrated in 1730 with his parents Michael Thomas and wife Ann Veronika (Lang). Six Thomas brothers and one sister emigrated to Frederick Co. See W&M-1015.

W&M-1529. Charles Wisner (1862-1944) and wife Cordelia (Mayne) (1865-1941) are buried at Mt. Olivet. His parents Charles (1822-1881) and wife Mary (1828-1882) are buried at the Catholic Cemetery in Frederick. A Johannes

Wisner emigrated from Switzerland in 1714 according to G. Franklin Wisner of Baltimore in 1918. There were later Wisner emigrants from Germany.

W&M-1529. John William Green (1876-1930) (Glade Cemetery) married Clara Virginia Jackson of Woodsboro. His parents Zachariah T. Green (1849-1900) and wife Amanda E. (Cline) (1844-1914) are buried at Utica. John's paternal grandparents were William Green (1820-1899) and Margaret S. (Duple) (1826-1904) who are buried at Grossnickle Meetinghouse.

In the 1800 census of Middletown Valley two Green households were headed by William over 45 years of age and Luke Green 16 to 26 years. In Libertytown District in 1800 lived Catherine Green over 45 years alone, also John Green (26-45 years) with 2 young daughters and 4 young sons. In the Frederick Co. Militia of 1812 were Benedict Green (d. 1869 at Frederick) who had wife Susan (c.1794-1882); Francis Green married Elizabeth Easterday (c.1774-1871); George Green (b. c.1788) of Woodsboro; Henry Green (b. 1791) went to Washington Co., IN; Capt. Joseph Green from Emmitsburg; Lawrence Green of Catoctin District, a substitute for George Harman; Lewis Green (d. 1826) who married Eliza Cary at Frederick in 1815; Lewis Green (c.1790-1879) drafted at Libertytown, died unmarried; Samuel Green Ensign under Capt. Andrew Smith 1808 and, under Capt. Samuel Ogle in 1813.

W&M-1530. Charles S. Houck (1874-1945) and wife Virginia (Cromwell) (1877-1957) are buried at Mt. Olivet along with his parents James (1844-1931) and Alice J. (Cramer) (1850-1932). The paternal grandparents of Charles were Ezra Houck (b. c.1803) and wife Catherine (1807-1850). See W&M-1375.

W&M-1530. Henry C. Fox (1844-1929) and wife Sarah E. (Poole) (1844-1911) are buried at McKaig Methodist Church, east of Frederick along with his parents John (1813-1902) and Julia Ann (Beall) (1816-1895).

There were 8 Fox families listed in the census of 1800 in eastern Frederick Co. Baltser, George and Peter Sr. all over 45 years of age; Catherine, Adam, Henry, Jacob and Peter Jr. were all 26 to 45 years in age. (LC)

In the Frederick Co. Militia of 1812 were Lieut. George Fox under Capt. Philip Smith; John Fox (c.1768-1856) (as substitute for Jacob Spoon) married Catherine Simon (c.1772-1869), both buried near Yellow Springs; Samuel Fox of First U. S. Rifles under Capt. William Smith (b. c.1793) discharged at New Orleans 1817.

W&M-1531. Daniel A. Bowers (1856-1916) and his parents Daniel W. (1817-1900) and Margaret S. (Riddlemoser) (1820-1899) are buried at Liberty Catholic Church. Daniel was born at Uniontown. A Philip Rippleogle and wife, over 45 years, are in the 1800 census of Liberty District.

W&M-1532. Samuel M. Strine (1857-1925) and wife Laura M. (Albaugh) (1865-1926) are buried at Mt. Hope Cemetery, Woodsboro. His parents Benjamin Strine (1819-1876) and Margaret (Winebrenner) (1820-1902) are buried at Rocky Hill Church.

Peter Strein and wife Christina had their daughter Maria Barbara baptized in 1773 at Rocky Hill and son William in 1778. John Adam Strein and wife Susanna had John William baptized there in 1784. Adam and Peter Strine both over 45 years of age, were the only Strine heads of families in eastern Frederick Co. in the census of 1800. A John Strine living on Tom's Creek is in court records of 1761.

In the Frederick Militia of 1812 were Peter Strine who served under Capt. Samuel Duvall and moved to Richland Co. Ohio and William Strine who served under Capt. John Galt and lived about 5 miles from Taneytown. Four generations from William (d. 1824) are in the Fogle and Strine Genealogy by Alma T. Fogle, 1976. (FH)

W&M-1533. Allen Z. Burrier (1850-1927) and wife Mary C. (Lease) (1850-1921) are buried at Liberty Chapel, along with his parents Jacob Jr. (1812-1892) and wife Eliza Ann (1828-1899). Allen's paternal grandparents were Jacob Burrier Sr. (1770-1851) and wife Catherine (1780-1854) who also are buried at Liberty Chapel. See W&M-1260.

In the census of 1800 of Liberty District were 5 Burrier households. Philip and wife were over 45 years of age. Adam, Jacob and John, all 26-45, were heads of households. George Burrier and wife were between 16 and 26 years of age.

W&M-1533. Dr. William F. Mercer (1839-1914) and his wife Jemima (Barthelow) (1842-1904) are buried at McKaig Methodist Church east of Frederick. W&M gives the spelling Mercier. Dr. Mercer's second wife Alice A. (Wagner) (1855-1937) also is buried at McKaig. Jemima's parents were Mary Ann (b. c.1820) and Elisha Barthlow (b. c.1808), shoemaker of Creagerstown District.

W&M-1534. Charles Albert Nicodemus (1858-1927) and wife Josephine (Brown)(1859-1933) are buried at Mt. Olivet Cemetery. He was a son of John Lewis (1828-1904) and wife Nancy (Cassell) (1831-1902) who also are buried at Mt. Olivet. For earlier Nicodemus families see W&M-970 and 1065.

James and Louisa E. Cassell farmed near Frederick in 1850. Other families in the county used the spelling Castle. In the 1800 census of Fredericktown District were households of Daniel Castle, over 45 years, Thomas Cassel, 26-45 and William Castle, 26-45.

W&M-1535. John Mathias Dinterman (1857-1941) and wife Anna Rebecca (Etzler) (1853-1954) are buried at Mt. Hope Cemetery at Woodsboro. His parents were George H. (1826-1896) and wife Susanna (1833-1897) and grandparents George Dinterman (1800-1883) and wife Mary (1797-1882) also buried at Mt. Hope. See also W&M-961 and 1512.

W&M-1535. Solomon David Devilbiss (1826-1902) and wife Susan Henrietta (Cronise) (1837-1926) are buried at Glade Reformed Cemetery, along with his parents David (1793-1859) and Catherine (Fulton) (1795-1855) daughter of Robert and Barbara. Other descendants of David are in W&M-1303; 1323; 1508.

W&M-1536. Martin Calvin Coblentz (1848-1914) and wife Ellen Frances (Brandenburger) (1852-1938), also his parents Henry (1807-1888) and Ann Magdalena (Routzahn) (1816-1872), are buried in Middletown Reformed Cemetery. Earlier Coblentz ancestors are given in W&M-776.

W&M-1537. C. Frank Burrier (1866-1941) and wife Anne E. (Zimmerman) (1865-1956) are buried at Mt. Olivet, as are his parents, Charles Daniel (1841-1892) and Catherine (Hoke) (1846-1935). Frank's paternal grandparents were

Daniel Burrier (1809-1898) and wife Lydia (1811-1886) who are buried at Israel Creek Cemetery north of Walkersville. See also W&M-1260 and 1533. Daniel was a son of Jacob (1770-1851) and Elizabeth (Crist). See also W&M-1260 and 1533.

W&M-1537. Charles Philip Kefauver (1854-1922) and wife Laura A. S. (Koogle) (1857-1931) are buried at Middletown Reformed Cemetery, along with his parents Jacob (1814-1882) and Lena (Coblentz) (1819-1903). For earlier Kefauvers see W&M-791 and 1296; for Coblentz see W&M-776.

W&M-1538. James W. Long (1857-1918) and wife Katherine (Perry) (1865-1956) are buried at Mt. Olivet. His parents Absalom (1830-1898) and wife Margaret A. (Harmis) (1831-1892) are buried at Glade Reformed Cemetery near Walkersville. See W&M-781 and 797 for earlier Longs. The parents of Margaret were Delila (b. c.1806) and Jacob Harmis (b. c.1803) a carpenter of Woodsboro District.

W&M-1539. Andrew Jackson Tabler (1831-1915) and first wife Martha Jane (Norwood) (1831-1915) are buried at Hyattstown Methodist Church. His 3rd wife was Delila (Lawson) (1839-1891) (daughter of John and Letha Lawson) who is buried at Lawson family graveyard near Browningsville. Andrew was a son of Lewis (1781-1847) and Mary Catherine (Leather) (1789-1867) who are buried at Hyattstown. John Leather (b. c.1790) farmed in Buckeystown District in 1850.

W&M-1540. Samuel L. Bowlus (1855-1930) and wife Jennie E. (Crampton) (1861-1930) are buried at Jefferson Union Cemetery. His parents were Capt. Stephen R. Bowlus (1822-1894) and wife Ann Caroline (Remsburg) (1824-1911) who are buried at Middletown Lutheran Church. See W&M-1255. The Bowlus family of Middletown Valley must not be confused with the family of Thomas and Eleanor Bowles of London and early Frederick. I wrote about famous son William Augustus Bowles, southern Indian Chief, in the Frederick News on Feb. 23, 1990.

W&M-1540. Hamilton Willard Shafer (1860-1919) and wife Sarah Margaret (Arnold) (1858-1939) are buried at Petersville Catholic Church. See also W&M-992 and 1146. Hamilton and Sarah fortunately were married in 1889.

W&M-1541. James Oliver Bussard (1851-1930) and wife Mary Elizabeth (Warrenfeltz) (1856-1905) are buried at Middletown Reformed Cemetery where also is buried his father John Wesley (1820-1893). His mother Catherine (Poffenberger) (1812-1889) is buried at St. John's Lutheran Church north of Myersville. J.M.H. found no gravestones of John Wesley Bussard (b. 1797) who married Susan Ann Delaughter (1820-1893). Susan (1795-1855) wife of Peter Bussard Jr. is buried at Shookstown west of Frederick. Peter Bussard Sr. (1761-1807) is buried at remote Poplar Grove Graveyard near Wigtown (M&C-I page 30.). The emigrant was Daniel Bussard. See W&M-860.

W&M-1542. Samuel D. Bussard (1859-1956) and wife Catherine Rebecca (Summers) (1866-1914) are buried in Middletown Lutheran Cemetery along with his parents Peter Hanson (1826-1905) and wife Charlotte M. (Curfman) (1829-1915). Samuel's paternal grandparents were John Wesley and Susan Bussard. See above and W&M-860.

W&M-1542. David Henry Roelkey (1854-1921) and wife Martha Alice (Renn) (1855-1919) are buried at Mt. Olivet as are his parents C. L. Peter Roelkey (1824-1892) and wife Mary Ellen (Anderson) (1828-1917). David's emigrant grandfather John Roelke (1782-1855) and wife Dorothea Justina (1791-1859) also are buried at Mt. Olivet.

W&M-1543. John P. Shafer (b. 1874) of W&M may be John F. Shafer (1874-1912) of J.M.H. buried at Middletown Reformed Church. His parents were Peter W. (1834-1910) and Anne Louisa Levy (Young) (1830-1918) buried at the same place. His paternal grandparents were John Shafer, III (1784-1835) and wife Elizabeth (Linebaugh (1796-1876) who also were buried at Middletown Reformed Church. The father of John III was John, Jr. (1753-1823) The father of Anne was Peter Young (b. c.1796-1868) buried at the same place. See also W&M-746.

W&M-1545. Charles M. Gall (1856-1932) and wife Mary J. (Warrenfeltz) (1856-1933) are buried at Thurmont U.B. Church, along with his parents Henry (1824-1900) and wife Catherine S. (Martz) (1805-1893). The paternal grandparents of Charles were William Gall (1791-1873) and wife Martha E. (1802-1886) who are buried at the same place. In 1800 in Frederick District were George Martz and wife, over 45 years.

W&M-1545. Clinton C. Nicodemus (1861-1944) and wife Sarah M. (Enoch) (1868-1951) are buried at Unionville Methodist Church where also are buried his parents Martin L. (c.1831-1898) and Lucinda (Carter) (1832-1897). A Joshua Carter (26-45 years) lived in Westminster District in 1800.

W&M-1546. Abram Washington Nusbaum (1828-1916) and first wife Margaret (Cashour) (1842-1870) are buried at Liberty Chapel where also are his parents Adam (1803-1877) and Rachel (Baumgardner) (1807-1885). Abram's paternal grandparents were Abraham Nusbaum (1771-1839) and wife Anna Margaret (1771-1856) who also are buried at Liberty Chapel. Abram W. married secondly Henrietta Molesworth (1848-1910) buried also at Liberty Chapel. See also W&M-1297. Margaret Cashour was a daughter of Martha (1816-1893) and William Cashour (1814-1857) who farmed in Liberty District. In Liberty District in 1800 lived John Nusbaum, over 45 years, and younger David and John Nusbaum with their families.

W&M-1547. Dr. Daniel Edwin Stone M.D. (1837-1924) and wife Rebecca (Owings) (1836-1920) are buried at New London Methodist Church (Central Chapel) north of New Market.

The signer of the Declaration of Independence referred to here was Thomas Stone who was admitted to practice as an attorney before the Frederick County Court in 1765 and lived several years in Frederick. See W&M-597.

W&M-1548. John E. Schell (1849-1932) and wife Ida M. (Fleming) (1867-1930) are buried at Mt. Olivet along with his parents Charles David (1822-1896) and wife Harriet (Lambrecht) (1825-1867). The German spelling Lambrecht became Lambright in Frederick Co. George Lambright (1782-1861) and wife Rachel (d. 1840) are buried at Mt. Olivet.

Other early Schells were Joseph (1796-1861) and wife Catherine A. (1808-1880) who are buried at Mt. Olivet. In the census of Fredericktown District in 1800 there were two Schell households. Henry Schell, over 45 years of age, lived with his wife, a daughter and 3 sons. Charles Schell and wife, both between 26 and 45, had 3 daughters and 6 sons. Records of (LW) reveal Henry and wife Elisabeth in 1789. Carl or Charles Schell in 1754 married Eva Margaretha Weiss born in Kandel, southern Pfalz. She died in Frederick in 1795. Her brothers George Heinrich and Johan Dieter Schell also came to America. I have seen the Weiss home well preserved in Kandel. Carl was a locksmith in Frederick.

W&M-1548. Edward S. Mobley (b. 1870) who married Zourie Schroeder of Frederick was a son of James Clarence Mobley (1850-1913) born in Washington Co. and wife Myra (Lykens) (1849-1923). George Lewis Mobley (1878-1956) a younger brother of Edward S., married Pleasant Gurley (1885-1921); they are buried at Mt. Olivet.

Edward's paternal grandfather was Edward Mobley of the Union Army and his great grandfather was Eli Mobley, wheelwright of Hagerstown. Descendant Jeffrey Mobley of Frederick married Susan Schildknecht. (M&C-II). (LC) John Mobley of Linganore Hundred is in Frederick Court records of 1751.

W&M-1549. Maurice A. Bowlus (b. 1871) married Mary A. Young. His parents were George W. Bowlus (1845-1923) and wife Amanda C. (Sigler) (1846-1920) who are buried at Middletown Lutheran Church. The paternal grandparents of Maurice were William Bowlus (1814-1852) and wife Ann Mary (1810-1895). See descents from Nicholas Paulus in W&M-1255. The parents of Amanda C. in the 1850 census were Jacob (b. c.1820) and Elizabeth Zeigler (b. c.1821) of Middletown District.

W&M-1549. Dr. Ira J. McCurdy M.D. (1869-1942) and wife Lucy (Eisenhauer) (d. 1958) are buried at Mt. Olivet. Earlier Eisenhauers at Frederick were John (1839-1910) and Balthasar recorded in the Catholic Cemetery.

W&M-1550. Thomas McGill Williamson (1872-1943) was a son of Joseph Alleyne (1845-1896) and wife Eleanor W. (McGill) (1844-1913). They are buried at Mt. Olivet. Eleanor W. was a daughter of Julia Ann (1818-1866) and Dr. Thomas J. McGill (1812-1886) who are buried at Petersville Episcopal Church.

W&M-1552. Calvin R. Coblentz (1863-1929) and wife Lizzie L. (Brandenburg) (1865-1953) are buried at the Middletown Reformed Cemetery as are his parents Philip (1812-1899) and wife Mary Ann (Kefauver) (1818-1870). See W&M-776 for earlier Coblentz families and W&M-866 for Brandenburgs.

W&M-1552. Dr. David Ferguson McKinney M.D. (1836-1915) and wife Mary E. (Trego) (1841-1924) are buried at Mt. Olivet. His parents are buried in Pennsylvania. The family of William and Eveline Trago lived in Frederick in 1850.

W&M-1553. William Devilbiss (1827-1909) and wife Mary C. (Kieffer) (1835-1929) are buried at Sam's Creek Methodist Church, also his parents Casper (1795-1868) and Ann (Barnett) (1805-1888). See W&M-1297. A Henry Keefer and wife both between 26 and 45 years, are in the 1800 census of Taneytown District.

W&M-1553. Dr. Brooke I. Jamison M.D. (b. 1882) was a son of Brooke I. (1846-1926) and wife Susan (Hilleary) (1843-1924) who are buried at Mt. Olivet.

The paternal grandparents of Dr. Brooke were John Ignatius (1818-1900) and wife Jane Emily (Jones) (1821-1908) who are buried at Urbana Catholic Church. In the census of 1800 in southern Frederick Co. was the household of Benedict Jamerson, 26-45 years, wife 16-26, also a daughter and a son under 10 years as well as 11 slaves. J. V. Jamison (b. 1851 at Urbana) son of John I. and Jane E. moved to Washington Co. where he has left descendants (Wms 1906).

The Brooke families of Brookeville and the Taneytown area were prominent in western Maryland history descending from Robert Brooke of London who emigrated in 1650. See published genealogies in M&C-II. One of the early tracts most cited in Carroll Co. deeds is Brooke's Discovery on Rich Lands, at later Taneytown. In the census of 1800 of Taneytown District were households of Raphael and Roger Brooke and their wives, all over 45 years, also Richard Brooke and wife both between 16 and 26. Many Brooke records are in the Catholic Archives at Mt. St. Mary's. (LC)

W&M-1555. George Hood (1815-1893) and wife C. Elizabeth (Duvall) (1820-1887) are buried at Prospect Cemetery near Mt. Airy. His parents were John Hood (1788-1850) and Tabitha (Wolf) (1792-1823) who also are buried at Prospect. In 1800 John Woolf (over 45 years) and family lived in Liberty District.

George Emory Hood (1859-1941) son of George and Elizabeth above, married Etta Pearl Haines (b. 1880). In the 1800 census Haines families lived in Westminster, Taneytown and Middletown Districts.

W&M-1556. Phillip Nusbaum Keefer (1849-1913) buried at Sam's Creek Methodist Church was a son of Lewis (1803-1880) and wife Rachel (Nusbaum) (1810-1873).

There were earlier Kiefers buried at Mt. Olivet including Christian (1751-1828) and Hiram Keefer (1803-1870). At Taneytown Reformed Church are buried Thomas Keefer (1797-1850) and Jacob Keefer (1780-1855); at Beaver Dam is Joseph Keefer (1805-1862); and at Haugh's Church Samuel Keefer (1808-1865).

In the census of 1800 in Fredericktown District lived families of Philip Keefer, over 45 years of age, and Philip Jr. between 26 and 45 years. In Taneytown District in 1800 was the household headed by Henry Keefer between 26 and 45 years. (LC)

W&M-1556. Jesse R. Wilson (1860-1914) and wife Medora or Dora (Duvall) (1864-1925) are buried at Prospect Methodist Church near Mt. Airy. His parents were Evan (1820-1902) and Rachel (Wolfe) (1822-1900) also buried at Prospect Church. See other Wilsons in W&M-725 and 1243. Serving in the Revolution were Ensign William Willson, also Lieuts. Edward, Thomas and Samuel Wilson.

W&M-1557. John H. Harn (1839-1916) and wife Mary A. C. (Long) (1848-1921) are buried at Unionville Methodist Church as are his parents Singleton W. (1802-1879) and Maria Cordelia (Harn) (1802-1887). In the area in 1800 were the families of John Harn and wife both over 45 years with 4 daughters and 6 sons; also Greenburg Harn and wife, both 26-45 years of age with one daughter and 4 sons.

W&M-1558. Charles McC. Hagan (1854-1916) and wife Elizabeth (Renner) (1854-1928) are buried at Mt. Olivet. His parents were Michael P. (1825-1883) (Frederick Catholic) and Mary M. (Wiles) (1834-1910) (Mt. Olivet). Earlier Hagans included Francis (1763-1825) buried at Frederick Catholic Church and Hugh Hagan (c.1744-1800) buried at Emmitsburg Catholic Church. Peter Hagen (1773-1850) buried at Frederick Catholic Cemetery was born at Carlingford Co., Southern Ireland, according to his gravestone. His wife Anna (c.1794-1847) is buried beside him. (LC)

W&M-1559. Frederick W. Obenderfer (1851-1938) and wife Susan Virginia (Getzendanner) (1855-1914) are buried at Mt. Olivet where also are his parents John Leonard (1815-1891) and wife Sabina (d. 1854). In 1800 German born John L. Obendorf and wife Susan lived in Frederick.

W&M-1560. William A. Hahn (1860-1951) (Mt. Olivet) married Alverta (Hobbs). His parents Adolph (1832-1910) and wife Caroline (Jacobs) (1827-1906) are buried also at Mt. Olivet. In 1800 William C. Hobbs, between 16 and 26 years and family lived in Frederick District. See also W&M-818 and 1511.

W&M-1560. Rudolph A. Neidhardt (1840-1919) and wife Caroline E. (Brengle) (1846-1927) are buried in Frederick Catholic Cemetery. His parents Joseph William (1809-1885) and wife Mary Louisa (1811-1899) are buried at Mt. Olivet. Daniel Brengle (1812-1842) and wife Caroline E. (1813-1891), both born in Germany, are buried at Mt. Olivet also.

W&M-1561. Jacob Notnagle (1854-1925) and wife Catharine (Hargett) (1858-1927) are buried at Mt. Olivet as are his parents Leonard (1822-1892) and Mary V. (Stephen) (1824-1901). A Notnagel couple both born in Germany were John Jacob (1814-1891) and wife Mary P. (Sahm) (1832-1900) who also are buried at Mt. Olivet.

W&M-1561. Oliver P. Bennett (1854-1920) and wife Helen (Besant) (1857-1944) are buried at the Catholic Cemetery in Frederick. The only Besant family in 1850 was that of James H. and Margaret A. of Buckeystown District. Oliver's parents William A. (1829-1902) and wife Ann M. (Lewis) (1837-1917) are buried at New London. Oliver's paternal grandfather was Tilghman Bennett (1808-1888) who is buried at Mt. Olivet.

Early Bennetts buried at Sam's Creek Methodist Church were Robert (1778-1856) and wife Elizabeth (1768-1846). Other Bennetts were in Frederick including Charlotte (1794-1861) buried in Frederick Reformed Cemetery. The only Bennett heads of families recorded in the 1800 census of Frederick Co. were in Libertytown District. Benjamin and wife, both over 45 years had no children at home, but owned 6 slaves. Lloyd and wife were between 26 and 45 and also were without children. They had one slave.

Richard Bennett was one of the earliest land owners in the Monocacy area. In 1721 William Fitzredmond surveyed the tract Hope at the mouth of Bennett's Creek including present Lilypons. The Hope tract was immediately assigned to Richard Bennett. In 1723 he had the tract enlarged to 3000 acres. Bennett sold off portions in 1738 and 1747. Suggesting that Richard actually lived in the Monocacy area, Charles Anderson of Monocacy was ordered by the Court of Prince Georges Co. to pay a debt of over 57 pounds to Richard Bennett.

(M&C-I) (T&D). The Court records of Frederick Co. between 1750 and 1763 include George, Jacob and Joseph Bennett. (LC)

W&M-1562. Ira E. Biser (1873-1935) (Mt. Olivet) married Irene C. Waters. His parents Jonathan (1828-1903) and wife Catherine (Hill) (1828-1926) are buried at Middletown Reformed Cemetery. Jonathan's lineage follows from (BL);

   (1) Jacob Beizer m. Catharina; emigrated 1746 (buried Middletown Reformed)

   (2) Frederick (1763-1823) (buried Burkittsville) m. Lydia (1786-1837)

   (3) John (1789-1835)

   (4) Jonathan, see above; also W&M-751

W&M-1563. Charles Sothoron Howard (b. 1861) married Frances Charlotte Dorsey (1872-1927) who is buried at Mt. Olivet, where also are his parents Charles Edward (1828-1869) and wife Joan Eliza (Grove) (1837-1910). The paternal grandparents of Charles S. were Edward Howard (1798-1877) and wife Ann H. (Buckey) (d. at 74 years) who also have gravestones at Mt. Olivet. John Howard surveyed a tract Rocky Hill of 150 acres in 1747. Ephraim Howard surveyed Howard's Paradise of 576 acres in 1789. See also W&M-1143.

W&M-1563. Dr. Harry S. Hedges M.D. (1863-1925) and wife Mary D. (Eichelberger) (1861-1945) of Martinsburg, WV are buried at Petersville Episcopal Church. Dr. Hedges ancestors lived in Berkeley Co., WV to which several sons of Joseph Hedges (d. 1732) moved from Frederick Co. See W&M-1061 and files of (FH).

W&M-1564. Aaron Veant (1843-1925) and wife Emily Catherine Baumgardner (1836-1898) are buried at Keysville where also are his parents John (1815-1886) and Susanna (Angel) (1813-1882). The family name was more often written Weant as in John Weant (c.1777-1858) and wife Catherine (1782-1853) who are buried at Taneytown Reformed Cemetery.

W&M-1564. Walper G. Musgrove (1853-1937) and wife Annie (Short) (1855-1950) are buried at Mt. Olivet. James (b. c.1825) and wife Susan Musgrove (b. c.1826) lived in Emmitsburg District in 1850.

W&M-1564. Dr. Wade Brown Watson D.D.S. (1878-1964) of Montgomery Co. and wife Eva (Moler) (d. 1953) are buried at Petersville Episcopal Church. Other Watsons are buried at Mt. Olivet. Phineas Watson (1768-1839) was born in Philadelphia; Catherine Watson (1777-1855) buried in Mt. Olivet may have been his wife. In the 1800 census of Frederick District William Watson and wife were over 45 years of age.

W&M-1565. Josephus Long (1834-1904) and wife Sarah E. (Holbrunner) (1840-1910) are buried at Mt. Hope Cemetery at Woodsboro. James Long (b. 1800) married Elizabeth (Bankard) (1801-1878).

In the 1800 census of northern Frederick were households of Henry, James and Matthias Long, all between 26 and 45 years of age. John Long and wife were between 16 and 26 years in 1800.

The earliest Langs or Longs in Silver Run Lutheran records were Adam and wife Anna Maria, baptism sponsors in 1777, also Peter and Elisabeth Margaret Long, sponsors in 1783.

W&M-1566. Josephus E. Harley (1837-1919) and wife Mary Theodoria (Duval) (1851-1928) are buried at Petersville Catholic Church. His parents Otho F. (1796-1871) and Catherine (Willard) (1804-1874) are buried at Burkittsville Union Cemetery. The paternal grandfather of Josephus namely Major Joshua Harley is in the census of 1800. He and wife both between 26 and 45 years of age had 6 children under 10 years and owned two slaves. The name of Joshua's wife Miss (Whitenight) of Virginia has been recorded in many different forms in courthouse and church records. Thomas Harley (1801-1883) born in Virginia is buried at Yellow Springs, northwest of Frederick.

W&M-1567. Milton S. Zimmerman (1857-1927) and wife Alice (Diehl) (1846-1921) are buried at Mt. Olivet. His parents Josiah B. (1828-1899) and wife Ellen B. (Holtz) (c.1827-1891) also are buried in Mt. Olivet. Ellen was a daughter of Catherine (1796-1859) and John Holtz (1788-1846) buried at Glade Reformed Cemetery.

Milton Zimmerman's great grandfather Michael (1750-1829) was born in Pennsylvania to George and Ann Catherine (Seidel). See W&M-979. Son Henry (1791-1875) and wife Charlotte (Thomas) (1790-1864) are buried at Church Hill on Ballenger Creek Road. They were parents of Josiah.

W&M-1568. Dr. Arlington Grove Horine M.D. (1862-1956) and wife Virginia M. (Ahalt) (1867-1942) are buried at Burkittsville Union Cemetery where also are his parents John Alpheus (1824-1915) and Frances E. (Grove) 1831-1887). Dr. Horine's grandparents Tobias Jr. (1800-1880) and wife Magdalena (Routzahn) (1802-1873) also are buried at Burkittsville. See W&M-1009 for Adam Horein Jr. emigrant.

W&M-1569. Jacob C. Shaff (1835-1916) was a son of George (1798-1874) and wife Julia Ann (Easterday) (1801-1862). They are buried at Jefferson Union Cemetery. Jacob's grandparents were Jacob (b. c.1770) and Margaret (Weaver). Jacob is in the 1800 census of Middletown Valley as is George Shaff and wife both over 45 years. A Casper Schaaf is in the Frederick Co. Court records of 1754. The children of George Schaaf and wife Susannah of the Monocacy Lutheran Congregation begin with Michael born in 1755. (M&C-II) For the later Schaff family of Switzerland and Mercersburg, PA see the Schaff Library of the United Church of Christ at Lancaster, PA and (Schley) (FH).

W&M-1570. Frederick Columbus Knott (1847-1924) and wife Catherine Elizabeth (Campbell) (1848-1924) are buried at Mt. Olivet. His parents were Francis A. (1812-1881) (Petersville Episcopal) and Ruth W. (Slagle) (1814-1892). (Mt. Olivet. They farmed near Petersville. (LC).

The ancestor of the Knott families of Frederick Co. was John Knott who emigrated from Yorkshire, England in 1642. Descendant Edward Knott married Elizabeth Sprigg Sweeney, a daughter of Allan Sweeney of Chaptico, St. Mary's Co. Edward was a planter in southern Maryland and an officer in the War of 1812. A son Aloysius Leo was born in Frederick Co. in 1835. He was educated at St. John's College at Frederick and after 1847 at St. Mary's College in Baltimore. A. L. Knott's career as a lawyer in Baltimore is given in NC Vol. 11.

In the 1800 census of Middletown Valley were families of Charles and John Slagle, both between 16 and 26 years of age.

W&M-1571. David R. Roop (1852-1936) was a son of Samuel (1816-1884) and wife Lydia Ann (1828-1894). They are buried at Pipe Creek Cemetery near Uniontown. David's grandparents Jacob Roop (1785-1860) and wife Sarah (Hartsock) (1787-1866) are also buried at Pipe Creek.

The local Roop families descend from Christian Rupp (1733-1810) who emigrated from Singheim (Sinsheim?) Baden, according to a genealogy by H. G. Englar (Westminster 1930) (W). (WP).

W&M-1571. Philip Summers (1849-1903) and wife Margaret A. M. (Zimmerman) (1854-1931) are buried at Middletown Lutheran Church as are his parents Henry W. (1826-1902) and Easter C. (Derr) (1832-1876).

Jacob Somer (1767-1850) and wife Elisabeth (Horine) (1769-1849) are buried at St. John's Lutheran Church, north of Myersville. Son George W. Summers (1802-1884) and wife Catherine E. (Michael) (1804-1875) are buried in Middletown Reformed Cemetery. Henry W. was their first child. See also W&M-964.

Henry W. Summers bought in 1868 a farm at Mt. Philip (near Mt. Zion Church) 4 miles southwest of Frederick. He probably was the grandfather of Mrs. Virgie (Summers) Moberly companion of my mother Edith (Fisher) Schildknecht (M&C-II).

There may have been a Summers of English speaking origin in early Frederick Co. A. William Summers was on the Frederick Co. Grand Jury in 1750. At that time German settlers seldom were granted such responsibilities.

W&M-1573. John D. Ahalt (1848-1916) and wife Harriet Janet (Willard) (b. 1879) have gravestones at Burkittsville Union Cemetery where also are buried his parents Samuel (1806-1889) and Mary Ann (Schlosser) (1815-1863) of near Myersville. For earlier Ahalts see W&M-988. The earliest Schlosser with a gravestone in Middletown Valley was Peter (1780-1850) buried at Middletown Lutheran Church.

W&M-1574. Charles Richmond Gregory (1848-1932) and wife Anna (Waters) (1857-1930) are buried at Petersville Episcopal Church. He was born at Williamsport, PA, she was from Georgetown D.C. (LC)

W&M-1574. George C. Crum (1865-1955) and wife Jennie (Martz) (b. 1871) have gravestones in Mt. Olivet where also are buried his parents Casper Jr. (1837-1922) and Mary (Wirtz) (1840-1908). Casper Sr. (b. c.1802), wife Christina (b. c.1809) and their four children emigrated from Germany about 1840. They lived in Battletown (W. Patrick St.); his will of 1879 discloses sons John, Henry, Casper, Lewis, Francis and George. A number of these are listed in (D).

W&M-1575. Frederick Tobias Main (1836-1916) and wife Mary Ann (Shafer) (1838-1910) are buried at Middletown Lutheran Cemetery where also are his parents Daniel (1812-1894) and Malinda (Horine) (1814-1859). See W&M-1481.

W&M-1576. Barton VanBuren Garrott (1840-1916) and wife Lydia M. (Atkinson) (1848-1932) are buried at St. Mark's Episcopal Church at Petersville where also are his parents Barton Garrott (1803-1880) and Mary Priscilla (Anderson) (1812-1891).

An earlier Barton Garret and wife, both over 45 years of age, are in the 1800 census of Middletown Valley. They owned 14 slaves. There were 5 other younger heads of Garret households there in 1800 namely Eanos, John D., John M. John P. and Joseph. All of them owned slaves. W&M-1577. Lewis Edward Horman (1871-1926) and wife Hattie (Cutsail) (1883-1924) are buried at Mt. Olivet Cemetery in Frederick where also are his parents William H. (1847-1933) and Mary E. (Haller) (1853-1937). See W&M-754. William H. was a son of George Harman (1792-1862), farmer of Creagerstown District, who is buried at Apples Church. Christian Harman and wife (both 26-45 years) lived in Emmitsburg District in 1800; a Jacob Harman and wife (both 26-45) then lived in Frederick District.

W&M-1577. William McClellan Roderick (1861-1929) and wife Clara V. (Mercer) (1864-1930) are buried at Mt. Olivet as are his parents William (1817-1877) and wife Eleanor (Lease) (1831-1920). See W&M-1191 and 1193. Eleanor's mother was Catherine Lease (1802-1887) buried at McKaig east of Frederick.

W&M-1578. Milton V. Summers (b. 1878) married Nannie M. (Grossnickle). He was a son of Joshua (1845-1922) and wife Mary E. (Leatherman) (1848-1928) who are buried at Middletown Reformed Church. Milton's paternal grandparents were George W. Summers (1802-1884) and wife Catherine (Michael) 1804-1875) who also are buried at Middletown Reformed Church. See also W&M-964.

W&M-1580. John C. Keller (b. 1855) was a son of Daniel (1823-1896) and wife Jane R. (Miller) (1833-1903) who are buried at Middletown Reformed Church. John's paternal grandparents were David Keller (1784-1863) and wife Hannah (1788-1865). David was the 7th child of John Jacob Keller (1743-1824) and wife Anna Maria (Humbert) (1747-1809) who farmed south of Myersville.

W&M-1582. William Warner Osburn (1871-1955) and wife Rose Schley (Chapline) (1876-1942) of Shepherdstown WV are buried at Mt. Olivet. For Schley families see W&M-700 and 745. For Chapline see W&M-913. (LC)

W&M-1583. In the account of Rev. Charles F. Steck the statement is not correct that the Frederick Lutheran Church is one of the oldest churches of Maryland founded in 1740. There is a little evidence of beginning of Lutheran organization by 1747. Monocacy Lutheran Church and Frederick Reformed Churches were earlier than the Frederick Lutheran Congregation. The Quaker Congregation of the Buckeystown area was organized about 1725. Other churches further east in Maryland were founded earlier.

W&M-1584. Oliver Z. Coblentz (1860-1946) and wife Georgetta M. (Boyer) (1869-1942) are buried at the Reformed Cemetery in Middletown, as are his parents Philip (1812-1899) and wife Mary Ann (Kefauver) (1818-1870). Oliver's paternal grandparents were John Philip Coblentz (1776-1853) and wife Elizabeth (Culler) (1778-1857) who also are buried at Middletown Reformed Cemetery. For earlier Coblentz ancestors see W&M-776 and 1552.

W&M-1584. Lewis C. Ogle (1865-1914) married Ella Martin of Thurmont area. He was a son of George W. (1831-1898) and wife Elizabeth (Hinea) (1837-1914) who are buried at Creagerstown. The grandparents of Lewis where Benjamin

Ogle (1809-1875) buried at Thurmont Catholic Church and wife Catherine (1809-1884) buried at Graceham.

Major Joseph Ogle and his relatives were among the most numerous and most prominent of early settlers in northern Frederick Co. John Ogle (c.1649-1684) emigrated as a youth from England and settled near New Castle, DE with wife Elizabeth (Peters) where their son Thomas married Mary Crawford. Their son Maj. Joseph Ogle (1707-1756) married Sarah Winters. Joseph served with Cresap in the "War with Pennsylvania" near later Wrightville, PA, after which he settled in the German Monocacy Settlement and first surveyed 250 acres near later Loy's Station. Children of Joseph and Sarah were John (b. 1731), Mary (1735), Sarah (1731), Elinor (1741), Joseph (1743), Benjamin (1747), Thomas (1749), William (1751) and James (1753). For son Thomas and wife Sybilla (Schley) to granddaughter Margaret Catherine Thomas who married Christian Burr Artz, see Donna V. Russell in Frederick News July 23, 1985. Maj. Joseph's son Benjamin married Rebecca Stille.

Maj. Joseph had two brothers who also settled in Frederick Co., namely Alexander (1730-1783) and Benjamin (1715-1777) who arrived here by 1741. Benjamin's sons Joseph, Jacob and Thomas Ogle moved westward to WV, OH and IL. It is probable that Benjamin was the grandfather of Benjamin Ogle (1809-1875) above. More about the Ogle families can be found in T&D and the files of (FH).

According to (NC) vol. 28, Sir John Ogle of Lancashire, England married Elizabeth Wollaston and emigrated to Ogleton near New Castle DE. in 1666. Son Thomas married Elizabeth Graham (widow). Their son Maj. Joseph had son John who had son Alexander who married Mary Williams. Alexander Jr. married Charlotte Schneider. Son Alexander Jackson married Harriet Forward. Their son John G. was born in 1851 at Somerset, Pennsylvania. Another Ogle lineage is in (NC) vol. 44.

W&M-1585. Robert L. Ogle (1869-1929) and wife Mollie E. (Stambaugh) (1869-1954) are buried at Mt. Hope Cemetery, Woodsboro. His parents George W. and Elizabeth Hinea are given above. Stambaughs have lived in Adams Co., Pa.

W&M-1586. Harvey B. Ogle (1874-1945) and wife Grace E. (Keilholtz) (1877-1938) are buried at Mt. Tabor Cemetery at Rocky Ridge. He is another son of George W. and Elizabeth (Hinea), see W&M-1584. Earlier Hineas were John H. (1795-1874) and Henry (c.1752-1824) both buried at Haugh's Church near Ladiesburg.

W&M-1586. Cornelius T. Zimmerman (1847-1926) and wife Rhudella (Zimmerman) (1844-1900) are buried at Mt. Olivet. His parents David M. and Susan R. (Snyder) later moved to Ohio.

A son of emigrant (John) George Zimmerman (1714-1795) was Michael (1750-1821) who married Eva Cronise and they lived near Carroll's Manor. Another Michael (1791-1867) is buried at Church Hill on Ballenger Creek Road. See W&M-979. For Cronise families see W&M-1054.

W&M-1587. Clarence L. Valentine (1880-1938) and wife Florence E. (Troxell) (1879-1934) are buried at Mt. Tabor Church, Rocky Ridge, where also are his parents Elias F. (1832-1910) and wife Mary S. (Wetzel) (1836-1863).

Valentine ancestors came from the *Valentine Family Genealogy* by Paul H. Valentine (Rochester N.Y. 1981): (CES)

(1) John George Valentine (1715-1783) m. Anna Margaret Mathias (b. 1734). He emigrated in 1749 from Mutterstadt near Ludwigshafen, Pfalz. Both are buried at Apples Church.

(2) Jacob (1753-1832) m. Anna Mary Freeze (1761-1824).

(3) William (1802-1877) m. Mary Magdalena Mehring (1801-1829); buried at Mt. Tabor Church Rocky Ridge.

(4) Elias Frederick m. Ann Enah Munshower (1836-1858). Elias F. 2m Mary Susan Wetzel. (LC)

W&M-1588. Harry F. Leatherman (1874-1953) and wife Mamie M. (Wiles) (1877-1913) are buried at Utica. His parents were Daniel Jr. (1821-1909 and second wife Josephine (Curtis) (1851-1920 who are buried at Utica where also is buried Daniel's first wife Caroline (Michael) (1823-1871). Harry's grandparents were Daniel (1797-1859) and wife Christina (Warrenfeltz) (1795-1857) who are buried at St. John's Lutheran Church north of Myersville. See also W&M-993 and 1147.

W&M-1590. Jacob S. Young (1845-1898) and wife Sarah E. (Herman) (1852-1916) are buried at Locust Grove Brethren Church near Linganore. He was a son of Daniel and Fanny (Shaffer). The 1800 census of eastern Frederick Co. gives heads of 9 different Young families.

W&M-1591. William Reese Derr (1846-1915) and wife Frances B. (Gittinger) (1847-1926) are buried at Mt. Olivet. His parents John (1798-1866) and Elisabeth (Lugenbeel) (1808-1883) also are buried at Mt. Olivet. John was a grandson of emigrant Sebastian Derr (c.1712-1802) (Mt. Olivet); see W&M-1246 and Wampler.

W&M-1591. John H. Martz (1874-1936) and wife Mary Magdalena (Koontz) (1875-1948) are buried at Mt. Olivet as are his parents Wilson N. (1837-1927) and wife Phoebe Ann Catherine (Whitmore) (1840-1922). Phoebe was a daughter of Nicholas (1795-1870) and Phoebe (Whitmore) (1799-1845) buried at Rocky Springs..

George D. Mertz of Wuerttemberg, Germany, and wife had son Maj. George (1786-1868) and wife Catherine (Reese) (1787-1858) who are buried at Mt. Olivet. Also there are buried their son David S. Martz (1814-1860) and his wife Harriet S. (Wachter) (1821-1906). See W&M-1010. Martz is a dialect form of Mertz or modern German Merz.

W&M-1593. John Philip Wachter (1852-1928) and wife Maryetta (Fout) (1855-1926) are buried at Charlesville Reformed Church. His parents Philip Jr. (1812-1886) and wife Susanna (1814-1899) are buried at Bethel Lutheran Church, north of Frederick. See W&M-724.

W&M-1594. John Dare (1796-1878) and wife Susan Hershberger (1806-1888) are buried at Jefferson Union Cemetery. He came from Bridgeton N.J.

W&M-1595. Bernard Hershberger (Hersperger on gravestone) (d. 1798) is buried at Jefferson Union Cemetery, the land for which he gave, according to his gravestone. His son Henry Hersperger (1760-1812) and wife Catherine (Remsberg) (1762-1824) as well as his grandson Henry II (1794-1859) and wife Julia A. (Scott) (1799-1878) are buried at Jefferson Union Cemetery.

W&M-1596. Ezra A. C. Buckey (1859-1930) and wife Ella (Collins) (1863-1931) are buried at Mt. Olivet Cemetery. His parents Richard Root Buckey (1831-1889) and Susan E. (Wolfe) (1834-1884) are buried at Mountain View Cemetery, Union Bridge. Ezra's grandfather Ezra Buckey (1803-1858) is buried at Beaver Dam Brethren Cemetery near Johnsville. He married Ann Root, of Thurmont, said to be related to Elihu Root.

There is no known relation between the local Buckeys of south German origin and Col. Henry Bouquet of Switzerland. However, the French form of the name, Bouquet, was used in early records of the Frederick Reformed Church and also occasionally around Minfeld, south Germany near the French border from which Mathias and Peter Bucki emigrated. Ezra was a descendant of emigrant Peter and wife Anna Maria (Schaefer) whose son George Peter was baptized at Frederick Reformed Church in 1771. See W&M-854.

W&M-1597. John H. Clem (1850-1928) and wife Wilhelmina S. (Stull) (1855-1947) are buried at Utica along with his parents Jacob (1819-1899) and wife Mary Matilda (Hiteshew) (1824-1863). The second wife of Jacob was Anna Catherine (1846-1896) who also is buried at Utica. See Clem chapter in M&C-I by Thomas R. Clem Sr. See also W&M-1022 and for Hiteshew W&M-407.

W&M-1598. George Waring Tyson (1851-1921) and wife A. Kate (Aubert) (1857-1935) are buried at Mt. Olivet as are his parents Jonathan Tyson (1802-1877) and Elizabeth W. D. (Bear) (1814-1886).

In 1753 John Tyson appears in Court records of Frederick, when the county included most of western Maryland. Dr. P. T. Tyson of Baltimore led development of copper mining in Frederick Co. especially near Libertytown.

Robert C. Tyson born in Thurmont in 1905 became Vice Pres. of U. S. Steel Corp. and Vice Pres. of New York Chamber of Commerce. He graduated at Princeton Univ. in 1927. Robert was a son of Robert Alexander and Effie May (Fleming) Tyson. His memberships and business activities are given in the book Gateway to the Mountains by George W. Wireman of Thurmont (Hagerstown 1969).

In the census of 1850 there was no Tyson family in Thurmont. However, in neighboring Emmitsburg District lived William Tyson (b. c.1805 in Baltimore) and wife Theressa (b. c.1809) with their 9 children.

W&M-1599. William H. Long (1865-1944) married Sarah E. (Fisher) (1866-1949) a distant relative of this writer (M&C-II). They farmed near Loy's Station north of Creagerstown. William's parents were Abraham Long (1828-1894) and Amanda (Mengis) (1835-1915) who are buried at Mt. Tabor Church at Rocky Ridge east of Thurmont. Abraham's ancestor Dr. John Long who emigrated from Germany as a child, married Sarah Keller. Near Littletown, PA. John farmed along with veterinary practice. A report of *Descendants of William*

Harvey Long and Sarah Elizabeth (Fisher) Long (1865-1962) has been prepared by Mildred Keilholtz and Elizabeth (Long) Auldridge. See also W&M-787.

W&M-1601. Rev. Jacob O. Williar (1867-1927) and wife Bertha C. (Ecker) (1871-1948) are buried at Locust Grove Brethren Church near Linganore. He was a son of Augustus (1821-1894) and Hannah Margaret (Pfoutz) (1829-1891) who are buried at the same place. Augustus Williar was born in Harbaugh Valley and farmed near Unionville. See W&M-1093 and 1407.

W&M-1601. William O. Michael (1867-1951) and wife Nannie D. (Zimmerman) (1869-1925) are buried at Mt. Olivet as are his parents William H. (1832-1904) and Jane E. (Specht) (1837-1904). William O. had paternal grandparents Henry S. Michael (1807-1875) and wife Mary E. (1811-1892) who also are buried at Mt. Olivet. Earlier buried at Mt. Olivet are Andrew Michael (1773-1851) and wife Jane (1781-1840). In Frederick District in the 1800 census were William Michael and wife both over 45 years of age. In Buckeystown District in 1800 were 5 Michael households. Andrew, William and Jacob, all 26-45 years of age. Andrew and Rebecca Michael were between 16 and 26 years in age.

W&M-1602. Franklin Easterday Michael (1861-1938) and wife Mary Elizabeth (Storr) (1866-1948) are buried at Mt. Hope Cemetery, Woodsboro. His parents Abraham (1828-1897) and wife Caroline M. (Hauck) (1830-1891) are buried at Bethel Lutheran Church, north of Frederick. Abraham Michael was a son of John (b. 1793) and Elizabeth (b. c.1797) of Frederick District in the census of 1850.

W&M-1603. Henry H. Brish (1863-1942) was a son of William H. (1824-1881) and wife Margaret S. (Wachter) (1840-1916) who are buried at Mt. Olivet Cemetery at Frederick. In Frederick District in the census of 1800 was the household of Henry Brist and wife of ages between 26 and 45 years. They had two children under 10 years. Earlier forms of the Brish name are in Frederick Reformed Church records. In 1789 David and wife Sophia Preuss were sponsors of a baptism. Maria Breusch married William McClain. Sophia Hemminger born 1742 at Nuertingen, Germany, married in 1759 David Preuach. She died at Frederick in 1785. (LW)

W&M-1604. Harry C. Hull (1878-1930) and wife Celeste (Day) (1882-1949) are buried at Mt. Olivet, as are his parents Henry Clay Hull (1844-1906) and Lavinia Ellen (Barrick) (1845-1911). The Barrick (earlier Berg) name is of German origin. See W&M-1091.

In Taneytown District in the 1800 census there were two Hull households of Andrew and wife, both over 45 years, and John Hull over 45 years with wife under 45 years. Henry C. Hull, a son of Julius E., was born in Pennsylvania, and wife Catherine (1802-1888) was born in Maryland. They are buried at Mt. Hope Cemetery at Woodsboro.

W&M-1604. Oliver Augustus Huffer (1863-1933) and wife Amanda Catherine (Arnold) (1866-1951) are buried at Middletown Lutheran Church. For his parents see his brother Howard W&M-101. For Arnold families see W&M-1188.

W&M-1605. George D. Gaver (1845-1918) and wife Martha E. (Hessong) (1848-1922) are buried at Grossnickle Brethren Meeting House as are his parents John P. Gaver (1817-1875) and wife Elizabeth (Cline) (1822-1897). The paternal grandparents of George were George Gaver (1791-1837) and wife Mary (Raymor) (1796-1865) who are buried at St. Johns Lutheran Church north of Myersville.

In the census of 1800 in Middletown Valley were two Gaber households of Peter and wife, over 45 years; and Samuel Gaber and wife of ages between 26 and 45. They had a daughter and 3 sons, all under 10 years.

The original German name was Geber. Like most early German emigrants the first Gebers probably sailed from Rotterdam, Holland.

W&M-1606. Roger M. Neighbors (1850-1834) and wife Annie M. (Breneman) (1853-1920) are buried at Mt. Olivet as are his parents Nathan O. Neighbors (c.1807-1879) and Eliza Ann (Christ) (1818-1875). The 1800 census includes Daniel Neihoof and Baltzer Nighhoof in Frederick District. Could they relate to Neighbors or Dahoffs?

W&M-1607. Peter M. Eader (b. 1844) married Sidney A. Bruchey (1849-1921). She is buried at Mt. Olivet where are also buried his parents Lewis B. Eader (1798-1873) and wife Catherine (Brengle) (1803-1890). Peter's paternal grandparents were David Eader (1774-1847) and wife Elizabeth (Stoner) (1777-1857) who also are buried at Mt. Olivet. Apparently Sidney was a daughter of miller Henry Bruchey (b. c.1827) and wife Ellenora R. (b. c.1828) of Frederick in the 1850 census. (LC)

W&M-1608. William Pinkney Maulsby Jr. (1843-1911) and wife Henrietta Hanson (Pigman) (1846-1931) are buried at Mt. Olivet. He was a son of Col. William Pinkney (1815-1894) and Emily C. (Nelson) (d. 1867) who also are buried at Mt. Olivet. See W&M-1122 for two different families of Nelsons. Emily was a descendant of Nelsons of Point of Rocks.

W&M-1609. Edward I. Angleberger (1860-1907) married Annie M. E. Michael (1858-1938). He is buried at Indian Springs Reformed Church northwest of Frederick and she at Mt. Olivet. Edward was a son of George W. Angleberger (b. 1814) and wife Louisa E. (King) (1824-1907) (buried at Indian Springs). Also buried near Indian Springs is Susanna Angleberger (1748-1846).

In the 1800 census of Frederick District was the household of Jacob Angleburgh of age over 45 years and wife between 26 and 45. They had 3 daughters and 3 sons.

W&M-1609. Colonel Layman (1870-1934) and wife Zoa C. (Freshour) (b. 1878) are buried at Lewistown Methodist Church. Colonel was a name given by his parents George W. (1829-1902) and wife Sophia R. (Favorite) (1832-1905) who also are buried at the Lewistown. By the 1850 census George W. is seen to be a son of Jacob Layman Jr. (1796-1837) buried at Lewistown Methodist Church and wife Savilla (b. c.1802). Jacob Layman Sr. (1769-1843) is buried at Utica. His gravestone states that he was from Dauphin Co., PA.

The German name Lehman became Layman, Leaman or Lemon, in Pennsylvania and Maryland. In the census of 1800 in Liberty District was the family headed by David Leaman in age between 26 and 45. In Westminster District in

1800 in the same age range were Nicholas and Peter Leamon. In northern Frederick Co. in 1800 the only Layman family listed was that of John and wife, both over 45 years.

W&M-1610. William Eugene Sponseller (1857-1933) and wife Annie E. E. (1857-1905) are buried at Mt. Olivet at Frederick. (W&M states that another wife was Cordelia (Harne)). William's parents were William H. (1823-1900) and wife Mary E. (Prince) (1825-1891) who are buried at Mt. Olivet. The paternal grandparents of William Eugene were Jacob Sponseller (1791-1873) and wife Catherine (Shopes) (1793-1870) who also are buried at Mt. Olivet.

Philip (c.1676-1752) and Anna Barbara (Mast) Spannseiler emigrated about 1732 from Kirnbach near Sinsheim, southeast of Heidelberg. Their descendants spread in Adams Co., PA, and Frederick Co. (See M&C-II). Son Andrew (1722-1799) married Elisabeth Lies or Lease (1721-1800) and they settled in Frederick Co. before 1790. Their son Jacob married Christina Kregelo (1761-1807) and they lived near New Market. A brother of Jacob Sponseller went to Washington Co. Six Sponsellers and Sponslers served in the War of 1812.

W&M-1611. Martin Luther Horine (1860-1944) and wife Mary E. (Hightmann) (1857-1933) are buried at Burkittsville Union Cemetery along with his parents Ezra S. (1832-1916) and wife Ann Eliza E. (House) (1836-1928). Ezra was a son of Tobias (1800-1880) and Magdalena (Routzahn) Horine (1802-1873), farmers of Petersville District. See also W&M-1009.

W&M-1611. John Alpheus Horine (1824-1915) and wife Frances E. (Grove) (1831-1883) are buried at Burkittsville Union Cemetery. He was a son of Tobias Jr. (1800-1880) and wife Magdalena (Routzahn) (1802-1873) who also are buried at Burkittsville. For early Horines see W&M-1009. Frances E. was a daughter of George Grove (b. c.1800) and wife Elizabeth (b. c.1804) who farmed in Middletown District in 1850. Grove families in Middletown Valley in 1800 were headed by Charles, George and Jacob.

W&M-1611. William H. Keller (1866-1941) and wife Amelia C. (Whitler) (1870-1951) are buried at Middletown Reformed Cemetery as are his parents William (1818-1876) and wife Ann Elizabeth (Derr) (c.1823-1903). The paternal grandparents of William H. were David Keller (1784-1863) and wife Hannah (1785-1965). See W&M-967 and Wampler.

W&M-1612. David A. Byers (1834-1910) and second wife Salina J. (Etzler) (1854-1934) are buried at Libertytown Fairmount Cemetery. His first wife was Sidney Ann (Shuman) (1837-1892) who was the mother of 12 children. The parents of David were Peter Byers and wife Rebecca (Marker) whose gravestones were not found by J.M.H.. In the 1800 census Daniel and Samuel Marker were young heads of families in Middletown Valley.

Other early Byers were Frederick (1797-1876) and wife Nancy (1803-1886) buried at Prospect Church near Mt. Airy and several buried at Emmitsburg. In the 1800 census Philip Byer, under 45 years of age, was the head of a large family in Frederick District. The early German spelling was Beyer.

W&M-1613. John Alfred Koons (1826-1890) and wife Georgina Celistia (Miller) (1835-1888) are buried at Haugh's Church north of Woodsboro. Ancestor Heinrich Kuhns or Kuntz probably was a Palatine German who embarked for America from the Netherlands. It may have been his son Henry (over 45 years in 1800 census) who had the 6 sons, including John Coones in Buckeystown District in 1800; also Abraham, Henry and George of age 26-45 years in Taneytown District in the 1800 census. George Koons (1753-1817) who married Susannah Shroyer (1760-1848) is buried at Taneytown Reformed Church. Their son Peter (1795-1876) and wife Mary Ann (Ott) (1803-1866) are buried at Haugh's Church. They were parents of John Alfred Koons.

Descendant Carroll H. Hendrickson Jr. pointed out that the will of Henry Koons (died 1821) gives his children as Abraham; Henry Jr.; Jacob; deceased John, George and William; Eve; Catherine; deceased Ann and Mary. Henry Sr., his sons George and Jacob, also Jacob Jr. were blacksmiths. Paul and Anna (Koons) Haugh had son William (1774-1845) who married Catherine Kemp (1777-1824). Their son David (1804-1878) and wife Abalonia (1803-1885) had daughter Mary Catherine Haugh (1833-1909) who married Daniel R. Hendrickson (1826-1898) (Mt. Olivet), a great grandfather of Carroll H. H. Jr.

In Adams Co. there have been numerous Kuhn families and fewer Kuhns and Kuntz (WB). A Georg Kuntz, linen weaver, emigrated in 1732 from Hatten in northern Alsace. He married in 1720 Catherina Jaeger (b. 1690) (B3). Cf Weiser MHM 2,11 (1979) and W&M-1517.

W&M-1614. Peter Koons (1795-1876) married Anna Maria Ott (1803-1866) daughter of John Jacob (c.1754-1822) and Anna Maria (1767-1812). Jacob, a shoemaker, and wife were buried in the Ott family graveyard near Miller's Bridge and Detour. Jacob Ott was a son of John and Maria Appalonia (Kolb) (Ott) (1723-1802). See article John Ott of Frederick County by J. Harold and Virginia Miller in W. MD Gen. Oct. 1986.

Another emigrant Ott family lived near Silver Run in Carroll Co. John Michael Ott, a cooper of Freckenfeld near Kandel in southern Pfalz, married in 1745 Maria Susanna Helck of Freckenfeld and had children Maria Catherine (b. 1746) and Johann Wendel (b. 1750) before they emigrated in 1751. Sons Francis and George were born in America. John Michael's will was probated in 1793. He was survived by wife Susanna. A descendant through Francis is Mrs. Pauline C. Howard of Sun City, AZ, who is collecting Ott family data.

W&M-1614. William Miller (1785-1851) and wife Mary Ann (Bloomenschein) (1782-1865) are buried at Glade Reformed Cemetery near Walkersville, where also are buried their son John W. Miller (1806-1875) and his wife Joann V. (Eichelberger) (1806-1881). The widow Mary of earlier Abraham Miller of Miller's Bridge sold land to Jacob Miller in 1773. Besides the early Millers of Millers Bridge (on Monocacy east of Thurmont) another prominent early Miller family was that of Abraham Miller (1707-1754) of Taskers Chance and the early Reformed Congregation at Frederick who moved to Miller's Mill (the later site of Lewistown). Abraham was granted a license for a tavern by the Frederick Co. Court in 1749. He was buried behind the Reformed Church Chapel (with town clock) on West Church St. in Frederick.

Heirs of Abraham of (what later became) Lewistown were Abraham Jr., Isaac, Jacob and widow Frances Shelhass who sold land at Lewistown to George Jacob Poe Jr. in 1769.

W&M-1615. Peter D. Koons (1860-1933) and wife Alice P. (Birely) (1863-1937) are buried at Haugh's Church near Ladiesburg, north of Woodsboro. At the same place are buried his parents John Alfred (1826-1890) and wife Georganna C. (Miller) (1845-1898) a daughter of Daniel (b. c.1815) and wife Susan (b. c.1818).

Peter Koon's younger brother James Alfred Koons (1867-1929) and wife Lillie M. (Smith) (1874-1929) are buried at Middleburg Methodist Church in Carroll Co. See also W&M-1613 and 1517.

W&M-1616. Joseph Maryland Koons (1869-1925) and wife Emma J. (Barrack) (1863-1938) widow of his brother Edward J. Koons, are buried at Haugh's Church, where also are buried his parents John A. and Georganna Koons discussed above.

W&M-1616. Harvey I. Leatherman (1871-1952) and wife Estella M. (Harshman) (1877-1952) are buried at Grossnickle Meetinghouse north of Myersville where also are his parents Adam (1826-1892) and Susan R. (Harshman) (1840-1907), descendants of Godfrey Leatherman (1748-1836) and wife Anna Elizabeth (Miller). Susan was a daughter of Rev. Christian Harshman (b. c.1779) and wife Catherine (b. c.1803) of Catoctin District.

W&M-1617. Allen George Fisher (1864-1950) married Cora May (Miller) (b. 1866). He is buried at Creagerstown as are his parents John M. (1828-1920) and Mary F. (Valentine) (1833-1898).

The W&M account omits one generation, that of Thomas Fisher Jr. The emigrant from Germany in 1751. Thomas Fisher Sr. married Eva King and their son Thomas Jr. married Catherine Warner. Isaac Fisher son of the latter couple is the ancestor of many Fishers now living in the area of Thurmont. For details see M&C-II, also W&M-829 and 1324.

W&M-1618. John Smith Jr. (1837-1909) and wife Mary Jane (Gilbert) (1836-1915) are buried at Mt. Hope Cemetery at Woodsboro. John Jr. was the seventh child born to John Smith (1797-1860) son of Middleton Smith, and the first child by second wife Elizabeth (Frock) (1812-1886). Middleton's will probated in 1836 reveals his wife Martha. See W&M-1237. There are 7 Smith families in the 1800 census of northern Frederick Co.

W&M-1619. Jeremiah Washington Whitmore (1859-1945) and wife Catherine Susanna Isabelle (Fox) (1858-1922) are buried at Apples Church on the north edge of Thurmont. He was a son of William Whitmore (1834-1894) and wife Sabina (Pittinger) (1837-1926) who also are buried at Apples Church. Jeremiah and Catherine were parents of Charlotte B. Whitmore who married Prof. James C. Biehl. See W&M-1418. For earlier Widmers see W&M-891.

W&M-1620. William Snively Flook (1846-1909) and wife Mary M. (Shaffer) (1847-1875) are buried in Middletown Reformed Cemetery. His parents were Daniel Biser Flook (1814-1870) and Elizabeth S. (Mumma) (1822-1897) who are buried in the same cemetery. The paternal grandparents of William were Jacob Flook Sr. (1760-1840) and wife Elizabeth (Biser) (1767-1842) who also are buried in the Reformed Cemetery at Middletown. See also W&M-829 and (BL).

W&M-1621. Peter H. Shafer (1828-1911) and wife Susan Elizabeth (Karn) (1832-1914) are buried at Burkittsville Union Cemetery, where also are his parents Henry (1793-1871) and wife Mary Magdalena (Willard) (1800-1864). Henry's parents were John Shafer, Jr. (1753-1823) and Anna Marie (Darner) (1754-1837) who are buried at the Reformed church in Middletown. For early Willards see W&M-1093 and 1407. Elizabeth's parents were carpenter George Karn (1794-1861) and wife Susanna (1804-1877) who are buried at Burkittsville Union Cemetery. In the 1800 census of Middletown Valley were households of Jacob Karnes, of age between 26 and 45, and Adam Kearn and wife, between 16 and 26 years.

W&M-1622. Benjamin William Saxten (b. 1879) was a son of Rev. John A. (1845-1931) and wife Josephine A. (Routzahn) (1849-1906) who are buried in Mt. Hope Cemetery at Woodsboro. Benjamin's paternal grandparents were William S. Saxten (1821-1904) and Mary J. (Stevens) (1824-1904) buried in the same cemetery. They came from Pennsylvania to the Woodsboro area in 1867.

The Author, Calvin E. Schildknecht

PRINCIPAL SOURCES AND LOCATIONS WITH ABBREVIATIONS

(AM) *Archives of Maryland* (FH), (GC), (H).

(AP) *Pennsylvania Archives*, 3rd. Series, 30 vols. (Tax, land and military records with index) (G), (GS), (GC).

(B1) *Eighteenth Century Emigrants, Vol. 1, Kraichgau or Neckar Area*, by Annette K. Burgert (PA German Society, 1983) (FH), (G).

(B2) Eighteenth Century Emigrants, vol. 2, Western Pfalz, by Annette K. Burgert (PA German Society, 1985) (FH), (G).

(B3) *Eighteenth Century Emigrants from Northern Alsace*, by Annette K. Burgert (Picton Press, Camden, ME, 1992) (FH), (G).

(BE) *Brethren Encyclopedia*, Donald F. Durnbaugh, ed. (1983) (GS) (H).

Bell, Herbert C., History of the Leitersburg District, (Leitersburg, MD, 1898) (GS), (H).

(BF) *Across the Years in Prince George's County* by Effie G. Bowie (Baltimore 1975) (H).

(BG) At Baltimore: Publications of the Society for the History of Germans in Maryland.

(BM) At Baltimore, The Maryland Historical Society.

(BL) *Beyser Family* by Margaret B. G. Lebherz (Baltimore 1987) (FH) (F).

(BP) At Baltimore, Enoch Pratt Library.

Census of 1800 of Frederick County (paperback) (MD Genealogical Society, Baltimore 1977). (F), (H).

Indexes to Census of Maryland and Pennsylvania 1790 to 1850 (G).

Census of 1850 of Frederick Co. as hardcover book called *Bridge in Time*, Mary F. Hitselberger and John P. Dern, editors (Redwood City, CA 1978) (FH) (H).

C.E.S. is Calvin Everett Schildknecht, files, Gettysburg, PA.

(CF) *Colonial Families of the United States* by G. N. McKenzie et al, editors, vols. 1-6 (Baltimore, 1966) (F).

(D) *General Directory of Frederick* City by Charles W. Miller (1886). (F).

(DV) *Devilbiss Genealogies*, 3 Vols. by Dr. D. Wilbur Devilbiss (Frederick, MD) (F).

(E) Emmitsburg Public Library.

(EM) At Emmitsburg, Archives of Mt. St. Mary's College.

(F) Frederick Public Library, E. Patrick St.

(FC) *Biographical Annals of Franklin Co., PA* by George O. Seilhamer (1905).(G)

(FH) At Frederick, the Library of the Historical Society of Frederick Co. on E. Church St.; Frederick News and Post newspapers on microfilm at (F) and clippings at (FH).

(FM) At Frederick Library of Latter Day Saints (Mormon) Church (including card files of J.M. Holdcraft on 57 rolls of film).

(G) At Gettysburg, PA, Library of the Historical Society of Adams Co. on the campus of the Lutheran Seminary. (Open Wednesday afternoons and Saturdays).

(GC) Gettysburg College, Musselman Library.

(GL) *Pastors and Congregations (Early Lutheran and Reformed)* by Charles H. Glatfelter (PA German Society, 1979) (FH) (G) (H).

(GM) *German Mercenaries Who Immigrated to Western Maryland* by Nancy Rice Kiddoo in Journal of the Pennsylvania German Society, vol. 23, #2, 43 (1989) (FH) (G).

(GP) At Gettysburg, Adams Co. Public Library.

(GS) At Gettysburg, the Library of the Lutheran Seminary.

(Grove), *History of Carrollton* by William J. Grove (Frederick, MD, 1922 and 1928) (FH) (HC).

(GZ) *Getzendanner/Giezendanner Genealogy* by Rev. David Cramer Getzendanner (Salem OR, 1979). (F), (FH).

(H) Hagerstown Public Library.

(HC) Hood College Library at Frederick.

(Helman), *History of Emmitsburg* by James A. Helman (1906) (F) (FH) (E) (H).

(HN) Hanover, PA, Public Library.

(IN) Inventories of Estates in Maryland in 18th Century (FH).

(J) *The Jews Beneath the Clustered Spires* by Paul and Rita Gordon (Frederick, 1971) (F) (FH) (H).

(JE) *Diary of Jacob Engelbrecht*, vols. 1-3 (1818-1878), William R. Quynn, editor (Historical Society of Frederick Co., 1976) (F), (FH), (H).

(JMH) *Names in Stone*, vols 1-3 by Jacob Mehrling Holdcraft (Monocacy Book Co., Redwood City CA, 1966 and 2nd. ed.), 75,000 Cemetery Inscriptions of Frederick Co. and nearby. (F) (FH), (H).

(JMH Files) Over 100,000 cards of genealogy in alphabetical order on microfilms at LDS Library at Frederick.

(JSM) *Genealogical Index to Frederick Co. MD (1730-1830)* by John S. Martin (Malvern, PA, 1992), 4 Vols. (F), (FH).

(K) At Kaiserslautern, South Germany, Library of the Heimatstelle Pfalz, renamed Institut fuer Pfaelzische Geschichte und Volkskunde (near City Art Museum).

(Kurier), *Der Kurier* a journal of the Mid-Atlantic Germanic Society.

(L) At Lancaster, PA, the Schaff Library at the Seminary of the United Church of Christ (former Reformed Church).

(LC) Library of Congress, Washington D.C. lists its genealogies with alternate spelling of family names in 3 vols. of LC directory (11th ed) (GC). See also genealogies in LC Supplements by Marion J. Kaminkow (Baltimore 1981 and 1987).

(LW) *Early Lutheran Records, Monocacy Vol. I* and *Frederick Vol. II* transcribed by Frederick S. Weiser (G), (F), (FH), (H), also early marriages and deaths published as book (National Genealogical Society, DC, 1972.)

(M) *Moravian Records*, Graceham, MD, transcribed by Henry J. Young (1942, reprinted 1988). (FH), (H).

(M&C) *Monocacy and Catoctin, Vol. I* (1985) and *Vol. II* (1989), C.E.S., editor (Family Line Publications, Westminster MD. (F), (FH), (H), (G).

(MHM) *Maryland Historical Magazine* (MD Historical Society, Baltimore) (F), (FH), (GC), (H).

(MS) (with numbers) Manuscripts at Maryland Historical Society.

(Myers): A large collection of books, files and reports of genealogist Margaret E. Myers of Frederick, willed to Hood College Library.

(N) *National Genealogical Quarterly* (Y).

(NA) *Colonial Maryland Naturalizations* by F. A. and F. L. Wyand (Genealogical Publishing Co., Baltimore 1975) (FH) (H).

(NC) *National Cyclopedia of American Biography* (Georgetown Univ. and Mt. St. Mary's College Libraries).

(NY) New York Public Library, 42nd. St., Genealogical Dept.

(P) *The Palatine Immigrant*, Journal of Palatines to America Society.

(PMH) *Pennsylvania Mennonite Heritage Magazine*, Lancaster, PA (G) (Y).

(R) *Rauenzahner to Routson* by John P. Dern and Marjorie Waidner, (Picton Press, Camden, ME, 1993) (F), (FH) (H).

(Reed and Burns) *In and Out of Frederick Town* by Amy L. H. Reed and Marie L. Burns (Frederick, 1985) (Occupations, lots, dates until 1764) (F) (FH) (H).

Revolutionary War, The Maryland Militia in the Revolutionary War by S. Eugene Clements and F. Edward Wright. Family Line Publications (Silver Spring, MD, 1987). (F) (H).

(S) *Staley Family* by Jim Burch (Hyattsville, MD 1993) (FH).

(Scharf), *History of Western Maryland* by J. Thomas Scharf (Philadelphia, 1882 and reprints, Baltimore) (F), (FH), (H).

(Schley), *Genealogy of Schley Family* by C. E. S. (F) (FH).

(S&H) *Pennsylvania Pioneers* by Ralph B. Strassburger and William J. Hinke (Norristown PA, 1934 and reprints) (F), (G), (GS), (H).

(ST) *Stoner Brethren* by Richard R. Weber (Columbia, MD, 1993)

(T) Tax Assessments in Frederick Co., 1798, on microfilm at (F).

(T&D) *Pioneers of Old Monocacy* by Grace L. Tracey and John P. Dern (Genealogical Publishing Co., Baltimore, MD, 1987) (F) (FH) (G) (H) cf. Notes from the Records of Old Monocacy by Grace Louise Tracey (1958) (FH) (BM).

(War of 1812) *Frederick County Militia in the War of 1812* by Sallie A. Mallick and F. Edward Wright (Family Line Publications, Westminster, MD 1992) (With genealogical notes) (F) (H).

(W) in Westminster, MD, Library of the Historical Society of Carroll County.

(WB) *History of Cumberland and Adams Counties* published by Warner, Beers Co., (Chicago 1886 and reprint) (G) (GC).

(Wampler) *The Derr Family* (1750-1986) Genealogy book by Roy H. Wampler (Gateway Press, Baltimore, 1987) (F) (FH) (H).

(Wentz), Dr. Abdel Ross Wentz, The Gettysburg Seminary, Vol. 2, Alumni Record (Harrisburg, 1964) (GS) (H).

(WMG) *Western Maryland Genealogy* (Middletown, MD) (FH) (H) (WP).

(W&M) *History of Frederick County* by T.J.C. Williams and Folger McKinsey (1910) (F) (G) (FH) (H).

(Williams 1906) *History of Washington County, MD* by T.J.C. Williams (Hagerstown, 1906 and reprint by Clearfield Co., Baltimore 1992) (H) (GS).

(WP) Westminster, MD, Public Library.

(Y) Library of the Historical Society of York County PA, at York, PA.

(Z) *Zimmerman Genealogy* by Margaret E. Myers vols. I & II (1988) (F) (FH).

INDEX OF FAMILY NAMES

Modern spellings are favored. Thus Smith references include Schmidt and Schmid.

Abbott 37, 92
Abell 38, 69, 226, 232
Ackler 67
Adams 13, 121, 201, 241
Addison 93, 191, 205, 229
Adlum 32
Ahalt 27, 111, 122, 125, 135, 143, 154, 164, 172, 175, 179, 202, 216, 248, 250, 270,. 271
Albaugh 15, 25, 39, 40, 53, 102, 135, 149, 174, 190, 193, 196, 201, 202, 205, 238, 241, 253, 259, 260, 261, 262
Albert 52
Albright 240, 241
Aldertse 170
Alexander 32, 55, 144, 190
Allen 138
Allison 138
Allnutt 157
Alvey 48
Ambrose 17, 91, 92, 132, 241
Amelung 14, 32, 78
Anders 46, 107, 152, 156, 168, 183, 187, 198, 214, 215, 259
Anderson 23, 63, 64, 82, 136, 137, 156, 183, 265, 268, 271
Andreas 154
Andruska 47
Angel 269
Angleberger 113, 151, 216, 246, 247, 277
Annan 90, 254, 255
Apple 11, 28, 75 129, 130, 163
Appleby 216
Appleman 93
Armacost 59
Arnet 92
Arnold 53, 91, 92, 148, 151, 152, 157, 172, 181, 188, 208, 215, 226, 249, 250, 251, 264, 276
Arter 73
Arthur 227
Artz 273
Asbury 14

Ashbaugh 140, 225
Atkinson 271
Atlee 103
Aubert 275
Auld 77, 194
Auldridge 276
Ausherman 92, 93
Axline 245
Ayers 159

Babcock 216
Babel 220
Babington 248
Bacon 100
Badger 187, 190
Baer 94, 98, 149
Bailey 148, 190, 256
Bainbridge 11, 33, 44, 90, 144
Baird 46
Baker 43, 85, 111, 150, 190, 204, 213, 217, 240, 241, 246, 252
Bale 115
Baltimore, Lord. See Calvert
Baltzell 52, 76, 94
Bankard 269
Bankert 220
Barber 204
Bard 12
Barker 113
Barnard 106, 110
Barnes 69, 106, 119, 124, 189, 246
Barnett 208, 253, 266
Barnhart 194
Barnheiser 224
Barnhold 215
Barrick 83, 108, 109, 112, 123, 154, 158, 162, 167, 170, 171, 175, 182, 191, 207, 208, 209, 219, 222, 245, 253, 255, 276, 280
Bartgis 28, 88, 160, 203
Barth 181
Barthelow 263
Bartholomaei 61
Barton 53, 255
Bast 251

Baugher 26, 40, 80, 121, 152, <u>261</u>
Baughman 38, 226
Baumgardner 34, 37, 86, 115, 204, 206, 207, 252, 265, 269
Bausman 141
Baust 148
Bayard 44
Bayer 89, 166
Bayley 13, 29
Beachley 9, 88, 150, 157, 203, 216, 248, 249
Beall 7, 32, 33, 80, 214, 240, 262
Bear 52, 108, 143, 275
Beard 12, 88, 157, 165, 198, 201, 215, 240
Beatty 7, 8, 32, 43, 45, 65, 215, 258
Beaver (Bieber) 46
Beavers 234
Bechtol (Bechtel) 11, 67, 103, 115, 207, 220, 221, 225, 236
Beck 124, 125, 166, 202
Beckenbaugh 14, 34, 71, 147, 236
Becker 167, 223
Beckley 239
Beckwith 171
Bedient 97
Beers 284
Beeson 58
Beighler 166
Bell 52, 113, 189, 227, 281
Belleson 254
Belt 44, 106
Benchoff 81
Bencker 86
Bender 175
Benner 79, <u>106</u>, 213
Bennett 43, 59, 134, 216, 268
Bentz 3, 7, 34, 41, 54, 66, 211, 225
Berg 154. See also Barrick
Berger 56
Bertz 237
Besant 268
Best 20, 22, 99, 240
Beyer 166
Beyers 166
Biddinger 259
Biehl 234, 280
Bielfeld 87

Biesecker 106
Biggs 7, <u>40</u>, <u>41</u>, 85, 105, 245, 256
Billmeyer 188
Binnie 181
Birely 32, <u>39</u>, 62, 77, 84, 86, 121, 130, 139, 141, <u>143</u>, 185, 198, 199, 227, 246, 280
Bischoff 169
Biser 34, 54, 66, 68, 70, 71, 79, 101, 103, <u>115</u>, 119, 137, <u>144</u>, 145, <u>146</u>, 158, 180, 199, 227, 231, 233, 269, 280, 281
Bittinger 12
Bittle 60, 94, 98, 117, 178, 224, 227
Bjorkman 201
Black 45, 88
Blackford 63
Blair 33
Blamey 76
Blessing <u>89</u>, 127, 154, 242, 258
Blickenstaff <u>89</u>, <u>90</u>, 133
Blizzard 146
Block 33
Blockson 207
Bloomfield 148
Blumenauer 117
Blumenschein 279
Bodner 83, 221
Boetzel 62
Bogen 32
Bogert 129
Boggs 229
Bogner 60, 61, 94, 95
Bohn 144, 179, 190
Boileau 188
Boller 58, 259
Bolling 138
Bond 238
Bonnet 18, 48
Boone 190, 193
Bopst 103, 142, 143, 177
Bordley 33
Boteler 122, <u>151</u>, 160
Bouquet 5, 86, 149, 275
Boutler 151
Bowerman 145
Bowers 74, 88, 104, 113, <u>159</u>, 160, 253, 255, 257, 262

Index

Bowie 281
Bowles 151, 264
Bowlus 34, 126, 137, 156, 178, <u>199</u>, <u>200</u>, 203, 264, 266
Bowman 113, 118, 165, 178
Boyer 66, 73, 89, 143, <u>166</u>, 177, 188, 224, 246, 249, 251, 272
Boyle 243
Braddock 9, 10, 11, 12, 16
Bradshaw 126, 167, 180
Braithwaite 22
Brandenburg 71, 85, <u>91</u>, 95, 107, 115, 145, 231, 247, 248, 254, 263, 266
Brane 86, 188, 199
Brashears 185
Braun 38, 105, 134
Brawner 11, 80
Bready 87, 151
Bream 144
Breneman 277
Brengle 7, 34, 50, 54, 118, 141, 184, 191, 196, 220, 241, 268, 277
Brewer 160
Brien 64, 78
Brightbill 100
Brightwell 133, 189, 196, 259
Brim 257
Brink 41
Brish 276
Brooke 65, 109, 158, 267
Brookey 34
Brown 7, 18, 19, 33, 41, 59, 75, 76, <u>93</u>, <u>94</u>, 95, 115, 117, 120, 128, 165, 167, 174, 178, 223, 225, 227, 232, 237, 242, 243, 263
Browning 91, 169, 214
Bruce 12
Bruchey 277
Brumbaugh 12, 17
Brunch 93
Brunner 11, 44, 51, 55, 57, 76, 102, <u>105</u>, 123, 140, 191, 199, 201, 208, 225, 229, 233, 240, 244
Buchanan 63
Buckey 5, 16, 40, <u>86</u>, <u>87</u>, 140, 149, 162, <u>165</u>, 166, 167, 169, 204, 209, 211, 235, 244, 255, 261, 269, 275
Buckingham 74, 97

Buhrman 76, 90, 93, 94, 98, 124, 152, 224
Bunce 14
Burall 246, 247
Burch 101, 284
Burgee 149, 245, 248
Burger 189, 212
Burgert 54, 61, 198, 214, 281
Burgess 83, 131, 196
Burkett 192
Burkhart 123, <u>228</u>, <u>229</u>
Burkholder 74, 90
Burnett 221
Burns 8, 14, 130, 200, 210, 284
Burnside 62
Burrier 133, 198, <u>201</u>, 263, 264
Bush 167, 238
Bushey 143
Bussard 64, 73, 89, 98, 99, 107, 118, 132, 209, 221, 225, 226, 237, 248, 261, 264
Butler 102, 151, 159
Butts 251
Buxton <u>139</u>, 249
Byerly 39, 104, 108, 226
Byers 89, 278

Cain 64
Caldwell 211
Calvert 8, 11, 12, 17, 23, 186
Cameron 82
Campbell 72, 162, 213, 256, 270
Carmack 107, 192, 258, 259
Carnes 158
Carpenter 39, 98
Carr 97
Carroll 8, 9, 12, 16, 24, 29, 30, 33
Carter 190, 216, 265
Cartwright 16
Carty 84, 95, 218
Cartzendafner 43
Cary 24, 158, 262
Casebier 75
Cash 160
Cashaw 202
Cashour 210, 265

Castle 47, 52, 86, 101, 103, 104, 116, 153, 164, 209, 217, 239, 251, 256, 263
Cease 258
Cecil 112
Chapline 11, 32, 33, 104, 147, 272
Charlton 29, 250
Chase 33, 64, 194
Chew 218
Childes 75
Chiles 206
Chilton 20
Chiswell 68, 69
Christian 217
Church 29
Claggett 54, 83, 90, 120, 139, 149, 201, 204, 205, 217, <u>218</u>
Clapp 200
Clarke 23, 214
Clary 194, 196, 197, 213
Clay 12
Clem <u>136</u>, 205, 239, 260, 275
Clements 284
Clemson 191
Cline 78, 134, <u>154</u>, 210, 242, 246, 247, 262, 277
Clugston 81
Coale 243
Coberly 61
Coblentz 34, 59, 67, 72, 115, 124, 131, 139, 151, 157, 164, 203, 205, 206, 207, 221, 225, 231, 236, 239, 251, 263, 264, 266, 272
Cochran 40, 109, 161, 255
Cocke 8
Coker 65
Colbert 159
Cole 21, 72, 91, 96
Coleman 64
Collard 163
Colliflower 41, <u>193</u>, <u>194</u>
Collinger 98
Collins 275
Compher 120
Condon 113
Contee 48
Conway 116
Cook 204, 251

Cookerly 207, 241
Cooling 21, 22
Coon (Kuhn) 34
Coontz 154
Copeland 110, 176
Copelin 219
Corem 258
Cornell 109
Cornog 63
Cost 122
Cover 97, 239
Cox 16
Crabb 32
Crabtree 3
Craig 233
Crapster 36, 87
Cramer 15, 39, 40, 41, 62, 76, <u>108</u>, <u>109</u>, 112, 121, 151, <u>160</u>, 1o62, 167, 169, 172, 177, 184, 186, <u>191</u>, 202, <u>203</u>, 208, 209, 210, 217, 225, 238, 251, 254, 255, 262
Craver 143
Crampton (earlier Cramphin) <u>193</u>, 249
Crawford 44, 85, 86, 273
Creager 9, 48, 92, 109, 166, 171, 208, 222, 238
Cresap 11, 12, 32, 65
Crewe 110, 202
Crise 182
Crist 123, 139, 264
Cromwell 159, 202, 262
Crone 16, 143, 178
Cronin 239
Cronise 122, 123, 130, 140, <u>144</u>, <u>145</u>, 181, 182, 184, 191, 201, 209, 210, 231, 240, 263, 273
Crooks 23, 74
Crouse 14, 112, 252
Crown 113
Crum 104, 117, <u>169</u>, <u>170</u>, 176, 183, 189, 212, 213, 261, 271
Crumpacker 53, 173, 197, 212
Culler 34, 85, <u>136</u>, 140, <u>153</u>, 154, 164, 169, 178, 185, 202, 206, 226, 230, 233, 236, 254, 272
Cummings 32
Cunningham 43

Curfman 225, 264
Currens 49
Curtis 274
Custard 113
Custer 90, 223
Cutsail 34, 178, 272
Cutshall 178, 193, 205

Damuth 227
Dance 220
Daniel 33
Danner 87, 108, 126, 245
Danson 157
Darby 64
Dare 274
Darling 113
Darner 54, 55, 126, 178, 214, 215
Darr 238
Daugherty 235
Davidson 146, 216
Davis 21, 63, 82, 98, 149, 177, 207, 215, 226, 239, 245, 246
Dawson 74, 115
Day 18, 160, 209, 276
Dayhoff 34
Dean 83, 159, 183
Deberry 184
Degen 241
Degrange 177
Delaplane 160, 195, 238
Delaplaine 3, 13, 22, 66, <u>139</u>, 185, 202, 241
Delashmutt 110, 113, 130, 158
DeLauder 137, 172, 221
Delauter 7, 11, 34, 89, 105, 264
Delozier 80
Delphey 176, 188
Demory 137
Denegre 41
Dennis 13, 75, 80, 206
Dern 145, 282
Derr 34, 43, 52, 56, 57, 83, 95, 118, 119, <u>128</u>, 130, 131, 135, 143, 146, 173, 178, 188, 192, <u>196</u>, 203, 208, 219, 244, 245, 253, 257, 271, 274, 278
Dertzbaugh 88, <u>134</u>, <u>135</u>
Detrick 112, 145, 198

Devilbiss 14, 57, 108, 115, 140, <u>162</u>, 163, 196, 203, 204, <u>207</u>-<u>209</u>, 210, 211, 213, 235, 253, 256, 263, 266, 282
Dickensheets 34, 166
Dickson 33, 147, 186
Deihl 79, 144, 174, 213, 245, 270
Dielman 74
Diffenbaugh 89
Diffendahl 34, 81, 176, 198
Digges 9, 11, 36, 242
Dill 43
Dillard 250
Diller 64, <u>162</u>
Dilworth 160
Dinckle 240, 241
Dinterman 118, 159, 212, 258, 263
Ditlo 34
Divine 174
Dixon 62, 83, 84, 110, 137, 150, 185, 188, 252
Dodderer 39, 62, 123, <u>124</u>, 253. See also Dudderar
Doehla 12
Dofler 34, 117
Dolan 159
Doll 34, <u>83</u>, <u>84</u>, 105, 108, 129, <u>151</u>, 234
Domer 66, 75
Donaldson 174
Donnelly 16, 80
Donsife 112, 168
Dorcas 183
Dorman 68
Dorner 99, 250
Dorff 92
Dorsey 43, 69, 99, 112, 149, 173, 242, 243, 269
Doty 75, 143
Doub 67, 71, <u>81</u>, <u>82</u>, 93, 100, 103, 117, 260
Dougherty 193
Douglass 64
Doull 32
Downey 68, 112, 145, 149
Doyle 97, 197
Dreyer 121
Droneburg <u>150</u>, 213

Drummond 257
Drye 28
Duple 262
Dubois 24, 30, 31, 170
Dubourg 29
Ducket 33
Dudderar 97, 110, 116, 133, 189, 194, 202
Duggan 49, 116
Dulany 4, 5, 8, 9, 10, 11, 12, 15, 16, 17, 24, 26, 32, 38, 110, 163, 186, 203
Dungan 3
Durnbaugh 224, 281
Durbin 112
Dutrow 34, 43, 68, 86, 124, 133, 166, 183, 205, 210, 218, 232, 255. See also Dodderer and Dudderar
Duvall 84, 114, 129, 155, 229, 267, 270
Dyer 140

Eader 158, 277
Eagle 139
Early 21, 22, 23
Easterday 34, 35, 51, 77, 89, 98, 127, 129, 233, 246, 249, 262, 270, 276
Ebbert 123
Eberly 131, 254
Ebert 158, 192, 246
Eby 73, 113, 137
Eccord 152
Eckenrode 156
Ecker 119, 133, 173, 190, 276
Eckstein 156
Edelin 32
Edmunds 214, 215
Edwards 21, 173
Effland 186
Eichelberger 121, 182, 220, 269, 279
Eickhofe 57
Eigenbrodt 34
Eisenhauer 15, 108, 266
Eisenhower 15, 228
Elder 7, 9, 16, 17, 24, 80, 158
Ellicott 37
Elliott 29, 78
Emery 226

Engelbrecht 5, 7, 19, 23, 34, 283
England 80, 87
Englar 120, 148, 152, 153, 256, 271
Engle 77, 102, 142, 247, 261
Englemann 245, 248
English 53
Enoch 265
Ensor 220
Ent 258
Erb 110, 211
Ernest 241
Etchison 73, 104, 136, 160, 161
Etzler 146, 162, 190, 203, 278
Eury 210
Evans 106, 112, 149, 154, 258
Everett 79, 214
Everhart 7, 13, 14, 15, 16, 96, 157
Evy 110
Eyler 68, 81, 122, 152, 168, 187, 192, 193, 205, 214, 222, 244, 254, 258
Eyster 258

Fabian 11
Fagan 172
Fahs 90
Fair 90
Faller 90
Farquhar 126
Farrell 16
Favorite 228, 277
Faw 12, 31
Fawley 141
Fay 145
Fearer 17, 67
Fearhake 34, 78
Feaster 178, 185, 193, 249
Fee 110
Feeser 84
Feinour 156
Feiser 34, 116, 192, 206
Felton 163, 216
Fendall 138
Fenwick 187
Ferree 39, 42, 72, 180, 195, 235
Ferrell 242
Fessler 69, 122
Fetterling 246

Index

Fickling 67
Fiegler 135
Fike 181
Finch 80
Finger 43, 213
Filicchi 29
Fillinger 106
Finch 16
Finefrock 34
Fineman 174
Fink 55, 120, 182
Firestone 46-47, 158
Firor 47, 238
Fischer 31, 32, 214
Fisher 43, 62, 79, 85, 106, 110, 114, 139, 188, 190, 209, 213, 214, 275, 280
Fister 136
Fitzgerald 38
Fitzhugh 189
Fitzredmond 268
Flanagan 191, 226
Flautt 93, 118, 194
Fleagle 191
Fleckener 196
Fleming 91, 156, 223, 230, 265, 275
Flickinger 114, 144, 198
Flight 260
Flook 14, 34, 79, 115, 125, 137, 182, 188, 231, 280
Flore 52
Floyd 60, 117, 126, 137, 178, 260
Fogle 51, 152, 168, 187, 212, 252, 254, 259, 263
Fogler 113
Foltz (Voltz) 14, 15, 109
Foote 20
Ford 99, 149
Foreman 40, 47, 239
Forney 42, 72
Forsyth 180
Fortney 39, 176, 234
Fout 77, 78, 170, 211, 274
Fowler 64
Fox 7, 20, 51, 68, 75, 91, 93, 95, 98, 152, 159, 165, 220, 240, 241, 252, 262, 280
Fraley 34, 172, 193, 260

Framback 24
Francis 260
Frankenfeld 24
Franklin 10, 11, 38, 282
Frazier 96, 112, 174
Frederick 215
Freeze 59, 274
French 186
Freshour 277
Frey 140, 212
Freyberger 123
Freyhoffen 56
Friend 23, 81
Frisk 11
Fritchie 7, 13, 19, 91, 143
Frizzell 220
Frock 192, 205, 259, 280
Frost 10
Fry(e) 96, 240, 245
Fuehrer 92
Fulmer 158
Fulton 120, 148, 193, 209, 263
Fundenberg 14, 34, 127, 145, 257
Funk 101, 137
Furgueson 67
Fuss 79, 144

Gaither 150, 179, 187, 246
Gall 76, 159, 261, 265
Gally 61
Galt 138, 196
Gambrill 33, 145, 241
Garber 149, 165, 167, 172, 182, 188, 260
Gardiner 63
Gardenour 93
Garret 272
Garrott 55, 189, 271, 272
Gartland 38
Gaugh 52, 192, 242
Gaver 53, 61, 78, 126, 137, 171, 209, 210, 224, 247, 248, 252, 277
Geasey 5, 58, 102, 261
Geesey 176, 234, 260
Geiger 129
Geisbert 52, 124
Geiselman 56, 59, 187
Geist 212

Gerhart 201
Gernand 47, 57, 75, <u>167</u>, 209, 251
Gerry 132
Getz 196
Getzend 245
Getzendanner 11, 34, 40, 72, <u>77</u>, <u>78</u>, 87, 101, 105, 134, 188, 198, 219, 222, 237, 244, 245, 268, 282
Gibson 44, 85
Gilbert 89, <u>174</u>, <u>175</u>, 186, 193, 229, 259, 280
Gilliland 121
Gilmore 129
Gilpin 78
Gilson 78
Gittinger 122, 220, 274
Gittings 33, 97
Gladhill 240, 241
Gladt 261
Glass 136
Glatfelter 282
Glaze 76, 136, 176
Goden 232
Goering 24
Goetz 163
Goldsborough 10, 22, 32, 68, 186, <u>194</u>, <u>195</u>
Good 13, 159
Goodman 102
Goodspeed 6
Gonso 14, 77
Gordan 75
Gordier 155
Gordon 32, 282
Gorman 216
Gorton 183
Grable 34, 82, 200
Grant 16, 22, 23, 200
Graf 100, 167, 180, 232, 241. See also Grove
Graham 8, 128, 189, 251, 273
Gray 121
Grayson 121, 138
Green 47, 51, 80, 81, 156, <u>158</u>, 226, 262
Greenberry 149, 194
Greenwald 154
Greenwood 208, 222, 253

Gregg 140
Gregory 271
Grier 64
Griesemer 86
Griffith 32, 68, 69, 77, 131, 173
Grimes 37, 52, <u>131</u>, 143, <u>149</u>, 191, 252, 259, 260
Grimm 156
Grinder 130, 160, 261
Groff 41, 97, 167, 192
Grosch 15, 32, 87, 225
Gross 96, 122, 182
Grosjean 155
Grossnickle 60, 64, 90, 91, 92, 96, 172, 218, <u>223</u>, 224, 225, 247, 258, 260, 272, 280
Grove 55, <u>97</u>, 115, 132, 156, 165, 167, 169, 179, <u>180</u>, 222, 241, 250, 260, 269, 270, 278, 282
Grubb 27, 162
Grumbine 191, 220
Gueting 230
Gumpf 130, 155
Gurley 244
Guth 19

Haas 87
Hackleton 28
Haff (Hoff) 49
Hagan 268
Hager 12, 13, 110
Hahn 34, 77, 131, 220, 238, 257, 259, 261, 268
Haifleigh 254
Haines <u>184</u>, 267
Hall 41, 98, 137, 163
Haller 34, <u>69</u>, 75, 84, 95, 117, 159, 244, 272
Hammaker 106
Hammett 76
Hammond 21, 109, 112, 113, 126, <u>186</u>, <u>187</u>, 201
Hane 134
Handly 205
Hankey 26, 75, 76, 176, 251
Hanks 163
Hann 140, 252
Hanna 160

Hanshaw 66, 92
Hanson 33
Harbaugh 9, 16, 25, 43, 48, 68, 81, 93, 121, 127, 128, 129, 156, 167, 178, 198, 202, 216, 238, 243
Hardey 180
Harding 44, 220, 241
Hardman 112, 171
Hargett 125, 130, 153, 155, 176, 200, 210, 222, 233, 236, 237, 261, 268
Harlan 107
Harley 179, 243, 244, 270
Harling 121
Harman 65, 228, 244, 272
Harmis 203, 259, 264
Harmon 54, 177, 202, 272
Harn(e) 133, 156, 207, 267, 278
Harner 85, 129
Harp 64, 79, 100, 126, 137, 172, 194, 224
Harris 76, 91, 227, 254
Harrison 215
Harry 210
Harshman 77, 218, 224, 280
Hart 12, 95
Hartly 139
Hartman 76, 96, 226
Hartsock 171
Harwood 120
Hassler 20
Hauer 13, 14, 19, 143
Haugh 112, 115, 144, 168, 185, 188, 254, 276, 279
Haupt 128, 173
Hausihl 11, 24, 26
Hauver 75, 94, 152, 156, 165, 224, 231
Hawk 138, 201
Hawman 177
Hax 211
Hayden 81
Hayes 87, 136, 150
Heaney 10
Hearn 195
Heater 163
Heaterale 253
Heberlig 183
Hechler 69
Heckathorn 34, 106

Hedges 72, 88, 102, 113, 147, 174, 211, 213, 269
Heffelbower 172, 188
Heffner 74, 88, 102, 122, 140, 198, 215, 250
Hehl 27
Heidelberger 227
Heighe 69
Heightman 131
Heinlein 76
Heinzman 37
Helck 279
Helfenstein 118
Heller 177
Helman 16, 282
Hemminger 276
Hemp 75, 248, 251
Henckel 130, 180
Hendricks 168, 170
Hendrickson 168, 256, 279
Hendrix 74
Hendry 190
Herman 27, 240, 274
Herring 157
Hershberger 72, 113, 236, 274, 275
Hershey 50
Hersperger 198, 244, 275
Hess 42, 80
Hesser 193
Hesson(g) 8, 67, 115, 125, 131, 201, 242, 277
Hett 53, 77
Heugh 33
Hickling 108
Hickman 157
Highbee 138
Hightmann 278
Hildebrand 101, 120, 135, 221
Hildebridle 34
Hill 20, 54, 97, 121, 147, 165, 217, 229, 269
Hilleary 148, 161, 168, 205, 266
Hindman 44
Hinea 164, 272, 273
Hink 284
Hinkle 82
Hinks 77, 213
Hite 9

Hiteshew 56, 75, 83, 96, 136, 161
Hitselberger 282
Hobbs 84, 243, 268
Hockensmith 67
Hoff 49, 78
Hoffman 7, 11, 40, 56, 86, 104, 144, 222, 254
Hogan 56, 137
Hogarth 75
Hohl 46
Hoke 76, 136, 138, 163, 175, 187, 263
Holbrunner 192, 269
Holdcraft 3, 4, 6, 45, 209, 256, 282, 283
Holmes 19
Holt 239
Holter 72, 157, 164, 169, 207
Holtz 84, 108, 114, 123, 160, 230, 270
Holtzapple 34
Holverstot 153
Homan 61
Hood 28, 129, 229, 267, 282
Hooker 21
Hooper 66, 113
Hoover 56, 110, 197, 224
Hopkins 68, 176, 187, 189
Hopwood 220
Horine 34, 119, 125, 131, 132, 154, 250, 270, 271, 278
Horman 244
Horn 150
Horner 128, 255
Horning 212
Hoskinson 155
Hospilhorn 127, 242
Hotz 135
Houck 9, 28, 58, 76, 112, 159, 183, 191, 225, 254, 262, 276
House 102, 104, 127, 130, 177, 179, 250, 278
Householder 89, 99, 122
Housman 148
Houx 255
Howard 40, 41, 87, 169, 176, 201, 205, 229, 233, 269, 279
Howell 19, 59
Hubbard 176
Huber 197, 198

Huff 167
Huffer 107, 122, 131, 135, 137, 172, 276
Huffman 222
Hughes 17, 67, 217
Hull 110, 176, 178, 193, 276
Humbert 71, 118, 119, 272
Hume 14
Humerick 193
Humm 77
Hummer 205, 226
Humrichhouse 197
Hunsecker 50
Hunt 168
Hunter 22, 23, 137
Hutzell 116
Hyatt 82, 121, 246
Hyde 204
Hyder 99, 114, 174
Hymes 137
Hyndman 76

Ijams 121
Inch 199
Ingle 191
Innis 33
Isanogle 74, 216

Jackson 14, 20, 74
Jacobs 166, 205, 251
Jaeger 279
James 29, 84, 85, 108, 150, 176
Jamison 38, 148, 187, 266, 267
Jansen 169, 170
Jarboe 54, 139, 180
Jefferson 222
Jenifer 33
Jenkin 82
Jenkins 242
Jesserang 16, 91
Jewell 157
Johns 206
Johnson 7, 11, 13, 17, 23, 27, 32, 33, 38, 63, 75, 98, 167, 172, 179, 185, 189, 226, 232, 251
Johnstone 95
Jolliffe 74

Index

Jones 3, 32, 54, 97, 116, 132, 194, 196, 197, 202, 213, 267
Jordan 115
Jourdan 74
Joy 147, 243
Julien 147, 211
Justice 259

Kailor 83
Kane 64
Kanode 212, 261
Karcher 118
Kallenberger 57
Karl 46
Karley 96
Karn 148, 156, 181, 221
Kauf 205
Kaufman 81, 183
Keedy 230
Keefer 267
Keene 176
Kefauver 34, 71, 72, 103, 104, 106, 118, 132, 147, 171, 202, 206, 207, 220, 221, 222, 224, 225, 236, 251, 254, 264, 272
Kehne 167
Keidel 19
Keilholtz 136, 273, 276
Keller 27, 60, 66, 70, 71, 75, 77, 91, 115, 119, 149, 165, 174, 191, 192, 221, 236, 248, 250, 254, 272, 275, 278
Kelly 49
Kemp 5, 11, 72, 73, 87, 91, 102, 121, 143, 148, 160, 187, 198, 199, 202, 211, 235, 236, 244, 247, 279
Kennedy 18, 19, 44
Kephart 171, 232
Kepler 54, 96, 150, 169, 251
Kepple 156
Kern 42
Kessebring 60
Kessler 161
Key 16, 33, 226
Keyser 40, 42
Kiddoo 55, 282
Kieffer 227, 266
Kimball 15

Kimber 237
Kimmell 84, 85
Kindley 73, 95, 149
Kiney 246
King 79, 82, 157, 213, 214, 223, 277
Kinna 214
Kinnamon 67
Kinzer 153
Kirch 155
Kiser 215, 233
Klein 207, 243
Kline 73, 74, 96
Kling 191, 259
Klipp 221
Knodle 126
Knott 167, 270
Knouff 49, 134, 145, 245
Kochher 65
Kohlenberg 34
Kolb 34, 164, 279
Koogle 83, 88, 131, 163, 166, 182, 214, 248, 249, 264
Koons 259, 279, 280
Koontz 32, 87, 126, 154, 193, 274
Korrell 212
Kortz 84
Kraft 26
Kramer 15, 109. See also Cramer
Krantz 73, 115, 233, 234
Krauth 94
Kreglo (Kregelo) 34, 135, 163, 278
Kreh 85, 211
Krise 43, 176
Kuhlman 24
Kuhn(s) 34, 81, 279, 280
Kump 83
Kunkel 226, 233
Kurtz 183, 257
Kuntz 279

La Barre 84
Lafayette 13, 14, 15, 30, 63, 195
Lakin 72, 95, 109, 124, 132, 148, 198
La Mar 76
Lamar 136, 179, 180
Lampe 100
Lambert 143, 184

Lambrecht 34
Lambright 265
Lamon 14
Landers 56, 57, 254
Landis 182
Langhorne 38
Lanham 249
Lantz 167
Lashorn 248
Lauber 16, 27
Lawrence 112
Lawson 245, 248, 264
Layman 34, 228, 277, 278
Layton 82
Lease 70, 79, 159, 169, 177, 191, 207, 240, 253, 263, 272, 278
Leather 144, 168, 247, 264
Leatherman 47, 51, 53, 68, 71, 89, 92, 95, 96, 104, 126, 128, 172, 224, 246, 260, 272, 274, 280
Leatherwood 260
Lebherz 115, 281
Le Compte 29
Ledwidge 203
Lee 19, 20, 21, 109, 229, 242
Leedy 206
Leggett 192
Legore 249
Lehman 34, 73, 199, 277
Leiter 101
Leitner 240
Lemon 228
Lenhart 128, 220
Leonard 219
Lescalleet 34
Leslie 16
Levy 62, 69, 70, 118, 171
Lewis 155, 156, 176, 183, 202, 242
Lichtleider 34, 123
Lieb 61
Liggett 227
Lighter 96, 156, 211, 235, 236
Lightner 114
Lilly 80
Lincoln 3, 21
Lindsay 63, 97, 119
Linebaugh 54, 68, 248, 265
Lingan 151, 160

Lingenfelter 34, 184, 241
Link 7, 136, 228
Linn 254
Linthicum 189, 245
Lischy 65
Livers 16, 24, 80, 81, 258
Locke 198
Lohr 40, 70
Long 53, 56, 70, 82, 86, 90, 127, 131, 134, 163, 188, 201, 207, 217, 222, 235, 261, 264, 269, 275, 276
Lookingbill 208
Lough 51, 100, 14, 178
Louthan 160
Lowenstein 223
Loy 11, 196, 241, 273
Luckenbill 34
Luckabaugh 244
Luckett 32, 193
Ludy 47, 68
Lugenbeel 62, 84, 95, 196, 210, 219, 274
Luke 48
Lusk 18
Lutz 69, 231
Lynn 32

Macht 127
Maddox 1
Madera 150
Magalis 137
Magaha 238
Magruder 32, 68, 201, 257
Main 142, 143, 145, 154, 157, 231, 250, 271
Mainhart 77
Maleve 24, 26
Mallick 284
Mann 158
Mantz 66, 117, 143, 189, 243
Markell 42, 43, 65, 108, 198, 241, 242
Marken 76, 88, 135
Marker 47, 48, 50, 91, 247, 278
Markey 41, 66
Marlin 1
Marshall 16
Martin 40, 49, 56, 58, 88, 116, 138, 233, 245, 259, 283

Martz 67, 132, 135, 152, 241, 265, 271, 274
Marye 10, 204
Mast 240, 278
Mathias 22, 107, 108, 130, 216, 274
Matthews 56, 130. See also Mathias
Maught 127, 249
Maulsly 187, 215, 277
Maxell 67
Maynard 68, 69, 149
Mayne 142, 261
Meade 21
Maeley 73, 233
Meals 59
Mears 158
Measell 47, 95, 101, 167, 216, 226, 240, 241, 251, 259
Medairy 204
Medtart 63
Mehring 34, 274
Mehrling 68, 85, 173
Meier 216
Melchers 90
Melins 16
Melsheimer 27
Melville 29, 30
Melvin 117
Menchy 125
Mengis 70, 275
Mentzer 173, 259
Mercer 67, 160, 230, 260, 263, 272
Mercier 179
Merckel 9, 66
Messner 66
Metcalfe 106
Meter 62, 147, 170
Metz 134
Metzger 64, 83, 94, 118, 135
Michael 9, 95, 110, 113, 119, 125, 154, 217, 225, 251, 257, 271, 272, 274, 276, 277
Michel 107, 108
Middaugh 215
Middleton 219
Miles 173
Millard 158
Miller 7, 11, 16, 43, 53, 56, 58, 62, 63, 68, 98, 99, 103, 106, 119, 121, 129, 144, 147, 153, 163, 173, 195, 202, 221, 228, 235, 243, 250, 251, 272, 279, 280, 282
Mills 18, 81, 144, 191
Mines 67
Minor 176, 234
Minot 181
Miss 221
Mitchell 20
Mobley 66, 266
Moffett 213
Moberly 54, 162, 210, 217, 271
Mohler 66
Molesworth 64, 113, 207, 214, 265
Monroe 30
Montague 38
Montgomery 17
Moore 12, 120, 136
Moose 52
Morgan 68, 84, 107, 206
Morrison 28, 78, 90
Morsell 82, 83, 207, 233, 245, 246
Mort 70, 233, 234, 243, 258
Moser 64-65, 76, 116
Motter 27, 76, 77, 90, 138, 141, 233, 255
Mount 45
Moxley 203
Moyer 130
Muhlenburg 26
Mull 122
Mullendore 131, 137, 172
Mullican 246
Mullinix 66, 136, 139
Mumma 20, 137, 280
Mummert 115
Munday 32
Munshower 274
Murdock 204, 217
Murphy 59, 64, 177
Murray 136, 141, 205
Musgrove 269
Musselman 282
Musseter 84, 121
Myers 58, 70, 72, 73, 76, 110, 120, 122, 141, 143, 169, 176, 199, 210, 234, 240, 241, 246, 283, 284
Mc Afee 93

Mc Aleer 38
Mc Allister 169
Mc Bride 116, 125, 165
Mc Cain 129
Mc Cann 76
Mc Cardell 11, 197
Mc Clain 64, 82, 190
Mc Clean 64
Mc Cleary 45, 85
Mc Clellan 20, 21
Mc Clure 39
Mc Conkey 201
Mc Coy 246, 253
Mc Culloh 78
Mc Curdy 107, 266
Mc Devitt 135, 233
Mc Donald 160, 258
Mc Duell 154, 168, 173
Mc Elfresh 34, 44, 165, 189, 216
Mc Gaha. See Magaha
Mc Gill 44, 75, 93, 106, 117, 161, 173, 266
Mc Glaughlin 34
Mc Glone 18
Mc Grath 8, 242
Mc. Gregor 257
Mc Intire 45
Mc Kaig 192
Mc Kenzie 282
Mc Kinney 266
Mc Kinnon 194
Mc Kinsey 2, 3, 4, 7, 19, 20, 21, 284
Mc Kinstry 150
Mc Kown 161
Mc Master 155
Mc Nair 255
Mc Pherson 12, 13, 17, 39, 44, 63, 64, 75, 77, 138, 186, 206
Mc Quire 233
Mc Sherry 38
Mc Sweeney 16
Mc Tavish 24
Mc Williams 255

Naff 67
Nagel 197
Naill 162, 204, 254
Nash 60, 186

Naylor 148
Neale 187
Needham 32
Neff 14, 120, 223, 241, 256
Neighbors 228, 277
Neidhart 162, 268
Neidig 184
Neihoof 277
Neikirk 72, 115, 221
Nelson 13, 23, 41, 114, 153, 163, 164, 187, 256, 277
Neuspiegel 129
Newcomer 180
Newman 88
Nicholson 33, 62
Nickel 3
Nickum 14
Nieke 9
Nicodemus 27, 53, 116, 120, 144, 148, 153, 169, 216, 232, 256, 257, 263, 265
Nichols 143
Nikirk 131
Niven 63
Nixdorff 34, 63, 77, 80
Noland 12
Norris 33, 49, 88, 99, 126, 150
Norwood 90, 95, 112, 144, 156, 187, 264
Notnagle 268
Null 130
Nunnemaker 46
Nusbaum 34, 165, 201, 202, 204, 207, 265, 267
Nusz 34
Nyberg 9

Obenderfer 268
Offutt 201
Ogdon 193
Ogle 9, 11, 80, 83, 106, 208, 236, 255, 272, 273
Ohler 41, 258
Oland 125, 143, 169, 209, 260, 261
Olson 92
Ordeman 157, 240, 245
Orndorff 204
Orrison 151

Osborn 105
Osburn 272
Oswald 93
Otis 39
Ott 168, 260, 279
Otto 259
Otterbein 25
Overholtzer 40, 70, 79
Owings 150, 265

Paca 33
Packard 215
Paggett 143, 151
Palmer 62, 67, 89, 187, 190, 195, 232, 248
Pampel 124
Parker 32, 110
Parr 11
Parrish 56
Parsons 88
Patterson 80
Payne 80, 129, 245
Pearre 62, 97, 113, 161
Peck 48, 101
Peddicord 148, 149
Peitzell 48, 167, 245
Pellentz 24
Penn 12
Pentzer 178, 243
Perky 46, 257
Perry 161, 218, 264
Pershing 67
Peters 13, 62, 146, 155, 273
Pfoutz 53, 131, 197, 254, 276
Pierce 194
Philips 70, 133
Phillips 53, 86, 121, 174
Philpot 73
Phleeger 210
Pickings 174
Pieterse 170
Pigman 277
Pinkney 277
Pittinger 34, 94, 197, 255, 256, 280
Pitzer 177, 229
Plank 106
Plummer 171

Poe 18, 252
Poffenberger 60-61, 89, 253, 264
Polsen 119
Pons 237
Poole 7, 149, 150, 163, 247, 262
Porter 143
Prather 32
Pratt 281
Preston 233
Price 13, 33, 90, 91, 157
Priest 20
Prince 278
Pritchard 257
Proffitt 159
Protzman 56, 68, 115
Pryor 94, 96, 178
Pugh 107
Purcell 218
Purdum 214
Purnell 28
Putman 60, 62, 83, 129, 147, 221, 235, 236
Pyfer 105

Quynn 7, 12, 159, 195

Railing 173
Rainsberger 58
Ralston 186
Ramsburg 7, 11, 12, 34, 44, 51, 55, 57-58, 60, 79, 99, 105, 116, 139, 140, 141, 144, 169, 171, 176, 177, 202, 208, 212, 228, 233, 235, 236, 237, 261
Ramsay 192
Rankin 129
Ranneberger 126
Raser 171
Rawlins 32, 143
Ray 148
Rayner (Roemer) 15, 34, 78, 87, 277
Read 43
Ream 113
Rebstock 101, 151
Recher 56, 68, 96, 115
Reck 27, 28
Reed 8, 14, 284

Reese 103, 132, 189, 205, 241, 251, 274
Reich 158, 167
Reichert 127
Reifsnider 77, 79, 107, 114, 184, 214
Remsburg 54, 57, 58, 60, 81, 87, 93, 97, 104, 107, 109, 114, 127, 131, 132, 133, 134, 140, 141, 148, 153, 171, 178, 181, 199, 203, 206, 225, 235, 237, 250, 275
Renn 45, 177, 265
Renner 56, 77, 89, 99, 268
Reno 20
Repp 107, 188, 200, 254
Reppert 15
Retgering 75
Reynes 232
Reynolds 21, 162, 191
Rhoads 11, 41, 73
Rhoderick 118, 165, 166, 182, 207, 272
Rhodes 127, 199
Rice 16, 27, 33, 85, 104, 116, 117, 125, 132, 153, 217, 249, 257
Richards 36, 258
Richardson 48
Ricksecker 156
Riddlemoser 198, 221, 262
Ridenour 92, 112
Rideout 3
Ridgely 38, 149, 179, 243
Ridgeway 115
Riemensperger 57, 99, 105, 134, 140, 225, 233. See Ramsburg and Remsburg
Rife 43, 133
Riggs 84, 155, 173, 206
Riley 59
Rinebeck 25, 128
Rinehart 53, 64, 82, 99, 175, 215
Riner 169
Ringer 115, 171
Ringgold 217, 226
Ringwalt 162
Rippleogle 262
Ritchie 41, 157, 215
Ritter 230
Rizer 71

Rizzuto 48
Roberson 156
Roberts 251
Robertson 255
Robinson 228
Roddy 133
Rodenpiller 27
Roelkey 156, 240, 265
Rogers 87, 107
Rohrback 51
Rohrer 34
Roop 271
Roosa 170
Roosevelt 170
Root 149, 201, 227, 275
Ropp 49, 124
Rosenour 227
Rosenstock 227
Ross 100, 163, 226
Rothenhoefer 125
Routson 158, 250, 283
Routzahn 34, 59-60, 71, 82, 86, 93, 94, 98, 119, 135, 144, 145, 146, 159, 202, 206, 210, 214, 224, 227, 235, 236, 248, 250, 263, 270, 278, 283
Rouzer 47, 56, 57, 59
Rowe 79, 218
Rowland 194
Rowler 46
Royer 53, 108, 213
Ruch 168
Rudisill 233
Rudy 157, 211, 212
Rumsey 17, 18
Runkle(s) 24, 184, 206, 210, 217
Rupp 23, 34, 53, 271
Ruse 245
Russell 26, 77, 132, 273
Rutherford 117
Ryan 162

Sadler 93
Saeger 43, 50
Sahm 268
Salmon 44, 51, 87, 169
Sanders 151, 241
Sanner 70, 116, 156, 157

Index

Sappington 38, 96, 234, 235, 243
Sauble 146
Sawyer 87
Saxten 190
Saylor 144, 149, 162, 164, 168, 179, 182, 223, 254
Schaaf 270
Schade 204
Schaeffer 55, 87, 102, 130, 133, 155, 158, 166, 199, 244, 245, 275. See also Shafer and Shaffer
Schaff 25, 127, 270, 283
Schaffner 52
Scharf 5, 13, 284
Scheinfew 190
Schell 265, 266
Schellman 143
Schildknecht 32, 34, 53, 70, 93, 116, 135, 214, 229, 266
Schildt 21, 22
Schindler 137
Schlisler 84
Schley 7, 9, 24, 32, 38-39, 54, 104, 106, 195, 211, 220, 227, 272, 273
Schlim 155
Schlosser 57, 104, 175, 271
Schmaul 245
Schnautigel 204
Schnebel 206
Schneider 167, 181, 273
Schober (Shover) 56
Scholl 13, 28, 122, 219, 229, 238
Schooley 35
Schopp 163
Schriver 93
Schroyer 53
Schuler 87
Schultz 8, 184, 208, 235
Schumacher 55
Schwartz 118
Schwenck 240
Scott 38, 275
Seabrook 17
Seachrist 258
Seagar 43, 50
Sebold 119
Seemahr 241
Sefton 243

Seidel 122, 123, 154, 181, 230, 240, 270
Seilhammer 282
Sell 72
Selman 174
Sensbauer 145
Sensenbaugh 260
Seton 29, 30
Seubold 61
Seward 248
Shafer 54-55, 96, 103, 126, 131, 169, 171, 172, 178, 181, 202, 231, 264, 265, 271
Shaff 140, 141, 143, 270
Shaffer 11, 54-55, 101, 103, 116, 122, 125, 126, 139, 143, 174, 250, 274, 280. See also Schaeffer
Shank 39, 89, 151, 175, 177, 188, 206, 236, 253, 259
Shankel 261
Shann 158
Shannon 161
Shaw 89, 178
Shawbaker 75, 116, 204
Shawn 110
Shearer 69, 110, 194
Sheetenhelm 70, 98, 159
Sheets 191
Sheffer 59, 82, 85, 99, 100, 118, 151, 204, 216, 250
Sheffield 220
Shelby 33
Shelhass 280
Shelman 141, 211
Shepherd 147
Sheridan 16, 22, 23, 200
Sherman 61
Shields 12
Shingle 52
Shipley 52, 124, 179, 207, 210, 229
Shoaf 163
Shoemaker 55, 88
Shook 192
Shopes 278
Shorb 7, 32, 101
Short 269
Shreve 164
Shrier 107

Shriner 88, 149, 189, 215, 219, 226, 245
Shriver 7, 39, 40, 42-43, 128, 129, 147, 195, 243
Shroyer 53, 54, 110, 279
Shryock 52
Shue 72, 157
Shuff 194, 218
Shull 238
Shuman 278
Shupp 172
Shutaire 56
Siedling 204
Sigler 125, 165, 238, 266
Simmons 48, 122, 232
Simon 262
Simpson 201, 202
Sines 231
Sinn 39, 110, 123, 252
Six 194, 196
Skinner 72
Slagle 270
Slick 243
Slifer 75, 181, 251
Smeltzer 14, 245
Smith 7, 11, 27, 32, 40, 42, 57, 59, 63, 64, 67, 77, 80, 84, 87, 88, 91, 92, 102, 110, 118, 127, 128, 133, 135, 141, 142, 144, 146, 147, 153, 154, 160, 168, 172, 173, 175, 177, 179, 185, 187, 188, 189, 190, 191-193, 198, 203, 205, 206, 210, 212, 214, 215, 216, 219, 230, 232, 243, 258, 259, 260, 280
Snader 99, 111
Snider 231
Snively 102
Snook 34, 54, 60, 99, 114, 140, 167, 174, 177, 191, 212, 226, 228, 229, 235
Snouffer 83, 213, 232
Snowden 160
Snyder 25, 105, 180, 184, 193, 221
Sollers 69
Souder 95
Spade 47, 68
Spahr 167
Spalding 16, 81, 82, 83, 245

Spaulding 207
Specht 271
Spessard 128
Spitler 78
Sponseller 177, 240, 241, 278
Spoon 262
Sprigg 270
Springer 174, 221
Spurrier 38, 139
Stackpole 23
Stafford 86
Stahr 29
Stalcop 147, 148
Staley 57, 67, 76, 92, 96, 99, 101-103, 113, 114, 151, 168, 173, 174, 204, 212, 215, 218, 230, 231, 241
Stalling 158
Stambaugh 188, 193, 194, 252, 273
Stansbury 53, 60
Staub 112, 177
Stauffer 184, 185, 200, 227, 245
Steck 272
Steelman 23, 27
Steinbrenner 97
Steiner 9, 44, 53, 57, 135, 140, 142, 167, 200. See also Stoner
Stem 152, 243
Stemple 34, 103
Stephens 173, 217, 252, 268
Stern 223
Stevens 112, 252
Stevenson 36
Steward 240
Stewart 90, 151, 240
Stickle 105
Stickley 58
Stiegel 15
Still 40
Stilley (Stille) 58, 102, 147, 273
Stimmel 52, 107, 203
Stine 77, 242
Stitely 131, 177, 191, 203, 243, 254, 259
Stockman 85, 117, 218, 236, 242, 251
Stocksdale 74
Stoddard 23
Stofflebean 127
Stoffrigan 240

Stokes 42, 226
Stone 33, 115, 158, 177, 265
Stonebraker 197
Stoner 53, 107, 113, 181, 196, 219, 231, 277, 284. See also Steiner
Storm 105
Storr 135
Stose 36
Stotelmyer 20
Stottlemyer 55, 56, 67, 68, 96, 115, 124, 218
Stouder 3
Stouffer 253
Stover 25, 228
Strassburger 284
Strausburg 112, 254
Strawbridge 25
Street 27
Stride 85
Strine 152, 262, 263
Strobel 69
Strodel 108
Strong 35
Strother 20
Struble 251
Stuart 19, 21, 38
Studebaker 90
Stull 9, 18, 71, 101, 114, 115, 129, 136, 162, 166, 174, 208, 210, 230, 231, 249
Stup 61, 73, 99, 116, 148, 233
Sulser 225
Suman 12, 216
Sumbrun 133. See also Zumbrun
Summers 34, 51, 62, 119, 125, 129, 150, 211, 217, 225, 243, 247, 248, 264, 271, 272
Suresch 60, 236
Swank 10
Sweadner 256
Sweeney 270
Swigart 126, 172
Swomley 26, 173, 223
Swope (Schwab) 46, 261

Tabler 62, 78, 167, 244, 264
Talbott 15, 63
Taney 14, 110

Tasker 11, 110, 186, 279
Taylor 11, 93, 161, 232
Teeter 37
Templin 192
Thomas 7, 11, 22, 23, 28, 31, 32, 40, 57, 69, 105, 106, 110, 117, 120, 123, 130, 132, 133, 134, 135, 136, 140, 141, 148, 151, 176, 178, 182, 183, 185, 213, 218, 219, 221, 222, 225, 229, 232, 233, 236, 237, 241, 261, 270
Thomson 64
Thompson 18, 64
Thornburgh 63
Thrasher 95
Thumb 168
Thurmons 119
Tierman 64, 78
Titlow 191
Titsworthy 7
Toms 54, 64, 83, 100, 103, 116, 117, 118, 137, 178, 183, 221, 224, 260
Touchstone 71
Townsend 23
Tracey 8, 284
Trail 22, 44, 107, 216
Trayer 173
Trego (Trago) 266
Tritapoe 177, 209
Tritt 178
Trout 11, 183, 241
Troutman 52, 71
Troxell 50, 51, 76, 123, 129, 216, 231, 241, 274
Truman 239
Trundle 40, 106, 143
Truxal 29
Tucker 66, 242
Turner 12, 20, 91, 137
Tyler 13, 32, 229
Tyson 37, 275

Unsult 9
Unverzagt 49
Updegraf 34
Urner 13, 49, 126, 189, 194
Utterback 233
Utz 49, 55

Vale 166
Valentine 47, 52, 79, 175, 190, 193, 274, 280
Vananda 96
Van Fossen 34
Van Meter 62, 147, 170
Van Sant 217
Van Vliet 170
Varlé 14
Veant 269
Vickory 73
Vincel 177
Virts 156
Voltz. See Foltz
Vosburg 236

Wachtel 118, 209
Wachter 45, 46, 102, 116, 125, 129, 132, 135, 166, 189, 205, 229, 230, 231, 233, 251, 274, 276
Wacker 181
Waesche 47, 48, 239
Wagaman 43, 64, 148
Wagner 144, 187, 237, 243, 263
Walcutt 73, 198
Waldeck 233
Walker 42, 52, 126, 162, 203, 246, 253
Wallace 22
Wallis 205
Walter 119, 124
Walters 51
Walton 24
Waltz 28, 194, 203
Wampler 89, 278, 284
Wantz 127
Ward 74, 80, 160
Warehime 228
Warfield 11, 202
Warford 33
Warner 43, 77, 79, 83, 132, 152, 213, 223, 280, 284
Warrenfeltz 47, 55, 57, 96, 115, 218, 219, 246, 264, 265, 274
Warring 186
Wasch 24
Washington 11, 13, 14, 17, 186, 222
Wastler 125

Waters 81, 94, 97, 98, 104, 130, 165, 243, 269
Watkins 45
Watson 44, 269
Watt 143
Way 102
Weagley 174
Weant 269
Weaver 40, 158, 175, 241, 270
Webb 17, 32, 106
Weber 53, 76, 284
Webster 67, 148, 205, 206, 230, 260
Weddle 257
Weidman 40
Weimer 26, 48, 214
Weiser 10, 283
Weller 7, 17, 25, 26, 34, 47, 59, 65, 76, 92, 155, 167, 182, 238
Wells 12, 45, 232
Welsh 77
Weltzheimer 141
Welty 45, 220, 242
Wentz 88, 284
Wertenbaker 34, 43, 53, 168
Wertheimer 96
West 83, 93, 129, 217
Westfield 62
Westlager 10
Wetzel 7, 11, 18, 117, 152, 187, 212, 244, 274
Weybright 111
Whaley 39
Wheeler 16, 80, 168
Whipp 74, 85, 133, 140, 200, 211, 228, 248
White 133
Whythill 33
Whitenight 270
Whitman 3, 71
Whitmore 26, 49, 53, 55, 68, 97, 127, 231, 234, 239, 274, 280
Whittacre 114, 200
Whittier 19
Wickham 11, 16, 32, 80, 260
Widerick 73, 166, 189, 205, 251
Wiener 151, 152, 163, 180, 181
Wiest 46
Wikard 196

Wilcoxon 128, 139, 161, <u>188</u>
Wildhagen 240
Wiles <u>45</u>, 49, 85, 158, 178, <u>226</u>, 250, 268, 274
Wilhide 35, <u>48-49</u>, 58, 59, 167, 172, 193, 194, 245, 259
Wilkinson 14
Will 97
Willard 34, 54, 67, 75, 81, 97, 128, <u>155</u>, <u>156</u>, 169, 175, 178, 179, 230, 231, 233, 243, 244, 270, 271, 276
Williams 1, 2, 3, 5, 7, 10, 23, 42, 45, 161, 238, 259, 273, 284
Williamson 266
Williar 146, 165, 167, 238, 244, 276
Willman 58, 83
Wills 115
Wilson 47, 50, 57, 78, 125, <u>138</u>, 147, 171, <u>195</u>, <u>196</u>, 219, 220, 238, 267
Wimberley 73
Winchester 28
Windred 11
Windsor 202
Winebrenner <u>41</u>, 44, 145, 160, 186, 203, 216, 217, 262
Winger 155
Wingerd 138
Winpigler 35, 120, 135
Winsett 232
Winters 102, 179, 273
Wintz 38, 196, 220
Wireman 275
Wirk 147
Wirtz 271
Wise (Weiss) 11, 20, 39, 123, 234, 170, 171, 175, 177, 207, 253, 266
Wiseman 97, 188
Wisner 252, 261, 262
Wisong 151
Wisotzkey 238
Witherow 42
Witmer 53
Witter 150
Wolf(e) 9, 56, 94, 96, 113, 123, 134, 141, 152, 162, 183, 219, 230, 231, 232, 233, 258, 259, 267, 275
Wollaston 272

Wood 10, 12, 17, 32, <u>43</u>, 52, 107, <u>131</u>, 147, 159, 189
Working 243
Worley 232
Worman 108, 135, 159, 219, 234, 235
Wort 145
Worthington 23, 43, <u>48</u>, 75, 168, 186, 201
Worthley 38
Wright 23, 112, 126, 174, 182, 198, 239, 284
Wyant 243, 283

Yaste 83, 188
Yeakle 133, 218
Yeast 45
Yerkes 155
Yinger 238
Yingling 35, 111, 180, 201
Young 7, 41, 42, 54, 71, 79, 106, <u>111</u>, 122, 123, 125, 152, 154, <u>163</u>, 172, 181, 215, 216, 247, 249, 253, 254, 255, 265, 266, 274, <u>283</u>
Youtsey 250, 252

Zacharias 50
Zavoiko 108
Zecher 215, 238
Zeiler 108
Zentz 40, 41, 92, 100, 105, 245
Ziegler 165, 266
Zittle 230
Zimmerman 7, 34, <u>39</u>, <u>40</u>, 45, 46, 67, 77, 95, 112, 115, <u>122</u>, <u>123</u>, 129, <u>130</u>, <u>141</u>, 145, 154, 155, 159, 173, 175, 177, 180, 181, 183, 207, 211, 213, 228, 229, 230, 231, 237, 240, 241, 244, 253, 263, 270, 271, 273, 276, 284
Zumbrun 116, 210
Zweizig 114

www.ingramcontent.com/pod-product-compliance
Lightning Source LLC
Chambersburg PA
CBHW070723160426
43192CB00009B/1288